国家卫生和计划生育委员会"十三五"英文版规划教材
全国高等学校教材

供临床医学专业及来华留学生（MBBS）双语教学用

Medical Statistics
医学统计学

Geoffrey R. Norman   David L. Streiner

主　编　郝元涛
Chief Editor   Yuantao Hao

副主编　赵　杨　　侯　艳　　陶育纯
Vice Chief Editor   Yang Zhao   Yan Hou   Yuchun Tao

人民卫生出版社

图字号 : 01-2015-1235

编者（以姓氏笔画为序）

王 玖   滨州医学院
Jiu Wang   Binzhou Medical University

王学梅   内蒙古医科大学
Xuemei Wang   Inner Mongolia Medical University

尹家祥   大理大学
Jiaxiang Yin   Dali University

邓 丹   重庆医科大学
Dan Deng   Chongqing Medical University

艾自胜   同济大学
Zisheng Ai   Tongji University

石武祥   桂林医学院
Wuxiang Shi   Guilin Medical University

李述刚   石河子大学
Shugang Li   Shihezi University

赵 杨   南京医科大学
Yang Zhao   Nanjing Medical University

郝元涛   中山大学
Yuantao Hao   Sun Yat-sen University

胡国清   中南大学
Guoqing Hu   Central South University

侯 艳   哈尔滨医科大学
Yan Hou   Harbin Medical University

贾 红   西南医科大学
Hong Jia   Southwest Medical University

顾 菁   中山大学
Jing Gu   Sun Yat-sen University

陶育纯   吉林大学
Yuchun Tao   Jilin University

曹明芹   新疆医科大学
Mingqin Cao   Xinjiang Medical University

潘发明   安徽医科大学
Faming Pan   Anhui Medical University

编写秘书

邵子杰   中山大学
Zijie Shao   Sun Yat-sen University

1995 年,我国首次招收全英文授课医学留学生,到 2015 年,接收临床医学专业 MBBS（Bachelor of Medicine & Bachelor of Surgery）留学生的院校达到了 40 余家,MBBS 院校数量、规模不断扩张;同时,医学院校在临床医学专业五年制、长学制教学中陆续开展不同规模和范围的双语或全英文授课,使得对一套符合我国教学实际、成体系、高质量英文教材的需求日益增长。

为了满足教学需求,进一步落实教育部《关于加强高等学校本科教学工作提高教学质量的若干意见（教高 [2001]4 号）》和《来华留学生医学本科教育（英文授课）质量控制标准暂行规定（教外来 [2007]39 号）》等相关文件的要求,规范和提高我国高等医学院校临床医学专业五年制、长学制和来华留学生（MBBS）双语教学及全英文教学的质量,推进医学双语教学和留学生教育的健康有序发展,完善和规范临床医学专业英文版教材的体系,人民卫生出版社在充分调研的基础上,于 2015 年召开了全国高等学校临床医学专业英文版规划教材的编写论证会,经过会上及会后的反复论证,最终确定组织编写一套全国规划的、适合我国高等医学院校教学实际的临床医学专业英文版教材,并计划作为 2017 年春季和秋季教材在全国出版发行。

本套英文版教材的编写结合国家卫生和计划生育委员会、教育部的总体要求,坚持"三基、五性、三特定"的原则,组织全国各大医学院校、教学医院的专家编写,主要特点如下:

1. 教材编写应教学之需启动,在全国范围进行了广泛、深入调研和论证,借鉴国内外医学人才培养模式和教材建设经验,对主要读者对象、编写模式、编写科目、编者遴选条件等进行了科学设计。

2. 坚持"三基、五性、三特定"和"多级论证"的教材编写原则,组织全国各大医学院校及教学医院有丰富英语教学经验的专家一起编写,以保证高质量出版。

3. 为保证英语表达的准确性和规范性,大部分教材以国外英文原版教科书为蓝本,根据我国教学大纲和人民卫生出版社临床医学专业第八轮规划教材主要内容进行改编,充分体现科学性、权威性、适用性和实用性。

4. 教材内部各环节合理设置,根据读者对象的特点,在英文原版教材的基础上结合需要,增加本章小结、关键术语（英中对照）、思考题、推荐阅读等模块,促进学生自主学习。

本套临床医学专业英文版规划教材共 38 种,均为国家卫生和计划生育委员会"十三五"规划教材,计划于 2017 年全部出版发行。

In 1995, China recruited overseas medical students of full English teaching for the first time. Up to 2015, more than 40 institutions enrolled overseas MBBS (Bachelor of Medicine & Bachelor of Surgery) students. The number of MBBS institutions and overseas students are continuously increasing. At the meantime, medical colleges' application for bilingual or full English teaching in different size and range in five-year and long-term professional clinical medicine teaching results to increasingly demand for a set of practical, systematic and high-qualified English teaching material.

In order to meet the teaching needs and to implement the regulations of relevant documents issued by Ministry of Education including "Some Suggestions to Strengthen the Undergraduate Teaching and to Improve the Teaching Quality" and "Interim Provisions on Quality Control Standards of International Medical Undergraduate Education (English teaching)", as well as to standardize and improve the quality of the bilingual teaching and English teaching of the five-year, long-term and international students (MBBS) of clinical medicine in China's higher medical colleges so as to promote the healthy and orderly development of medical bilingual teaching and international students education and to improve and standardize the system of English clinical medicine textbooks, after full investigation, People's Medical Publishing House (PMPH) held the writing discussion meeting of English textbook for clinical medicine department of national colleges and universities in 2015. After the repeated demonstration in and after the meeting, PMPH ultimately determined to organize the compilation of a set of national planning English textbooks which are suitable for China's actual clinical medicine teaching of medical colleges and universities. This set will be published as spring and autumn textbooks of 2017.

This set of English textbooks meets the overall requirements of the Ministry of Education and National Health and Family Planning Commission, the editorial committee includes the experts from major medical colleges and universities as well as teaching hospitals, the main features are as follows:

1. Textbooks compilation is started to meet the teaching needs, extensive and deep research and demonstration are conducted across the country, the main target readers, the model and subject of compilation and selection conditions of authors are scientifically designed in accordance with the reference of domestic and foreign medical personnel training model and experience in teaching materials.

2. Adhere to the teaching materials compiling principles of "three foundations, five characteristics, and three specialties" and "multi-level demonstration", the organization of English teaching experts with rich experience from major medical schools and teaching hospitals ensures the high quality of publication.

3. In order to ensure the accuracy and standardization of English expression, most of the textbooks are modeled on original English textbooks, and adapted based on national syllabus and main content of the eighth round of clinical medicine textbooks which were published by PMPH, fully reflecting the scientificity, authority, applicability and practicality.

4. All aspects of teaching materials are arranged reasonably, based on original textbooks,the chapter summary, key terms (English and Chinese), review questions, and recommended readings are added to promote students' independent learning in accordance with teaching needs and the characteristics of the target readers.

This set of English textbooks for clinical medicine includes 38 species which are among "13th Five-Year" planning textbooks of National Health and Family Planning Commission, and will be all published in 2017.

全国高等学校临床医学专业第一轮英文版规划教材 · 教材目录

PREFACE

To meet the urgent needs to enhance and standardize the bilingual education of Clinical Medicine in China for both the Chinese and international students, the *People's Medical Publishing House* decided to publish a series of textbooks in English, also called the *Series of Clinical Medicine Textbooks in English for the "13th Five-Year" Planning. Medical Statistics* is one of the 38 textbooks. From the discussions with the *People's Medical Publishing House*, foreign publishers, and experts in the education of Medical Statistics, this textbook was made possible by a combined effort in following the *MEDICAL STATISTICS: The Bare Essentials (4th Edition)* as well as the principles and requirements of the curriculum for the 5-year Clinical Medicine Program in China.

This textbook includes five parts: 1) data characterization and basic statistics, 2) t-test and analysis of variance, 3) non-parametric statistics, 4) regression and correlation, and 5) common problems in Medical Statistics. This structure is in line with other textbooks of Medical Statistics and constitutes an integral and important components of medical education. By adapting a vivid and reader-friendly writing style, this textbook strives to achieve the best educational outcome. Moreover, this textbook cites many real life examples to teach the principles and applications of statistical methods, operational steps and interpretation of results the best, so the knowledge could be implied into future clinical practice.

Furthermore, we have made some modifications and adjustments to the original textbooks by: 1) shortening length to improve concision, 2) removing sessions that were rarely introduced in the 5-year Clinical Medicine Program in China, such as the Possion regression, 3) adding contents, such as the comparisons between regression and correlation, that are commonly introduced in the Chinese-version textbooks of Medical Statistics, 4) combining some sessions and adjusting the orders of some chapters, and 5) adding a summary session to each chapter. This textbook not only includes the main contents of the Chinese Medical Statistics textbook, but also covers the requirements in Medical Statistics of the medical licensing examination. Therefore, this textbook can be used for 5-, 7- or 8-year Clinical Medicine Program and other medical related majors, as well as for international MBBS training.

Time has flied since the editor-in-chief meeting in August, 2015 in Wuhan, and the editorial board meeting in January, 2016 in Guangzhou. I would like to thank the dedicative work of all editors. I would like to thank Professor Jiqian Fang of the Sun Yat-sen University for his instructive suggestions. We appreciate graduate students Zijie shao, Xinwei Wang, Yun Huang, Xiao Lin etc. of the Sun Yat-sen University, who have done a lot of serious and meticulous work on the editing and layout of this textbook. We are grateful to the Office of Academic Affairs at the Sun Yat-sen University for their financial support.

Due to our limited knowledge and experience, there may be deficiencies and/or errors in this textbook. We are looking forward to your valuable comments and suggestions to improve future versions.

Yuantao HAO
July 2018, Guangzhou

CONTENTS

REPRISE

CHAPTER THE FIRST **The Basics**

In this chapter, we will introduce you to the concepts of variables and to the different types of data: nominal, ordinal, interval, and ratio.

STATISTICS: SO WHO NEEDS IT?

The first question most beginning students of statistics ask is, "Why do we need it?" Leaving aside the unworthy answer that it is required for you to get your degree, we have to address the issue of how learning the arcane methods and jargon of this field will make you a better person and leave you feeling fulfilled in ways that were previously unimaginable. The reason is that the world is full of variation, and sometimes it's hard to tell real differences from natural variation. Statistics wouldn't be needed if everybody in the world were exactly like everyone else; if you were male, 172 cm tall, had brown eyes and hair, and were incredibly good looking,[1] this description would fit every other person. This means that there is no any male like dwarf or giant for tall, blue or black for eyes, black or yellow for hairs, bad or general for looking in the world. You don't need to know how many males taller or shorter than you by statistics, because every male is 172 cm tall. You also don't need to know how many males' looks better than you by statistics, because every male is incredibly good looking, not just for you.

Fortunately, this is not the case; people are different in all of these areas, as well as in thousands of other ways. The downside of all this variability is that it makes it more difficult to determine how a person will respond to some newfangled treatment regimen or react in some situation. We can't look in the mirror, ask ourselves, "Self, how do you feel about the newest brand of toothpaste?" and assume everyone will feel the same way.

POPULATION AND SAMPLE

It is because of this variability among people, and even within any one person from one time to another, that statistics were born. As we hope to show as you wade through this tome, statistics allow us to describe the "average" person, to see how well that description fits or doesn't fit other people, and to see how much we can generalize our findings from studying a few people[2] to the population as a whole. So statistics can be used in two ways: to describe data, and to make inferences from them.

In statistics, the aim of study is to estimate the characteristics of population based on the information from samples. The two terms are important

---

[1] *Coincidentally, this perfectly describes the person writing this section.*

[2] *As we'll see later, "a few" to a statistician can mean over 400 000 people, as in the Salk polio vaccine trial. So much for the scientific use of language.*

for the following chapters.

Population is any entire collection of people, animals, items or events about which we wish to describe or draw conclusions about.

It is the entire group we are interested in. It is not always convenient or possible to examine every member of an entire population. For instance, the population for a study of infant health might be all children born in the UK in the 1980's. A measurable characteristic of a population, such as a mean or standard deviation, is called a parameter.

Sample is a group of units selected from a larger group (population). By studying the sample it is hoped to draw valid conclusions about the larger group.

A sample is generally selected for study because the population is too large to study or be performed in its entirety. The sample should be representative of the general population. This is often best achieved by random sampling. Also, before collecting the sample, it is important that the researcher carefully and completely defines the population, including a description of the members to be included. If the sample is random and large enough, you can use the information collected from the sample to make inferences about the population. As the above-mentioned example, the sample might be all babies born on 7th May in any of the years. The measurable characteristic of a sample is called a statistic.

DESCRIPTIVE AND INFERENTIAL STATISTICS

Descriptive statistics are concerned with the presentation, organization, and summarization of data.

The realm of descriptive statistics, which we cover in this section, includes various methods of organizing and graphing the data to get an idea of what they show. Descriptive statistics also include various indices that summarize the data with just a few key numbers.

The bulk of the book is devoted to inferential stats.

Inferential statistics allow us to generalize from our sample of data to a larger group of subjects.

For instance, when a dermatologist gives a new cream, attar of eggplant, to 20 adolescents whose chances for true love have been jeopardized by acne, and compares them with 20 adolescents who remain untreated (and presumably unloved), he is not interested in just those 40 kids. He wants to know whether all kids with acne will respond to this treatment. Thus he is trying to make an inference about a larger group of subjects(population) from the small group(sample) he is studying. We'll get into the basics of inferential statistics in Chapter 5; for now, let's continue with some more definitions.

VARIABLES

In the first few paragraphs, we mentioned a number of ways that people differ: gender,[3] age, height, hair and eye color, responsiveness to treatment, and life expectancy. In the statistical parlance you'll be learning, these factors are referred to as *variables*.

A *variable* is simply what is being observed or measured.

Variables come in two flavors: independent and dependent. The easiest way to start to think of them is in an experiment, so let's return to those acned adolescents. We want to see if the degree of acne depends on whether or not the kids got attar of eggplant. The outcome (acne) is the dependent variable, which we hope will change in response to treatment. What we've manipulated is the treatment (attar of eggplant), and this is our independent variable.

The *dependent variable* is the outcome of interest, which should change in response to some intervention.

The *independent variable* is the intervention, or what is being manipulated.

---

[3] *Formerly referred to as "sex."*

Sounds straightforward, doesn't it? That's a dead giveaway that it's too simple. Once we get out of the realm of experiments, the distinction between dependent and independent variables gets a bit hairier. For instance, if we wanted to look at the growth of vocabulary as a kid grows up, the number of different words would be the dependent variable and age the independent one. That is, we're saying that vocabulary is dependent on age, even though it isn't an intervention and we're not manipulating it. So, more generally, if one variable changes in response to another, we say that the dependent variable is the one that changes in response to the independent variable.

Both dependent and independent variables can take one of a number of specific values: for gender, this is usually limited to either male or female; hair color can be brown, black, blonde, red, gray, artificial, or missing; and a variable such as height can range between about 25 to 40 cm for premature infants to about 200 cm for basketball players and coauthors of statistics books.

TYPES OF DATA

Discrete versus Continuous Data

Although we referred to both gender and height as variables, it's obvious that they are different from one another with respect to the type and number of values they can assume. One way to differentiate between types of variables is to decide whether the values are **discrete** or **continuous**.

Discrete variables can have only one of a limited set of values. Using our previous examples, this would include variables such as gender, hair and eye color, and which treatment a person received. Another example of a discrete variable is a number total, such as how many times a person has been admitted to hospital; the number of decayed, missing, or filled teeth; and the number of children. Despite what the demographers tell us, it's impossible to have 2.13 children—kids come in discrete quantities.

Discrete data have values that can assume only whole numbers.

The situation is different for continuous variables. It may seem at first that something such as height, for example, is measured in discrete units: someone is 172 cm tall; a person slightly taller would be 173 cm, and a somewhat shorter person would measure in at 171 cm. In fact, though, the limitation is imposed by our measuring stick. If we used one with finer gradations, we may be able to measure in 1/2 cm increments. Indeed, we could get really silly about the whole affair and use a laser to measure the person's height to the nearest thousandth of a millimeter. The point is that height, like weight, blood pressure, serum rhubarb, time, and many other variables, is really continuous, and the divisions we make are arbitrary to meet our measurement needs. The measurement, though, is artificial; if two people appear to have the same blood pressure when measured to the nearest millimeter of mercury, they will likely be different if we could measure to the nearest tenth of a millimeter. If they're still the same, we can measure with even finer gradations until a difference finally appears.

Continuous data may take any value, within a defined range.

We can illustrate this difference between discrete and continuous variables with two other examples. A piano is a "discrete" instrument. It has only 88 keys, and those of us who struggled long and hard to murder Paganini learnt that A-sharp was the same note as B-flat. Violinists ("fiddlers" to y'all south of the Mason-Dixon line), though, play a "continuous" instrument and are able to make a fine distinction between these two notes. Similarly, really cheap digital watches display only 4 digits and cut time into 1minute chunks. Razzle-dazzle watches, in addition to storing telephone numbers and your bank balance, cut time into $\frac{1}{100}$-second intervals. A physicist can do even better, dividing each second into 9 192 631 770 oscillations of a cesium atom. Even this, though, is only an arbitrary division.

Many of the statistical techniques you'll be learning about don't really care if the data are discrete or continuous; after all, a number to them is just a number. There are instances, though, when the distinction is important. Rest assured that we will point these out to you at the appropriate times.

Nominal, Ordinal, Interval, and Ratio Data

We can think about different types of variables in another way. A variable such as gender can take only two values: male and female. One value isn't "higher" or "better" than the other; we can list them by putting male first or female first without losing any information. This is called a nominal variable.

A nominal variable consists of named categories, with no implied order among the categories.

The simplest nominal categories are what Feinstein (1977) calls "existential" variables—a property either exists or it doesn't exist. A person has cancer of the liver or doesn't have it; someone has received the new treatment or didn't receive it; and, most existential of all, the subject is either alive or dead. Nominal variables don't have to be dichotomous; they can have any number of categories. We can classify a person's marital status as Single/Married/Separated/Widowed/Divorced/Common-Law (six categories); her eye color into Black/Brown/Blue/Green/Mixed (five categories[4]); and her medical problem into one of a few hundred diagnostic categories. The important point is that you can't say brown eyes are "better" or "worse" than blue. The ordering is arbitrary, and no information is gained or lost by changing the order.

Because computers handle numbers far more easily than they do letters, researchers commonly code nominal data by assigning a number to each value: Female could be coded as 1 and Male as 2; or Single=1, Married=2, and so on. In these cases, the numerals are really no more than alternative names, and they should not be thought of as having any quantitative value. Again, we can change the coding by letting Male=1 and Female=2, and the conclusions we draw will be identical (assuming, of course, that we remember which way we coded the data).[5]

A student evaluation rating consisting of Excellent/Satisfactory/Unsatisfactory has three categories. It differs from a variable such as hair color in that there is an ordering of these values: "Excellent" is better than "Satisfactory," which in turn is better than "Unsatisfactory." However, the difference in performance between "Excellent" and "Satisfactory" cannot be assumed to be the same difference as exists between "Satisfactory" and "Unsatisfactory." This is seen more clearly with letter grades; there is only a small division between a B+ and a B, but a large one, amounting to a ruined summer, between a D− and an F+. This is like the results of a horse race; we know that the horse who won ran faster than the horse who placed, and the one who showed came in third. But there could have been only a 1-second difference between the first two horses, with the third trailing by 10 seconds. So letter grades and the order of finishing a race are called ordinal variables.

An ordinal variable consists of ordered categories, where the differences between categories cannot be considered to be equal.

Many of the variables encountered in the health care field are ordinal in nature. Patients are often rated as Much improved/Somewhat improved/Same/Worse/Dead; or Emergent/Urgent/Elective.[6] Sometimes numbers are used, as in Stage I through Stage IV cancer. Don't be deceived by this use of numbers; it's still an ordinal scale, with the numbers (Roman, this time, to add a bit of class) really representing nothing more than ordered categories. Use the difference test: Is the difference in disease severity between Stage I and Stage II cancer the same as exists between Stages II and III or between III and IV? If the answer is No, the scale is ordinal.

If the distance between values is constant, we've graduated to what is called an **interval variable**.

---

[4] *"Bloodshot" is usually only a temporary condition and so is not coded.*

[5] *Other examples of numbers really being nominal variables and not reflecting measured quantities would be telephone numbers, social insurance or social security numbers, credit card numbers.*

[6] *This is similar to the scheme used to evaluate employees: Walks on water/Keeps head above water under stress/Washes with water/Drinks water/Passes water in emergencies.*

An *interval variable* has equal distances between values, but the zero point is arbitrary.

Why did we add that tag on the end, "the zero point is arbitrary," and what does it mean? We added it because, as we'll see, it puts a limitation on the types of statements we can make about interval variables. What the phrase means is that the zero point isn't meaningful and therefore can be changed. To illustrate this, let's contrast intelligence, measured by some IQ test, with something such as weight, where the zero is meaningful. We all know what zero weight is.[7] We can't suddenly decide that from now on, we'll subtract 10 kilos from everything we weigh and say that something that previously weighed 11 kilos now weighs 1 kilo. It's more than a matter of semantics; if something weighed 5 kilos before, we would have to say it weighed –5 kilos after the conversion—an obvious impossibility.

An intelligence score is a different matter. We say that the average IQ is 100, but that's only by convention. The next world conference of IQ experts can just as arbitrarily decide that from now on, we'll make the average 500, simply by adding 400 to all scores. We haven't gained anything, but by the same token, we haven't lost anything; the only necessary change is that we now have to readjust our previously learned standards of what is average.

Now let's see what the implications of this are. Because the intervals are equal, the difference between an IQ of 70 and an IQ of 80 is the same as the difference between 120 and 130. However, an IQ of 100 is not twice as high as an IQ of 50. The point is that if the zero point is artificial and moveable, then the differences between numbers are meaningful, but the ratios between them are not.

If the zero point is meaningful, then the ratios between numbers are also meaningful, and we are dealing with (not surprisingly) a **ratio variable**.

A *ratio variable* has equal intervals between values and a meaningful zero point.

Most laboratory test values are ratio variables, as are physical characteristics such as height and weight. A person who weighs 100 kilos is twice as heavy as a person weighing 50 kilos; even when we convert kilos to pounds, the ratio stays the same: 220 pounds to 110 pounds.

That's about enough for the difference between interval and ratio data. The fact of the matter is that, from the viewpoint of a statistician, they can be treated and analyzed the same way.

Notice that each step up the hierarchy from ordinal data to ratio data takes the assumptions of the step below it and then adds another restriction:[8]

Variable type	Assumptions
Nominal	Named categories
Ordinal	Same as nominal plus ordered categories
Interval	Same as ordinal plus equal intervals
Ratio	Same as interval plus meaningful zero

Although the distinctions among nominal, ordinal, interval, and ratio data appear straightforward on paper, the lines between them occasionally get a bit fuzzy. For example, as we've said, intelligence is measured in IQ units, with the average person having an IQ of 100. Strictly speaking, we have no assurance that the difference between an IQ of 80 and one of 100 means the same as the difference between 120 and 140; that is, IQ most likely is an ordinal variable. In the real world outside of textbooks, though, most people treat IQ and many other such variables as if they were interval variables. As far as we know, they have not been arrested for doing so, nor has the sky fallen on their heads.

Despite this, the distinctions among nominal, ordinal, interval, and ratio are important to keep in mind because they dictate to some degree the types of statistical tests we can use with them. As we'll see in the later chapters, certain types of graphs and what are called "parametric tests" can be used with interval and ratio data but not with nominal or ordinal data.

---

[7] It's a state aspired to by "high fashion" models.

[8] A good mnemonic for remembering the order of the categories is the French word NOIR. Of course, this assumes you know French. Anglophones will just have to memorize the order.

By contrast, if you have nominal or ordinal data, you are, strictly speaking, restricted to "nonparametric" statistics. We'll get into what these obscure terms mean later in the book.

PROPORTIONS AND RATES

So far, our discussion of types of numbers has dealt with single numbers—blood pressure, course grade, or counts. Sometimes, though, we deal with fractions. Even though this is stuff we learned in grade school, there's still some confusion, owing, at least in part, to the sloppy English used by some statisticians. But, being purists, we'll try to clear the air.

A **proportion** is a type of fraction in which the numerator is a subset of the denominator. That is, when we write ⅓, we mean that there are three objects, and we're talking about one of them. Percentages are a form of proportions, where the denominator is jigged to equal 100. This may seem so elementary that you may wonder why we bother to mention it. There are two reasons. First, we'll later encounter other fractions (e.g., odds) where the numerator is not part of the denominator; and second (here's where statisticians often screw up), people sometimes call a proportion a "rate."

But, strictly speaking, a **rate** is a fraction that also has a time component. If we say that 23% of children have blue eyes (a figure we just made up on the spot), that's a proportion. But, if we say that 1 out of every 1000 people will develop photonumerophobia this year, that's a rate, because we're specifying a time interval.

So, with that as background, on to statistics!

Relative ratio is always used to measure the relative effect that expressed the outcome in one group relative to that in the other, and consists of **risk ratio** and **rate ratio** (odd ratio).

The *risk ratio* (or relative risk) is the ratio of the risk of an event in the two groups, whereas the odds ratio is the ratio of the odds of an event. For both measures a value of 1 indicates that the estimated effects are the same for both interventions.

Risk ratios (or relative risk, RR) describe the multiplication of the risk that occurs with use of the experimental intervention and simply divided the cumulative incidence in interventional group by the cumulative incidence in the non-interventional group (control group).

For example, a risk ratio of 3 for a treatment implies that events with treatment are three times more likely than events without treatment. Alternatively we can say that treatment increases the risk of events by $100 \times (RR-1)\% = 200\%$. Similarly a risk ratio of 0.25 is interpreted as the probability of an event with treatment being one-quarter of that without treatment. This may be expressed alternatively by saying that treatment decreases the risk of events by $100 \times (1-RR)\% = 75\%$. This is known as the relative risk reduction.

Odds ratios (OR) are closely related to risk ratios, but they are computed as the ratio of the incidence rate in an interventional group to the incidence rate in a control group.

For instance, women who used postmenopausal hormones had 0.47 times the rate of coronary artery disease (CAD) compared to women who did not use postmenopausal hormones. Rate ratios are often interpreted as if they were risk ratios, e.g., postmenopausal women using hormone replacement therapy (HRT) had 0.47 times the risk of CAD compared to women not using HRT, but it is more precise to refer to the ratio of rates rather than risk. To understand what an odds ratio means in terms of changes in numbers of events it is simplest to first convert it into a risk ratio, and then interpret the risk ratio in the context of a typical control group risk, as outlined above. The formula for converting an odds ratio to a risk ratio is provided $RR = OR/1 - ACR \times (1-OR)$, where ACR (assumed control risk) is the assumed control risk that can achieved from a meta-analysis.

Crude rates, as measures of morbidity or mortality, can be used for population description and may be suitable for investigations of their variations over time; however, comparisons of crude rates are often invalid because the populations may be different with respect to an important characteristic such as age, gender, or race (potential confounders).

To overcome this heterogeneity, an adjusted (or standardized) rate is used in the comparison; the adjust mentre moves the difference in composition with respect to a confounder.

Standardized rate is a summary measure to describe any rates from samples (subpopulation) in a population with adjusting the confounding factors like age in order to provide a less distorted comparison.

Direct and indirect techniques are commonly used to compute "age-adjusted" summary rates that facilitate comparisons among population. Direct standardization applies a standard age distribution to the populations being compared in order to compute summary rates indicating how overall rates would have compared if the populations had the same age distribution.

THE INDICATORS OF DEATH STATISTICS AND MORBILITY STATISTICS

In biostatistics, three types of rates are commonly mentioned: crude, specific, and adjusted (or standardized). Crude rates are computed for an entire large group or population; they disregard factors such as age, gender, and race, Specific rates consider these differences among subgroups or categories of diseases. Adjusted or standardized rates are used to make valid summary comparisons between two or more groups possessing different age distributions.

Crude death rate is defined as the number of deaths in a calendar year divided by the population on a specific time of that year (which is always an estimate).

The quotient is often multiplied by 1000 or other suitable power of 10,resulting in a number between 1 and 100 or between 1 and 1000. For example, the 1990 population of Seattle was 23 000 000 (as estimated by Jan 1) and there were 190 237 deaths during 1990, leading to crude death rate= (190 327/23 000 000)×1000=8.3death per 1000 persons per year.

Age-specific death rate is the total number of residents deaths of a specified age or age group in a specified geographic area (country, state, county, etc.) in a calendar year divided by the population of the same age or age group in the same geographic area and multiplied by the quotient.

Cause-specific death rate is the total number of resident deaths of a specific cause or resident deaths in a specific geographic area (country, state, county, etc.).

Cause-specific death rates may be adjusted for the age and sex composition, or other characteristics of the population. When that is done, for instance, in the case of age adjustment, it is called an age-adjusted rate.

Proportionate mortality describes the proportion of deaths in a specified population over a period of time attributable to different causes.

Each cause is expressed as a percentage of all deaths, and the sum of the causes must add to 100%. These proportions are not mortality rates, because the denominator is all deaths rather than the population in which the deaths occurred.

Cause-specific proportional mortality is the number of deaths from a specific cause within a population in a specific period of time divided by deaths from all causes in the same time period.

Incidence rate (sometimes called incidence) is the number of newly diagnosed cases of a disease divided by the number of persons initially at risk in a given time period (e.g. in a calendar year).

For example, if a population contains 200 women who do not have breast cancer at the beginning of the study period and 10 are diagnosed with breast cancer in the one-year observation, then we would say that the incidence of breast cancer in this population was 0.05 (or 10/2000) .

Prevalence rate (sometimes called prevalence) is the total number of diseased cases at the time of investigation divided by the total number of persons examined in the same time period.

For instance, if a measurement of breast cancer is taken in a population of 40 000 people and 1200 were recently diagnosed with breast cancer and 3500 are living with cancer, then the prevalence of breast cancer is 0.118. ((1200+3500)/40 000).

Case fatality rate (or case fatality risk, case

fatality ratio or fatality rate) is expressed as the proportion of cases diagnosed as having a specified disease who die as a result of that illness within a given period.

This case fatality rate (CFR) is a measure of the severity of a disease and is most frequently applied to a specific outbreak of acute disease in which all patients have been followed for an adequate period of time to include all attributable deaths. For instance, 9 deaths among 100 people diagnosed with the same disease in a community, The case fatality rate, therefore, would be 9%.

Cure rate is the total number of cases who are cured due to the treatment divided by the total number of cases who received the same treatment in the same time period.

THE BASIC STEPS OF STATISTICS

Statistics is more than just a collection of numbers and sets of formulas. It is a way of thinking about ways to gather and analyze data to achieve study objective. The identifying the question or hypothesis we are interested in always comes first. The gathering part comes before the analyzing part; the first thing a statistician or a learner of statistics does when faced with data is to find out how the data were collected. Not only does how we should analyze data depend on how data were collected, but formulas and techniques may be misused due to the improperly data collection. Therefore, the typical steps for statistics are displayed as follows:

1. A *study design* is a specific plan or protocol for conducting the study, which allows the investigator to translate the conceptual hypothesis into an operational one.

It have similar components: defined the hypothesis to be tested (original hypothesis); a defined population from which groups of subjects are studied; outcomes that are measures; decide which study design will be the most appropriate to test that specific study hypothesis (e.g. survey, observational studies, experimental studies).

2. *Data collection* is the process of systematically gathering and measuring information on variables of interest.

There are various methods of data collection, such as registry data, questionnaire, personal interviewing, telephone and direct observation. Depending on the types of study design, these methods can be used separately or combined.

3. *Data sorting* (sometimes also called data scrubbing) is the process of amending or removing data in a database that is incorrect, incomplete, improperly formatted, or duplicated.

It is always a two-step process including detection and then correction of errors in a data set. Common sources of errors come from missing data, typing errors on data entry, column shift, coding errors, measurement and interview errors, while most errors will be detected using descriptive statistics, scatter plots and histograms, which would be illustrate in the following chapters.

4. *Data analysis* consists of procedure and techniques to examine, extract, compile, model raw data with the purpose of drawing conclusions about population.

It uses proper procedure and techniques and check the assumptions behind the procedures and techniques. Furthermore, make conclusion and discuss the limitations (e.g. what are the answers to the original hypothesis; what are the limitations of the study; what conclusions does the study not make; what new questions arise from this study).

SUMMARY

✧ You can get known the concepts of some statistical jargon, such as population and sample, descriptive and inferential statistics, and variables. There are two ways to differentiate types of data, one is discrete versus continuous data, and another includes nominal, ordinal, interval and ratio data. Three types of rates are commonly mentioned: crude, specific, and adjusted (or standardized) in biostatistics. The typical steps for statistics are study design, data collection, data sorting and data analysis.

GLOSSARY

population　总体

sample　样本

descriptive statistics　统计描述

inferential statistics　统计推断

variable　变量

dependent variable　应变量

independent variable　自变量

discrete data　离散数据

continuous data　连续数据

nominal variable　名义变量

ordinal variable　有序变量

interval variable　区间变量

ratio variable　比率变量

risk ratio (RR)　危险比

odds ratio (OR)　优势比

crude death rate　粗死亡率

age-specific death rate　年龄别死亡率

cause-specific death rate　死因别死亡率

cause-specific proportional mortality　死因构成

incidence rate　发病率

prevalence rate　患病率

case fatality rate (CFR)　病死率

cure rate　治愈率

study design　研究设计

data collection　数据收集

EXERCISES

1. For the following studies, indicate which of the variables are *dependent* (DVs), *independent* (IVs), or neither.

   a. ASA is compared against placebo to see if it leads to a reduction in coronary events.

   The IV is _____　　The DV is _____

   b. The relationship between hypocholesterolemia and cancer.

   The IV is _____　　The DV is _____

   c. We know that members of religious groups that ban drugs, alcohol, smoking, meat, and sex (because it may lead to dancing) live longer than the rest of us poor mortals, but is it worth it? How do they compare with us on a test of quality of life?

   The IV is _____　　The DV is _____

   d. One study (a real one, this time) found that bus drivers had higher morbidity rates of coronary heart disease than did conductors. it leads to a reduction in coronary events.

   The IV is _____　　The DV is _____

2. State which of the following variables are *discrete* and which are *continuous*.

   a. The number of hair-transplant sessions undergone in the past year.

   b. The time since the last patient was grateful for what you did.

   c. Your anticipated before-taxes income the year after you graduate.

   d. Your anticipated after-taxes income in the same year.

   e. The amount of weight you've put on in the last year.

   f. The number of hairs you've lost in the same time.

3. Indicate whether the following variables are *nominal, ordinal, interval,* or *ratio.*

   a. Your income (assuming it's more than $0).

   b. A list of the different specialties in your profession.

   c. The ranking of specialties with regard to income.

   d. Bo Derek was described as a "10." What type of variable was the scale?

   e. A range of motion in degrees.

   f. A score of 13 out of 17 on the Schmedlap Anxiety Scale.

   g. Staging of breast cancer as Type Ⅰ, Ⅱ, Ⅲ, or Ⅳ.

   h. ST depression on the ECG, measured in millimeters.

   i. ST depression, measured as "1"±1 mm, "2"=1 to 5 mm, and "3"≤5 mm.

   j. ICD-9 classifications: 0295=Organic psychosis, 0296=Depression, and so on.

   k. Diastolic blood pressure, in mmHg.

   l. Pain measurement on a seven-point scale.

4. Indicate whether the following are proportions or

rates:

a. The increase in the price of household good last year.

b. The ratio of males to females.

c. The ratio of new cases of breast cancer last month to the total number of women in the population.

d. The ratio of the number of women who have breast cancer to the total number of women in the population.

5. A cohort study is conducted to determine whether smoking is associated with an increased risk of bronchitis in adults over the age of 40. The findings are as follows: The frequency of bronchitis in the smokers is 27 per 1000 person-years; The frequency of bronchitis in the non-smokers is 3 per 1000 person-years. What is the rate ratio?

a. 0.1111.

b. 0.999.

c. 9.

d. 0.0333.

e. 9 per 1000.

f. 11 per thousand.

6. A cohort study examined the association between smoking and lung cancer after following 400 smokers and 600 non-smokers for 15 years. At the conclusion of the study the investigators found a risk ratio=17. Which of the following would be the best interpretation of this risk ratio?

a. There were 17 more cases of lung cancer in the smokers.

b. Smokers had 17% more lung cancers compared to non-smokers.

c. Smokers had 17 times more risk of lung cancer than non-smokers.

d. Smokers had 17 times the risk of lung cancer compared to non-smokers.

e. 17% of the lung cancers in smokers were due to smoking.

CHAPTER THE SECOND Looking at the Data

A First Look at Graphing Data

Here we look at how to make better tables, different ways of graphing data, how to make the graphs look both accurate and esthetic, and how not to plot data.

WHY BOTHER TO LOOK AT DATA?

Now that you've suffered through all these pages of jargon, let's actually do something useful: Learn how to look at data. With the ready availability of computers on every desk, there is a great temptation to jump right in and start analyzing the bejezus out of any set of data we get. After all, we did the study in the first place to get some results that we could publish and prove to the Dean that we're doing something. However, as in most areas of our lives (especially those that are enjoyable), we must learn to control our temptations in order to become better people.

It is difficult to overemphasize the importance and usefulness of getting a "feel for the data" before starting to play with them. If there isn't a Murphy's Law to the effect that "There will be errors in your data," then there should be one. You do not look at the data just in case there are errors; they are there, and your job is to try to find as many as you can. Sometimes the problem isn't an error as such; very often, a researcher may use a code number such as 99 or 999 to indicate a missing value for some variable, and then forget to tell you this little detail when he asks you to analyze his data. As a result, you may find that some people in his study are a few years older than Methuselah. Graphing the data beforehand may well save you from one of life's embarrassing little moments.

A second purpose for looking at the data is to see if they can be analyzed by the statistical tests you're planning to use. For example, some tests require the data to fit a given shape, or that a plot of two variables follow a straight line. Although there are specific tests of these assumptions, the power of the "calibrated eyeball test" should not be underestimated. A quick look often gives you a better sense of the data than a bunch of numbers.

MAKING BETTER TABLES

There are various ways of organizing and presenting data; simple tables and graphs, however, are still very effective methods. Although there are different ways of presenting data in graphs, this is not the only way that data can be portrayed. There are times, though, when only a table of numbers will do—when we have many variables to show at the same time, or when we want the reader to see the actual numbers. It may seem at first glance as if tables were the simplest thing in the world to construct: just write the names of the variables as the headings of the columns, the subjects along the left to indicate the rows, and fill in the blanks. Table 2-1 is such a table, and it is typical of many you'll see. The countries are listed alphabetically, and the numbers are given with as much accuracy as possible.

Now, quickly—which is the largest country? The smallest? The one with the highest GNP? The lowest infant mortality rate (IMR)? If you think that was hard, imagine how hard it would be if we had listed all of the countries in Africa.[1]

Why was such a seemingly easy task so hard? The main reason is that there are too many numbers; not

---

[1] *Don't bother to check; there are 56 of them.*

TABLE 2-1   Demographic characteristics of the countries in South America

Country	Area (km²)	Population	Per capita GNP (US$)	Births/ 1000	Deaths/ 1000	IMR*
Argentina	2 776 661	28 438 000	2134	20	9	32
Bolivia	1 098 582	5 600 000	600	36	13	123
Brazil	8 506 663	110 098 992	2434	27	7	67
Chile	756 946	11 275 400	1979	21	6	18
Colombia	1 138 339	27 520 000	1190	27	7	54
Ecuador	283 561	8 354 000	1040	31	7	63
Guyana	214 970	820 000	324	31	12	49
Paraguay	406 752	2 973 000	1180	36	6	49
Peru	1 285 215	17 031 221	1850	29	8	69
Suriname	142 823	354 860	3020	27	5	40
Uruguay	186 925	2 899 000	2736	17	10	34
Venezuela	912 050	14 313 000	2058	30	6	38

*IMR = infant mortality rate/1000 live births.

that there are too many columns but that we have "unnecessary" accuracy. Don't get us wrong; accuracy is good but, like a child, only in its place. If the exact numbers are important for archival purposes then, fine, maintain as many significant digits as you can come up with, but stick the table in an appendix. For most purposes, however, so many digits give an illusion of accuracy that is often misleading. For example, the population of Brazil is given as 110 098 992.[2] By the time you finish reading that number, it's already wrong. Even assuming that the census was correct when it was taken (a dubious assumption at best in developed countries, and most likely a myth in developing ones), it was out of date almost as soon as it was recorded. If the population increases by 3% a year, then there are nearly seven additional people every minute, or almost 10 000 a day. Between the time the census was taken (and don't forget it was probably taken over a period of weeks or months), recorded by the central government, reported in an official document, reproduced in the atlas, and read by you, years may have elapsed. That number is no longer correct—if it ever was to begin with—but the last three digits give the illusion of precision.

"Inaccurate precision" can be found all over the place. If we report that the average age of one group is 43.02 years, and for another group is 44.76 years, is that last decimal place really meaningful? Bear in mind that 0.01 years represents less than four days. Making the problem worse, we probably asked people their age to the nearest year, so they were introducing a loss of accuracy from the very outset (assuming that they didn't lie about their age[3]). Finally, without glancing up the page or at the table, do you remember the exact population of Brazil? Probably not; if you're like most people, you'll remember that it was somewhat over 110 million, but that final "90 992" has gone by the board. The moral of this story is to round, and then round again—keep enough digits to highlight important differences, and no more.

In Table 2-2, we've done some rounding. Now let's try the same exercise again: Which is the largest country? The smallest? The one with the highest GNP? The lowest IMR? That was much easier, wasn't it? Getting rid of unnecessary digits made the table much easier to comprehend. However, we can go even further. Keeping the countries in alphabetical order makes sense if this table is referred to often,

---

[2] All of whom squeeze into one stadium every Sunday to watch the soccer match.

[3] Isn't it somewhat passing strange that people will lie about their age, but not about their year of birth?

TABLE 2-2   Data from Table 2-1, with rounding introduced

Country	Area (100 000 km²)	Population (1 000 000)	Per capita GNP (US$100)	Births/ 1000	Deaths/ 1000	IMR*
Argentina	28	28	21	20	9	32
Bolivia	11	6	6	36	13	123
Brazil	85	110	24	27	7	67
Chile	8	11	20	21	6	18
Colombia	11	28	12	27	7	54
Ecuador	3	8	10	31	7	63
Guyana	2	0.8	3	31	12	49
Paraguay	4	3	12	36	6	49
Peru	13	17	19	29	8	69
Suriname	1	0.3	30	27	5	40
Uruguay	2	3	27	17	10	34
Venezuela	9	14	21	30	6	38

*IMR = infant mortality rate/1000 live births.

or for a number of different purposes. But if there is one major point you want to make, such as focusing on the IMR, it would be even better to list the countries in order, ranging from the one with the highest IMR to the lowest (or vice versa). Then, ask yourself, Are the other columns really necessary? If you want to relate the IMR to the size of the country or to other indices of health such as the birth and death rates, then keep them; otherwise, out they go

(or into an appendix). This also means that it may be worthwhile to reorder the columns; if IMR is the most important point of the table, list it first. If you want to relate it primarily to other health indices, then the birth and death rates are next, followed by the country's per capita income and size.

Finally, use spaces to highlight clusters, as in Table 2-3 in which information is arranged logically for you. For example, Bolivia seems to be in its own

TABLE 2-3   Data from Table 2-2, reordered and with spaces

Country	IMR*	Births/ 1000	Deaths/ 1000	Per capita GNP (US$100)	Population (1 000 000)	Area (100 000 km²)
Bolivia	123	36	13	6	6	11
Peru	69	29	8	19	17	13
Brazil	67	27	7	24	110	85
Ecuador	63	31	7	10	8	3
Colombia	54	27	7	12	28	11
Guyana	49	31	12	3	0.8	2
Paraguay	49	36	6	12	3	4
Suriname	40	27	5	30	0.3	1
Venezuela	38	30	6	21	14	9
Uruguay	34	17	10	27	3	2
Argentina	32	20	9	21	28	28
Chile	18	21	6	20	11	8

*IMR = infant mortality rate/1000 live births.

class, with an IMR that is quite a bit higher than that of the next country. Then, there appears to be a group of countries with a gradation of similar IMRs, and Chile is by itself, with the lowest IMR.[4] Those divisions are totally arbitrary; if you feel that there should be a break between Paraguay and Suriname, for instance, you can put one in; we're flexible.

HISTOGRAMS, BAR CHARTS, AND VARIATIONS ON A THEME

Perhaps the most effective and most convenient way of presenting data is through the use of graphs. Graphs convey the information, the general pattern in a set of data, at a single glance. Therefore, graphs are often easier to read than tables, the most information graphs are simple and self-explanatory. Of course, to achieve that objective, graphs should be constructed carefully. Like tables, they should be clearly labelled and units of measurement and/or magnitude of quantities should be included. Graphs must tell their own story; they should be complete in themselves and require little or no additional explanation.

The Basic Theme: The Bar Chart

Perhaps the most familiar types of graphs to most people are **bar charts** and **histograms** (we'll tell you what the difference is in a little bit). In essence, they consist of a bar whose length is proportional to the number of cases. To illustrate it, let's conduct a "gedanken experiment."[5] Imagine we do a study in which we survey 100 students and ask them what their most boring course was in college. We can then tabulate the data as is shown in Table 2-4.

The first step is to choose an appropriate length for the *Y*-axis, where we'll plot (at least for now) the number of people who chose each alternative. The largest number in the table is 42, so we will choose some number somewhat larger than this for the top of the axis. Because we'll label the tick points every

TABLE 2-4 Responses of 100 students to the question, "What was your most boring introductory course?"

Course	Number of students
Sociology	25
Economics	42
History	8
Psychology	13
Calculus	13

10 units, 50 would be a good choice. If we had used the number 42, we would have had to label the axis either every 7 units (which are somewhat bizarre numbers[6]), or every even number, which would make the axis look too cluttered. So, our graph would look like Figure 2-1.

At first glance, this doesn't look too bad! However, we can make it look even better. It's obvious that the data are nominal; the order is arbitrary, so we can change the categories around without losing anything. In fact, we gain something if we rank the courses so that the highest count is first and the lowest one is last. Now the relative standing of the courses is more readily apparent. (As a minor point,

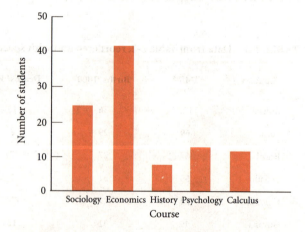

FIGURE 2-1 Bar chart of the five least popular courses.

---

[4] It's probably no coincidence that they also produce the finest wine in South America. On the other hand, have you ever tasted Bolivian wine? We rest our case.

[5] This is a German term, popularized by Albert Einstein, meaning "thought experiment." It is used here simply for purposes of pretentiousness.

[6] Tast! Count by sevens, starting at 1 and ending at 64. See what we mean?

it's often better to put the tick marks outside the axes rather than in. When the data fall near the Y-axis, a tick mark inside the axis may obscure the data point, or vice versa.) Making these two changes gives us Figure 2-2.

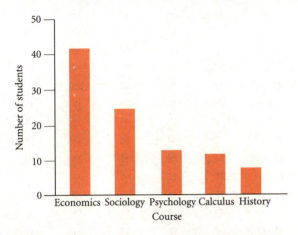

FIGURE 2-2   redrawn so that the categories are in order of preference and the tick marks are outside the axes.

This is the way most bar charts of nominal data looked until recently. Within recent years, though, things have been turned on their ear—literally. If the names of the categories are long, things can look pretty cluttered down there on the bottom. Also, some research (Cleveland, 1984) has shown that people get a more accurate grasp of the relative sizes of the bars if they are placed horizontally. Adding this twist (pun intended), we'll end up with Figure 2-3.

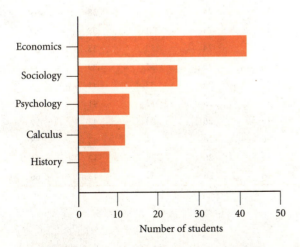

FIGURE 2-3   redrawn so that the bars are horizontal.

Variation 1: Dot Plots

Another variant of the bar chart that is particularly useful when there are many categories is the dot plot, as shown in Figure 2-4. Instead of a bar, just a heavy dot is placed where the end of the bar would be. When there are many labels, smaller dots that extend back to the labeled axis are often used to make the chart easier to read.

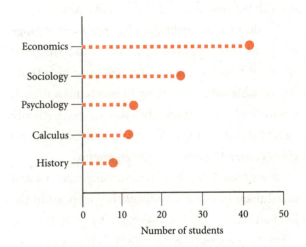

FIGURE 2-4   redrawn as a point graph.

Graphing Ordinal Data

The use of bar charts isn't limited to nominal data; it can be used with all four types. However, a few other considerations should be kept in mind when using them with ordinal, interval, and ratio data. The first, which would seem obvious, is that because the values are ordered, you can't blithely move the categories around simply to make the graph look prettier. If you were graphing the number of students who received Excellent/Satisfactory/Unsatisfactory ratings, it would confuse more than help if you put them in the order: Satisfactory/Excellent/Unsatisfactory just because most students were in the first category.

Graphing Interval and Ratio Data

A few other factors have to be considered in graphing interval and ratio data. Let's say we have some data on the number of tissues dispensed each day by a group of 75 social workers. We look at our data, and we find that the lowest number is 10 and the highest is 117. The difference between the highest and lowest value is 107 (This difference is called the **range**. We'll define it a bit more formally later in the next chapter). If we have one bar for each value, we'll run into a few problems. First, we have more possible values than data points, so some bars will have a "height" of zero units, and many others will be only one or two units high. This leads to the second problem, in that it will be hard to discern any pattern by eyeballing the data. Third, the X-axis is going to get awfully cluttered. For these reasons, we try to end up with between 10 and 20 bars on the axis.[7]

To do this, we make each bar represent a range of numbers; what we refer to as the **interval width**. If possible, use a width that most people are comfortable with: 2, 5, 10, or 20 points. Even though a width of 6 or 7 may give you an aesthetically beautiful picture, these don't yield multiples that are easily comprehended. Let's use an example.

If we took 100 fourth-year nursing students and asked them how many bedpans they emptied in the last month, we'd get 100 answers, as in Table 2-5. The main thing a table like this tells us is that it's next to impossible to make sense of a table like this. We're overwhelmed by the sheer mass of numbers, and no pattern emerges. In fact, it's very hard even to figure out what the highest and lowest numbers are; who's been working like a Trojan and who's been goofing off. To make our lives (and all of the next steps) easier, the first thing we should do is to put the data in rank order,[8] starting with the smallest number and ending with the highest. Two notes are in order. First, you can go from highest to lowest if you wish, it makes no difference. Second, most computers have a simple routine, usually called SORT, to do the job for you. Once we do this, we'll end up with Table 2-6.

With this table we can immediately see the highest and lowest values and get at least a rough feel for how the numbers are distributed; not too many between 1 and 10 or between 60 and 70, and many in the 20s and 30s. We also see that the range (66–1) = 65; far too large to graph when letting each bar stand for a unique number. An interval width of 10 would

TABLE 2-5   Number of bedpans emptied by 100 fourth-year nursing students in the past month

Student	Data				
1~5	43	45	16	37	33
6~10	41	24	11	34	51
11~15	14	29	55	9	25
16~20	31	24	24	28	16
21~25	35	36	14	15	18
26~30	36	27	42	7	43
31~35	45	32	42	46	14
36~40	57	16	27	34	12
41~45	32	30	26	25	1
46~50	58	26	19	17	35
51~55	32	17	31	22	16
56~60	42	28	26	36	51
61~65	52	28	15	38	49
66~70	21	11	66	37	35
71~75	37	41	11	27	43
76~80	7	20	56	13	61
81~85	38	38	39	54	31
86~90	26	24	43	38	33
91~95	34	12	52	47	25
96~100	26	17	7	22	54

TABLE 2-6   Data from Table 2-5 put in rank order

1	17	26	35	43
7	17	27	35	43
7	17	27	35	43
7	18	27	36	45
9	19	28	36	46
11	20	28	36	46
11	21	28	37	47
11	22	29	37	49
12	22	30	37	51
12	24	31	38	51
13	24	31	38	51
14	24	31	38	52
14	24	32	38	52
14	25	32	39	54
15	25	33	41	56
15	25	33	41	56
16	26	33	42	57
16	26	34	42	58
16	26	34	42	61
16	26	34	43	66

---

[7] Note that this dictum is based on esthetics, not statistics.

[8] No pun is intended; it really is called "rank" order, even when the data aren't as smelly.

give us 7 boxes (not quite enough for our esthetic sense), whereas a width of 2 would result in 33 boxes (which is still too many). A width interval of 5 yields 14 boxes (which is just right). To help us in drawing the graph, we could make up a summary table, such as Table 2-7, which gives the interval and the number of subjects in that interval.

TABLE 2-7   A summary of Table 2-6, showing the intervals, midpoints, counts, and cumulative total

Interval	Midpoint	Count	Cumulative total
0~4	2	1	1
5~9	7	4	5
10~14	12	9	14
15~19	17	11	25
20~24	22	8	33
25~29	27	15	48
30~34	32	12	60
35~39	37	14	74
40~44	42	9	83
45~49	47	5	88
50~54	52	6	94
55~59	57	4	98
60~64	62	1	99
65~69	67	1	100

There are a few things to notice about this table. First, there are two extra columns, one labelled *Midpoint* and the other labelled *Cumulative Total*. The first is just what the name implies: It is the middle of the interval. Because the first interval consists of the numbers 0, 1, 2, 3, and 4, the midpoint is 2. If there were an even number of numbers, say 0, 1, 2, and 3, then the midpoint would again be in the middle. This time, though, it would fall halfway between the 1 and 2, and we would label it 1.5. The other added column, the Cumulative Total, is simply a running sum of the number of cases; the first interval had 1 case, and the second 4, so the cumulative total at the second interval is (1+4)= 5. The 9 cases in the third interval then produce a cumulative total of (5+9)=14. This is very handy because, if we didn't end up with 100 at the bottom, we would know that we messed up the addition somewhere along the line. The other point to notice

is the interval. The first one goes from 0 to 4, the second from 5 to 9, and so on. Don't fall into the trap of saying an interval width of 5 covers the numbers 0 to 5; that's actually 6 digits.

Another point to notice is that we've paid a price for grouping the data to make it more readable, and that price is the loss of some information. We can tell from Table 2-7 that 1 person emptied between 0 and 4 bedpans, but we don't know exactly how many. In the next interval, we see that 4 people emptied between 5 and 9 pans, but again we're not sure precisely how many future nurses dumped what number of bedpans. The wider the interval, the more information is lost.

So, with these points in mind, we're almost ready to start drawing the graph. There's one last consideration, though: how to label the two axes. Looking at the count column in Table 2-7, we can see that the maximum number of cases in any one interval is 15. We would therefore want the Y-axis to extend from 0 to some number over 15. A good choice would be 20, because this would allow us to label every fifth tick mark. Notice that on the X-axis, we've labeled the middle of the interval. If we labeled every possible number, the axis would look too cluttered; the midpoint cuts down on the clutter and (for reasons we'll explore further in the next chapter) is the best single summary of the interval. Our end product would look like Figure 2-5.

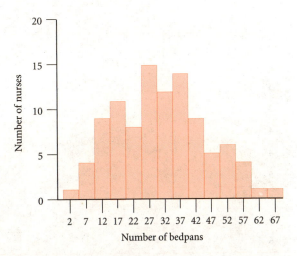

FIGURE 2-5   Histogram showing the number of bedpans emptied during the past month by each of 100 nursing students.

This figure differs from Figure 2-2 in a subtle way. In the earlier figure, because each category was different from every other one, we left a bit of a gap between bars. In Figure 2-5, the data are interval, so it makes both statistical as well as esthetic sense[9] to have each bar abutting its neighbors. Now we can finally tell you the difference between bar charts and histograms:

Bar charts: There are spaces between the bars.
Histograms: The bars touch each other.

STEM-LEAF PLOTS AND RELATED FLORA

All these variants of histograms and bar charts are the traditional ways of taking a mess of data such as we found in Table 2-5 and transforming them into a graph such as Figure 2-5. The steps were as follows:

1. Rank order the data.

2. Find the range (the highest value minus the lowest).

3. Choose and appropriate width to yield about 10 to 20 intervals.

4. Make a new table consisting of the intervals, their midpoints, the count, and a cumulative total.

5. Turn this into a histogram.

6. Lose some information along the way, consisting of the exact values.

Tukey (1977) devised a way to eliminate steps 1 and 6 and to combine 4 and 5 into one step. The resulting diagram, called a **Stem-and-Leaf Plot**, thus consists of only three steps:

1. Find the range.

2. Choose an appropriate width to yield about 10 to 20 intervals.

3. Make a new table that looks like a histogram and preserves the original data.

Let's take a look and see how this is done, at the same time explaining these somewhat odd-sounding terms. The "leaf" consists of the least significant digit of the number, and the "stem" is the most significant. So, for the number 94, the leaf is "4" and the stem is "9". If our data included numbers such as 167, we would make the "16" the stem. Using the data from Table 2-6 and the same reasoning we did for the histogram, we would again opt for an interval width of 5. We then write the stems we need, vertically, as in Table 2-8 (it's best to do this on graph paper, for reasons that will be readily apparent if you'll just be patient).

TABLE 2-8   First step in constructing a Stem-and-Leaf Plot: Writing the stems

Stem	Leaf
0	
0	
1	
1	
2	
2	
3	
3	
4	
4	
5	
5	
6	
6	

[9] Is "esthetic sense" an oxymoron?

No, you are not seeing double. Table 2-8 really does have two 0s, two 1s, and so on. The reason is that, because we've chosen an interval width of 5, the first 0 will contain the numbers 0 to 4. Strictly speaking, the 0 is the stem of the numbers 00 (zero) to 04 (four). The second interval covers the numbers 5 (05) to 9 (09); the first 1 is the stem for the numbers 10 to 14, the second for the numbers 15 to 19, and so on. Now, we go back to our original data and write the leaf of each number next to the appropriate stem. For example, the first number in Table 2-5 is 43, so we put a 3 (the leaf) next to the first 4. The second number, reading across, is 45 so we put a 5 next to the second 4, because this stem contains the intervals 45 to 49. If you did what we told you to earlier, and used graph paper, each leaf would be put in a separate and adjacent horizontal box. Table 2-9 shows a plot of the first 10 numbers, and Table 2-10 is the stem-and-leaf plot of all 100 numbers.

TABLE 2-9   Stem-and-Leaf Plot of the first 10 items of Table 2-5

Stem	Leaf															
0																
0																
1	1															
1	6															
2	4															
2																
3	3	4														
3	7															
4	3	1														
4	5															
5	1															
5																
6																
6																

TABLE 2-10   Stem-and-Leaf Plot of all the data in Table 2-5

Stem	Leaf															
0	1															
0	9	7	7	7												
1	1	4	4	4	2	1	1	3	2							
1	6	6	5	8	6	9	7	7	6	5	7					
2	4	4	4	2	1	0	4	2								
2	9	5	8	7	7	6	5	6	8	6	8	7	6	5	6	
3	3	4	1	2	4	2	0	2	1	1	3	4				
3	7	5	6	6	5	6	8	7	5	7	8	8	9	8		
4	3	1	2	3	2	2	1	3	3							
4	5	5	6	9	7											
5	1	1	2	4	2	4										
5	5	7	8	6												
6	1															
6	6															

If you turn Table 2-10 sideways, you'll see it has exactly the same shape as Figure 2-5. Moreover, the original data are preserved. Let's take the third line down, the first stem with a 1. Reading across, we can see that the actual numbers were 11, 14, 14, 14, 12, 11, 11, 13, and 12. If we want to be a bit fancier, we can actually rank order the numbers within each stem. Computer programs that produce stem-leaf plots (see the end of this chapter) do this for you automatically. Most journals still prefer histograms or bar charts rather than stem-leaf plots, but this is slowly changing. In any case, it's simple to go from the plot to the more traditional forms.

Line Graphs

A line graph is similar to a bar graph, but the horizontal axis represents time. The most suitable application to use line graphs is a binary characteristic which is observed repeated over time. The measures are observed in a consecutive year, so that a line graph is suitable to illustrate how certain proportions change over time. In a line graph, the proportion associated with each year is represented by a point at the appropriate height; the points are then connected by straight lines.

For example, between the years 1986 and 1989, the crude death rates for women in the United States were as listed in Table 2-11. The change in crude death rate for U.S. women can be represented by the line graph shown in Figure 2-6. In addition to their use with proportions, line graphs can be used to describe changes in the number of occurrences and with continuous measurements.

TABLE 2-11   Crude death rates between 1986 and 1989 in U.S.

Year	Crude death rate per 100 000
1986	809.6
1987	813.3
1988	819.2
1989	831.1

Box Plot

In descriptive statistics, a box plot is a convenient way of graphically depicting the location, spread and direction of skewness from groups of numerical

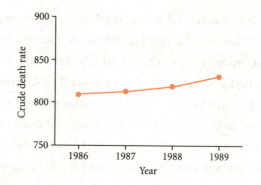

FIGURE 2-6   Crude death rate between 1986 and 1989 in U.S..
The line graph shown in Figure 2-6 displayed the trend in rates of malaria reported in U.S. between 1986 and 1989 (proportions× 100 000 as above).

data through their quartiles.It can also allow for identification of the outliers, which are those out of the lines extending vertically from the boxes (*whiskers*) indicating variability outside the upper and lower quartiles, hence the terms as box-and-whisker plot and box-and-whisker diagram. Outliers may be plotted as individual points. Box plots are non-parametric: they display variation in samples of a statistical population without making any assumptions of the underlying statistical distribution. The spacings between the different parts of the box indicate the degree of dispersion (spread) and skewness in the data, and show outliers.Types of box plots:the bottom and top of the box are always the first and third quartiles, and the band inside the box is always the second quartile (the median). But the ends of the whiskers can represent several possible alternative values, e.g the minimum and maximum of all of the data; the lowest datum still within 1.5 interquartile range (IQR) of the lower quartile, and the highest datum still within 1.5 IQR of the upper quartile (often called the Tukey boxplot shown in Figure 2-7); one standard deviation above and below the mean of the data; the 9th percentile and the 91st percentile; the 2nd percentile and the 98th percentile.

Imagine if you will a course in Academish IA7 for young, contractually limited, tenureless, assistant profs. As one exercise, they are required to open a dictionary to a random page, pick the three longest words, and practice and rehearse them until they roll off their lips as if Mommy had put them there.

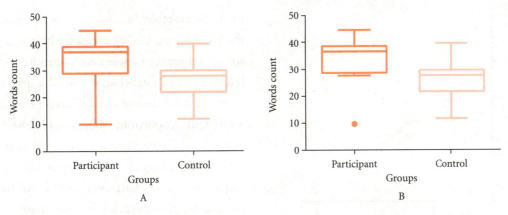

FIGURE 2-7   Box plot (Min and Max and Tukey) of words that could not be understood.
In Figure 2-7A, the whiskers indicated the minimum and maximum of all of the data, the bottom and top of the box are always the first and third quartiles, and the band inside the box is the median, while Figure 2-7B is Tukey box plot with the whiskers of 1.5 interquartile range (IQR) of the lower quartile and 1.5 IQR of the upper quartile.

Of course, not wanting to pass up on a potential publication, graduate students are required to attend a lecture from one of the graduands and some other prof from the control group and count all the words that could not be understood.

Error Bar Graph

Error bars are a graphical representation of the data variability and are used to indicate the error, or uncertainty of measurements. They give a general description of how precise the measurement is away from the reported statistics. Error bars often represent one standard deviation, one standard error. These quantities are not the same and so the measure selected should be stated explicitly in the graph or supporting text. Error bars can be expressed in a plus and/or minus sign ($\pm$), plus the upper limit of the error and minus the lower limit of the error.

See Table 2-12 after the data are analyzed, the graduands ($n_1=11$) used a mean and standard deviation of 33.82 and 9.44 obscure words, respectively. A comparable group ($n_2=11$) who didn't take the course used a mean 26.64 and standard deviation 7.30 such words in their lectures. Did the course succeed? In Figure 2-8, the height of bars indicated the means for two groups and the error bar is the standard deviation of data from each group.

TABLE 2-12   Box plot of words that could not be understood

Participant	Controls
35	22
31	25
29	23
45	12
28	29
39	30
41	28
37	30
39	33
38	21
10	40

Scatter Plot

Scatter plots are similar to line graphs because they use horizontal and vertical axes to plot data points as shown in Figure 2-9. However, it shows how much one variable is affected by another. The relationship between two variables is called their correlation. If the data points make a straight line going from the origin out to high x-and y-values, then the variables have a positive correlation, while if the line goes from

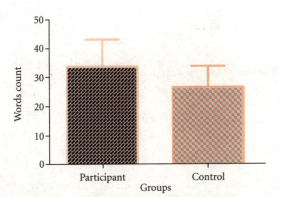

FIGURE 2-8   Error bar chart of words that could not be understood.

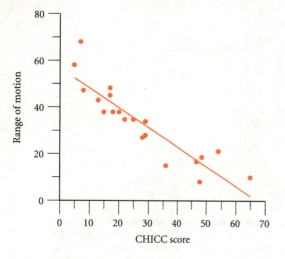

FIGURE 2-9   Scatter plot.

a high-value on the *Y*-axis down to a high-value on the *X*-axis, the variables have a negative correlation. A perfect positive correlation is given the value of 1. A perfect negative correlation is given the value of −1. If there is absolutely no correlation present the value given is 0. The closer the number is to 1 or −1, the stronger the correlation, or the stronger the relationship between the variables. The closer the number is to 0, the weaker the correlation.

Pie Chart

Pie chart is another popular type of graph. In practice, when it comes to pie chart, there is only one group but we want to decompose it into several categories. A pie chart consists of a circle which is divided into wedges that correspond to the magnitude of the proportions for various categories. pie chart shows the differences between the sizes of various categories or subgroups as a decomposition of the

total. For example, In Table 2-4, for use in presenting the boring introductory courses, where we can easily see the difference between each introductory course. In other words, a bar chart is a suitable graphic device when we have several groups, each associated with a different proportion; whereas a pie chart is more suitable when we have one group that is divided into several categories. The proportions of various categories in a pie chart should add up to 100%. Like bar charts, the categories in a pie chart are usually arranged by the size of the proportions as in Figure 2-10. They may also be arranged alphabetically or on some other rational basis.

HOW *NOT* TO GRAPH

As the old joke goes, "We have some good news and some bad news." The good news is that every spreadsheet program, slide presentation program, and statistics program now can make graphs for you at the press of a button; you simply have to enter the data. The bad news is that, almost without exception, they do it extremely badly. Many of the choices are worse than useless, and most default options are just plain wrong. In this section, we'll discuss some very useless and misleading (albeit very pretty) ways of presenting data.

Do You Really Need a Graph?

Before we begin to discuss bad graphs, let's decide whether a graph is even needed. Take a look at Figure 2-11. It shows the number of males and females in some study. In other words, it conveys one bit of information—the proportion of males is 54%. (Even

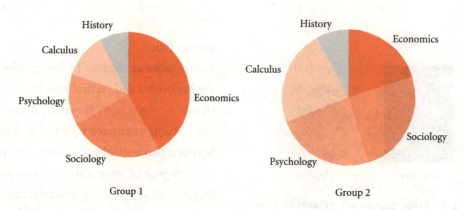

Group 1   Group 2

FIGURE 2-10   Comparing two groups using pie charts.

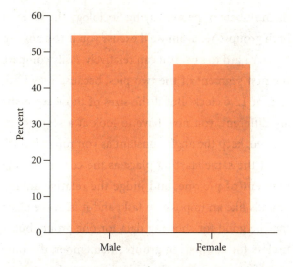

FIGURE 2-11 The proportion of males and females in a study.

though you haven't gotten too far into this book yet, we bet you can figure out that the proportion of females is 46%.) Do you need a graph, something that takes up about ¼ of a page, to tell you that? We can convey the same information in one sentence, which takes about 15 seconds to write and 2 seconds to read; we don't have to waste 30 minutes drawing a figure. Use graphs to show relationships, not to report numbers.

The Case of the Missing Zero

Dr.X[10] wants to be considered for early promotion. To support his petition, he submits a graph, shown in Figure 2-12, to show that the amount of grant money he has received has risen dramatically in the past year. So, should he be promoted?

Not if this graph is any indication of the quality of his work. From the picture, it looks as though there has been almost a threefold increase in his funding (the actual value is about 275%). The reality is that it went from a measly $11 000 to a paltry $15 000, an increase of only 37%. The problem is with the Y-axis. Instead of starting at zero, it begins at $10,000, so that small differences are magnified. We see examples of this every day on TV or in the newspapers; it looks as though the temperature or the stock market is fluctuating wildly, because the axis doesn't start at zero.

One way to check on this distortion is to use the Graph Discrepancy Index (GDI), which is simply:

$$GDI = \frac{\text{Size of the effect in the graph}}{\text{Size of the effect in the data}} - 1 \quad (2\text{-}1)$$

In this case, it's (275/37) −1=6.43. That's a tad higher than the recommended value of the GDI, which is 0.05 (Beattie and Jones, 1992). Gotcha, Dr. X!

3-D or Not 3-D, That is the Question

The bar charts and histograms that we've shown you so far look pretty drab and ordinary. Wouldn't it be nice if we jazzed them up a bit by making them look three dimensional, or used fancier objects instead of just rectangles, or if we added shading, or converted them to pie charts? No, it would not be nice; it will just be confusing.

Let's take Figure 2-2 and make it look sexy by adding some of the features we've just mentioned.

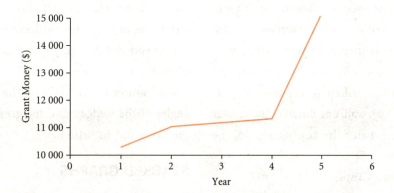

FIGURE 2-12 Grant money per year for Dr. X.

---

[10] *We're using a pseudonym to protect his identity. His real name is Dr. Y.*

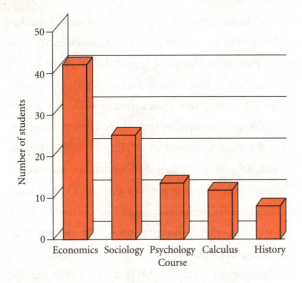

FIGURE 2-13   A 3-D version of Figure 2-2.

Golly gee, Figure 2-13 looks hot! But quickly now, how many students said Economics? You're excused if you said 39. You'd be wrong—the real answer is 42—but we'll excuse you, because we're nice guys. The problem is that the leading edge of the bar, which is where your eye is drawn, is just below the 40. The true value is actually indicated by the back edge of the bar, which confuses both the eye and its owner. For bars farther from the left side of the graph, we have to follow an imaginary line to the Y-axis, make a turn, and then follow another imaginary line to where the legend is—a process that's prone to error at every step. Compounding the problem, the back of the bar is not flush with the back wall, so the top of the bar is not at 40—you have to continue an invisible line until it hits the wall, two units above the top. As if that isn't enough, the major purveyor of software (which will remain unnamed, but they make PowerPoint, Word, and other products) is inconsistent in this regard. Graph exactly the same data with PowerPoint and with Excel and you'll get different results—one puts the bars against the back wall, one doesn't. The greater the 3-D effect, the greater the confusion. So, the bottom line is, lose the 3-D.

Pie in the Sky, Not in a Graph

Now let's take the same data to make a pie chart and use it to compare two groups, as in Figure 2-10. Are the numbers of people saying Sociology the same in both groups? Yet again we'll excuse you if you answer, "That's hard to say." You can relatively easily compare the first segment of the two pies, because they both start at 12 o'clock. But if the sizes of those segments are different, you now have to look at a segment of pie two, keep the angle constant as you rotate it until it's at the same starting place as the corresponding segment of pie one, and judge the relative angles. Sounds like an impossible task, and it is. A pie chart may be good for showing data for one group, but is useless for comparing groups. Remember, the only place for a pie chart is at a baker's convention.

"But," we hear you say, "you can simply put numbers inside or next to the wedges, and that will remove any ambiguity." Let's keep in mind the difference between a table and a graph. A graph is ideal for giving the reader a very quick grasp of relationships that exist in the data; is there a trend over time, or does one group differ from another? If the precise numbers are important, use a table. Don't mix up these two functions: communicating a picture, or reporting data.

The Worst of Both Worlds

Take a look at Figure 2-14. Quickly now, answer two questions: (a) put the segments in rank order; and (b) tell us how much bigger is segment D than segment C. If you struggled to put A through C in order, and couldn't easily say how much bigger D is, then we would say, "Gotcha!" The answers are: (a) segments A, B, and C are all equal, and (b) D is twice as big as each of them. Had the data been presented as a bar chart, the answers would have been obvious. The reason you had difficulty is that not only is this a pie chart, but it's a 3-D pie chart, thus incorporating the worst features of each. Tilting the graph distorts the angles of the wedges, and the greater the 3-D effect, the worse the distortion.

STACKED GRAPHS

For a change, we're not making some sort of sexist joke.[11] Rather, we're talking about graphs, much

---

[11]*Although heaven knows we can think of quite a few.*

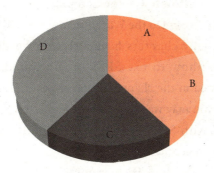

FIGURE 2-14   A 3D-pie chart.

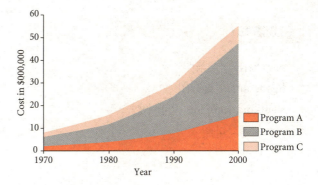

FIGURE 2-16   A stacked line graph.

beloved by newspapers and magazines, where different values of a variable are placed on top of one another. Figure 2-15 is a stacked bar graph showing the marital status in three groups. As with a pie chart, we have no trouble comparing the groups with respect to the proportion married or single, because they have a common axis (the top or bottom of the graph). But, what about those who are widowed? To compare the groups, we have to try to keep the height of the segment in our mind while shifting the bases until they all line up, and then see if the heights are comparable; not an easy task by any means. These data would either be better presented in a table, or using separate bars for each category of marital status.

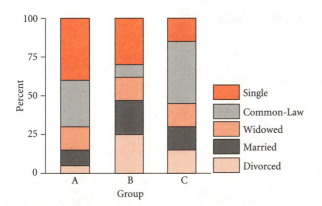

FIGURE 2-15   A stacked bar chart.

In Figure 2-16, we show the annual cost of three programs over time in a stacked line chart. This type of graph is fine if we want to see what's happening to the *total* cost of the three, but it's terrible for looking at the contributions of each. Which program

is growing the fastest? The reality is that Programs A and B are increasing geometrically each decade (e.g., 2, 4, 8, 16), whereas C is only increasing arithmetically (2, 4, 6, 8). Hard to tell, isn't it? The bottom line—don't use it.

Conclusion

We'll close with a beautiful quote from Howard Wainer (1990): "Although I shudder to consider it, perhaps there is something to be learned from the success enjoyed by the multi-colored, three-dimensional pie charts that clutter the pages of USA Today, Time, and Newsweek. I sure hope not much."

SUMMARY

✧ Simple tables and graphs are usually used to organize and present data. The commonly used graphs have bar charts, histograms, stem-leaf plots, pie chart and line chart. Bar charts is suitable for all four types and histograms is suitable for interval and ration data. Stem-leaf plots is more simple than traditional graphs, the "leaf" consists of the least significant digit of the number, and the "stem" is the most significant. Pie chart is more suitable when we have one group that is divided into several categories. Line chart is most suitable for a binary characteristic which is observed repeated over time. For graphing data, you shall know that more simple, more clear, more complex, more confuse.

GLOSSARY

bar charts　直条图

histograms　直方图

stem-and-leaf plot　茎叶图

pie chart　饼图

line chart　线图

EXERCISES

Let's take another look at some of the variables we used in the exercises for Chapter 1, as well as a few others to minimize boredom. This time, though, indicate what type of graph you'd use to present the data (bar chart, histogram, frequency polygon, or something else). Just to keep you on your toes, there is sometimes more than one correct answer.

1. Number of hair transplant sessions per person.
2. Time since the last patient indicated his/her gratitude.
3. The number of patients with 0, 1, or 2+ vessels with > 75% stenosis.
4. Before-taxes income.
5. Income for the different specialties in your profession.
6. Range of wrist motion for 100 patients.
7. Schmedlap Anxiety Inventory scores for 128 people.

How to Get the Computer to Do the Work for You

Note: Many chapters have a section on the end showing how to use SPSS to run the analyses mentioned in the chapter. If you've never used SPSS before, you may want to look at Chapter 29, "Getting Started with SPSS," before you begin. It's a basic tutorial on getting started.

Histograms

- From **Graphs**, choose **Bar**
- The default is **Simple**; keep it and then click the Define button
- Click the name of the variable you want to graph from the list on the left, and click the arrow next to **Category Axis**
- You can name the axes by clicking the but-ton marked **Titles**
- Click OK

Stem-and-Leaf Plots

- From **Analyze**, choose **Descriptive Statistics → Explore**
- Click the Plots button
- Choose **Stem-and-Leaf** and click the Continue button
- Click the name of the variable you want to graph from the list on the left, and click the arrow next to **Dependent List**
- Click OK

CHAPTER THE THIRD
Describing the Data with Numbers

Measures of Central Tendency and Dispersion

In this chapter, we discuss how to summarize the data with just a few numbers: measures of central tendency (such as the mean, median, and geometric mean), and measures of dispersion (such as the range, interquartile range, and standard deviation).

SETTING THE SCENE

Graphing the data is a necessary first step in data analysis, but it has two limitations. First, if someone asks you to describe the essence of what you found, all you can do is find a blank or even used but have blank place paper, and draw a graph. Second, there's not much we can do with the results, except show them; we can't easily compare the results of two or more different groups or see if they differ in important ways.[1]It would be helpful if we could summarize the results with just a few numbers. Not surprisingly, those numbers exist. The two most important are measures of central tendency and of dispersion. (We will later discuss two other indices, called "skewness" and "kurtosis.")

However, before we introduce these two terms, a brief diversion is in order to introduce some of the shorthand notation that is used in statistics.

A SLIGHT DIGRESSION INTO NOTATION

A specific data point—that is, the value of a variable for one subject—is represented by the capital letter X. The small letter x is used to denote something different, which we'll get to later in this chapter. In Table 2-2 for subject 1, $X=43$. We denote the *mean* (see below for definition) of a variable by putting a bar over the capital letter X: $\overline{X}$. When speaking to another statistician, we can say either the "mean" or the "X bar."[2]

The number of subjects in the sample is represented by n. There is no convention on whether to use uppercase or lowercase, but most books use a lowercase n to indicate the sample size for a group when there are two or more and use the upper case N to show the entire sample, summed over all groups. If there is only one group, take your pick and you'll find someone who'll support your choice. If there are two or more groups, how do we tell which one the n refers to? Whenever we want to differentiate between numbers, be they sample sizes, data points, or whatever, we use subscript notation. That is, we put a subscript after the letter to let us know what it refers to—n_1 would be the sample size for group 1, X_3 the value of X for subject 3, and so on.

To indicate adding up a series of numbers, we use the symbol $\sum$, which is the uppercase Greek letter sigma. (The lowercase sigma, σ, has a completely different meaning, which we'll discuss shortly.) If there is any possible ambiguity about the summation, we can show explicitly which numbers are being added, using the subscript notation:

$$\sum_{i=1}^{n} X_i \qquad (3\text{-}1)$$

---

[1]*Even more important, there wouldn't be any work for statisticians, and they'd have to find an honest profession.*

[2]*"X bar" means "the arithmetic mean (AM)"; it is not the name of a drinking place for divorced statisticians (see the glossary at the end of the book).*

We read this as, "Sum over X-sub-*i*, as *I* goes from 1 to *n*." This is just a fancy way of saying "Add all the *X*s, one for each of the *n* subjects."

X refers to a single data point. X_i is the value of *X* for subject *i*. n_j is the number of subjects (sample size) in group *j*. *n* is the total sample size. $\overline{X}$ is the arithmetic mean. $\sum$ means to sum.

Later in this book, we'll get even fancier, and even show you some more Greek. But for now, that's enough background and we're ready to return to the main feature.

MEASURES OF CENTRAL TENDENCY

The Mean

Just to break the monotony, let's begin by discussing interval and ratio data and work our way down through ordinal to nominal. Take a look at Figure 3-1, where we've added a second group to the bedpan data from the previous chapter. As you can see, the shape of its distribution is the same as the first group's, but it's been shifted over by 15 units. Is there any way to capture this fact with a number?[3] One obvious way is to add up the total number of bedpans emptied by each group. For the first group, this comes to 3086.[4] Although we haven't given you the data, the total for the second group is 4586. Equivalent

to the every nurse in group 2 emptied 15 bedpans more than group 1. This immediately tells us that the second group worked harder than the first (or had more patients who needed this necessary service).

However, we're not always in the position where both groups have exactly the same number of subjects. If the students in the second group worked just as hard, but they numbered only 50, their total would be only 2293 or so. It's obvious that a better way would be to divide the total by the number of data points so that we can directly compare two or more groups, even when they comprise different numbers of subjects. So, dividing each total by 100, we get 30.86 for the first group and 45.86 for the second. What we've done is to calculate the *average* number of bedpans emptied by each person. In statistical parlance, this is called the **arithmetic mean** (**AM**), or the **mean**, for short.

The reason we distinguish it by calling it the arithmetic mean is because there are other means, such as the harmonic mean and the geometric mean. However, when the term *mean* is used without an adjective, it refers to the AM. If there is any room for confusion (and there's *always* room for confusion in this field), we'll use the abbreviation. Using the notation we've just learned, the formula for the mean is:

$$\overline{X} = \frac{\sum_{i=1}^{n} X_i}{n} \tag{3-2}$$

We spelled out the equation using this formidable notation for didactic purposes. From now on, we'll use conceptually more simple forms in the text unless there is any ambiguity. Because there is no ambiguity regarding what values of *X* we're summing over, we can simplify this to:

The Arithmetic Mean

$$\overline{X} = \frac{\sum X}{n} \tag{3-3}$$

The mean is the measure of *central tendency* for interval and ratio data.

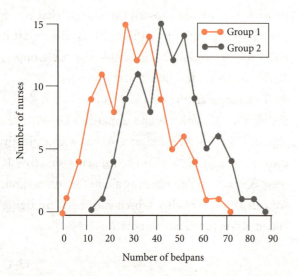

FIGURE 3-1 **Graphs of two groups, with the second shifted to the right by 15 units.**

---

[3]*By now, you should have learned that we never ask a question unless we know beforehand what the answer will be.*
[4]*If you don't believe us, you can add up the numbers in Table 2-2!*

A measure of central tendency is the "typical" value for the data.

One of the ironies of statistics is that the most "typical" value, 30.86 in the case of Group 1 and 45.86 for Group 2, never appears in the original data. That is, if you go back to Table 2-2, you won't find anybody who dumped 30.86 bedpans, yet this value is the most representative of the groups as a whole.[5]

The Geometric Mean

Some data, such as population growth, show what is called exponential growth; that is, if we were to plot them, the curve would rise more steeply as we move out to the right, as in Figure 3-2. Let's assume we know the value for X_8 and X_{10} and want to estimate what it is at X_9. If the value of X_8 is 138, and it is 522 for X_{10}, then the AM is $(138+522) \div 2 = 330$. As you can see in the graph, this overestimates the real value. On the other hand, the dot labelled *Geometric mean* seems almost dead on. The conclusion is that when you've got exponential or growth-type data, the geometric mean is a better estimator than is the AM.

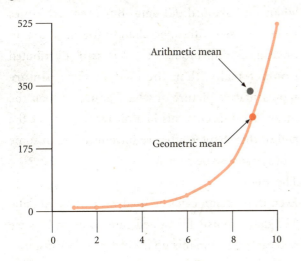

FIGURE 3-2 The difference between the arithmetic and geometric means.

The formula for the geometric mean is:
The Geometric Mean

$$GM = n\sqrt{\prod_{i=1}^{n} X_i} \qquad (3\text{-}4)$$

This looks pretty formidable, but it's not really

that bad. The Greek letter π (pi) doesn't mean 3.14159; in this context, it means *the product* of all those Xs, So:

$$\sum_{i=1}^{3} X_i = X_1 + X_2 + X_3 \qquad (3\text{-}5)$$

$$\prod_{i=1}^{3} X_i = X_1 \times X_2 \times X_3 \qquad (3\text{-}6)$$

Then, the n to the left of the root sign ($\sqrt{}$) means that if we're dealing with two numbers, we take the square root; if there are three numbers, the cube root; and so on. In the example we used, there were only two numbers, so the geometric mean is:

$$GM = \sqrt[2]{138 \times 522} = \sqrt{72\,036} = 268.4 \qquad (3\text{-}7)$$

Most calculators have trouble with anything other than square roots. So you can use either a computer or, if you're really good at this sort of stuff, logarithms. If you are so inclined, the formula using logs is:

$$GM = \text{antilog}\,\frac{1}{n}\sum_{i=1}^{n}\log X_i \qquad (3\text{-}8)$$

Be aware of two possible pitfalls when using the GM, owing to the fact that all of the numbers are multiplied together and then the root is extracted: (1) if any number is zero, then the product is zero, and hence the GM will be zero, irrespective of the magnitude of the other numbers; and (2) if an odd number of values are negative, then the computer will have an infarct when it tries to take the root of a negative number.

The Harmonic Mean

Another mean that we sometimes run across is the *harmonic mean*; its formula is:

$$HM = \frac{n}{\displaystyle\sum_{i=1}^{n}\frac{1}{X_i}} \qquad (3\text{-}9)$$

So, the **harmonic mean** of 138 and 522 is:

$$HM = \frac{2}{\dfrac{1}{138}+\dfrac{1}{522}} = 218.29 \qquad (3\text{-}10)$$

Despite its name, it is rarely used by musicians

---

[5]*This is like the advice to a nonswimmer to never a cross a stream just because its average depth is four feet.*

(and only occasionally by statisticians). Usually, the only time it is used is when we want to figure out the average sample size of a number of groups, each of which has a different number of subjects. The reason for this is that, as we can see in Table 3-1, it gives the smallest number of the three means, and the statistical tests are a bit more conservative.[6] When all of the numbers are the same, the three means are all the same. As the variability of the numbers increases, the differences among the three means also increase, and the AM is always larger than the GM, which, in turn, is always larger than the HM.

TABLE 3-1   Different results for arithmetic, geometric, and harmonic means

Data	Arithmetic mean	Geometric mean	Harmonic mean
10, 10, 10, 10	10	10	10
9, 10, 10, 11	10	9.97	9.95
5, 10, 10, 15	10	9.31	8.57
1, 2, 18, 19	10	5.11	2.49

The Median

What can we do with ordinal data? It's obvious (at least to us) that, because they consist of ordered categories, you can't simply add them up and divide by the number of scores. Even if the categories are represented by numbers, such as Stage I through Stage IV of cancer, the "mean" is meaningless.[7] In this case, we use a measure of central tendency called the **median**.

The *median* is that value such that half of the data points fall above it and half below it.

Let's start off with a simple example: We have the following 9 numbers: 1, 3, 3, 4, 6, 13, 14, 14, and 18. Note that we have already done the first step, which is to put the values in rank order. It is immaterial whether they are in ascending or descending order. Because there is an odd number of values, the middle one, 6 in this case, is the median; four values are lower and four are higher.

If we added one more value, say 17, we'd have

an even number of data points, and the median would be the AM of the two middle ones. Here, the middle values would be 6 and 13, whose mean is (6+13)÷2=9.5; this would then be taken as the median. Again, half of the values are at or below 9.5 and half located at or above. (On a somewhat technical level, this approach is logically inconsistent. We're calculating the median because we're not supposed to use the mean with ordinal data. If that's the case, how can we then turn around and calculate this mean of the middle values? Strictly speaking, we can't, yet we do.)

If the median number occurs more than once (as in the sequence 5 6 7 7 7 10 10 11), some purists calculate a median that is dependent on the number of values above and below the dividing line (e.g., there are two 7s below and one above). Not only is this a pain to figure out, but also the result rarely differs from our "impure" method by more than a few decimal places.

As we've said, the median is used primarily when we have ordinal data. But there are times when it's used with interval and ratio data, too, in preference to the mean. If the data aren't distributed symmetrically, then the median gives a more representative picture of what's going on than the mean. We'll discuss this in a bit more depth at the end of this chapter, after we introduce you to some more jargon; so be patient.

The Mode

Even the median can't be used with nominal data. The data are usually named categories and, as we said earlier, we can mix up the order of the categories and not lose anything. So the concept of a "middle" value just doesn't make sense. The measure of central tendency for nominal data is the **mode**.

The *mode* is the most frequently occurring category.

If we go back to Table 2-1, the subject that was endorsed most often was Economics, so it would be the mode. If two categories were endorsed with the

---

[6] Although why you'd want to be more conservative in this (or any) regard escapes us.

[7] It also seems ridiculous to write that the mean stage is II.LXIV (that's 2.64, for those of you who don't calculate in Latin).

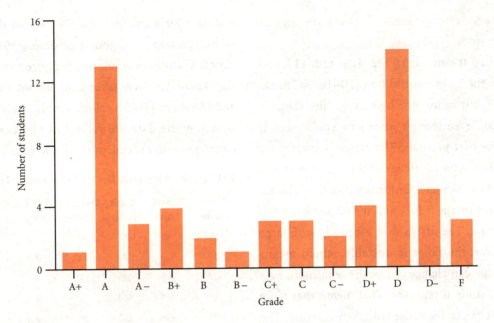

FIGURE 3-3   A bimodal distribution of course grades.

same, or almost the same[8] frequency, the data are called bimodal. This happened in one course I had in differential equations: If you understood what was being done, the course was a breeze; if you didn't, no amount of studying helped. So, the final marks looked like those in Figure 3-3—mainly As and Ds, with a sprinkling of Bs, Cs, and Fs. If there were three humps in the data, we could use the term *trimodal*, but it's unusual to see it in print because statisticians have trouble counting above two. However, you'll sometimes see the term *multimodal* to refer to data with a lot of humps[9] of almost equal height.

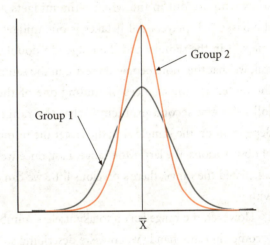

FIGURE 3-4   Two groups, differing in the degree of dispersion.

MEASURES OF DISPERSION

So far we've seen that distributions of data (i.e., their shape) can differ with regard to their central tendency, but there are other ways they can differ. For example, take a look at Figure 3-4. The two curves have the same means, marked $\overline{X}$, yet they obviously do not have identical shapes; the data points in Group 2 cluster closer to the mean than those in Group 1. In other words, there is less **dispersion** in the second group.

A *measure of* dispersion refers to how closely the data cluster around the measure of central tendency.

The Range

When ordinal data comprise named, ordered categories, you can say only how many categories were used. However, if the ordinal data are numeric, such as the rank order of students within a graduating class, we can use the **range** as a measure of dispersion.

---

[8]*The quantity "almost the same" is mathematically determined by turning to your neighbor and asking, "Does it look almost the same to you?"*

[9]*Another technical statistical term.*

The *range* is the difference between the highest and lowest values.

If we had the numbers 102, 109, 110, 117, and 120, then the range would be (120–102)=18. Do not show your ignorance by saying, "the range is 102 to 120," even though we're sure you've seen it in even the best journals. The range is always one number. The main advantage of this measure is that it's simple to calculate. Unfortunately, that's about the only advantage it has, and it's offset by several disadvantages. The first is that, especially with large sample sizes, the range is unstable, which means that its value can change drastically with more data or when a study is repeated. That means that if we add new subjects, the range will likely increase. The reason is that the range depends on those few poor souls who are out in the wings—the midgets and the basketball players. All it takes is one midget or one stilt in the sample, and the range can double. It follows that the more people there are in the sample, the better are the chances of finding one of these folks. So, the second problem is that the range is dependent on the sample size; the larger the number of observations, the larger the range. Last, once we've calculated the range, there's precious little we can do with it.

However, the range isn't a totally useless number. It comes in quite handy when we're describing some data, especially when we want to alert the reader that our data have (or perhaps don't have) some oddball values. For instance, if we say that the mean length of stay on a particular unit is 32 days, it makes a difference if the range is 10 as opposed to 100. In the latter case, we'd immediately know that there were some people with very long stays, and the mean may not be an appropriate measure of central tendency, for reasons we'll go into shortly.

The Interquartile Range

Because of these problems with the range, especially its instability from one sample to another or when new subjects are added, another index of dispersion is sometimes used with ordinal data, the **interquartile range** (sometimes referred to as the **midspread**). To illustrate how it's calculated, we'll use some

real data for a change. Table 3-2 shows the length, width, breadth, and gonad grade for 35 littleneck clams, *Protothaca staminea*, harvested in Garrison Bay. These data were taken from a book by Andrews and Herzberg (1985), called, simply, *Data*. And yes, we know the data are ratio, but you can use this technique with ordinal, interval, and ratio data.

TABLE 3-2   Vital statistics on 35 littleneck clams

Clam number	Length (mm)	Width (mm)	Breadth (mm)	Gonad grade	
31	91	77	42		
30	169	141	81	0	
29	305	264	172		
28	330	268	188	3	
23	420	282	265	3	
18	335	288	193	3	
26	393	333	209	2	
16	394	338	253	3	
24	402	340	216		$Q_L = 340$
25	410	349	253	3	
27	389	356	249	3	
15	455	385	269	3	
11	459	394	282	2	
9	452	395	282	3	
12	449	397	278	3	
14	471	401	271	2	
22	465	402	299	2	
5	487	407	286	3	Median = 407
7	485	408	298	3	
13	472	408	281	2	
4	512	413	302	3	
21	474	414	317	3	
10	468	417	272	3	
17	475	422	287	3	
6	481	427	315	2	
8	479	430	314	3	
34	509	433	284	3	$Q_U = 433$
20	486	436	275	3	
35	511	447	285	3	
33	519	456	312	3	
19	508	464	298	3	
3	505	471	338	3	
2	517	477	334	3	
1	530	494	337	3	
32	537	498	345		

For this part, we'll focus on the data for the width; to save you the trouble, we've rank ordered the data on this variable and indicated the median and the upper and lower quartiles.[10] Remember that the median divides the scores into two equal sections, an upper half and a lower half. There are 35 numbers in Table 3-2, so the median will be the eighteenth number, i.e. Clam number 24, which is 407. Now let's find the median of the lower half, using the same method. It's the ninth number, i.e. Clam number 24, which is 340, and this is the lower quartile, symbolized as Q_L. In the same way, the upper quartile is the median of the upper half of the data; in Table 3-2, Q_U is 433. So, what we've done is divide the data into four equal parts (hence the name **quartile**).

The *interquartile range* is the difference between Q_L and Q_U and comprises the middle 50% of the data.

Because the interquartile range deals with only the middle 50% of the data, it is much less affected by a few extreme scores than is the range, making it a more useful measure.

Variations on a Range

The interquartile range, which divides the numbers into quarters, is perhaps the best known of the ranges, but there's no law that states that we have to split the numbers into four parts. For example, we can use *quintiles* that divide the numbers into five equally sized groups, or *deciles* that break the data into 10 groups. Having done that, we can specify a range that includes, for example, the middle 30% (D_6–D_4), 50% (D_7–D_3), or 70% (D_8–D_2) of the data. The choice depends on what information we want to have: narrower intervals (e.g., D_6–D_4) contain less of the data but fall closer to the median; wider ranges (e.g., D_7–D_3) encompass more of the data but are less accurate estimates of the median.

The Mean Deviation

An approach that at first seems intuitively satisfying with interval and ratio data would be to calculate the mean value and then see how much each individual value varies from it. We can denote the difference between an individual value and the mean either by $(X-\bar{X})$ or by the lowercase letter, x. Column 1 of Table 3-3 shows the number of coffee breaks taken during 1 day by 10 people[11]: their sum, symbolized by $\sum X$, is 90. Dividing this by n, which is 10, yields a mean of 9. Column 2 shows the results of taking the difference between each individual value and 9. The symbols at the bottom of Column 2, $\sum(X-\bar{X})$, signify the sum of the differences between each value and the mean. We could also have written this as $\sum x$. Adding up these 10 deviations results in—a big zero. This isn't just a fluke of these particular numbers; by definition, *the sum of the deviations of any set of numbers around its mean is zero*. So, clearly, this approach isn't going to tell us much. We can get around this problem by taking the absolute value of the deviation; that is, by ignoring the sign. This is done in Column 3, when taking the absolute value of a number is indicated by putting the number between the vertical bars: $|+3| = 3$, and $|-3| = 3$. The sum of the absolute deviations is 42. Dividing this by the sample size, 10, we get a mean deviation of 4.2; that is, the average of the absolute deviations. To summarize the calculation:

TABLE 3-3   Calculation of the mean deviation

Column 1 number of coffee breaks X	Column 2 raw deviation $X-\bar{X}$	Column 3 absolute deviation $|X-\bar{X}|$	Column 4 squared deviation $(X-\bar{X})^2$
1	−8	8	64
3	−6	6	36
4	−5	5	25
7	−2	2	4
9	0	0	0
9	0	0	0
11	2	2	4
12	3	3	9
16	7	7	49
18	9	9	81
$\sum X = 90$	$\sum(X-\bar{X}) = 0$	$\sum|X-\bar{X}| = 42$	$\sum(X-\bar{X})^2 = 272$

---

[10] *These data are kosher, although the subject matter isn't. However, we couldn't find any data on hole sizes in bagels or the degree of heartburn following Mother's Friday night meal.*

[11] *Judging from the numbers, obviously civil servants.*

$$\text{Mean deviation (MD)} = \frac{\sum |X - \bar{X}|}{n} = \frac{\sum |x|}{n} \quad \text{(3-11)}$$

This looks so good, there must be something wrong, and in fact there is. Mathematicians view the use of absolute values with the same sense of horror and scorn with which politicians view making an unretractable table statement. The problem is the same as with the mode, the median, and the range; absolute values, and therefore the mean deviation (MD), can't be manipulated algebraically, for various arcane reasons that aren't worth getting into here.

The Variance and Standard Deviation

But all is not lost. There is another way to get rid of negative values: by squaring each value.[12] As you remember from high school, two negative numbers multiplied by each other yield a positive number: $-4 \times (-3) = +12$. Therefore, any number times itself must result in a positive value. So, rather than taking the absolute value, we take the square of the deviation and add these up, as in Column 4. If we left it at this, then the result would be larger as our sample size grows. What we want, then, is some measure of the average deviation of the individual values, so we divide by the number of differences, which is the sample size, n. This yields a number called the **variance**, which is denoted by the symbol S^2.

$$S^2 = \frac{\sum (X - \bar{X})^2}{n} = \frac{\sum x^2}{n} \quad \text{(3-12)}$$

This is more like what we want, but there's still one remaining difficulty. The mean of the 10 numbers in Column 1 is 9.0 coffee breaks per day, and the variance is 27.2 squared coffee breaks. But what the #&$! is a squared coffee break? The problem is that we squared each number to eliminate the negative signs. So, to get back to the original units, we simply take the square root of the whole thing and call it the **standard deviation** abbreviated as either SD or S:

The Standard Deviation

$$S = \sqrt{\frac{\sum (X - \bar{X})^2}{n}} = \sqrt{\frac{\sum x^2}{n}} \quad \text{(3-13)}$$

The result, 5.22 (the square root of 27.2), looks more like the right answer. So, in summary, the SD is the square root of the average of the squared deviations of each number from the mean of all the numbers, and it is expressed in the same units as the original measurement. The closer the numbers cluster around the mean, the smaller S will be. Going back to Figure 3-4, Group 1 would have a larger SD than Group 2.

Do NOT use the above equation to actually calculate the SD. To begin with, you have to go through the data three times: once to calculate the mean, a second time to subtract the mean from each value, and a third time to square and add the numbers. Moreover, because the mean is often a decimal that has to be rounded, each subtraction leads to some rounding error, which is then magnified when the difference is squared. Computers use a different equation that minimizes these errors. Finally, this equation is appropriate only in the highly unlikely event that we have data from every possible person in the group in which we're interested (e.g., all males in the world with hypertension). After we distinguish between this situation and the far more common one in which we have only a sample of people (see Chapter 5), we'll show you the equation that's actually used.

Let's look for a moment at some of the properties of the variance and SD. Say we took a string of numbers, such as the ones in Table 3-3, and added 10 to each one. It's obvious that the mean will similarly increase by 10, but what will happen to S and S^2? The answer is, absolutely nothing. *If we add a constant to every number, the variance (and hence the SD) does not change.*

The Coefficient of Variation

One measure much beloved by people in fields as diverse as lab medicine and industrial/ occupational psychology is the **coefficient of variation** (CV). It is defined simply as follows:

$$CV = \frac{SD}{\bar{X}} \times 100\% \quad \text{(3-14)}$$

Because both SD and $\bar{X}$ are expressed in the same

---

[12] *Erasing the minus sign is not considered to be good mathematical technique.*

units of measurement, the units cancel out and we're left with a pure number, independent from any scale (Simpson et al., 1960). This makes it easy to compare a bunch of measurements, say from different labs, to see if they're equivalent in their spread of scores.

But, there are a couple of limitations of the CV. First, although the SD enters into nearly every statistical test that we'll discuss, in one form or another, we can't incorporate CV into any of them. Second, and perhaps more telling, CV is sensitive to the scale of measurement (Bedeian and Mossholder, 2000). If we *multiply* every value by a constant, both $\overline{X}$ and SD will increase, leaving CV unchanged; this is good. However, if we *add* a constant to each value, $\overline{X}$ will increase but, as we said in the previous section, SD will not. Consequently, CV will decrease as the mean value increases. The bottom line, then, is that CV *may* be a useful index for ratio-level data where you cannot indiscriminately add a constant number, but should definitely *not* be used with interval-level data, where the zero is arbitrary and constants don't change anything.

Skewness and Kurtosis

We've seen that distributions can differ from each other in two ways; in their "typical" value (the measure of central tendency), and in how closely the individual values cluster around this typical value (dispersion). With interval and ratio data, we can use two other measures to describe the distribution; **skewness** and **kurtosis**. As usual, it's probably easier to see what these terms mean first, so take a look at the graphs in Figure 3-5. They differ from those in Figure 3-4 in one important respect. The curves in Figure 3-4 were symmetric, whereas the ones in Figure 3-5 are not; one end (or tail, in statistical parlance) is longer than the other. The distributions in this figure are said to be **skewed**.

Skewness refers to the symmetry of the curve.

The terminology of skewness can be a bit confusing. Curve A is said to be **skewed right**, or to have a **positive skew**; Curve B is **skewed left**, or has a

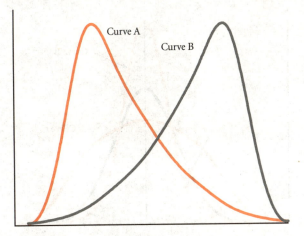

FIGURE 3-5 Two curves, one with positive and one with negative *skew*.

negative skew. So, the "direction" of the skew refers to the direction of the longer tail, not to where the bulk of the data are located. **skewness** is not easy to calculate by hand, but most statistical software will be happy to do it for you. A value of 0 indicates no skew; a positive number shows positive skew (to the right), and a negative number reflects negative, or left, skew.[13]

The three curves in Figure 3-6 are symmetric (i.e., their skew is 0), but they differ with respect to how flat or peaked they are, a property known as **kurtosis**. The middle line, Curve A, shows the classical "bell curve," or "normal distribution," a term we'll define in a short while. The statistical term for this is **mesokurtic**. Curve B is more peaked; we refer to this distribution as **leptokurtic**. By contrast, Curve C is flatter than the normal one; it's called **platykurtic**. The same as **skewness, you** may get **kurtosis by** statistical software quickly. The normal distribution (which is mesokurtic) has a kurtosis of 3. However, many computer programs subtract 3 from this, so that it ends up with a value of 0, with positive numbers reflecting leptokurtosis, and negative numbers, platykurtosis. You'll have to check in the program manual[14] to find out what yours does.

Kurtosis refers to how flat or peaked the curve is.

Although kurtosis is usually defined simply in terms of the flatness or peakedness of the distr-

---

[13]*At least some things in statistics make sense.*

[14]*Usually something we do only as a last resort, when everything else has failed.*

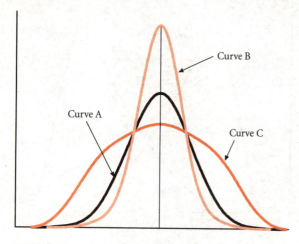

FIGURE 3-6   Three distributions differing in terms of *kurtosis*.

ibution, it also affects other parts of the curve. Distributions that are leptokurtic also have heavier tails; whereas platykurtic curves tend to have lighter tails. However, kurtosis doesn't affect the variance of the distribution.

So Who's Normal?

Many of the tests we'll describe in this book are based on the assumption that the data are normally distributed. But how do we know? A good place to start is just looking at a plot of the data. Are they symmetrically distributed, or is there a long tail to one side or the other? Sometimes we're reading an article and don't have access to the raw data, only some summary information. Then we can use a couple of tricks suggested by Altman and Bland (1996). First, we know that the normal curve extends beyond two SDs on either side of the mean. So, for data that can have only positive numbers (e.g, most lab results, demographic information, scores on paper-and-pencil tests), if the mean is less than twice the SD, there's some skewness present. Passing the test doesn't guarantee normality, but failing it definitely shows a problem. We can use the second trick if there are a number of groups, each with a different mean value of the variable. If the SD increases as the mean does, then again the data are skewed. If they're your own data you're looking at, then you should think of one of the transformations described in Chapter 19 to normalize them.

A more formal way to check for normality is to look at the tests for skewness and kurtosis that we discussed in the previous section. If both are less than 2.0, it's fairly safe to assume that the data are reasonably normal. However, a better way would be a direct test to see if the data deviate from normality. There are actually a few different statistics for this, but rest assured, we won't spell out the formulae for them. As with the computations for skewness and kurtosis, only a statistician would think of doing them by hand. The *Wilks-Shapiro Normality Test*, as the name implies, assesses the data you have against a normal population. The *Anderson-Darling Normality Test* is a bit more flexible, and lets you evaluate the data against a number of different distributions. In both cases, the number that's produced doesn't mean much in its own right; we just look at the *P* level. Because the tests are looking at *deviation* from normality, we want the *P* level to be greater than .05; if it's less, it means there's too much difference.

So which one do we use? That's extremely simple to answer—whichever one your computer program deigns to give you.

When Do We Use What(and Why)

Now that we have three measures of central tendency (the mode, the median, and the mean), and four measures of dispersion (the range, the interquartile range, and the SD), when do we use what? To help us decide, we'll invoke four criteria that are applied to evaluating how well *any* statistical test—not just descriptive stats—works:

Sufficiency. How much of the data is used? For measures of central tendency, the mean is very sufficient, because it uses all of the data, whereas the mode uses very little. Looking at measures of dispersion, the SD uses all the data, the range just the two extreme values.

Unbiasedness. If we draw an infinite number of samples, does the average of the estimates approximate the parameter we're interested in, or is it biased in some way? As we'll see when we get to Chapter 5, most of statistics (like most of science) is about generalizing from things you studied (the *sample*) to the rest of the world (the *population*). When we do a study on a bunch of patients with multiple sclerosis, we are assuming, correctly or incorrectly, that the sample we studied is representative of all MS patients (the population). We're further assuming that the estimates we compute are *unbiased* estimates of the same variables in the population (the parameters). The mean is an unbiased estimator of the population value, as is the SD where the denominator is $n - 1$. However, if we use Equation (3-13), where the denominator is just n, the estimate would be biased, in that it would systematically underestimate the population value. We'll explain why this is so in Chapter 6.

Efficiency. Again drawing a large number of samples, how closely do the estimates cluster around the population value? Efficient statistics, like the SD, cluster more closely than does the range or IQR.

Robustness. To what degree are the statistics affected by outliers or extreme scores? The median is much more robust than the mean; multiplying the highest number in a series by 10 won't affect the median at all, but will grossly distort the mean, especially if the sample size is small.

Applying these criteria, we can use the guidelines shown in Table 3-4.

TABLE 3-4   Guidelines for use of central tendency and measure of dispersion

Type of data	Measure of central tendency	Measure of dispersion
Ordinal	Median	Interquartile range
	Mode	Range
Interval	Mean	SD*
	Median	Interquartile range
	Mode	Range
Ratio	Mean	SD
	Median	Interquartile range
	Mode	Range

*SD—standard deviation.

For each listing, the most appropriate measures are listed first. If we have interval data, then our choice would be the mean and SD. Whenever possible, we try to use the statistics that are most appropriate for that level of measurement; we can do more statistically with the mean (and its SD) than

with the median or mode, and we can do more with the median (and the range) than with the mode.

Having stated this rule, let's promptly break it. The mean is the measure of central tendency of choice for interval and ratio data when the data are symmetrically distributed around the mean, but not when things are wildly asymmetric; a synonym is "if the data are highly skewed." To use the terminology we just introduced, we'd say the mean is not a *robust* statistic. Let's see why. If the data are symmetrically distributed around the mean, then the mean, median, and mode all have the same value, as in Figure 3-7.

This isn't true for skewed distributions, though. Figure 3-8 shows some data with a positive skew, like physicians' incomes. As you can see, the median is offset to the right of the mode, and the mean is even further to the right than the median. If the data

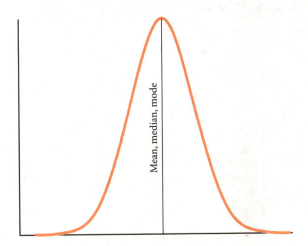

FIGURE 3-7   The mean, median, and mode in a symmetric distribution.

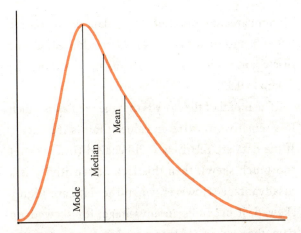

FIGURE 3-8   The mean, median, and mode in a skewed distribution.

were skewed left, the picture would be reversed: the mode (by definition) would fall at the highest point on the curve, the median would be to the left of it, and the mean would be even further out on the tail. The more skewed the data, the further apart these three measures of central tendency will be from one another.

Another way data can become skewed is shown in Figure 3-9. If we ignore the oddball off to the right, both the mode and the median of the 17 data points are 4, and the mean is 3.88. All these estimates of central tendency are fairly consistent with one another and intuitively seem to describe the data fairly well. If we now add that eighteenth fellow, the mode and median both stay at 4, but the mean increases to 6.06. So the median and the mode are untouched, but the mean value is now higher than 17 of the 18 values.

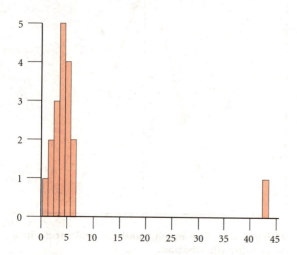

FIGURE 3-9   Histogram of highly skewed data.

Similarly, the range of the 17 data points on the left is 5, and their SD is 1.41. After adding that one discrepant value, the range shoots up to 42 and the SD up to 9.32.

The moral of the story is that the median is much less sensitive to extreme values than is the mean. If the data are relatively well behaved (i.e., without too much skew), then this lack of sensitivity is a disadvantage. However, when the data are highly skewed, it becomes an advantage; for skewed-up data, the median more accurately reflects where the bulk of the numbers lie than does the mean.

SUMMARY

✧ The commonly used measures of central tendency have mean, geometric mean and median. mean is suitable for symmetric distribution of data, especially for normal distribution of data; geometric mean is suitable for exponential or growth-type data; median is suitable for various types of data, but frequently used for asymmetric distribution of data, existed extreme values of data, ordinal data.

✧ The commonly used measures of dispersion have range, interquartile range, variance, standard deviation and coefficient of variation. range is suitable for various types of data, but rarely be used because of crude and unstable; interquartile range is suitable for various types of data, but frequently used for asymmetric distribution of data, existed extreme values of data, ordinal data; variance and standard deviation are both suitable for symmetric distribution of data, especially for normal distribution of data, but variance for mathematical proof, standard deviation for real application; coefficient of variation is just for comparison of the variation of different measurements with different units or bigger difference of means.

✧ Skewness and kurtosis can describe the shape of distribution of data. Skewness refers to the symmetry of the curve, kurtosis refers to how flat or peaked the curve is.

GLOSSARY

arithmetic mean   算术均数
geometric mean   几何均数
harmonic mean   调和均数
median   中位数
mode   众数
range   极差

interquartile range 四分位数间距
variance 方差
standard deviation 标准差
coefficient of variation 变异系数
skewness 偏度
kurtosis 峰度

EXERCISES

1. Coming from a school advocating the superiority (moral and otherwise) of the SG-PBL approach (that stands for Small Group—Problem-Based Learning and is pronounced "skg-pble"), we do a study, randomizing half of the stats students into SG-PBL classes and half into the traditional lecture approach. At the end, we measure the following variables. For each, give the best *measure of central tendency* and *measure of dispersion*.

   a. Scores on a final stats exam.

   b. Time to complete the final exam (there was no time limit).

   c. Based on a 5-year follow-up, the number of articles each person had rejected by journals for inappropriate data analysis.

   d. The type of headache (migraine, cluster, or tension) developed by all of the students during class (i.e., in both sections combined).

2. Just to give yourself some practice, figure out the following statistics for this data set (we deliberately made the numbers easy, so you don't need a calculator): 4 8 6 3 4.

   a. The *mean* is _____.

   b. The *median* is _____.

   c. The *mode* is _____.

   d. The *range* is _____.

   e. The *SD* is _____.

3. A study of 100 subjects unfortunately contains 5 people with missing data. This was coded as "99" in the computer. Assume that the true values for the variables are:

   $\overline{X}$=45.0   SD=5.6

   Minimun=16   Minimun=65

   If the statistician went ahead and analyzed the data as if the 99s were real data, would it make the following parameter estimates *larger, smaller*, or *stay the same*?

   a. The mode.

   b. The median.

   c. The mean.

   d. The standard deviation.

   e. The range.

How to Get the Computer to Do the Work for You Descriptive Statistics

- From **Analyze**, choose **Descriptive Statistics →Frequencies…**
- Click on the variables you want to calculate, and click the arrow button next to the **Variable(s)** box
- Click the Statistics button
- Check the boxes you want (will likely include **Mean, Median, Quartiles, Standard Deviation, Skewness,** and **Kurtosis**)
- Click OK

Testing for Normality

- From **Analyze**, choose **Descriptive Statistics → Explore…**
- Choose the variables you want to analyze and click the arrow button next to the **Dependent List** box
- Click the Plots button and check **Normality plots with tests**, then Continue
- Click OK

CHAPTER THE FOURTH
The Normal Distribution and Binomial Distribution

The normal distribution is ubiquitous in statistics. Here, we discuss what it is, why it's useful, and how to use it. Binomial Distribution is also introduced in this chapter.

SETTING THE SCENE

A survey of contraceptive practices found that the most widely used method is the phrase, "Not tonight, dear, I've got a headache," uttered by one or the other partner. Based on a survey of 2000 people, it was found to be used an average of 100 times a year, with a standard deviation (SD) of 15. Can we determine what proportion of the public uses this reason at least 115 times a year; or fewer than 70 times a year; or between 106 and 112 times annually?

Before you can answer these important questions, you'll need to have some more information, starting with what we mean by a "normal distribution." We've made passing mention of it in the earlier chapters without really defining what it is. Now the moment of truth has come, and we'll tell you what is meant by a normal distribution and why you really want to know about it.

The normal curve has appeared in several previous figures, although it wasn't explicitly labelled as such. It's often referred to by a couple of other names, such as a bell curve or a Gaussian distribution. The term "bell curve" comes from its shape;[1] "Gaussian" from its discoverer.[2,3] So the alternative terms make sense and reflect attributes of the curve—its shape and history. Unfortunately, the standard term doesn't make sense; there's nothing inherently "normal" about this distribution, nor "abnormal" about other types.

WHY WE CARE ABOUT THE NORMAL DISTRIBUTION

There are several reasons why the normal curve is important. First, many of the statistical tests we'll be discussing in this book assume that the data come from a normal distribution. Second, with normally distributed data, the mean and variance aren't dependent on each other; if we increase the mean of a normal distribution, its variance should remain the same. This isn't true for many other types of distributions. Third, it's held that many natural phenomena are in fact approximately normally distributed. That is, if we were to measure the height, weight, blood pressure, or urine dehydroepiandrosterone level in a larger number of people ("large" meaning at least 1000) and make frequency polygons of our findings, they would each approximate the normal curve. Each measure, naturally, would have a different mean, but all of the curves would be roughly symmetric around their means and resemble that general shape. The only fly in the ointment is that the resemblance may be more illusory than real. Lippman (in Wainer and Thissen, 1976) put it well; he said, "Everybody believes in the theory of errors (the normal distribution). The experimenters because they think it is a mathematical theorem. The mathematicians because they think it is an

---

[1] And has led to the "gong phenomenon" —ask a statistician any question, and the first thing he or she will do is draw bell curve.

[2] Although rumor has it that, when lying on his back, Karl Friedrich Gauss himself resembled a Gaussian curve.

[3] A pity Alexander Graham Bell spent all his time on the phone. If he had discovered this curve, we would have only one name to remember.

experimental fact." On an empirical level, Micceri (1989) looked at the distributions of scores from well over 400 widely used psychological measures, such as achievement and aptitude tests, and found that distributions that were strictly normal were as rare as hen's teeth.[4]

The fourth reason that the normal distribution is important is that, whatever the distribution of the data, if we drew a large number of samples of reasonable size (we'll define "reasonable" shortly), then the distribution of the means of those samples will always be normally distributed. Now for the real heart of the matter—the data don't have to be normally distributed for this to be true because of what's called the Central Limit Theorem.

The *Central Limit Theorem* states if we draw equally sized samples from a **non-normal** distribution, the distribution of the means of these samples will *still* be normal, as long as the samples are large enough.

How large is "large"? Again, it all depends. If the shape of the population is pretty close to normal, then "large" can be as small as 2. If the population is markedly different from normal, then 10 to 20 may be large enough. To play it safe, though, we usually say that anything over 30 is enough under almost all circumstances.

We can illustrate this with another gedanken experiment. Imagine that we had a die that we rolled 600 times, and we recorded the number of times each face appeared. If the die wasn't loaded (and neither were we), no face would be expected to appear more often than any other. Consequently, we would expect that each number would appear one-sixth of the time, and we would get a graph that looks like Figure 4-1. This obviously is not a normal distribution; because of its shape, it's referred to as a rectangular distribution.

Now, let's roll the die twice and add up the two numbers. The sums could range from a minimum of 2 to a maximum of 12. But this time, we wouldn't expect each number to show up with the same frequency. There's only one way to get a 2 (roll a 1 on

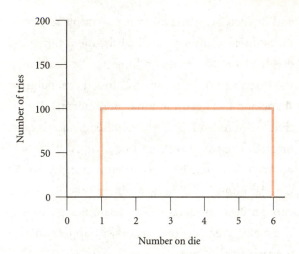

FIGURE 4-1   Theoretical distribution from rolling a die 600 times.

each throw) or a 12 (roll a 6 each time), but two ways to roll a 3 (roll a 1 followed by a 2, or a 2 followed by a 1), and five ways to roll a 6. So, because there are more ways to get the numbers in the middle of the range, we expect that they will show up more often than those at the extremes. This tendency becomes more and more pronounced as we roll the die more and more times.

We did a computer simulation of this; the results are shown in Figure 4-2. The computer "rolled" the die twice, added the numbers, and divided by 2 (i.e., took the mean for a sample size of 2) 600 times; then it "rolled" the die four times, added the numbers,

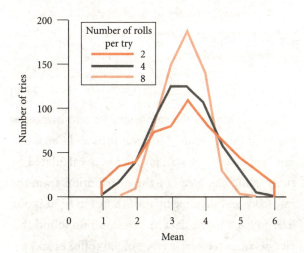

FIGURE 4-2   Computer simulation of averaging the sum of rolling the die 2, 4, and 8 times, each done 600 times.

---

[4] *Thus you can say that, in some sense, normal curves are abnormal.*

and divided by 4 (the mean for a sample size of 4) for 600 trials; and again rolled the die 8 times and divided by 8. Notice that rolling the die even twice, the distribution of means has lost its rectangular shape and has begun to look more normal. By the time we've rolled it 8 times, the resemblance is quite marked. This works with any underlying distribution, no matter how much it deviates from normal. So, the Central Limit Theorem guarantees that, if we take enough even moderately sized samples ("enough" is usually over 30), the means will approximate a normal distribution.

STANDARD SCORES

Before we get into the intricacies of the normal distribution, we have to make a minor detour. If hundreds of variables were normally distributed, each with its own mean and SD, we'd need hundreds of tables to give us the necessary specifications of the distributions. This would make publishers of these tables ecstatic, but everyone else mildly perturbed. So statisticians have found a way to transform all normal distributions so that they (the distributions, not the statisticians) use the same scale. The idea is to specify how far away an individual value is from the mean by describing its location in standard deviation (SD) units. When we transform a raw score in this manner, we call the results a standard score.

A *standard score*, abbreviated as z or Z, is a way of expressing any raw score in terms of SD units.

The standard score

$$z = \frac{(X - \bar{X})}{s} = \frac{x}{s} \qquad (4\text{-}1)$$

Adding a bit to the confusion, Americans pronounce this as "zee scores," whereas Brits and Canadians say "zed score."[5] A standard score is calculated by subtracting the mean of the distribution from the raw score and dividing by the SD. Just to try this out, let's go back to the data in Table 3-2; we found that civil servants took an average of 9.0 coffee breaks per day, with a SD of 5.22. A raw score of 1 coffee break a day corresponds to:

$$z = \frac{(1 - 9)}{5.22} = -1.53 \qquad (4\text{-}2)$$

that is, −1.53SD units, or 1.53SD units below the mean. We can do the same thing with all of the other numbers, and these are presented in Table 4-1.

TABLE 4-1   Data in Table 3-3 transformed into standard scores

X	Z
1	−1.53
3	−1.15
4	−0.96
7	−0.38
9	0
9	0
11	0.38
12	0.57
16	1.34
18	1.72

In addition to allowing us to compare against just one table of the normal distribution instead of having to cope with a few hundred tables, z-scores also have other uses. They allow us to compare scores derived from various tests or measures. For example, several different scales measure the degree of depression, such as the Beck Depression Inventory (BDI; Beck et al., 1961) and the Self-Rating Depression Scale (SDS; Zung, 1965). The only problem is that the BDI is a 21-item scale, with scores varying from a minimum of 0 to a maximum of 63; whereas the SDS is a 20-item scale with a possible total score between 25 and 100. How can we compare a score of, say, 23 on the BDI with a score of 68 on the SDS? It's a piece of cake, if we know the mean and SD of both scales. To save you the trouble of looking these up, we've graciously provided you with the information in Table 4-2.

What we can now do is to transform each of these raw scores into a z-score. For the BDI score of 23:

$$z = \frac{23 - 11.3}{7.7} = 1.52 \qquad (4\text{-}3)$$

---

[5]*This further confirms G. B. Shaw's statement that the United States and Britain are two countries separated by a common language. Canada is one country divided by two languages.*

TABLE 4-2 Mean and standard deviations of two depression scales

Beck Depression Inventory	Self-Rating Depression Scale
	Mean
11.3	52.1
	SD
7.7	10.5

Similarly, for the SDS score of 68:

$$z = \frac{68 - 52.1}{10.5} = 1.51 \qquad \textbf{(4-4)}$$

So, these transformations tell us that the scores are equivalent. They each correspond to z-scores of about 1.5; that is, 1½ SD units above the mean. Let's just check these calculations. In the case of the BDI, the SD is 7.7, so 1½ SD units is $(1.5 \times 7.7) = 11.6$. When we add this to the mean of 11.3, we get 22.9, which is (within rounding error) what we started off with, a raw score of 23. This also shows that if we know the mean and SD, we can go from raw scores to z-scores, and from z-scores back to raw scores. Isn't science wonderful?

There are a few points to note about standard scores that we can illustrate using the data in Table 4-1. First, the raw score of 9, which corresponds to the mean, has a z-score of 0.0; this is reassuring, because it indicates that it doesn't deviate from the mean. Of course, not every set of data contains a score exactly equal to the mean; however, to check your calculations, any score that is close to the mean should have a z-score close to 0.0. Second, if we add up the z-scores, their sum is 0 (plus or minus a bit of rounding error). This will always be the case if we use the mean and SD from the sample to transform the raw scores into z-scores. It is the same reason that the mean deviation is always 0; the average deviation of scores about their mean is 0, even if we transform the raw scores into SD units (or any other units). A third point about standard scores is that if you take all the numbers in the column marked z in Table 4-1 and figured out their SDs, the result will be 1.0. By definition, when you convert any group of numbers into z-scores, they will always have a mean of 0.0 and a standard deviation of 1.0 (plus or minus a fudge factor, for rounding error).

However, we don't have to use the mean and SD of the sample from which we got the data; we can take them from another sample, or from the population. We do this when we compare laboratory test results of patients against the general (presumably healthy) population. For instance, if we took serum rhubarb levels from 100 patients suffering from hyperrhubarbemia[6] and transformed their raw scores into z-scores using the mean and SD of those 100 scores, we would expect the sum of the z-scores to be 0. But if we used the mean and SD derived from a group of normal[7] subjects, then it's possible that all of the patients' z-scores would be positive.

THE NORMAL CURVE

Now armed with all this knowledge, we're ready to look at the normal curve itself, which is shown in Figure 4-3. Notice a few properties:

1. The mean, median, and mode all have the same value.
2. The curve is symmetric around the mean; the skew is 0.
3. The kurtosis is also 0, although you'll have to take our word for this.

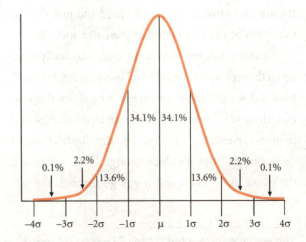

FIGURE 4-3 The normal curve.

---

[6] *A nonfatal disorder that makes people long and green and turns their hair red.*

[7] *Here, "normal" means healthy, not bell-shaped.*

4. The tails of the curve get closer and closer to the X-axis as you move away from the mean, but they never quite reach it, no matter how far out you go. In mathematical jargon, the curve approaches the X-axis asymptotically.

5. For reasons we'll discuss in Chapter 5, we've used μ (the Greek mu) for the mean and σ (lower-case sigma) for the SD.

These properties are true for theoretical normal curves; that is, those which exist only in the imaginations and dreams of statisticians. Reality deviates from this to some degree; any set of real numbers will show a slight degree of skew and kurtosis, and the mean, median, and mode will not be exactly the same. Most importantly, the curve will eventually touch the X-axis, unless we have an infinite set of data points.[8] For all intents and purposes, though, most of the action takes place between the lines labelled -3σ and $+3\sigma$, so the discrepancy between theoretical and real normal curves bothers only the purists.[9]

Let's now take a look at the numbers inside the curve. What they tell us is that 34.1% of the area under the normal curve falls between the mean (μ) and one SD above the mean ($+1\sigma$); because the curve is symmetric, it follows that another 34.1% falls between μ and -1σ. So, roughly two-thirds of the area (actually 68.2%) is between $+1\sigma$ and -1σ. Going a bit further, 13.6% of the area is between $+1\sigma$ and $+2\sigma$ (and between -1σ and -2σ); therefore, 47.7% of the area is between the μ and $+2\sigma$,[10] and just slightly over 95% of the curve falls between $+2\sigma$ and -2σ.

All this raises two questions: first, who really cares about the area under this odd-looking curve; and second, how did we get these numbers? To answer the first question, we'll return to those intrepid nurses and their never-empty bed pans. The distribution wasn't quite normal, but it's close enough.[11] We calculated the mean to be 30.83, and if you go through the cal-

culations, you'll find that the SD=14.08. So, putting this together with the numbers in Figure 4-3, we know that 68% of the nurses emptied between (30.83–14.08) and (30.83+14.08), or between 16.75 and 44.91 (let's say 17 and 45) bedpans. The vast majority—95% of them—emptied between [30.83–(2×14.08)] and [30.83+(2×14.08)], or between about 3 and 59 pans. Anyone who dumped fewer was really slacking off, and those who cleaned 60 or more were working harder than about 97% of their mates.

The important point is that, if our data are relatively close to being normally distributed, the properties of the normal curve apply to our data. So the normal curve can give us information about the data we've collected, not just about some theoretical line on a piece of paper.

The second question is about where those numbers came from. That's easy; look at Table A in the back of the book, titled Area of the Normal Curve. Where those numbers came from is a bit more difficult. There is an equation, which we won't bother you with, that can be solved to give the area between the mean and any value of σ. We "simply" solved this a few hundred times and put the results in the table. To simplify your life yet again, we've reproduced a part of it in Table 4-3. Now, how to read it.

TABLE 4-3   A portion of the table of the normal curve

z	Area below	z	Area below
0.00	0.0000	1.00	0.3413
0.10	0.0398	1.10	0.3643
0.20	0.0793	1.20	0.3849
0.30	0.1179	1.30	0.4032
0.40	0.1554	1.40	0.4192
0.50	0.1915	1.50	0.4332
0.60	0.2257	1.60	0.4452
0.70	0.2580	1.70	0.4554
0.80	0.2881	1.80	0.4641
0.90	0.3159	1.90	0.4713
1.00	0.3413	2.00	0.4772

---

[8] However, to misquote Albert Einstein, "There are only two things that are infinite—the universe and human stupidity—and I'm not sure about the universe."

[9] By now, you should know that "purist" is one term that will never be assigned to us.

[10] That's 34.1 + 13.6 for those of you whose calculator batteries died.

[11] Another one of those precise statistical terms.

Table 4-3 has two columns, one labelled "z" and one labelled "Area below." There are a few things to notice about the table: first, the z is in SD units. Tables in other books may refer to it as x/σ or as σ. They all mean the same thing; 0.1 is one-tenth of a SD. Second, Table A starts at 0.00 and goes up to 4.00 (we've given only a few values up to 2.00 in Table 4-3); because the curve is symmetric, it doesn't make sense to waste ink and paper going from 0.00 to −4.00. We'll show you how to deal with negative z values in a minute. Last, be careful reading tables of the normal curve in other books. Many show the curve the same way it is here, giving the area between mean ($z=0.00$) and the value of z (or σ, or x/σ, or however, it's labelled). Other books give the area to the left of z; these are easy to spot because the area equivalent to $z=0.00$ is 0.5000 rather than 0.0000, as it is here. Finally, a few tables give the area to the right of z. So be sure to check which type of table you are using.[12]

Now, let's start using it. Notice that the number next to a value of z of 1.00 is 0.3413; not coincidentally, it's the same number as in Figure 4-3, showing the percent of the area between μ and $+1\sigma$. This shows first, how we got the number, and second, that the total area under the curve is 1.0000 units, so that an area of 0.341 is 34.1% of the total area.

To really give the normal curve a good workout, let's return to the problem posed in Setting the Scene, and try to determine how many times the phrase, "Not tonight, dear, I've got a headache," has been used.

1. How many people used this excuse up to 115 times? First, we have to transform 115 to a z-score, using the format of Equation (4-1):

$$z = \frac{115 - 100}{15} = 1.00 \qquad (4\text{-}5)$$

Table 4-3 tells us that the area of the curve between the mean and +1.00 SD is 0.3413. This means that 34.13% of the people use this delightful phrase between 100 and 115 times. But we're interested in all of the people who said it 115 times and less, so we'll have to add the 50% of the area that falls below the mean, as in Figure 4-4. So the answer is 84.13% of 2000, or 1683 people.[13]

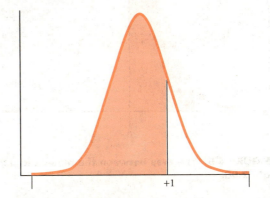

FIGURE 4-4   The area below a z of 1.00.

2. How many people said this fewer than 70 times in 1 year? Again, we start off by converting this to a z-score:

$$z = \frac{70 - 100}{15} = -2.00 \qquad (4\text{-}6)$$

As we mentioned, the table does not include negative z-scores. What we do is ignore the sign, but keep it in our minds. Looking up 2.00 in the table, we find 0.4772. This is the area between the mean and +2.00, and also between the mean and −2.00; because the sign was negative, we use this latter figure. It corresponds to the shaded area in Figure 4-5. But this isn't the area we're interested in; we want to know the area below 70. Because the total area between the extreme left and the mean is half the area of the curve, or 0.5000, the area to the left of the shaded portion is (0.5000−0.4772), or 0.0228; that is, 2.28% of the people.

What this also shows is that it is very helpful to draw a rough sketch of the normal curve and the area that the table shows; it helps clarify in our mind the portion that we're interested in. This isn't just for neophytes; usoldtimers do it all the time.[14] Just one more for practice.

---

[12] Although we couldn't begin to imagine why you would want to look at, much less own, any other statistics book.

[13] So that's why the U.S. birth rate is falling!

[14] Perhaps a reflection of our increasing decrepitude. We have also been told that the correct phrase is "we oldtimers." But, usoldtimers prefer "us oldtimers."

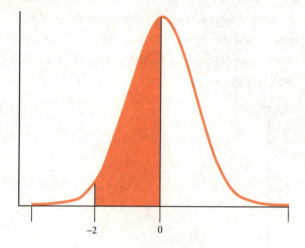

FIGURE 4-5   The area between the mean and a z of –2.00.

3. How many people use this phrase between 106 and 112 times a year? As usual, we begin by changing the raw numbers into z-scores, which in this case are +0.40 and +0.80, and making a rough sketch (Figure 4-6). Table 4-3 tells us that the area between the mean and +0.80 is 0.2881, and the mean and +0.40 is 0.1554. We're interested in the area between these; the difference is 0.1327, or 13.3% of the 2000 people.

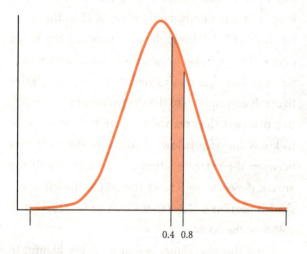

FIGURE 4-6   The area between a z of +0.40 and +0.80.

This finishes our discussion of the normal distribution. It is not the only one used in statistics; there are many others with names such as Poisson, exponential, Gompertz, and the like. However, we're not going to discuss them for two reasons. First, unless you plan on doing some very fancy stuff with statistics, the normal curve will get you through almost everything. Second, we don't know how to use them, so why should you?[15]

MEDICAL REFERENCE RANGE

What is the Reference Range?

In medical practice, a physician or other health professional may use the reference range of some measurement to evaluate whether the individual is "normal" on the corresponding measurement. Thus the reference range is also called the normal range.

A *reference range,* or reference interval, is a range of values for a physiologicmeasurement in most of healthy persons.

In the above definition of the reference range, "most of" may be 90%, 95% or 99%, among which, the 95% is commonly used. "Healthy", or say, "normal" individual does not mean "absolutely healthy". An individual may considered to be "normal" or "healthy" if he/she does not suffer from some diseases or exposed to some environmental factors which may influence the measurement.

Some important reference ranges in medicine include reference ranges for blood tests and reference ranges for blood pressures.

How to Calculate the Reference Range?

To calculate the reference range, a sample of "normal" and homogeneous individual need to be randomly sampled from the target population.

The reference range can be either two-or one-sided. If a measurement is considered to be of clinical significance if it is either too high or too low, a two-sided reference range should be calculated. A reference range with only the upper limit can be used if the measurements considered as unnormal only if it is too high, such as blood lead level. If the measurement is considered to be un-normal of if it is too low, such as IQ and vital capacity, a reference range with only the lower limit should be used.

If the measurement is normally distributed in the normal population, one can use the equations in Table 4-4 to calculate the reference range.

---

[15]*Actually, since we originally wrote this, we've added a discussion of the Poisson distribution, showing that even old farts can learn new things.*

TABLE 4-4   Calculation of the Reference Range

Level	If the variable is normally distributed			Otherwise		
	Double sided	Single sided		Double sided	Single sided	
		Lower limit	Upper limit		Lower limit	Upper limit
90%	$\overline{X}\pm1.64SD$	$\overline{X}-1.28SD$	$\overline{X}+1.28SD$	$P_5\sim P_{95}$	P_{10}	P_{90}
95%	$\overline{X}\pm1.96SD$	$\overline{X}-1.64SD$	$\overline{X}+1.64SD$	$P_{2.5}\sim P_{97.5}$	P_5	P_{95}
99%	$\overline{X}\pm2.58SD$	$\overline{X}-2.33SD$	$\overline{X}+2.33SD$	$P_{0.5}\sim P_{99.5}$	P_1	P_{99}

Let's go back to the sample in "Setting the Scene". If we consider a people to be not normal if he/she use the phrase "Not tonight, dear, I've got a headache." too many or too few times, we should calculate a double sided 95% reference range by Equation (4-7).

$$100\pm1.96\times15= (70.6, 129.4) \qquad \textbf{(4-7)}$$

One may argue it is perfect if one does not use the phrase at all. Then the upper limit of the single sided reference range should be

$$100+2.33\times15=134.95 \qquad \textbf{(4-8)}$$

If the measurement is not normally distributed, one can use the percentiles method to calculate the reference range. This is also included in Table 4-4.

THE BINOMIAL DISTRIBUTION

Question: What do these statements (taken from Bloch, 1979) have in common? Circle the correct answer:

"Any wire cut to length will be too short."

"Any error in any calculation will be in the direction of most harm."

"If you miss one issue of any magazine, it will be the issue that contained the article, story, or installment you were most anxious to read."

"For a bike rider, it's always uphill and against the wind."

Answers:

a. They're all cynical.

b. They're all correct.

c. They all express the probabilities of dichotomous events.

d. All of the above.

In case you didn't know, the correct answer is

d, "All of the above." I was first introduced to this apparent breakdown of the laws of probability when my kids were small and learning to put on their shoes. You would expect that if they didn't know right from left, and put their shoes on at random, they'd get it wrong only half the time. This is not what happened; it seemed that they put their left shoes on their right feet at least 89% of the time. Now, is there some way to tell how often this deviation from chance would be expected to occur?

Again, a give-away question; of course there is. What we're dealing with here is called the **binomial distribution**.[16]

What is the Binomial Distribution?

As you no doubt recall, the normal curve describes how a continuous variable (such as blood pressure or IQ) would be distributed if we measured it in a large number of people. The curve can also be used to give us the probability of a given event, such as a diastolic pressure 95. However, the examples we just gave are not continuous, but have only two possible outcomes: The wire either will be too short, or it won't be too short; the missing issue either will be the one containing the last installment of the mystery story, or it won't be, and so on. What we would like to have is something equivalent to the normal distribution, but that can be used to both describe and give us the probabilities for dichotomous events. Not surprisingly, we have such an animal; it's called the binomial distribution.

The *binomial distribution* shows the probabilities of different outcomes for a series of random events, each of which can have only one of two values.

---

[16]*Or, if you prefer, contrary children —your choice.*

Let's start off with the easiest case, where each of the two values is equally likely. The usual example, used in every other textbook, is flipping a coin and seeing how many times it comes up heads in 10 flips. For that reason, we'll avoid that example assiduously and stick with a kid putting on his shoes.

If we let the kid try to put his shoes on once, there are two possible outcomes: right (R) or wrong (W), each of which should occur 50% of the time.[17] If there are two attempts at getting shod, then the possible outcomes are (1) R on both tries; (2) W on both tries; (3) R on the first and W on the second; and (4) W on the first and R on the second. It's easy enough in this instance to figure out the probability of getting it wrong both times: there are four equally possible outcomes, one of which is the combination WW, so the chances are 1 in 4. The other way to figure it out is to use the multiplicative law: the probability of W on the first try is 0.50, as it is on the second (i.e., the probability of getting it wrong on the second try, conditional that the first try was wrong). Consequently, the probability of W on both trials is 0.50×0.50=0.25, which is what we got before.

We could do the same thing for 3, 10, or 100 tries, but these methods are laborious. For example, we could ask the question: If a kid puts his shoes on 10 times, what's the probability that he will get it wrong on exactly 7 of those tries? If we tried to solve this by making a table of the possible outcomes, we'd quickly get bogged down. On the first try, there are two possible results—right or wrong. For each of these outcomes, there are two possible results for the second try—again, right or wrong, yielding the four different patterns we just discussed. On each trial, the number of possibilities doubles, so that by the time we reach 10 trials, there are 2^{10}, or 1024 possibilities.

However, there's an easier way to figure things out, which is called the **binomial expansion**. Although we're trying to avoid equations as much as possible, this one comes in quite handy, so bear with us. We'll have to define a few more terms in addition to the ones we use in discussing combinations and permutations:

p is the probability on each try of the outcome of interest (0.5 in this example) occurring;

and q is $(1-p)$

Now, the formula for the binomial expansion is:

$$\frac{n!}{r!(n-r)!}p^r q^{n-r} \qquad (4\text{-}9)$$

The first part is the formula for the number of combinations of n objects taken r at a time. We can also write Equation (4-9) as:

$$\binom{n}{r}p^r q^{(n-r)} \qquad (4\text{-}10)$$

because the term $\binom{n}{r}$ is simply a shorthand way of writing:

$$\frac{n!}{r!(n-r)!} \qquad (4\text{-}11)$$

These equations may look fairly scary, but actually they're not hard to handle. The only difficult part is calculating the factorials, but nowadays, many pocket calculators can do it for you. Putting the numbers from our example into Equation (4-9) gives us:

$$\frac{10!}{7!(10-7)!} \times 0.5^7 \times 0.5^{(10-7)}$$
$$= \frac{10!}{7!3!} \times 0.5^7 \times 0.5^3 = 0.1172 \qquad (4\text{-}12)$$

So, the probability is just under 12% that the kid would get it wrong 7 times out of 10, if he were really putting the shoes on at random.

Now, let's get a bit fancier. What's the probability that he does it wrong at least 7 times out of 10 (instead of exactly 7 out of 10)? This means getting it wrong 7, 8, 9, or 10 times out of 10 trials. To calculate the cumulative probability of any of these outcomes, we figure out the individual probabilities and then add them up. We already figured out the probability of 7 out of 10. Next, 8 out of 10 looks like:

$$\frac{10!}{8!(10-8)!} \times 0.5^8 \times 0.5^{(10-8)} = 0.0439 \qquad (4\text{-}13)$$

---

[17] *This assumes the kid really doesn't know right from left, and the attempts are truly random. It doesn't apply if the kid does know, but does it wrong to get you annoyed; that is, it doesn't apply about 97% of the time.*

9 out of 10 is:

$$\frac{10!}{9!(10-9)!} \times 0.5^9 \times 0.5^{(10-9)} = 0.0098 \quad \textbf{(4-14)}$$

and for 10 out of 10

$$\frac{10!}{10!0!} \times 0.5^{10} \times 0.5^0 = 0.0010 \quad \textbf{(4-15)}$$

Adding these up gives us 0.1719, or just over 17%. So, the binomial expansion has allowed us to figure out that the kid has a 12% chance of putting his shoes on wrong in 7 out of 10 tries and a 17% chance that he'll get it wrong 7 or more times out of 10.

So far, we've dealt with situations that have a 50:50 chance of happening, but we're not limited to this. For example, let's say that the bug committee at the hospital has really been effective and has knocked the incidence of nosocomial infections down to 20% following abdominal surgery. If we have 15 of these hapless abdominal surgery patients on our wards, what's the probability that 5 of them will develop an infection from the hospital? In this case, $n=15$, $r=5$, $p=0.20$, and $q=0.80$. Putting these into the equation gives us:

$$\frac{15!}{5!(15-5)!} \times 0.2^5 \times 0.8^{(15-5)} = 0.1032 \quad \textbf{(4-16)}$$

So the probability that 5 of the 15 patients will develop a hospital-acquired infection is 10.32%.

What we've learned in this section is how to extend the binomial expansion beyond the case where each alternative has a 50% chance of occurring to the more general situation where the two outcomes have different probabilities.

Learning a Bit More About the Binomial Distribution
Staying with this example for a minute, how many people with nosocomial infections would we expect to see on our 15-bed unit? It is almost intuitive that, given 15 patients and an incidence of .20, we would expect that, most of the time, 3 infected patients would be on the unit simultaneously (i.e., 20% of 15). In Figure 4-7, we've plotted the probabilities of having anywhere between 0 and 15 nosocomial patients on the ward at the same time. This was done using Equation (4-9) by setting $r=0$, then $r=1$, up through $r=15$. This figure, then, shows the binomial

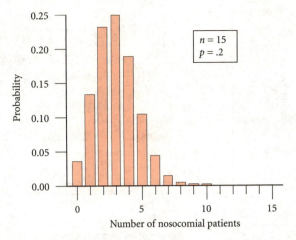

FIGURE 4-7   The binomial distribution for $n=15$, $p=0.2$, and r going from 0 to 15.

distribution for $p=0.2$ and $n=15$. Notice that the distribution isn't quite symmetrical; it's skewed somewhat toward the right.

What happens when we change the probability and the number of trials (in this case, each patient can be thought of as one trial)? In Figure 4-8, we've kept n at 15, but we changed p from 0.2 to 0.3. You would expect that the average number on the ward at any one time would increase (30% of 15=4.5), and sure enough the graph has shifted to the right a bit. It also looks as if the data are spread out some more, and there's a bit less skew.

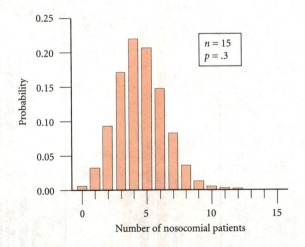

FIGURE 4-8   Changing p from 0.2 to 0.3.

If we keep p at 0.2 but increase n from 15 to 30, we would again expect a shift to the right, with an expected average of 6 (Figure 4-9). Mirabiledi-

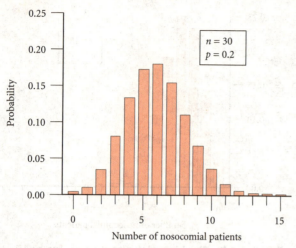

FIGURE 4-9 **Keeping _p_ at 0.2, and changing _n_ from 15 to 30.**

ctu,[18] the data behave just as we predicted, and again, there seems to be a greater spread in the scores.

So let's summarize what we've seen so far. First, as _p_ gets closer to 0.5, the graph becomes more symmetric. When it is exactly equal to 0.5, the graph is perfectly symmetric. When _p_ is less than 0.5, the distribution is skewed to the right; it's skewed left when _p_ is greater than 0.5 (we haven't shown that, but trust us). Second, the closer _p_ is to 0.5, the greater the variability in the scores. Third, there isn't just one "binomial distribution"; there's a different one for every combination of _n_ and _p_.

We learned in the previous chapters how to figure out the mean, SD, and variance of continuous data. We can do the same for binomial data, and thus numerically describe the properties of the binomial distribution that we just saw graphically. As we would expect from the graphs, these properties depend on _n_ and _p_ (and therefore also on _q_, which you remember is $1-p$). What we have, then, is:

Properties of the Binomial Distribution

$$\text{Mean} = np \qquad (4\text{-}17)$$
$$\text{Variance} = npq \qquad (4\text{-}18)$$
$$\text{SD} = \sqrt{npq} \qquad (4\text{-}19)$$

THE BINOMIAL AND NORMAL DISTRIBUTIONS

If we go back and compare Figure 4-7 with Figure 4-9, it looks as though increasing the sample size with the same value of _p_ makes the graph seem more normally distributed. Yet again, your eyes don't deceive you; as n increases, the binomial distribution looks more and more like the normal distribution. Let's pursue this a bit further. In Figure 4-10, we show a binomial distribution with $p=q=0.5$. The left graph is for _n_=5, the middle shows _n_=10, and the right part shows _n_=20. As you can see, the graph looks more and more normal as _n_ increases; by the time _n_=30, the figure is

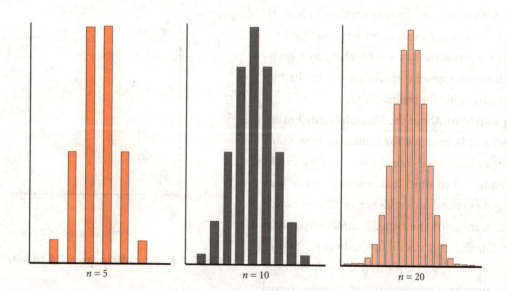

FUGURE 4-10 **The binomial distribution for _n_=5, _n_=10, and _n_=20, with _p_=_q_=0.5.**

[18]_Virgil, 17 BC (personal communication)._

virtually indistinguishable from the normal distribution. What this means is that, if we're dealing with binomial distributions where n is 30 or more, we don't have to worry about using Equation (4-9) to figure out probabilities; we can approximate the binomial distribution by using the normal curve. In fact, when $p=0.5$, we can use the normal curve when n is as low as 10; however, the more p deviates from 0.5, the worse the approximation to the normal distribution, so using the normal curve only when n is at least 30 is fairly safe.

To illustrate how we can use the normal distribution to approximate the binomial one, let's stick with the example of patients who leave the operating room minus an appendix but with an infection, and we'll figure out how likely it will be that we'd have five such people on our unit at one time. Now, one difference between the normal and binomial distributions is that the former is intended to be used with continuous variables (those which can assume any value between the highest and lowest ones), and the latter with discrete variables. Consequently, we have to consider the discrete value of 5 people as actually covering the exact limits of 4.5 to 5.5.[19] The next step is to convert these two numbers (4.5 and 5.5) to standard scores, using the formula we encountered in this chapter. Remember that the mean for a binomial distribution is np, and its standard deviation is $\sqrt{npq}$. This means that in our case, the mean is $15 \times 0.2 = 3.0$, and the SD is $\sqrt{15 \times 0.2 \times 0.8} = 1.55$. Plugging these values into the equation, we get:

$$z_1 = \frac{5.5 - 3.0}{1.55} = 1.61 \qquad z_2 = \frac{4.5 - 3.0}{1.55} = 0.97 \qquad \textbf{(4-20)}$$

We look these two numbers up in a table of the normal distribution and find that $z1.61=0.4463$, and $z0.97=0.3340$. The difference between them is 0.1123, meaning that the probability of finding five nosocomial patients on the ward at the same time is about 11%. This approximation isn't bad, especially considering that in this case, p deviates from 0.5

quite a bit and n is less than 30; it's fairly close to what we found before, 0.1032.

SUMMARY

1. The Normal distribution is one of the most important distributions in Biostatistics. Many natural phenomena are approximately normally distributed.

2. The Normal curve is a bell-shape liked curve. It is symmetric around the mean with both skew and kurtosis are 0s.

3. The area under the Normal curve can be found by using the standard score and Table A.

4. A Reference Range is the range of some measurement which includes most of the "normal" people.

5. Binomial distribution can be used to describe the probabilities of obtaining different number of events for n independent random experiments, each of them has only two possible outcomes with probabilities of p and $1-p$.

6. For a Binomial Distribution with $p = 0.5$, we can use the normal curve to approximate it when n is as low as 10. When p deviates from 0.5, using the normal curve only when n is at least 30.

GLOSSARY

normal distribution　正态分布

Gaussian distribution　高斯分布

central limit theorem　中心极限定理

standard score　标准化得分

area of the normal curve　正态分布曲线下面积

binomial distribution　二项分布

binomial expansion　二项式展开

reference range　参考值范围

normal range　正常值范围

---

[19] *We'll ignore the fact that no one but a gross anatomist has ever seen 4.5 or 5.5 people and simply remind you that we did the same thing in Chapter 3 when we were discussing the median.*

EXERCISES

1. The entire first-year class in Billing Practices 101 takes the Norman-Streiner Test of Real or Imagined Licentiousness (the NoSTRIL; often referred to as the NoSE). The results were:

	Males	Females
Mean	60	40
SD	12	10
N	138	97

Unlike the students, the scores were fairly normal for both men and women. Based on these data, figure out the following:

1) If a male gets a score of 70, what's his z-score?

2) What's the z-score for a female with a score of 35?

3) What score for females is equivalent to a male's score of 78?

4) What proportion of women get scores between 30 and 45?

5) What proportion of men get scores over 68?

6) What score demarcates the upper 10% of women?

2. According to the weather report, the probability of rain is 10% each day for the next 7 days. If you go camping for 3 days, what is the probability that it will rain every day? And what is the probability that it will rain more than 2 days?

3. The natural recovery rate for some disease is 20%. For a set of 10 patients, what are the probabilities of at most 2 natural recoveries and at least 8 natural recoveries?

4. Blood samples were collected from 360 healthy males randomly sampled from a town in east China. Their average haemoglobin (HGB) is 134.5g/L, and standard deviation is 0.71g/L. What is the 95% reference range of HGB level for the healthy males in that town?

SUGGESTED READINGS AND WEBSITES

Fang JQ. Medical Statistics and Computer Experiments. World Scientific. 2005.

CHAPTER THE FIFTH **Statistical Inference**

In this chapter, we discuss the problem of comparing a sample to a population of values with a known mean and standard deviation.

SETTING THE SCENE

As male baby boomers age, they have every reason to become increasingly preoccupied with their, uh, "apparatus." Various drug companies regularly remind them that their sexual prowess could once again return to the halcyon[1] days of yore through the ingestion of little pills of various colors. As if that wasn't bad enough, increasing exposure to various parts of the male anatomy in the ever-more permissive media is a constant reminder that, with all the libido in the world, they still might just not measure up (so to speak). However, modern pharmacology has come to the rescue yet again; through the simple expedient of a little, long, and narrow pill derived from natural ingredients found in bamboo, the fastest growing stalk on earth, you can reach new lengths of satisfaction. Scientific studies have proved it.

BASIC CONCEPTS

When you approach the average man on the street and ask what statistics means to him, the answer is simple. If he is less than 30, the only statistic of interest is 900 - 600 - 900 (36 - 24 - 36 before metric); between ages 30 and 60, statistics are the inflation rate and the Dow Jones averages; and over 60, it's vital statistics and mortality rates that count.

However, in research, these descriptive statistics, the type we discussed in Chapter 3, count for little. What we spend the most time on is the stuff of **inferential statistics:** *t*-tests, chi-squares, ANOVAs, life tables, and their ilk. The basic goal of these statistics is not to describe the data—that's what the previous statistics do—but to determine the likelihood that any conclusion drawn from the data is correct.

*Inferential statistics are used to determine the probability (or likelihood) that a conclusion based on analysis of data from a sample is true. To be more precise, it could **estimate** the population parameter via calculated sample statistic—the mean or standard deviation calculated from the sample.*

The fly in the ointment that leads to all sorts of false conclusions and keeps all us statisticians employed is **random error**. Any measurement based on a sample of people, even though they are drawn at random from the **population** (more on this later) of all individuals of interest, will differ from the true value by some amount as a result of random processes. So, whenever you compare two treatments, or look for an association between two variables, some differences or association will be present purely by chance. As a result, unless you take the role of chance into account, every experiment will conclude that one treatment was better or worse than another.

To explore how chance wrecks things, imagine trying to determine the average height of all statisticians. It would be difficult and unfundable to try to measure all of us, so you would likely **sample** us somehow; perhaps by sending a letter to the department heads at some northwestern colleges or steering delegates at the annual statisticians' conference into your booth with offers of beer and pizza. If you were unlucky enough to get one of your esteemed authors in your sample (a good possibility with a six-pack for bait), we guarantee that your estimate will be in trouble. You see, Streiner is about 5'8", a bit on the short side, whereas Norman is 6'5",

---

[1]*Ironic in this context that Halcyon is a sleeping pill. One man's pleasure …*

a basketball reject. That doesn't matter too much unless you want to make an **inference** that the height you measured is an accurate reflection of all statisticians. If you got Streiner, your estimate would be too low; if you got Norman, you'd be too high. If you pick us both, you'll likely be about right. **If you wanted to generalize from the sample to the population of statisticians, there is a good chance that your estimate may be too high or too low** just as a result of the operation of chance in determining who walks through the door of the hospitality suite.

The goal of inferential statistics is to be highly specific about these chances. Instead of saying, as we just did, that there is some chance that the estimate will be a bit off, we want to do just like Gallup and state that "the true height will lie within plus or minus 2 inches of what we measured 95% of the time."

THE MEANING OF THE MAGICAL *P* VALUE

In part, this generalization is strengthened by the methods of sampling and the chances that the generalization will be successful are enhanced if involving a process of **random sampling**, Generally speaking, samples are on average a little bit different from populations as *sample* describes the individuals in the study while the *population* describes the hypothetical (and usually) infinite number of people you wish to generalize. So what? Well, so quite a bit. We're often in a situation where we want to claim that something we did to our sample—our treatment—actually worked. That is, in the most simple of scientific worlds, we might pick a sample from somewhere, flip a coin to get them into two groups, do something to one group leaving the other alone, then calculate the means of both groups after one got the treatment. And if the gods shine upon us and our elixir, we'll find that the mean of our treated group is indeed a bit better. But the trouble is that, if we did the experiment a bunch of times with an elixir that did nothing, half the time the experimental group would look better, and half the time it would look worse, just by chance. Putting it another way, if the therapy were completely ineffective, the probability that we would observe a difference in favor of the treatment *of any size* is exactly 50%.[2]

On the other hand, if the difference in favor of the treated group were huge, we would probably be saying to ourselves something along the line of, "Jeepers, that's one heck of a big difference. Sure seems pretty unlikely that you could get such a humungous difference just by chance if there were no real effect of treatment." In other words, if all we ask is that there is a difference in favor of the treatment, the likelihood this could arise by chance is 50%. But as the difference gets bigger and bigger, the chance that this could arise by chance given the vagaries of random fluctuation, become lower and lower.

That's what all of statistics is really about; putting a number on trivial versus humungous. You've seen the number if you read the journals, "the difference was 22.7%, $p<0.001$." And the little "$p<0.001$" says that, based on the author's knowledge of inferential statistics and/or the money he spent on a PhD, he can state with confidence that the chance this difference, or one larger, could arise by chance is less than 0.001, or less that 0.1%

That is, inferential statistics is entirely directed at working out, with arcane math and many tables, the probability that an effect could arise purely by chance. That seems like a truly magical feat. How can you, without knowledge of the true value, estimate how far you might be away from it? But it really isn't all that mysterious. It depends on only two variables—the extent to which individual values differ from the average, often expressed as a *standard deviation* (SD), and the sample size. If relatively little variation is found about the mean of the sample, it is likely that the sample mean will lie fairly close to the true value. Also, if we have a large sample size,

---

[2]*As we write, there is a popular TV commercial running that states boldly, "50% of all Canadians are at increased risk of heart disease from high cholesterol. Ask your doctor about Leptostatin." Yes, and 50% are at decreased risk from low cholesterol. That's why statistics can empower you.*

regardless of the variation, all the differences in individual values will tend to cancel themselves out, and our estimate will be close to truth.

A Bit More of Nomenclature

Of course, as we start inferring, we have suddenly doubled the number of variables we have on hand. We now have *sample* means and *population* means, *sample* SDs and *population* SDs, *sample* variances and *population* variances, and so on. As one strategy to keep things straight, statisticians, a long time ago, created two sets of labels. Sample values are labeled with the usual Roman letters, as we have been doing all along, and population parameters are labeled with Greek letters. Undoubtedly this was a good idea back in those wondrous days of yore when every school person had to survive courses in Latin and Greek. Nowadays, the only people who know Greek are Greek scholars, Greek fraternity members, and Greeks, so the convention confuses. However, one of us had the benefit of a Greek fraternity[3] (but thankfully no Greek course), so all will now be enlightened. Table 5-1 is a small sprinkling of Greek and Roman letters, and their names:

TABLE 5-1 sprinkling of Greek and Roman letters, and their names

Greek letter	Name	Roman letter	Statistical term
α	alpha	a	Type I error (see below)
β	beta	b	Type II error (see below)
γ	delta	D	Difference
π	pi	p	Proportion
μ	mu	M	Mean
σ	sigma	s	standard deviation

So, the little squiggles aren't all that mysterious; most stand for the same quantity in the sample and the population. Sample means begin with M, population means begin with Greek m, or mu (μ) . . . and so on.

So these wrap up for the basics and now we would jump right into the theorem and essentials behind statistical inference.

ELEMENTS OF STATISTICAL INFERENCE

Times are tough for male boomers. Those carefree sixties, the days of free love and free spirits (and other more leafy intoxicants), are long gone. And somehow, most of their libido went with it. To make matters worse, the issue is no longer restricted to inner thoughts; it has now become medicalized. Nightly television ads are a constant reminder that you have a disease—"erectile dysfunction syndrome"—that is cured by a little blue pill, if only you screw up your courage and fess up to your doctor. Added to that, the increasing barrage of explicit images of well-endowed males on late night TV, movies, and all, does nothing to reassure the aging male that he's not merely on the small side of normal.

However, just as Pfizer's little blue pill solved the problem, pharmacologic help has come from an unlikely source. Researchers in a small company situated 234 km northwest of Port Moresby, New Guinea, many years ago noted that the local men were apparently remarkably well endowed by rubbing a potion derived from the boiled oil of bamboo stalks on the area. They managed to refine the ingredient in bamboo into a small red pill, with the trade name of Mangro. The label says that it's "Guaranteed to add half an inch after six weeks or your money refunded."

While the temptation is powerful, you, decide to put the claim to the test. You design a trial and swing it with ease past the ethics committee. While no one would want to be in the control group, you enlist 100 males in the study and just administer the real drug to them. Six weeks later, the results are in: an average erect length of 6.7 inches (170.0 mm).

Then you find it on internet—*the definitive penis size survey results* (www.sizesurvey.com/result.htm). Now in its sixth edition, the survey has gathered data on flaccid and erect lengths from over 3100 subjects, and has carefully compiled the data. We take the distribution of erect penile length of the whole sample as a good comparison on penile length of males who aren't taking the drug, shown in Figure 5-1. Overall,

---

[3] *The other author will be happy to furnish Hebrew equivalents on request.*

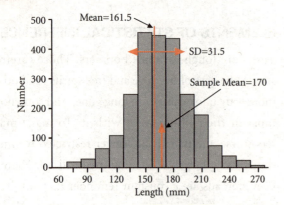

FIGURE 5-1   Distribution of erect penile length for 3100 subjects.

the mean of all 3100 subjects is 161.5 mm (6.4 inches), with a standard deviation of 31.5 mm (1.25 inches). With 3100 subjects, that's as close as we're ever going to get to a population, so we assume the population mean is 161.5 mm. and SD is 31.5 mm. So our guys, with an average length of 170.0 mm, have gained a total of 8.5 mm, about a third of an inch. Not quite up to the claim, but still, not so small that you would walk away from it altogether.

The distribution looks remarkably bell shaped. In Figure 5-2, we've replaced the original data with a normal curve with a mean of 161.5 and standard deviation of 31.5, and displayed our sample mean. Looking at the distribution, that puts the study

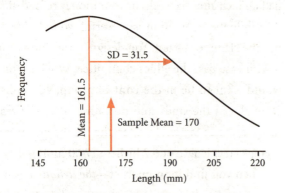

FIGURE 5-2   Normal distribution of the data in Figure 5-1.

participants up around the 60th percentile; 40% bigger, 60% smaller.

The obvious question is, "Is this a real difference, or did you just happen to locate 100 guys who were, on average, just a little bit bigger than normal?" In short, did the drug work, or could the difference you found be simply explained by chance; that is, by the sample you ended up with? Putting it slightly differently again, what's the probability that you could get a difference between your sample of 100 people and the population in the definitive survey of a third of an inch, just by chance? That, dear reader, is what *all* of inferential statistics is about—figuring out the chances that a difference could come about by chance. All the stuff that fills the next 200 pages and all the other pages in all the other stats books, all the exams that have struck terror in the hearts of other stats students (but not you!), is all about working out the chances that a difference could come about by chance.

Of course, if ordinary people realized that was all there is, people like us couldn't make all the big bucks, so we have to put a veneer of scientific credibility on it. We turn the whole thing into a scientific hypothesis. However, statisticians are a cynical lot, so we actually start with a hypothesis that the drug didn't work, called a *null hypothesis*.[4]

H_0: There is no difference between the penile length of males treated with Mangro and untreated males.

Of course, if this is true, then the chances of cashing in on the drug are non-existent and our chances of retiring early on the profits are equally small. So there is also a parallel hypothesis that the drug did work, called the alternative hypothesis, and labelled H_1. It states that the penile length of treated males is bigger than untreated males.[5]

---

[4]In this case, null means "the hypothesis to be nullified"; it doesn't mean "nothing." In the majority of cases, the null hypothesis does state that nothing is going on (i.e., the nil hypothesis), but it can also take different forms.

[5]Actually, there are two kinds of alternative hypotheses—one that says they're bigger, and one that says they're different—either bigger or smaller. We'll explain all this later.

THE STANDARD ERROR AND THE STANDARD DEVIATION OF THE MEAN

If you look at Figure 5-1, you're likely thinking to yourself that this is one study where the null hypothesis wins hands down. A third of an inch just doesn't look very impressive, to either scientist or consumer. However, and it's a very big however, the question we're asking as scientists is not whether a particular penile length could be ⅓ of an inch bigger than the mean by chance, but whether the *mean* of a sample of 100 erect phalli could be bigger than the population by ⅓".

Suppose the treatment doesn't work; that the null hypothesis is true. That means that our study is simply repeating the original survey, only with 100 guys, not 3000. It would be the same as if we went out on the street,[6] sampled 100 guys, measured them up, computed their mean, and put it on a piece of graph paper. If we now do this a number of times, plotting the mean for each of our samples, we would start to build up a distribution like Figure 5-1. However, we're now no longer displaying the original observations; we're displaying means based on a sample size of 100 each. Every time we sample 100 guys, we get a few who are big, some who are small, and a bunch who are about average. The big ones cancel out the little ones, so the sample mean should fall much closer to 161.5 than any individual observation.

Putting it another way, what we're really worried about are the chances that a *sample mean* could be equal to or greater than 170.0 mm if the sample came from a distribution of *means* with mean 161.5. So, we have to work out how the means for sample size 100 would be distributed by chance if the true mean was 161.5.

One thing is clear. The sample means will fall symmetrically on either side of 161.5, so that the mean of the means will just be the overall mean, 161.5. And from our discussion above, another thing is clear—the distribution of the sample means will be much tighter around 161.5 than was the distribution of the individual lengths. That's because, as we've said, when we're plotting the individual measurements, we'll find big guys and small ones. But, when we're plotting the *average* of 100 folks, the big ones will average out with the little ones.

If this doesn't seem obvious, think about the relation with sample size. If we did the study with a very small sample size, say by taking two guys at a time, sometimes they would both be on the big size of average, sometimes they would both be on the small side, but most of the time one small guy is going to be balanced by one large guy. So if we average their two observations, they'll be a bit closer to 161.5 than each alone. If we increase the sample size to, say, five, then there's a pretty good chance that the five guys will be spread out across the size range, the extremes will cancel out, and the mean will be closer still to 161.5. And as the sample size gets bigger and bigger, there's an increasing chance that extreme values will cancel out, so the mean will get closer and closer to the population value of 161.5.

Of course, this whole exercise is a bit bizarre. We find ourselves in the unenviable position of having to do a study where we go and grab (not literally) 100 guys at a time, measure their members, and send them packing, and doing this again and again, all in the cause of finding out how the means for sample size 100 are distributed, in order to figure out how likely it is to find a mean of 170.0 or more on a single study.

But here's where statistics students get their Ph.D.s. They work out for us just how those means will be distributed theoretically. For this case, it's not really all that complicated. We've already figured out that the bigger the sample size, the tighter the distribution (the closer the individual means will be to the population mean of 161.5). It's also not too great a leap of faith to figure out that the less dispersed the original observations (i.e., the smaller the standard deviation), the tighter the means will be to the population mean. In other words, we expect that

---

[6] *We're not telling which street, and we hope the cops don't find out.*

under the null hypothesis, the distribution of means for a given sample size will be directly related to the original standard deviation, and inversely related to the sample size. And that's just about the way it turns out. The width of the distribution of means, called the **Standard Error of the Mean** [which is abbreviated as SE(M) or SE_M], is directly proportional to the standard deviation, and inversely proportional to the square root of the sample size:

Standard Error of the Mean

$$\text{SE(M)} = \frac{\sigma}{\sqrt{Sample\ Size}} = \frac{\sigma}{\sqrt{n}} \qquad (5\text{-}1)$$

Of course, we usually don't know σ, because we very rarely have access to the entire population, so in most cases, we estimate it with the sample SD. In this case, the SE(M) is $31.5/\sqrt{100} = 3.15$ mm. This formula tells us, based on a single sample, how spread out the means will be for a given value of σ and n. Fortunately for us (and for the measures), we don't have to repeat the study hundreds of times to find out.

So, the SD reflects how close *individual observations* come to the sample mean, and the SE(M) reflects, for a given sample size, how close the *means* of repeated samples will come to the population mean. Of course, all this is assuming that the repeated samples are random samples of the population we began with, normal males; the **null hypothesis** still holds.

THE CRITICAL VALUE, DECISION REGIONS, ALPHA AND TYPE I ERRORS

All the preceding discussion suggests that Figure 5-2 is working from the wrong distribution. What we really need to know is the distribution of means for a sample size of 100 under the null hypothesis that they all come from the untreated population with a true mean of 161.5. We also know that the distribution will have a standard deviation (the standard error of the mean) of 3.15. This distribution is portrayed in Figure 5-3, where we have stretched the X-axis. The solid line is the distribution of *means* and the dotted line above it the distribution of individual values.

We're getting there. We now have an idea about how means for a sample size of 100 would be distributed, just by chance, if the null hypothesis were true. Of course we don't know whether it's true or false—that's our goal. But if we think about our situation for a minute, it's easy to see, at least in qualitative terms, how we can go from a computed sample mean to a probability that it could arise by chance. If the difference between the sample mean and 161.5 is very small compared to the width of the distribution, say 1.5 (so the sample mean is at 163.0), then it likely did arise by chance and we would be unlikely to conclude the treatment worked and reject the null hypothesis. Quantitatively, we would say that the

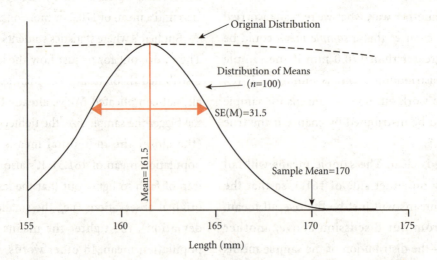

FIGURE 5-3 The distribution of means of *n*=100 from the population in Figure 5-1.

probability that the difference arose by chance was large. Conversely, if the difference between sample and population means were large, say 15 (a sample mean of 176.5), then the sample mean is way out on the tail of the distribution so the probability of observing it by chance is very small, and we would likely conclude it was a real difference.

Taking this one step further, we can see that there is a relationship between the magnitude of the difference and the likelihood it arose by chance. The larger the difference, the lower the likelihood it could arise by chance. We could let it go at that, and just compute the actual probability; in fact, in a few pages we'll do just that. But for the moment we want to push the logic just a bit further.

Let's acknowledge that, at the end of the day, we want a clear statement that either the drug worked or it didn't. This must be related to the probability the difference arose by chance. To turn it into a decision situation, all we need do is to declare *a priori* that below a given probability of occurrence, we'll assume that the difference is real, and *reject the null hypothesis*. And anyone who has ever read a journal article using stats knows what that number is: 0.05. We call this "alpha" or α. Of course, another way of saying it is that there is a probability of 0.05 (i.e., alpha) that we'll mistakenly assume there is a difference when there isn't:

Alpha (α) is the probability of concluding that there is a difference when there is not, and the sample actually came from the H_0 distribution.

We'll delve into the history of the magic 0.05 a bit later, but for the moment, continuing this line of reasoning, declaring this number as the *critical value* that decides between "real" differences and chance differences has some consequences. What it means, in effect, is shown in Figure 5-4. Below a certain critical value of the difference, which corresponds to a probability in the tail of the null hypothesis distribution of 0.05, we'll accept that there is no difference; i.e., accept the null hypothesis (or, to be pedantic about it, fail to reject it, since we can never prove the nonexistence of something). Conversely, in another region corresponding to differences greater

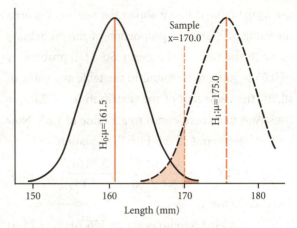

FIGURE 5-4   Testing if our result differs from a mean of 175.

than the critical value, we'll reject the null hypothesis and conclude that there is a difference. This then establishes an "Accept H_0" region and a "Reject H_0" region.

In the case of the present study, what we need to do is work out the location on the X-axis that corresponds to the critical value, where there is 5% of the distribution to the right. That's not hard, since others wiser than we have worked it all out in advance. A first step is to transform the raw data into standard error (SE) units, called a *z* **transformation**. We simply compute how many SEs away from the mean a particular value is. In the present example, the mean is 161.5 and the SE is 3.15. So a value of 164.65 is 1 SE above the mean; a value of 167.8 is 2 SEs above the mean. The actual formula is:

$$z = \frac{(x - \mu)}{\sigma / \sqrt{n}} \qquad (5\text{-}2)$$

where μ (called *mu*, Greek for "m") is the population mean and σ (*sigma*, Greek for s) is the population **standard deviation (SD)**. By using *z* transformation, we bring you the *z* distribution where we study how skewed away from the mean a particular value is and how this distribution of change is characterized. For a large population, *z* distribution of mean of this particular value always complies with the rule of normality. That's what CLT (central limit theorem) tells us! (See Chapter 4 and remember it). If we go to Table A in the Appendix, we see that it shows the relation between a particular value, expressed in standard error units, and the probability. Critical to use of the table is that it shows the relation between the value of X and the proportion of the probability curve to the right of the mean. So a tail probability of 0.05 is going to be found in the table at a value of [0.50 (the right half of the distribution) − 0.05] = 0.45. And that corresponds to a z value of 1.65. Now we just have to put all this into the equation:

$$z = 1.65 = \frac{X - 161.5}{31.5 / \sqrt{100}} = \frac{X - 161.5}{3.15} \qquad (5\text{-}3)$$

and solving for X:

$$X = 161.5 + (1.65 \times 3.15) = 166.70 \qquad (5\text{-}4)$$

So if our experiment yields a sample mean larger than 166.70, the likelihood it could have arisen by chance is less than 0.05, 1 in 20, and it's statistically *significant*. That is, any sample mean to the right of the critical value in Figure 5-4 is significant; anything to the left is not. In the present case, the observed mean of 170 is to the right of the critical value, so, despite our initial reservations, the result was unlikely to arise by chance. We therefore **reject the null hypothesis** and declare a significant difference. That's what "significant" means—the chance that a difference this big or bigger could have arisen by chance if the null hypothesis were true is less than 1 in 20. No more and no less.

This is the approach that was advocated by Jerzy Neyman and Egon Pearson about a century ago. The critical idea is that you don't associate a probability directly with the calculated sample mean. Instead, you use knowledge of the population mean, the SD, and the sample size to create an Accept and a Reject region, using a preordained value of the tail probability. You then do the study, compute the sample mean, and either it falls to the left or to the right of the critical value, so you accept or reject H_0; you declare that the difference was or was not statistically significant. And you stop.

However, don't lose sight of that 1 in 20 probability. The decision all hinged on a likelihood of 1 in 20 that the difference could arise by chance. This means, of course, that for every 20 studies that report a significant difference at the 0.05 level, one is wrong. In short, there is a 1 in 20 chance that we will reject the null hypothesis when it is true. This is called "making a Type I error."

Why Type I? To distinguish it from Type II, of course. That's next on the agenda.

THE ALTERNATIVE HYPOTHESIS AND β ERROR

Things might not have turned out the way they did. The sample mean, after the experiment was over, could have actually ended up to the left of the critical value, in the "Accept H_0" region. There are two ways this could arise:

1. The most obvious is simply that Mangro doesn't work, so that any difference that arises is due to chance. The sample mean comes from the null hypothesis distribution, and so most (95%) of the time, it will lie in the Accept H_0 region. If this is the case, then we conclude there is no difference and we're right, there is none. All is well with the world.

2. On the other hand, Mangro might well work. We might have done the experiment exactly the same way, but this time the sample mean was not so large, say 165.0. In this case, we would conclude there was no significant difference as well. But in fact it did work, so when we conclude that it didn't we have made a mistake.

This can come about in many ways. It may be that the treatment effect is smaller than we thought, but still non-zero. Or the variability in individual observations (the SD) was larger. Or we did the study with a smaller sample size so that, although everything else was the same, the SE(M) is larger. Regardless of the cause of the problem, we would be making a mistake. As you might suspect, it's called a Type II error: concluding there is no difference (accepting the null hypothesis) when there is one—the null hypothesis should be rejected.

It clearly matters, and not only because we don't like making mistakes. It's also harder to publish negative results, so pragmatically, accepting H_0 is a hard way to get ahead. In any case, having put all that time and money into the study, it would be nice to know which alternative—the treatment doesn't work, or it does work, but Ma Nature conspired against us—is the truth.

But how can we tell these two apart? After all, all we have is a sample mean and a hypothetical null distribution. Actually, no. We have a sample mean and *two* hypothetical distributions; one corresponding to the distribution of means under the null hypothesis that the treatment didn't work and a second, sitting off to the right, under the **alternative hypothesis, H_1**, that it *did* work. That is, if we are going to assume that there is a difference, this is tantamount to saying that the sample mean no longer comes from the H_0 distribution—that's the distribution of sample means if the treatment did not work. Instead, we're saying that the sample mean actually comes from a distribution of sample means resulting from a non-zero treatment effect. That is, there is now a second distribution, the H_1 distribution, centered around some treatment effect, which we'll call Δ (delta). This is shown in Figure 5-5.

Now we cannot actually tell them apart. We can never really conclude whether the treatment didn't work, or it did work but we missed it. But with this picture, showing the distribution of sample means under both assumptions, what we can do is compute the probability that the alternative hypothesis is true, for a particular configuration of treatment effect, standard deviation, and sample size. It's just the area of the H_1 distribution to the left of the critical value, as shown in Figure 5-5.

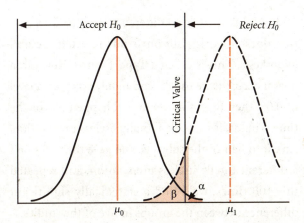

FIGURE 5-5   The null and alternate hypotheses.

To do that, we need one more piece of information. We know where the H_0 distribution is—centered on 0.0 treatment effect, obviously. In this case, that's at 161.5 cm. We know the width of the H_0 distribution—it's $\sigma/\sqrt{n}$. We can easily make a small additional assumption that, wherever the H_1 distribution is, it has the same width. (This is called the assumption of **homoscedasticity**, don't ask us why.) But we also have to make an assumption about where the H_1 distribution is centered.

How in the world can we do that? After all, we did the experiment to find out what the treatment effect was. But on reflection, right now our best guess is that it's zero, given the way the data turned out. So we have to make a blatant guess. The logic goes like this:

"Darn drat.[7] The study didn't work. I wonder if this is because we just didn't have enough power to detect a difference." (Power is a good word here. We'll explain it in a minute.) By this we mean, to reiterate, maybe the SD is too large, the sample size too small, or the treatment effect too small, to get us a significant difference. OK. Suppose we assume a plausible value of the treatment effect. Does the configuration put the H_1 distribution far enough to the right that there isn't much tail of it to the left of the critical value? If we can locate the plausible value, the center of the H_1 distribution, then it's trivial to figure out how much of the tail might hang to the left of the critical value. Essentially, we have Figure 5-5, where we've planted the H_1 distribution some distance to the right of the H_0 distribution (but not necessarily to the right of the critical value).

How do we do that? Well, in the present case, it's fairly straightforward. Mangro was guaranteed to add ½"—about 13 mm. So we should, to give the inventors credit, reassure ourselves that if, indeed, it delivered on the ½", we could deliver on a 0.05 significant difference. All we have to do is create a figure like 5-5, with the H_1 distribution at 161.5 + 13 = 174.5 mm. The standard error (standard deviation of the means) is still 3.15, and the critical value is at 166.70. We have all the pieces we need. The critical value is at:

$$z = \frac{174.5 - 166.70}{3.15} = \frac{7.80}{3.15} = 2.47 \qquad (5\text{-}5)$$

That then means that the probability of having a sample mean to the left of the critical value, if H_1 is true, is the probability corresponding to a z of 2.47, which is, from Table A, 0.0068 (that is, 0.5 − 0.4932). This is the β error, the likelihood of saying there is no difference when, in fact, there is. Or more formally, the probability of accepting H_0 when H_1 is true. Since it's kind of small, we're happy to go with it.

Beta (β) is the probability of concluding that there is no difference when there is, and the sample actually came from the H_1 distribution.

On the other hand, we began this bit by asking whether we had enough **power** to detect a difference. That is formally defined as $(1 - \beta)$, the probability of accepting the alternative hypothesis when it's true. And in this case, it turns out to be $(1.0 - 0.007) = 0.993$.

Power $(1-\beta)$ is the probability of concluding that there is difference when there is.

So if you're using this approach (and you may not, stay tuned), you write the paper with two critical elements. In the Methods section, at some point you say, "we used an alpha of 0.05."[8] And in the Results section, when you're talking about what happened, you say that either "The difference was statistically significant" or "The difference was not statistically significant." You **do not** say "The difference was highly significant." That's like saying "we *really* rejected the null hypothesis."

We've come to the end of the road. We've discussed all aspects of the Neyman-Pearson convention, based on the testing of hypotheses. Two in particular: H_0: it didn't work; and H_1: it did work. This, in turn, leads to four different conclusions: (a) the stuff really works, and our study showed that it worked; (b) it works, but our study concluded that it didn't; (c) it doesn't do anything, and that's what our study said;

and (d) it doesn't do anything, but we concluded that it did. The first part of each of the four phrases—it works or it doesn't work—is, in fact, beyond our ken. This is something that only an omnipotent being would know; it is "truth" in the Platonic sense[9] that we can get glimpses of through our studies, but never know definitely. We can show the four conclusions in a two-way table, as in Table 5-2. The columns show "reality," while the rows show what we found in our study. Cell A describes the situation in which there really is a difference, and that's also what our study showed. Congratulations are in order; we've come to the right conclusion. As you can see in the table, this box reflects the *power* of the study—the probability of finding a difference when it's there, which is $1 - \beta$. Similarly, Cell D shows another place where we've come to the correct answer—there really is no difference because of the intervention, and that's also what our study said. Unfortunately, that leaves two boxes to be filled.

TABLE 5-2   The results of a study and the types of errors

Study Results	Truth				
	Difference			**No Difference**	
Difference	✓			Type I Error	
	$(1-\beta)$	A	B	α	
No Difference	Type II Error	C	D	✓	
	β			$(1-\alpha)$	

In Cell B, there is no difference (i.e., the intervention doesn't work), but our study rejected the null hypothesis. This is called a **Type I** error. How often does it occur? If we use the commonly accepted α level of 0.05, then by definition, it will happen 5% of the time. That is, if we took a totally useless preparation, gave it to half of the subjects, and gave the other half a different totally useless preparation, and repeated this 100 times, we'd find a statistically significant difference between the groups in five of the studies.

Cell C shows the opposite situation—the stuff really works, but our study failed to reject H_0. With

---

[8]*Of course you used 0.05; doesn't everybody? It's like saying the sun rose in the east this morning.*

[9]*That refers to the Greek philosopher; it is not describing a chaste relationship between individuals, even if one has used Mangro.*

great originality, statisticians call this a **Type II** error,[10] and its probability of occurring is denoted by β. By tradition, we'd like β to be 0.15 to 0.20 (meaning that the power of the study was between 80 and 85%). There are many factors that affect β—the magnitude of the difference between the groups, the variability within the groups, and α. But, the factor that we have the most control over is the sample size; the larger the study, the more power (and the smaller is β); the smaller the study the less power. So, if you did a study and the results look promising, but they didn't reach statistical significance, the most likely culprit is that there were too few subjects.[11]

On "Proving" the Null Hypothesis

One final bit of philosophical logic. All along, we've used the phrases "accept the null hypothesis" and "fail to reject the null hypothesis" more or less interchangeably, since to the average reader they differ only in pomposity. However, to serious statisticians and philosophers of science (both of which categories exclude present company), there is a world of difference, and by treating them as synonyms we have offended them terribly.

It really is illustrated with the example. When we did the study with a sample size of 100, we found that there was a significant difference, so we rejected H_0 and concluded the treatment worked. Exactly the same data, only a smaller sample size, and we might come to the opposite conclusion. But the fact is, there really was a difference between the groups; it's just that we couldn't find it. Hence the logic that we "failed to reject the null hypothesis" acknowledges that there may well be a treatment effect, but we have insufficient evidence to prove it. It's logically analogous to the old philosophical analysis of the statement, "All swans are white," which can never be proven correct because you can never assemble all swans to be sure.[12]

To be a bit more formal about it, you can never prove the non-existence of something (although we'll try to in Chapter 19). The lack of evidence is not the same as the evidence of a lack. Our study may not have found an effect because it was badly designed, we used the wrong measures, or, more likely, the sample size was too small (and hence the power was low). The next study, which is better executed, may very well show a difference. Hence, all we can do in the face of negative findings is to say that we haven't disproven the null hypothesis, *yet*.

Where Did That 5% Come From?

We promised you we'd explain why the magic number for journal editors is a *p* level of 0.05 or less, so here we go. The historical reason is that the grand-daddy of statistics, Sir Ronald Fisher, sayeth unto the multitudes, "Let it be 0.05," and it was 0.05. We'll see in a bit that, as with most historical "truths," this isn't quite right. But at another level, 5% does seem to correspond to our gut-level feeling of the dividing between chance and something "real" going on![13]

Try this out with some of your friends. Tell them you'll play a game—you'll flip a coin and if it comes up heads, each of them will pay you $1.00; whereas if it comes up tails, you'll pay each of them $1.00. You keep tossing and, *mirabile dictu*, it keeps coming up heads. How many tosses before your friends think the game is rigged?

If we were doing it with our friends, they would say "One or fewer." But, with a less cynical audience, many will start becoming suspicious after four heads in a row, and the remainder after five. Let's work out

---

[10]This table doesn't show the all-too-frequent Type III error—getting the correct answer to a question no one is really asking.

[11]It doesn't make any sense to calculate the power of a study if you found a significant difference—if you found significance, you obviously had sufficient power. As our kids would say, "Duh!"

[12]Also analogous to the verdict of the O.J. Simpson trial, and all criminal trials, where he was found "not guilty," and was not found "innocent" (which then led on to a civil suit). That means that he was presumed innocent until proven guilty, and there was not sufficient evidence to prove him guilty. So the trial failed to reject the hypothesis of innocence. The Scots have a better solution; they say "Not proven."

[13]James Bond said, in one of the early books in the series, "Once is happenstance, twice is luck, three times is an enemy conspiracy." As we'll see, he was off by one or two events.

the probabilities. For one head (and no cheating), the probability of a head is 1 in 2, or 50%. Two heads, it's 1 in 2^2, or 25%; three heads is 1 in 2^3, or 12.5%; four heads is 1 in 2^4, or 6.25%; and the probability of five heads in a row is 1 in 2^5, which is just over 3%. So 5% falls nicely in between; Sir Ronnie was probably right.

Ritual and Myth of $p<0.05$

Having just fed you the party line about the history and sanctity of $p<0.05$, let's take much of it back. First, Fisher did in fact talk about a null hypothesis (which, by the way, he said need not always be the "nil" hypothesis of nothing going on), but never talked about "accepting" or "rejecting" it; he simply said we should work out its exact probability. Second, he said that we should go through the rigamarole of running statistical tests and figuring out probabilities only if we know very little about the problem we're dealing with (Gigerenzer, 2004); otherwise, just look at the data. Finally, he was actually the author of the heretical words:

No scientific worker has a fixed level of significance at which from year to year, and in all circumstances, he rejects hypotheses; he rather gives his mind to each particular case in the light of his evidence and his ideas (Fisher, 1956).

Which mirrors what the famous philosopher and skeptic David Hume said way back in 1748: "A wise man proportions his belief to the evidence," and Carl Sagan turned into his battle cry of "Extraordinary claims require extraordinary proof."

That is, do we need the same level of evidence to believe that non-steroidal anti-inflammatory drugs help with arthritis as the claim that extract of shark cartilage cures cancer? There have been roughly 10 papers by every rheumatologist in the world demonstrating the first, and not a single randomized trial showing the second. Insisting that the same p level of 0.05 applies in both situations is somewhat ridiculous.

So where does that leave us? Should we test for $p<0.05$ or not? We'd love to say that saner heads have now prevailed, and we consider the strength of the evidence, and speak of values as near significant or highly significant, not just whether the probability is less than or greater than 1 in 20. Unfortunately, if anything, things are more rigid. To quote a recent JAMA editorial review when we tried to get away with it:

JAMA reserves the term "trend" for results of statistical tests for trend, and does not use it to describe results that do not reach statistical significance. We also do not use similar terms such as "marginal significance" or "borderline significance." Instead, such findings should just be described as "no statistically significant association" or the equivalent, with relevant confidence intervals and p-values provided.

In brief, if you want to pass Miss Manner's rules of statistical etiquette, you can't talk about "trends," "near significant result," "highly significant result," and so on. It is or it ain't.[14]

WHEN CAN YOU PEEK? EXPLORATORY DATA ANALYSIS, STOPPING RULES, AND STATISTICAL ETIQUETTE

The Bridge argument was not Tukey's only or largest contribution to the science of statistics.[15] Indeed, most have forgotten the bridge argument or never came across it in their education. Tukey also invented a number of methods we've reviewed in this book: the Stem-and-Leaf Plot, the Box-and-Whisker Plot, jackknife estimation, and some post-hoc tests are all attributed to him. Some claim that he even invented two computer terms: bit—short for "binary digit"—and software, although the latter is disputed. But what he is best known for is exploratory data analysis (which the cognoscenti call EDA), which he described as:

If we need a short suggestion of what exploratory data analysis is, I would suggest that

---

[14]Having said that, we're both guilty of exactly this kind of bet-hedging on occasion. Do as we say, not as we do.

[15]Or to the world: among other things, Tukey also worked on designing the U-2 spy plane and the H-bomb; not all statisticians are useless drudges.

1. *It is an attitude AND.*
2. *A flexibility AND.*
3. *Some graph paper (or transparencies, or both).*

Tukey strongly felt that the statistician's job was to really understand what his data were telling him before any *p* values were produced. In fact, another one of his (many) quotes is that "Exploratory data analysis … does not need probability, significance or confidence." To that end, his book, *EDA*, introduced the community to all sorts of strategies to get to really know what Ma Nature was trying to tell the researcher (some of which we described in Chapter 3). Only after the data have been suitably explored are you justified in proceeding to the now appropriate statistical test.

This seems all eminently reasonable. So what led to communal apoplexy? Well, the statistician's golden rule (one of many) is "In the final analysis, thou shalt not mess with thy data before the final analysis." There are two issues underlying the commandment. The first relates to *p* values yet again. Strictly speaking, every time you do a statistical analysis, you have a 0.05 chance of rejecting H_0 incorrectly. So if you sneak a peek at the data after half the subjects have been enrolled, there goes one 0.05. And if you take another look two weeks later, there's another 0.05. And on it goes. You have committed a cardinal sin and "lost control of your alpha level," and may end up in numerical purgatory for eternity.

Of course, one solution is to just look at the data, as Tukey would have us to. Graph it, scatter plot it, survival curve it, or whatever, but don't compute a *p* value. That's OK, isn't it? Yeah, but…

So you're in the middle of the NIH-funded trial of date pits and toenail cancer, and you look at the survival curves. Fifty percent of the placebo group are goners, but 75% of the pit group are alive and kicking. Trouble is, there are only 12 patients in each group so far. Now you have a problem. It's unethical to keep the trial going and deny an effective therapy to the patients in the placebo group. It's also unethical to do a *p* value early. So what can the poor ethical researcher do? One strategy is called "stopping rules," where, if the risk reduction is greater than *X*,

you're entitled to declare a victor and call the whole thing off and save a few placebo group lives in the process. Trouble is, it's hard to separate real benefit from chance; after all, $p < 0.001$ does happen one time in a thousand, and there is good evidence that trials stopped early do overestimate the benefit. So a controversy continues to rage, with little sign of resolution. We will explore no further; suffice it to say that, while statistical methods have evolved to deal with these issues, they remain controversial.

But there's another, even more catastrophic, danger lurking in them thar hills. Imagine a different trial now; one where we are looking at quality of life as a primary endpoint. We use a bunch of standard measures—the EQ5-D, the SF-36, the GHQ, or whatever—and we administer them every three months for two years of follow-up. Now suppose we sneak the peek at 18 months and discover that at 3, 6, 9, 12, and 15 months none of the measures showed a difference, but at 18 months there was a significant difference for the EQ5-D but none of the others. Care to guess how the journal article will be written?

Lest you think we're making this up, sadly there's much evidence that this kind of data culling is not a rare phenomenon. One review (Lexchin et al., 2003) found that studies funded by drug companies were four times as likely to show a significant difference favoring the drug as those not funded by companies. A follow-up study (Lexchin, 2012) showed a number of reasons for this: the studies may use an inappropriate dose of the comparator drug to reduce efficacy or increase side effects, selective nonreporting of negative studies, liberal statistical tests, reinterpreting the data, multiple publication of favorable trials, and, as we suggested above, only publishing the outcomes that favored the drug. This review found that, in 164 trials, there were 43 outcomes that did not favor the drug, and half (20) of them were unreported. In the remaining 23, five were reported as significant in the publication but not in the report.

Steps have been taken in the last decade or so to reduce the bias. Not surprisingly, the biggest concern is the clinical trial, where the most money can be made (or lost). Nowadays, if you want to publish your trial in *BMJ* or *The Lancet*, not only must you swear on a stack of Harrison's that you have no (or some) financial interest in the outcome, but you must have registered your trial when you began, telling the world exactly what you would do to whom and how. But long before CONSORT statements, statistics courses cautioned students to specify the analysis in detail at the time of the proposal and never, Never, NEVER depart from the initial plan.

And that is why Tukey is both worshipped and reviled. Exploratory data analysis, with or without *p* values, where you conduct the first analysis to determine how to conduct the later analysis, breaks all the rules. Well, all *those* rules. Which brings us to another school of thought altogether that falls in line with Tukey's approach. This second perspective is that the good scientist is sensitive to the story her data tells her. She pokes the data every way she can think of to understand the data better. Only when she is certain of the underlying trends does she punch the *p* value button. In short, selective use of some variables and transformations is not only condoned; it is viewed as essential. Moreover, early analysis, while the study is underway, is also encouraged, so that you don't waste time and people pursuing hypotheses that ultimately turn out to be dumb ideas. Two quotes, both from Fred Mosteller, a famous statistician, say it all:

Although we often hear that data speak for themselves, their voices can be soft and sly (Mosteller et al., 1983, p. 234).

The main purpose of a significance test is to inhibit the natural enthusiasm of the investigator (Mosteller and Bush, 1954, pp. 331–332).

Who is right? Well this won't be the last time we will answer with an unequivocal "It depends." On the one hand, in a typical clinical trial, the goal is really not to advance understanding—it's to find out whether the therapy works or not. And the stakes are high—millions of dollars may hang in the balance. So this is not the place for fudge factors.

On the other hand, science is a detective story. As Mary Budd Rowe, professor of philosophy of science said: "Science is a special kind of story-telling with no right or wrong answers, just better and better stories."

As anyone who has read *The Double Helix* (Watson, 1968) will attest, when it's done right it's a huge mystery story. But somehow, as we keep adding layers of bureaucracy to the research game, maybe, just maybe, we're throwing out the baby with the bathwater. This week, we sent an article to *BMJ*, and it came back with the ominous note that it had been "desubmitted"[16] for lack of dotted i's and crossed t's. Turns out that in *BMJ* guidelines, they now want you to submit the original grant proposal if at all possible, and if you have departed in any way from what you said you would do four years ago, you must explain why. Boy, isn't *that* a cue to follow the leads! Tukey is turning over in his grave.

MULTIPLICITY AND TYPE I ERROR RATES

Until now, we have been discussing statistical tests as if they were hermits, living on their own in splendid isolation. In fact, they're more like cockroaches—if you see one, you can bet there'll be plenty of others. It's extremely unusual for a paper to report only one test or *p* level, and that can be a problem. The problem has a name: **multiplicity**, which simply means multiple statistical tests within a single study. Actually, multiplicity situations are like cockroaches in many regards: they're ubiquitous, pesky, and difficult to deal with. First, let's outline what the problem is.

In the world of mathematics, the probability of at least one test being significant is 1 minus the probability that none are significant (this rule is known to be the law of 'at least one'). It's just simple math algebra and easy enough to memorize. In one, Bennett et al. (2010) showed a subject a series of photographs of people expressing specific emotions in social situations, and the subject had to identify the emotion. The approach was very technical, using

---

[16]*So much for the King's English.*

"a 6-parameter rigid-body affine realignment of the fMRI timeseries, coregistration of the data to a T_1-weighted anatomical image, and 8 mm full-width at half-maximum (FWHM) Gaussian smoothing" (we don't know what they're talking about either). After searching 8064 voxels produced by the fMRI, they found three with significant signal changes during the photo condition compared to rest. The only fly in the ointment was that the "subject" was a salmon, and a dead one at that. In the other study, Austin et al. (2006) searched through 223 of the most common diagnoses in a large database and found that people born under the astrological sign of Leo had a higher probability of gastrointestinal hemorrhage, and those born under Sagittarius had a higher probability of fractures of the humerus, compared to the other signs combined.

The problem, as you've probably guessed by now, is the large number of statistical tests that were run, compounded by the fact that none of the hypotheses were specified beforehand; they were fishing expeditions, pure and simple (and not just because the subject in one study was a salmon). Admittedly, these are extreme cases, with many variables, and were conducted to illustrate the difficulties that are encountered under such circumstances, but the question is still valid: Is it necessary to adopt a more stringent cutoff for p when a study involves more than one test of significance? The question is simple, but the answer is far from straightforward. One leading epidemiologist (Rothman, 1990) argues that you should never correct for multiple tests, because it will lead to too many Type II errors; while others, like Ottenbacher (1998) are just as vociferous that you always should because not correcting leads to too many Type I errors. Moyé (1998) puts it well: "Type I error accumulates with each executed hypothesis test and must be controlled by the investigators." So what should we do?

Not surprisingly, your devoted authors have jumped head-first into this fray (Streiner and Norman, 2011). To begin with, let's differentiate among various situations where multiplicity may rear its ugly head. The first is when we have done a study involving two or more groups, and we want to see if they differ at baseline. If it's a randomized controlled study (RCT), don't bother to test at all. The p level under such circumstances is meaningless, since the probability that any differences could have arisen by chance is 100%; after all, what else *could* account for any differences if the subjects are divided randomly? If it's not an RCT, then the main purpose for testing baseline differences is to see if we should correct for them. (We'll have more to say about dealing with baseline differences in Chapters 14 and 15). Here, it's probably better to have Type I errors rather than Type II, because it doesn't cost much to control for differences that may not actually exist. So, correcting for multiplicity isn't necessary.

The second situation is when we may have a limited number of outcomes, and we have specified them beforehand. A good example of this is factorial ANOVA (see Chapter 7), which may routinely test five or 10 hypotheses. Typically, the researcher may be interested in only one or two, each relating to a different hypothesis, so it doesn't make sense to correct for all of the tests that will be ignored. Here, we tend to side with Rothman and not correct. It may result in some false positive results, but that's likely better than closing off potentially useful research areas with false negative conclusions.

The final area is when we haven't specified hypotheses *a priori* (a fancy way of saying we're on a fishing expedition). This often arises when people have measured a number of variables and then examine the table of correlations to find out which relationships are significant. Our advice here would be that you definitely have to correct for multiplicity; how to do so is discussed in Chapter 7, under Post-Hoc Comparisons.

STATISTICAL INFERENCE AND THE SIGNAL-TO-NOISE RATIO

The essence of the z-test (and as we will eventually see, the essence of all statistical tests), is the notion of a **signal**, based on some observed difference between groups, and a **noise**, which is the variability in the measure between individuals within the group. If the signal—the difference—is large enough as compared with the noise within the group, then it is reasonable to conclude that the signal has some effect. If the signal does not rise above the noise level, then it is reasonable to conclude that no association exists. The basis of all inferential statistics is to attach a probability to this ratio.

Nearly all statistical tests are based on a signal-to-noise ratio, where the *signal* is the important relationship and the *noise* is a measure of individual variation.

To bring home the concept of signal-to-noise ratio, we'll make a brief diversion into home audio. Pour yourself a glass of finest red wine, embrace yourself the sofa cushion, enjoy yourself a piece of nice orchestra masterpiece via playback from CDs. So good? That is because CDs could deliver all the rap noise at a zillion decibels—completely distortion-free.

All that hissing and wowing was **noise**, brought about by scratches and dents on the album or random magnetization on the little tape. This was magically removed by digitizing the signal and implanting it as a bit string on the CD, letting the **signal**—the original music (or rap noise or heavy metal noise)—come booming on through. In short, two decades of sound technology can be boiled down to a quest for higher and higher signal-to-noise ratios so worse and worse music can be played louder and

louder without distortion.

Although we are referring to music, we are simply using this as one example of a small signal detected above a sea of noise. When it comes to receiving the radio signal from Voyager 2 as it rounds the bend at Uranus, signal-to-noise ratio of the radio receiver is not just an issue of entertainment value; it's a measure of whether any information will be detected and whether all those NASA bucks are being well spent.

You might imagine the signals from Voyager 2 whistling through the ether as a "blip" from space. This is superimposed on the random noise of cosmic rays, magnetic fields, sunspots, or whatever. The end result looks like Figure 5-6. Now, if we project these waves onto the *Y*-axis, we get a distribution of signals and noises remarkably like what we have already been seeing. The signals come from a distribution with an average height about +1.1 microvolts (μV), and the noises around another distribution at + 0.7 μV. If we now imagine detecting a blip in our receiver and trying to decide if it is a signal or just a random squeak, we can see that it may come from either distribution. Of course, if it is sufficiently high, we then conclude that it is definitely unlikely to have occurred by chance. Conversely, if it is very low, we do not hear it at all above the noise, and we falsely conclude that no signal was present. That is, there are always four possibilities: (1) concluding we heard

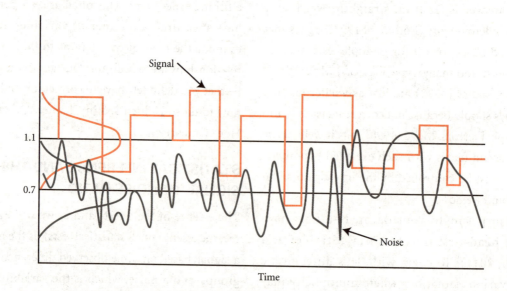

FIGURE 5-6   Spectra of radio signal and noise.

a signal when there was none, (2) concluding there was a signal when there was, (3) concluding no signal when there was one, and (4) concluding there was no signal when there was none. Two of these are correct decisions (2 and 4), and two are wrong ones (1 and 3). Our problem is to determine which our decision is.

TWO TAILS VERSUS ONE TAIL

You might have noticed that, all through the phallus example, we were preoccupied with the right side of the H_0 distribution. For obvious reasons, we were really not interested in a treatment that made things shorter. As a consequence, we worried only about committing a Type I error on the high side. This kind of test, focusing only on one side, is called, with astounding logic, a **one-tailed** test:

A *one-tailed test* specifies the direction of the difference of interest in advance.

On the other hand, given the dubious provenance of the therapy, there exists the possibility, ever so slight, that it might make them shrink, not grow. If so, we would surely be interested in such a consequence, if for no other reason than to fend off lawsuits. That is, we might reframe the alternative hypothesis, so that instead of asking whether the Mangro group is *larger* than the population, we might ask whether it is *different* from the population, in either direction. If we do this, then we are equally concerned about Type I errors in either direction, albeit for very different reasons. Consequently, we have to think about the H_0 distribution with a critical value on both sides, which is called, as an obvious extension a **two-tailed** test.

A *two-tailed test* is a test of any difference between groups, regardless of the direction of the difference.

If we frame it formally, for a one-tailed test, the two hypotheses are:

$$H_0: \mu_A < \mu_B \qquad (5\text{-}6)$$
$$H_1: \mu_A \geq \mu_B \qquad (5\text{-}7)$$

or, if the direction is the other way around:

$$H_0: \mu_A > \mu_B \qquad (5\text{-}8)$$
$$H_1: \mu_A \leq \mu_B \qquad (5\text{-}9)$$

where A and B refer to the two groups.

For a two-tailed test, the null and alternate hypotheses are:

$$H_0: \mu_A = \mu_B \qquad (5\text{-}10)$$
$$H_1: \mu_A \neq \mu_B \qquad (5\text{-}11)$$

Aside from the philosophy, it is not immediately evident what difference all this makes. But remember that the significance or nonsignificance of the test is predicated on the probability of reaching some conventionally small criterion (usually 0.05). If this occurs only on one side of the distribution, then from Table A in the book Appendix, we see that this probability occurs at a *z* value of 1.645 (i.e., 1.645 SDs from the mean). By contrast, if we want the *total* probability on both sides to equal 0.05, then the probability one side is 0.025, which corresponds to a *z* value of 1.96. So, to achieve significance with a one-tailed test, we need only achieve a *z* value of 1.645; if it is a two-tailed test, we must make it to 1.96. Clearly the two-tailed test is a bit more stringent.

You would think that one-tailed tests would be the order of the day. When we test a drug against a placebo, we don't usually care to prove that the drug is worse than the placebo.[17] If we want to investigate the effects of high versus low social support, we wouldn't be thrilled to find that folks with high support are more depressed. In fact, except for the circumstance where you are testing two equivalent treatments against each other, it is difficult to find circumstances where a researcher isn't cheering for one side over the other.

However, there is a strong argument against the use of one-tailed tests. We may well begin a study hoping to show that our drug is better than a placebo, and we expect, for the sake of argument, a 10% improvement. Taking the one-tail philosophy to heart, imagine our embarrassment when the drug turns out to have lethal, but unanticipated, side effects, so that it is 80% worse. Now we are in the awkward situation of concluding that an 80% difference in this direction is *not significant*, where a 10% difference in the other direction was. Strictly speaking, in fact, we don't even have the right to analyze whether this difference

---

[17] *And trying too hard to prove this is a surefire way to cut oneself off from the filthy lucre of the drug companies.*

was statistically significant; we would have to say it resulted from chance. Oops![18]

So that is the basic idea. One-tailed tests are used to test a *directional* hypothesis, and two-tailed tests are used when you are *indifferent* as to the direction of the difference. Except that everybody uses two-tailed tests all the time.

CONFIDENCE INTERVALS

More and more, politicians are showing that they have no judgment of their own; whatever opinions they express are simply the results of the latest poll.[19] Polling is now a regular feature of most daily newspapers. And every poll somewhere contains the cryptic phrase, "This poll is accurate to ± 2 percentage points 95% of the time." Often we wonder what mere mortals make of that bit of convoluted prose. We know what they're supposed to make of it; it's what is called the **95% confidence interval** (CI or CI_{95}).[20]

It is a different kind of logic from what we've seen until now. Instead of focusing on two hypothetical means and bobbing back and forth, we go from the opposite direction, and say, "Well, it's all over. We did the study, and we got a treatment effect of 123.45. We know that this isn't 100% correct, because we're dealing with a sample, not the population. But, we're pretty confident that the truth lies around there somewhere. In fact, we're 95% confident that the mean lies between 121 and 125." Or, putting it another way, if we did the study a thousand times, on 950 occasions the means would lie between 121 and 125.

Now the question is how can we figure out what the bounds of 95% probability would be. Let's go back to Mangro and work it out. Recall that the calculated mean of the study sample was 170 mm,

and the standard error of the mean was 3.15 mm. What we now want to do is establish an upper and lower bound so that we're 95% confident that the true mean of the treated population lies between these bounds.

Let's look at the lower bound first. We want to find out where the population mean would have to be located in order that 2.5% [½ of (100 − 95)] of the sample means for $n=100$ would be greater than 170. The SE for a sample size 100 is 3.15. From the normal distribution, a 2.5% probability corresponds to a *z* value of 1.96. Therefore, the lower bound must be $(170 − 1.96 × 3.15) = 170 − 6.17 = 163.83$. So, if the true population mean was 163.83, there is a 2.5% chance of observing a sample mean greater than 170.

Using a similar logic, we calculate the upper bound as $(170 − 1.96 × 3.15) = 176.17$, meaning that if the true population mean were 176.17, there is a 2.5% chance of seeing a sample mean of 170 or less.

All this is evident from Figure 5-7, which shows that the left-hand curve—the distribution of sample means for a population mean of 163.83—ends up with a tail probability of 2.5% above 170; and the right-hand curve—the distribution of sample means with a population mean of 176.17—has 2.5% below the sample mean of 170.0.

There is also a consistency between this and the results of our hypothesis-testing exercise. Since the lower bound is actually larger than the original untreated population mean (161.5), it must be the case that the probability of seeing a sample mean of 170 is lower than 0.025, so the result is significant (both two-tailed, as in this case, and one-tailed as we first calculated it). Conversely, the upper bound of 176.17 is actually greater than our alternative hypothesis of 175, so the probability of observing a sample mean of 170 with a population mean of

---

[18]*This is not as farfetched as it may sound. Nobody expected pure oxygen to produce blindness in neonates, or that clofibrate would kill more people with high cholesterol than it saved, but that's what happened.*

[19]*Regrettably, with the notable exception of "Dubya" Bush, whose pronouncements clearly show he has lots of independent judgment; unfortunately, all of it bad.*

[20]*Confidence interval is the interval estimate of a population parameter under a specific confidence level and a calculated standard error. Confidence level can be denoted as $100×(1−α)\%$ and the mostly used confidence level in medical science is 0.95.*

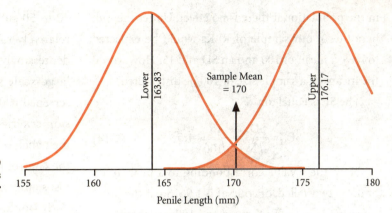

FIGURE 5-7   A 95% CI about a sample mean of 170, showing the distributions corresponding to the upper and lower bounds.

175 is greater than 0.025, and we do not reject the alternative hypothesis. All this is shown in Figure 5-8, where the lower bound of the CI is to the right of the null hypothesis line at 161.5, but the upper bound is beyond (to the right) of the alternative hypothesis line at 175.

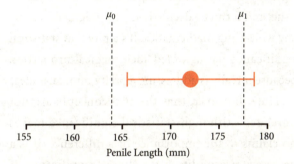

FIGURE 5-8   Another way of showing the 95% CI.

Putting it all together, the actual confidence interval will be written as:

$$CI_{95} = 170.0 \pm 1.96 \times \frac{31.5}{\sqrt{100}} = 170.0 \pm 6.17 \quad \textbf{(5-12)}$$
$$= (163.83, 176.17)$$

To formalize all this into an equation, the 95% confidence interval is:

$$CI = \overline{X} \pm z_{\alpha/2}\frac{s}{\sqrt{n}} = \overline{X} \pm (z_{\alpha/2} \times SE_M) \quad \textbf{(5-13)}$$

From this equation, it is evident that a relationship exists between the CI and the sample size and SD. The smaller the sample size or the larger the SD, the larger the CI; the larger the sample size or the smaller the SD, the smaller the CI. And considering the relationship between the CI and the null hypothesis, if the population mean falls within

the CI, the sample doesn't differ significantly from it. In the next chapter, we'll go into more detail on using the CIs from two groups to do "eyeball" tests of statistical significance.

STATISTICAL SIGNIFICANCE VERSUS CLINICAL IMPORTANCE

It may have dawned on you by now that statistical significance is all wrapped up in issues of probability and in tables at the ends of books. Whatever actual differences were observed were left far behind. Indeed, this is a very profound observation. Statistical significance, if you read the fine print once again, is simply an issue of the probability or likelihood that there *was* a difference—*any* difference of *any* size. If the sample size is small, even huge differences may remain non- (not in-) significant. By the same token, with a large sample size, even tiddly little differences may be statistically significant. As our wise old prof once said, "Too large a sample size and you are *doomed* to statistical significance."

As one example, imagine a mail-order brochure offering to make your rotten little offspring smarter so they can go to Ivy League colleges. Suppose the brochure even contains relatively legitimate research data to support its claims that the product was demonstrated to raise IQs by an amount significant "at the 0.05 level."

How big a difference is this? We begin by noting that IQ tests are designed to have a mean of 100 and SD of 15. Suppose we did a study with 100 RLKs (rotten little kids) who took the test. Just like the earlier example, we know the distribution of scores in the population if there is no effect. Under the null hypothesis, our sample of RLKs would be expected to have a mean of 100 and an SD and 15. How would the means of a sample size of 100 be distributed?

The SE is equal to:

$$SE_M = \frac{SD}{\sqrt{N}} = \frac{15}{\sqrt{100}} = 1.5 \qquad (5\text{-}14)$$

Now, the z value corresponding to a probability of 0.05 (two-tailed, of course) is 1.96. So, if the difference between the RLK mean and 100 is δ, then:

$$\frac{\delta}{1.5} = 1.96 \qquad (5\text{-}15)$$

so δ= (1.96 × 1.5) = 2.94 IQ points. That is, for N= 100, a difference of only 3 points would produce a statistically significant difference.

This is not the thing of which carefree retirement, supported by rich and adoring offspring, is made! Working the formula out for a few more sample sizes, it looks like Table 5-3. It would seem important, before finding that little cottage in the Florida swampland, to investigate how large the sample was on which the study was performed.

TABLE 5-3   Relation between sample size and the size of a difference needed to reach statistical significance when SD = 15

Sample size	Difference	Sample size	Difference
4	14.70	100	2.94
9	9.80	400	1.47
25	5.88	900	0.98
64	3.68		

Of course, like everything else, "large" and "small" in terms of sample size are relative terms. By and large (and small), if the study deals with measured quantities such as blood sugar, clinical ratings, aptitude tests, or depression scores, any difference worth worrying about can be attained with about 30 to 50 subjects in each group. By contrast, with relatively rare events such as death,[21] it may take depressingly large samples.[22] For example, the first large-scale sample of cholesterol-lowering drugs screened 300 000 men to get 4000 who fit the inclusion criteria. They were followed for 7 to 10 years, then analyzed. There were 38 heart-related deaths in the control group and 30 in the treatment group— just significant at the 0.05 level.

It would seem important to clearly outline the difference between statistical significance and clinical importance. As we have shown (we hope), statistical significance simply addresses the likelihood that the observed difference is, in truth, not actually zero. Statistical significance *says nothing about the actual magnitude or the importance of the difference*. The importance of the difference, often called **clinical significance** or **clinical importance**,[23] is a separate issue, and it can be decided only by judgment, not by any whiz-bang mathematics. It's a pity that statistical significance has assumed such magical properties, because it really is addressing a pretty mundane idea.

Note, however, that the two concepts are not unrelated. Although statistical significance makes no claims to the importance of a difference, it is a necessary precondition for clinical significance. If a difference is not statistically significant, it might as well be zero, or, for that matter, it might as well be in the opposite direction. Trying to argue that a difference that is not statistically significant (i.e., may be equal to zero) is still clinically important is illogical and, frankly, dumb.

Statistical significance is a necessary precondition for a consideration of *clinical importance* but says nothing about the actual magnitude of the effect.

EFFECT SIZES

Now that we've told you that there's a difference

---

[21]*Yes, we know, death has a 100% prevalence. But in a follow-up period sufficiently short that the investigators themselves have some certainty of survival, death can be relatively rare.*

[22]*There is an up side. With large samples, there is a need for multicenter trials, resulting in a need for international collaborative meetings in exotic locales.*

[23]*Presumably to make clinicians feel that there is a role for them just about the time that they are totally intimidated by the whole thing.*

between statistical significance and clinical importance, the question arises, how do you determine if a result is clinically important? One way is to simply turn to your colleague and ask, "OK, Charlie, do you think this is clinically important?" There are a couple of problems with this approach. First, it assumes that Charlie knows the answer, but he may be as much in the dark as you are. Second, there may not be much difficulty if the outcome is in units we can understand, such as the number of deaths in the treatment and control groups, or decreases in weight for people on a diet. But very often, we are dealing with scores on a scale. Is a three-point difference between groups on a pain scale clinically important? Without any other information, about all we can say is, "I dunno, whadda you think?" What we need is an index that can express differences between groups or relationships among variables using a common yardstick.[24] That common index is called the **effect size**, or ES.

Borrowing a definition from Vacha-Haase and Thompson (2004), we can define an ES as:

A statistic that quantifies the degree to which results diverge from the expectations (e.g., no difference in group means, no relationship between two variables) specified in the null hypothesis.

Many physicians, physiotherapists, lab medicine types, and others go through their entire career without ever encountering an ES. This doesn't (necessarily) make them benighted souls who have been deprived of a solid education. Rather, it reflects the type of measures they encounter in their work. Variables such as blood pressure, range of motion, or serum whatever are measured in commonly accepted units that all practitioners are familiar with (or at least should be). If $PaCO_2$ changes from 50 mmHg to 40 mmHg, that's all you really need to know—it moved from a level indicating acidosis into the normal range. The need to express change or differences between groups arises only when we're dealing with measures that use arbitrary scales. This applies to almost all paper-and-pencil questionnaires, and since there are literally tens of thousands of these, ESs won't be out of a job.

We're not going to go into the messy details of how you calculate ESs just yet; whenever possible, we'll spell it out when we discuss the different statistical tests. For now, suffice it to say that ESs come in two different flavors: those for tests that look at *differences* between groups, and those that evaluate the *proportion of variance* in one variable that is explained by another variable.[25] For historical reasons, the first class is known as *d* type effect sizes, and the second as *r* type. There is no upper limit for *d* type ESs, although in practice, it's unusual to find them greater than 1.0. For *r* type ESs, the upper limit is 1.0.

SAMPLE SIZE ESTIMATION

As we already indicated, a lot of clinical research is horrendously expensive. To keep the cost of doing the study down, it has become *de rigueur* to include a sample size calculation in the grant proposal. Essentially, this begins with the clinicians guessing the amount of the minimum *clinically* significant difference worth detecting. Then the statistics are messed around so that this minimum clinical difference corresponds to the statistical difference at $p=0.05$.

Returning to the example of the RLKs, suppose we decide, about the time the encyclopedia salesman is shoving his foot further into the door, that the minimum difference in IQ we would shell out for is 5 points. How big a sample would *Encyclopedia New found landia (E.N.)* need to prove that its books will raise IQ levels by 5 points?

Now the picture is like Figure 5-9. We know where the mean of the null distribution is, at 100 points. We know where the mean of the population of RLKs who had the dubious benefit of *E.N.* is—a 5-point gain, at IQ 105. Finally, we must keep in mind that the normal curves we have drawn in the figure

---

[24]*That's a meter stick for the 97% of the world that doesn't live in the U.S., Liberia, or Myanmar.*

[25]*Don't worry if you don't fully understand the distinction just yet. All will be revealed in the fullness of time.*

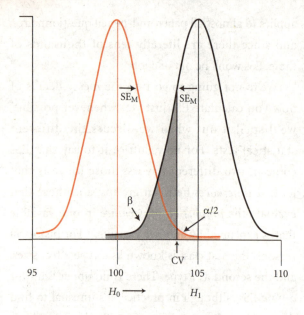

FIGURE 5-9   Mean IQ of sample of RLKs against the null and alternative hypotheses.

correspond to the distribution of *means* for repeated experiments, where the values are distributed about either 100 (if *E.N.* had no effect) or 105 (if *E.N.* had an effect). Of course, we don't know what distribution our *E.N.*-exposed RLKs come from; that's the point of the experiment. Either way, we know how wide the normal curves are—they correspond to an SD of $15 \div \sqrt{n}$. The challenge is to pull it all together and solve for *n*.

Imagine that the experiment was completed in such a way that it just achieved statistical significance at the 0.05 level, by the skin of its chin. Then the **critical value** (CV) corresponding to this state is 1.96 SEs to the right of the null mean. We will call this distance z_α, the z value corresponding to the alpha error. Now we have to decide how much we want to risk a Type II error, the area of the H_1 curve to the left of this point. Suppose we decide that we will risk a beta error rate of 0.10; this, then, puts the critical value at 1.28 SEs to the left of the alternative hypothesis mean. By analogy, this will be called z_β, the z value on the alternative curve corresponding to the beta error. IMPORTANT NOTE: The z-value for β is always based on a one-sided test. This doesn't contradict what we said about two-tailed tests because that applies only to the α level. The reason can be seen in Figure 5-9, where the tail of the H_1 distribution

overlaps that of H_0 on only one side.

We can formalize this with a couple of equations:

$$\frac{(CV - 100)}{s/\sqrt{n}} = z_\alpha = 1.96 \qquad (5\text{-}16)$$

Similarly:

$$\frac{(105 - CV)}{s/\sqrt{n}} = z_\beta = 1.28 \qquad (5\text{-}17)$$

where CV is the critical value between the H_0 and H_1 curves. Adding the two equations together, we get rid of CV.

$$\frac{(105 - 100)}{s/\sqrt{n}} = z_\alpha + z_\beta = 3.24 \qquad (5\text{-}18)$$

If, for the sake of generality, we call (105–100) the difference Δ, the algebra becomes:

$$\frac{\Delta}{s/\sqrt{n}} = (z_\alpha + z_\beta) \qquad (5\text{-}19)$$

so that

$$\sqrt{n} = \frac{(z_\alpha + z_\beta)\, s}{\Delta} \qquad (5\text{-}20)$$

and squaring everything up:

$$n = \left[\frac{(z_\alpha + z_\beta)\, s}{\Delta} \right]^2 \qquad (5\text{-}21)$$

We should put this equation in big, bold type because it, and variations on it, are the things of which successful grant proposals are made. The same strategy will be used in subsequent chapters to derive sample size estimates for a variety of statistical tests. To save you the agony of having to work out this formula every time you want to see how many subjects you need to compare two means, we've given you these in Table B in the Appendix at the end of the book. Obviously, we couldn't do this for every possible value of σ and Δ. What we've done is to present N for different *ratios* of σ ÷ Δ.

Note that the ratio of the difference between groups to the SD is called the **effect size** (ES). The effect size is like a z-score, and it tells you how big the difference is in SD units. If the difference you're looking for is 5 points and the SD is 15 points, then the ES is 5 ÷ 15 = 0.33. So the ratio in the sample size equation, σ/Δ, is the inverse of the effect size.

For completeness, we'll put the numbers of Figure 5-8 back in:

$$n = [(3.24 \times 15) \div 5]^2 = 95 \text{ subjects} \qquad (5\text{-}22)$$

What is the distinction between the αs and βs in this calculation and the one before? Really only one of timing. In the previous example, the experiment was finished and did not show a difference. In this case, we are in the position of designing a trial, and so we based our calculations on a critical value for the sample mean that corresponded to the difference required to just reject the null hypothesis. If the experiment had turned out at that critical value, we then would have been able to determine exactly the probability of rejecting the null hypothesis when it was true (α, the Type I error) and the probability of rejecting the alternative hypothesis (accepting the null hypothesis) when it was true (β, the Type II error). It was these values that were used in the sample size calculation.

IMPORTANT NOTES

Misunderstanding of P Value

In Chapter 20, we give you some rules for how to report the results that you worked so hard to obtain. But here, we'll give you a foretaste[26] of what's to come. We can lay blame for many of the problems at the feet of the ubiquitous computers; the people who program them may know a lot about how to make electrons fly around to give us the right answer (most of the time), but don't know diddly-squat about logic. Other mistakes, though, are due to the people who (mis)interpret what the computer spit out. What's wrong with these statements?

   a) "The results were highly significant ($p<0.0000$)."

   b) "The results were of borderline significance ($p=0.058$)."

   c) "The effect was stronger in Study A ($n= 273, p= 0.013$) than in Study B ($n= 14, p= 0.042$)."

   d) "The results, based on this study of 13 individuals, were highly significant ($p=0.00002357$)."

   a) There are actually two things wrong with this statement. First, if we're going to use the logic of null hypothesis significance testing, results are either significant or they're not. Statisticians don't differentiate among "significant," "highly significant," and "really, Really, REALLY significant." They is or they ain't. The second problem is that there are precious few things with a probability of zero—reincarnation is one, and there are three others mentioned in Chapter 20, which was all we could think of. There are even fewer than four that have a probability *less* than zero. In fact, if you can think of even one, let us know, and the next edition of this book will be dedicated to you.

   b) See above. They is or they ain't. Reserve the term "borderline" for geography and psychiatric diagnoses.

   c) Using the same logic, there are two things wrong with this statement, too. The first is simply trying to compare "levels" of significance by using the relative sizes of the p values. The second is that the effect may actually have been stronger in Study B than in Study A, but the p level is higher because the sample size was so much smaller. If you want to compare results, use some estimate of effect size, not p.

   d) Do you really have the sample size to justify this much "accuracy"? We didn't think so either. If you have fewer than 100 subjects, two decimal places will do nicely, thank you, for reporting both the p level and the estimates of parameters. You can go up to three decimal places, but only if your sample size is larger than 1000 or so.

Relationship between statistical inference and confident interval

Taking a glance at the subsequent sections, you will find the confident interval plays such an important part in your work of report. Not only should you report on the estimated mean or ratio of population you've comprehended in this section, but also should you say something about the regression coefficient and so on. Let's capture a fragment from one of the paper as an example.

"The results show that the mean the paper as an

---

[26]*Although given the topic of this chapter's example, perhaps we should call it a foreplay.*

fident interval plays sn=31) was (16.00±/ml0)U/ml and for the control group(n=30)was (20.00±/ml0)U/ml; the difference between the two groups was 4.00U/ml, and the **95% CI** of the two population means was(0.0304,7.9696)U/ml."

It should be noted that:

a) The significance levels and confidence limits provide complementary information and both should be reported, where possible.

b) In this case the **95%CI** is abbreviation of the 95% confidence interval. We represent CI with Alpha as "100%b(1-α)CI" normally. The critical value could be different according to different clinical problems and we use the background knowledge to decide one that is most reasonable.

c) The wider the CI we take, the smaller the critical value is. Which means the accuracy of parameter estimation is low. Conversely, if the CI is narrower, the accuracy of parameter estimation would be higher.

d) Suppose we are testing H_0:μ=μ_0 vs. H_1:μ≠μ_0. H_0 is rejected with a two-sided level α test only if the 100%o(1-α)CI forμ does not containμ_0. H_0 is accepted with a two-sided level α test only if the 100%-(1-α)CI for μ does containμ_0.

Graphing with confidence

One way to enhance the visual presentation of data is to combine what we learned in Chapter 2 on graphing with what we just learned about CIs. We saw a simple example of this in Figure 5-8, which showed the population mean, plus a sample mean and its 95% CI. We can extend this by plotting a number of means, each with its CI, as in Figure 5-10. Once we've introduced you to the niceties of significance testing, we'll show you how to do "eyeball" tests of significance by using graphs like these. A word of caution, though. There's no convention about drawing error bars in graphs; some people plot the SD, others show 1 SE (which is the 68% CI), and still others the 95% CI. If you're drawing the figure, be sure to indicate which one you're using; if you're

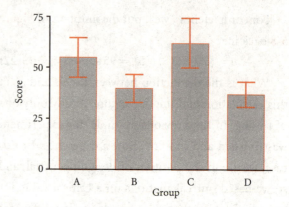

FIGURE 5-10   Showing a number of means and their 95% CIs.

reading the graph, be sure to check which one the authors used.[27]

AN IN-DEPTH VIEW ON STATISTICAL INFERENCE

Actually, what we've been describing in these first five chapters, and indeed what we'll discuss in the remainder of this book, is only one way to approach statistics—what's called the **frequentist** approach. But there's also another way, which differs not only in terms of the techniques used, but more importantly, in the philosophical approach to statistics—the **Bayesian** approach. It may seem odd to see the word "philosophical" in a book about statistics—what can be less philosophical than adding and squaring numbers—but in fact there are philosophical questions of truth and epistemology that are central, if usually unstated, in statistics.

Let's start off by discussing what we mean by the "frequentist" approach. We begin with a hypothesis, which is usually the nil hypothesis that nothing is going on. (This is indeed **the Neyman-Pearson approach**) The next step is to gather data, the more the better. We then run some statistical test to determine the probability (P) of the data (D), given the hypothesis (H). Putting this into statistical notation, we are trying to determine $P(D|H)$. In doing so, we are making some assumptions (here comes the epistemology): (i) the hypothesis is fixed—it's either

---

[27]*If the authors didn't indicate which one was used, then throw the paper away; you don't know how else they may have screwed up.*

true or it's false; and (ii) the data are random—draw another sample and the parameter estimates will change. This also implies that the population mean (or any other parameter we're interested in) is unknown and unknowable; we can estimate it, and even draw confidence intervals around our estimate, but we will never be certain of it. The term "frequentist" arises from what we've said—we're making predictions about the *frequency* with which data will appear given the hypothesis; and drawing conclusions about the truth or falsity of the hypothesis given the *frequency* of the data. Also, there is another approach we haven't quite mentioned yet since we are too afraid to confuse you back then. The particular approach is **the fisher approach** on which Fisher simply said "Here's the difference I observed. What's the likelihood that this could have arisen by chance if there really was no difference?" There've been debates on this two approaches and you could read more from Lenhard (2006) below.

Let's think about this for a moment. Truth be told, we're not really interested in $P(D|H)$; what we really want to know is $P(H|D)$—what's the probability that the hypothesis is true, given the data? This is where Bayesian statistics comes into play. And let's take a history lesson on all the above-mentioned approaches first.

A Little Bit More History on frequentist approach

For the two frequentist approach, they don't seem so different. Neyman and Pearson declare two hypotheses—it's different and it's not different—and then reject one or the other based on where the sample mean lies. Fisher, by contrast, determines the exact probability that a particular sample mean could arise by chance. But they're all based on the same distributions and the same data. What's the big deal? Beats us. Seems pretty mundane. But this was the stuff of one of the longest standing debates in science. Believe it or not, this particular battle between the two camps ranged from 1933 when Neyman and Pearson published their counterpoint to Fisher until at least 1968, six years after Fisher's death, when Egon Pearson was still writing letters to *Biometrica* quoting an even earlier statistician, William Gossett (Student),

in defense of his position.

If nothing else, the debate has great entertainment value. All parties were British, and like most Brits who rose through the public (i.e., private) school system to the hallowed halls of Oxbridge, they were trained in the art of rhetoric before they were potty trained. Here's an exchange, minuted by the Royal Statistical Society in 1935:

Dr Pearson said while he knew that there was a widespread belief in Professor Fisher's infallibility, he must, in the first place, beg leave to question the wisdom of accusing a fellow-worker of incompetence without, at the same time, showing that he had succeeded in mastering his argument [cited in Lenhard (2006)].

And just to show that the polemics were not one-sided, here is Fisher on Pearson:

[The unfounded presumptions] would scarcely have been possible without that insulation from all living contact with the natural sciences, which is a disconcerting feature of many mathematical departments (Fisher, 1955).

Just what could have caused such longstanding vitriol? Well, in part, no doubt, it's just British academe flexing its rhetorical muscle. But in fact there are some very subtle and profound differences between the two positions. We won't begin to explore the subtleties, but if you want to read further, Lenhard (2006) has reviewed the longstanding feud in some detail. We will, however, highlight two critical differences.

The first, as Lenhard points out in his review of the Neyman-Pearson critique, is that Fisher's position lacks some symmetry. A test can accept or reject the null hypothesis, but it puts nothing in its place. At best, that's a risky strategy, a bit like turning down a job offer without having a better one. The Neyman–Pearson approach, instead, leads naturally to rejecting the null hypothesis and therefore to accepting the alternative hypothesis, or not rejecting the null hypothesis and looking carefully at power to do so.

That then leads to the second fundamental difference. In the Neyman-Pearson perspective, it's all a case of model testing. You test two models—

null hypothesis and alternative hypothesis—and determine, based on the experiment's results, which model better fits the data. By contrast, the Fisher perspective begins, as we described at the beginning of the chapter, with a hypothetical infinite population of results consistent with the null hypothesis, and we draw a sample from the population, which becomes our study. We do something to the folks in the sample, and probably we don't do something (or do something else) to another sample, then calculate the difference between the two. And if it is sufficiently unlikely to have arisen by chance, as determined by Fisher's p value, we then conclude that the difference could not have arisen by chance, and we reject the null hypothesis.

You know all of this by now; we've drummed it in again and again. But we want to return to the idea of a hypothetical infinite population. As we said earlier in this chapter, "*no one* has ever made a truly random sample from a list of everyone of interest (the population)." We weren't the first people to notice this small speed bump on the road to truth, beauty, and wisdom. But eventually, a better idea about the whole logic of inference came along.

It took about 50 years for that better idea, which emerged from the work of two American statisticians—Jerome Cornfield and John Tukey. Tukey was most famous for a book called *Exploratory Data Analysis* (1977), which proposed the radical concept of simply looking at the data—an idea which induces apoplexy in mainstream statisticians, and which we will return to in due course. He is less famous for a bit of philosophy he and Cornfield put together that directly confronts Fisher's dilemma, called the "Cornfield Tukey Bridge Argument" (Cornfield and Tukey, 1956).

It's likely easiest to explain it by taking an example from the laboratory. When the EPA (Environmental Protection Agency) wants to prove that such and such a noxious agent "causes" cancer, they first try to find a species of rat or mouse that has been bred to be highly susceptible to cancer. They then expose small groups of rats (typically around 40) to absurdly high levels of the agent, and hang around to see how many get cancer. With luck, about half will. With more luck, more will get cancer in the high exposure group than the low or no exposure groups. With even more luck, the difference will be statistically significant. And if it is, they approach the *New York Times* and ban the agent as a "probable human carcinogen."

The bridge argument goes like this. Imagine a river with an island in the middle. One span of the bridge goes from the near bank to the island, and the next span goes to the far bank. The short span to the island is the statistical "$p<0.05$" bit, where after comparing one group of mice to another, you then generalize to all mice in a famous hypothetical population just like yours.[28] And we worry and fret endlessly about this short span. Did they really sample randomly? Did they follow up everyone? Did they blind the observers? Did they do the stats right? And on and on.

All this ignores the long span from the island to the far side of the river. This is the scientific inference that mice are enough like people (in terms of exposure to nasty things) to justify concluding an effect on humans even though you never studied them. And it rests on theoretical grounds—similar metabolism, similar anatomy, or whatever—not on statistical grounds. Another name for the short and long spans, seen in books on research design, are "internal validity" (the short span) and "external validity" (the long span).

It's almost axiomatic that increasing internal validity reduces external validity—the more inclusion and exclusion criteria, for example, the less the patients in the study resemble those in real life; the more control we exercise over how the treatment is delivered, the more it deviates from how it's really given. The distance from one bank to the other is constant; all we can do is move the island closer to

---

[28] *In fact, the EPA goes one better. If the poison causes cancer in one species (rats, in the case of formaldehyde) but not in another (mice) they ignore the latter group, and extrapolate from the group that showed an effect. No wonder we're all carcinophobic.*

one bank or the other. Tukey had a last word on this:

Far better an approximate answer to the right question, which is often vague and imprecise, than an exact answer to the wrong question, which can always be made precise (Tukey, 1962).

The same issue arises when a psychologist does a reaction time experiment on a bunch of first-year psychology students who don't really want to be there, but have to, for course credit.[29] If she's done her stats really well, she'll have no difficulty whatsoever convincing the peer reviewers that the effects apply to all human brains, not just 18-year-old, testosterone-soaked ones.[30] But one might well ask what tapping a key when a light flashes on a computer screen has to do with hitting the brakes in time to avoid an accident on a highway. Maybe it is the same; maybe it's not. But we need more knowledge, not more statistics, to find out.

It's actually a huge issue in science. Just as the EPA concluded that formaldehyde was a "probable human carcinogen" at domestic exposure of about 50 parts per *billion* on the basis of seeing that susceptible rats exposed to 15 parts per *million* for their whole lives got nasal cancer, we routinely make inferences about how things work that go well beyond our experiments. Not just in terms of the study sample; also in choice of experimental conditions. Psychologists (OK, some psychologists) go out of their way to develop materials that are sensitive to the manipulations they want to investigate, but then extrapolate far beyond these materials.

And now doctors, let's stop and wipe that smugness off your clinical faces, please. You too must plead guilty as charged. When you do a clinical trial, the standard routine is to develop a list of inclusion and exclusion criteria as long as your right arm so that you'll end up with a sample of patients as close to genetically identical rats as you can. And as far from typical patients as imaginable. You want them to have squeaky clean arteries, no excess fat, no hypertension, no diabetes, nonuttin' except a really

high total cholesterol. Think I'm kidding? The LRC-CPPT trial (Lipids Research Clinics Program, 1984) screened 300 000 men just like that to find 4000 who would take the crud (cholestyramine) morning noon and night for 7 to 10 years. And when the dust settled, they were looking at 38 heart attack deaths in one group and 30 in the other − $p < 0.05$ (just). Now do we wonder why clinicians constantly complain that "those patients aren't like mine"?

That's what Cornfield and Tukey are talking about. In the LRC trial, the first bridge, the really short one, was the statistical one from the 4000 guys they studied to other similar "guys" from some hypothetical population. The really long bridge was from those atypical guys to the more typical at-risk patient who walks into the family doc's office, with his large gut, smoking two packs a day, a father who died young of an MI, and elevated blood sugar. And their point is that it's really a case of "*buyer beware.*" You have to decide, based on your understanding of biology, physiology, pharmacology, as well as a bit of statistics, whether the results of that big multicenter trial are of use to you or not. That's why proclamations of the death of basic science in medical school curricula are a bit premature. As more and more practice guidelines impose recommendations based on findings from atypical samples, it is more and more incumbent on the doc to decide about the applicability of those guidelines to her patients. In our view, reasoned departure from guidelines is a sign of a good, not a bad, doctor.

And all these examples do make the debate between Fisher and Pearson about sampling from an infinite hypothetical population a bit like ancient monks debating how many pins you can stick in the head of an angel.

Yet another piece of History on Bayesian approach

Let's take another trip into history yet. The Reverend Thomas Bayes was a Dissenter—that is, someone who did not support the Church of England. His monograph, describing what is now called **Bayes'**

---

[29] At least it's a step up from rats and pigeons of the behaviorist era.

[30] OK. No sexism here. And estrogen-soaked.

Theorem, was published in 1764, three years after his death; a sterling example of perish and then publish.[31] But according to Sharon McGrayne (2011), who wrote a delightful history of Bayes and his theorem, it should more accurately be called Laplace's theorem, or at least the Bayes-Laplace theorem, as Pierre-Simon Marquis de Laplace developed Bayes' rather sketchy thoughts into something mathematicians could work with. Mc Grayne's description of Bayes' original thought experiment neatly encapsulates the Bayesian approach.

Imagine sitting with your back turned to a perfectly flat table, on which is a cue ball, and your job is to figure out whether the ball is to the right or to the left of center. Knowing nothing, your best initial guess is that it's right in the middle. Now a colleague throws another ball randomly onto the table and tells you whether it landed to the left or to the right of the cue ball. If it landed to the left, you may revise your initial hypothesis slightly by thinking the cue ball is a bit to the right of center, leaving more space on the left for the second ball to land. If the next five tosses also result in hits to the left of the cue ball, your hypothesis changes some more, moving the ball even further to the right and is strengthened. In other words, your hypothesis about "truth" changes in light of new data. Although this appears sensible, realize how different it is from the frequentist approach: now (i) the hypothesis changes, and (ii) the data are real (they're all you have).

Fortunately (if you're a frequentist) or unfortunately (if you're a Bayesian), Ronald Fisher was vehemently anti-Bayesian and his beliefs (or prejudices), coupled with his legendary temper and vitriolic tongue, succeeded in driving the Bayesian approach out of the social and medical sciences.[32] What accounts for his vitriol? In part, it was due to the Bayesians themselves. Let's summarize Bayes in a greatly simplified form:

$$P_{Posterior} = P_{Prior} \times Data \qquad (5\text{-}23)$$

That is, our revised hypothesis ($P_{Posterior}$) is our prior hypothesis (P_{Prior}) modified by new data. The problem is, where did that prior estimate come from?

There are two ways of determining prior probabilities—objective and subjective. Nowadays, few people would have difficulty with the objective, data-based method—as we'll see in a bit, it's widely used in applying the results of diagnostic tests—but it's the subjective way that leaves frequentists frequently fidgety, because it depends on the person's beliefs, which may or may not have anything to do with reality. For example, when Bem (2011) published a series of nine studies "proving" the existence of extrasensory perception (ESP), few people believed the results, because their prior probability of the reality of ESP was so low that even data from nine studies (or even from a century of research) couldn't change it. In fact, given the generally poor quality of much of the ESP research, this probably makes sense.

But what about when the data are solid, but the subjective prior probabilities are way off? That's when we (or rather, them Bayesians) run into difficulties. Despite solid research, people still believe that high-tension wires cause leukemia (or is it brain tumors this week?); cell phones cause brain tumors (or is it leukemia?); the MMR vaccine leads to autism; global climate change is a myth; and that the Toronto Blue Jays will win the World Series this year. As you can see, Bayes' Theorem, or rather the Bayesian approach, can result in rejecting strong evidence or accepting weak evidence, based on one's subjective prior probabilities.

Parenthetically, a study by Leibovici (2001) nicely illustrated how the same data can lead to outright dismissal of the results or enthusiastic embracing of them, depending on prior beliefs. His findings showed that intercessory prayer for patients with bloodstream infections resulted in a shorter stay

---

[31] *One frequentist said, "Bayesian statisticians do not stick closely enough to the pattern laid down by Bayes himself; if they would only do as he did and publish posthumously we should all be saved a lot of trouble" (Kendall, 1968).*

[32] *Interestingly, his proposal to use varying levels of statistical significance, depending on the situation and what we already know, and which we cited earlier in this chapter, reflects a very strong Bayesian influence.*

in hospital and duration of fever—*even though the intervention was carried out four to ten years after the hospitalization.* The study was real, although meant to be satirical, but it led to over 90 letters to the editor, divided between those who thought the research was junk, and those who took it as proof of a divine being.

Current Uses of Bayes' Theorem

In her book, McGrayne highlights many areas where Bayesian statistics has had a major impact, ranging from breaking the German Enigma code during World War II to setting rates for insurance policies. In the health sciences, its widest use now is in determining how test results influence the probability of a given disorder. Here, it takes the simplified form[33] of:

$$P(D|T) = \frac{P(T|D) \times P(D)}{P(T|D) \times P(D) + P(T|\overline{D}) \times P(\overline{D})} \quad (5\text{-}24)$$

where:

- $P(D|T)$ means the probability of the disorder, given a positive test result.
- $P(T|D)$ is the probability of a positive test result, given that the disease is present (the **sensitivity** of the test).
- $P(T|\overline{D})$ the probability of a positive test result, given that the disease is absent (1–the **specificity** of the test).
- $P(D)$ is the probability or prevalence of the disorder (i.e., the prior probability); and $P(\overline{D})$ the probability that the disease is absent [i.e., $1-P(D)$].[34]

In a later chapter, we will introduce you to one of the many diseases your intrepid authors have discovered: Somaliland Camelbite Fever (SCF). Not content with merely discovering hitherto unknown scourges of humanity, we have also developed a test to diagnose it—the Streiner-Norman Assessment of the Camelbite Kondition, or SNACK. Its test characteristics are average and comparable to most diag-

nostic tests: a sensitivity of 0.80 and a specificity of 0.90. Now imagine that a person comes into your office, complaining of bad breath and an uncontrollable urge to spit; indicators of possible SCF. If the SNACK test comes back positive, can you conclude that this person suffers from SCF?

The answer is, "It all depends," and what it depends on is the prior probability that the person has SCF. Let's assume that your practice is located in Somaliland, where the prevalence of the disease is high, verging on 75% of the population. Your best estimate of the prior probability is the prevalence, so if we plug the numbers into Equation (5-23), we'll get:

$$P(D|T) = \frac{0.80 \times 0.75}{0.80 \times 0.75 + 0.10 \times 0.25} = 0.96 \quad (5\text{-}25)$$

meaning that our **posterior probability** is 96% that the poor wretch has SCF. In other words, Bayes' Theorem has resulted in an increase in the confidence of our hypothesis, from 75% to 96%.

Now let's assume that your practice is on Fifth Avenue in New York City, a location renowned for the brass plaques of rich society doctors, but not particularly a hot-spot of SCF; in fact, the prevalence is only 1% among people with those symptoms (the other 99% of people with those symptoms tend to be cab drivers). Putting those numbers into the equation, we find:

$$P(D|T) = \frac{0.80 \times 0.01}{0.80 \times 0.01 + 0.10 \times 0.99} = 0.07 \quad (5\text{-}26)$$

so that our prior probability has increased, but even so, 93% of positive tests will in fact be false positives, and it's more probable that the person is a taxi driver.

From the viewpoint of Bayesian statistics, there are two major points. First, the same data led to two completely different conclusions, because our prior probabilities were different in the two situations. Second, our hypotheses (the probabilities that the patient has SCF) changed in light of the data—strengthened in both cases, but not enough in our

---

[33]*Yes, this really is a simple form of the formula, since there are only two outcomes—the person does or does not have the disorder. The equation becomes much more formidable when there are more outcomes, and especially if the outcome is a random variable.*

[34]*If you need help with the concepts of sensitivity and specificity, you can't do better than to consult Streiner and Norman (2014).*

second example to put the patient on a diet of hay and dried grass. This is completely different from the frequentist perspective that hypotheses are constant, and the interpretation of the data is not influenced by our prior beliefs.

SUMMARY

✧ You can use a z-test to determine the statistical significance of the difference between a sample and a population with known mean and SD. The z-test, like all statistical tests, relates the magnitude of an observed difference to the probability that such a difference might occur by chance alone. The notion of statistical significance is embodied in this probability. But statistical significance does not, of itself, reveal anything about the importance of the observed difference.

GLOSSARY

inference statistics   统计推断

standard error of the mean(SEM)   标准误

standard deviation of the mean (SDM)   均数标准差

p value   P 值

null hypothesis   无效假设 / 零假设 / 无差异假设

alternative hypothesis   备择假设 / 差异假设

alpha   检验水准

z transformation   z 分布

power   检验功效

Type Ⅰ error   一类错误

Type Ⅱ error   二类错误

one-tailed test   单侧检验

two-tailed test   双侧检验

confident interval   置信区间

effect size（ES）   效应大小

EXERCISES

1. A report of a clinical trial of a new anticocaine drug,

Snortstop, versus a placebo, noted that the new drug gave a higher pro-portion of successes than the placebo. The report ended with the statement that the statistical test was significant ($p < 0.05$). In light of this information we may conclude:

a. Fewer than 1 patient in 20 will fail to benefit from the drug.

b. The chance that an individual patient will fail to benefit is less than 0.05.

c. If the drug were effective, the probability of the reported finding or one more extreme is less than 1 in 20.

d. If the drug were ineffective, the probability of the reported finding or one more extreme is less than 0.05.

e. The power of the test exceeds 0.95.

2. In a small, randomized, double-blind trial of a new treatment in patients with acute myocardial infarction, the mortality in the treated group was half that in the control group, but the difference was not significant. We can conclude that:

a. The treatment is useless.

b. There is no point in continuing to develop the treatment.

c. The reduction in mortality is so great that we should introduce the treatment immediately.

d. We should keep adding cases to the trial until the Normal test for comparison of two proportions is significant.

e. We should carry out a new trial of much greater size.

3. Consider two randomized trials of the effect of anabolic steroids on commuters' times in the "100 meter train dash." Both studies used the same populations and experimental design. The only difference is that the first study used a total of 10 office workers per group, whereas the second used 100 per group. For the first study, the means (SDs) of the two groups were 12.0 (3.0) seconds for the placebo group and 16.0 (3.0) seconds for the group that received anabolic steroids. Answer the following questions regarding the expected results of the second study:

	Larger	Smaller	Stay the same	Can't tell from the data
SD	_____	_____	_____	_____
SE of mean	_____	_____	_____	_____
Statistical test	_____	_____	_____	_____
p-value	_____	_____	_____	_____

4. In a two-group design comparing the effects of diet restriction and exercise on quality of life of obese patients, researchers used a quality-of-life instrument, the CPQ (Couch Potato Questionnaire) with 5 sub-scales (Emotional Function, Social Function, Physical Function, Self-Esteem, Eating Attitudes). Because of concern about the use of multiple tests, the alpha level (probability of declaring a difference under the null hypothesis) was set at 0.01 instead of the usual 0.05. What effect will this have on the power to detect a true difference between the two groups on the Eating Attitudes subscale?

   a. Increase power.

   b. Decrease power.

   c. Stay the same

   d. Insufficient data to tell.

5. Second only to terminal zits, the biggest concern of every nubile adolescent in the 21st century is "Quality of Life." So the local teener's health office developed a questionnaire to assess satisfaction with social interactions, depression, self-esteem, mirror avoidance, and time spent in closets.

Because of concerns about using multiple t-tests, the investigators used a Bonferroni correction; α was divided by 5, so only p levels less than 0.01 were considered significant. What effect will this have on:

   a. The Type I error rate.

   b. The Type II error rate.

   c. Power.

   d. Degrees of freedom.

6. You have just completed a study of a patent medicine for basketball players, designed to make them jump higher, spin around faster, and fool the opposition by looking like they're going backwards and forwards at the same time. It's called MJ³ Elixir and is endorsed by Magic Johnson, Michael Jackson, and Michael Jordan. Testing the first part only, you find that a sample of 16 collegiate players fed the elixir for 2 weeks can jump an average height of 56 cm. Population data gathered by university physed coaches across the country show a normal jump height of 50 cm, SD 15 cm.

   a. What is the probability that this difference could have occurred by chance?

   b. Suppose the true benefit was 10 cm. What is the power of the study to detect this difference?

   c. How large a sample would you need to have a 90% power of detecting this difference (using alpha = 0.05 as a critical value)?

CHAPTER THE SIXTH   *t*-test

In this chapter, we will introduce *t*-test and learn when, why and how to appropriately perform a *t*-test. The *t*-test is to compare means, it consists of three types of *t*-tests, i.e., one-sample *t*-test, two-group *t*-test, paired *t*-test. One-sample *t*-test is used for comparing sample results with a fixed number. Specifically, in this type of test, a single sample is collected, and the resulting sample mean is compared with a value of interest, sometimes a "gold standard", that is not based on the current sample. The purpose of the one-sample *t*-test is to determine whether there is sufficient evidence to conclude that the mean of the population from which the sample is taken is different from the fixed value. Two-group *t*-test is used to determine whether the unknown means of two populations are different from each other on account of independent samples from each population. Paired *t*-test is appropriate for data in which the two samples are correlated or related in some way.

ONE SAMPLE *t*-TEST

t DISTRIBUTION

Definition of *t*-distribution

If a stochastic variable follows a normal distribution $N(\mu, \sigma^2)$ with a population mean of μ and overall standard deviation of σ, then a common normal distribution can be transformed into standard normal distribution, i.e. $N(0,1^2)$ through *u*-transformation ($\frac{X-\mu}{\sigma}$, also known as Z transformation). Similarly, if a sample mean $\overline{X}$ follows a normal distribution $N\left(\mu, \sigma\frac{2}{X}\right)$ with an population mean of μ and overall standard deviation of $\sigma_{\overline{x}}$, it also can be transformed into standard normal distribution $N(0,1^2)$, i.e. *u*-distribution, in the same way.

In practical condition, $\sigma_{\overline{x}}$ is usually unknown, which can be replaced by $S_{\overline{x}}$. Then $\frac{\overline{X}-\mu}{S_{\overline{x}}}$ obeys *t*-distribution instead of a standard normal distribution:

$$t = \frac{\overline{X}-\mu}{S_{\overline{X}}} = \frac{\overline{X}-\mu}{S/\sqrt{n}}, \quad v = n-1 \qquad (6\text{-}1)$$

Where v is degree of freedom (*df*), representing the number of variables which can be of any value in mathematics. For example, $X+Y+Z=20$, there're three variables, but only two of them can select any value. Therefore, the degree of freedom is v. In Statistics, degree of freedom can be calculated as: $v=n-m$. Where n stands for the number of values when calculating a certain statistic, m stands for the number of other independent statistics needed for the calculation of this certain statistic. For instance, in the calculation of statistic t, the number of values is n. $\overline{X}$ is needed for the calculation of S, so the other independent statistic includes only $\overline{X}$, which means the degree of freedom is $v=n-1$.

The *t*-distribution was originally published by British Statistician W.S. Gosset in 1908 by her penname "Student", so it's also called Student's *t*-distribution. This discovery initiated a new epoch in small sample statistical inference. *t*-distribution is mainly used for interval estimation of overall mean and *t*-test etc.

Graphics and features of *t*-distribution

t-distribution only has one parameter, which is degree of freedom v. Graphics of *t*-distribution is a cluster of curves, the shape of which varies in pace with the variation of degree of freedom v. When $v \to \infty$, *t*-distribution approaches standard normal distribution, but when degree of freedom v is relatively small, it obviously differs from standard normal distribution.

From the graphics above, we can find the characteristics of *t*-distribution as follows:

(1) Unimodal distribution, centered about 0, bilaterally symmetrical.

(2) The curve shape of *t*-distribution depends on the value of degree of freedom v. The smaller v is, the more dispersed *t*-value is, the shorter the peak of the curve is and the higher the tail curls.

(3) When v approaches ∞, $S_{\bar{X}}$ approaches $\sigma_{\bar{X}}$, *t*-distribution approaches standard normal distribution. When degree of freedom reaches ∞, *t*-distribution becomes standard normal distribution. Therefore, standard normal distribution is a special case of *t*-distribution.

Same as the curve of standard normal distribution, the relation between the area under the curve of *t*-distribution (i.e. Probability P or α) and lateral axis *t*-value is the most concerned part in statistical application. In consideration of convenience, statisticians complied *t* boundary value table reflecting the relation between different degrees of freedom v and their according probability.

t TABLE

In *t*-boundary value table, the horizontal subheading is the degree of freedom v and the vertical subheading is the tail probability or one-tailed probability. The sum of two sides of tail area is called two-tailed probability, *i.e.* the shadow part of the legend in the upper right-hand corner of the table. The numbers in table represents the according *t*-critical value when v and α are determined, in which the *t*-critical value according with one-tailed probability is represented by $t_{\alpha,v}$ and the *t*-critical value in accordance with two-tailed probability is represented by $t_{\alpha/2,v}$. Since *t*-distribution is bilaterally symmetrical and centered about 0, there's only positive *t*-value in the table. We can get the probability *P*-value by getting absolute value of *t*-value regardless of positives or negatives when looking up the table.

From the legend in the upper right-hand corner of the table and change regulation of the numbers in table, we can find:

(1) Under the circumstances of same degree of freedom, the larger $|t|$ is, the smaller the probability *P*-value is.

(2) When $|t|$ remains the same, two-tailed probability P is twice of the one-tailed probability when they have the same degree of freedom. For example, $t_{0.10/2,10} = t_{0.05,10} = 1.812$.

With respect to two-tailed or one-tailed P values for different degrees of freedom, Critical value of the *t*-distribution will be obtained. For example, from table C in the Appendix, for 10 degrees of freedom, the two-tailed tabulated $P = 0.05$ value is 2.228, the one-tailed tabulated $P = 0.05$ value is 1.812, the two-tailed tabulated $P = 0.01$ value is 3.169, the one-tailed tabulated $P = 0.01$ value is 2.764.

ONE SAMPLE *t*-TEST

The one-sample *t*-test is used for comparing sample results with a fixed value. To be specific, in this type of *t*-test, we will collect a single sample, and the result of sample mean is compared with a value of interest, sometimes a "gold standard," that is not based on the current sample.

The purpose of the one-sample *t*-test is to determine whether there is sufficient evidence to conclude that the mean of the population from which the sample is taken is not the same as the specified value.

Related to the one-sample *t*-test is a confidence interval on the mean. The confidence interval is usually applied when you are not testing against a specified value of the population mean but instead want to know a range of plausible values of the unknown mean of the population from which the sample was selected.

When performing a one-sample *t*-test, you may or may not have a preconceived assumption about the direction of your findings. Depending on the design of your study, you may decide to perform a one- or two-tailed test.

Two-tailed t-tests: The basic hypotheses for the one-sample t-test are as follows: where μ denotes the mean of the population from which the sample was selected, and μ is a value that does not depend on the current sample.

H_0: $\mu=\mu_0$ (the population mean is equal to the hypothesized value μ_0)

H_1: $\mu\neq\mu_0$ (the population mean is not equal to μ_0)

One-tailed t-tests: If you are only interested in rejecting the null hypothesis that the population mean differs from the hypothesized value in a direction of interest, you may want to use a one-tailed(sometimes called a one-sided)test. If, for example, you want to reject the null hypothesis only when there is sufficient evidence that the mean is larger than the value hypothesize under the null hypothesis, the hypothesis become the following:

H_0: $\mu=\mu_0$ (the population mean is equal to the hypothesized value μ_0)

H_1: $\mu>\mu_0$ (the population mean is greater than μ_0)

If, for example, you want to reject the null hypothesis only when there is sufficient evidence that the mean is less than the value hypothesize under the null hypothesis, the hypothesis becomes the following:

H_0: $\mu=\mu_0$ (the population mean is equal to the hypothesized value μ_0)

H_1: $\mu<\mu_0$ (the population mean is greater than μ_0)

AN OVERVIEW

In the hypothesis testing of quantitative data, the most common way is to perform t-test (or Student t-test). In practical condition, we should figure out the purpose, applicable conditions and matters needing attention of various test methods.

When σ is unknown and the sample size n is relatively small (such as $n<60$), the sample of t-test should be drawn randomly from the population of normal distribution theoretically. Besides, in the comparison of two sample means, population variance of two samples should be equal ($\sigma_1^2=\sigma_2^2$),

which is called homogeneity of variance. In practical application, even if the real condition deviates slightly from the conditions above, it won't affect the results significantly. When the sample size n is relatively large, t-value is close to u-value, someone calls it u-test or z-test. In fact, this is an exception of t-test.

One sample/group t-test refers to the comparison given the sample mean $\overline{X}$ (meaning the population mean μ is unknown) and population mean μ_0 (normally theoretical value, standard value or stable value after a large amount of observations etc.). The test statistic can be calculated using Formula (6-1).

Example 6-1

Hb of 36 workers engaging works with plumbum were tested, the mean of Hb was 130.83g/L, and standard deviation is 25.74g/L. It is known that the average Hb of normal adult man is 140g/L. Is there difference on Hb between worker with plumbum and normal adult man?

It may be due to:(1) The two population mean are difference, (2) The sampling error. Question: which is the truth?

This belongs to problem of hypothesis test! Basic theory and approaches of hypothesis test. In hypothesis test (significance test), the question of interest is simplified into two competing claims / hypotheses between which we have a choice; the null hypothesis, denoted H_0. and the alternative hypothesis, denoted H_1.These two competing claims/hypotheses are not however treated on an equal basis, special consideration is given to the null hypothesis. We have two common situations: with respect to Basic theory, under the null hypothesis, how possible to occur the current situation and even more unfavorable situation to? --calculate a probability (P-value). If it is less possible for the current situation or even more unfavorable situation to occur, then reject; otherwise, not reject, given a small α, compare P and α(α is called the significance level of the test).

Concrete steps as followings:

(1) Set hypothesis and the significance level of test

Null hypothesis (H_0): the statement being tested

in a test of significance

Alternative hypothesis (H_1): the statement we hope or suspect is true instead of One-sided and two-sided alternatives. Significance level α, often $\alpha=0.05$

(2) Select an appropriate test and calculate the test statistic: It is a random variable with a distribution that we know if X follows a normal distribution $N(\mu,\sigma^2)$ then $t=\dfrac{\bar{x}-\mu}{\dfrac{S}{\sqrt{n}}}\sim$ t distribution

(3) determine P value, and make decision: The probability, computed assuming that H_0 is true, that the test statistic would take a value as extreme or more extreme than that actually observed is called the P value of the test.

Above example 6-1 belongs to this type of question, and the detailed steps of hypothesis test are:

Establish hypothesis test, determine test level

(1) H_0: $\mu=\mu_0=140$ g/L, which means the mean hemoglobin content of male workers engaged in lead work is the same as that of normal male adults;

H_1: $\mu\neq\mu_0=140$ g/L, which means the mean hemoglobin content of male workers engaged in lead work is not the same as that of normal male adults;

$$\alpha=0.05$$

(2) Calculate test statistic: In this example, $n=36$, $\bar{X}=130.83$ g/L, $S=25.74$ g/L, $\mu_0=140$ g/L. According to Equation(6-1):

$$t=\frac{130.83-140}{25.74/\sqrt{36}}=-2.138, \quad v=36-1=35$$

(3) Determine P value, make an inferred conclusion: Suppose $v=35$, $|t|=|-2.138|=2.138$, then we can look up in the t-boundary value table. Since $t_{0.05/2.35}<2.138<t_{0.02/2.35}$, so $0.02<P<0.05$. According to $\alpha=0.05$, we can refuse H_0, accept H_1, and the difference has statistical significance. Together with the subject, we can find the male workers who are engaged in lead work have lower average hemoglobin content than normal male adults.

SAMPLE SIZE AND POWER

Sample size calculations for one-sample t-test are the essence of simplicity. We use the original sample size calculation introduced in Chapter 5:

$$n=\left[\frac{(Z_\alpha+Z_\beta)\sigma}{\delta}\right]^2 \qquad (6\text{-}2)$$

where δ is the hypothesized difference, s is the SD of the difference, and z_α and z_β correspond to the chosen a and b levels. The only small fly in the ointment is that we must now estimate not only the treatment difference, but also the SD of the difference within subjects—which is almost never known in advance. But look on the bright side—more room for optimistic forecasts.

How to Get the Computer to Do the Work for You
Descriptive Statistics

- From Analyze, choose Compare Means→One-Sample t-Test
- Click on the variable(s) to be analyzed from the list on the left, and click the arrow to move it (them) into the box marked Test Variable(s)
- Enter the value which defines Test Value and press the <Tab> key
- Click <kbd>Continue</kbd>
- Click <kbd>OK</kbd>

TWO-GROUP *t*-TEST

*The *t*-test is used for comparing the means of two groups and is based on the ratio of the difference between groups to the standard error of the difference.*

SETTING THE SCENE

To help young profs succeed in academia, you have devised an orientation course where they learn how to use big words when little ones would do. And, to help yourself survive in academia, you decide to do some research on it. So, you randomize half your willing profs to take the course and half to do without, then measure all the obscure words they mutter. How can you use these data to tell if the course worked? In short, how can you determine how much of the variation in the scores arose from differences between groups and how much came from variation within groups?

Perhaps the most common comparison in all of statistics is between two groups—cases vs. controls, drugs vs. placebos, boys vs. girls. Reasons why this comparison is ubiquitous are numerous. First, when you run an experiment in biomedicine, in contrast to doing an experiment in Grade 7 biology, you usually do something to some poor souls and leave some others alone so that you can figure out what effect your ministrations may have had. As a result, you end up looking at some variable that was measured in those lucky folks who benefited from your treatment and also in those who missed out.[1]

Note that we have implied that we measure something about each hapless subject. Perhaps the most common form of measurement is the FBI criterion—dead or alive. There are many variations on this theme: diseased or healthy; better, same, or worse; normal or abnormal x-ray; and so on. We do *not* consider this categorical type of measurement in this section. Instead, we demand that you measure something more precise, be it a lab test, a blood pressure, or a quality-of-life index, so that we can consider means, SDs, and the like. In the discussion below, we examine **Interval** or **Ratio** variables.

AN OVERVIEW

As we indicated in Chapter 5, all of statistics comes down to a signal-to-noise ratio. To show how this ap-plies to the types of analyses discussed in this section, consider the following example.

A moment's reflection on the academic game reveals certain distinct features of universities that set them apart from the rest of the world. First, there is the matter of the dress code. Profs pride themselves on their shabbiness. Old tweed jackets that the rest of the world gardens in are paraded regularly in front of lecture theaters. The more informal among us, usually draft dodgers with a remnant of the flower child ethos, tramp around in old denim stretched taut over ever-expanding derrieres.

But even without the dress code, you can tell a prof in a dark room just by the sound of his voice. We tend, as a group, to try to impress with obscure words in long, meandering sentences.[2] It's such a common affliction that one might be led to believe that we take a course in the subject, and foreigners on the campus might do well to acquire a Berlitz English-Academish dictionary.

Imagine if you will a course in Academish IA7 for young, contractually limited, tenureless, assistant profs. As one exercise, they are required to open a dictionary to a random page, pick the three longest words, and practice and rehearse them until they roll off their lips as if Mommy had put them there.

Of course, not wanting to pass up on a potential publication, the course planners design a rand-

---

[1] *Or maybe the lucky folks who missed out, and the poor souls who "benefited" from your treatment.*

[2] *The long, obscure word for that is sesquipedalianism, which literally means a foot and a half.*

omized trial; graduate students are required to attend a lecture from one of the graduands and some other prof from the control group and count all the words that could not be understood. After the data are analyzed, the graduands ($n_1 = 10$) used a mean of 35 obscure words. A comparable group ($n_2 = 10$) who didn't take the course used a mean 27 such words in their lectures. Did the course succeed? The data are tabulated in Table 6-1.

TABLE 6-1   Number of incomprehensible words in treatment and control groups

	Participants	Controls
	35	22
	31	25
	29	23
	28	29
	39	30
	41	28
	37	30
	39	33
	38	21
	33	29
Sum	350	270
Mean	35.0	27.0
Grand Mean	31.0	

It is apparent that some overlap occurs between the two distributions, although a sizeable difference also exists between them. Now the challenge is to create some method to calculate a number corresponding to the **signal**—the difference between those who did and did not have the course, and to the **noise**—the variability in scores among individuals within each group.

The simplest method to make this comparison is called **Student's *t*-test**. Why it is called Student's is actually well known. It was invented by a statistician named William Gossett, who worked at the Guinness brewery in Dublin around the turn of the century. Perhaps because he recognized that no Irishman, let alone one who worked in a brewery, would be taken seriously by British academics, he wrote under the

pseudonym "Student." It is less clear why it is called the "*t*"-test. There is some speculation that he did most of his work during the afternoon breaks at the brewery. Student's Stout test probably didn't have the same ring about it, so "tea" or "*t*" it became.[3]

EQUAL SAMPLE SIZES

To illustrate the *t*-test, let's continue to work through the above example. From the table, the profs who made it through Academish IA7 had a mean of 35 incomprehensible words per lecture; the control group only 27. One obvious measure of the signal is simply the difference between the groups or $(35 - 27) = 8.0$. More formally:

$$Numerator = \left| \overline{X}_1 - \overline{X}_2 \right| \qquad (6\text{-}3)$$

where the vertical lines mean that we're interested in the absolute value of the difference; because it's totally arbitrary which group we call 1 and which is 2, the sign is meaningless. Under the null hypothesis (i.e. that the course made no difference), we are presuming that this difference arises from a distribution of differences with a mean of zero and a standard deviation (s) that is, in some way, related to the original distributions.

There are two differences between the *t*-test and the *z*-test. The first is that, although the *t*-test can be used with only one group, to see if its mean is different from some arbitrary or population value, its primary purpose is to compare two groups; whereas the *z*-test is used mainly with one group. The second, and more important, difference is that for the *t*-test, the standard deviation is unknown; whereas in the case of the *z*-test, discussed in Chapter 5, the SD of the population, σ, was furnished to us (remember, we had a survey of 3000 or so penile lengths, so we were given the mean and SD of the population).

This is not the case here, so the next challenge is to determine the SD of this distribution of differences between the means: the amount of variability in this estimate that we would expect by chance alone. Because we are looking at a difference between two

---

[3]*Actually, all Guinness employees were forbidden to publish. Too bad Guinness doesn't run universities.*

means, one strategy would be to simply assume that the error of the difference is the sum of the error of the two estimated means. The error in each mean is the *standard error* (SE), $s \div \sqrt{n}$, as we demonstrated in Chapter 5. So, a first guess at the error of the difference would be:

$$Standard\ error_{difference} = SE_d = \frac{s_1}{\sqrt{n_1}} + \frac{s_2}{\sqrt{n_2}}$$

$$(6\text{-}4)$$

This is almost right, but for various arcane reasons we won't bother to go into, we can't add SDs; the sum doesn't come out right. But, we can add variances, and then take the square root of the answer to get back to our original units of measurement. So, what we end up with is:

$$SE_d = \sqrt{\frac{s_1^2}{n_1} + \frac{s_2^2}{n_2}} \qquad (6\text{-}5)$$

Because the sample sizes are equal (i.e. $n_1 = n_2$), this equation simplifies a bit further to:

$$SE_d = \sqrt{\frac{s_1^2 + s_2^2}{n}} \qquad (6\text{-}6)$$

In the present example, then, we can calculate the variances of the two groups separately, and these are equal to:

$$s_1^2 = \frac{(35-35)^2 + (31-35)^2 + \ldots + (33-35)^2}{10-1}$$

$$= \frac{186}{9} = 20.67$$

$$s_1^2 = \frac{(22-27)^2 + (25-27)^2 + \ldots + (29-27)^2}{10-1}$$

$$= \frac{144}{9} = 16.0$$

$$(6\text{-}7)$$

Then the denominator of the test is equal to $\sqrt{(20.67+16.0) \div 6.} = 1.915$.

We can see what is happening by putting the whole thing on a graph, as shown in Figure 6-1. The distribution of differences is centered on zero, with an SE of 1.915. The probability of observing a sample difference large enough is the area in the right and left tails. If the difference is big enough (i.e. sufficiently different from zero), then we can see that it will achieve significance. The *t*-test is then obtained by simply taking the signal-to-noise ratio:

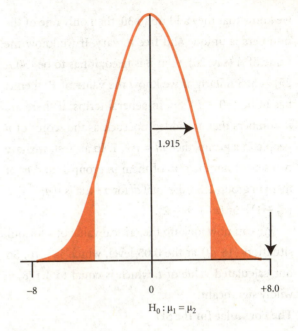

FIGURE 6-1   Testing if the mean difference is greater than zero.

$$t = \frac{(\overline{X}_1 - \overline{X}_2)}{\sqrt{\dfrac{s_1^2 + s_2^2}{n}}} = \frac{8}{1.915} = 4.178$$

$$(6\text{-}8)$$

We can then look this up in Table C in the Appendix and find a whole slew of numbers we don't know how to handle. The principal problem is that, unlike the situation with the *z*-test, there is a different *t* value for every degree of freedom, as well as for every α level. Instead of finding that, if α = 0.05, then *t* = 1.96, as we could expect if it behaved like a *z*-test, we find that now, *t* can range anywhere from 1.96 to 12.70. The problem is that, because we have estimated both the means and the SDs, we have introduced a dependency on the degrees of freedom. As it turns out, for large samples, *t* converges with *z*—they are both equal to 1.96 when α = 0.05. However, *t* is larger for small samples, so we require a larger relative difference to achieve significance.

Degrees of Freedom

We talked about that magical quantity, **degrees of freedom** (*df*), but haven't yet told you what it is or how we figure it out. Degrees of freedom can be thought of as the number of *unique* pieces of information in a set of data, given that we know the sum. For example, if we have two numbers, *A* and *B*, and we know that they add up to 30, then only one of the numbers is unique and free to vary. If we know the value of A (say, 25), then B is fixed; it has to be (30 − 25) = 5. Similarly, if we know the value of B, then A has to be (30 − B). So, in general terms, if there are *n* numbers that are added up, such as the scores of *n* people in a group, then $df = n - 1$. In a *t*-test, we have two sets of numbers: n_1 of them in group 1, and n_2 of them in group 2. So, the total *df* for a *t*-test is $[(n_1 - 1) + (n_2 - 1)]$, or $(n_1 + n_2 - 2)$.

We can now look up the critical value of *t* for our situation (18 *df*) at the 0.05 level, which is 2.10. So our calculated value of *t*, which is equal to 4.178, is wildly significant.

The Formulae for the SD

If you were paying attention, you would have noticed that the equation we just used to calculate the variance [Equation (6-5)] differs slightly from the equation we used in Chapter 3, when we introduced the concept of variance and the SD; in particular, the denominator is $N - 1$, rather than just N. Equations (3-12) (for the variance) and (3-13)(for the SD) are used to calculate these values for the **population**; whereas the equivalent formulae with $N - 1$ in the denominator are used for **samples** (the usual situation). Why the difference? The answer is based on three factors, all of which we've already discussed. First, the purpose of inferential statistics is to estimate the value of the parameter in the population, based on the data we have from a sample. Second, we expect that the sample parameter (the mean, in this case) will differ from the population value to some degree, small as it may be. Finally, any set of numbers will deviate less from their own mean than from any other number. Putting this all together, the sample data will deviate less from the sample mean than they will from the population mean, so that the estimate of the variance and SD will be biased downward. Dividing the squared deviations by $N - 1$ rather than by N compensates for this, and leads to an **unbiased** estimate of the population parameter.

The question is why we divide by $N - 1$ as a fudge factor rather than, say, $N - 2$ or some other value. We're not going to go into the messy details.

Suffice it to say that if we took a very large number of independent samples from the population (about a billion or so), we'd find that the mean of those variances isn't σ^2 the population variance, but rather σ^2 times $(n - 1)/n$. So, if we multiply each of the obtained values by $n/(n - 1)$, we'll end up with the unbiased estimate that we're looking for. That's why there's a 1 in the denominator, rather than a different number.

TWO GROUPS AND UNEQUAL SAMPLE SIZES: EXTENDED *t*-TEST

If there are unequal sample sizes in the two groups, the formula becomes a little more complex. To understand why, we must again delve into the philosophy of statistics. In particular, when we used the two sample SDs to calculate the SE of the difference, we were actually implying that each was an equally good estimate of the population SD, σ.

Now, if the two samples are different sizes, we might reasonably presume that the SD from the larger group is a better estimate of the population value. Thus it would be appropriate, in combining the two values, to **weight** the sum by the sample sizes, like this:

$$\sigma^2 (est.) = \frac{n_1 s_1^2 + n_2 s_2^2}{n_1 + n_2} \tag{6-9}$$

This is close, but by now you have probably gotten into the habit of subtracting 1 every time you see an *n*. This is not the place to stop, so:

$$\sigma^2 (est.) = \frac{(n_1 - 1)s_1^2 + (n_2 - 1)s_2^2}{n_1 + n_2 - 2} \tag{6-10}$$

This is the best guess at the SD of the difference. But we actually want the SE, which introduces yet another $1 \div n$ term. In this case, there is no single *n*; there are two *n* terms. Instead of forcing a choice, we take them both and create a $(1 \div n_1 + 1 \div n_2)$ term. So, the final denominator looks like:

$$Denominator =$$

$$\sqrt{\frac{(n_1 - 1) s_1^2 + (n_2 - 1) s_2^2}{n_1 + n_2 - 2} \times \left(\frac{1}{n_1} + \frac{1}{n_2} \right)} \tag{6-11}$$

And the more general form of the *t*-test is:

$$t = \frac{(\overline{X}_1 - \overline{X}_2)}{\sqrt{\dfrac{(n_1 - 1)s_1^2 + (n_2 - 1)s_2^2}{n_1 + n_2 - 2} \times \left(\dfrac{1}{n_1} + \dfrac{1}{n_2}\right)}}$$

(6-12)

Although this looks formidable, the only conceptual change involves weighting each SD by the relevant sample size. And of course, the redeeming feature is that computer programs are around to deal with all these pesky specifics, leaving you free. From here we proceed as before by looking up a table in the Appendix, and the relevant *df* is now $(n_1 + n_2 - 2)$.

Pooled versus Separate Variance Estimates

The whole idea of the *t*-test, as we have talked about it so far, is that the two samples are drawn from the same population, and hence have the same mean *and* SD. If this is so, then it makes good sense to pool everything together to get the best estimate of the SD. That's why we did it; this approach is called a **pooled estimate**.

However, it might not work out this way. It could be that the two SDs are wildly different. At this point, one might rightly pause to question the whole basis of the analysis. If you are desperate and decide to plow ahead, some computer packages proceed to calculate a new *t*-test that doesn't weight the two estimates together. The denominator now looks like:

$$SE = \sqrt{\frac{s_1^2}{n_1} + \frac{s_2^2}{n_2}}$$

(6-13)

This looks very much like our original form and has the advantage of simplicity. The trade-off is that the *df* are calculated differently and turn out to be much closer to the smaller sample of the two. The reason is not all that obscure. Because the samples are now receiving equal weight in terms of contributing to the overall SE, it makes sense that the *df* should reflect the relatively excess contribution of the smaller sample. This strategy is called the **harmonic mean** (abbreviated as $\overline{n}_h$), and comes about as:

$$\overline{n}_h = \frac{2}{\dfrac{1}{n_1} + \dfrac{1}{n_2}}$$

(6-14)

In short, if n_1 was 4 and n_2 was 20, the arithmetic

mean would be 12; the harmonic mean would be $2 \div (^1/_4 + ^1/_{20}) = 6.67$, which is closer to 4 than to 20. So the cost of the separate variance test is that the *df* are much lower, and it is appropriately a little harder to get statistical significance.

THE CALIBRATED EYEBALL

We promised you in the previous chapter that we would show you how to do statistical "tests" with your eyeball, so, honorable gentlemen that we are, here goes. What we do is plot the means of the groups with their respective 95% CIs; that's done in the left side (Part A) of Figure 6-2 for the data in Table 6-1.

Remember that the CI is:

$$CI = \overline{X} \pm t_{\alpha/2} \times SE = \overline{X} \pm t_{\alpha/2} \times \frac{SD}{\sqrt{N}}$$

(6-15)

We're using the *t* distribution rather than the normal curve because the sample size is relatively small. N is 10, so *t* with *df* = 9 is 2.26. For the Participants, Equation (6-7) tells us that s^2 is 20.67, so the SD is $\sqrt{20.67} = 4.55$. Plugging those numbers into the formula gives us:

$$CI = 35.0 \pm 2.26 \times \frac{4.55}{\sqrt{10}} = 35.0 \pm 3.25$$
$$= (31.75, 38.25)$$

(6-16)

and (24.14, 29.86) for the Controls.

What we see in Figure 6-2 is that the confidence intervals don't overlap; in this case, they don't even come close. We conclude that the groups are significantly different from each other, which is reassuring, because that's what the formal *t*-test told us. On the other hand, the error bars in the right side (Part B) of the figure show considerable overlap, so the difference is not statistically significant. From this, we can follow Cumming and Finch (2005) and establish a few rules:

(1) If the error bars don't overlap, then the groups are significant at $p \le 0.01$.

(2) If the amount of overlap is less than half of the CI, the significance level is ≤ 0.05.

(3) If the overlap is more than about 50% of the

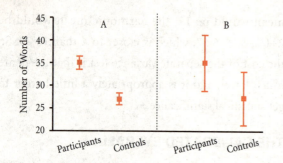

FIGURE 6-2 Means and 95% CIs when two groups do (left side) and do not (right side) significantly differ.

CI, the difference is not statistically significant.[4]

Note that this works only for two independent groups. If there are more than two, or if the data consist of two measurements on the same individuals (e.g. before and after treatment, as we'll discuss in a later chapter), you shouldn't use this.

EFFECT SIZE

The **effect size** for the difference between two means is:

Effect Size for Two Means

$$ES = \frac{\bar{X}_1 - \bar{X}_2}{SD} \qquad (6\text{-}17)$$

meaning that the ES is expressed in SD units. That is, if the ES is 1.0, it means that the difference between the groups is one standard deviation. Using the data in Table 6-1, we would get:

$$ES = \frac{35.0 - 27.0}{5.85} = 1.37 \qquad (6\text{-}18)$$

showing that the groups differ by 1.37 SDs. In this example, we used the pooled SDs from both groups, and the ES is also referred to as **Cohen's d** (Rosenthal, 1994). The advantage of *d* is that it uses data from both groups, which increases the accuracy of the estimate. The disadvantage is that the intervention may change not only the mean but also the SD, so the pooled estimate may be biased. That's the reason that another estimate of the ES, **Glass's Δ** (Glass, 1976), uses the SD only from the control group. As yet, there is no consensus which is better, but most

people seem to use *d*.

For obvious reasons, both of these indices are referred to as the **standardized mean difference**. Whichever measure is used, we still rely on Cohen's (1988) criteria: an ES of 0.2 is considered to be small (of negligible practical or clinical importance); one of 0.5 is moderate (of moderate practical or clinical importance); and 0.8 is large (of crucial practical or clinical importance). There are two things to bear in mind, though. First, these criteria apply only to *d* or Δ; we'll later encounter other indices of ESs that use different standards for small, moderate, and large.

Second, and more importantly, even Cohen himself said that they were just conventions, and should not be applied blindly but only in relation to what's known in a specific field and the importance of the finding. Meyer et al. (2001) calculated ESs from over 800 studies; those reporting the relationship between smoking and lung cancer, and the reduction of heart attacks from the use of ASA were less than 0.001. But, no reputable physician would advise her patients to replace the ASA they're taking with cigarettes on the basis that both ESs are vanishingly small and therefore unimportant. Thompson (2001) said it best: "If people interpreted effect sizes with the same rigidity that α=0.05 has been used in statistical testing, we would merely be being stupid in another metric."

Another way to interpret the standardized mean difference is that with *d* = 0.2, just over 85% of the scores in the distributions of the two groups overlap. When *d* = 0.5, the overlap is 67%; and with a *d* of 0.8, 52.6% of the scores overlap (Henson, 2006). If you want to convert a *d*-type ES into an *r*-type so you can compare them, the formula is:

$$r = \frac{d}{\sqrt{d^2 + \dfrac{N^2 - 2N}{n_1 n_2}}} \qquad (6\text{-}19)$$

where $N = n_1 + n_2$.

Often in reading articles, we come across naked values of *t* without any ES associated with it. We can easily figure out *d* using the formula:

---

[4]*If you thought that if the bars don't overlap, p is ⩽0.05 (rather than ⩽0.01), and that any overlap means nonsignificance, don't be ashamed; so do a majority of established researchers (Belia, et al., 2005).*

$$d = t \times \sqrt{\frac{1}{n_1} + \frac{1}{n_2}} \qquad \text{(6-20)}$$

SAMPLE SIZE AND POWER

Sample size estimates for the *t*-test closely follow the formulism developed in Chapter 5. However, note one small wrinkle. Because there are two groups, a factor of 2 sneaks into the equation. So the new formula for the sample size requirements for a two-group comparison looks like:

$$n = 2\left[\frac{(z_\alpha + z_\beta)\sigma}{\Delta}\right]^2 \qquad \text{(6-21)}$$

For example, if we wanted to compare a clam juice group and a placebo group, and our dependent variable was the misery of psoriasis, measured as percent of body area, we would proceed as follows:

1. *What is known about the extent of psoriasis in my patient population?*

For the sake of argument, let's assume that the mean extent is 42% and the SD is 15%.[5]

2. *How big a treatment effect do I think I will get?*

This is never known. If it were, you wouldn't need to do the study. So, make it up. If the sample size is more than you can manage in a year, double the treatment effect. If it's too small, and you can't justify enough funding, halve the treatment effect. Usually, though, it's the smallest difference that you would say is *clinically important*. Even if a smaller difference were statistically significant, you wouldn't change your practice because of it. So, for the sake of argument, let's say 20% in relative terms, so .20 × 42 = 8.4% in absolute terms.

3. *How big a Type I and Type II error do you want?*

Unfortunately, you can never diddle with the α level (unless you try one-tailed tests, but this should be used only as a last resort when all else fails). However, you can pick out β levels of 0.05, 0.10, or 0.20, or even 0.50 if you are really desperate. So, for the sake of argument, let's say α = 0.05, so z_α = 1.96; and β = 0.10, so z_β = 1.28.

Now we put it all in the old sausage machine, and crank:

$$n = 2\left[\frac{(1.96 + 1.28)15}{8.4}\right]^2 \qquad \text{(6-22)}$$
$$= 66.94 \text{ (say 67) per group}$$

If 67 per group is too large or too small, diddle away.

To save you the agony of having to buy batteries for your calculator, Table D in the Appendix gives you the sample sizes you need. The first column is labeled *d*, which is the ratio of δ ÷ σ. That's upside down from the way it appears in the formula, but it's simply another way of expressing the ES that's in Equation (6-21). In this case, 8.4 ÷ 15 is about 0.5. So, looking up a two-sided α of 0.05 and β of 0.20, you'll find 63 subjects per group, which is pretty close.

Table E goes the other way. If you've stumbled across a study that reports a non-significant *t*-test, you can check if the groups really were equivalent or if a high probability of a Type II error existed. Use the article to find out the sample size (if the two groups are different, use the harmonic mean), the difference between the means that they actually found (δ), and the SD (σ). Then, with an α of your choosing, you can look up the power of the test. For example, if the previous study was done with only 30 subjects per group, look across the row with 30 in column 1 until you get to the two-tailed α = 0.05. There's one column with *d* = 0.4, and one for *d* = 0.6, so we'll use a number half way between. For *d* = 0.4, the power is 0.346; for *d* = 0.6, power is 0.648. The mean of the two is 0.497, so for an effect size of 0.5, there was only a 50% probability that the study would have found a difference if it were actually there. This is too low for our blood (we usually want power to be at least 0.80), so we'd conclude that this study was too small and that the negative results were probably a Type II error.

The moral of the story is that a sample size calculation informs you about whether you need 20 or 200 people to do the study. Anyone who takes it more literally than that, unless the data on which it is based

---

[5] *If these data are not available, make them up. For the sake of the granting agency, though, try to back it up with some data from the literature.*

are very good indeed, is suffering from delusions.

One last word about power. The *t*-test and all related statistics, such as the *z*-test and the analyses of variance (which will be discussed in later chapters), are based on the assumption that the data are normally distributed. The concern is that if the data aren't normally distributed, the value of the test will still be correct, but the significance level wouldn't be accurate. Well, put your mind at ease. Sawilowsky and Hillman (1992) found that even with a "radically nonnormal distribution,"[6] the tabled significance levels are accurate, except when the *ns* are small, and the groups differ in sample size.

In this latter situation (small *ns*, different sample sizes), consider using a non-parametric test such as the Mann-Whitney *U* test, which we describe in Chapter 9; it will be even more powerful than the *t*-test (Zimmerman, 2011).

REPORTING GUIDELINES

Reporting the results of a *t*-test includes three elements: (1) the value of the test, (2) the degrees of freedom, and (3) the *p* level. Reporting just the *p* level, although allowed by some journals, is very poor practice. The format differs from one journal to the next, so—even though it may sound like an act of desperation—read the instructions to authors or flip

through a recent issue. Some typical ways of reporting the results would be:

$$t = 4.18, df = 18, p<0.001$$
$$t(18) = 4.18, p<0.001$$
$$t_{18} = 4.18, p<0.001$$

Two other points: If the computer prints out the exact probability, use it rather than "<0.05" or "<0.01." Second, if the computer prints out $p = 0.0000$, *don't* copy that into your manuscript; write "$p<0.001$."

How to Get the Computer to Do the Work for You
Descriptive Statistics

- From **Analyze**, choose Compare Means → **Independent-Samples *t*-Test**
- Click on the variable(s) to be analyzed from the list on the left, and click the arrow to move it (them) into the box marked **Test Variable(s)** [Note: One *t*-test will be performed for each variable listed.]
- Click on the grouping variable from the list on the left, and click the arrow to move it into the box marked **Grouping Variable**
- Click the Define Groups button
- Enter the value which defines the first group into Group 1 and press the <**Tab**> key
- Do the same for Group 2 and press <**Tab**>
- Click Continue
- Click OK

PAIRED *t*-TEST

One common analysis problem results from situations where individuals are measured at the beginning of a period of time (e.g. at the start of treatment) and again later (at the end of treatment). This design requires a new test, the paired *t*-test, which explicitly accounts for systematic variance between subjects.

SETTING THE SCENE

In a blatant attempt to cash in on the North American preoccupation with girth, Dr. Casimir from Chittagong designs yet another diet plan. To add a dash of science to the whole affair, he does a study where he weighs a bunch of chubbies before and after they indulge in the plan. He dumps the data on your desk, promising endless riches if you analyze it right. Somehow it seems that you must pair up the beginning and ending observations on each patient. How do you proceed?

All this stuff about randomizing folks to groups, although now *de rigeur* for medical research, goes

against a lot of intuition. A much more natural experiment is to measure something, do something to

---

[6]*That is, one skewed to the left; if it's skewed to the right, we presume it's referred to as a "conservatively nonnormal distribution."*

make it better, and then measure it again. It seems nonsensical to do it to some folks and not to others, and then measure everybody only after it is all over.

For example, when we reach middle age, we tend to get most of our exercise stepping up and down on the bathroom scales each morning.[7] The point of the exercise is to compare today's weight with yesterday's. Our hope is that by resisting the third donut at coffee or walking to the mailroom, some magical transformation will take place so that the belt will move in a notch or two.

If we were serious about combating this growing girth, we might even consider enlisting in an experiment. One possibility is Marine Basic Training at Parris Island, but they wouldn't want middle-aged academics for all sorts of reasons, of which big bellies are the least. A more likely option is some local group, such as Stomach Starers or Girth Gazers. And there we would go once a week, to pay for our pounds of flesh with our pounds of cash, to suffer public humiliation inflicted by the sadistic scales.

The measure of the success or failure of this treatment is based entirely on the comparison of this week's measurement with last week's. Although we may derive some perverse pleasure out of comparing ourselves with other pathetic creatures in the group, the comparison is based on weight loss (or more likely, not lost), not absolute weight. It is small consolation to the formerly petite housewife of 70 kg (154 lb) that the football alumnus and current used car salesman beside her tops in at 140 kg (308 lb). Even if we were to enroll a bunch of these folks in an experiment where they were randomly assigned to a treatment and control group, no scientist (or for that matter, no 6-year-old) in his or her right mind would simply weigh them all after the course of treatment.

Forgive us for being so pedantic, but *why* exactly is it so evidently right to measure change in weight within an individual instead of final weight between groups of individuals? In particular, in view of the

inevitable statistical sleight of hand to be inflicted on the unsuspecting data in the search for the magical *p*, why is change better than terminal measure?

The reason is that, when it comes to weight, stable differences *between* individuals are far greater than any likely difference resulting from treatment *within* individuals. This is not simply a reflection that some of us are gaunt and some gross. Recall again that your esteemed authors differ somewhat in height. Stretch is 6'5"; Shrimp is 5'8". Both have approximately the same size of self-induced life preserver about the midriff. But the big guy weighs about 200 lb and the little fella about 160 lb. Arguably, both could afford to lose about 15 lb.

Suppose, by some miracle, they achieved this lofty goal, whereas comparable authors in a control group didn't. To be more precise, Stretch lost 16 lb, Shrimp lost 14. Their counterparts across the way lost 1 and gained 1. Then if we looked simply at post-test weights, using a straight *t*-test, the difference between the groups would be 15 lb. However, the variability in this difference, which goes into the denominator, includes all the differences among individuals, amounting to 20 lb. By contrast, if we examine change scores, the numerator is still 15 lb, but the denominator includes the variability of the differences within the groups, which is 1 or 2 pounds. So the net effect is a large gain in precision and a corresponding increase in statistical power.

This, then, is the basic idea that we pursue here. We begin by examining two measurements per person, but eventually we explore the situation where there are any number of measures, and they may be a result of more than one factor. Pretesting and post-testing are only one example of these within-subject, or **repeated measures**, designs.

As we have seen, the main advantage of these strategies is the potential gain in statistical power. It is also possible to correct for baseline differences between groups, such as may occur if randomization

---

[7] *It's not really that simple. You know you have become obsessed with the problem when you spend a few minutes each day exploring different positions of feet, arms, and so on to see what results in minimum weight. Actually, we have found that leaving one foot off the scale works better; leaving both feet off works best of all.*

were inadequate or intact groups were used. But we should point out that this is not the universal panacea it would appear from our contrived example, and we will eventually explore situations where you can lose, as well as gain, power and sensitivity.

Having explored the theoretical issues around the issues of excess *avoirdupois*,[8] perhaps we can proceed to an actual example. The simplest example of a repeated-measures design involves two measurements on a series of subjects, such as those weighing in before and after a round of dieting.

It goes like this. We all know that the closer you get to the equator, the hotter the food gets. It's a puzzlement until you apply basic physics to the issue. Spicy food makes your body hotter, which makes you sweat, which evaporates, which absorbs heat from your flesh, which cools you off.[9] If this is so, then there may be real benefit, in calorie loss, of a fiery hot curry diet. First, most folks can't eat it anyway. Second, if they do, then the fire in their bellies raises their body temperature, which in turn results in a net energy loss to the environment. Voilá! The fat literally burns off!

So, enter Casper Casimir, the charming chap from Chittagong, with *Captain Casper Casimir's Choice Curried Calorie-Consuming Cuisine for Cold Canadian Consumers* (the C[11] Diet). All the prospective clients weigh in. For the treatment, they consume, to the best of their ability, suicide-level vindaloos, curries, and Rogan Josh's, at which point they sweat the pounds off. They undergo a second weigh-in after a month. The data are given in Table 6-2. We have taken the liberty, in the right-hand column, of calculating the difference for each individual (*after* minus *before*). We have also calculated the mean and SD of the prediet and postdiet weights and also the weight differences, as shown at the bottom of the table. Note that the SD of preweights and postweights are quite large, about 25 kg, reflecting the large stable differ-

TABLE 6-2   Pretest and post-test weights of 12 Casimir subjects

Subject	Pre-test	Post-test	Difference
1	65	62	4
2	88	86	4
3	125	118	4
4	103	105	4
5	90	91	4
6	76	72	4
7	85	81	4
8	126	122	4
9	97	95	4
10	142	145	4
11	132	132	0
12	110	105	
Mean	103.3	101.2	
SD	24.0	24.8	3.03

ences among *Homo sapiens*. However, the SD of the differences is much smaller, only 3.03 kg.

Now, if we follow the logic of statistics, our null hypothesis is that no loss in weight has occurred. In terms of the individual differences, this is equivalent to the null hypothesis that the true *difference* in the population is zero. Our best estimate of this difference is the calculated difference, 2.08. Moreover, the estimated SD of the differences is the calculated SD, 3.03. The statistical question is, What is the likelihood that a difference of 2.08 or greater could have occurred by chance in a sample of size 12 drawn from the population with a mean difference of 0 and an SD of 3.03?

The approach is to determine a signal-to-noise ratio, naturally. Here the signal is the observed difference (*d*), 2.08, and the noise is the *SE* of the difference, $3.03/\sqrt{12}$. So the test, called a **paired *t*-test**, is equal to:

$$t = \frac{d}{s/\sqrt{n}} \qquad (6\text{-}23)$$

In this case, it equals $2.08 \div (3.03 \div \sqrt{12}) = 2.38$.

Now, the critical value of a one-tailed *t*-test with 11 *df* (12 data 1 mean) at the 0.05 level is equal to

---

[8]*Showing off our Canadian bilingualism, this bizarre word is printed on many scales, but means, literally, "have some weight." We sure do.*

[9]*It's the same reason that mad dogs and Englishmen go out in the noonday sun and is also the origin of that classic ex-pat line "There's nothing like a nice cuppa tea (pronounced TAY) on a hot summer day."*

1.80. Casimir will undoubtedly proclaim to the world that the C^{11} diet is "scientifically proven" and cite papers to back up his claim. Of course, you recall Chapter 5 and are a little more suspicious of one-tailed tests.

For illustration, if we were intent on randomizing to two groups at all costs, we could have gone ahead with an independent sample *t*-test. For the sake of argument, assume that the pretest values were instead derived from a control group of 12 who were destined to pass up the benefits of the curry plan. If they must maintain their wicked ways, it is likely that they would be the same as the treatment group before the treatment began. We could then compare the treatment group after treatment to the control group with an independent sample test as we did in the next chapter (Chapter 7, so hold on for now):

$$t = \frac{2.08}{\sqrt{(24.8^2 + 24.0^2) \div 12}} = 0.216 \qquad \textbf{(6-24)}$$

Given all the previous discussion, you should not be surprised to see that this *t*-test is minuscule and doesn't warrant a peek at Table C in the Appendix.

Therein lies the power of repeated observations. In the situation where small differences resulting from treatments are superimposed on large, stable differences between individuals, it can't be beat.

So why do all these randomized trials, where folks are assigned to one group or another and measured at the end of the study? There are three reasons, all of which go against the simple paired observation design: one a design issue, one a logistic issue, and one a statistical issue. We'll take them in that order.

The design problem is that a simple pretest-post-test design does not control for a zillion other variables that might explain the observed differences. Maybe the local union went on strike and the study subjects had to cut back on the food bill. Maybe "20/20" came out with a new Baba Wawa piece on the beneficial effect of kiwi fruit for dieters.[10] All of these are alternative "treatments" that might have contributed to the observed weight loss. For these reasons, most textbooks on experimental design mention this design only to dismiss it out of hand.

The logistic problem is more complicated. In many situations a pretest is not possible or desirable. If the outcome is mortality rates, it makes little sense to measure alive/dead at the beginning of the study. If it is an educational intervention, it is often dangerous to measure achievement at the beginning because the pretest measurement may be very much a part of the intervention, telling students what you want them to learn as well as anything you teach to them. Or it may be far too costly to measure things at the beginning.

Finally, there is a statistical issue. If *no* large, stable between-individual differences exist, not only will you not gain ground with a paired comparison, but you could possibly *lose* statistical power. The reason is that the difference score involves two measurements, each with associated error or variability. Comparing groups on the basis of only post-treatment scores introduces error from (1) within-subject variation and (2) between-subject variation. Taking differences introduces within-subject variation *twice*. If within-subject variation exceeds between-subject variation, the latter test will have less power than has the former.

To illustrate this point a bit more, and also to confront the design issue, let's consider a slightly more elaborate design. As we indicated, the difficulty with the pre-post design is that any number of agents might have come into play between the first and second measurement, and we have no justification for taking all the credit. One obvious way around the issue is to go back to the classical randomized experiment: randomizing folks to get and not get our ministrations, and then measuring *both* groups before and after the treatment. Now the data might look like that in Table 6-3.

First of all, this is not exactly a classic randomized controlled trial; that would only measure weights after treatment and then compare treatment and

---

[10]*Who can forget the great grapefruit diet? Seduce the population, make zillions of dollars off the suckers, take a mistress who then shoots you full of holes, and lose about 5 pounds instantly as the blood drains away. And you never gain the weight back!*

TABLE 6-3   Pretest and post-test weights of 12 Casimir subjects and 12 controls

Subject	Experimental			Control		
	Pretest	Post-test	Difference	Pretest	Post-test	Difference
1	65	62	−3	68	70	+2
2	88	86	−2	122	123	+1
3	125	118	−7	84	83	−1
4	103	105	+2	95	97	+2
5	90	91	+1	106	106	0
6	76	72	−4	71	72	+1
7	85	81	−4	87	86	−1
8	126	122	−4	147	152	+5
9	97	95	−2	129	131	+2
10	142	145	+3	136	138	+2
11	132	132	0	105	104	−1
12	110	105	−5	99	100	+1
MEAN	103.3	101.3	−2.1	104.1	105.2	+1.1
SD	24.0	24.8	3.03	25.2	26.2	1.73

control groups with an unpaired *t*-test. The calibrated eyeball indicates that such a test is not worth the trouble; the mean in the treatment group is 101.17 kg and in the control group is 105.16 kg. The difference amounts to 4 kg, but the SDs are about 25 kg in each group. Nonetheless, for completeness, we'll go ahead and do it.

$$t = \frac{101.17 - 105.17}{\sqrt{(24.83^2 + 26.19^2) \div 12}} = 0.384$$

$$(6\text{-}25)$$

However, an alternative approach that takes advantage of the difference measure is to simply ask whether the average weight **loss** in the treatment group is different from the average weight loss in the control group.[11] If we call the weight loss D, the null hypothesis comparing treatment (T) and control (C) groups is:

$$H_0 : \Delta_T = \Delta_C \qquad (6\text{-}26)$$

Having framed the question this way, the obvious test is an unpaired *t*-test on the *difference* scores:

$$t = \frac{-2.1 - 1.1}{\sqrt{(3.03^2 + 1.73^2) \div 12}} = 3.145 \qquad (6\text{-}27)$$

This is significant at the 0.05 level (*t*[22] 2.07). The test of significance for the difference score is

considerably higher than is the *t*-test for the post-test scores, even though the absolute difference was smaller (3.2 instead of 4.0), because the between-subject SD (about 24 to 26) is much larger than the within-subject SD (1.7 to 3.5).

OTHER USES OF THE PAIRED *t*-TEST

The example that we just used, of testing the effect of the C[11] diet by measuring people before and after an intervention, is probably the most common way that the paired *t*-test is used. But, there are other situations where the paired *t*-test is not only handy, but mandatory. One problem with the study of teaching Academish 1A7 is that we're trusting randomization to result in both groups being similar at baseline in their ability to say "hegemonic phallocentric discourse" and other such phrases without breaking into uncontrollable peals of laughter. Randomization works in the long run (say, an infinite number of people per group, which would make the lecture hall quite crowded), but is no guarantee of group similarity for smaller studies. We also know that gender has an effect on language,[12] as does area of specialization[13] and perhaps a couple of other factors, such as

---

[11] *Of such things, Nobel prizes are not made. Nor are we implying that this is something you might not have thought of yourself.*

[12] *So does sex, but we're not allowed to discuss that in a book of this nature.*

[13] *Have you ever tried to have a conversation with a business major?*

age. We could improve the design by selecting people from the pool of controls by *matching* each person to someone in the experimental group of the same age, gender, and from the same academic department, thus insuring that the groups are relatively similar at the beginning.

Why can't we just charge ahead and use a Student's *t*-test? The reason is the same as the rationale for using the paired *t*-test in the C[11] example; subject 1 in the experimental group is, because of the matching, much more similar to subject 1 in the control group than to any other, randomly selected person. So, the situation is closer to that of one person being tested under two different conditions than of two unrelated people in different groups. We lose power if we ignore the similarity, in much the same way that we lose power if we treat a repeated measures design as if it consisted of two different groups.

But, there's a caveat. We also lose degrees of freedom, as we just discussed in the C[11] example. We hope that this is more than compensated for by the reduction in between-subject variance, but this means we have to select our matching variables carefully. If subjects are matched on variables that are unrelated to the outcome, such as eye color or height, then the *df* is reduced with no gain in variance reduction.

EFFECT SIZE

When we discussed the ES for the independent *t*-test, we mentioned that there are a few choices, which vary in terms of which estimate of the SD is used in the denominator. Similarly, there are four ways to calculate a *d*-type effect size for a paired *t*-test, and which one you use depends on what assumptions you're willing (or are forced) to make (Kline, 2004). Although some of these have their roots in the standard statistical literature, others have been reincarnated in a slightly different guise in clinical research (often with the authors being unaware of the index's

previous life), primarily in the form of responsiveness to change, which has been suggested in the quality-of-life literature as an important measurement characteristic, right up there with reliability and validity (e.g., Kirshner and Guyatt, 1985; but see Streiner and Norman, 2014, for the truth of the matter). Since it's in the latter domain where you're most likely to encounter these things, we'll show you the parallels.

The reason there's more than one coefficient relates directly back to the previous section, where we discussed the difference between the paired and unpaired *t*-tests. When you calculate an ES with paired (usually pre-post) data, you can use either the SD *between* people measured either before or after the intervention, or the SD *within* people (i.e., the SD of the differences, $SD_{Difference}$). While it usually makes little sense in a statistical test to use the SD between people in the measurement of an ES,[14] both are defensible; they're just different. If you use $SD_{Between}$ in the denominator, you're comparing average change with the variability among people (i.e., the treatment effect is large enough to move a patient up 1 SD). If you use $SD_{Difference}$, you're looking at average change compared with the variability of possible changes (Norman et al., 2006).

As we'll see, even that doesn't exhaust the possible permutations. Using the comparison with $SD_{Between}$, the first we'll look at is called **Hedges's g** and is simply:

$$G = \frac{Mean\ Difference}{s_p} \qquad (6\text{-}28)$$

where s_p is the pooled SD from the two conditions (pre and post) or the two matched groups. The problem is that this formula assumes homogeneity of variance, and this may not be the case if the intervention changes the variance,[15] or the two matched groups have different variances.

The second approach, called **Glass's△**, gets around this by using only the preintervention or the

---

[14]*Actually, as we'll see at the end of this chapter, sometimes it makes a great deal of sense.*

[15]*Which is highly likely. Different people respond differently to treatment, so the SD of the post-test is usually larger than the SD of the pretest (assuming treatment increases a person's score).*

comparison group's SD (s_c).[16] This avoids one problem, but the penalty is that the estimate of the SD is based on only half the number of observations, so it may be less accurate.

$$\Delta = \frac{Mean\ Difference}{s_c} \qquad \textbf{(6-29)}$$

A third possibility, recommended by Cohen (1988) for pre-post designs, is to use the SD of the difference score. This has been reincarnated in the quality-of-life literature by Liang (2000) and McHorney and Tarlov (1995) and is often called the *Standardized Response Mean.*

$$Cohen's\ d = \frac{Mean\ Difference}{SD_{Difference}} \qquad \textbf{(6-30)}$$

If you're comparing the change in the treatment group with the change in the control group, as in the example shown in Table 6-2, then things get more complicated. You can use (a) the pooled $SD_{Difference}$ of both groups (which uses all the data but doesn't recognize the confounding with treatment mentioned in rubric 9); (b) the $SD_{Difference}$ of just the control group (Guyatt's *responsiveness*) which ignores the interaction with treatment; or (c) the $SD_{Difference}$ of the treatment group, which is likely the least biased measure, but uses only half the data.

What's the relation between the two families of coefficients? Well, if there were no correlation between the pretreatment and post-treatment scores, the $SD_{Difference}$ would just be. In fact, though, there often is a substantial correlation, which has the effect of reducing the $SD_{Difference}$ relative to s_p. (If the correlation were 1, then everyone's postintervention score would be just the baseline score plus a constant, and the $SD_{Difference}$ would be 0.) The relationship between the two SDs is:

$$SD_{Difference} = s_p\sqrt{21(1-r_{12})} \qquad \textbf{(6-31)}$$

A long stare at this equation yields an important insight that goes beyond just how to compute an ES. As we've already indicated, if the correlation is 1,

then $SD_{Difference}$ is 0, and you're way further ahead to use difference scores in the design, since the paired *t*-test is infinite. If the correlation is 0, then the $SD_{Difference}$ is larger than s_p, and you actually lose ground by using change scores. In fact, the equation shows that the break-even point is a correlation of 0.5; above that you'd do better to use change scores, below and you're actually further ahead to just look at post-treatment scores.

Just remember when you use Equation (6-29) that the ES is given in units of the SD of the *difference* score, not in the SD of the original scale. To avoid confusion, it's probably best to report both. In all cases, we still use the same criteria: an ES of 0.2 is small; 0.5 is moderate; and 0.8 is large.

THE CALIBRATED EYEBALL

In Chapter 5, we presented three rules for an eyeball test of significance for two independent groups, simply by plotting the means and 95% CIs. Here's the fourth rule, applicable to the paired *t*-test:

DON'T DO IT!

The reason is that we're not interested in the CIs around the individual means, but rather the single CI around the difference score. The problem is that the width of this difference CI (*wd*) depends on the correlation[17] (*r*) between the pretest and post-test scores:

$$W_d = W_{Pre} + W_{Post} - 2rW_{Pre}W_{Post} \qquad \textbf{(6-32)}$$

the higher the correlation, the smaller w_d. Because we can't see that correlation by just eyeballing the data, comparing the CIs of the two means is meaningless (Cumming and Finch, 2005).

SAMPLE SIZE CALCULATION

Sample size calculations for paired *t*-tests are the essence of simplicity. We use the original sample size calculation introduced in Chapter 5:

---

[16]*Note that here, Δ is the name of a test, whereas in other circumstances it is used to represent the difference between groups. Similarly, d can either be another symbol for the difference between groups, or it can refer to a class of ES estimates. For that reason, we're using "mean difference" rather than d in the formulae. As you can see, statistics is a rigorous way of eliminating confusion and ambiguity.*

[17]*We'll define correlation formally in Chapter 11. Suffice it to say for now that it's a measure of relationship; are high pretest scores associated with high post-test scores?*

$$n = \left[\frac{(Z_\alpha + Z_\beta)\sigma}{\delta} \right]^2$$

where δ is the hypothesized difference, s is the SD of the difference, and z_α and z_β correspond to the chosen a and b levels. The only small fly in the ointment is that we must now estimate not only the treatment difference, but also the SD of the difference within subjects—which is almost never known in advance. But look on the bright side—more room for optimistic forecasts.

REPORTING GUIDELINES

Would you be surprised if we said they're exactly the same as for the unpaired *t*-test that we told you about in the above section? If you are surprised, go back and reread both chapters.

How to Get the Computer to Do the Work for You
Descriptive Statistics

* From **Analyze**, choose **Compare Means→Paired-Samples *t*-Test**
* Click on the two variables to be analyzed from the list on the left [e.g. the before and after scores], and click the arrow to move them into the box marked **Paired Variables**
* Click **OK**

SUMMARY

* ◇ The *t*-test, where the test statistic follows a Student's *t* distribution if the null hypothesis is true, is a common method for constructing test statistics and their corresponding critical value. It applies to the comparisons of sample means, including one sample *t*-test, two-group *t*-test, paired *t*-test, and it is the bread and butter of statistical data analysis. Confidence interval and hypothesis are two different methods for *t*-test, their conclusion is the same.

* ◇ The one-sample *t*-test is served for comparing sample results with specified value. To be specific, one-sample *t*-test is collected a single sample, the single sample mean is compared with a known value, and it is considered as the simplest types of *t*-test.

* ◇ Two-group *t*-test, is the easiest approach to the comparison of two means. The distinction between the *t*-test and the *z*-test, discussed in the previous chapter, is that the *t*-test estimates both the means and the SD, which introduces a dependency on sample size. Despite its computational ease, the *t*-test is *not* appropriate when there are more than two groups or when individuals in one group are matched to individuals in another.

* ◇ The comparison of differences between treatment and control groups using an unpaired *t*-test on the difference scores (between initial and final observations, or between matched subjects) is the best of both worlds—almost. The basic strategy is to use pairs of observations to eliminate between-subject variance from the denominator of the test. The test is used in pre-post designs, and a variant of the strategy is useful in the more powerful pre-post, control group designs. The advantage of the test exists as long as the subjects or pairs have systematic differences between them. If this is not the case, then the test can result in a loss, rather than a gain, in statistical power.

GLOSSARY

one sample *t*-test　单样本 *t* 检验

two-group *t*-test　成组 *t* 检验

paired *t*-test　配对 *t* 检验

test statistic　检验统计量

standard normal deviate　标准正态离差

confidence interval　可信区间

t-distribution　*t* 分布

two-tailed test　双侧检验

one-tail test　单侧检验

null hypothesis　无效假设

alternative hypothesis　备择假设

hypothesis testing　假设检验

EXERCISES

1. As we discussed, at least three kinds of *t*-tests can be applied to data sets—unpaired *t*-tests, paired *t*-tests, and unpaired *t*-tests on difference scores. For the following designs, select the most appropriate.

   a. Scores on this exercise before and after reading Chapter 5.

   b. Crossover trial, with joint count of patients with rheumatoid arthritis, each of whom undergoes (1) 6 weeks of treatment with gold, and (2) 6 more weeks with fool's gold (iron pyrites). Order is randomized.

   c. School performance of only children versus children with one brother or sister.

   d. School performance of younger versus older brother/sister in two-child families.

   e. School performance of older brother/ sister in one-parent versus two-parent families.

   f. Average intelligence of older and younger siblings, reared apart and reared together.

2. You may recall that we did a *t*-test on hair restorers. Let's return to the data, but add a piece of information:

   subjects were related. Subjects 1 and 6, 2 and 7, and so on are brothers. How does this change the analysis?

Drug		Placebo	
Subject	Hairs	Subject	Hairs
1	12	6	5
2	14	7	10
3	28	8	20
4	3	9	2
5	22	10	12
Mean	15.8		9.8
SD	8.59		6.21

3. Answer True or False: When comparing the means of two samples using the *t*-test:

   a. The null hypothesis is that the means are equal

   b. The null hypothesis is that the means are not significantly different

   c. The sample sizes must be equal

   d. The SEs of the means must be equal

   e. The data must be normally distributed

4. Let's look at hair loss, the last bastion of male vanity (and a personal issue with your intrepid authors). Till recently, most patent hair restorers contained ethyl alcohol as the main active ingredient, presumably to ease the anguish. Now, a legitimate drug has changed all that. But does it really work? We take 10 chrome-domes, randomize them to two groups, and have them rub the active drug or a placebo into the affected part for 6 weeks.

   A blind (technically, not literally) observer counts hairs per cm^2 on the dome, and we calculate the means and SDs. The data look like this:

Drug		Placebo	
Subject	Hairs	Subject	Hairs
1	12	5	5
2	14	7	10
3	28	8	20
4	3	9	2
5	22	10	12
Mean	15.8		9.8
SD	8.59		6.21

   Calculate the following quantities:

   a. Difference between the means

   b. SE of the difference

   c. *t*-test

   d. Is this result significant?

5. Okay, so you tried and failed to grow hair. Maybe the sample wasn't big enough (and you can get even more money to do a bigger and better study).

   a. How much power did you have to detect a difference of 100% (i.e. the treatment mean is 19.6, the control mean is 9.8)?

   b. How big a sample size would you need to detect a true difference of 50% with α of 0.05 and β of 0.10?

6. The height of 16 students selected at random from a school had a mean 118 cm and variance 85cm. Test at 5% level of significance the hypothesis that the students are on the average less 125

cm in all.

Calculate the following quantities:

a. Normality test

b. Confidence interval of the sample

c. *t*-test

d. Is this result significant?

7. The life expectancy of people in the year 2013 in certain city of china is expected to be 73 years. A survey was conducted in 10 districts of certain city of china and the data obtained are given below.

68 72 78 71 73 74 69 70 72 67

a. How did you carry out the statistical analysis?

b. Did you conform the expect view?

8. A certain bolt is designed to be 4 inches in length. The lengths of a random sample of 15 bolts are shown as follows:

4.00 3.95 4.01 3.95 4.00 3.98 3.97 3.97

4.01 3.98 3.99 4.01 4.02 4.02 3.98

a. Please examine the normality of the data

b. Which statistical method will be carried out?

c. Comment on the above result

SUGGESTED READINGS AND WEBSITES

[1] Posten HO. The robustness of the two-sample *t*-test over the Pearson system. Journal of Statistical Computation and Simulation,1978:6,295-311.

[2] Hays WL. Statistics, 3rd ed. New York: Holt, Rinehart, and Winston,1981.

[3] Cohen J. Statistical power analysis for the behavioral sciences. 2nd ed. Journal of the American Statistical Association,1988,84(334):19-74.

[4] Sawilowsky SS, Einstein FS,Behrens-Fisher. The probable difference between two means when $\sigma_1^2 \neq \sigma_2^2$. Journal of Modern Applied Statistical Methods, 2002,1(2),461-472.

[5] Watkins AE,Scheaffer RL,Cobb GW. Statistics in action: Understanding a world of data. Emeryville,CA: Key College Publishing,2004.

[6] Moore D, McCabe G. Introduction to the practice of statistics. 7th ed. New York, NY: Freeman.

CHAPTER THE SEVENTH   Analysis of Variance

SETTING THE SCENE

The t-test is usually used to compare with two sample means, but it is unsuitable for multi-group comparison of several sample means. For example, there are three medicines of dropping blood pressure, which are allocated to three groups of hypertension patients, what is difference between the average blood pressure reduction values of three groups. Analysis of variance (ANOVA)is a powerful set of techniques to test differences among means of three or more samples, which also named as F test due to the initial techniques of the analysis of variance were developed by the statistician and geneticist Fisher RA in the 1920s and 1930s.

There are several types of ANOVA, such as one-way ANOVA (or one factor), two-way ANOVA (or two factors), multi-factor ANOVA, repeated measures ANOVA, and so on. This chapter will introduce one-way ANOVA and two-way ANOVA, as well as multiple comparisons between the groups.

One–way ANOVA is a simple method of ANOVA, which allows us to compare means in several groups of observation, all of the groups are independent but possibly with a different mean for each group. So, we use one-way ANOVA to introduce fundamentals of ANOVA. We create a sum of squares representing the differences between individual group means and a second sum of squares representing variation within groups.

FUNDAMENTALS OF ANOVA

Why not choose *t*-test but ANOVA for comparing means among several groups? Say, for A, B and C, three group sample means comparisons, if we were to Compare their means with a *t*-test, a problem would arise. We can do only two at a time, so we end up comparing A with B, A with C, B with C. There are 3 possible comparisons, each of which has a 0.05 chance of making type I error by chance, so the overall chance of making I error approaches 1-(1-0.05)³, that is 0.14, far away more than α=0.05. To increase number of comparisons, the probability of overall type I error becomes increasing, according to the formals: 1-(1-0.05)k, k is the number of comparisons.

ANOVA allows us to compare several sample means at the same time. The basic idea of ANOVA is that it divides the total variance into two or more parts depending on study design and source of variation, and different sources of variation are expressed as different **sum of squares (SS)** respectively, then average variation for each effect sources sum of squares ratio by degree of freedom, that is **mean of squares (MS)**, then hypothesis test statistic *F* value is constructed to make conclusion whether is difference among the several population means.

Example 7-1

The studies have suggested that there is an association between oral cancer and DNA expression level of the gene polymorphism of oral exfoliated cells. The data of one study is shown in Table 7-1. The question is that if DNA expression level is different among different peoples.

In Table 7-1, values of sample mean are 10.68, 15.27, 19.36, 22.06 respectively. The purpose of hypotheses test is to deduce if several population means are significantly different basing on sample's information and sample error. Now, what is of the hypothesis? A test of great importance is whether or not all the means are equal. Formalizing it a bit, the null hypothesis is:

$$H_0 : \mu_1=\mu_2=\mu_3=\mu_4 \qquad (7\text{-}1)$$

and our alternative hypothesis is simply:

$$H_1 : \text{Not all the } \mu\text{'s are equal.} \qquad (7\text{-}2)$$

If H_0 is not rejected, we should stop right here. If H_0 is rejected, then we might like to find out which is best highest or lowest in four groups.

This is where the complicated formula comes in. Thinking in terms of signals and noises, what we need is a measure of the overall difference among the means of the groups and a second measure of the overall variability within the groups. We approach this by first determining the sum of all the squared

TABLE 7-1   DNA expression level of the gene polymorphism of oral exfoliated cells in different groups

subject	healthy control	oral mucosa hyperplasia	early-stage oral cancer	later-stage oral cancer
1	11.9	13.9	17.8	27.2
2	13.4	17.2	23.4	22.9
3	9.1	16.5	17.1	19.9
4	10.7	14.7	23.2	23.9
5	13.7	14.6	20.6	23.1
6	12.2	13.0	23.5	21.1
7	12.8	12.0	13.4	15.6
8	5.2	16.4	19.4	27.2
9	8.6	14.1	18.8	19.5
10	9.2	20.3	16.4	20.2
Mean	10.68	15.27	19.36	22.06
Stand deviation	2.66	2.40	3.36	3.58
Grand mean	16.84			

differences between group means and the overall mean. Then we determine a second sum of all the squared differences between the individual data and their group mean. These are then massaged into a statistical test.

THE PARTS OF THE ANALYSIS

Sums of Squares

With the t-test, our measure of the signal was the difference between the means. As we just saw, though, we can't do that when we have more than two groups, so what do we use? Another way of thinking about what we did with the t-test was that we got the **grand mean** of the two groups (which we abbreviate as $\overline{X}..$ for reasons we'll explain shortly), and then saw how much each individual mean deviated from it:

$$(\overline{X}_1 - \overline{X}..) - (\overline{X}_2 - \overline{X}..) = \overline{X}_1 - \overline{X}_2 \quad \textbf{(7-3)}$$

We use the same logic with the analysis of variance (ANOVA); we figure out the grand mean of all of the groups, and see how much each group mean deviates from it. As we saw when we were deriving the formula for the SD in Chapter 3, though, this will always add up to zero, unless we square the results. We also need to take into account how many subjects there are in each group. We call the results the **Sum of Squares (Between)**, because it is literally the sum of the squared differences between the group means

and the grand mean. So what we have is:

$$SS(between) = n\sum(\overline{X}_{.k} - \overline{X}..)^2 \quad \textbf{(7-4)}$$

Where n is the number of subjects in each group. If the groups have different sample sizes, you would use the harmonic mean of the sample sizes, as explained in Chapter 3.

Time to explain those funny dot subscripts in Equation (7-3) and (7-4). Each person's value is represented as X. Now, we need some way of differentiating Subject 1's value from Subject 2's, and so on, so we have one subscript (i) to indicate which subject we're talking about. But, we in essence have four Subject 1s—one from each of the groups, so we need another subscript (k) to reflect group membership. A dot replacing a subscript means that we're talking about all of the people referred to by that subscript. So, $\overline{X}_{.k}$ is the mean of all people in Group k, and $\overline{X}..$ is the mean of all people in all groups (i.e., the grand mean).

Using Equation (7-4), we'll get:

SS (Between)= $10[(10.68 - 16.84)^2 + (15.27 - 16.84)^2 + (19.36 - 16.84)^2 + (22.06 - 16.84)^2] = 740.093$

Similarly, the Sum of Squares (Within) is the sum of all the squared differences between individual data and the group mean **within** each group. It looks like:

Sum of Squares (Within)= $(11.9 - 10.68)^2 + (13.4 - 10.68)^2 + \ldots + (13.9 - 15.27)^2 + (17.2 - 15.27)^2 + \ldots +$

$(17.8-19.36)^2 + (23.4-19.36)^2 + \dots + (27.2-22.06)^2 +$
$(22.9-22.06)^2 + \dots + (20.2-22.06)^2 [40 \text{ terms}]$ $\hspace{2em}$ (7-7)

After much anguish, this turns out to equal 332.765. Again, the algebraic formula, for the masochists in the crowd, is:

$$SS(within) = \sum_i \sum_k (X_{ik} - \bar{X}_{.k})^2 \hspace{2em} (7\text{-}5)$$

Where the first summation sign, the one with the i under it, means to add over all of the subjects in the group, and the second summation sign means to add across all the groups.

Finally, the Sum of Squares (Total) is the difference between all the individual data and the grand mean. It is the sum of SS (Between) and SS (Within). But in longhand:

Sum of Squares (Total)$= (11.9-16.84)^2 + (13.4-16.84)^2 + \dots + (13.9-16.84)^2 + (17.2-16.84)^2 + \dots + (17.8-16.84)^2 + (23.4-16.84)^2 + \dots + (27.2-16.84)^2 + (22.9-16.84)^2 + \dots + (20.2-16.84)^2$ [40 terms] $=$ 1076.858.

To check the result, this should be equal to the sum of the Between and Within Sums of Squares, 740.093+332.765=1076.858; and the algebraic formula is:

$$SS(total) = \sum_i \sum_k (X_{ik} - \bar{X}..)^2 \hspace{2em} (7\text{-}6)$$

There are two things to note. First, because summation is usually obvious from the equation, from now on, we'll just use a single Σ without a subscript, even when two or more are called for, and let you work things out. Second, the equations look a little bit different if there aren't the same number of subjects in each group, but we'll let the computer worry about that wrinkle.

Degrees of Freedom

The next step is to figure out the degrees of freedom (*df* or df or d.f.) for each term, preparatory to calculating the Mean Squares. Remember that in the previous chapter, we defined df as the number of unique bits of information. For the Between-Groups Sum of Squares, there are four groups, whose sum must equal the Grand Mean. So, the df (Between) is equal to $4 - 1 = 3$. More generally, for k groups:

$$df(\text{Between}) = k-1$$

We follow the model for the *t*-test for the Within-Groups Sum of Squares, where we figured out the *df* for each group, and then added them together. Here, each of the four groups has 10 data points, so *df* is $4 \times (10 - 1) = 36$. In general, then:

$$df(\text{Within}) = k\,(n-1) \hspace{2em} (7\text{-}8)$$

Finally, for the Total Sum of Squares, there are 40 data points that again must add up to the Grand Mean, so $df = 39$. Again, generally, the formula is:

$$df(\text{Total}) = nk - 1 \hspace{2em} (7\text{-}9)$$

It's no coincidence that the *df* for the individual variance components (between and within) add up to the total *df*. This is always the case, and it provides an easy check in complex designs.

Mean Squares

Now we can go the next, and last, steps. First we calculate the Mean Square by dividing each Sum of Squares by its *df*. This is then a measure of the average deviation of individual values from their respective mean (which is why it's called a *Mean Square*), since the *df* is about the same as the number of terms in the sum. Finally, we form the ratio of the two Mean Squares, the *F*-ratio, which is a signal-to-noise ratio of the differences between groups to the variation within groups. This is summarized in an ANOVA table such as Table 7-2. We can then look up the calculated *F*-ratio to see if it is significant. Do not worry about complex formulas and calculation, all analysis are conducted by SPSS Software.

TABLE 7-2 The ANOVA summary table

Source of variation	Sum of squares	df	Mean square	F value
Between	740.093	3	246.698	26.689
Within	332.765	36	9.243	
Total	1076.858	39		

The critical values of the *F*-test at the back of the book are listed under the *df* for both the numerator and the denominator. When you publish this piece (good luck!!), the *F*-ratio would be written as *F* 3,36 or, if you can't afford the word processor, $F(3,36)$ or $F(3/36)$. Either way, the calculated ratio turns out to be significant because 26.689 is very much greater than the published F-value for 3 and 36 df, 2.86. So the conclusion of statistical deduce is that H_0 is rejected, that is, not all the population means are equal. At this point, we know that at least two are different from each other, but it can't say yet which they are; we'll get to that when we discuss *post-hoc comparisons*.

EXPECTED MEAN SQUARES AND THE DISTRIBUTION OF *F*

If you peruse the table of *F-ratios* in the back, one fact becomes clear—you don't see *F-ratios* anywhere near zero. Perhaps that's not a surprise; after all, we didn't find that any *t*-values worth talking about were near zero either. But it actually should be a bit more surprising, if you consider where the *F-ratio* comes from. After all, the numerator is the signal—the difference between the groups—and the denominator is the differences within the groups. If no difference truly exists between the groups, shouldn't the numerator go to zero?

Surprisingly, no. Imagine that there really was no difference among the groups. All the µs are therefore equal. Would we expect the Sum of Squares (Between) to be zero? As you might have guessed, the answer is "No." The reason is because whatever variation occurred within the groups as a result of error variance would eventually find its way into the group means, and then in turn into the Sum of Squares (Between) and the Mean Square. As it turns out, in the absence of any difference in population means, the expected Mean Square (Between) [usually abbreviated as $E(MS_{bet})$] is exactly equal to the variance (within), σ_{err}^2.

Conversely, if no variance exists within groups, then the only variance contributing to the Mean Square is between groups, and the expected Mean Square (Between) $= n \times \sigma_{bet}^2$.

Putting it together, then, the expected value of the Mean Square (Within) is just the error variance, σ^2; and the expected value of the Mean Square (Between) is equal to the sum of the two variances:

$$E(MS_{bet}) = \sigma_{err}^2 + n\sigma_{bet}^2 \qquad \textbf{(7-10)}$$

So when there is no true variance between groups,

the σ_{bet}^2 drops out and the ratio (the F-ratio) equals 1.

As we go to hairier and hairier designs, the formulae for the expected mean squares will also become hairier (to the extent that this is the last time you will ever see the beast derived exactly), but one thing will always remain true: In the absence of an effect, we expect the relevant F-ratio to equal 1. Conversely, if we go to a really simple design and do a one-way ANOVA on just two groups, the calculated F-ratio is precisely the square of the t-test.

Does this mean that you'll never see an F-ratio less than 1? Again, the same answer, "No." Because of sampling error, it sometimes happens that when nothing is going on—there's no effect of group membership—you'll end up with an F that's just below 1. Usually it's in the high 0.90s.

ASSUMPTIONS OF ANOVA

One-way ANOVA, as well as the t-test and all other ANOVAs, makes two assumptions about the data. The first is that they are normally distributed, and the second is that there is homogeneity of variance across all of the groups. The first assumption, normality, is rarely tested formally because, as Ferguson and Takane (1989) state, "Unless there is reason to suspect a fairly extreme departure from normality, it is probable that the conclusions drawn from the data using an F-test will not be seriously affected". That is, the Type I and Type II errors aren't inflated if the data are skewed (especially if the skew is in the same direction for all groups); and deviations in kurtosis (the distribution being flatter or more peaked than the normal curve) affect power only if the sample size is low.

There's another very good reason not to worry about it. If we go back to Chapter 5 and the logic of statistical inference, what we're actually looking at with ANOVA, t-tests, and any other statistic focused on differences between means, is the distribution *of the means*. From the **Central Limit Theorem** (Chapter 4), the means will be normally distributed, regardless of the original distribution, especially when there are at least 30 or so observations per group.

The assumption of homogeneity of variance,

which also goes by the fancy name of *homoscedasticity*, is assessed more often because most computer programs do it whether we want it or not, but the results are rarely used. The reason is that one-way ANOVA is fairly robust to deviations from homoscedasticity (which is called, for obvious reasons, *heteroscedasticity*), especially if the groups have equal sample sizes, and the populations (not the samples) are normally distributed. Just how robust is anybody's guess, but as with the assumption of normality, it's rarely worth worrying about, especially if the ratio of the largest to the smallest variance is less than 3 (Box, 1954).

COMPLETED RANDOMIZED DESIGN

What is the Completed Randomized Design?

The simplest type of analysis of variance is that known as one-way analysis, in which only one source of variance, or factor, is investigated. It is an extension to three or more samples of the *t*-test procedure for use with two dependent samples. The completed randomized design is typical single factor design that only one primary factor with several level is take into account. The subjective(for example, the hypertension patients) are assigned completely at random to several treatment in different level (different drugs treatment groups), and measurements to determine treatment effectiveness are to be made comparisons (hypertension reduction values of several groups), to find out the optimal treatment. In observational research, comparison the difference of the certain variable among several independent groups also be regarded as one factor design, and its hypotheses test is same as completely randomized design. For example 7-1, the difference of DNA level among four groups is effected on different populations, besides by random error of individual variation and measurement error.

In one-way ANOVA, the total variance of the variable interested in our study is divided into variance among groups and variance within groups. The total variance is expressed as the total sum of squares (SST), that is the sum of squares of the deviations of individual observations from the mean

of all the observations taken together, and the degree of freedom of the total variance is $N-1$, N is the total sample size. The variance among groups is expressed as the among groups sum of squares (SSA), that is computed for each group the squared deviation of the group mean from the grand mean and multiply the result by the size of the group, then added these results overall group, and the degree of freedom of the variance among groups is $k-1$, k is the number of groups. The variance within groups is expressed as the within groups sum of squares (SSW), that is computed within each group the sum of squared deviations of the individual observations from their mean, then added them together, and the degree of freedom of the variance within groups is $N-k$. Three equations must be met in one-way ANOVA, as following,

$$SST = SSA + SSW \qquad (7\text{-}11)$$

$$df(Total) = df(Among\ groups) + df(Within\ groups) \qquad (7\text{-}12)$$

$$The\ meas\ squares = \frac{the\ sum\ of\ squares}{the\ degree\ of\ freedom}$$

$$(7\text{-}13)$$

And the among groups mean square is to reflect the mean effective of treatment groups and random error (that is random measurement error and random sampling error), while the within groups mean square is only to reflect the mean effective of random error. Assume $H_0: \mu_1=\mu_2=\mu_3=\mu_4$ is true, that is mean effective of treatment groups is negligibly small, the ratio of F value is near 1. If F value is larger enough than 1, H_0 will be rejected.

The calculations that we perform may be summarized and displayed in table such as Table 7-3, which is called the ANOVA table.

The Hypothesis Test Steps for the ANOVA Analysis of Randomized Design

Now, let's give another example to show the hypothesis test steps for the ANOVA of randomized design, as following:

EXAMPLE 7-2

To evaluate drug safety and tolerability in phase I clinical trial, 30 healthy volunteers were randomized into three groups that they were injected drug with 0.5U, 1U, 2U, these was 10 members in each group, then partial thromboplastin time in 48 hours of each healthy volunteer was measured by lab examination for clinical trial evaluation. We wish to know if the different doses of drugs have different effects on the mean level of thromboplastin time (Table 7-4).

According to the raw data, the thromboplastin times of 30 healthy volunteers are different values due to individual variation and different dose drug intervention. They have different sample means for three groups. We assume that three populations of measurements are normally distributed with equal variances. List the steps of hypothesis test for one-way ANOVA:

(1) Set up the hypotheses test, and decide the significance level.

H_0: $\mu_1=\mu_2=\mu_3$

H_1: Not all μ's are equal.

$\alpha=0.05$

(2) Calculate the statistic, list the statistic in the ANOVA table (Table 7-5) computed by SPSS software

(3) Determine the P Value, and make a statistical decision.

The F value is more far away 1, the P value will be small, and P=0.005 is shown precisely by SPSS software. Since the P value is very small, we reject H_0, and accept H_1. it is statistical significant difference among three population means of the thromboplastin times. Multiple comparisons will be made to know which is different between each two groups we want to compare.

A word of Caution

The conditions of one-way ANOVA for completely randomized design are as following: there are several independent sample group for mean comparisons, there are all normal distribution populations where samples come from, and their population variance are homogeneous, which is the most important assumption of three. If the data available for analysis do not meet the assumptions for one-way analysis of variance as discussed here, one may wish to consider the use of the Kruskal-Wallis procedure, a nonparametric method discussed at the back of chapter.

TABLE 7-3   Analysis of Variance Table for the completely Randomized Design

Source of variance	Sum of squares	Degree of freedom	Mean squares	The ratio of F value
Among groups	$SSA=SS\,(between)=n\sum(\bar{X}_{.k}-\bar{X}..)^2$	$k-1$	$MSA=SSA/(k-1)$	$F=\dfrac{MSA}{MSW}$
Within groups	$SSW=SS(within)=\sum_i\sum_k(X_{ik}-\bar{X}_k)^2$	$N-k$	$MSW=SSW/(n-k)$	
Total	$SST=SS(total)=\sum_i\sum_k(X_{ik}-\bar{X}..)^2$	$N-1$		

TABLE 7-4   The thromboplastin times in three volunteer groups of different drug doses

Dose	The thromboplastin time (s)										n	$\bar{x}\pm s$
0.5U	36.8	34.4	34.3	35.7	33.2	31.1	34.3	29.8	35.4	31.2	10	33.62±2.26
1U	40.0	35.5	36.7	39.3	40.1	36.8	33.4	38.3	38.4	39.8	10	37.83±2.21
2U	32.9	37.9	30.5	31.1	34.7	37.6	40.2	38.1	32.4	35.6	10	35.10±3.31
Total											30	35.52±3.11

TABLE 7-5   The ANOVA table for Example 7-2

Source of variation	Sum of squares	df	Mean square	F value	P value
Between	91.225	2	45.612	6.524	0.005
Within	188.757	27	6.991		
Total	279.982	29			

RANDOMIZED BLOCKED DESIGN

What is The Randomized Blocked Design?

The randomized blocked design is extend at the base of matched pair design *t*-test. When we want to find out difference among several drug cure for hypertension patients, but hypertension patients are not homogeneous because of different age and the state of serious illness, which is not compare drug cure outcome directly. First, the subjects of hypertension patients will be subdivided into homogeneous groups called blocks, in each block the subjects have the same or similar conditions on age and state of illness, and the number of experimental units in a block is equal to the number of drug treatments being studies. The treatments are then assigned at random to the experimental units within each block. It should be emphasized that each treatment appears in every block, and each block receives every treatment.

EXAMPLE 7-3

18 patients of primary hypertension are matched into 6 blocks in each block three patients have similar at the state of illness and age within 3 year old, then 3 patients of each block are randomly assigned to A, B, C treatment groups. The platelet levels of patients are measure on increasing after one month treatment. The data about platelet level increment are shown in Table 7-6. We want to know if the treatment effect on platelet level.

TABLE 7-6   The patients' platelet level increment after three treatment groups($\times 10^{12}$/L)

Block	Drug A	Drug B	Drug C	Block mean
1	3.8	6.3	8.0	6.03
2	4.6	6.3	11.9	7.60
3	7.6	10.2	14.1	10.63
4	8.6	9.2	14.7	10.83
5	6.4	8.1	13.0	9.17
6	6.2	6.9	13.4	8.83
Group mean	6.20	7.83	10.52	
Grand mean				8.88

The randomized blocked design is two-way factors design, one factor is treatment factor which the study is interested in, and another factor is blocking or confounding factor which the study want to control. This two factor design has not interaction between the treatment and blocking due to no repeated observations for each crossover level of two factors.

The randomized blocked design is to isolate and remove from the error term the variation attributable to the blocks. When blocking is used effectively, the error mean squares in the ANOVA table will be reduced, the ratio of *F* value will be increased, and the change of rejected the null hypothesis will be improved.

The total variance of the randomized blocked design is divided into three part sum of squares: the variance among groups, the variance among blocks and the variance of random error (within groups). *xij* is expressed as each individual value, *i* is the number of blocks from 1 to *b*, and *j* is the number of treatment from 1 to *k*. Sample size is *b×k*. The ANOVA table for randomized blocked design is shown as Table 7-7. The sum of squares among groups is to explain treatment group effective and random error, the sum of squares among blocks is to explain blocking group effective and random error, and the sum of squares within groups is to only explain random error. The complex computation will be finished by SPSS software.

The Hypothesis Test Steps for the ANOVA Analysis of Randomized Blocked Design

Now, let's give the Example 7-3 to show the hypothesis test steps for the ANOVA of randomized blocked design, as following:

(1) Set up the hypotheses test, and decide the significance level.

For treatment effective:

H_0: $\mu_1 = \mu_2 = \mu_3$

H_1: Not all μ's are equal.

For blocking effective:

H_0: $\mu_1 = \mu_2 = \ldots = \mu_6$

H_1: Not all μ's are equal.

$\alpha = 0.05$

(2) Calculate the statistic, list the statistic in the ANOVA table (Table 7-8) computed by SPSS software

TABLE 7-7 The ANOVA table for randomized blocked design

Source of variance	Sum of squares	Degree of freedom	Mean squares	The ratio of F value
Among groups	$SSG = b\sum(\overline{X}_k - \overline{X}..)^2$	$k-1$	$MSG = SSG/(k-1)$	$F = \dfrac{MSG}{MSE}$
Among blocks	$SSB = k\sum(\overline{X}_b - \overline{X}..)^2$	$b-1$	$MSB = SSB/(b-1)$	$F = \dfrac{MSB}{MSE}$
Error (Within groups)	$SSE = SST - SSG - SSB$	$(b-1)(k-1)$		
Total	$SST = \sum_i\sum_j(\overline{X}_{ij} - \overline{X}..)^2$	$N-1$		

TABLE 7-8 The ANOVA table for Example 7-3

Source of variation	Sum of squares	df	Mean square	F value	P value
Among groups	129.003	2	64.502	79.338	<0.001
Among blocks	50.132	5	10.026	12.333	0.001
Error	8.130	10	0.813		
Total	187.265	17			

(3) Determine the P Value, and make a statistical decision.

Whether for treatment or blocking, the P values of two are smaller than 0.05, the two H_0 are all rejected. It is statistical significant difference among three population means of platelet level increment, and the population means in different blocks are statistical significant too. Note that we can further use Post Hoc test to identify which treatment group is more effective than others.

MULTIPLE COMPARISONS

When the analysis of variance leads to a rejection of the null hypothesis, the question naturally need to answer which pairs of means are different. In general, methods used to find out the group differences after the null hypothesis has been rejected are called post hoc test. There are a lot of multiple comparison tests to investigate differences between levels of the independent variable, such as Fisher's *LSD* (Least Significant Difference), Tukey's *HSD* (Honestly Significant Difference), the Scheffé Method, the Neuman-Keuls Test, Dunnett's *t*, and others. In this chapter, we introduce several commonly used procedure.

Bonferroni Correction

Why not just do a bunch of *t*-tests? Two reasons: (1) it puts us back into the swamp we began in, of losing control of the α level; and (2) we can use the Mean Square (Error) term as a better estimate of the within-group variance. This does point to one of the simplest strategies devised to deal with multiple comparisons (of any type). Recognizing that the probability of making a Type I error on any one comparison is 0.05, one easy way to keep things in line is to set an alpha level that is more stringent. This is called a **Bonferroni correction**. All you do is count up the total number of comparisons you are going to make (say k comparisons), then divide 0.05 by k. If you have four comparisons, then the alpha level becomes $0.05 \div 4 = 0.0125$.

You shouldn't use Bonferroni if there are more than five groups. The reason is that it should more appropriately be called the Bonferroni overcorrection because it does over compensate. In an attempt to overcome the extremely conservative nature of the Bonferroni correction, a number of alternatives have been proposed. The most liberal ones, proposed by Holm (1979) and Hochberg (1988), use critical values that change with each test, rather than the fixed value of α/T (where T is the number of tests), which Bonferroni uses. Both of the tests start off by arranging the p levels in order, from the smallest (p_1) to the largest (p_T). In the Holm procedure, we start off with the smallest (most significant) p level, and compare it with α/T. If our p level is smaller than this, then it is significant, and we move on to the next p value in our list, which is compared with α/($T-1$). We continue doing this until we find a p value larger than the critical number; it and all larger *p*s are nonsignificant.

Let's run through an example to see how these procedures work. Assume we have the results of five tests, and their *p* values, in order, are:

$$p_1 = 0.008 \quad p_2 = 0.011 \quad p_3 = 0.030$$
$$p_4 = 0.040 \quad p_5 = 0.045$$

In the Holm method, we would compare p_1 against $\alpha/5 = 0.010$. Because it is smaller, p_1 is significant, and we move on to p_2, which is compared against $\alpha/4 = 0.0125$. It too is significant, so we test p_3 against $\alpha/3 = 0.0167$. It's larger, meaning that p_3 through p_5 are not significant.

The Studentized Range

Common to all the remaining methods is the use of the overall Mean Square (Within) as an estimate of the error term in the statistical test, so we'll elaborate a bit on this idea. You remember in the previous chapter that we spent quite a bit of time devising ways to use the estimate of σ derived from each of the two groups to give us a best guess of the overall SE of the difference. In ANOVA, most of this work is already done for us, in that the Mean Square (Within) is calculated from the differences between individual values and the group mean across all the groups. Furthermore, as we showed already, the Mean Square (Within) is the best estimate of σ^2. So the calculation of the denominator starts with Mean Square (Within). We first take the square root to give an estimate of the SD. Finally, we must then divide by some *n*s to get to the SE of the difference. In the end, the denominator of the test looks like:

$$Denominator = \sqrt{MS_{within} \times \left(\frac{1}{n_1} + \frac{1}{n_2} \right)} \quad (7\text{-}14)$$

If the sample sizes are the same in both groups, this reduces further to:

$$Denominator = \sqrt{\frac{2 \times MS_{within}}{n}} \quad (7\text{-}15)$$

For reasons which may, with luck, become evident, we're going to call this quantity **q′**. It really represents a critical range of differences between means resulting from the error in the observations. We could, for example, create a *t*-test using this new denominator:

$$t = \frac{\overline{X}_1 - \overline{X}_2}{q'} \quad (7\text{-}16)$$

So, in Example 7-1, if we want to compare the difference between oral mucosa hyperplasia and healthy control, we would first compute the denominator:

$$q' = \sqrt{\frac{2 \times 9.243}{10}} = 1.360 \quad (7\text{-}17)$$

Then, we could proceed with a *t*-test:

$$t = \frac{|15.27 - 10.68|}{1.360} = 3.375 \quad (7\text{-}18)$$

This is just an ordinary *t*-test, except that we computed the denominator differently, using the Mean Square (Within) instead of a sum of variances, which we called **q′**. This does introduce one small wrinkle. Since we are using all the data (in this case, 40 observations) to compute the error, we modify the degrees of freedom to take this into account; so, we compare this with a critical value for the *t*-test on 36 *df*, which turns out to be 2.03.

In fact, almost all the post-hoc procedures we will discuss are, at their core, variants on a *t*-test. However, since by definition they involve multiple comparisons (between Group A and Group B, Group A and Group C, etc.), they go about it another way altogether, turning the whole equation on its head, and computing the difference required to obtain a significant result. That is, they begin with a range computed from the Mean Square (Within), multiply it by the appropriate critical value of the particular test, and then conclude that any difference between group means which is larger than this range is statistically significant. Sticking with our example of a *t*-test for the moment, we would compute the range by multiplying 1.360 by the critical value of the *t*-test (in this case, 2.03). Then, any difference we encounter that is larger than this, we'll call statistically significant by the *t*-test.

Regrettably, before we launch into the litany of post-hoc tests, one more historical diversion is necessary. It seems that, when folks were devising these post-hoc tests, someone decided early on that the factor of 2 in the square root was just unnecessary baggage, so they created a new range, called the **Stu-**

dentized range. This has the formula:

$$q = \sqrt{\frac{MS_{within}}{n}}, \text{ that is, } q = \sqrt{\frac{9.243}{10}} = 0.961$$

(7-19)

And that's where **q** and **q′** come about. Why they bothered to create a new range, one will never know. After all, it doesn't take a rocket scientist to determine that q′ is just $\sqrt{2} = 1.4141$ times q. Since most of the range tests use q, we have included critical values of q in Table M in the Appendix.

Fisher's Least Significant Difference (*LSD*)

Fisher's *LSD*, which is a multiple comparison test, is on the opposite wing in terms of conservatism, and it is actually nothing more than a computational device to save work; goodness knows how this got into the history books. You begin with the critical value of t, given the *df*. In this case, we have 36 *df*, so a significant t (at 0.05) is 2.03. We worked out before that the denominator of the calculated t-test is 1.360, so any difference between means greater than 1.360×2.03 = 2.761 would be significant. So 2.761 becomes the *LSD*, and it is not necessary to calculate a new t for every comparison. Just compare the difference to 2.761; if it's bigger, it's significant. The formula for the *LSD* is therefore:

$$LSD = t_{n-2}\sqrt{\frac{2 \times MS_{within}}{n}} = t_{n-2} \times q'$$

(7-20)

Where *df* is the degrees of freedom association with the MS_{within} term. The comparison between oral mucosa hyperplasia and healthy control is still statistically significant. For completeness, the *LSD* also found the comparison *between early-stage oral cancer and healthy control* to be significant, but the comparison between early-stage oral cancer and later-stage oral cancer not to be significant.

One would be forgiven if there were some inner doubt surfacing about the wisdom of such strategies. Fisher's *LSD* does nothing to deal with the problem of multiplicity because the critical value is set at 0.05 for each comparison; all it does is save a little calculation. But, since computers do the work in any case, that's not a consideration, and we should avoid using *LSD* for anything except recreational activities.

Tukey's Honestly Significant Difference

This time the test statistic is changed to something closer to the square root of an *F* statistic. It has its own table at the back of some stats books (but not this one). In the present example, with 4 and 36 *df*, the statistic q equals 3.79. Tukey then creates another critical difference, called the **Honestly Significant Difference**, or **HSD**:

$$HSD = q_{(k,M)}\sqrt{\frac{MS_{(within)}}{n}}$$

(7-21)

When *n* is, as before, the sample size in each group, *k* is the number of groups (4 in this case), and *M* is the *df* for the within term, equal to $k(n-1)$. This time around, then, the HSD equals:

$$HSD = 3.79\sqrt{\frac{9.243}{10}} = 3.64$$

(7-22)

The comparison *between early-stage oral cancer and healthy control* to be still significant, and the comparison between early-stage oral cancer and later-stage oral cancer still not to be significant.

Note that this test, like the one that follows, uses the q statistic. Second, these tests (including the *LSD*), don't start with a difference between means and then compute a test statistic, but, rather, start with a test statistic, and compute from it how big the difference between means has to be in order for it to be significant. This involves looking up the critical value of the q statistic in Table M, which turns out to involve not just the mean, SD, and sample size, but also the number of means, *k*.

This isn't at all unreasonable. After all, the more groups there are, the more possible differences between group means there are, and the greater the chance that some of them will be extreme enough to ring the 0.05 bell. So, the test statistic for the HSD and the next test, which we've called q up until now, takes all this into account.

Unlike the previous tests, which were either multiple comparisons (Bonferroni, Holm, Hochberg, and *LSD*) or range tests (the Studentized Range), the HSD is both. After identifying means that are significantly different, it gives a table showing subsets of homogeneous means, as in Table 7-9. The means are listed in numerical order (it doesn't matter if they're

TABLE 7-9 Tukey's HSD range test for the data in Table 7-1

Group	Subset 1	Subset 2	Subset 3
healthy control	10.68		
oral mucosa hyperplasia		15.27	
early-stage oral cancer			19.36
later-stage oral cancer			22.06

ascending or descending), and a line is placed under the means that don't differ from each other. You can use this technique with any range-type post-hoc test.

The Neuman-Keuls Test

For reasons known only to real statisticians,[1] the **Neuman-Keuls** test appears to have won the post-hoc popularity contest lately. It, too, is a minor variation on what is becoming a familiar theme. We begin by ordering all the group means from highest to lowest.

Now in order to apply the N-K test, we have to introduce a new concept, called the **step**. Basically, we need to know how many steps (means) we have to traverse to get from one mean of interest to the other mean of interest, and what the difference is between the means; we've worked this out in Table 7-10. So, to get from *healthy control* to *later-stage oral cancer*, we have four steps; to go from *early-stage oral cancer* to *later-stage oral cancer*, only one. For $\alpha = 0.05$, four means, and 36 degrees of freedom, the tabled value equals 3.81, so any difference between means greater

TABLE 7-10 Differences between means for different steps, with critical values of *q*

	Mean	Differences		
		1 step	2 steps	3 steps
Healthy control	10.68			
		4.59		
Oral mucosa hyperplasia	15.27		8.68	
		4.09		11.38
Early-stage oral cancer	19.36		6.79	
		2.70		
Later-stage oral cancer	22.06			
Critical *q*		2.763	3.328	3.661

than a critical value of:

$$Critical\ (\overline{X}_i - \overline{X}_j) = 3.81 \times q = 3.81 \times 0.961$$
$$= 3.661 \qquad (7\text{-}23)$$

Since the from healthy control to *later-stage oral cancer* comparison is bigger than 3.661, it is declared significant. Now, to discuss two two-step comparisons. From the table, the critical *q* is 3.464, so any difference larger than $3.464 \times 0.961 = 3.328$ is significant. So, *the from healthy control to oral mucosa hyperplasia comparison* is quite significant. Since neither comparison is significant, there is no point in continuing, as none of the one-step comparisons would be significant. Just to prove the point, for the one-step comparisons, the critical *q* is 2.875, so any comparison greater than $2.875 \times 0.961 = 2.763$ is significant; and none is.

Tukey's Wholly Significant Difference

Tukey's HSD is the way to go if you have a large number of groups (say, six or more) and you want to make all possible comparisons. The downside is that it tends to be somewhat conservative with respect to Type I and Type II errors. On the other hand, the N-K can be a bit too liberal. Tukey's **Wholly Significant Difference** (**WSD**, also known as Tukey's b) tries to be like Momma Bear, and be "just right." If you have *k* groups, use WSD if you want to do more than $k-1$ but fewer than $k \times (k-1)/2$ comparisons; otherwise, use the N-K.

Dunnett's *t*

Yet another *t*-test. We include it for two reasons only. The big one is that it is the right test for a particular circumstance that is common to many clinical studies in which you wish to compare several treatments with a control group. That is, the study is now designed to compare multiple treatments with a control group.

Dunnett's test is the essence of simplicity, doing essentially what all the others did. We compute a critical value for the difference using a test statistic called, as you might expect, Dunnett's *t*, and another standard error derived from Mean Square (Within), only this time with the $\sqrt{2}$ back in—that is, a q'

---

[1]*Thereby counting us out.*

range. So the critical value looks like:

$$Critical\ (\bar{X}_i - \bar{X}_c) = t_d \sqrt{\frac{2\,MS_{within}}{n}} \qquad (7\text{-}24)$$

Dunnett's main contribution was that he worked out what the distribution of the t statistic would be (for reasons of space, you won't find it in the back of this book). Not surprisingly, like the Studentized range, it is dependent on the number of groups and the sample size. For the present situation, with four groups and a total sample size of 40 (so that $df = 40 - 4 = 36$), the td is 2.54. So, with a Mean Square (Within) of 9.243 the critical value is:

$$Critical\ (\bar{X}_j - \bar{X}_c) = 2.54 \times \sqrt{\frac{2 \times 9.243}{10}} = 3.45$$

$$(7\text{-}25)$$

On this basis, hyperplasia and cancer patient comparing with health control, exceeds this critical value and is declared significantly different from health control.

THE STRENGTH OF RELATIONSHIP

The logic behind ANOVA is that we want to see if one variable (in this case, type of condom) is related to another one (here, satisfaction). The F-ratio tells us if the association is statistically significant, but it doesn't give us any information about the *strength* of the relationship. As it happens, we can pull this information out from the ANOVA summary table. We can express the strength of the relationship in terms of a variable called **eta-squared** and written η^2.

$$\eta^2 = \frac{SS_{factor}}{SS_{total}} \qquad (7\text{-}26)$$

which in the case of a one-way ANOVA is:

$$\eta^2 = \frac{SS_{between}}{SS_{total}} = 1 - \frac{SS_{within}}{SS_{total}} \qquad (7\text{-}27)$$

In our Example 7-1,

$$\eta^2 = \frac{740.093}{1072.858} = 0.69 \qquad (7\text{-}28)$$

so that almost 69% of the variance in DNA level can be explained by different groups; 31% of the variance results from other factors.

η^2 is an r-type effect size that will always yield a number between 0 and 1 and is interpreted as the *proportion* of the variance in the dependent variable that can be attributed to the independent variable. According to Stevens (2001), an η^2 of 0.01 would be considered small; 0.06 would be moderate; and 0.14 would be large.

SUMMARY

✧ Analysis of variance (ANOVA) is one of the most commonly used statistical methods in comparing means among several groups. It can answer whether there are significant difference among groups and which pair two groups are significant different.

✧ The conditions of ANOVA are that several samples come from normal distribution populations, observations are independent each other, and several population variance are homogenous. If the condition are violated, we either transform data so as to achieve normality or use non-parametric tests.

✧ In the analysis of variance for completely randomized design, the total variance is divided into the variance among groups and within groups; and in the analysis of variance for randomized blocked design, the total variance is divided into the variance among groups and among blocks and random error.

✧ The post hoc tests are common methods of multiple comparisons for means. Such as *LSD*, Bonferroni Correction, *SNK* test, Dunnett's *t*, and so on, all of these can be finished by SPSS software.

GLOSSARY

sum of squares　平方和

mean squares　均方差

analysis of variance　方差分析

analysis of variance for completely randomized design　完全随机设计方差分析

analysis of variance for randomized blocked design 随机区组设计方差分析

EXERCISES

1. Select the answer to each of the following statements from the list below. Note that each statement may have more than one answer.
   a. Sum of squares (between)
   b. Sum of squares (within)
   c. Mean square (between)
   d. Mean square (within)
   e. Degrees of freedom (between)
   f. Degrees of freedom (within)
   g. *F*-ratio
   h. Probability of *F*
   A. Related to the size of the effect _____
   B. Related to the random variation within each group _____
   C. Increases with the number of groups _____
   D. Increases with the number of subjects in each group _____
   E. Decreases with the number of subjects per group _____
   F. Decreases as the signal-to-noise ratio gets bigger _____

2. One dilemma facing all lovers of fiery food is that different culinary establishments have different standards. "Suicide" wings in one joint don't rate more than a "Medium" in another—or so it seems.
   It's a slow day in the lab, so let's put this one to the test. We locate 3 different road-houses and 12 fearless undergraduates. We randomize diners to diners (so to speak) and they sally forth, late at night, armed to the teeth with clipboards, Tums, and Pepto-Bismol. They screw up their collective courages, order the platter of "Suicide," and then, if they remain conscious, rate fire on the ubiquitous 10-point scale.
   The data look like this:

Rater	Roadhouse		
	A	B	C
1	4	7	7
2	4	8	9
3	7	6	10
4	5	7	10
Mean	5.0	7.0	9.0
SD	1.41	0.82	1.41

Now is your chance to flex your computational muscles.
   a. Construct an ANOVA table and see if there is really a difference in suicide ratings among roadhouses.
   b. Where does the difference lie? Do post-hoc comparisons using Scheffé and Fisher's *LSD* methods.

3. To research a drug with tumor suppressor role, a batch mice were developed cancer, then they were randomly divided into four groups according completely random design. A, B, C as three experimental groups that were separately injected 0.5, 1.0 and 1.5 ml of drug with 30% concentration, control group without drugs. After a period of time, the tumor weight of four groups mice were weighed. The data are as follows. Ask: have tumor suppressor any difference with difference drug doses?

Table   **research result with tumor suppressor in different drug doses**

control group	3.6	4.5	4.2	4.4	3.7
group A(0.5ml)	3.0	2.3	2.4	1.1	4.0
group B(1.0ml)	0.4	1.8	2.1	4.5	3.6
group C(1.5ml)	3.3	1.2	1.3	2.5	3.1
control group	5.6	7.0	4.1	5.0	4.5
group A(0.5ml)	3.7	2.8	1.9	2.6	1.3
group B(1.0ml)	1.3	3.2	2.1	2.6	2.3
group C(1.5ml)	3.2	0.6	1.4	1.3	2.1

4. To explore clinical commonly three ways treat sudden deafness effect, 30 new patients upon age from low to high were divided into 10 blocks by researchers, three patients of each group were randomly assigned to three treatment group that they were accepted treatment by drugs, acupuncture and hyperbaric oxygen. After a period of time, hear-ascend situation (unit: db) were measured. Ask: have therapeutic effect any difference between three methods?

Table   three groups hear-ascend after treatment

block	drug	acupuncture	hyperbaric oxygenation
1	11.87	15.51	18.25
2	13.52	24.42	18.81
3	13.06	7.71	9.79
4	15.78	15.43	23.66
5	3.10	4.86	12.25
6	6.04	18.99	19.07
7	12.08	17.21	17.02
8	7.84	17.80	9.66
9	6.47	15.18	11.73
10	8.32	6.64	10.22

5. Juvenile rat will be injected estrogen with three different doses, observing effects of uterus weight after a period of time. The experiment design is as follows: screening 4 nest rats with different species, 3 per litter, they were randomly assigned to intervention group with three different estrogen doses. The results are as follows. Ask: have rats uterus weigh any difference between estrogen doses?

Table   Juvenile rat uterus weigh after injecting different estrogen doses

nest	uterine weights		
	0.2μg/100g	0.4μg/100g	0.8μg/100g
1	106	116	145
2	42	68	115
3	70	111	133
4	42	63	87

How to Get the Computer to Do the Work for You
One-way ANOVA

- From **Analyze**, choose **Compare Means One-Way ANOVA**

- Click on the variable(s) to be analyzed from the list on the left, and click the arrow to move it (them) into the box marked **Dependent List** [Note: One ANOVA will be performed for each variable listed.]
- Click on the grouping variable from the list on the left, and click the arrow to move it into the box marked **Factor**
- Click the Post Hoc button and select those tests you want [we recommend *LSD*, **Tukey**, and **Tukey's-b**], then click Continue
- Click the Options button and click on **Descriptives** and **Homogeneity-of-Variance**
- To run planned comparisons, click on Contrasts; fill in the first coefficient and click Add. Continue until there are contrasts for all of the groups, and be sure the Coefficient Total on the bottom is 0.000 when you're done. If you want another set of contrasts, click Next; otherwise, click Continue.
- If you want to test for linear or quadratic trend, click on Contrasts, check the box labeled Polynomial, and use the down arrow to select the degree (linear, quadratic, cubic). Then click Continue.

Two-way ANOVA for randomized blocked design

- From **Analyze**, choose **General Linear Model**
- Click on the variable(s) to be analyzed from the list on the left, and click the arrow to move it (them) into the box marked **Dependent List**.
- Click on the grouping variable from the list on the left, and click the arrow to move it into the box marked **Factor**.
- Click the Model button and select those two factors Main effect to the right window.
- Click the Post Hoc button and select those tests you want [we recommend *LSD*, **Tukey**, and **Tukey's-b**], then click. Continue

CHAPTER THE EIGHTH

Tests of Significance for Categorical Frequency Data

Here we introduce statistical methods used to deal with categorical frequency data of the form. We begin with Chi-squared distribution, test of goodness of fit, the chi-squared (χ^2) test, and then consider some special cases: small numbers (the Fisher Exact Test), paired data (McNemar's chi-squared), two factors (Mantel-Haenszel chi-squared), and finally the general case involving many factors (log-linear analysis). And several measures of association used for contingency tables are introduced. The phi coefficient and Cramer's V are directly related to the chi-squared test of significance. Kappa and weighted kappa are popular measures of "agreement beyond chance," the former for nominal scales where no gradation of disagreement is found, and the latter for when degrees of disagreement do exist. The equivalence between kappa and the intraclass correlation (ICC) coefficient is discussed.

CHI-SQUARED DISTRIBUTION, TEST OF GOODNESS OF FIT

Chi-squared distribution

Suppose that Z is a standard normal random variable with mean = 0 and variance=1, $Z \sim N(0,1)$. Its probability density is high in the middle and low on the left and right sides on the interval of $(-\infty, +\infty)$, and symmetrical about 0. However, Z^2 is different, its possible value range is $(0, +\infty)$, the possibility of a smaller value is larger, the possibility of a larger value is smaller. The corresponding probability density curve is shown in Figure 8-1 ($v=1$).

If $Z_1, ..., Z_k$ are independent standard normal random variables, then the distribution of $Z_1^2 + Z_2^2 + \cdots + Z_k^2$ is Chi-squared distribution with k degrees of freedom. This is usually denoted as $\chi^2_{(k)}$. Besides, $\chi^2_{(1)}$, Figure 8-1 shows us the Chi-square distribution curve with $df=3,5$. The graph of a Chi-square distribution is asymmetrical with only values greater than 0. The larger the degrees of freedom is, the better

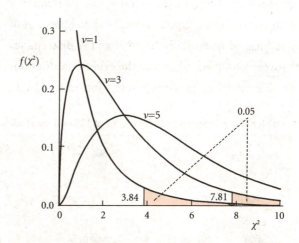

FIGURE 8-1 Probability density curve of Chi-squared distribution (df=1,3,5).

the symmetric is. When the degrees of freedom is large enough, the distribution curve approaches a normal distribution. The population mean of the Chi-square distribution is equal to its degree of freedom. The Chi-squared distribution for df with α and its corresponding Chi-squared value of $\chi^2_{\alpha,v}$ can be found in Chi-squared critical value tables (appendix).

Suppose that $\chi^2_{(v_1)}$ and $\chi^2_{(v_2)}$ are Chi-squared distribution random variables, with $v_1 > v_2$, it can be proved that $\chi^2_{(v_1)} + \chi^2_{(v_2)}$ are also Chi-squared distribution random variable with $df\ v_1 + v_2$. $\chi^2_{(v_1)} - \chi^2_{(v_2)}$ are also Chi-squared distribution random variable with $df\ v_1 - v_2$.

The Chi-squared distribution is used in the common Chi-squared tests for goodness of fit of an observed distribution to a theoretical one, the independence of two criteria of classification of qualitative data, and in confidence interval estimation for a population standard deviation of a normal distribution from a sample standard deviation. Many other statistical tests also use this distribution, like Friedman's analysis of variance by ranks.

Test of goodness of fit

The goodness of fit of a statistical model describes how well it fits a set of observations. In practical work we often need to know whether a sample observed frequency is consistent with a theoretical frequency, i.e. to determine whether the sample is drawn from a theoretical distribution. A Chi-squared goodness of fit test is used to test whether a frequency distribution fits an expected distribution. Measures of goodness of fit typically summarize the discrepancy between observed values and the expected values under the model in question. χ^2 test is introduced by an example test of goodness of fit test as follows.

A representative sample of 120 college students whose body weights are distributed as follows.

50.2	56.7	57.8	58.8	54.4	57.4	48.4	55.2
41.6	60.8	52.9	51.0	47.4	49.3	55.3	50.3
45.9	49.3	52.7	57.3	39.0	52.7	45.7	53.8
48.6	44.3	60.6	55.3	50.8	54.2	57.1	52.1
55.2	50.6	48.2	55.8	48.6	48.9	56.4	53.4
45.8	49.0	46.2	45.0	49.1	52.9	47.5	50.0
41.6	49.4	54.9	51.7	59.4	49.5	53.8	39.2
52.4	46.1	48.6	50.6	51.9	54.3	51.3	50.0
54.1	51.8	45.3	52.2	53.8	55.2	54.7	43.7
51.4	53.5	51.8	58.6	51.0	51.9	56.4	50.6
57.1	46.3	45.5	49.8	49.8	56.1	55.1	39.5
54.5	49.1	48.5	57.5	53.9	41.7	50.4	47.0
45.2	49.2	51.1	43.3	49.0	47.1	55.1	51.1
52.0	49.8	38.9	46.4	43.0	38.5	43.0	45.8
46.0	52.8	50.5	53.7	43.9	50.7	43.8	40.2

Whether the data of the college students' weight is drawn from normal distribution?

Firstly, let's use the sample mean and the sample standard deviation as the estimates of the population mean and standard deviation of the population distribution respectively(Table 8-1). For this sample,

$$\overline{X} = 50.35, S = 5.00$$

The hypothesis of testing is:

H_0:the data follow a normal distribution with mean μ=50.35 and standard deviation σ=5.00.

TABLE 8-1   A frequency distribution of 120 college students' body weights and statistic calculation for goodness of fit

body weight (1)	Observed frequency O_i (2)	$\Phi\left(\dfrac{l_i - \mu}{\sigma}\right)$ (3)	$\Phi\left(\dfrac{u_i - \mu}{\sigma}\right)$ (4)	P_i (5)=(4)-(3)	Expected frequency E_i (6)	$\dfrac{(O_i - E_i)^2}{E_i}$ (7)
38.0~	5	0.0068	0.0192	0.0124	1.488	8.28908
40.0~	4	0.0192	0.0475	0.0283	3.396	0.10743
42.0~	6	0.0475	0.1020	0.0545	6.54	0.04459
44.0~	9	0.1020	0.1922	0.0902	10.824	0.30737
46.0~	9	0.1922	0.3192	0.1270	15.24	2.55496
48.0~	19	0.3192	0.4721	0.1529	18.348	0.02317
50.0~	22	0.4721	0.6293	0.1572	18.864	0.52134
52.0~	16	0.6293	0.7673	0.1380	16.56	0.01894
54.0~	15	0.7673	0.8708	0.1035	12.42	0.53594
56.0~	10	0.8708	0.9370	0.0662	7.944	0.53212
58.0~	3	0.9370	0.9732	0.0362	4.344	0.41582
60.0~	2	0.9732	0.9901	0.0169	2.028	0.00039
total	120					13.35113

H_1: the data don't follow a normal distribution with mean $\mu=50.35$ and standard deviation $\sigma=5.00$.

(1) Suppose $X=(X_1, X_2, \ldots X_n)$ is sample which is drawn from normal distribution, such as 120 values listed in this example, here $n=120$.

(2) Determine the range of the data, divide the range by k classes$(l_i, u_i), 2, \ldots, k$, see in the column 1 in Table 8-1, here $k=11$.

(3) Find the total frequency O_i for each class, list in the column 2 in Table 8-1.

(4) P_i is the probability of values in k_i class if H_0 is true, then

$$P_i = P(l_i \leqslant X < u_i) \quad i=1,2,\ldots,k$$

By standardized normal convert for l_i and u_i, we can get the corresponding probability

$$P_1 = P(38.0 \leqslant X < 40.0)$$
$$= \Phi\left(\frac{40.0-50.35}{5.00}\right) - \Phi\left(\frac{38.0-50.35}{5.00}\right)$$
$$= 0.0192 - 0.0068 = 0.0124$$

$$P_2 = P(40.0 \leqslant X < 42.0)$$
$$= \Phi\left(\frac{42.0-50.35}{5.00}\right) - \Phi\left(\frac{40.0-50.35}{5.00}\right)$$
$$= 0.0475 - 0.0192 = 0.0283$$

and so on. We can calculate $P_3, P_4, P_5, P_6, P_7, P_8, P_9, P_{10}, P_{11}$, see n in column 5 of Table 8-1.

(5) T_i is the expected frequency in k_i class if H_0 is true, then $E_i=nP_i (i=1,2,\ldots,k)$, see n in column 6.

If the sample observed frequency is consistent with the theoretical frequency, the difference between the O_i and E_i will become smaller when observed number n is bigger.

So the difference between O_i and E_i can reflect whether the sample frequency distribution is consistent with the theory of distribution which is determined by H_0. K.Pearson proposed to use the statistic χ^2 to measure their differences firstly,

$$\chi^2 \sum \frac{(O_i - E_i)^2}{E_i} \tag{8-1}$$

and proved that if H_0 is true and the observed number n is large enough, the statistic χ^2 approximately obey the χ^2 distribution with k−1 df. If there is s sample statistic to replace population parameter when calculating E_i, then the df is $v=k-1-s$.

The value of χ^2 statistic reflect the difference between the sample actual frequency distribution and the theory of distribution, obviously χ^2 value is always positive. If H_0 is true, the observed frequency will be consistent with the expected frequency and the χ^2 value is unlikely to be large. On the contrary, if there is big difference between the observed frequency and the expected one, the χ^2 value will be larger and the P value will be smaller, and we will suspect the true of H_0 and we will reject H_0.

For example, in Table 8-1, the χ^2 value and df is as follow

$$\chi^2 = \sum_{i=1}^{12} \frac{(O_i - E_i)^2}{E_i} = 13.35$$
$$v = k - 1 - s = 12 - 1 - 2 = 9$$

And looking at the chi-square critical value table (Appendix χ^2 distribution), $\chi^2_{0.10,9} = 14.68$, $13.35 < \chi^2_{0.10,9}$, so $P > 0.10$. At the level of $\alpha=0.10$, the null hypothesis (H_0) cannot be rejected, we can think that the data follow a normal distribution with mean $\mu=50.35$ and standard deviation $\sigma=5.00$.

Notice is as follows when using χ^2 test of goodness of fit:

(1) Besides along with the degree of difference between the actual observed frequency and expected one, χ^2 value also will tend to be associated with their group number, fitting results may vary with different grouping. Therefore, when considering the χ^2 value, we must take into count the number of groups. The general requirement is that the expected frequency in each group should not less than 5 when grouping, or group combination with smaller frequencies will be needed.

(2) Enough sample size is necessary in χ^2 test of goodness of fit. If the sample size is not big enough, sometimes χ^2 test can be used after continuity correction. The continuity correction formula is

$$\chi^2 = \sum \frac{(|O_i - T_i| - 0.5)^2}{T_i} \tag{8-2}$$

THE CHI-SQUARED TEST

A few years ago, a report (Eidson et al., 1990) indicated that several people in New Mexico had succumbed to a rare but particularly nasty disease, eosinophilia-myalgia syndrome (EMS). The only circumstance they appeared to have in common was that they were health food freaks and had all been imbibing large quantities of an amino acid health food called tryptophan, which is supposed to be good for everything from insomnia to impotence. You, Hercules Parrot, have been assigned to the case by your masters at CDC Atlantis. Did tryptophan do it, and how will you prove it? In particular, how do you perform statistics on counts of bodies?

You may have heard that the best of all research designs is a **randomized controlled trial**, whereby subjects are assigned at random to a treatment or control group and no one knows until it's over who was in what group. What you heard is true, but it's also impossible to apply in this situation. If we really thought people might die from tryptophan exposure, it's unlikely (we hope) that any ethics committee would let us expose folks to the stuff just for the sake of science. The next best design is a **cohort** study. Here, you assemble cohorts of folks who, of their own volition (smoking), or from an accident of nature (radon) or their jobs (Agent Orange), have been exposed to a substance, match them up as best you can to another group of folks who are similar in every way you can think of but exposure, and then check the frequency of disease occurrence in both. That might work here, except that probably hundreds of thousands of health food freaks are gobbling up megavitamins and all sorts of other stuff, and (1) very few of them actually appear to have come down with eosinophilia-myalgia syndrome (EMS), and (2) it would be hard to trace all of them. So you end up at a third design, a **case-control** study, in which you take a bunch of folks with the disease (the cases) and without the disease (controls), and see how much of the exposure of interest each group has had. Although this approach has its problems, it is about the only practical approach to looking at risk when the prevalence is very low.

Off you go, to find cases and controls. You scour hospital records and death certificates around the country, and you eventually locate 80 people with EMS. You also locate some controls, who were hospitalized for something else or died of something else. Because there are lots of the latter, you stop at

200. You then administer a detailed questionnaire to their next of kin or by way of seance, ascertaining exposure to all sorts of noxious substances—vitamins, honey, ginseng root, lecithin, and (of course) tryptophan. After the dust settles, 42 of the EMS group and 34 of the control group took tryptophan regularly. Is this a statistically significant difference? That, of course, is what this chapter is all about.

(a) 2×2 CONTINGENCY TABLE

To begin to tease out a strategy for approaching the data, we'll put the data into a form alike: a **2 × 2 contingency table**. It's called "2 × 2" because it has two rows and two columns and "contingency" because the values in the cells are contingent on what is happening at the marginals (be patient; we'll get to that in a minute) (Table 8-2).

TABLE 8-2   Association between tryptophan exposure and eosinophilia myalgia syndrome (EMS)

		EMS	Normal	TOTAL
Tryptophan	Yes	42	34	76
	No	38	166	204
	TOTAL	80	200	280

Now, what we are trying to get at is whether any association exists between tryptophan use and EMS. As usual, the starting point is to assume the null hypothesis (no association) and then try to reject it. The question is, "What would the 2 × 2 table look like if there were no association?" We began with 80 patients and 200 controls. Were there no association, we would expect that exactly the same *proportion* of patients as controls would have gobbled tryptophan. Our best guess at the proportion of tryptophan users is based on the *marginal* totals, and it equals $76 \div 280 = 0.271$. So, the number of EMS patients who ate tryptophan, under the null hypothesis of no association, is $80 \times (76 \div 280) = 21.7$; and the number of controls is $200 \times (76 \div 280) = 54.3$. In a similar manner, the number of EMS folks who abstained is $80 \times (204 \div 280) = 58.3$, and the number of control abstainers is 145.7. If there were no association, then, Table 8-3 would result.

TABLE 8-3   Expected values of the table assuming no association

		EMS	Normal	TOTAL
Tryptophan	Yes	21.7	54.3	76
	No	58.3	145.7	204
	TOTAL	80	200	280

The extent to which the observed values differ from the expected values is a measure of the association, our *signal* again. But if you work it out, it equals zero, just as it did when we determined differences from the mean in the ANOVA case. So we do the standard statistical game and square everything. The signal now looks like:

$$\text{Signal} = (42 - 21.7)^2 + (34 - 54.3)^2 + (38 - 58.3)^2 + (166 - 145.7)^2$$

If we were to follow the now familiar routine, the next step would be to use the individual values within each cell to estimate the noise. The ratio of the squared difference between the observed and expected frequency to the expected mean is a signal-to-noise ratio. It's called **chi-squared**, for reasons now lost in antiquity. Formally, then:

$$x^2 = \sum \frac{[O_i - E_i]^2}{E_i} \qquad (8\text{-}3)$$

where O_i is the observed frequency and E_i is the expected frequency. And in this case, it equals:

$$x^2 = \frac{(42 - 21.7)^2}{21.7} + \frac{(34 - 54.3)^2}{54.3} +$$
$$\frac{(38 - 58.3)^2}{58.3} + \frac{(166 - 145.7)}{145.7}$$
$$= 36.4$$

That looks like a big enough number, but it's not clear where we should go looking to see whether it's big enough to be statistically significant. As it turns out, chi-squared has a table all to itself (Table F in the Appendix). Once again, it's complicated a bit by the *df*. For this table, *df* is 1. To demonstrate this, keep the marginal frequencies fixed and put the number in one cell. Now, for the cells to add up to the correct marginal totals, all other cells are predetermined: the marginal total minus the filled-in value. So you have only one cell free to vary; hence, one *df*. In the gen-

eral case of a ($r \times c$) contingency table (*r* rows and *c* columns), there are ($r - 1$) $\times$ ($c - 1$) *df*. This particular value is highly significant (the value of chi-squared needed for significance at $p = 0.05$ for one *df* is 3.84), proving conclusively that health food is bad for your health.

A nice rule of thumb is that the value of χ^2 needed for significance at the 0.05 level is about equal to the number of cells. In this case, we would have said 4, which differs a bit from the true value of 3.84. For a 5 $\times$ 2 table, our guess would be 10; the actual value is 9.49.

(b) R×C CONTIGENCY TABLE

But that's not the end of the story. Careful tracking of EMS cases showed that many were turning up all over the United States but virtually none in Canada or Europe. Although Americans were more likely to junk out on health foods and other "alternative" therapies than were the staid Brits, it was well known that Canadians were also popping the stuff with gay abandon. So perhaps the illness was caused by a contaminant that snuck into one batch from one manufacturer, not by the stuff itself. This cause was pinpointed in a study by Slutsker et al. (1990). They located 46 cases with EMS who also took tryptophan; 45 of the 46 ate stuff from one manufacturer in Japan (sold through 12 wholesalers and rebottled under 12 different brand names). There were 41 controls who took tryptophan but didn't get EMS; 12 of them ate tryptophan from the Japanese manufacturer, the other controls from other manufacturers. This difference (45/46 to 12/41) is so significant that only a sadist or a software manufacturer would demand a statistical test.

Another study, this time in Minnesota (Belongia et al., 1990), managed to track the nasties down to a single contaminant. To do this, they first located 52 cases with a high eosinophil count and myalgia. They then formed two control groups: (1) a volunteer group of folks who had been taking tryptophan but weren't sick, located by public announcements ($n = 33$), and (2) a control group of people who had also taken tryptophan and were located by a random telephone survey ($n = 24$). They then interviewed everybody to see what brand of tryptophan they were using. Only 30 cases, 26 volunteers, and 9 random controls could locate the bottle. They rapidly focused the problem down to a single manufacturer. The data are presented in Table 8-4.

TABLE 8-4   Source of tryptophan by group

Group	Manufacturer			TOTALS
	Showa Denko K.K.	Other	Unknown	
Cases	29	1	22	52
Random controls	5	4	15	24
Volunteers	16	10	7	33
TOTALS	50	15	44	109

And once again, the time has come to crunch numbers. The approach is just the same as with the 2×2 table. This time, the analysis is analogous to a one-way ANOVA for parametric statistics. First, you estimate the expected value in each cell by multiplying the row and column marginal totals and dividing by the grand total. So for row 1 and column 1, this equals $(50 \times 52) \div 109 = 23.8$. Working through the expected values results in Table 8-5.

TABLE 8-5   Expected values for Table 8-4

Group	Manufacturer			TOTALS
	Showa Denko K.K.	Other	Unknown	
Cases	23.8	7.2	21.0	52
Random controls	11.0	3.3	9.7	24
Volunteers	15.1	4.5	13.3	33
TOTALS	50	15	44	109

From this, we can calculate a chi-squared as we did before, simply by taking the difference between observed and expected values, squaring it, dividing by the expected value, and adding up all nine terms. The answer is 22.40, and the *df* are $(3 - 1) \times (3 - 1) = 4$; moreover, the result is highly significant, at $P < 0.0001$. To close the corporate noose around Showa Denko, the investigators then showed that (1) the manufacturer cut back on the amount of activated charcoal at one filtration stage, (2) bypassed some other filter, and (3) 17 of the 29 cases had consumed tryptophan out of one particular batch. The con-

taminant also showed up on liquid chromatography. In short, the goose was neatly fried.

Another way of looking at the chi-squared test of association is that it is a test of the null hypothesis that the *proportion* of EMS cases among tryptophan users (usually abbreviated as π_t) was the same as the proportion among nonusers (π_n); that is, it is a test of two or more proportions. There is, in fact, a *z*-test of the significance of two independent proportions. We haven't bothered to include it for the simple reason that z^2 is exactly the same as chi-squared. However, it's easier to figure out sample size requirements based on proportions, so we'll come back to this concept when we tell you how to figure them out.

That's the story for chi-squared—almost. Things work out well as long as (1) you only have four cells, and (2) the frequencies are reasonably good. When you have more cells, as in the example of myalgia, or when the numbers are small, then some fancier stuff is required.

DECONSTRUCTING CHI-SQUARED

In the previous example, we showed that the overall chi-squared was significant, but we skipped over a problem—what was significantly different from what? This is similar to the situation after finding a significant *F*-ratio in a one-way ANOVA: we still don't know which groups differ from the others. In the case of ANOVA, we would use one of the post-hoc tests, such as Tukey's or Scheffé's, but we don't have that option with χ^2. What we have to do is **decompose** the χ^2 table into a number of smaller subtables, and see which ones are significant.

At first glance, it would seem as if we could have nine 2×2 subtables: Showa Denko versus Other for Cases versus Controls, Cases versus Volunteers, and Controls versus Volunteers; Showa Denko versus Unknown for the same three group comparisons; and the three group comparisons for Other versus Unknown. But the rules of the game say otherwise; the number of subtables we are allowed and how they are constructed must follow certain conventions. These were summarized by Iversen (1979)—kind of like the Hoyle of χ^2 decomposition. The rules are as follows:

1. The degrees of freedom, summed over all of the subtables, must equal the degrees of freedom of the original table.

2. Each frequency (i.e., cell count) in the original table must be a frequency in one and only one subtable.

3. Each marginal total, including the grand total, must be a marginal total in one and only one subtable.

Are you sufficiently confused yet? Let's work this out for the data in Table 8-4 and see what it looks like. This should either dispel the confusion or make you turn to hard liquor. According to the first rule, we can have subtables with a total of four degrees of freedom, since the original table had *df* = 4. This means we can have four 2 × 2 tables, or one 3 × 2 and two 2 × 2 tables. The easiest breakdown to interpret (although not necessarily the most informative) is a series of 2 × 2 tables. It's easiest to start with the upper left corner, so that's what we'll do. For reasons that will become obvious as we go along, we'll arrange the table so that the row and column we're most interested in (Showa Denko and Cases) are the last ones, rather than the first. The first subtable, then, is shown in Table 8-6A. Now, according to the second rule, none of those four cell counts can appear in any other table, and the marginal totals must appear in some other table. We can satisfy these rules (in part, so far), by combining columns 1 (Other) and 2 (Unknown) and comparing this to column 3 (Showa-Denko) for the Controls and Volunteers; this is shown in Table 8-6B. Notice also that some of the row marginals from the original table are now frequencies in Table 8-6B, in accordance with rule 3. In Table 8-6C, we do the same thing, only this time we're combining the first two rows (Controls and Volunteers) and comparing them with the Cases; in Table 8-6D, we combine both rows and columns. If you want to check, you will see that each of the 16 numbers in Table 8-4 (nine cell frequencies, three row totals, three column totals, and the grand total) appears once and only once in one of the subtables. Now, that wasn't hard, was it?

TABLE 8-6 Decomposing the data from Table 8-4 into a series of 2 × 2 subtables

A	Group	Other	Unknown	Total
	Controls	4	15	19
	Volunteers	10	7	17
	TOTALS	14	22	36

B	Group	Other + unknown	Showa Denko	Total
	Controls	19	5	24
	Volunteers	17	16	33
	TOTALS	36	21	57

C	Group	Other	Unknown	Total
	Controls + Volunteers	14	22	36
	Cases	1	22	23
	TOTALS	15	44	59

D	Group	Other + unknown	Showa Denko	Total
	Controls + Volunteers	36	21	57
	Cases	23	29	52
	TOTALS	59	50	109

This is one of a number of possible sets of 2 × 2 tables. It may make more sense, for example, to combine Unknown with Showa-Denko than with Other, or to combine Controls with Cases rather than Volunteers. Because you're limited in the number of tables you can make, it's important to think about which comparisons will provide you with the most useful information.

Strictly speaking, the subtables shouldn't be analyzed with the usual method for χ^2, because it doesn't account for the frequencies in the cells that aren't included. But, people do it anyway, and the results are relatively accurate, if the total N in the subtable is close to the N of the original table. If you want to be extremely precise, the equation you need is in Agresti (1990). But be forewarned—it's formidable! We'll take the easy route and just do χ^2 on the four of them. It turns out that all four subtables are significant. This tells us that the Other and Unknown preparations produce different results for the Cases and Volunteers. The most important analysis, from our perspective, however, is of Table 8-6D—Showa-Denko versus everything else and Cases versus everyone else. The numbers in this table really clinch the case.

EFFECT SIZE

After devoting an entire heading to effect size for chi-squared, we're actually not going to discuss it; at least not yet. Stay tuned until the later section, where we discuss measures of association for categorical data. There, you'll find out about the phi coefficient (φ) and Cramer's V, which are the indices of effect size for chi-squared.

SMALL NUMBERS, YATES' CORRECTION, AND FISHER'S EXACT TEST

(a) Yates' Correction for Continuity

When the *expected* value for any particular cell is less than 5, then the usual chi-squared statistic runs into trouble. Part of this is simply instability. Because the denominator is the expected frequency, addition or subtraction of one body can make a big difference when the expected values are small. But the chi-squared tends towards liberalism because it approximates categories with a continuous distribution. However popular this is politically, it is anathema to statisticians. One quick and dirty solution is called **Yates' Correction**. All you do is add or subtract 0.5 to each difference in the numerator to make it smaller before squaring and dividing by expected values. So the **Yates' corrected chi-squared** is:

$$\chi^2 = \sum \frac{[|O_i - E_i| - 0.5]^2}{E_i} \qquad (8\text{-}4)$$

The vertical lines around the *O* and *E* are "absolute value" signs, so you make the quantity positive, then take away half and proceed as before.

Having said all this, it turns out that Yates' correction is a bit too conservative. So half the world's statisticians recommend using it all the time, and half recommend never using it. In any case, the impact is small unless frequencies are very low, in which case an exact alternative is available.

(b) Fisher's Exact Test

Imagine that we have proceeded with the original investigation of whether tryptophan causes the disease and we're using a stronger design—a *cohort* study. You put more signs up in the health food stores, this time asking for people who are taking tryptophan, not people who are sick. You then locate a second group of folks who weren't exposed to the noxious agent tryptophan, perhaps by hitting up the local greasy spoon.

Now, fortunately for the populace (but unfortunately for you), tryptophan isn't all that nasty, so very few people actually come down with EMS. If we had 100 of each group, the data might look like Table 8-7. The expected value for both cells in the first column is 5, so we can't use chi-squared on this. The alternative is called **Fisher's exact test**, which is as follows. Instead of calculating a signal-to-noise ratio and then looking it up in the back of the book, we dredge up some of the basic laws of probability to calculate the exact probability of the data under the hypothesis of no association.

TABLE 8-7   **Association between tryptophan use and EMS**

		EMS	Normal	TOTALS
Tryptophan	Yes	8	92	100
	No	2	98	100
	TOTALS	10	190	280

Data from Slutsker L et al. (1990). Eosinophilia-myalgia syndrome associated with exposure to tryptophan from a single manufacturer. *Journal of the American Medical Association*, **264**:213–217.

To understand how this one works, we'll really stretch the analogy. Cast your mind back to the Civil War, when families were torn asunder, etc. You remember from your history books the famous Battle of Bull Roar, don't you? Let's just briefly remind you.

Bull Roar was a small town in West Virginia. One hot summer night, recruiters from both the Union and the Confederacy descended on the town, hit all the local pubs, stuffed the boys into uniforms, and handed them all muskets. The next day, they assembled in a field on the edge of town. Thirteen wore the blue of the North, and 11 wore the gray of the South. They opened fire, and when the smoke blew away, four Union men and three Confederates lay dead on the ground. At this point, the survivors all took off their uniforms, went into the pubs in their underwear, and got thoroughly sozzled.

The statistical question is, "Given only the information in the marginals—that is, there were 24 able-bodied males, of whom 13 were in blue uniforms and 11 in gray; and 7 ended up dead and 17 alive—what is the chance that things could have turned out the way they did?" We might, as we are wont to do in this chapter, put it all into a 2 × 2 table (Table 8-8).

TABLE 8-8   Statistics from the Battle of Bull Roar

		Alive	Dead	TOTALS
Army	Union	9 ... a	4 ... b	13 $(a + b)$
	Confed	c ... 8	d ... 3	11 $(c + d)$
	TOTALS	17 $(a + c)$	7 $(b + d)$	24

To make things easier, we'll begin by illustrating the field of battle graphically (Figure 8-2). Now let's look at the Union men first. What is the chance that 4 of the 13 should die? Think of it one shot at a time. The first fatal bullet might have taken out any 1 of 13 men, so there are 13 ways that the first bullet could have done its dirty work. Now one man is dead—what about the second bullet? There are 12 men to choose from, so 12 possibilities. Similarly, there are 11 possibilities for the third bullet, and 10 for the fourth. So in the end, there are 13 × 12 × 11 × 10 possible ways the bullets could have found their mark. However, once the lads are dead on the field, we no longer care in which order they were killed. Again, by the same logic, any one of the four could have been taken out by the first bullet, then three possibilities for the second bullet, and so on. So the overall number of ways that 4 of the 13 Union men

could have been killed is (13 × 12 × 11 × 10) ÷ (4 × 3 × 2 × 1). A convenient way of writing this algebraically is through the use of factorials. So, the number of ways to bump off 4 men out of 13 is:

$$nC_k = \frac{n!}{(n-k)!\,k!} = \frac{13!}{9!4!} = \frac{13 \times 12 \times 11 \times 10}{4 \times 3 \times 2 \times 1}$$
$$= 715$$

(8-5)

where k is the number of events (deaths) and n is the total number of individuals. Similarly, the number of ways losses on the Confederate side could have occurred are equal to 11! ÷ (8! 3!) = 165.

However, we are ultimately interested in the association between Union/Confederate and Alive/Dead. To get at this, we have to begin with the nonassociation and figure out how many ways a total of 7 men could have been shot out of the 24 who started. We put them all in one long row, regardless of the color of their uniform, and do the same exercise. The answer, using the same logic as before, is 24! ÷ (7! 17!) = 346 104.

That means that there were a total of 346 104 ways of ending up with 7 dead souls out of the 24 with we began. That is, if we were to line up all the soldiers in a row with the 13 Union guys on the left and the 11 Rebels on the right and fire 7 rounds at them, there are a total of 346 104 ways to take out 7 soldiers. Some of these possibilities are 6 dead Union soldiers and 1 dead Confederate soldier, 5 dead Confederate soldiers and 2 dead Union soldiers, and on and on.

Now, how many possibilities have the right combination of 4 and 3? Well, imagine the Confeder-

FIGURE 8-2   Aftermath of the Battle of Bull Roar.

ates shoot first, so there are just 4 Unionists on the ground. We have already worked out that the number of ways you can kill 4 Union people of 13 is 715. Now, for each one of these possibilities, we can now let the Union guys open fire, and kill 3 Confederates—as before, 165 possible configurations. So the total number of patterns that correspond to 4 and 3 dead, after we have got everyone back in a single line, is just $715 \times 165 = 117\,975$. This is out of the total number of possibilities of 346 104. So, the overall probability of getting the distribution of deaths that occurred at Bull Roar is $117\,975/346\,104 = 0.34$. Now, if we put all the factorials together, we can see that the formula for the probability that things came out as they did is:

$$p = \frac{\dfrac{13!}{9!\,4!} \times \dfrac{11!}{8!\,3!}}{\dfrac{24!}{17!\,7!}} \qquad (8\text{-}6)$$

More generally, this can be expressed in terms of as and bs as:

$$p = \frac{\dfrac{(a+b)!}{a!\,b!} \times \dfrac{(c+d)!}{c!\,d!}}{\dfrac{N!}{(a+c)!\,(b+d)!}} \qquad (8\text{-}7)$$

This simplifies to:

$$p = \frac{(a+b)!\,(c+d)!\,(a+c)!\,(b+d)!}{N!\,a!\,b!\,c!\,d!} \qquad (8\text{-}8)$$

This then is the probability of a particular configuration in a 2×2 table. So going back to our original EMS example, the probability of occurrence of the events in Table 8-7 is:

$$\text{Prob}\,(2) = \frac{10! \times 190! \times 100! \times 100!}{100! \times 8! \times 2! \times 92! \times 98!} = 0.0401 \qquad (8\text{-}9)$$

where the '(2)' means that the count in the cell with the fewest number of subjects is two. We'll see why that's important in a moment.

We're not quite done. The probability used in the statistical test is the entire probability in the tail (i.e., the likelihood of observing a value *as* extreme or even *more* extreme than the one observed). In the discrete case we are considering, this corresponds to tables with stronger associations, which means more extreme values in the cells. There are only two possibilities with more extreme values; 1 case in the control group and 0 cases in the control group.

The corresponding 2×2 tables are shown in Table 8-9. For one occurrence the formula is:

$$\text{Prob}\,(1) = \frac{10! \times 190! \times 100! \times 100!}{200! \times 9! \times 1! \times 91! \times 99!} = 0.0085 \qquad (8\text{-}10)$$

And for no occurrences this probability equals:

$$\text{Prob}\,(0) = \frac{10! \times 190! \times 100! \times 100!}{200! \times 10! \times 0! \times 90! \times 100!} = 0.0008 \qquad (8\text{-}11)$$

Putting it all together, the overall probability of observing this strong an association or stronger is $0.0410 + 0.0085 + 0.0008 = 0.0503$. But, that's only one tail of the distribution; the two-tailed probability is (about) double that, or about 0.10. When we're doing the calculations by hand, we can stop at an earlier step if the sum of the probabilities (two-tailed) exceeds 0.05. So, this particular investigation doesn't make it to the *New England Journal of Medicine*.

To summarize, Fisher's exact test is used when the expected frequency of any cell in a 2×2 table is less than 5. You construct the 2×2 tables for the actual data and all more extreme cases, then work out the probability for each contingency table using the binomial theorem, shown above. The exact probabilities are then added together to give the probability of the observed association or any more extreme.

TABLE 8-9   Most extreme associations between tryptophan use and EMS

P(1)		EMS	Normal	totals	P(0)		EMS	Normal	TOTALS
Tryptophan	Yes	9	91	100	Tryptophan	Yes	10	90	100
	No	1	99	100		No	0	100	100
	TOTALS	10	190	200		TOTALS	10	190	200

PAIRED AND MATCHED OBSERVATIONS: MCNEMAR CHI-SQUARED

Perhaps you noticed that we began this chapter by telling you that we were going to use a real example, and we then went back to some imaginary data. There was a good reason for this peculiar action. The original study that implicated tryptophan (Eidson et al., 1990) used a slightly more complicated design—complicated in the sense of analysis at any rate. They located 11 individuals who had EMS based on objective criteria and then matched them with 22 controls on the basis of age and sex. The magical word "match" means that we have to try another approach to analysis, equivalent to a paired *t*-test. The approach is called the **McNemar chi-squared**; it is logically complex but computationally trivial. Because the logic is tough enough with simple designs, we will pretend that the investigators just did a one-on-one matching and actually located 22 cases. If we ignored the matching, the data could be displayed as usual (Table 8-10).

TABLE 8-10   Study 3—matched design association between tryptophan use and EMS (shown unmatched)

		Tryptophan use		
		Yes	**No**	**TOTALS**
EMS	Yes	22	0	22
	No	2	20	22
	TOTALS	24	20	44

Data from Eidson M et al. (1990). L-tryptophan and eosinophilia-myalgia syndrome in New Mexico. *Lancet*, **335**:645–648.

Matched or not, clearly this is one case where the *p* value is simply icing on the cake; however, we will proceed. The logic of the matching is that we frankly don't care about those instances where both case and control took tryptophan, or about those instances where neither took it. All that interests us is the circumstances where either the case took it and the control didn't, or vice versa. So we must construct a different 2 × 2 table reflecting this logic (Table 8-11). The first thing to note is that the total at the bottom right is only 22; the analysis is based on 22 *pairs*, not 44 people. Second, note that the four cells display the four possibilities of the pairs—both used it, both didn't use it, cases did but controls didn't, and controls did but cases didn't.

TABLE 8-11   Study 3—matched design association between tryptophan use and EMS (shown matched)

		Control (without EMS) used tryptophan		
Case (with EMS) used tryptophan	Yes	2	20	22
	No	0	0	0
	TOTALS	2	20	22

Data from Eidson M et al. (1990). L-tryptophan and eosinophilia-myalgia syndrome in New Mexico. *Lancet*, **335**:645–648.

Finally, as we said, we're interested in only the two off-diagonal cells because those are where the action will be. The reason is that if *no* association existed between being a case or a control and tryptophan exposure, we would expect that there would be just as many instances where cases used tryptophan and controls didn't as the opposite. We have 20 instances altogether, so we would expect 10 to go one way and 10 the other. In short, for the McNemar chi-squared, the expected value is obtained by totaling the off-diagonal pairs and dividing by two. It is now computationally straightforward to crank out a chi-squared based on these observed and expected values. There is one wrinkle—McNemar recognized that he would likely be dealing with small numbers most of the time, so he built a Yates'-type correction into the formula:

$$\chi^2_M = \frac{(|\,20-10\,|-0.5)^2}{10} + \frac{(|\,0-10\,|-0.5)^2}{10}$$
$$= 18.05 \tag{8-12}$$

with one *df*. To no one's surprise, this is significant at the 0.0001 level. Because of the particular form of the expected values, the McNemar chi-squared takes a simpler form for computation. If we label the top left cell *a*, the top right *b*, the bottom left *c*, and the bottom right *d*, as we did in Table 8-8, the McNemar chi-squared is just:

$$\chi^2_M = \frac{(|\,b-c\,|-1)^2}{(b+c)} \tag{8-13}$$

To summarize, then, the McNemar chi-squared is the approach when dealing with paired, matched, or pre-post designs. Unfortunately, despite its computational simplicity, it is limited to situations with only two response categories and simple one-on-one matching. That's why we modified the example a bit. To consider the instance of two controls to each case, we must look at more possibilities (e.g., one exposed case and one control case, and both controls). It's possible, but a bit hairier.

TWO FACTORS: MANTEL-HAENSZEL CHI-SQUARED

We have dealt with all the possibilities where we have one independent categorical variable. Chi-squared, with a 2 × 2 table, is equivalent to a *t*-test, and with more than two categories is like one-way ANOVA. The McNemar chi-squared is the analogue of the paired *t*-test. The next extension is to consider the case of two independent variables, the parallel of two-way ANOVA. The strategy is called a **Mantel-Haenszel chi-squared**.

Unfortunately, none of the real data from the EMS studies are up to it, so we'll have to fabricate some. Stretch your biochemical imagination a bit and examine the possibility (admittedly remote) that some other factors interact with tryptophan exposure from the bad batch to result in illness. For example, suppose EMS is actually caused by a massive allergic response to mosquito bites that occurs only when excess serum levels of tryptophan are present. Well now, gin and tonic (G and T) was originally developed by the British Raj to protect the imperialist swine from another mosquito-borne contagion (malaria) while concurrently providing emotional support (in the form of inebriation).

To test the theory (and to deal with the possible response bias resulting from folks in the G and T group saying they are feeling great when they are past feeling anything), we create six groups by combining the two independent variables: Gin and Tonic, Tonic Only, or No Drinks, with half of each group having taken tryptophan and the other half a placebo (in ANOVA terms, a 3 × 2 factorial design). We can't afford any lab work, so we use symptoms as dependent variables: insomnia, fatigue, and sexual dysfunction. When we announced the study in the graduate stu-

dent lounges, we had no trouble recruiting subjects and got up to 500 per group, despite the possible risk. However, the dropout rates were ferocious. The No Drink group subjects were mad that they didn't get to drink; the G and T group got so blotto they forgot to show up; and the Tonic Only group presumed they were supposed to be blotto and didn't come either. In the end, the data resulted in Table 8-12.

TABLE 8-12   **Association between tryptophan, gin and tonic, and EMS**

	EMS symptoms		
	Yes	**No**	**TOTALS**
Gin and tonic			
Trypt	16	131	147
Placebo	4	101	105
TOTALS	20	232	252
CHI-SQUARED = 4.16, $p <0.05$			
Tonic only			
Trypt	29	85	114
Placebo	7	79	86
TOTALS	36	164	200
CHI-SQUARED = 9.39, $p <0.005$			
Nothing			
Trypt	66	22	88
Placebo	88	72	160
TOTALS	154	94	248
CHI-SQUARED = 9.65, $p < 0.005$			
Totals			
Trypt	111	238	349
Placebo	99	252	351
TOTALS	210	490	700
CHI-SQUARED = 1.08, ns			

Before we plunge into the statistical esoterica, take really close look at the table. Within each 2 × 2 subtable there is a strong association between tryptophan use and symptoms, with about three times as many people with symptoms per 100 in each stratum. The risk of symptoms among tryptophan-exposed individuals in the Tonic Only group is 29 ÷ 114 = 25.4/100; in the Placebo and Tonic Only group, it's 8.14/100. So the relative risk is 25.4 ÷ 8.14 = 3.12. But because of the peculiarities of the data—mainly the excess of symptoms in the "Nothing" group, and the factor of two between Tryptophan and Placebo in those who stayed in the trial (160 vs 88)—when they are combined (shown at the bottom of Table 8-12), the association disappears.

Clearly, one way *not* to examine the association between tryptophan and symptoms, when there are strata with unequal sample sizes, is to add it all together, which makes the effect completely disappear. Instead, we must use some strategy that will recognize the interaction between the two factors, and so must stay at the level of the individual 2×2 tables.

We can start as we have before, by considering the expected value of an individual frequency, contrasting this with the observed value, and squaring the lot up. For example, the expected frequency in the G and T, Tryptophan, YES cell is:

$$\text{Exp} = \frac{(a+b)(a+c)}{N} = \frac{20 \times 147}{252} = 11.67$$

(8-14)

You probably thought that a reasonable way to proceed now is simply to calculate a chi-squared by doing as we have already done—summing up all the $(O - E)^2 \div E$ for all 12 cells. We thought so too, but Mantel and Haenszel didn't. First, the variance in this situation is *not* just the expected value, as it was when we did the original chi-squared. Here, the variance of the expected value of each frequency is:

$$\text{Var(Exp)} = \frac{(a+b)(a+c)(c+d)(b+d)}{N^2(N-1)}$$

(8-15)

The next step is to add up the $(O - E)$ differences for all the individual frequencies in the a (top left) cells across all subtables and square the resulting total. We then throw in a Yates' correction, just for the heck of it. This is the numerator for the M-H chi-squared and is an overall measure of the *signal*, the difference between observed and expected values, analogous to the mean square (between) in ANOVA.

$$\text{Numerator} = \left[\sum (O_i - E_i) - 0.5 \right]^2$$
$$= [(16 - 11.67) + (29 - 20.52) +$$
$$(66 - 54.64) - 0.5]^2$$
$$= 23.67^2 = 560.26$$

Similarly, the variances of the values in each subtable are added together to give the *noise* term, analogous to the mean square (within) in ANOVA:

$$\sum \frac{(a+b)(a+c)(c+d)(b+d)}{N^2(N-1)}$$
$$= 4.49 + 7.27 + 13.41 = 25.17$$

(8-16)

where N is the total sample size for each subtable (252 200, and 248). Finally, the ratio of the two sums is the M-H chi-squared, with $(k-1)$ *df*, where k is the number of subtables in the analysis; in this case, three. This M-H chi-squared equals $560.26 \div 25.17 = 22.25$, and it is significant at the 0.001 level.

Although useful for analyzing stratified data, the MH chi-squared also appears in the analysis of life tables because, at one level, a life table is nothing more than a series of 2×2 tables (e.g., treatment/control by alive/dead) on successive years over the course of the study. This is described in more detail in Chapter 10.

When we first introduced χ^2, we said that both variables are measured at the nominal level, such as sex, group membership, or the presence or absence of some outcome. Well, that's only partially true. The ordinary, run-of-the-mill Pearson's χ^2 is like this, so if a variable has more than two levels, such as tryptophan manufacturer, we'd get exactly the same answer if we changed the order of the rows or columns around in the table—the true property of a nominal level variable. So what do we do if both of the variables are ordinal, or if one is ordinal and the other is dichotomous? In this case, we're looking for a *linear trend*, to see if a higher level of one variable is associated with a higher or lower level of the other, and we'd lose information if we ignore this.

Let's get away from "healthy" additives for a while and turn our attention to more pressing issues—such as testing the hypothesis that believing professional wrestling is staged or not is related to your education level. So, we stop 100 people on the street, ask them about the highest grade they completed, and whether or not they think that the outcome of a pro wrestling matched is fixed ahead of time. The results of our scientific survey are presented in Table 8-13, with education classified as (1) attended or fin-

TABLE 8-13 Belief in the honesty of professional wrestling by educational level

Highest Education Received	Are the results honest?		total
	Yes	No	
High School	21	10	31
College	24	24	48
Graduate or Professional	8	13	21
Total	53	47	100

ished high school, (2) attended or finished college, or (3) attended or finished graduate or professional school.

Now, if we ignored the ordinal level of education, and ran an ordinary χ^2, we'd get a value of 4.751 which, with $df = 2$, is not statistically significant. Let's pull another test out of our bag of tricks, called the **Mantel-Haenszel chi-squared** (χ^2_{MH}), which is also known as the **test for linear trend** or the **linear-by-linear test**. We'd find its value, with $df = 1$, is 4.620, which is significant at $p = 0.032$. We would conclude that there's a significant trend, with higher education being associated with a greater degree of skepticism, which we wouldn't have seen with a Pearson's χ^2.

Calculating χ^2_{MH} is quite easy. We run a Pearson's correlation (r) between the two variables, and then:

$$\chi^2_{MH} = (N-1)r^2 \qquad \textbf{(8-17)}$$

which we would then look up in a table of the critical values of the χ^2 distribution (Table F in the Appendix) with $df = 1$. Pearson's correlation between education and belief is 0.216, so

$$\chi^2_{MH} = (99) \times 0.216^2 = 4.619 \qquad \textbf{(8-18)}$$

As you can see from the example, the increase in significance level isn't due to a higher value of the χ^2, but to fewer degrees of freedom: $(r-1) \times (c-1)$ for Pearson's χ^2, and 1 for χ^2_{MH}, irrespective of the number of levels of either variable. So the more levels there are, the greater the gain when you use χ^2_{MH}.

Did we just violate something or someone by figuring out Pearson's r on ordinal data? Not really; Pearson is robust and can handle this easily. If you're a purist and insist on using a non-parametric correlation, such as Spearman's ρ instead, you'd get a value of 0.217 rather than 0.216. But, if it makes you feel better, go ahead and spear away. While you're doing

that, we'll return to the tragedy of tryptophan.

MANY FACTORS: LOG-LINEAR ANALYSIS

In particular, in the last example, we examined the combined effects of tryptophan and gin and tonic on EMS symptoms. But the astute ANOVA'er might have noticed that we could have, but didn't, look at the effects of gin and tonic separately. As a result, we cannot separate out the main effect of gin from the interaction between gin and tonic. A better design would be to have four groups—Gin and Tonic, Gin only, Tonic only, and Nothing, with half of each group exposed to tryptophan and half to placebo.

We had a good reason for not doing it this way. This would have introduced three factors in the design (Tryptophan, Gin, Tonic) and the M-H chi-squared, like the parametric two-way ANOVA, is capable of dealing only with two independent variables. To deal with multiple factors, we must move up yet again in the analytical strategy: the approach to analysis called **log-linear analysis**. We work out a way to predict the expected frequency in each cell by a product of "effects"—main effects and interactions—and then take the logarithm of the effects to create a linear equation (hence, log-linear). It ends up, yet again, as a regression problem using estimates of the regression parameters. Everything seems to be a linear model, or if it's not, we poke it around until it becomes one!

For relative simplicity, we'll add an extra group to Table 8-12 to separate out the two drinking factors (Table 8-14). In log-linear analysis, we first collapse the distinction between independent and dependent variables. You and I know that Symptoms of EMS is the dependent variable, but from the vantage point of the computer, it's just one more factor leading to vertical or horizontal lines in the contingency table. Table 8-14 could be displayed with any combinations of factors on the vertical and horizontal axis, and it is only logic, not statistics, that distinguishes between independent and dependent variables. Ultimately we care about the association between EMS and Tryptophan, Gin, and Tonic, but this, like a correlation, has no statistical directionality.

TABLE 8-14   **Association between tryptophan, gin, tonic, and EMS**

Tonic	Gin		EMS symptoms		
			Yes	No	totals
Yes	Yes	Trypt	16	131	147
		Placebo	4	101	105
		TOTALS	20	232	252
Yes	No	Trypt	29	85	114
		Placebo	7	79	86
		TOTALS	36	164	200
No	Yes	Trypt	32	33	65
		Placebo	23	64	87
		TOTALS	55	97	152
No	No	Trypt	66	22	88
		Placebo	88	72	160
		TOTALS	154	94	248

We begin by determining what an *effect* is. Let's start by assuming there was *no* effect of any of the variables at all. In this case, the expected value of each cell is just the total divided by the number of cells, $852 \div 16 = 53.25$.

The next level of analysis presumes a main effect of each factor; this explains the different marginals. This is introduced by multiplying the expected value by a factor reflecting the difference in marginal totals. We would begin by determining the marginal proportion with Gin present, $(252 + 152) \div 852 = 0.47$, and the proportion with Gin absent (0.53). If Gin had no marginal effect, these proportions would be 0.50 and 0.50, so we multiply the Gin-present cells by $0.47 \div 0.50 = 0.94$, and the Gin absent cells by $0.53 \div 0.50 = 1.06$.

Working this through for the top left cell, where all effects are present, to account for all the marginal totals, the initial estimate must also be multiplied by the overall probability of Tonic $(252 + 200) \div 852 = 0.53, 0.53 \div 0.50 = 1.06$; the overall probability of Tryptophan $(147 + 114 + 65 + 88) \div 852 = 0.48, 0.48 \div 0.50 = 0.96$; and the overall probability of Symptom $(20 + 36 + 55 + 154) \div 852 = 0.31, 0.31 \div 0.50 = 0.62$. so, the expected value in this cell is $53.25 \times 0.94 \times 1.06 \times 0.95 \times 0.62 = 31.58$. If we call β_{G1} (there is no logical reason to call these things β's—that's just what ev-

erybody calls them) the main effect of the Gin factor, where the subscript (1) indicates the first level; β_{P1} the effect of the Pop (Tonic) factor; β_{S1} the main effect of EMS at the first level; and β_{T1} the main effect of tryptophan, then algebraically the expected value of cell (1,1,1,1) with no association is:

$$f_{1111} = N \times \beta_{G1} \times \beta_{P1} \times \beta_{T1} \times \beta_{S1}$$
$$= 53.25 \times 0.94 \times 1.06 \times 0.96 \times 0.62 = 31.58$$

(8-19)

where N is the expected frequency in each cell assuming no main effects, just the total count divided by the number of cells ($852 \div 16 = 53.25$). Going the next step, if we assume that there *is* an association between Gin and Symptoms, but there *is not* an association between Pop and Tryptophan and Symptoms, then this would amount to introducing another multiplicative factor to reflect this interaction, a factor that we might call β_{GS11}. We won't try to estimate this value because there is a limit to our multiplication skills, but algebraically, the expected value in the top left cell of such a model would look like:

$$f_{1111} = N \times \beta_{G1} \times \beta_{P1} \times \beta_{T1} \times \beta_{S1} \times \beta_{GS11}$$

(8-20)

There is no reason to stop here. Several models could be tested, including No Effects (the expected value in each cell is 53.25), then one or more main effects only, then one or more two-way interactions, then the three-way interactions, and finally the four-way interaction.

However, as yet, we have not indicated how we test the models. Here is the chicanery. Recall once again your high school algebra, where you were told (and then forgot) that the logarithm of a *product* of terms is the *sum* of the logarithms of the terms. So if we take the log of the above equation, it becomes:

$$\log[f_{1111}] = \log N + \log\beta_{G1} + \log\beta_{P1} + \log\beta_{T1} + \log\beta_{S1} + \log\beta_{GS11}$$
$$= \theta + \lambda_{G1} + \lambda_{P1} + \lambda_{T1} + \lambda_{S1} + \lambda_{GS11}$$

(8-21)

Again, unfortunately, there isn't much rationale for the Greek symbols. The first thing looking like an "O" with a bird dropping in the center is called *theta*. The others are called *lambda* and are the Greek "L"— for *log-linear*, we suppose.

We have now reduced the beast to a regression problem. The usual analytical approach is to fit the models in hierarchical fashion, so that first the main effects model is fitted, then the two-way interactions model, then the three-way interactions model, and on to the full model. Of course, just as in regression, when new terms are introduced into the model, the magnitudes of all the estimated parameters change. One additional constraint is imposed on the analysis: all the λs for a particular effect must add to zero. Thus, when an effect has two levels, as is the case in our example, the λs will be something like +0.602 and −0.602. In turn, because each of the estimated parameters is the logarithm of a factor that multiplies the initial expected cell frequency, it is also possible to determine the expected cell frequencies at any stage by listing the parameter estimates, taking antilogs, and then multiplying the whole lot together. Computer packages that run log-linear analysis will do this for you, of course.

At each stage of the analysis, a chi-squared is calculated, based on the differences between the observed frequencies and the frequencies estimated from the model. If the model fits the data adequately,

we get a nonsignificant chi-squared, indicating no significant differences between the predicted and the observed data. Where do the degrees of freedom come from? Two effects: first, note that, in this case, all variables are at two levels, so each effect is a 2×2 or a $2 \times 2 \times 2$ table, and any combination of 2×2 tables has one df; second, there are 4 main effects, 6 two-way interactions, 4 three-way interactions, and 1 four-way interaction (Table 8-15), so these are the total df: 15.

For the present data, the analysis of zero, first, and higher order interactions results in Table 8-16. It is clear that the test of first-order interactions (i.e., main effects) is significant (L.R. chi-squared = 130.90), simply implying that the marginals are not equal; the two-way interactions are also highly significant (L.R. chi-squared = 290.69). However, fortunately for us, no evidence of a significant three-way or four-way interaction is found (fortunate because we wouldn't know how to interpret it if it was there). So we conclude that the model with two-way interactions fits the data (i.e., it is the model with the lowest order significant interactions, and no significant chi-squareds exist beyond it), so we stop.

TABLE 8-15   Test of individual interactions in log-linear analysis

Effect	df	Partial association		Marginal association	
		Chi-squared	P	Chi-squared	p
S	1	124.77	<0.0001		
T	1	0.68	0.41		
G	1	2.27	0.13		
P	1	3.18	0.07		
ST	1	31.27	<0.0001	4.44	<0.05
SG	1	39.85	<0.0001	57.94	<0.0001
SP	1	165.54	<0.0001	163.99	<0.0001
TG	1	5.39	<0.05	4.64	<0.05
TP	1	52.88	<0.05	32.51	<0.0001
GP	1	2.45	0.11	32.51	<0.0001
STG	1	0.00	0.98	26.99	<0.0001
STP	1	0.63	0.43	0.53	0.46
SGP	1	0.25	0.61	0.23	0.27
TGP	1	1.34	0.24	0.12	0.73
STGP	1	0.13	0.71	0.78	0.38

TABLE 8-16   Test of interactions in log-linear analysis

Level	L.R. χ^2	df	p	Pearson χ^2	p
1	130.90	4	<0.0001	102.15	<0.0001
2	290.69	6	<0.0001	290.14	<0.0001
3	4.43	4	0.351	4.30	0.367
4	0.16	1	0.686	0.17	0.684

So what is an "L.R. chi-squared"? The L.R. is shorthand for likelihood-ratio, which is defined as:

$$\chi^2_{LR} = 2 \sum (Observed) \left(\ln \times \frac{Observed}{Expected} \right)$$

$$(8\text{-}22)$$

where *ln* means the natural logarithm (i.e., to base e). Actually, SPSS gives you both a run-of-the-mill Pearsonian χ^2 as well as Fisher's χ^2_{LR}, and they're usually fairly similar. The advantage of χ^2_{LR} is that the difference between the ones at succeeding levels shows the contribution of the next level (with degrees of freedom equal to the difference in *df*).

The next step is to examine the individual terms to determine which of the main effects and interactions are significant. For the present data, these are shown in Table 8-15. Looking at the main effects, we see that only S is significant, which means that the frequencies in the Symptom and No Symptom summed cells are not equal. Who cares? More interesting is that all the two-way interactions with Symptoms are significant, so an association does exist between symptoms and tryptophan, gin, and tonic. Tryptophan makes you sicker, tonic makes you better, and gin makes you better. The remaining two-way interactions are not of any particular interest, indicating only that there happen to be interactions among the independent variables. Finally, none of the three-way or four-way interactions are significant.

Note that, in Table 8-15, we show both a *marginal and a partial association. The marginal* association is based on frequencies at the marginals and is analogous to a test of a simple correlation. Conversely, the partial association takes into account the effect of the other variables at this level, so it is analogous to the test of the partial correlation.

Not surprisingly, at a conceptual level, the analysis resembles multiple regression, in that it reduces to an estimation of a number of fit parameters based on an assumed linear model, with the exception that, in log-linear analysis, you generally proceed in hierarchical fashion, fitting all effects at a given level. For those with an epidemiological bent, there is one final wrinkle. The estimated effect is exactly equal to the log of the *odds ratio*. Thus an effect of -1.5 for G and T implies that the odds ratio (the odds of disease with G and T present to the odds of disease with G and T absent) is equal to exp $(-1.5) = 0.22$. Similarity to factorial ANOVA also exists in the unique ability of the log-linear analysis to handle multiple categorical variables.

DIFFERENCE BETWEEN INDEPENDENT PROPORTIONS

Let's take another look at the data in Table 8-2. We analyzed them using χ^2 and found a significant association between tryptophan exposure and EMS. One problem with χ^2, though, is that all we get is a probability level; we can't draw any confidence intervals (CIs) around the difference. A different approach is to look at the *proportions* in each group of people who developed EMS. We can derive CIs for the individual proportions, and also for the difference between them.

In the EMS group, 42 people had taken tryptophan and 38 had not, so p_1, the proportion in Group 1 who took the stuff is 42 / (42 + 38) = 0.525. Similarly, the proportion in the second (Normal) group, p_2, is 34 / (34 + 166) = 0.170. If we want to have CIs around the proportions, we begin with the **standard error of a proportion**, which is:

$$SE = \sqrt{p(1-p)/n}$$

$$(8\text{-}23)$$

and the 95% CI is then:

$$95\%CI = p \pm 1.96 \sqrt{(1-p)/n}$$

$$(8\text{-}24)$$

So, for the EMS group, we get:

$$0.525 \pm 1.96 \sqrt{(0.525 \times 0.475)/80}$$
$$= 0.525 \pm (1.96 \times 0.056) = (0.416, \ 0.634)$$

$$(8\text{-}25)$$

The **standard error of the difference in proportions** is:

$$SE_{diff} = \sqrt{p(1-p)\left(\frac{1}{n_1} + \frac{1}{n_2}\right)}$$

$$(8\text{-}26)$$

where p is the pooled proportion (i.e., $[42 + 34]$ / $[80 + 200] = 0.271$), so that for this example:

$$\sqrt{0.271 \times 0.729 \left(\frac{1}{80} + \frac{1}{200}\right)} = 0.059 \quad (8\text{-}27)$$

and (finally) the test for the difference in the proportions is:

$$z = \frac{p_1 - p_2}{SE_{diff}}$$

$$(8\text{-}28)$$

This turns out to be:

$$\frac{0.525 - 0.170}{0.059} = 6.017 \quad (8\text{-}29)$$

which is highly significant, as was the χ^2. This isn't surprising, since both tests are using the same data in the same way.

Which one you use depends on whether you just want a significance level, or also want the CIs.

MEASURES OF ASSOCIATION FOR CATEGORICAL DATA

Having succeeded in deriving several approaches to do significance testing for categorical data, the next step is to work out some measures of association. In parametric statistics, once statistical significance was established, we examined nondimensional measures indicating how much association was present. Pearson's product moment coefficient and spearman's rank correlation coefficient did nicely for two variables, the multiple *correlation coefficient* handled multiple independent variables, and the eta-squared did the same for ANOVA situations. All were based on the underlying concept of proportion of variance in dependent variable accounted for by the independent variables.

All is not so straightforward in nonparametric statistics. Just as with the tests of significance, which

were an inventors' paradise with two-man teams all over the countryside striving for immortality, nonparametric measures of association are similarly littered with surnames, although these tend to be of solo practitioners. We will mention only a few of the more common ones, attributable to Cohen, Yule, and Cramer. Left for obscurity are the dozens of more esoteric tests.

MEASURES OF ASSOCIATION FOR 2 × 2 AND HIGHER TABLES

In an effort to reform the public schools and catch up with education in the rest of the world, a study is initiated to see if school psychologists can detect potential criminals so that taxpayers' dollars won't be wasted in the schools and can be diverted directly to the prisons.

In fact, terms such as "criminal" or "juvenile delinquent" have acquired a pejorative meaning in our opening scenario, as if the bearer had actually done something wrong rather than just finding himself or herself in unfortunate circumstances. This labeling gets in the way of rehabilitation. Clearly, in these politically correct times, it's an occasion for a new, neutral label for such unlucky folks. So we use "youthful legally challenged" (YLC for short) instead of juvenile delinquent.

Along these lines, if we could only identify these kids early, perhaps they might never stray at all. School psychologists should be in an ideal position to do this. Let's do a study to see if they are good at primary prevention.

The design is straightforward. We locate a sample of a couple hundred kids, both YLCs from the local reformatory and normals (oops, there we go again. Calling them "normals" implies that the YLCs aren't normal. Let's call them "others"). We ask the psychologists at their schools (former or current, depending on the kid) to review the files and predict whether they were likely to end up on the other side of the bars. The data is arranged in Table 8-17.

Now, it would be easy enough to apply a statistical test to determine if the relationship is significant. The appropriate test is the chi-squared, which equals

TABLE 8-17   **Association between predicted and actual criminal status**

Predicted Bars-Bound?	Status		Totals
	YLC	Other	
Yes	36	24	60
No	40	100	140
Totals	76	124	200

17.61, significant at the 0.001 level. But a larger question is involved, namely: Is it worth putting a lot of effort into attempting to catch these kids early and do counseling, handholding, or whatever is necessary to keep them off the streets if the association is not all that strong? In short, we would like a measure of the *strength* of the association, equivalent to a correlation coefficient, before we decide to throw taxpayers' money at this social problem.

The Phi Coefficient, Contingency Coefficient, Yule's Q and Cramer's V

The most obvious approach is to pretend that the data are actually interval and go ahead and calculate a Pearson correlation. If the kid is identified by the psychologist as a troublemaker, he gets a "1," if not, a "0"; if he ends up a YLC, he gets a "1," if not, a "0." And so we stuff 200 (x,y) pairs into computer, where each pair looks like (1,1), (1,0), (0,1), or (0,0), and see what emerges. As it turns out, this results in some simplifications to the formula. We won't go through all the dreary details, but will just give you a glimpse. Remember that the numerator of the Pearson correlation was:

$$\text{Numerator} = N\sum XY - \sum X\sum Y$$

Now for the shenanigans. If we call the top left cell a, the top right one b, the bottom left c, and the bottom right cell d, then the first observation is that the sum of XY is equal only to a because this is the only cell where both X and Y are equal to 1. Second, the sum of X (the rows) is just $(a + b)$, and the sum of Y is $(a + c)$, again because this is where the 1s are located. Finally, N is equal to $(a + b + c + d)$, the total sample size. The equation now becomes:

$$\text{Numerator} = (a+b+c+d)(a) - (a+b)(a+c)$$
$$= (a^2 + ab + ac + ad) - (a^2 + ab + ac + bc)$$
$$= ad - bc$$

Similar messing around with the formula for Pearson correlation results in a simplication of the denominator, so that the final formula of the *phi coefficient* is equal to:

$$\Phi = \frac{ad - bc}{\sqrt{(a+b)(a+c)(c+d)(b+d)}} \quad (8\text{-}30)$$

Put the numbers in the formula, then Phi is equal to 0.297.

We'll let you be the judge whether this correlation is high enough (or low enough) to merit trying to inspire a change in behavior.

Because the phi coefficient falls directly out of the 2×2 table, if the associated chi-squared is significant, so is the phi coefficient (and vice versa). In fact there is an exact relationship between phi and chi-squared:

$$\Phi = \sqrt{\frac{x^2}{N}} \quad (8\text{-}31)$$

This relationship, and some variations, is the basis of several other coefficients. Pearson's *contingency coefficient*, not to be confused with the product-moment correlation, looks like:

$$\text{Contingency Coefficient} = \sqrt{\frac{x^2}{(N + x^2)}} \quad (8\text{-}32)$$

and in fact ϕ is the effect size (ES) indicator for the χ^2. However, there's one problem with blindly using ϕ as an ES, and that is that its maximum value is 1 only when the row margins and the column margins are equal to 50%. In fact, the maximum possible value of ϕ for the data in Table 8-17 is 0.84. A better index of ES may be the ratio of ϕ to ϕ_{Max}, which, in this case, is $0.297 \div 0.84$ and is a somewhat more impressive 0.35.

Cramer's V is based on the chi-squared as well, but it is a more general form for use with $C \times R$ contingency tables. It is written as:

$$\text{Cramer's V} = \sqrt{\frac{x^2}{[N \times \text{minme}C - 1, R - 1]}} \quad (8\text{-}33)$$

where the denominator means "N times the minimum of $(C - 1)$ or $(R - 1)$." For a 2×2 table, this is the same as phi.

Yule's Q is another measure based on the cross-product of the marginals, and it has a particularly simple form:

$$Q = \frac{ad - bc}{ad + bc} \qquad (8\text{-}34)$$

Choice among these alternatives can be made on cultural or aesthetic grounds as well as any other because they are all variations on a theme that give different answers, with differences ranging from none, through slight, to major.

Cohen's Kappa

A second popular measure of association in the biomedical literature is **Cohen's kappa** (Cohen, 1960), the formula is equal to:

$$\kappa = \frac{(f_0 - f_e)}{(N - f_e)} \qquad (8\text{-}35)$$

Where f_o means the *observed frequency, and* f_e means the *expected frequency.* If you prefer to work with proportions, then divide each number by N, and use the formula:

$$\kappa = \frac{(p_0 - p_e)}{(1.0 - p_e)} \qquad (8\text{-}36)$$

where p_o is the observed proportion and p_e the expected.

Kappa is usually used to examine inter-observer agreement on diagnostic tests (e.g., physical signs, radiographs) but need not be restricted to such purposes. However, to show how it goes, we'll create a new example.

One clear problem with our above study is that we were left with a number of prediction errors, which may be due either to individual psychologists' inability to agree on their predictions (an issue of reliability); or because they may agree based on the evidence available at the school, but this evidence is simply not predictive of future behavior (an issue of validity). Disagreement among observers will reduce the association, so it might be useful to examine the extent of agreement on this classification. This is straightforward. We assemble the files for a bunch of kids (e.g., $n = 300$), and get two psychologists to independently classify each kid as rotten or not. We then examine the association between the two categorizations, which are displayed in Table 8-18.

TABLE 8-18   Inter-rater agreement on criminal status

Observer 2 Bars-bound?	Observer 1 Bars-bound?		Totals
	YLC	Other	
Yes	78	42	120
No	48	132	180
Totals	126	174	300

Then we can use kappa to measure the agreement of on this classification. To begin, let's take a closer look at the data. How much agreement would we expect between the two shrinks just by chance? That is, if the psychologists don't know beans about the students' behaviors, they would still agree with each other a number of times, just by chance. Thus, the proportion of agreements would be non-zero.

The chance agreement is calculated by working out the expected frequencies for the *a* and *d* cells, using the product of the marginals as we did with the chi-squared test. This equals $(120 \times 126 / 300) = 50.4$ for cell *a* and $(180 \times 174 / 300) = 104.4$ for cell *d*, for a total chance agreement of 154.8. Then we simply plug *expected frequency* (f_e) and the *observed frequency* (f_o) for the two cells into the Formula (8-35), so the **Cohen's kappa** is equal to 0.380.

So, even though the observed agreement was a fairly impressive 70%, much of this was due to chance agreement, and the kappa is a less impressive 0.380.

Although kappa appears to start from a different premise than the phi coefficient, there are more similarities than differences after the dust settles. The numerator of kappa turns out also to equal (*ad-bc*), the same as phi. The denominators are different, but this amounts to a scaling factor. In fact, in this situation, phi is also equal to 0.380.

Standard error of kappa and significance test. To test the significance of kappa, it is first necessary to derive the standard error (SE; or the variance) of kappa, assuming that it is equal to zero. In its most general form, including multiple categories and multiple raters, this turns out to be a fairly horrendous equation. However, for a 2×2 table, it is a lot easier:

$$var(\kappa) = \frac{p_o - p_0^2}{N[1 - p_e]^2} \qquad (8\text{-}37)$$

In the present case, p_o is 0.70, p_e is 0.516, and N is 300, so the variance is equal to 0.003.

Once the variance has been determined, the significance of kappa can be determined through a z-statistic:

$$z = \frac{\kappa}{\sqrt{var\,(\kappa)}} \qquad \text{(8-38)}$$

which in this case equals $0.380 / \sqrt{0.003} = 6.952$—which is significant. In turn, the confidence interval about kappa is just 1.96 times the square root of the variance, or ± 0.107.

A problem with (and possible solution to) kappa. In Table 8-18, both observers were saying that roughly the same proportion of kids were destined to wear those bizarre and outlandish clothes (42% for Observer 1, 40% for Observer 2). We encounter a problem with kappa when the proportions between raters or between a rater and a measurement scale differ considerably. For example, let's say that Observer 1 believed that most kids could be redeemed and that only 10% of the most serious cases were prison-bound; while Observer 2 is a tough-nosed SOB, who foresees redemption in only 50%. We could conceivably end up with the situation shown in Table 8-19, where they both evaluate 100 cases. Cell a can't have more than 10 people in it, nor can cell d have more than 50 because of the marginal totals.

TABLE 8-19   When the observers have very different assignment probabilities

Observer 2 Bars-bound?	Observer 1 Bars-bound?		Totals
	YLC	Other	
Yes	10	40	50
No	0	50	50
Totals	10	90	100

The raw agreement is 0.60, and kappa is a paltry 0.20. But let's look at this table another way. Of all the cases who Observer 1 said were destined for the big house, Observer 2 agreed; and similarly, of all the people Observer 2 said were bound for jail, Observer 1 agreed. So, that kappa of 0.20 seems like a gross underestimate of how much they come to the same conclusion. For this reason, Loeber and Dishion

(1983) introduced a variant of kappa called **Relative Improvement Over Chance** (RIOC) that compensates for the difference in base rate between the two observers (or an observer and a measurement tool). The simplified equation (Copas and Loeber, 1990) is:

$$\textbf{RIOC} = \frac{Na - [(a + c)\,(a + b)]}{N \min\,[(a + c)\,(a + b)] - [(a + c)\,(a + b)]}$$

$$\text{(8-39)}$$

where min means the smaller value of $(a + c)$ or $(a + b)$. So, in this case, it becomes 1.00, indicating that there is as much agreement as the differences in the marginal totals allow.

Things are rarely this extreme, but even so, that's quite a difference—0.20 versus 1.00. So, which is right? The former is too conservative when the marginal totals are unequal, and the latter too liberal by not "penalizing" the observers for being so discrepant regarding their base rates. So, we'd be tempted to report both and let the readers see the table.

Generalization to multiple levels and dimensions. Kappa, unlike phi, can be generalized to more complex situations. The first is multiple levels; for example, we might have decided to get the counselors to identify what kind of difficulty the kids would end up in violent crimes, "white collar" crimes, drugs, and so on. Kappa can be used; it is just a matter of working out the expected agreement by totaling all the cells on the diagonal, then the expected agreement by totaling all the expected values, obtained by multiplying out the marginals. The ratio is then calculated according to the above formula.

Kappa can also be used for multiple observers, which amounts to building a $2 \times 2 \times 2$ table for three observers, a $2 \times 2 \times 2 \times 2$ table for four observers, and so on. You can still work out the observed and expected frequencies on the diagonal (only this time in three-dimensional or four-dimensional space) and calculate the coefficient. Beware, though, that this is now a measure of *complete* agreement among three, four, or more observers and ignores agreement among a majority or minority of observers.

Finally, kappa can be used for ordinal data, without resorting to ranking. For this, we go to the next section.

PARTIAL AGREEMENT AND WEIGHTED KAPPA

Let's continue to unfold the original question. In the first analysis, we found a relatively low and non-significant relationship between the prediction and the eventual status. In the next analysis, we explored the agreement on observer rating of criminal tendencies, which was only moderate. One way we might improve agreement is by expanding the categories to account for the degree of criminal tendency. Criminality, like most biomedical variables (blood pressure, height, obesity, rheumatoid joint count, serum creatinine, extent of cancer), is really on an underlying continuum. Shoving it all into two categories throws away information. We should contemplate at least four categories of prediction, for example "Saintly," "Slightly Crooked," "Street Thug," and "Serial Killer." If we again employ two observers, using the same design, the data would take the form of Table 8-20.

The first thing to note is that the overall agreement, on the diagonal, is now 44 ÷ 170, or 26%, which is pretty awful. If we went ahead and calculated a kappa on these data, using the previous formula, it would be less than zero. But there is actually a lot of "near agreement" in the table; 103 additional observations (8 + 14 + 27 + 5 + 29 + 20) agree within one category; combining these would yield an agreement of (44 + 103) ÷ 170 = 0.865, which is much better. The challenge is to figure out some way to put all these instances of *partial* agreement together into some overall measure of agreement.

Cohen (1968) dealt this problem a body blow with the idea of a **weighted kappa**, whereby the cells are assigned a weight related to the degree of dis-agreement. Full agreement, the cells on the diagonal, are weighted zero. (This does not mean that these very important cells are ignored. Stay tuned). The weights on the off-diagonal cells are then varied according to the degree of disagreement. The weights can be arbitrary and assigned by the user. For example, we might decide that a disagreement between Slightly Crooked and Street Thug is of little consequence, so this disagreement gets weighted 1; a difference between Saintly and Slightly Crooked gets a weight of 2; and a difference between Serial Killer and Street Thug is as severe as any of the greater disagreements (e.g., Serial Killer and Saintly) and all get weighted 4. We might do that—but we had better marshal up some pretty compelling reason why we chose these particular weights because the resulting kappa coefficient will not be comparable with any other coefficients generated by a different set of weights. (There is one exception. If the sole reason is to do comparisons *within* a study—for example, to show the effects of training on agreement—this is acceptable.)

The alternative is to use a standard weighting scheme, of which there are two: Cicchetti weights, which apparently are used only by Cicchetti (1972); and **quadratic weights**, which are used by everybody. For obvious reasons, we focus our attention on the latter. Actually the scheme is easy—the weight is simply equal to the square of the amount of disagreement. So, cells on the diagonal are weighted 0; one level of disagreement (e.g., Serial Killer vs Street Thug) gets a weight of $1^2 = 1$; two levels of disagreement (e.g., Serial Killer vs Somewhat Crooked) gets weighted $2^2 = 4$, and so on up.

To see how this all works, we begin with the formula for kappa, in Equation (8-36), and then sub-

TABLE 8-20   Inter-rater agreement on criminal status

Observer 1	Observer 2				
	Saintly	Slightly crooked	Street thug	Serial killer	totals
Saintly	1	5	8	1	15
Slightly crooked	8	10	29	5	52
Street thug	4	14	21	20	59
Serial killer	1	4	27	12	44
TOTALS	14	33	85	38	170

stitute $q = (1-p)$ for everything. In other words, the formula is rewritten in terms of *disagreement* instead of agreement. The revised formula is now:

$$\kappa = \frac{q_e - q_o}{q_e} = 1 - \frac{q_o}{q_e} \qquad (8\text{-}40)$$

It is now a matter of incorporating the various weighting schemes into the q's. No problem—just sum up the weighted disagreements, both observed and expected (by taking the product of the related marginals divided by the total), over all the cells (i,j), which are off the diagonal: where w_{ij} are the weights for the cells. These are then popped back into the original equation, and that gives us weighted kappa.

$$q_o = \sum w_{ij} \times p_{o_{ij}} \qquad (8\text{-}41)$$

$$q_e = \sum w_{ij} \times p_{e_{ij}} \qquad (8\text{-}42)$$

To demonstrate how this all works, let's calculate the example in Table 8-20. In Table 8-21, we have worked out the expected frequencies by taking the product of the marginals and dividing by the total. (Note that we did this calculation only for the off-diagonal cells. Why make work for ourselves when we don't use the data in the diagonal cells?) In Table 8-22, we have shown what the quadratic weights for each cell look like.

TABLE 8-21   Expected frequencies for rater agreement

Observer 1	Observer 2			
	Saintly	Slightly crooked	Street thug	Serial killer
Saintly	—	2.91	7.50	3.35
Slightly crooked	4.28	—	26.00	11.62
Street thug	4.85	11.45	—	13.19
Serial killer	3.62	8.54	22.00	—

TABLE 8-22   Quadratic weights for rater agreement

Observer 1	Observer 2			
	Saintly	Slightly crooked	Street thug	Serial killer
Saintly	—	1	4	9
Slightly crooked	1	—	1	4
Street thug	4	1	—	1
Serial killer	9	4	1	—

Now we can put it all together. Keep in mind that the tables show the *frequencies* and we need the *proportions*, so we will have an extra "170" kicking around in the summations. Now the **observed weighted disagreement** is:

$$q_o = 1 \times \frac{5}{170} + 4 \times \frac{8}{170} + 9 \times \frac{1}{170} + 1 \times \frac{8}{170} +$$
$$1 \times \frac{29}{170} + \ldots + 1 \times \frac{27}{170}$$
$$= 1.206$$

and the **expected weighted disagreement** is:

$$q_e = 1 \times \frac{2.91}{170} + 4 \times \frac{6.61}{170} + 9 \times \frac{4.23}{170} +$$
$$1 \times \frac{4.28}{170} \ldots + 1 \times \frac{19.41}{170}$$
$$= 1.604$$

So the weighted kappa in this case is: $\kappa = 1 - \dfrac{q_o}{q_e} =$

$$1 - \frac{1.206}{1.604} = 0.248$$

Although this is not terribly impressive, it is an improvement over the unweighted kappa for these data, which would equal -0.018. The general conclusion is that the weighted kappa, which takes partial agreement into account, is usually larger than the unweighted kappa.

RELATION BETWEEN KAPPA AND THE IN-TRACLASS CORRELATION

One reason Cicchetti was fighting a losing battle is that the weighted kappa using quadratic weights has a very general property—it is mathematically (i.e., exactly) equal to the ICC correlation. We know that the ICC evaluates correlation between all the observations within the same variable or class. The ICC is useful only for interval-level data, and kappa is based on frequencies and nominal or ordinal data.

But just suppose we didn't tell the computer that. We call *Saintly* a 4, *Slightly* a 3, *Street* a 2, and *Serial* a 1. We then have a whole bunch of pairs of data, so the top left cell gives us one (4,4) and the bottom right cell gives us a total of 12 (1,1)s. There are, of course, 170 points in all. We then do a repeated-measures ANOVA (way out of this book's range, please refer to more sophisticated statistical textbook) where Observer is the within-subject factor with two levels. We calculate an ICC. The result is *identical* to weighted kappa. It also follows that, if we were to analyze a 2 × 2 table with ANOVA, using numbers equal to 0 and 1, unweighted kappa would equal this ICC when calculated like we did above (Cohen, 1968).

Who cares? Well, this eases interpretation. Kappa can be looked on as just another correlation, explaining some percentage of the variance. And there is another real advantage. If we have multiple observers, we can do an intraclass correlation and report it as an average kappa instead of doing a bunch of kappas for observer 1 vs observer 2, observer 1 vs 3, etc.

SAMPLE SIZE ESTIMATION

As we found in earlier situations, sample size procedures are worked out for the simpler cases such as those with two proportions, but not for any of the more advanced situations. The method for two proportions is a direct extension of the basic strategy introduced in Chapter 5. Imagine a standard RCT where the proportion of deaths in the treatment group is π_T and in the control group is π_C. (With a few sad exceptions, π_T is less than π_C.)

We consider two normal curves, one corresponding to the null hypothesis that the two proportions are the same ($\pi_T - \pi_C = 0$), and the second corresponding to the alternative hypothesis that the proportions are different ($\pi_C - \pi_T = \delta$). We're almost set. However, we first have to figure out the SD of the two normal curves. You may recall that the SD of a proportion is related to the proportion itself. In this case, the SD of the proportion π is equal to:

$$SD(\pi) = \sqrt{\frac{\pi(1-\pi)}{n}} \qquad (8\text{-}43)$$

and the variance is just the square of this quantity. Now the two bell curves are actually derived from a *difference* between two proportions, so the variances of the two proportions are added. For the H_1 curve on the right, then, the SD is:

$$SD(\delta) = \sqrt{\frac{\pi_T(1-\pi_T) + \pi_C(1-\pi_C)}{n}} \qquad (8\text{-}44)$$

Finally, the H_0 curve is a little simpler because the two proportions are the same, just equal to the average of π_T and π_C.

$$SD(O) = \sqrt{2\frac{\pi(1-\pi)}{n}} \qquad (8\text{-}45)$$

The whole lot looks like Figure 8-3, which, of course, bears an uncanny resemblance to the equivalent figure in Chapter 5 (Figure 5-6). We can then do as we did in Chapter 5, and solve for the critical value. The resulting sample size equation looks a little horrible:

$$n = \left[\frac{Z_\alpha\sqrt{2\pi(1-\pi)} + Z_\beta\sqrt{\pi_T(1-\pi_T) + \pi_C(1-\pi_C)}}{(\pi_T - \pi_C)}\right]^2 \qquad (8\text{-}46)$$

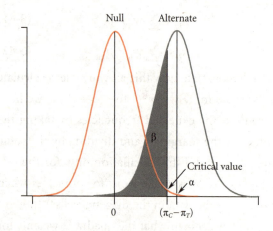

FIGURE 8-3 Visualizing the sample size calculation for two independent proportions.

What a miserable mess this is! Now the good news. If you would like to forget the whole thing, that's fine with us because we have furnished tables (Appendix Table K) that have performed all this awful calculation for you. These tables are based on a slightly different, and even more complicated, formula, so they will not yield exactly the same result.

For the situation where you wish to test the significance of a single proportion, the formula is a bit simpler. One good example of this is the paired design of the McNemar chi-squared, where the null hypothesis is that the proportion of pairs in each off-diagonal cell is 0.5. In this case, the SDs are a bit simpler, and the formula looks like:

$$n = \left[\frac{Z_\alpha\sqrt{\pi_1(1-\pi_1)} + Z_\beta\sqrt{\pi_0(1-\pi_0)}}{(\pi_1 - \pi_0)}\right]^2 \qquad (8\text{-}47)$$

where π_1 is the proportion under the alternative hypothesis, and π_0 is the proportion under the null hypothesis (in this case, 0.5). Unfortunately, there is no table for this, so get out the old calculator.

To show you how it's done, we refer to an ad we recently saw on TV where it was loudly proclaimed that, "In a recent survey, 57% of consumers preferred Brand *X* to the leading competitor." Pause a moment, and warm up the old C.R.A.P. Detectors. This means that 43% preferred the competitor, and the split is not far from 50–50. They also don't say how many times they did the "study" or how many people were involved. More particularly, we might ask the essential statistical question, "How large a sample would they need to ensure that the 57–43 split did not arise by chance alone?"

Looking at the formula above π_1 is 0.57, and π_0 is 0.50, so the equation looks like (assuming $\alpha = 0.05$ and $\beta = 0.10$):

$$n = \left[\frac{1.96\sqrt{0.57(1-0.57)} + 1.28\sqrt{0.50(1-0.50)}}{(0.57 - 0.50)} \right]^2$$

$$= 410$$

(8-48)

Any bets how many consumers they really used?

Sample size calculations for phi, kappa, and weighted kappa are surprisingly straightforward. To test the significance of a phi coefficient (i.e., to determine whether phi is different from zero), we simply use the sample size formula for the equivalent chi-squared because both are based on the same 2×2 table.

For kappa, you must first consider a bit of philosophical decision making. If the point of the study is to determine whether kappa is significantly different from zero, we can use the formula in Equation (8-49) to derive an SE for kappa and then insert this into the usual formula for sample size:

$$N = \left[\frac{(z_\alpha + z_\beta)\,\mathrm{SE}(\kappa)}{\kappa_{est}} \right]^2$$

(8-49)

where κ_{est} is the estimated value of kappa. However, this philosophical stance presumes that a kappa of zero is a plausible outcome. If you are looking at observer agreement, an agreement of zero is hopefully highly implausible (although it happens only

too often). In this case, you are really hoping that your estimate of the agreement is somewhere near the true agreement. In short, you want to establish a *confidence interval* around your estimated kappa. The formula for the SE of kappa [Equation (8-49) again] is a likely starting point, and it is necessary only to decide what is a reasonable confidence interval, δ (say, 0.1 on either side of the estimate, or 0.2), then solve for N. Of course, the fact that you have to guess at the likely value for both p_o and p_e in these equations gives you lots of freedom to come up with just about any sample size you want. The formula is now:

$$N = \frac{z_\alpha^2}{\delta^2}\, \frac{p_o(1 - p_o)}{(1 - p_e)^2}$$

(8-50)

The sample size for weighted kappa would require too many guesses, so a rule of thumb is invoked: the minimum number of objects being rated should be more than $2c^2$, where c is the number of categories (Soeken and Prescott, 1986; Cicchetti, 1981). So in our example, with four categories, we should have $2 \times 4^2 = 32$ objects.

SUMMARY

✧ We have considered several statistical tests to be used on frequencies in categories. The ubiquitous chi-squared deals with the case of two factors (one independent, one dependent) only, as long as no frequencies are too small. In the case of low frequencies, you use the Fisher exact test. For 2×2 tables with paired or matched designs, the McNemar chi-squared is appropriate. Finally, we considered the MH chi-squared for three factor designs, and log-linear analysis for still more complex designs.

✧ This chapter has reviewed three popular coefficients to express agreement among categorical variables. The phi coefficient is a measure of association directly related to the chi-squared significance test. Kappa is a measure of agreement particularly suited to 2×2

tables; it measures agreement beyond chance. Weighted kappa is a generalization of kappa for multiple categories, used in situations where partial agreement can be considered. Unless there are compelling reasons, weighted kappa should use a standard weighting scheme. When quadratic weights are used, weighted kappa is identical to the intraclass correlation.

GLOSSARY

Chi-squared distribution χ^2 分布

test of goodness of fit 拟合优度检验

Chi-Squared test χ^2 检验

non-parametric test 非参数检验

non-parametric statistics 非参数统计

2×2 contingency table 2×2 列联表

deconstructing chi-squared χ^2 分割

Yates' correction for continuity Yates 连续性校正

Fisher's exact test Fisher 确切概率法

Mcnemar chi-squared Mcnemar χ^2 检验

Mantel-Haenszel chi-squared Mantel-Haenszel χ^2 检验

test for linear trend 线性趋势检验

log-linear analysis 对数线性分析

standard error of a proportion 率的标准误

sign test 符号检验

sample size estimation 样本量估计

the Phi coefficient Phi 系数

contingency coefficient 列联系数

Yule's Q Yule's Q 值

Cramer's v Cramer's V 值

cohen's kappa cohen's kappa 系数

standard error of kappa kappa 系数的标准误

partial agreement 部分一致性

weighted kappa 加权 kappa 系数

observed weighted disagreement 实际加权不一致率

intraclass correlation 组内相关性

sample size 样本量

EXERCISES

1. In a small randomized double-blind trial of attar of eggplant for acne, the ZR (medical talk for "zit rate") in the treated group was half that of the control group. However, a chi-squared test of independent proportions showed that the difference was not significant. We can conclude that:

   a. The treatment is useless

   b. The reduction in ZR is so large that we should start using the treatment immediately

   c. We should keep adding cases to the trial until the test becomes significant

   d. We should do a new trial with more subjects

   e. We should use a t-test instead of the chi-squared

2. The data below are from a study of previous failure in school, academic or behavioral problems, and dropout.

Previous failure		Dropout	
	Problems	Yes	No
Yes	Yes	32	45
	No	18	99
No	Yes	75	181
	No	84	832

How would you analyze it?

3. A case-control study was performed to examine the potential effect of marijuana as a risk factor for brain cancer. A total of 75 patients with brain cancer were matched to 75 controls. All subjects were questioned about previous marijuana use.

Case	Control	
	Yes	No
Yes	(A)	(B)
No	(C)	(D)

Of the cases, 50 said they had used marijuana, and 35 of their matched controls reported marijuana use. No use of marijuana was reported by 25 cases and 20 controls.

If the data were analyzed with a McNemar chi-squared, what would be the observed frequency in the upper right corner (cell B) in the table below?

4. Is it really true that "If you don't wear your long underwear, you'll catch your death of cold, dearie!"? We know colds are caused by viruses, but surely all those grannies all those years couldn't have all been wrong.

5. Let's put it to the test. One cold, wintry week in February, half the kids in the student residence have their longjohns confiscated for science. After a week, the number of colds looks like this:

Longjohns	Control		
	Yes	**No**	
Yes	1	19	20
No	5	15	20
	6	34	40

Analyze the data with:

a. Chi-squared
b. Yates' corrected chi-squared
c. Fisher exact test

6. Consider a study of inter-rater agreement on the likelihood that psychiatric patients have von Richthofen's disease (VRD, characterized by the propensity to take off one's shirt in the bright sunlight—the "Red Barin' Sign"). Two psychiatrists indicate whether or not patients have VRD, rated as Present or Absent.

Suppose we now did a second study where they did the same rating, only this time on a four-point scale, from "Definitely Present" to "Definitely Absent." What would happen to the following quantities?

	SMALLER	SAME	LARGER	UNDEFINED
a. Raw agreement	___	___	___	
b. Unweighted kappa	___	___	___	___
c. Weighted kappa	___	___	___	___
d. Phi coefficient	___	___	___	___

7. The following 2 × 2 table displays agreement between two observers on the presence or absence of the dreaded "Red Barin' Sign" (see above for explanation):

		Observer 1		
		Present	**Absent**	
Observer 2	Present	87	23	110
	Absent	63	227	290
		150	250	400

Calculate

a. Phi
b. Contingency coefficient
c. Cramer's V
d. Cohen's kappa

CHAPTER THE NINTH

Tests of Significance for Ranked Data

SETTING THE SCENE

You heard that clam juice works wonders for psoriasis. Going one better, you arrange a randomized trial of Bloody Caesars (reasoning that the booze will ease the physical and psychic pain while the clam juice works its miracles). At the end, a bunch of dermatologists examine photographs of the patients and put them in rank order from best to worst. How, Dr. Skinflint, will you analyze this lot?

Dr. Skinflint, a locally renowned dermatologist, recalls reading somewhere that clam juice works wonders for the misery of psoriasis. He speculates that a combination of clam juice and ethyl alcohol might ease the symptoms while reducing the lesions. So he arranges a randomized trial of Bloody Caesars (BC) against Virgin Marys (VM). At the conclusion of the trial, he photographs all the patients and places the pictures together in random order, then he distributes the set of photos to a group of dermatologists, who are asked to simply rank the pictures from best to worst. The idea then is to examine the ranks of the patients in the BC group against the patients in the VM group.

A comment on the rank ordering. We know a couple of possible alternative approaches to measurement. The photographs could be placed on an interval scale by, for example, measuring the extent of body surface involvement. However, this might not adequately capture other aspects, such as the severity of involvement. Moreover, this could lead to a badly skewed distribution: many patients with only a small percentage of body surface area involved, and a few patients in which nearly all the skin is involved can bias parametric tests. Alternatively, some objective staging criteria, such as is used for cancer, might be devised, but this would simply lead to another ordinal scale, which must be analyzed by ranking individual subjects. Similarly, rating individuals on 7-point scales would be regarded by some (but

not us) as ordinal level measurement, thus requiring non-parametric statistics. For all these reasons, proceeding directly to a subjective ranking may well represent a viable approach to measurement.

The question is now how to analyze the ranks, which are clearly ordinal level measurement. We cannot use statistics that employ means, SD, and the like. To clarify the situation, if 20 patients were in the trial, the ranks would extend from 1 (the best outcome) to 20 (the worst). If the treatment were successful, we would expect that, on the average, patients in the BC group would have higher ranks (lower numbers) than those in the VM group. Suppose Table 9-1 shows the data. It is evident that treatment has some effect. If no effect occurred, the BCs and the VMs would be interspersed, and the average rank of

TABLE 9-1   Ranks of 20 psoriasis patients treated with BC and VM

Rank	Treatment	Rank	Treatment
1	BC	11	BC
2	BC	12	VM
3	BC	13	VM
4	BC	14	BC
5	VM	15	BC
6	BC	16	VM
7	VM	17	BC
8	BC	18	VM
9	VM	19	VM
10	VM	20	VM

BC = Bloody Caesars; VM = Virgin Marys.

the BCs and the VMs would be the same. This does not seem to be happening; the BCs appear to be systematically higher in the table than do the VMs. The question is how one puts a p value on all this.

ONE SAMPLE

The Wilcoxon signed-ranks test is a nonparametric procedure employed in a hypothesis testing situation involving a single sample in order to determine whether a sample is derived from a population with a median of θ. If the Wilcoxon signed-ranks test yields a significant result, the researcher can conclude there is a high likelihood the sample is derived from a population with a median value other than θ.

A physician states that the median number of times he sees each of his patients during the year is five. In order to evaluate the validity of this statement, he randomly selects ten of his patients and determines the number of office visits each of them made during the past year. He obtains the following values for the ten patients in his sample: 9, 10, 8, 4, 8, 3, 0, 10, 15, 9. Do the data support his contention that the median number of times he sees a patient is five?

The data are summarized in Table 9-2. In Column 3, The d_i score is referred to as a difference score between a subject's score and the hypothesized value of the population median, $\theta=5$. Column 4 contains the ranks of the difference scores. In ranking the difference scores for the Wilcoxon signed-ranks test, the following guidelines are employed: (1) The absolute values of the difference scores (d_i) are ranked. It should be emphasized that in the test it is essential that a rank of 1 be assigned to the difference score with the lowest absolute value, and that the highest rank be assigned to the difference score with the highest absolute value. (2) Any difference score that equals zero is not ranked. (3) When there are tied scores present, the average of the ranks involved is assigned to all difference scores tied for a given rank. (4) After ranking the absolute values of the difference scores, the sign of each difference score is placed in front of its rank, and then the sum of the ranks that have a positive sign and the sum of the ranks that have a negative sign are calculated, respectively.

TABLE 9-2   The times a physician sees each of his patients

Subject	X_i	$d_i = X_i - \theta$	Rank of $|d_i|$	Signed rank of $|d_i|$
1	9	4	5.5	5.5
2	10	5	8	8
3	8	3	3.5	3.5
4	4	−1	1	−1
5	8	3	3.5	3.5
6	3	−2	2	−2
7	0	−5	8	−8
8	10	5	8	8
9	15	10	10	10
10	9	4	5.5	5.5

$$\sum R+ = 44$$

$$\sum R- = 11$$

The absolute value of the smaller of the two values $\sum R+$ versus $\sum R-$ is designated as the Wilcoxon t-test statistic. The T value is interpreted by employing Table of Critical T Values for Wilcoxon's Signed-Ranks and Matched-Pairs Signed-Ranks Tests. In order to be significant, the obtained value of T must be equal to or less than the tabled critical T value at the prespecified level of significance. Therefore, $P=0.091>0.05$.

A summary of the analysis follows: With respect to the median number of times the doctor sees a patient, we can conclude that the data do not reject that the sample of 10 subjects comes from a population with a median value of 5.

TWO INDEPENDENT GROUPS

For this simple case with two groups, the **Mann-Whitney U test** will be used, which is also called the **Wilcoxon Rank Sum** test. The test focuses on the sum of the ranks for the two groups separately, which explains **Rank Sum**, but not U. Anyway, as you see in Table 9-3, the calculation is the essence of simplicity. The summed rank for the BC group is 81 and for the VM group, 129. [Actually we didn't have to calculate the second one for two reasons: (1) the sum of all ranks is $N(N+1) \div 2 = 210$, so we can get it by subtraction, and (2) we don't need it anyway.] The

TABLE 9-3   Ranks of 20 psoriasis patients treated with BC and VM

Rank	Treatment	Rank of BC group	Rank of VM group
1	BC	1	
2	BC	2	
3	BC	3	
4	BC	4	
5	VM		5
6	BC	6	
7	VM		7
8	BC	8	
9	VM		9
10	VM		10
11	BC	11	
12	VM		12
13	VM		13
14	BC	14	
15	BC	15	
16	VM		16
17	BC	17	
18	VM		18
19	VM		19
20	VM		20
	SUMMED RANK	81	129

BC = Bloody Caesars; VM = Virgin Marys.

larger the difference between the two sums, the more likely the difference is real. The next step is easier still—you turn to the back of the book (as long as the sample size per group is less than 10) and look up 81. You find that the probability of a rank sum (W or U, depending on where your allegiance lies) as *low* as 81 is 0.0376 (using a one-tailed test).

What do you do if there are more than 10 per group? Believe it or not, parametric statistics rear their heads yet again. It turns out that the normal distribution and z-test can be used as an approximation. If the total sample size is N and m are in the higher ranked group, then the expected value of the rank sum is $m(N + 1) \div 2$, or 105. So, we can construct a z-test with a numerator of the observed rank sum minus the expected rank sum. The question is the form of the denominator, the SE of the difference. This turns out, after much boring algebra, to equal $\sqrt{mn(N+1)/12}$, where m and n are the two group sizes, with $m + n = N$. The z-test (with a continuity correction) then equals:

$$z = \frac{|U - m(N+1)/2| - 0.5}{\sqrt{mn(N+1)/12}} \quad (9\text{-}1)$$

which is this case is:

$$z = \frac{|81 - (10)(21)/2| - 0.5}{\sqrt{(10)(10)(21)/(12)}} = \frac{23.5}{\sqrt{175}}$$

$$= \frac{31}{13.23} = 1.776 \quad (9\text{-}2)$$

Looking this value up in Table A (in the Appendix) of the normal distribution, we find that a z of 1.776 results in a one-tail probability of .0379, very close to the tabulated value up above. As is frequently the case, nonparametric tests are devised because of a concern for bias in the parametric tests. However, except for some limiting cases, the parametric test turns out to be quite a precise approximation.

MORE THAN TWO GROUPS

Following our usual progression, we can next consider the extension to three groups—the equivalent of one-way ANOVA. The strategy is a lot like the Wilcoxon (Mann-Whitney) test. However, instead of examining the total rank in each group, we calculate the average rank. And instead of doing a t-test on the ranks, we do a one-way ANOVA on the ranks. Once again, terms such as $N(N + 1)$ and factors of 12 start kicking around, simply because of the use of ranks.

The test is the **Kruskal-Wallis One-Way ANOVA**. To illustrate, suppose we throw an intermediate group into our original design. They are fed just clamato juice, what might be called a Virgin Caesar (VC), to see whether the vodka is having any real beneficial effect on the skin of the BC group as opposed to that group's souls. We now have 30 patients, and in Table 9-4 we have shown the ranks of the patients in each group. It is clear that these contrived data are working according to plan: the BC group has a mean rank of 10.1; the VC group, a mean rank of 15.6; and the VM group a rank of 20.8. If no difference existed, we would have expected that the average rank of each group would be about halfway, or 15. [Actually, it's $(N + 1) \div 2 = 15.5$, because the ranks start counting at 1.]. But is it significant?

To address the question (cued by the title of the test), obviously, the first thing to do is to calculate a

TABLE 9-4   Ranks of patients in the BC, VC, and VM trial

Bloody Caesar	Virgin Caesar	Virgin Mary
1	4	8
2	7	12
3	9	15
5	11	16
6	14	21
10	17	22
13	20	27
18	23	28
19	25	29
24	26	30
SUM 101	156	208
MEAN 10.1	15.6	20.8

mean square (between groups), exactly as we have been doing since Chapter 7. This looks like:

$$MS_{bet} = \sum n_j (\bar{R}_j - \bar{R}_.)^2 = \sum n_j \left(\bar{R}_j - \frac{N+1}{2} \right)^2 \quad (9\text{-}3)$$

Where n_j is the sample size in each group; $\bar{R}_j$ the group mean; and $\bar{R}_.$ the overall mean. So, in this case it equals:

$$MS_{bet} = 10(10.1 - 15.5)^2 + 10(15.6 - 15.5)^2 + 10(20.8 - 15.5)^2 = 572.6 \quad (9\text{-}4)$$

In the normal course of events, we would now have to work out a mean square (within), but because of the use of ranks again, this takes a particularly simple form: $N(N + 1)/12$. Writing the equation slightly differently to show what it looks like using the sums rather than the means of the ranks for each group, the final ratio (**the Kruskal-Wallis, or K-W test**) looks like:

$$K\text{-}W = \frac{12}{N(N+1)} \sum \frac{R_j^2}{n_j} - 3(N+1) \quad (9\text{-}5)$$

So what we end up with is:

$$K\text{-}W = \frac{12}{(30)(31)} \times \left(\frac{101^2}{10} + \frac{156^2}{10} + \frac{208^2}{10} \right) - 3(30+1) = 7.388 \quad (9\text{-}6)$$

Strictly speaking, this value should be divided by yet another equation that corrects for the effects of ties; in essence, making K-W a bit larger and hence more significant. But we're not going to show it to

you for two reasons: first, because the computer does it quite well, thank you; and second, unless there are more than about 25% of the numbers that are tied, the effect of the corrections is negligible.

For small samples, the K-W test statistic has to be retrieved from the back of someone else's book. However, if more than five subjects are in each group, then it looks like a chi-squared distribution with $(k - 1)$ df, where k is the number of groups. Because you shouldn't have fewer than five subjects per group anyway, you don't need the special table.

Multiple Comparisons

When we discussed the one-way ANOVA, we listed a large number of post-hoc analyses that are used when we find a significant F-ratio. Fortunately, or not, there's only one such test for the Kruskal-Wallis. Any difference between mean ranks is significant if it's larger than:

$$z_{\alpha/k(k-1)} \times \sqrt{\frac{N(N+1)}{12} \left(\frac{1}{n_i} + \frac{1}{n_j} \right)} \quad (9\text{-}7)$$

Where k is the number of groups.

For the data in Table 9-4, since $k(k - 1) = 6$ and we're using the traditional α of 0.05, we look up a z value of $(0.05 / 6) = 0.0083$ in the table of the normal distribution and find it's about 2.39. So, we're looking at a critical value of:

$$2.39 \times \sqrt{\frac{30 \times 31}{12} \left(\frac{1}{10} + \frac{1}{10} \right)} = 9.41 \quad (9\text{-}8)$$

The only difference that's larger than this is between Bloody Caesar and Virgin Mary (20.8 − 10.1), so only it is statistically significant.

ORDERED MEDIANS: THE JONCKHEERE TEST

For our purposes, and for the tests to be significant, it doesn't matter if the ordering of the groups is A > B > C, or B > A = C, or any of the other possible combinations; as long as at least two groups differ significantly, we declare victory. But there are times when our theory lets us make more precise predictions, and we can use more powerful tests. If we believe that both clam juice and vodka have healing properties, then we'd predict that clam juice + vodka (BC) would be better than clam juice alone (VC), and that clam juice would be superior to a drink that has neither ingredient (VM). As long as our data are at least ordinal, we can use the **Jonckheere Test for Ordered Alternatives** (abbreviated as J) to test for this.

We begin by arranging the groups in the hypothesized order of their medians or mean ranks, from lowest to highest. It's important to keep in mind that the ordering must be based on our *a priori* hypothesis; it's intellectually dishonest to first look at the results, and then arrange the groups in order of their observed medians or mean ranks. Fortunately for the publisher, Table 9-4 is already in the predicted order, so he doesn't have to spend any more (of our) money printing the table again. The next step is simple, but tedious. For each entry, we count how many values in the succeeding groups are higher. So, for subject 1 in the BC group (Rank = 1), there are 10 higher values in the VC group and 10 in the VM group. For the last subject in that group (Rank = 24), there are 2 higher values in VC and 4 in VM. We do this for all people, and the results are presented in Table 9-5. There are three things to notice about the table. First, if we have k groups, then there will be $k \times (k - 1) / 2$ columns. Second, it's a lot easier to do this if the numbers in each column are in rank order; and finally, the bottom row is the sum of the values.

To compensate us for all the counting we had to do, the J test itself is the essence of simplicity; we just add up all the values of U:

$$J = \sum U_i \qquad (9\text{-}9)$$

which in this case is 224. But our luck doesn't last too long. To test the significance of J, we use a z-like test, so we have to figure out the mean and variance of J. The mean is:

$$\mu_J = \frac{N^2 - \sum n_i^2}{4} \qquad (9\text{-}10)$$

the variance is:

$$\sigma_J^2 = \frac{1}{72}[N^2(2N+3) - \sum n_i^2(2n_i+3)] \qquad (9\text{-}11)$$

and the test statistic is:

$$J^* = \frac{J - \mu_J}{\sigma_J} \qquad (9\text{-}12)$$

For these data,

$$\mu_J = \frac{30^2 - (10^2 + 10^2 + 10^2)}{4} = 150 \qquad (9\text{-}13)$$

and

$$\sigma_J^2 = \frac{1}{72}[30^2(2 \times 30 + 3) - 3(10^2 \times 23)]$$
$$= 691.67 \qquad (9\text{-}14)$$

so that

$$J^* = \frac{224 - 150}{\sqrt{691.67}} = 2.814 \qquad (9\text{-}15)$$

which we look up in a table of the distribution of the normal curve. Because the hypothesis is an ordered one, we use a one-tailed test, so that the critical value for $\alpha = 0.05$ is 1.645, rather than the more usual 1.960. Since J^* is larger than this (it actually corresponds to a p level of 0.0025), the test is significant.

REPEATED MEASURES: WILCOXON SIGNED RANK TEST AND FRIEDMAN TWO-WAY ANOVA

The final step in this walk through the ranked clones of the parametric tests is to consider the issue of matched or paired data.

Suppose some cowboy scientist, Gene Auful, was let loose in the university molecular biology lab and managed to create some clones of graduate students from samples of blood they unwittingly donated to the Red Cross. The little darlings were raised by foster parents, and in due course, 20 years later, the clones

TABLE 9-5 **The number of times a score from** Table 9-4 **is smaller than scores from succeeding groups**

BC<VC	BC<VM	VC<VM
10	10	10
10	10	10
10	10	9
9	10	9
9	10	8
7	9	6
6	8	6
4	6	4
4	6	4
2	4	4
U_1 71	U_2 83	U_3 70

end up as graduate students in the same labs (the experiment is working!). Recognizing that here are the makings of the ultimate nature-nurture experiment, one of the measures we put in place is a measure of achievement and likelihood of success, arrived at by getting the graduate faculty to sit around a table with all the files of both original and clone students and ranking them. One measure of successful clones would be that they, on the average, are ranked just as highly on ability to succeed. The data are in Table 9-6.

TABLE 9-6   Ranking of graduate students and their clones on success

Pair	Rank of original	Rank of clone	Signed difference	Signed ranked difference
A	1	3	+2	+3.5
B	8	2	−6	−10.0
C	6	14	+8	+12.0
D	9	10	+1	+1.5
E	5	12	+7	+11.0
F	20	17	−3	−6.0
G	7	26	+19	+15.0
H	4	13	+9	+13.0
I	11	15	+4	+8.0
J	22	27	+5	−9.0
K	25	23	−2	−3.5
L	24	21	−3	−6.0
M	16	19	+3	+6.0
N	18	30	+12	+14.0
O	29	28	−1	−1.5

There are 15 pairs, and we have listed the rank order of the original and the clone, ranging from 1 to 30, where (this time) 1 is best and 30 is worst. It seems that the clones are actually a bit inferior because their average rank appears higher than that of the originals. This is confirmed in the fourth column, which is the first step to the **Wilcoxon Signed Ranks test**, where we have calculated the difference of ranks for each pair. Next, we rank the differences in column five, so that the smallest differences have the first rank (ignoring the sign, but carrying it through). You will notice some funny-looking numbers in the right column. We have three 6s, two 2.5s, and two 1.5s, but no 5s, 7s, or 1s. The problem is caused by having three differences of 3, which should take up the ranks of fifth, sixth, and seventh; two differences of 2, which should be third and fourth; and two differences of 1, which should be first and second. Because we don't know which is which, to avoid any infighting, we give them all (or both) the average rank: 6, 3.5, or 1.5.

Finally, we sum the ranks of the positive and negative differences. The positive sum is (3.5 + 12 + 1.5 + 11 + 15 + … + 14) = 84, and the negative sum turns out to be 36; as before, they sum to $N(N+1) \div 2 = 120$.

Now, under the null hypothesis that no difference exists between original and clone, we would anticipate that the average rank of the originals and the clones would be about the same. If so, then the differences between rankings would all be small, and the sum of the rankings for both the positive and the negative differences would be small. If either of the summed differences is large, this indicates a substantial difference between the average original rank of the individuals in the matched pairs and so would lead to rejection of the null hypothesis.

Once again, we rush expectantly to the back of the book, only to be disappointed. However, in Siegel and Castellan (1988), a T of 84 (that's what the sum refers to) is not quite significant ($p = 0.094$). And once again, the table stops at a sample size of 15 matched pairs. For larger samples, there is (you guessed it) an approximate z-test, based on the fact that, once again, this statistic is approximately normally distributed, with a mean and SD based on the number of pairs, N. The formula is:

$$z = \frac{T - N(N+1)/4}{\sqrt{N(N+1)(2N+1)/24}} \qquad (9\text{-}16)$$

In the present case, z equals 1.842, and the associated p value is 0.066, not quite the same as the exact value calculated from the table, but close enough.

The extension of this test to three or more groups, the equivalent of repeated-measures ANOVA, is the **Friedman test**. We won't spell it out in detail because (1) it follows along a familiar path of summed ranks, and (2) the applications are rare. Briefly, it considers matched groups of three, four, or however many, each of which is assigned to a different treatment. It calculates the rank of each member of the trio or quartet. If one treatment is clearly superior, then that member of the group would be ranked first every time. If another treatment is awful, the member receiving that treatment would always come in last. And if the null hypothesis were true, all the ranks would be scrambled up. You then calculate the total of the ranks under each condition and plug the average ranks into a formula, again involving sum of squares and Ns. For a small sample, you look it up in a table; for a large sample, you approximate it with an F distribution. For more information, see Siegel and Castellan, yet again.

MEASURES OF ASSOCIATION FOR RANKED DATA

Measures of Association for Ranked Data frequently used is called The Spearman rank correlation coefficient, and is designated by ρ(RHO) or r_s. The calculations are made on the ranks of the observations, rather than, as with Pearson's correlation coefficient, r, on the observations themselves. r_s is interpreted in the same way as r. The Spearman rank correlation coefficient is obtained using the same formula for r in Chapter 11 (hold on for now, more to come in the next chapter!) but inserting the ranks rather than the measured values. However, because the difference between the adjacent ranks is always 1 this formula can be simplified to become

$$r_s = 1 - \frac{6\sum d_i^2}{n(n^2 - 1)} \tag{9-17}$$

where d_i is the difference between the rankings of the same item in each series. If two items in one or other of the series of measurements tie, that is, have the same rank, such as third equal, then the ranks are added and the sum divided by the number of items sharing the same rank.

Significance test of the Spearman correlation coefficient is a t-test,

$$t = \frac{r_s}{\sqrt{\frac{1.0 - r_s^3}{n - 2}}} \tag{9-18}$$

Seventeen patients with a history of congestive heart failure participated in a study to assess the effects of exercise on various bodily functions. During a period of exercise the following data were collected on the percent change in plasma norepinephrine (Y) and the percent change in oxygen consumption (X), shown in Table 9-7. On the basis of these data can one conclude that there is an association between two variables? Let $\alpha = 0.05$

$$r_s = 1 - \frac{6\sum d_i^2}{n(n^2 - 1)} = 0.697, \quad p = 0.02$$

On the analysis, we can make the conclusion that the two variables are positively related.

SAMPLE SIZE AND POWER

We did Medline, Statline, PsychInfo, and Edline searches, and we even called a few 1~900 numbers, but we were unable to come up with any formulas for sample size calculations on rank tests. What should we do if the granting agency demands them? Determine the sample size from the equivalent para-

TABLE 9-7 **The effects of exercise on various bodily functions**

Subject	X	Rank of X	Y	Rank of Y	d	Subject	X	Rank of X	Y	Rank of Y	d
1	500	17	525	17	0	10	50	1	60	1	0
2	475	16	130	7.5	8.5	11	175	7	105	6	1
3	390	15	325	15	0	12	130	5	148	9	-4
4	325	13.5	190	12	1.5	13	76	3	75	3	0
5	325	13.5	90	4	9.5	14	200	8.5	250	13	-4.5
6	205	11	295	14	-3	15	174	6	102	5	1
7	200	8.5	180	11	-2.5	16	201	10	151	10	0
8	75	2	74	2	0	17	125	4	130	7.5	-3.5
9	230	12	420	16	-4						

metric test, and leave it at that. For a long time, it was assumed that nonparametric tests were less powerful than parametric ones, so some people suggested adding a "fudge factor." More recent work, however, has shown that you don't lose any power with these tests and, when the data aren't normal, they may even be more powerful than their parametric equivalents.

SUMMARY

◈ In this chapter, we dealt with several ways to do statistical inference on ranks. We should remind you that, although the examples used rankings as a primary variable, in circumstances where the distributions are very skewed or the data are suspiciously non-interval, such as staging in cancer, the data can often be converted to ranks and analyzed with one of these nonparametric tests.

◈ Why not use ranking tests all the time and avoid all the assumptions of parametric statistics? The main reason is simply that the technology of rank tests is not as advanced (there really is no Streiner-Norman two-way ANOVA by ranks), so the rank tests are more limited in potential application. A second reason is that they tend to be a *little* bit conservative (i.e., when the equivalent parametric test says $p = 0.05$, the rank test says $p = 0.08$); however, they are not nearly as conservative as are tests for categories such as chi-squared when applied to interval-level data.

GLOSSARY

tests of significance for ranked data   等级资料的显著性差异检验

Wilcoxon rank sum test   Wilcoxon 秩和检验

Mann-Whitney U test   Mann-Whitney U 检验

Kruskal-Wallis one-way ANOVA   Kruskal-Wallis H 秩和检验

Wilcoxon signed ranks test   Wilcoxon 符号秩和检验

Friedman two-way ANOVA   Friedman 随机区组秩和检验

the Spearman rank correlation coefficient   Spearman 秩相关系数

the Jonckheere test   Jonckheere 检验

EXERCISES

1. A college English instructor reads in an educational journal that the median number of times a student is absent from a class that meets for fifty minutes three times a week during a 15-week semester is 5. During the fall semester she keeps a record of the number of times each of the 10 students in her writing class is absent. She obtains the following values: 9, 10, 8, 4, 8, 3, 0, 10, 15, 9. Do the data suggest that the class is representative of a population that has a median of 5?

2. Is it really true that "Gentlemen Prefer Blondes?" To test this hypothesis, we assemble 24 Playboy playmate centerfolds from back issues—8 blondes, 8 brunettes, and 8 redheads. To avoid bias from extraneous variables, we use only the top third of each picture. We locate some gentlemen (with great difficulty) and get them to rank order the ladies from highest to lowest preference. The data look like this:

Rank

Blondes	Brunettes	Redheads
1	4	5
2	7	6
3	9	13
8	10	16
11	15	20
12	18	21
14	19	23
17	22	24

Proceed to analyze it with the appropriate test.

3. In retaliation, the ladies decide to do their own pin-up analysis to address another age-old question related to the encounters between the sexes (oops—genders). Is it true that bald men are

sexier? To improve experimental control over the sloppy study done by the gents, they work out a way to control for all extraneous variables. They go to one of those clinics that claim to make chromedomes into full heads of hair and get a bunch of before-after pictures. They get some ladies to rank the snapshots from most to least sexy and then analyze the ranks of the boys with and without rugs. It looks like this:

Ranking

Subject	Bald	Rug
A	3	1
B	12	15
C	11	6
D	8	4
E	19	13
F	5	2
G	20	7
H	10	9
I	17	14
J	16	18

Go ahead and analyze this one too.

4. One last kick at the cat. The gentlemen, most of whom are predictably thinning, express displeasure at the results of the ladies' study, and assault it on methodological grounds (naturally). They claim that men who would go and buy rugs are not representative of all bald men. So the ladies proceed to repeat the study, only this time ripping out Playgirl centerfolds (top third again), and getting ranks. Now the data look like:

Bald	Hairy
5	1
6	2
8	3
9	4
12	7
14	10
15	11
18	13
19	16
20	17

Analyze appropriately.

5. In a study of the relationship between age and the EEG, data were collected on 20 subjects between ages 20 and 60 years, shown in the next table. The investigator wishes to know if it can be concluded that this particular EEG output is inversely correlated with age.

Age and EEG Output Value for 20 Subjects

Subjects	Age	EEG Output Value
1	20	98
2	21	75
3	22	95
4	24	100
5	27	99
6	30	65
7	31	64
8	33	70
9	35	85
10	38	74
11	40	68
12	42	66
13	44	71
14	46	62
15	48	69
16	51	54
17	53	63
18	55	52
19	58	67
20	60	55

How to Get the Computer to Do the Work for You
Independent Test for Ranked Data

- From **Analyze**, choose **Nonparametric Tests**
- Then select the appropriate option for the desired test *Mann-Whitney U (Wilcoxon Rank Sum Test)*
- **2 Independent Samples**
  Kruskal-Wallis one-way ANOVA
- **K Independent Samples**
  Wilcoxon Signed Rank Test
- **2 Related Samples**

Friedman Two-Way ANOVA

- **K Related Samples**

Jonkheere's Test

Association Analysis for Ranked Data

- From **Analyze,** choose **Correlate, and then** select **Bivariate Correlations,** last click **Spearman**
- **Forget it; you'll have to do it by hand.**

CHAPTER THE TENTH   Survival Analysis

Survival analysis is a technique used when the outcome of interest is the time it takes for some outcome to occur, such outcome may be the death, recurrence of a disease, or hospitalization. It can handle situations in which people enter the trial at different times and are followed for varying durations; it also allows us to compare two or more groups, and to examine the influence of different covariates.

SETTING THE SCENE

In some parts of the developed world, such as southern California and Vancouver, it is commonly believed that, if you eat only "natural" foods, exercise (under the direction of a personal trainer, of course), live in a home built according to the principles of FengShui, have a bottle of designer water permanently attached to your hand, and follow other precepts of the Yuppie life, you need never die. To test this supposition, people were randomly assigned to one of two conditions: Life As Usual (LAU) or an intervention consisting of Diet, Exercise, Anti-oxidant supplements, Tai-Chi, and Hydration (the DEATH condition). Because of the difficulty finding Yuppies who didn't follow this regimen to begin with, recruitment into the trial had to extend over a 3-year period. Participants were followed until the trial ended 10 years later. During this time, some of the participants died, others moved from La-La Land to rejoin the rest of humanity, and some were still alive when the study ended. How can the investigators maximize the use of the data they have collected?

WHEN WE USE SURVIVAL ANALYSIS

In most studies, people are recruited into the trial, where they either get or don't get the intervention that is destined to change the world. They are then followed for a fixed period of time, which could be as short as a couple of seconds (e.g., if we want to know if a new anesthetic agent works faster than the old one) or a few decades (e.g., to see if reduced dietary fat decreases the incidence of breast cancer). At the end of that time, we measure the person's status on whatever variable we're interested in. Sometimes, though, we are less interested in *how much* of something a person has at the end, and more concerned with *how long* it takes to reach some outcome. In our example, the outcome we're looking at is the length of time a person survives (hence the name of the statistical test), although the end point can be any binary state (whether a disease recurs or not, if a person is readmitted to hospital, and so on). Complicating the picture even more, many of these

trials enroll participants over an extended period of time in order to get a sufficient sample size. The Multiple Risk Factor Intervention Trial (MRFIT), for instance, involved nearly 13 000 men recruited over a 27-month period (MRFIT, 1977). Because of this *staggered entry*,[1] when the study finally ends (as all trials must, at some time), the subjects will have been followed for varying lengths of time, during which several outcomes could have occurred:

1. Some subjects will have reached the designated end point. In this example, it means that the person dies, much to his or her surprise. In other types of trials, such as chemotherapy for cancer, the end point may the reappearance of a malignancy.

2. Some subjects will have dropped out of sight: they moved without leaving a forwarding address; refused to participate in any more follow-up visits; or died of some cause unrelated to the study, such as being struck by lightning or a car.[2]

3. The study will have ended before all the subjects reach the end point. When the trial ends 10

---

[1]*This means that subjects are enrolled over a period of time. In a study of alcohol abuse, the phrase may have a secondary (and perhaps more accurate) definition.*

[2]*If they are killed by an enraged spouse after the discovery of an affair with the personal trainer, this criterion may not hold.*

years after its inception, some participants are still alive. They may die the next day or live for another 50 years, but we won't know, because the data collection period has ended.

Figure 10-1 shows how we can illustrate these different outcomes, indicating what happened to the first 10 subjects in the *DEATH* group. Subjects A, C, D, and F died at various times during the course of the trial; they're labelled *D* for Dead. Subjects B, G, and I were lost to follow-up, and therefore have the label *L*. The other subjects, E, H, and J (labelled *C*) were still alive at the time the trial ended. These last three data points are called "right censored."[3] Note that Figure 10-1 shows two different types of time: the X-axis shows *calendar* time, and each line shows *survival* time (Newman, 2001). To be more quantitative about the data, Table 10-1 shows how long each person was in the study and what the outcome was.

When we get around to finally analyzing the data, people who were lost and those who were censored will be lumped together into one category because, from the perspective of the statistician, they are the same. In both cases, we know they survived for some length of time and, after that, we have no idea. It

TABLE 10-1 Outcomes of the first 10 subjects

Subject	Length of time in trial (months)	Outcome
A	61	Died
B	111	Lost
C	29	Died
D	46	Died
E	92	Censored
F	22	Died
G	37	Lost
H	76	Censored
I	14	Lost
J	45	Censored

doesn't matter what name we call them, but to be consistent with most other books, we'll refer to them as lost.

SUMMARIZING THE DATA

So, how can we draw conclusions from these data regarding the survival time of people in the *DEATH* condition? What we need is a method of summarizing the results that uses most, if not all, of the data and isn't overly biased by the fact that some of the data are censored. Rather than giving you the right answer immediately, we'll approach it in stages. The

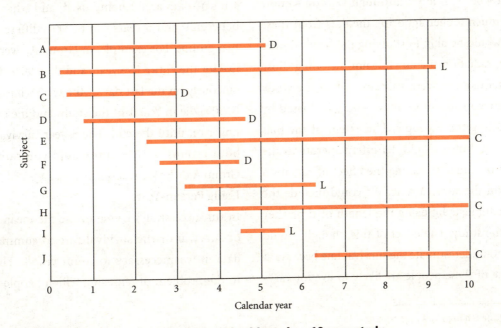

FIGURE 10-1 Entry and withdrawal of subjects in a 10-year study.

---

[3]*That means that the data toward the right of the graph were cut off because the study ended before the subjects reached the designated end point; it doesn't mean they were silenced by conservative moralists.*

first two ways of summarizing the data (**Mean Survival** and **Survival Rate**) are intuitively appealing but have some problems associated with them, which the third method (using Person-Years) neatly sidesteps.

Mean Survival

One tactic would be to look at only those subjects for whom we have complete data, in that we know exactly what happened to them. These subjects would be only those who died: subjects A, C, D, and F.

$$\text{Mean Survival} = \frac{\text{Time to Outcome}}{\substack{\text{Number of Subjects Who} \\ \text{Reached the Outcome}}} \quad \textbf{(10-1)}$$

Their **mean survival** was $(61 + 29 + 46 + 22)/4 = 39.5$ months after entering the trial.[4] The major problem with this approach is that we've thrown out 60% of the subjects. Even more seriously, we have no guarantee that the six people we eliminated are similar to the four whose data we analyzed; indeed, it is most likely they are *not* the same. Those who were lost to follow-up may be more transient, for either good or bad (they may be more upwardly mobile and were promoted to jobs in other parts of the country; or lazy bums who moved to avoid paying the rent), less compliant; or whatever. Those who were right censored were still alive, although we don't know for how much longer. Ignoring the data from these subjects would be akin to studying the survival rates following radiation therapy but not including those who benefited and were still alive when the study ended; any conclusion we drew would be biased by not including these people. The extent of the bias is unknown, but it would definitely operate in the direction of underestimating the effect of radiation therapy on the survival rate.[5] We could include the censored subjects by using the length of time they were in the study. The effect of this, though, would again be to underestimate the survival rate because at least some of these people are likely to live for varying lengths of time beyond the study period.

Survival Rate

Another way to summarize the data is to see what proportion of people are still alive. The major problem is "survived" *as of when*? The survival rate after one month would be pretty close to 100%; after 60 years, it would probably be 0%.[6] One way around this is to use a commonly designated follow-up time. Many cancer trials, for instance, look at survival after five years. Any subjects who are still around at five years would be called "survivors" for the 5-year **survival rate**, no matter what subsequently happened to them.

$$\text{Survival Rate} = \frac{\text{Number of Subjects Surviving at Time } (t)}{\text{Total Number of Subjects}}$$

$$\textbf{(10-2)}$$

This strategy reduces the impact of "the censored ones," although it doesn't eliminate it. Those subjects who were censored *after* five years don't bother us any more because their data have already been used to figure out the 5-year survival rate. Now the only people who give us any trouble are those who have been followed for less than 5 years when the study ended. However, the major disadvantage is still that a lot of data aren't being used, and what happens between 0 and 5 years can be very different for the two groups. For example, in Group A, everyone can live for the entire five years and then 90% die simultaneously on the last day of the trial; while in Group B, 90% die in Year 1 of the study, and the other 10% linger on until the end. The 5-year survival rate for both groups is 10%, but would you rather be in Group A or B? We rest our case.

Using Person-Years

In (unsuccessfully) trying to use the mean duration of survival or the survival rate to summarize the data, it was necessary to count *people*. This led us to the problem of choosing which people to count

---

[4] *Obviously, life is a high-risk proposition.*

[5] *We recently uncovered a Web page that contained this egregious error. They looked at 391 dead rock musicians, and discovered that they lived an average of only 39.6 years. Their conclusion was that the Lord was punishing them for messing around with drugs and loose women. They forgot to count the many thousands of rock stars who were still alive (including Keith Richards, who only looks dead).*

[6] *Despite the underlying assumption in the DEATH condition, the mortality rate is 100% if we wait long enough.*

or not count when the data were censored. Because we divide the length of survival or the number of survivors by whichever number we finally decide to include, this has been referred to as the "denominator problem."

A different approach is to use the *length of time* each person was in the study as the denominator, rather than to use individual people; that is, the total number of **person-years** of follow-up in the study. Actually, it doesn't have to be measured in years; we can use any time interval that best fits our data. If we were looking at how quickly a new serotonin reuptake inhibitor reduced depressive symptoms, for example, we could even talk in terms of person-*days*. The major advantage of this approach is that it uses data even from people who were lost for one reason or another. If we add up all the numbers in the middle column of Table 10-1, we would find a total of 503 person-months, during which time 4 people died. This means that the mortality in the *DEATH* group is $(4 \div 503) = 0.0080$ deaths per person-month. The major problem with this approach is the assumption that the risk of death is constant from one year to the next. We know that, in this case at least, it isn't. The risk of dying increases as we get older; in the *LAU* group, due to the aging of the body, and in the *DEATH* group, probably from drinking all that bottled water.[7]

SURVIVAL ANALYSIS TECHNIQUES

What we *can* do is figure out how many people survive for at least one year, for at least two years, and so on. We're not limited to having equal intervals; they can be days for the first week, then weeks for the next month, and then months thereafter. This approach, called either the **survival-table** or, more commonly, the **life-table** technique, has all the advantages of the person-years method (i.e., making maximum use of the data from all of the subjects), without its disad-

vantage of assuming a constant risk over time. There are two ways to go about calculating a life table: the **actuarial approach** and the **Kaplan-Meier approach**. They're fairly similar in most details, so we'll begin with the older (although now less frequently used) actuarial approach.

THE ACTUARIAL APPROACH

The first step in both approaches involves redrawing the graph so that all of the people appear to start at the same time. Figure 10-2 shows the same data as Figure 10-1; however, instead of the *X*-axis being *Calendar Year*, it becomes *Number of Years in the Study*. Now, both the *X*-axis and the lines represent survival time. The lines are all the same length as in Figure 10-1; they've just been shifted to the left so that they all begin at Time 0.

From this figure, we can start working out a table showing the number of people **at risk** of death each year, and the probability of them still being around at the end of the year. To begin with, let's summarize the data in Figure 10-2, listing for each year of the study (1) the number of subjects who are still up and kicking (those at risk),[8] (2) the number who died, and (3) the number lost to follow-up. We've done this in Table 10-2.

Getting from the graph to the table is quite simple. There were 10 lines at the left side of the interval 0 to 1 year, so 10 people were at risk of dying. No lines terminate during this interval, so we know that no one died and no one was lost. Between years 1 and 2, one line ends with a *D* and one with an *L*, so we enter one Death and one Loss in the table. This means that two fewer subjects begin the next time interval, so we subtract 2 from 10, leaving 8 at risk. As a check, we can count the number of lines at the left side of the Year 2~3 interval, and see that there are 8 of them. We continue this until either the study ends or we run out of subjects. As we said previously, we're treating those who were censored and those

---

[7] *In fact, the risk of contracting Salmonella or E. coli 0157:H7 is much higher among people using unpasteurized juices or honey; eating "natural" foods may lead to unnatural deaths.*

[8] *It is indeed a sobering thought that being alive merely means you are at risk of death.*

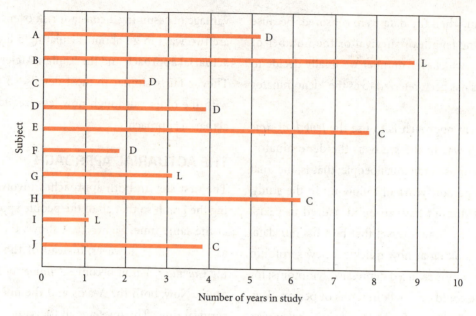

FIGURE 10-2   Redrawn so all subjects have a common starting date.

who were lost identically; both are placed in the Lost column.

The next step is to figure out the probability of dying each year. This would be relatively simple to do if all we had to deal with were subjects who were alive at the start of each study year and the number who died. In that case, the probability of death would simply be:

$$Pr\,(Death) = \frac{Number\ Who\ Died}{Number\ at\ Risk\ of\ Death}$$

$$(10\text{-}3)$$

To simplify writing our equation, let's use the symbols:

q_i = Probability of death in Year i

$p_i = 1 - q_i$ (i.e., the probability of survival in Year i)

D_i = Number of persons who died in Year i

R_i = Number of subjects at risk starting Year i

So, we can rewrite Equation (10-3) as:

$$q_i = \frac{D_i}{R_i} \qquad (10\text{-}4)$$

But, back to our machinations. What do we do with the people who were lost *during* the year? If we gather follow-up data only at discrete intervals, we wouldn't know exactly when they were lost and thus aren't sure for what length of time they were at risk.

Do we say that they were at risk for the whole year, or should we drop them entirely at the beginning of the year? For example, Subject G in Figure 10-2 dropped out of sight some time between the start of Year 3 and the start of Year 4. We can either attribute a full year of risk to this subject (Year 3 to Year 4), or limit his time at risk to the end of Year 3. To say he was at risk for the entire year assumes he lived all 12 months. In reality, he may have died one minute after New Year's Eve.[9] In this case, we have "credited" him with 12 ex-

TABLE 10-2   Number of subjects at risk, who died, and were lost each year

Number of years in study	Number of subjects at risk	Number of subjects who died	Number of subjects lost
0~1	10	0	0
1~2	10	1	1
2~3	8	1	0
3~4	7	1	2
4~5	4	0	0
5~6	4	1	0
6~7	3	0	1
7~8	2	0	1
8~9	1	0	1
9~10	0	0	0

---

[9]*Obviously, because he was overdosing on bottled water, when he should have been drinking red wine and benefiting from its cardio-protective effects.*

tra months of life, which would then underestimate the death rate. On the other hand, to drop him entirely from that year throws away valid data; we know that he at least made it to the beginning of Year 3, if not to the end.

What we do is make a compromise. If we don't know exactly when a subject was lost or censored, but we know it was sometime within the interval, we count him as half a person-year (or whatever interval we're using). That is, we say that half a person got through the interval, or putting it slightly differently and more logically, the person got through half the interval. In a large study, this compromise is based on a fairly safe assumption. If deaths occur randomly throughout the year, then someone who died during the first month would be balanced by another who died during the last, and the mean duration of surviving for these people is six months. On average, then, giving each person credit for half the year balances out. So, if we abbreviate the number of people lost (i.e., truly lost or censored) each year as L_i, we can rewrite Equation (10-3) as:

$$\text{Pr(death)} = \frac{\text{Number Who Died in Year } i}{\text{Number at Risk at Start of Year } i - \dfrac{\text{Lost or Censored}}{2}}$$

$$\text{(10-5)}$$

or, in statistical shorthand:

$$q_1 = \frac{D_1}{R_1 - \dfrac{L_i}{2}} \qquad \text{(10-6)}$$

Let's assume that these 10 people were drawn from a larger study, with 100 people in each group. The (fictitious) data for subjects in the *DEATH* condition are in Table 10-3. Now, using Equation (10-6) with the data in Table 10-3, we can make a new table (Table 10-4), giving (1) q_i, the probability of death occurring during each interval, (2) the converse of this, p_i, which is the probability of *surviving* the interval, and (3) S_i, the *cumulative probability* of survival (which is also referred

to as the **survival function**).[10] Let's walk through a few lines of Table 10-4 and see how it's done.

TABLE 10-3   Data for all subjects in the *DEATH* trial

Number of years in study	Number of subjects at risk	Number of subjects who died	Number of subjects lost
0~1	100	5	2
1~2	93	4	4
2~3	85	5	1
3~4	79	3	3
4~5	73	7	2
5~6	64	5	4
6~7	55	7	3
7~8	45	10	5
8~9	30	8	2
9~10	20	7	5

TABLE 10-4   Life-table based on data in Table 10-3

Number of years in study	Probability of death (q_i)	Probability of surviving (p_i)	Cumulative probability of surviving (S_i)
0~1	0.0505	0.9495	0.9495
1~2	0.0440	0.9560	0.9078
2~3	0.0592	0.9408	0.8541
3~4	0.0387	0.9613	0.8210
4~5	0.0972	0.9028	0.7412
5~6	0.0806	0.9194	0.6814
6~7	0.1308	0.8692	0.5922
7~8	0.2353	0.7647	0.4529
8~9	0.2759	0.7241	0.3280
9~10	0.4000	0.6000	0.1968

The first line of Table 10-3 (0~1 years in the study) tells us that there were 5 deaths and 2 losses. Using Equation (10-6), then, we have:

$$q_{(1)} = \frac{5}{100 - \dfrac{2}{2}} = \frac{5}{99} = .0505 \qquad \text{(10-7)}$$

So the probability of death during Year 1 is slightly over 5%. Therefore, the probability of surviving that year, p_1, which is $(1 - q_1)$, is 0.9495.[11] The second

---

[10]*In some texts (and in the previous editions of this one), this was abbreviated as Pi. Some people (including us), however, had problems differentiating pi from Pi, so we've adopted the other commonly used symbol, Si, where S stands for Survival.*

[11]*Although having only 100 subjects would not normally support accuracy to four decimal places, we use four because these quantities will be multiplied with others many times. Fewer decimal places will lead to rounding errors which would be compounded as we march along.*

year began with 93 subjects at risk (100 minus the 5 who died and 2 who were lost); 4 died during that year, and 4 were either truly lost or censored. Again, we use Equation (10-6), and get:

$$q_{(2)} = \frac{4}{93 - \frac{4}{2}} = \frac{4}{91} = .0440 \qquad \textbf{(10-8)}$$

The probability of surviving Year 2 is (1 − 0.0440) = 0.9560. The **cumulative probability** of surviving Year 2 (S_2) is the probability of surviving Year 1 (S_1, which in this case is 0.9560) times the probability of surviving Year 2 (p_2, which is 0.9560), or 0.9078.

What is the difference between p_2 and S_2? The first term (which is 1 minus the probability of dying in Year 2) is a **conditional probability;** that is, it tells us that the probability of making it through Year 2 is 95.60%, *conditional upon having survived up to the beginning of Year 2.* However, not all the people made it to the start of the year; five died during the previous interval and two were lost. Hence the *cumulative* probability, S_2, gives us the probability of surviving the second year *for all subjects who started the study,* whereas p_2 is the probability of surviving the second year only for those subjects who started Year 2.

Now we continue to fill in the table for the rest of the intervals. If some of the intervals have no deaths, it's not necessary to calculate q_i, p_i, or S_i. By definition, q_i will be 0, p_i will be 1, and S_i will be unchanged from the previous interval. Once we've completed the table, we can plot the data in the S_i column (the *survival function*), which we have done in Figure 10-3. This is called, for obvious reasons, a **survival curve.**

THE KAPLAN-MEIER APPROACH TO SURVIVAL ANALYSIS

The **Kaplan-Meier** approach (KM; Kaplan and

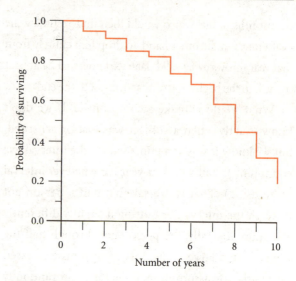

FIGURE 10-3   Survival curve for the data in Table 10-4.

Meier, 1958), which is also called the **product-limit method** for reasons that will be spelled out later, is similar to the actuarial one, with four exceptions. First, rather than placing death within some arbitrary interval, the *exact* time of death is used in the calculations. Needless to say, this presupposes that we know the exact time.[12] If all we know is that the patient died after the 2-year follow-up visit but before the 3-year visit, we're limited to the actuarial approach.[13] Second, instead of calculating the survival function at fixed times (e.g., every month or year of the study), it's done only when an outcome occurs. This means that some of the data points may be close together in time, whereas others can be spread far apart. This then leads to the third difference; the survival curve derived from the actuarial method changes only at the end of an interval, whereas that derived from the KM way changes whenever an outcome has occurred. What this means is that, with the actuarial approach, equal steps occur along the *time* axis (X); but with the KM method, the steps

---

[12]Note that "exact" is an inexact term. It may mean knowing the time of death within hours, if we are dealing with an outcome that may occur soon after enrollment (e.g., a trial of a treatment for hemorrhagic fever), or within weeks for diseases such as cancer or cystic fibrosis.

[13]Patients are notorious for not letting investigators know when they die. This is one of the hazards of clinical research and explains why investigators such as B. F. Skinner preferred using pigeons. Other reasons include the fact that, if you don't like the results, you can have squab for dinner and start again the next day with a new batch of subjects.

are equal along the *probability* (*Y*) axis. You can usually tell what type of graph you're looking at—if the steps along the *X*-axis are equal, it's from an actuarial analysis; if the steps aren't of equal length but most are of equal height, it's from a KM analysis.

Last, subjects who are lost to follow-up because they are truly lost or due to censoring are considered to be at risk up to the time they drop out. This means that, if they withdraw at a time between two events (i.e., deaths of other subjects), their data are used in the calculation of the survival rate for the first event but not for the second. If we go back to Figure 10-2, one event occurred when Subject C died; the next when Subject D left us to sing with the choir invisible. Between these two times, Subject G dropped out of sight. So, Subject G's data will be used when we figure out the survival rate at the time of C's death, but not D's.

To show how this is done, let's go back and use the data for the 10 subjects in Table 10-1. The first step is to rank order the length of time in the trial, flagging the numbers that reflect the outcome of interest (death, in this case), and indicate which ones are from people who were lost or censored. We've done this by putting an asterisk after the value for people who were lost or censored because of the termination of the study.

14* 22 29 37* 45* 46 61 76* 92* 111*

Our life table (Table 10-5) would thus have only four rows; one for each of the four people who shucked their mortal coils. As a small point, notice that we used the subscript *i* in each column of Table 10-4. In Table 10-5 we've used *t* to indicate that we're measuring an exact *time*, rather than an *interval*.

One person was lost before the first person died, so the number at risk at 22 months (the time of the first death) is only 9. At 46 months, 2 people had died and 3 were lost, so the number at risk is 5, and so on. Because we know the exact time when people were lost to the trial, we don't have to use the fancy-shmancy correction in Equation (10-6) to approximate when they dropped out of sight. We can use Equation (10-4) to figure out the death rate, q_t, as we did in Table 10-5.[14]

So, which technique do we use, the actuarial or the KM? When you have fewer than about 50 subjects in each group, the KM approach is likely somewhat more efficient, from a statistical perspective, because you're using exact times rather than approximations for the outcomes. The downside of KM is that withdrawals occurring between outcomes are ignored; this is more of a problem when $N > 50$. However, in most cases the two approaches lead to fairly similar results, so go with whichever one is on your computer.[15]

The Hazard Function

Closely related to the term q_i, the probability of dying in interval i, is something called the **hazard function**. The hazard function is the potential of occurrence of the outcome at a specific time, t, for those people who were alive up until that point.

Those in the area of demographics refer to this as

TABLE 10-5 Kaplan-Meier life-table analysis of the data in Table 10-1

Time (months) (*t*)	Number at risk (R_t)	Number of deaths (D_t)	Death rate (q_t)	Survival rate (p_t)	Cumulative survival rate (S_t)
22	9	1	0.1111	0.8889	0.8889
29	8	1	0.1250	0.8750	0.7778
46	5	1	0.2000	0.8000	0.6222
61	4	1	0.2500	0.7500	0.4667

---

[14]*The calculations for the KM method involve multiplying (i.e., getting the product) of the terms up to the limit of the last outcome; hence its alias, the product-limit method.*

[15]*And how's that for statistical pragmatism?*

the *force of mortality*. Whatever it's called, the hazard is a *conditional* value; that is, it is conditional on the supposition that the person has arrived at time *t* alive. So, the hazard at the end of Year 4 doesn't apply to all people in the group; only those who began Year 4. It isn't appropriate to use for those who died before Year 4 began. When we plot the hazard for each interval of the study, we would call this graph the **hazard function**, which is usually abbreviated $h(t)$.

There are a couple of things to note about the hazard function. First, we've used terms like "potential of occurrence" and "conditional value" and studiously avoided the term *probability*. The reason is that the hazard is a rate (more specifically, a ***conditional failure rate***) and not a proportion. A proportion can have values only between 0 and 1, while the hazard function has no upper limit. Confusing the picture a bit, the hazard *can* be interpreted as a proportion with the actuarial method; but not with the KM approach. Second, the cumulative probability of surviving (S_i), and hence the survival curve, can only stay the same or decrease over time. On the other hand, the hazard and the hazard function can fluctuate from one interval to the next. The hazard function for people from the age of 5 or so until the end of middle age[16] is a flat line; that is, it's relatively constant over the interval. On the other hand, the hazard function over the entire life span of a large group of people is a U-shaped function: high in infancy and old age, and low in the intermediate years. There are other possible hazard functions. For example, for leukemic patients who aren't responsive to treatment, the potential for dying increases over time; this is called an **increasing Weibull function.** Conversely, recovery from major surgery shows a high perioperative risk that decreases over time; this is described as a **negative Weibull** function (Kleinbaum, 1996). However, the risk of giving you more information than you really want increases rapidly the more we talk about different hazard functions, so we'll stop at this point.

[16] *A term defined as five years older than us.*

SUMMARY MEASURES

There are a few measures we can calculate at this point to summarize what's happening in each of the groups. Once we've plotted the survival curve, it is a simple matter to determine the **median survival time**. In fact, no calculation is necessary. Simply draw a horizontal line from the *Y*-axis where the probability of surviving is 50% until it intersects the curve, and then drop a line down to the *X*-axis. In this case, it is 8 years, meaning that subjects in the *DEATH* group live on average 8 years after entering the trial. The median survival time is also the time up to which 50% of the sample survives only if there were no censored data. Needless to say, we can complement the median survival time (which is a measure of central tendency, like the median itself) with an index of dispersion. As you well remember, the measure of dispersion that accompanies the median is the inter-quartile range, and we do that here by drawing two additional lines; one where the probability of surviving is 25% and the other where it is 75%.

Another summary measure involves the hazard, which, as we've described, can change over time. The **average hazard rate** ($\overline{h}$) is the number of outcomes divided by the survival times summed over all the people in the group:

Average Hazard Rate

$$\overline{h} = \frac{Number\ of\ Outcomes}{\sum t_n} \tag{10-9}$$

where t_n means the survival time for each of the *n* people. Using the data in Table 10-1, where there were four deaths, $\overline{h}$ would be:

$$\overline{h} = \frac{4}{61+111+29+\ldots+45} = \frac{4}{503} = 0.008$$

$$\tag{10-10}$$

THE STANDARD ERROR

It's possible to calculate an SE for the survival function, just as we can for any other parameter. (Just to remind you, the survival function consists of the data in the S_i

column of Table 10-4, which are plotted as a curve in Figure 10-3; or the S_t column of Table 10-5.) However, we're limited to estimating it at a specific time, rather than for the function as a whole; that is, there are as many SEs as there are intervals (with the actuarial method) or times (with the KM approach). There are also several formulae, all of which are approximations of the SE and some of which are quite complicated. The formula most widely used in computer programs is the one by Greenwood, because it is the most accurate:

The SE of the Survival Function

$$SE(S_i) = S_i \sqrt{\sum \frac{D_i}{R_i(R_i - d_i)}} \qquad \textbf{(10-11)}$$

The equation is exactly the same for the KM approach; just use the terms with the subscript t rather than i. Let's go back to Tables 10-3 and 10-4 to figure out the numbers. For Year 0~1, $S_i = 0.9495$, and $R_i = 100$, and there were 5 deaths, so:

$$SE(S_1) = 0.9495 \sqrt{\frac{5}{100(100-5)}} = 0.0218$$
$$\textbf{(10-12)}$$

That was easy. Unfortunately, once we get beyond the first interval, the math gets a bit hairy, which is fine for computers but not for humans. For this reason, Peto and colleagues (1977) introduced an approximation that isn't too far off and is much more tractable if we ever want to second-guess the computer:

$$SE(S_i) = \sqrt{\frac{S_i(1-S_i)}{R_1}} \qquad \textbf{(10-13)}$$

Plugging in the same numbers we get:

$$SE(S_1) = \sqrt{\frac{0.9495(1-0.9495)}{100}} = 0.0219$$
$$\textbf{(10-14)}$$

which, as you can see, isn't very far off the mark. For Year 9~10, $S_{10} = 0.1968$ and $R_{10} = 20$:

$$SE(S_{10}) = \sqrt{\frac{0.1968(1-0.1968)}{20}} = 0.0889$$
$$\textbf{(10-15)}$$

$SE(S_{10})$ is larger than $SE(S_1)$ because the sample size is smaller. In general, then, as the intervals or times increase, so do the SEs, because the estimates of the survival function are based on fewer and fewer subjects.

ASSUMPTIONS OF SURVIVAL ANALYSIS

During our discussion so far, we've made several assumptions; now let's make them explicit.

1. *An identifiable **starting point**.* In this example, the starting point was easily identifiable, at least for those in the *DEATH* group: when subjects were enrolled in the study and began their five-part regimen. When the study looks at survival following some intervention under the experimenter's control, there's usually no problem in identifying the start for each subject. However, if we want to use this technique to look at the natural history of some disorder, such as how long a person is laid up with low-back pain, we may have a problem specifying when the problem actually began. Is baseline when the person first came to the attention of the physician; when he or she first felt any pain; or when he or she did something presumably injurious to the back? There are difficulties with each of these. For instance, some people run to their docs at the first twinge of pain, whereas others avoid using them at all costs. The other proposed starting points rely on the patients' recall of events, which we know is notoriously inaccurate.[17]

Having a person enter a trial in the midst of an episode is referred to as **left censoring**,[18] because now it is the left-hand part of the lines that have been cut off. Survival analysis has no problem dealing with right censoring, but left censoring is much more difficult to deal with, and so should be avoided if it's at all possible. This injunction is similar to the recommendations for evaluating the natural history of a disorder—the participants should form an *inception cohort* (Guyatt et al., 1993, 1994). The impor-

---

[17] *For some examples of just how bad recall of health events can be, see the extremely good and highly recommended book, Health Measurement Scales (2014). Oh, by the way, did we mention that it's by Streiner and Norman?*

[18] *By analogy to right censoring, left censoring would also mean making all those rabid ultra-conservative radio talk show hosts finally shut up and get a real job.*

tant point is that, whatever starting point is chosen, it must be applied uniformly and reproducibly for all subjects.

2. *A binary **end point***. Survival analysis requires an end-point that is well-defined and consists of two states that are mutually exclusive and collectively exhaustive (Wright, 2000). This isn't a problem when the end point is death.[19] However, we have problems similar to those in identifying a starting point if the outcome isn't as "hard" as death (e.g., the re-emergence of symptoms or the reappearance of a tumor). If we rely on a physician's report or the patient's recall, we face the prospect that a multitude of other factors affect these, many of which have nothing to do with the disorder. The more we have to rely on recall or reporting, the more error we introduce into our identification of the end point and hence into our measurement of survival time.

A second problem occurs if the end point can occur numerous times in the same person. Examples would include hospitalization, recurrence of symptoms, admission to jail, falling off the wagon following a drinking abstinence program, binge eating after a weight-loss program, and a multitude of others. The usual rule is to take the *first* occurrence of the outcome event, and then unceremoniously toss the subject out of the study. If the person is readmitted to the study and is thus represented in the data set more than once, this would violate the assumption that the events are *statistically independent* and would play havoc with any hypothesis testing (Wright, 2000).[20]

3. ***Loss to follow-up*** *should not be related to the outcome*. We've been assuming that the reason people were lost to follow-up is that they dropped out of the study for reasons that had nothing to do with the outcome (the assumption of **independent censoring**). They may have moved, lost interest in the study, or died for reasons that are unrelated to the interven-

tion. If the reasons *are* related, then our estimation of the survival rate will be seriously biased, in that we'd underestimate the death rate and overestimate survival.

Determining if the loss is or isn't related to the outcome is a thorny issue that isn't always as easy to resolve as it first appears. If we're studying the effectiveness of a combination of chemotherapy and radiation therapy for cancer, with the end point being a reappearance of a tumor, what do we do with a person who dies because of a heart attack, or who commits suicide, or even dies in an automobile accident?

At first glance, these have nothing to do with the treatment. But, could the myocardial infarction have been due to the cardiotoxic effects of radiation? Could the person have committed suicide because she believed she was becoming symptomatic again and didn't want to face the prospect of a lingering death? Was the accident due to decreased concentration secondary to the effects of the treatment? It's not as easy to determine this as it first appeared. You may want to look at Sackett and Gent (1979) for an extended discussion on this point.

Note that this isn't an issue for people who are lost because of right censoring; only for those who drop out or who are lost to follow-up for other reasons.

4. There is no secular trend. When we construct the life table, we start everyone at a common time. In studies that recruit and follow patients for extended periods, there could be up to a five-year span between the time the first subject actually enters and leaves the trial and when the last one does. We assume that nothing has happened over this interval that would affect who gets into the trial, what is done to them, and what factors influence the outcome. If changes have occurred over this time (referred to as secular changes[21] or trends), then the subjects recruited at the end may differ systematically, as may

---

[19] *This state, however, may be hard to recognize in some tenured professors and long-serving politicians, when signs of life may appear only when the bar opens in the afternoon.*

[20] *There are programs that can handle this, but they're highly specialized and not found in the major commercial packages.*

[21] *We presume as opposed to "ecclesiastical changes," which affect only members of the clergy.*

their outcomes, from those who got in early. This could have resulted from changes in diagnostic practices (e.g., the introduction of a more sensitive test or a change in the diagnostic criteria), different treatment regimens, or even a new research assistant who codes things differently.

COMPARING TWO (OR MORE) GROUPS

The survival curve in Figure 10-3 shows us what happened to people in the *DEATH* group. But, we began with the question of comparing the *DEATH* regimen with life as usual. Does adhering to all those precepts of Yuppiedom actually prolong life, or does it just make it feel that way? Because we anticipate that many people in the *LAU* group may become subverted by the blandishments of the promise of eternal life and drop out of the study, we oversampled and got 250 subjects to enroll in the *LAU* group. The data for both groups are presented in Table 10-6. The first four columns are the same as in Table 10-3, and the last three columns give the data for the subjects in the *LAU* condition.

The first thing we should do is draw the survival curves for the two groups on the same graph so we can get a picture of what (if anything) is going on (Figure 10-4). This shows us that *DEATH* may be living up to its name; rather than making people

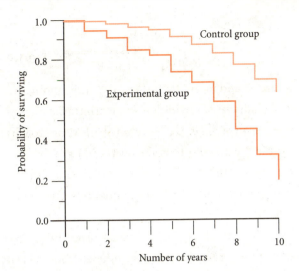

FIGURE 10-4 Survival curves for both groups in the *DEATH* study, from Table 10-6.

immortal, diet, exercise, bottled water, and the like may actually be hastening their demise.[22] The survival curve for the *DEATH* group seems to be dropping at a faster rate than that for the *LAU* group. But is the difference statistically significant?

THE *z*-TEST

One approach to answering the question would be to compare the two curves at a specific point. To do this, using our old standby of the *z*-test, we have to assume that the cumulative survival rates of the two groups are normally distributed. So:

TABLE 10-6 Data for both groups in the *DEATH* trial

Number of years in study	Experimental group			Control group		
	At risk (R_1)	Died (D_1)	Lost (L_1)	At risk (R_2)	Died (D_2)	Lost (L_2)
0~1	100	5	2	250	0	2
1~2	93	4	4	248	3	5
2~3	85	5	1	240	5	4
3~4	79	3	3	231	1	5
4~5	73	7	2	225	10	4
5~6	64	5	4	211	8	6
6~7	55	7	3	197	9	5
7~8	45	10	5	183	12	9
8~9	30	8	2	162	15	5
9~10	20	7	5	142	13	8

---

[22]*If the acronym DEATH didn't alert you to our views about a "lifestyle" based on the precepts of the Age of Aquarius, suely these fictitious results will.*

The z-test

$$z = \frac{S_{i_\tau} - S_{i_c}}{\sqrt{[SE(S_{i_\tau})]^2 + [SE(S_{i_c})]^2}} \quad \textbf{(10-16)}$$

where S_{i_τ} and S_{i_c} are the values of S (the cumulative probability of surviving) at some arbitrarily chosen interval i (or time, t, if we used the KM approach) for the Treatment (T) and Control (C) groups; and the SEs are the standard errors at that time for the two groups, calculated using Equations (10-11) or (10-13).

This method is quite easy to calculate and is very useful if we are interested in the difference in survival rates at one specific time, such as 5-year survival in cancer. An added advantage is that it is simple to determine the **Relative Risk (RR)** at this point. The RR is the ratio of the probability of having the outcome occur among subjects in one group versus the other. In this example, it would be the risk of expiring for people in the *DEATH* group relative to the *LAU* group. The formula for determining the RR is:

The Relative Risk at Interval i:

$$RR = \frac{1}{1} \frac{S_{i_T}}{S_{i_c}} \quad \textbf{(10-17)}$$

The z-test can also be applied to evaluate the significance of the RR.

The RR compares the survival functions of the two groups. We can similarly compare the hazard functions at a specific time. As the name implies, the **hazard ratio** (HR) is simply the ratio of the hazards at time i for the Treatment and Control groups:

The Hazard Ratio

$$HR = \frac{h_{i_T}}{h_{i_c}} \quad \textbf{(10-18)}$$

Although the HR isn't an odds ratio, it's interpreted in much the same way (Kleinbaum, 1996). An HR of 1 means the hazards are identical in both groups; an HR of 3 means the hazard in the Experimental group is 3 times that of the Control; and an HR of 0.5 means the hazard for the Experimental group is half that of the Control group. Because the RR deals with the survival function and the HR with the hazard function, as one goes up, the other goes down.

THE MANTEL-COX LOG-RANK TEST AND OTHERS

This approach, however,[23] has two problems. The first involves intellectual honesty; you should pick your comparison time *before* you look at the data, ideally, before you even start the trial. Otherwise, there is a great temptation to choose the time that maximizes the difference between the groups. The second problem is more substantive, and involves the issues we discussed early in the chapter when we introduced the Survival Rate—we've ignored most of the data by focusing on one time point and, more specifically, we don't take into account that the groups can reach the same survival rate in very different ways. A better approach would be to use all of the data. This is done by using the **Mantel-Cox log-rank** (or log-rank) **test**, which is a modification of the **Mantel-Haenszel chi-squared** we ran into earlier (Cox, 1972; Mantel, 1966).[24] Although it is a nonparametric test, it is more powerful than the parametric z-test because it is a whole-pattern test that uses all of the data. Indeed, one of the strengths of the log-rank test is that it makes no assumptions about the shape of the survival curves, and doesn't require us to know what the shapes are (Bland and Altman, 2004).

As with most chi-squared tests, the log-rank test compares the *observed* number of events with the number *expected*, under the assumption that the null hypothesis of no group difference is true. That is, if no differences existed between the groups, then at any interval (or time), the total number of events should be divided between the groups roughly in proportion to the number at risk. For example, if Group A and Group B have the same number of subjects, and there were 12 deaths in a specific interval,

---

[23]*Why does there always seem to be a "however" whenever something appears simple?*

[24]*We can't use the **Mantel-Haenszel** chi-squared because it assumes that the chi-squared tables we're summing across are independent. They aren't truly independent in survival analysis because the number of people at risk at any interval is dependent on the number of people at risk during the previous intervals. That's a long answer for a question you didn't ask.*

then each group should have about 6 deaths. On the other hand, if Group A is twice as large as B, then the deaths should be split 8 : 4.

If we go back to Table 10-6, we see that there are 350 people at risk during the first interval: 100 in the *DEATH* group, and 250 in the *LAU* group. Because 28.6% of the subjects are in the *DEATH* regimen, and there were a total of 5 deaths during this interval, we would expect that $5 \times 0.286 = 1.43$ deaths would have occurred in this group, and 3.57 among the controls.[25] The shortcut formula for calculating the expected frequency for Group k (where $k = 1$ or 2) at interval i is:

$$E_{i_k} = D_i \times \frac{R_{i_k}}{R_{i_1} + R_{i_2}} \qquad (10\text{-}19)$$

Where D_i is the total number of deaths.

Using this in the example we just worked out:

$$E_{i_1} = 5 \times \frac{100}{100 + 250} = 1.43$$
$$E_{i_2} = 5 \times \frac{250}{100 + 250} = 3.57 \qquad (10\text{-}20)$$

Doing this for each interval, we get a new table listing the observed and expected frequencies, as in Table 10-7.[26] As a check on our (or the computer's)

math, the total of the observed deaths $(61 + 76)$ should equal the sum of the expected ones $(28.06 + 108.93)$, within rounding error. The last step, then, is to figure out how much our *observed* event rate differs from the *expected* rate. To do this, we use (finally!) the **Mantel-Cox chi-squared**:

The Mantel-Cox Chi-Squared

$$\chi^2_{MC} = \frac{(O_1 - E_1)^2}{E_1} + \frac{(O_2 - E_2)^2}{E_2} \qquad (10\text{-}21)$$

with 1 *df*. (Some texts subtract ½ from the value $|(O - E)|$ before squaring. As we discussed, though, we question the usefulness of this correction for continuity.) If we had more than two groups, we would simply extend Equation (10-21) by tacking more terms on the end and using $k - 1$ *df*, where k is the number of groups.[27] Let's apply this to our data in Table 10-7:

$$\chi^2_{MC}(1) = \frac{(61 - 28.06)^2}{28.06} + \frac{(76 - 108.93)^2}{108.93}$$
$$= 38.67 + 9.95 = 48.62 \qquad (10\text{-}22)$$

which is highly significant.

The RR can be figured out with the formula:

The Overall Relative Risk

TABLE 10-7   Calculating a log-rank test on the data in Table 10-6

Number of years in study	At risk			Dead			Expected	
	Exper (R_{i_1})	Cont (R_{i_2})	Total (R_i)	Exper (D_{i_1})	Cont (D_{i_2})	Total (D_i)	Exper (E_{i_1})	Cont (E_{i_2})
0~1	100	250	350	5	0	5	1.43	3.57
1~2	93	248	341	4	3	7	1.91	5.09
2~3	85	240	325	5	5	10	2.62	7.38
3~4	79	231	310	3	1	4	1.02	2.97
4~5	73	225	298	7	10	17	4.16	12.84
5~6	64	211	275	5	8	13	3.03	9.97
6~7	55	197	252	7	9	16	3.49	12.51
7~8	45	183	228	10	12	22	4.34	17.66
8~9	30	162	192	8	15	23	3.59	19.41
9~10	20	142	162	7	13	20	2.47	17.53
TOTALS				$O_1 = 61$	$O_2 = 76$		$E_1 = 28.06$	$E_2 = 108.93$

---

[25] We'll not deal with the existential question of how there can be a fraction of a death.

[26] In reality, we let the computer do this for us. After all, that's why they were placed on this earth.

[27] Don't even think of asking why this is also called the log-rank test, as no logs or ranks appear in it. But since you did ask, there is a version that does use logs and ranks, but the results are equivalent.

$$RR = \frac{O_T / E_T}{O_C / E_C} \qquad (10\text{-}23)$$

For our data, this works out to be:

$$RR = \frac{61 / 28.06}{76 / 108.93} = 3.12 \qquad (10\text{-}24)$$

Because the chi-squared value was significant, we can go ahead and look at the RR. By convention, we disregard any RR under 2 as not being anything to write home about. This RR of 3.12 tells us that sticking to a strict healthy regimen is bad for your health—let's go out and eat ourselves silly to celebrate!

The Mantel-Cox chi-squared is probably the best test of significance when one group is consistently higher than the other across time. If the survival curves cross at any point, even at the very beginning before going their separate ways, it's unlikely to be significant (Bland and Altman, 2004). When the group differences are larger at the beginning of the study than later on, the **Breslow test** (which is a generalized Wilcoxon test) is more sensitive; and the **Tarone-Ware test** (Tarrone and Ware, 1977) is best if the differences aren't constant over time or if the curves intersect (Wright, 2000).

ADJUSTING FOR COVARIATES

After having gone to all this trouble to demonstrate the log-rank test, it would be a pity if we could use it only to compare two or more groups. In fact, it does have more uses, mainly in testing for the possible effects of covariates. If we thought, for example, that men and women may react to the regimen differently, then we could divide the two groups by sex and do a survival analysis (either actuarial or KM) for these two (or more[28]) strata. If the covariate were continuous, such as age, we could split it at the median or some other logical place (despite our constant injunctions to not turn continuous variables into categorical or ordinal ones). *Taking the covariate into consideration involves an "adjustment" that takes place at the level of the final chi-squared, where we use the strata-adjusted expected frequencies.* Let's assume

that we divided each group by sex and had the computer redo the calculations for Table 10-7 two times: once for females divided by experimental condition (*DEATH* vs *LAU*), and again for males split the same way. Table 10-8 shows what we found. Using these new figures in Equation (**10**-21) gives us:

$$\chi^2_{MC} = \frac{(61 - 25.92)^2}{25.92} + \frac{(76 - 111.08)^2}{111.08} = 58.59 \qquad (10\text{-}25)$$

TABLE 10-8   Survival time of the two groups stratified by sex

Sex	Experimental		Control	
	Observed deaths	Expected deaths	Observed deaths	Expected deaths
Females	28	12.01	34	49.99
Males	33	13.91	42	61.09
TOTALS	61	25.92	76	111.08

which is larger than the unadjusted log-rank test, telling us that the *DEATH* way of life did indeed affect the two sexes differently.

There are a few problems with this way of going about things, though. First, each time we split the groups into two or more strata, our sample size in each subgroup drops. Unless we have an extremely large study, then, we're limited as to the number of covariates we can examine at any one time. The second problem, which we mentioned in the previous paragraph, is that we may be taking perfectly good interval or ratio data and turning them into nominal or ordinal categories (e.g., converting age into <40 and ≥40 years). This is a good way to lose power and sensitivity. Last, although we can calculate the statistical significance of adjusting for the prognostic factor(s) (that is, the covariates), we don't get an estimate for the *magnitude* of the effect.

What we need, then, is a technique that can (1) handle any number of covariates, (2) treat continuous data as continuous, and (3) give us an estimate of the magnitude of the effect; in other words, an equivalent to an analysis of covariance for survival data. With this build-up, it's obvious that such a statistic is around and is the next topic we tackle. This tech-

---

[28]*We know; we know. To do this, we'd have to differentiate between "sexual orientation" and "gender." However, we're not going there.*

nique is called the **Cox proportional hazards model** (Cox, 1972).

Let's go back to the definition of the hazard:

The hazard at time t, h_t, is the potential of an event at time t, given survival (no event) up to time t.

The proportional hazards model extends this to read:

The proportional hazard is the potential of an event at time t, given survival up to time t, and for specific values of prognostic variables, X_1, X_2, etc.

In the example we did illustrating the Mantel-Cox chi-squared, it would be the probability of death at time t (or interval i), given that the person was male or female. With our new, enhanced technique, the prognostic variable can be either discrete (e.g., sex) or continuous (such as age), and we can have several of them (age *and* sex).[29] So, to be more precise, instead of having just one X, we can have several, X_1, X_2, and so on, with each X representing a different prognostic variable. However, let's stick to just one variable now to simplify our discussion.

The major assumption we make is that the effects of the prognostic variables depend on the *values* of the variables and that these values *do not vary over time*; in other words, they are **time-independent** prognostic variables. That is, we assume that the values of the Xs for a specific person don't change over the course of the study. Gender (for the vast majority of people, at least) remains constant, as does the presence of most chronic comorbid disorders. Age is a bit tricky; it naturally increases as the trial goes on, but it does so at a constant rate for all participants; and its effect on survival depends primarily on its value at baseline. So, it's usually considered to be a time-independent variable (Kleinbaum, 1996). On the other hand, if people's weights fluctuate considerably, and this fluctuation differs among people and affects the outcome, then weight is **time-dependent** prognostic variable, and the proportional hazards assumption wouldn't be met. Later, we'll discuss how

to assess this assumption.

The proportional hazard consists of two parts: a constant, c, which depends on t and tells us how fast the curve is dropping; and a function, f, that is dependent on the covariate, X. Needless to say, f gets more complex as we add more covariates to the mix. Putting this into the form of an equation, we can say:

The proportional hazard at time t for some specific value of X = (some constant that depends on t) times (some function dependent on X)

and writing it in mathematical shorthand, we get:

The Proportional Hazard

$$h(t \mid X) = c(t) \times f(X) \qquad \textbf{(10-26)}$$

where the symbol $(t \mid X)$ means a value of t given (or at some value of) X.

Now let's start using it with some data. To keep the number of subjects manageable, we'll use the 10 subjects in the *DEATH* group we first met in Table 10-1. In Table 10-9, we've added one covariate, Age, and ranked the subjects by their time in the study, because we'll use the KM method.

The first death occurred at 22 months and was Subject F (let's call her the **index case** for this calculation). All of the other people were in the study at least 22 months, with the exception of Subject I, who was lost to follow-up after 14 months. The next step is to figure out the probability of Subject F dying at 22 months, versus the probabilities for the other people at risk. She was a tender 28 years of age, so her probability of death at 22 months after starting the regimen is $c(22) \times f(28)$.

We[30] now repeat this procedure in turn for all of the other people who died, each of them in turn becoming the index case. In each calculation, we include in the denominator only those people who were still in the study at the time the index case went to his or her eternal reward; that is, those still at risk. We don't include those who were already singing with the angels or those whose data were censored before the time the index case died.

---

[29] *No, the two are not mutually incompatible.*

[30] *Or, more accurately, the computer, as no rational being would ever want to do this by hand, except to atone for some otherwise unpardonable sin, such as reading another stats book.*

When we're finally done with these mind-numbing calculations, what we've got[31] for each person is some expression, or function, involving the term *f*. Multiplying all of the expressions together gives us the overall probability of the observed deaths. Now the fun begins.

TABLE 10-9   Outcomes of the first 10 subjects

Subject	Length of time in trial (months)	Age (years)	Outcome
I	14	24	Lost
F	22	28	Died
C	29	53	Died
G	37	55	Lost
J	45	47	Censored
D	46	68	Died
A	61	64	Died
H	76	72	Censored
E	92	75	Censored
B	111	60	Lost

Those of you who are still awake at this juncture may have noticed that we've been talking about the term *f* without ever really defining it. Based on both fairly arcane statistical theory as well as real data,[32] the distribution of deaths over time can best be described by a type of curve called **exponential**, and is shown in Figure 10-5. This occurs when the hazard function is a flat line; more events occur early on when there are more people at risk, and then the number tapers off as time goes on because there are fewer people left in the study. In mathematical shorthand, we write the equation for an exponential curve as:

$$y = e^{-kt} \qquad (10\text{-}27)$$

where *e* is an irrational number[33] which is the base of the natural logarithm and is roughly equal to 2.71828. Another way of writing this to avoid superscripts is: $y = \exp(-kt)$. What this equation means is that some variable *y* (in this case, the number of deaths)

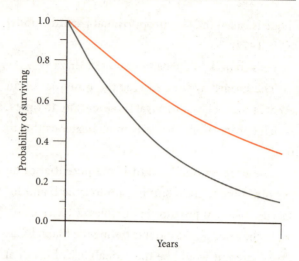

FIGURE 10-5   Two examples of exponential curves.

gets smaller over time (that's why the minus sign is there). The *k* is a constant; it's what makes the two curves in Figure 10-5 differ from one another. All of this is an introduction for saying that the *f* in our equation is really $\exp(-kX)$; *X* is the specific value of the covariate we're interested in (age, in this case), and we've gone through all these calculations simply to determine the value of *k*.

The computer now goes through its gyrations and comes up with an answer. Let's say it tells us that *k* is −0.02, with an associated *p* level of 0.03. First, the *p* tells us that the effect of age is significant: older people have a different rate of dying than those who are less chronologically challenged.[34] Knowing the exact value of *k*, we can compare the RRs at any two times. For example, to compare those who are 40 years old with those who are 60, we simply calculate:

$$RR = \frac{\exp[-(-0.02) \times 40]}{\exp[-(-0.2) \times 60]} - \frac{e^{0.8}}{e^{1.2}} = 0.67$$

$$(10\text{-}28)$$

This gives us the press-stopping news that people who are 40 years of age had only two-thirds the risk of dying as those who are 60 years old.

When we have more than one covariate, we have a number of *k* terms, one for each. If we were to

---

[31] Aside from a headache.

[32] For a change, both theory and facts give the same results.

[33] An irrational number is simply one that cannot be created by the ratio of two numbers. No aspersions are being cast on its mental stability.

[34] For such findings, Nobel prizes are rarely awarded.

write out the exponent for, say, three predictors, it would look like:

$$y = e^{-(k_1X_1 + k_2X_2 + k_3X_3)t} \quad (10\text{-}29)$$

$k_1X_1 + k_2X_2 + k_3X_3$ is basically a multiple regression, where the ks are equivalent to the βs, and with a time factor, t, thrown in.

So, to reiterate, the proportional hazards model allows us to adjust for any number of covariates, whether they are discrete (e.g., sex or use of FengShui) or continuous (e.g., age or amount of red wine consumed every day). Another reason for the popularity of the Cox model is that it is **robust**. Even if we don't know what the shape is of the hazard function (e.g., exponential, Weibull), the Cox model will give us a good approximation; that is, it's a "safe" choice (Kleinbaum, 1996). The only drawback is that, to get relatively accurate estimates of the standard errors associated with the coefficients, larger sample sizes are needed than for the actuarial or KM methods (Blossfeld et al., 1989; Cox, 1972).

TESTING FOR PROPORTIONALITY

So, how do we know if our data meet the assumption of proportional hazards? There are a couple of ways; visual and mathematical. One visual method consists of plotting the hazard functions for the groups over time. If the lines are parallel, the assumption is met; if they diverge or cross, as in Figure 10-6, we don't have proportionality.

Another visual technique is a **log-log** (or **log-minus-log**) plot. For mathematical reasons, we won't bother to go into here,[35] we take the logarithm of the survival function (S), change the sign of the result

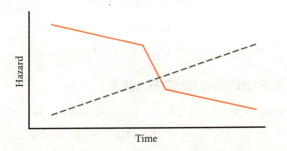

FIGURE 10-6   Because the hazard functions cross, the assumption of proportional hazards is not met.

(because it will be negative, and you can't take the log of a negative number), and then take the log of that again (hence the name "log-log" and the reason for the "minus" in the alias) for two or three values of the covariate and plot the results. If the log-log plot of the data is close to the log-log plot of the expected line of the survival curve for each group, we're fine; otherwise, we have problems.

Appealing and simple as these techniques are (at least if you're a computer), there are a couple of problems. First, how parallel is parallel; or how close is close enough? If the lines are perfectly parallel or if they cross, the answer is fairly obvious. For anything in between, though, we have to make a judgment call, and one person's "close enough" may be another person's "that ain't gonna cut it." Fortunately, Kleinbaum (1996) says the assumption of proportional hazards is "not satisfied *only* when plots are strongly discrepant" (p. 146). A second problem is that these approaches are fine if the covariate has only two or three values. When we're dealing with a continuous covariate, such as age, we have to divide it into a few categories, with all the problems that entails.

The mathematical approach uses a **goodness-of-fit chi-squared** (χ^2_{GOF}) test, with $df = 1$. As with all χ^2 tests, it evaluates how closely the data conform to expected values. With the traditional χ^2, the expected values are those that arise under the null hypothesis that there's no association between two variables, so we naturally want χ^2 to be large, and p to be less than 0.05. With χ^2_{GOF}, though, we're seeing how far the data deviate from some theoretical model that we've proposed, so we *don't* want it to be significant; in fact, the less significant, the better.

So, which do we use? Actually, it's a good idea to use all. If the graphs look sort of parallel and close, and χ^2_{GOF} is not significant, we're in good shape. If they disagree, use your judgment.

CONFIDENCE INTERVALS

We've calculated a lot of different parameters in this section: differences in proportions surviving, hazard

---

[35]*If you want the messy details, see the excellent book by Kleinbaum (1996).*

ratios, and the like. Jealous creatures that they are, each of them demands its own CI, so we'll dip into Gardner and Altman's (1989) book again and dig out a few of them.

In Equation (10-11), we calculated the SE for the survival function at time i. The 95% CI around it is the old standby:

$$S_i \pm 1.96 \times SE_{S_i} \qquad (10\text{-}30)$$

For the difference between survival proportions at any time, we naturally have to start with the SE for the difference between two proportions, P_1 and P_2, each with a given number of people at risk, R_1 and R_2:

$$SE_{Diff} = \sqrt{\frac{S_1(1-S_1)}{R_1} + \frac{S_2(1-S_2)}{R_2}}$$

$$(10\text{-}31)$$

and the 95% CI is:

$$(S_1 - S_2) \pm 1.96 \times SE_{Diff} \qquad (10\text{-}32)$$

For the hazard ratio (h), it's a bit messier. First, we have to calculate two new values, X and Y:

$$X = \frac{O_1 - E_1}{V} \text{ and } Y = \frac{1.96}{\sqrt{V}} \qquad (10\text{-}33)$$

where V is:

$$V = \sum \frac{R_{i_1} R_{i_2} D_i (R_i - D_i)}{R_i^2 (R_i - 1)} \qquad (10\text{-}34)$$

and finally (Yes!), the CI is:

$$e^{(X-Y)} \text{ to } e^{(X+Y)} \qquad (10\text{-}35)$$

SAMPLE SIZE AND POWER

As is usual in determining the required sample size for a study, we have to make some estimate of the magnitude of the *effect size* that we wish to detect. For the *t*-test, the effect size is the ratio of the difference between the groups divided by the SD. In survival analysis, the effect size is the ratio of the hazards, q, at a given time, such as five or 10 years. If we call this ratio δ (delta), then the number of events (deaths, recurrences, readmissions, or whatever) we need in each group can be figured out with an equation proposed by George and Desu (1974):

$$d = \frac{2(z_\alpha + z_\beta)^2}{(\ln \delta)^2} \qquad (10\text{-}36)$$

where the term "$\ln\delta$" means the natural logarithm of

δ. To save you the hassle of having to work through the formula, we've provided sample sizes for various values of δ in Table L in the book's appendix.

Remember that these aren't the sample sizes at the *start* of the study; they're how many people have to have *outcomes*. To figure out how many people have to enter the trial, you'll have to divide these numbers by the proportion in each group you expect will have the outcome. So, if you're planning on a two-tailed α of 0.05, a β of 0.20, and δ of 2, Table L says you'll need 33 events per group. If you expect that 25% of the subjects in the control group will experience the outcome by the time the study ends, then you have to start with $(33 \div 0.25) = 132$ subjects. A different approach to calculating sample sizes, based on the *difference* in survival rates, is given by Freedman (1982), who also provides tables.

To determine the power of a trial after the fact, we take Equation (10-36) and solve for z_β. For those who care, this gives us:

$$z_\beta = \frac{(\ln\delta)\sqrt{d} - z_\alpha\sqrt{2}}{\sqrt{2}} \qquad (10\text{-}37)$$

A minor problem arises if the number of outcomes (d) is different in the two groups. If this happens, the best estimate of the average number of events in the two groups can be derived using the formula for the harmonic mean:

$$d = \frac{2}{\dfrac{1}{d_1} + \dfrac{1}{d_2}} \qquad (10\text{-}38)$$

For example, if Group 1 had 13 events at the end, and Group 2 had 20, we would have:

$$d = \frac{2}{\dfrac{1}{13} + \dfrac{1}{20}} = 15.76 \qquad (10\text{-}39)$$

So we would use 15.76 (or 16) for d.

REPORTING GUIDELINES

The most crucial information you want to report is the survival curve. If there are two or more groups, be sure that the lines for them are clearly distinguishable (don't use different colors for a journal article; journals don't do color). When you're comparing groups, you should report (1) the hazard ratio; (2) its confidence interval; (3) the statistical test between the groups (e.g., the log-rank test); (4) its exact p level; and (5) some indication of the survival in each group, such as the median survival time or the survival probabilities at a particular time.

SUMMARY

✧ In this chapter, time-to-event data was introduced, including **censored data**. The survival time data and the presence of censored observations are non-normality. The Kaplan-Meier method and life table are used to **calculate** the survival rate and median survival time and to plot the survival curve. The log-rank test and Breslow test are used to compare the survival curves between two or more groups. If we want to study the effects of several risk factors on survival, then the Cox proportional-hazards model can be used to adjust covariates. But the Cox model require the **data to meet the assumption of proportional hazards.**

GLOSSARY

survival analysis   生存分析
covariates   协变量
lost to follow-up   失访
mean survival   平均生存时间
censored   删失
survival rate   生存率
life-table   寿命表
product-limit method   乘积极限法
Kaplan-Meier approach   Kaplan-Meier 方法
cumulative probability of survival   累积生存概率
survival function   生存函数
conditional probability   条件概率

survival curve   生存曲线
hazard function   风险函数
median survival time   中位生存时间
average hazard rate   平均风险率
relative risk (RR)   相对危险度
hazard ratio (HR)   风险比
odds ratio   优势比
Mantel-Cox log-rank test   Mantel-Cox 对数秩检验
Mantel-Cox chi-squared   Mantel-Cox 卡方检验
Cox proportional hazards model   Cox 比例风险模型
exponential curves   指数曲线
goodness-of-fit   拟合优度

EXERCISES

Television executives are becoming worried that, at one point or another, all TV talk-show hosts become afflicted with a case of terminal megalomania and think they are as powerful as the Assistant Junior Vice President in Charge of Washroom Keys. To slow the onset of this insidious condition, the executives try an experiment. They hire a group of television psychologists[36] to give half of the 20 hosts a course in Humbleness 101[37] and have the other half serve as the controls. The outcome is any 5-minute interval where the host says "I," "me," or "my" more than 15 times; a sure sign that the course did not work or that its effects are wearing off.

Because the course is a grueling one, the company can take in only one or two people each month over the 2 years of the study. Also, some of the hosts are killed off by irate viewers, crashes in their Lamborghinis, or enraged Assistant Junior Vice Presidents in Charge of Washroom Keys. The data for the experiment are shown in the accompanying table.

1. Draw an actuarial curve for these data.

2. What test would you use to determine whether

---

[36]*They used to be pet psychologists until the market went to the dogs.*

[37]*The motto of this company is, "The most important thing is sincerity. Once you learn to fake that, the rest is easy."*

Outcomes for subjects in both groups	TV host	Treatment/control	Month of entry	Month of conclusion	Outcome
	1	T	2	24	Still humble
	2	C	3	18	Megalomaniacal
	3	T	4	24	Still humble
	4	T	4	20	Megalomaniacal
	5	C	5	8	Megalomaniacal
	6	T	5	23	Dead
	7	C	6	22	Still humble
	8	C	6	9	Megalomaniacal
	9	T	8	23	Megalomaniacal
	10	T	8	24	Still humble
	11	C	9	22	Still humble
	12	C	11	24	Still humble
	13	T	11	20	Megalomaniacal
	14	C	13	15	Dead
	15	T	14	24	Still humble
	16	C	16	24	Still humble
	17	T	19	23	Still humble
	18	T	21	24	Still humble
	19	C	20	21	Megalomaniacal
	20	C	22	24	Still humble

your treatment works?

3. What would your data look like if you simply approached it with a **contingency table** chi-squared?
4. What is the SE at 6 to 7 months for the control group?
5. What is the relative risk at 18 months? (If you cheated on your homework and didn't work out the table for the experimental group, $p_E = 0.567$.)

How to Get the Computer to Do the Work for You Actuarial Method

- From **Analyze**, choose **Survival → Life Tables**
- Click on the variable in the left column that indicates the time since entry into the study, and click the arrow to move it into the **Time** box
- Fill in the boxes in the **Display Time Intervals** area. In the first box (**0 through ❑**), fill in the last interval you want analyzed. In the second box (**by ❑**), enter 1 if you want to analyze every interval, 2 for every other interval, and so on
- Click on the variable in the left column that indicates the outcome for that case, and move it into the **Status** area with the arrow button

- Click the [Define Event] button
- The default is **Single Value.** Enter the number that indicates that an outcome has occurred (all other values will be treated as censored data)
- If you have two or more groups, you can analyze each group separately by moving the variable that defines group membership into the **Factor** box
- By clicking the [Options] button, you can elect to display the survival function or the hazard function, or both
- Click [Continue] and then [OK]

Kaplan-Meier Method

- From **Analyze**, choose **Survival → Kaplan-Meier**
- The rest is identical to the Actuarial Method

Cox Proportional Hazards Method

- From **Analyze**, choose **Survival → Cox Regression**
- Then follow the instructions for the Actuarial Method, except now you can enter the name of the covariate(s) into the **Covariates** box or analyze categorical data by strata by entering the name of the variable into the **Strata** box

SUGGESTED READINGS AND WEBSITES

[1] Kleinbaum DG,Klein M. Survival Analysis: A Self-Learning Text. 3rd ed. Statistics for Biology and Health. 2012, 76(3):507-508.

[2] Hosmer DW, Lemeshow S. Applied Survival Analysis: Regression Modeling of Time to Event Data. Wiley-Interscience, 1999. http://www.ats. ucla.edu/stat/examples/asa/.

[3] Institute for Digital Research and Education. Introduction to Survival Analysis in SAS. https:// stats.idre.ucla.edu/sas/seminars/sas-survival/.

[4] Prinja S, Gupta N, Verma R. Censoring in Clinical Trials: Review of Survival Analysis Techniques. Indian J Community Med. 2010,35(2): 217-221.

[5] Short course-Statistical methods for population-based cancer survival analysis. http://cansurv. net/links.html.

[6] Kleinbaum DG,Klein M. Survival Analysis: A Self-Learning Text. 2nd ed. Springer, New York, 2005.

[7] LEE ET, Wang JW. Statistical Methods for Survival Data Analysis. 3rd ed. Wiley, New York, 2003.

[8] Hosmer DW, Lemeshow S. Applied Survival Analysis: Regression Modeling of Time to Event data, Wiley, New York, 1999.

[9] Allison PD. Survival Analysis using SAS®: A Practical Guide. 2nd ed. SAS Publishing, Cary, NC,2010.

CHAPTER THE ELEVENTH
Simple Regression and Correlation

The previous section dealt with ANOVA methods, which are suitable when the independent variable is nominal categories and the dependent variable approximates an interval variable. However, there are many problems in which both independent and dependent variables are interval-level measurements. In these circumstances (with 1 independent variable) the appropriate method is called simple regression and is analogous to one-way ANOVA.

SETTING THE SCENE

Lead is a kind of neurotoxic heavy metal elements, intrauterine lead exposure is more important to affect children's development than after birth. How do we investigate the relationship between infant lead content in umbilical blood and lead content in parturiens. Apparently the level of blood lead in pregnant women and umbilical cord are both continuous variables. You could categorize one or the other into High, Medium, and Low and do an ANOVA, but this would lose information. Are there better ways?

BASIC CONCEPTS OF REGRESSION ANALYSIS

At present, the harm of lead to children's health has aroused the concern of the society. The development of fetus nervous system is the most rapid, but also the most vulnerable to be damaged in the period before the birth. This relationship wasn't well known until an observant doctor in Guangdong province noticed this affliction among her patients and decided to do a scientific investigation.

But how to start the research design? After reviewing the literature on this phenomenon, she decided that the fetus blood lead content could be captured by blood lead in pregnant women. Now we define the gravidas blood lead as X; and the fetus blood lead content as Y.

X and Y are very nice variables; both have interval properties. Thus we can go ahead and add or subtract, take means and SDs, and engage in all those arcane games that delight only statisticians. But the issue is, How do we test for a relationship between X and Y?

Let's begin with a graph. We enlisted 20 pregnant women and measured their and their baby's blood lead content. The data might look like Figure 11-1. At first glance, it certainly seems that some relationship exists between X and Y—the higher the X, the higher the Y. It also seems to follow a straight-line relationship—we can apparently capture all the relationship by drawing a straight line through the points.

Before we vault into the calculations, it might be worthwhile to speculate on the reasons why we all agree[1] on the existence of some relationship between

---

[1]*One good reason is that the teacher says so. When we were students, this never held much appeal; strangely, now it does.*

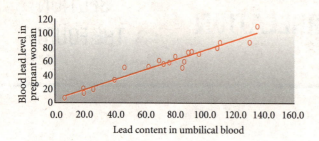

FIGURE 11-1 *Relation between range of X and Y in 20 pregnant women.*

the two variables. After all, the statistics, if done right, should concur with some of our intuitions. One way to consider the question is to go to extremes and see what conditions would lead us to the conclusion that (1) no relationship or (2) a perfect relationship exists.

Examine, if you will, Figure 11-2. Seemingly, the relationship depicted in the upper graph is as perfect as it gets. To the untrained eye (yours, not ours), Y is perfectly predictable from X—if you know one, you can calculate another. By contrast, even a geneticist would likely give up on the lower graph because of the lack of

an apparent association between the two variables.

Two reasons why we might infer a relationship between two variables are (1) the line relating the two is not horizontal (i.e., the slope is not zero). In fact, one might be driven to conclude that the stronger the relationship, the more the line differs from the horizontal. Unfortunately, although this captures the spirit of the game, it is not quite accurate. (2) Perhaps less obviously, the closer the points fall to the fitted line, the stronger the relationship. That's why we concluded there was a perfect linear relationship on the top left of Figure 11-2. The straight-line relationship between X and Y explained all the variability in Y.

Actually, both observations contain some of the essence of the relationship question. If we contrast the amount of variability captured in the departures of individual points from the fitted line with the amount of variability contained in the fitted function, then this is a relative measure of the strength of association of the two variables.

To elaborate a little more, consider Figure 11-3, where we have chosen to focus on the narrow window of the blood lead level of baby between 80.0 and 140.0, which were extracted from the original data of Figure 11-1. Now the signal (there's that ugly word again!) is contained in the departure of the fitted data from the grand mean of 75.1. The noise is contained in the variability of the individual data about the corresponding fitted points.

If this is not starting to look familiar, then you must have slept through Section II.[2] We could apply

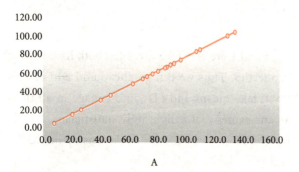

A

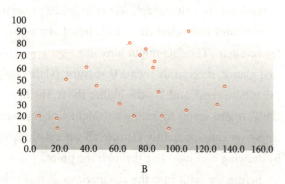

B

FIGURE 11-2 *Relation between X and Y (enlarged).*

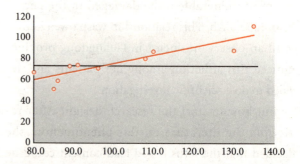

FIGURE 11-3 **Relation between two variable (enlarged).**

[2]*A not uncommon experience among readers of statistics books; however, we had hoped the dirty jokes would reduce the soporific effect of this one.*

the same, now almost reflex, approach of calculating a Sum of Squares (Signal) based on deviations of the fitted points from the grand mean and a Sum of Squares (Noise) based on deviations of individual data from the corresponding fitted points.

One mystery remains, however, before we launch into the arcane delights of sum-of-squaring everything in sight. In several locations we have referred to the fitted line rather glibly, with no indication of how one fits such a line. Well, the moment of reckoning has arrived. For openers, you must retrieve the linear model from the depth of your minds, namely:

$$Y = \beta_0 + \beta_1 X + \varepsilon$$

Where Y and X both are interval variables. The term β_0 is the intercept, also known as the value of Y when X is equal to zero, and β_1 is the slope, or regression coefficient, the amount of average change in Y when X changes the value of a unit. And ε is the random error in the study.

Let's refit the linear equation by using the sample data in many cases and also change "β_0" and "β_1" to "b_0" and "b_1":

$$\hat{Y} = b_0 + b_1 X$$

That funny-looking thing over Y goes by the technical name of "hat"? so we would say, "Y hat equals…" It means that for any given value of X, the equation yields an estimate of the Y, rather than the original value. So, a $\hat{Y}$ over any variable signifies an estimate of it.

Still, the issue remains of how one goes about selecting the value of b_0 and b_1 to best fit the line to the data. The strategy used in this analysis is to adjust the values in such a way as to maximize the variance resulting from the fitted line, or, equivalently, to minimize the variance resulting from deviations from the fitted line. Now although it sounds as if we are faced with the monumental task of trying some values, calculating the variances, diddling the values a bit and recalculating the values, and carrying on until an optimal solution comes about, it isn't at all that bad. The right answer can be determined analytically (in other words, as a solvable equation) with calculus.

Unfortunately, no one who has completed the second year of college ever uses calculus, including ourselves, so you will have to accept that the computer knows the way to beauty and wisdom, even if you don't.[3] For reasons that bear no allegiance to Freud, the method is called regression analysis[4] and the line of best fit is the regression line. A more descriptive and less obscure term is **least-squares analysis** because the goal is to create a line that results in the least square sum between fitted and actual data. Because the term doesn't sound obscure and scientific enough, no one uses it.

According to least-squares principles, it is not difficult to get the values of the two statistics in the linear equation above:

$$b = \frac{\sum (x_i - \bar{x})(y_i - \bar{y})}{\sum (y_i - \bar{y})^2} \qquad a = \bar{y} - b\bar{x} \qquad \textbf{(11-1)}$$

Where $\bar{x}$ and $\bar{y}$ is the mean of x and y respectively. Furthermore, the numerator denotes cross-product of X deviations and Y deviations, but the denominator only denotes the sum of square of y.

The regression line is the straight line passing through the data that minimizes the sum of the squared differences between the original data and the fitted points. It is simple and often provide an adequate and interpretable description of how the inputs affect the output.

Now that that is out of the way, let's go back to the old routine and start to do some sums of squares. The first sum of squares results from the signal, or

---

[3]*The key to the solution resides in the magical words maximum and minimum. In calculus, to find a maximum or minimum of an equation, you take the derivative and set it equal to zero, then solve the equation, equivalent to setting the slope equal to zero. The quantity we want to maximize is the squared difference between the individual data and the corresponding fitted line. To get the best fit line, this sum is differentiated with respect to both b_0 and b_1, and the resulting expression is set equal to zero. This results in two equations in two unknowns, so we can solve the equations for the optimal values of the b.*

[4]*The real reason it's called regression? is that the technique is based on a study by Francis Galton called regression Toward Mediocrity in Hereditary Stature.? In today's language, tall people's children regress? to the mean height of the population. (And one of the authors is delighted Galton discovered that persons of average height are mediocre; he always suspected it).*

the difference between the fitted points and the horizontal line through the mean of X and Y.[5] In creating this equation, we call $\hat{Y}$ the fitted point on the line that corresponds to each of the original data; in other words, $\hat{Y}$ is the number that results from plugging the X value of each individual into the regression equation.

$$SS_{regression} = \sum(\hat{Y}_i - \bar{Y})^2 \quad \text{(11-2)}$$

This tells us how far the predicted values differ from the overall mean, analogous to the Sum of Squares (Between) in ANOVA. The value reflects the linear effects of X on Y.

The second sum of squares reflects the difference between the original data and the fitted line. This looks like:

$$SS_{residual} = \sum(Y_i - \hat{Y}_i)^2 \quad \text{(11-3)}$$

This is capturing the error between the estimate and the actual data, analogous to the Sum of Squares (Within) in ANOVA. It should be called the error sum of squares, or the within sum of squares, but it isn't— it's called the Sum of Squares (Residual), expressing the variance that remains, or residual variance, after the regression is all over.

To make this just a little less abstract, we have actually listed the data used in making Figure 11-1 in Table 11-1. On the left side is the calculated X for each of the afflicted, in the middle is the corresponding Y, and on the right is the fitted value of the Y based on the analytic approach described above (i.e., plugging the X in the equation and estimating Y).

As an example of the looks of these sums of squares, the Sum of Squares (Regression) has terms such as:

$$SS_{reg} = (4.5-75.1)^2 + (14.5-75.1)^2 + ... + (84.5-75.1)^2 \quad \text{(11-4)}$$

and the Sum of Squares (Residual) has terms such as:

$$SS_{res} = (6-4.5)^2 + (19-14.5)^2 + ... + (110-84.5)^2 \quad \text{(11-5)}$$

To save you the anguish, we have worked out the

TABLE 11-1 Range of motion (Y) and lead content in umbilical blood (X) in 20 pregnant women

subject	X	Y	Fitted Y
1	6.1	6.0	4.5
2	18.5	19.0	14.5
3	19.0	13.0	9.9
4	25.0	18.5	14.1
5	39.0	32.0	24.5
6	46.0	50.0	38.4
7	62.0	51.0	39.1
8	69.0	60.0	46.0
9	72.0	55.3	42.4
10	76.0	57.0	43.7
11	80.0	66.0	50.7
12	85.0	50.0	38.4
13	86.0	58.0	44.5
14	89.0	72.0	55.3
15	91.0	73.0	56.0
16	96.0	70.0	53.7
17	108.0	79.0	60.7
18	110.0	86.0	66.0
19	130.0	87.0	66.8
20	135.0	110.0	84.5

Sum of Squares (Regression) and Sum of Squares (Residual) and have (inevitably) created an ANOVA table, or at least the first two columns of it (Table 11-2).

TABLE 11-2 ANOVA table for X against Y (step 1)

Source	Sums of Squares	df	Mean Square	F
Regression	13 153.0			
Residual	810.1			

However, the remaining terms are a bit problematic. We can't count groups, so it is a little unclear how many df to put on each line. It's time for a little logic. The idea of df is the difference between the number of data values and the number of estimated parameters. The parameters were means up until now, but the same idea applies. We have two param-

---

[5]*The reason for examining differences from the horizontal line is clear if we project the data onto the Y-axis. The horizontal through the mean of the Ys is just the Grand Mean, in our old ANOVA notation, and we are calculating the analogue of the Sum of Squares (Between). Another way to think of it is—if no relationship between X and Y existed, then the best estimate of Y at each value of X is the mean value of Y. If we plotted this, we'd get a horizontal line, just as we've shown.*

eters in the problem, the slope and the intercept, so it would seem that the regression line should have 2 df. The residual should have $(n-2-1)$ or 17, to give the usual total of $(n-1)$, losing 1 for the grand mean. Almost, but not quite. One of the parameters is the intercept term, and this is completely equivalent to the grand mean, so only 1 df is associated with this regression, and $(n-1-1)$ with the error term. Analysis of variance (ANOVA) table for simple linear regression model can be shown as Table 11-3:

TABLE 11-3   Analysis of variance (ANOVA) table for simple linear regression model

Source	df	Sums of Squares	Mean Squares	F-Statistic
Regression	1	SS_R	$MS_R = SS_R/1$	$F = MS_R/MS_E$
Error	$n-2$	SS_E	$MS_E = SS_E/(n-2)$	
Total	$n-1$	Variation in y (SS_T)		

Now that we have this in hand, we can also go on to the calculation of the Mean Squares and, for that matter, can create an F-test. So the table now looks like Table 11-4. The p-value associated with the F-test, in a completely analogous manner, tells us whether the regression line is significantly different from the horizontal (i.e., whether a significant relationship exists between the X and Y). In this case, yes.

B'S, BETAS AND TESTS OF SIGNIFICANCE

While the ANOVA of regression in Table 11-4 gives an overall measure of whether or not the regression line is significant, it doesn't actually say anything about what the line actually is—what the computed value of b_0 and b_1 are. Typically, these values are presented in a separate table, as shown in Table 11-5.

TABLE 11-4   ANOVA table for X against Y (step 2)

Source	Sums of Squares	df	Mean Square	F
Regression	13 153.0	1	13 153.0	292.2
Residual	810.1	18	45.0	

TABLE 11-5   Regression Coefficient and Standard Errors for X against Y

Parameter	b	SE (b)	β	t	P
Constant (b_0)	4.179	3.363		1.243	0.23
Slope (b_1)	0.713	0.042	0.971	17.095	0.000

The first column of numbers is just the estimates of the coefficients that resulted from the minimization procedure described in the last section. The second, labeled Standard Error (or SE), requires some further discussion. For the slope, which is what we usually are most worried about, it turns out that the SE is related to the Mean Square (Residual), MS_{Res}. The square root of MS_{Res}, called $S(Y|X)$ (the standard error of Y given X), is just the standard deviation of the deviations between the original data and the fitted values; the bigger this is, the more error there is going to be in the estimate of the slope. But there are a couple of other things coming into play. First, as usual, the larger the sample size, the smaller the SE, with the usual $1/\sqrt{n}$ relation. And the more dispersion there is in the X-values, the better we can anchor the line, so this error term in inversely related to the standard deviation of the X-values. The actual formula is:

$$SE(\beta_1) = \frac{\sqrt{MS_{Res}}}{S_x\sqrt{(n-1)}} \qquad (11\text{-}6)$$

where S_x is the standard deviation of the X-values. The SE associated with the intercept is similar, but a bit more complicated. Since we rarely care about it, we'll not go into any more detail.

*The column labelled β (beta) is called a **Standard Regression Coefficient**; like a z-score, this expresses the coefficient in standard deviation units. We'll talk more about it in the next chapter. Finally, the table contains a t-test, which actually has the same form as all the other t-tests we've encountered; it's just the ratio of the coefficient to its SE.*

There's another consistency lurking in the table as well. After all, the test of the significance of the regression line is the test of the significance of the slope. Fortunately, it works out this way. The F-test from Table 11-4 is just the square of the t-test, and the p-values are exactly the same.

THE REGRESSION LINE: ERRORS AND CONFIDENCE INTERVALS

While we're pursuing the idea of errors in slopes and intercepts, there are a couple of other ways to think about it. If we think about the graph of the data in

Figure 11-1, we can imagine that the fitted line, with its associated errors, actually looks more like a fitted band, where the true value of the line could be anywhere within the band around our computed best fit. Further, while it's tempting to think that this band might just be like a ribbon around the fitted line, with limits as two other parallel lines above and below the fitted line, this isn't quite the case. There is error in both the slope and intercept; this means that as the slope varies, it's going to sweep out something like a Japanese fan around the point on the graph corresponding to the mean of X and Y. In other words, we have the best fix on the line where most of the points are, at the center, and as we move toward the extremes we have more and more error.

Putting the two ideas together, then, the confidence interval around the fitted line is going to be at a minimum at the mean and spread out as we get to high and low values (where there are fewer subjects), as shown by the dotted red lines in Figure 11-4. The actual equation is a pretty complicated combination of things we've seen before: the SE of the residuals, $S(Y \mid X)$, the sample size, and an expression involving the standard deviation of the Xs. The standard error of the line at any point X, is

$$SE(X) = S(Y \mid X) \sqrt{\frac{1}{N} + \frac{(X - \bar{X})^2}{(n-1)S_x^2}} \qquad (11\text{-}7)$$

where S_x^2 is the variance of the X-values. So, the SE is at a minimum when X is at the mean, equal to $S(Y \mid X)/\sqrt{n}$, and it gets bigger proportional to the square of the distance from X to the mean.

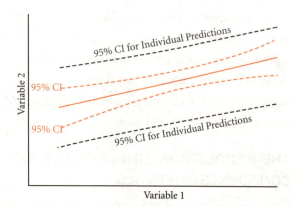

FIGURE 11-4   *The 95% CI around the regression line (red) and the 95% CI for predicting the score of a single individual (black).*

The confidence interval is just this quantity multiplied by the t-value, on either side of the fitted line:

$$CI_{95\%} = \hat{Y}_i \pm t_{n-2,\,1-\alpha/2} SE(X) \qquad (11\text{-}8)$$

So this fancy formula ends up describing a kind of double-trumpet-shaped zone around the fitted line, which is the $(1-\alpha)\%$ confidence interval around the line. Technically this formula should be used for infinite populations.

If you go back to Figure 11-4, you'll see another CI, much broader, around the regression line. This is the CI for predicting the DV for a single individual. It's wider than the CI for the line for the same reason that the CIs are wider at the ends—sample size. There's more error associated with the prediction of the score for one person with a given set of values of the predictor variable(s) than for a group of people with the same values.

THE COEFFICIENT OF DETERMINATION AND THE CORRELATION COEFFICIENT

However, we have been insistent to the point of nagging that statistical significance says nothing about the magnitude of the effect.

For some obscure reason, people who do regression analysis are more aware of this issue and spend more time and paper examining the size of effects than does the ANOVA crowd. One explanation may lie in the nature of the studies. Regression, particularly multiple regression, is often applied to existing data bases containing zillions of variables. Under these circumstances, significant associations are a dime a dozen , and their size matters a lot .By contrast, ANOVA is usually applied to experiments in which only a few variables are manipulated, the data were gathered prospectively at high cost, and the researchers are grateful for any significant result, no matter how small.

We have a simple way to determine the magnitude of the effect—simply look at the proportion of the variance explained by the regression. This number is called the **coefficient of determination** and usually written as R^2 for the case of simple regression. The formula is:

$$R^2 = \frac{SS_{reg}}{SS_{reg} + SS_{res}} \qquad (11\text{-}9)$$

This expression is just the ratio of the signal (the sum of the squares of Y accounted for by X) to the signal plus noise, or the total sum of squares. Put another way , this is the proportion of variance in Y explained by X. For our example, this equals $13\ 153 \div (13\ 153 + 810.1)$, or 0.942. (If you examine the formula for eta^2 in Chapter 7, this is completely analogous.)

R^2, the *coefficient of determination*, expresses the proportion of variance in the dependent variable explained by the independent variable.

The square root of this quantity is a term familiar to all, long before you had any statistics course—it's the **correlation coefficient:**

$$r = \pm \sqrt{\frac{SS_{reg}}{SS_{reg} + SS_{res}}} \qquad (11\text{-}10)$$

Note the little $\pm$ sign. Because the square of any number,it is positive or negative, is always positive, the converse also holds: the square root of a positive number[6] can be positive or negative. This is of some value; we call the correlation positive if the slope of the line is positive (more of X gives more of Y) and negative if, such as in the present situation, the slope is negative. So the correlation is $\sqrt{0.942} = 0.971$. One other fact, which may be helpful (e.g., looking up the significance of the correlation in Table G in the Appendix), is that the *df* of the correlation is the number of pairs 2.

The *correlation coefficient is* a number between −1 and +1 whose sign is the same as the slope of the line and whose magnitude is related to the degree of linear association between two variables.

We choose to remain consistent with the idea of expressing the correlation coefficient in terms of sums of squares to show how it relates to the familiar concepts of signal and noise. However, this is not the usual expression encountered in more hidebound stats texts. So there is a complete formula as follows:

$$r = \frac{\sum(X_i - \bar{X})(Y_i - \bar{Y})}{\sqrt{[\sum(X_i - \bar{X})^2][\sum(Y_i - \bar{Y})^2]}} \qquad (11\text{-}11)$$

Because we can write $(X_i - \bar{X})$ as x_i, and $(Y_i - \bar{Y})$ as y_i, this can also be written as:

$$r = \frac{\sum xy}{\sqrt{\sum x^2 \sum y^2}} \qquad (11\text{-}12)$$

However messy this looks, some components are recognizable. The denominator is simply made up of two sums of squares, one for X and one for Y. If we divide out by an N here and there, we would have a product of the variance of X and the variance of Y, all square-rooted. The numerator is a bit different— it is a cross-product of X deviations and Y deviations. Some clarification may come from taking two extreme cases. First, imagine that X and Y are really closely related, so that when X is large (or small) Y is large (or small)—they are *highly correlated*. In this case, every time you have a positive deviation of X from its mean, Y also deviates in a positive direction from its mean, so the term is $(+) \times (+) = +$. Conversely, small values of X and Y correspond to negative deviations from the mean, so this term ends up as $(-) \times (-) = +$. So if X and Y are highly correlated (positively), each pair contributes a positive quantity to this sum., if X and Y are negatively correlated, large values of X are associated with small values of Y, and vice versa. Therefore each term contributes a negative quantity to the sum.

Now imagine there is no relationship between X and Y. Now, each positive deviation of X from its mean would be equally likely to be paired with a positive and a negative deviation of Y. So the sum of the cross-products would likely end up close to zero, as the positive and negative terms cancel each other out offset each other. Thus, this term expresses the extent that X and Y vary together, so it is called the **covariance** of X and Y, or **cov** (X,Y).

The *covariance* of X and Y is the product of the deviations of X and Y from their respective means.

The correlation coefficient, then, the covariance

---

[6]Note that the coefficient of determination should not be less than zero because it is the ratio of two sums of squares. It can happen, when no relationship exists, to have an estimated sum of squares below zero; this is due simply to rounding error. Usually, it is then set equal to zero.

of X and Y, standardized by dividing out by the respective SDs. So, another way of representing it is:

$$r = \frac{\text{cov}(X,Y)}{\sqrt{\text{var}(X) \times \text{var}(Y)}} \qquad \textbf{(11-13)}$$

Incidentally, of historical importance, this version was derived by another one of the field's granddaddies, Karl Pearson. Hence it is often called the **Pearson Correlation Coefficient**. This name is used to distinguish it from several alternative forms, in particular the Intraclass Correlation. Its full name, used only at black-tie affairs, is the Pearson Product Moment Correlation Coefficient. Whatever it's called, it is always abbreviated r.

INTERPRETATION OF THE CORRELATION COEFFICIENT

Because the correlation coefficient is so ubiquitous in biomedical research people have developed some cultural norms about what constitutes a reasonable value for the correlation. One starting point that is often forgotten is the relationship between the correlation coefficient and the proportion of variance we showed above—the square of the correlation coefficient gives the proportion of the variance in Y explained by X. So a correlation of 0.7, which is viewed favorably by most researchers, explains slightly less than half the variance; and a correlation of 0.3, which is statistically significant with a sample size of 40 or 20 (see Table G in the Appendix), accounts for about 10% of the variance.

Having said all that, the cultural norms now reestablish themselves. In some quarters, such as physiology and some epidemiology, any correlation of 0.15, which is statistically significant with a sample size of about 400, is viewed with delight. To maintain some sanity, we have demonstrated for you how correlations of different sizes actually appear.[7] In Figure 11-5, we have generated data sets corresponding to correlations of 0.3, 0.5, 0.7, and 0.9. Our calibrated eyeball says, even at 0.9, a lot of scatter occurs about the line; conversely on the contrary, 0.3 hardly merits any consideration.[8]

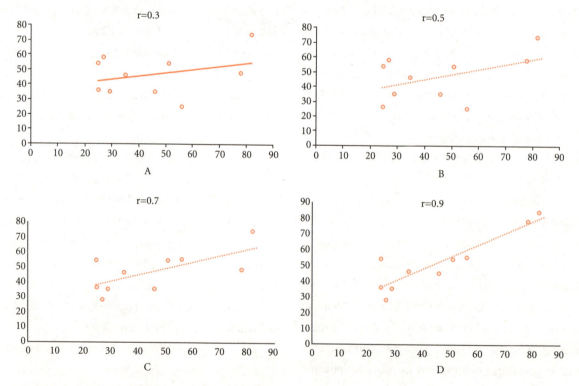

FIGURE 11-5   Scatter plots of with correlations

---

[7] *If people took Section I seriously, this demonstration would not be necessary. However they don't, so it is.*

[8] *We 'fess up. You don't have to track our own CVs very far back to find instances where we were waxing ecstatic in print about pretty low correlations. Those are the circles we move in.*

There's a third way to get some feel for the magnitude of a correlation. If we take only those people who score above the median on X, where do they fall on Y? If the correlation between X and Y is 0, then the score on one variable doesn't affect the score on the other, so we'd expect that half of these people would be above the median on Y, and half would be below. Similarly, if the correlation were 1.0, then all of the people who are above the median on X would also be above the median on Y. Unfortunately, the relationship isn't linear between $r = 0$ and $r = 1$; the actual relationship is shown in Figure 11-6.

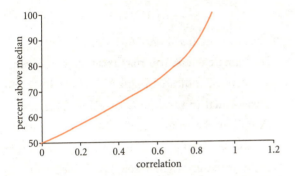

FIGURE 11-6   Percentage of people above the median on one variable who are above the median on the second variable, for various magnitudes of the correlation.

Bear in mind when you're trying to make sense of the relative magnitudes of two correlations that r is not scaled at an interval level. A correlation of 0.6 is larger than one of 0.3, but it is not twice as large. However, the *coefficient of determination* (r^2 for a simple correlation, R^2 for simple and multiple regression) is on ratio scale, so that an r^2 of 0.50 is twice as large as an r^2 of 0.25. In the next section, we'll discuss a transformation that puts r on a ratio scale.

One last point about the interpretation of the correlation coefficient. If there is one guiding motto in statistics, it is this: CORRELATION DOES NOT EQUAL CAUSATION! Just because X and Y are correlated, and just because you can predict Y from X, and just because this correlation is significant at the 0.0001 level, does not mean that X causes Y. It is equally plausible that Y causes X or that both result from some other things, such as Z. If you compare country statistics, you find a correlation of about -0.9 between both infant rate and the number of computers per capita. However much fun it is to speculate that the reason is because to buy some clothes and to send email to whoever has online mail, most people would recognize that the underlying cause of both is degree of development.

Simple as the idea is, it continues to amaze us how often it has been ignored, to the later embarrassment (we hope) of the investigators involved. For example, among all the risk factors of hypercholesterolemia, one researcher found that hypocholesterolemia was associated with a higher incidence of stomach cancer and warned about lowering your triglyceride levels too much. It turned out that he got it bass-ackwards—the cancer can produce hypocholesterolemia. Closer to home, several studies showed an association between an "ear crease" in the earlobe and heart disease. Lovely physiologic explanations have been made of the association—extra vascularization, an excess of androgens, etc. However, in the end, it turned out that both ear creases and coronary artery disease are strongly associated with obesity, and the latter is a known and much more plausible risk factor.

CONFIDENCE INTERVALS, SIGNIFICANCE TESTS, AND EFFECT SIZE

Making r Normal

With other parameters we've calculated, such as the mean, it's fairly straightforward to figure out the SE and then the 95% CI. Would that life were that simple here. Unfortunately, as we've said, Pearson's r is not measured on an interval scale and therefore is not normally distributed, which can lead to two problems: the CIs won't be accurate; and for large correlations, the upper bound of the CI may exceed 1.0. We have to proceed in three steps: (1) transform the r so that its distribution is normal; (2) figure out the SE and CI on the transformed value; and (3) "untransform"[9] the answers so that they're comparable with the original correlation. Fisher worked out the equation for the

---

[9] *No, there isn't such a word, but there should be.*

transformation, so not too surprisingly, it's called *Fisher's z'*. We can either use Equation (11-14) and do the calculations (it's not really that hard with a calculator), or use Table P in the Appendix:

$$z' = \frac{1}{2} \log_e \frac{1+r}{1-r} \qquad (11\text{-}14)$$

and the SE of z' is simply:

$$SE_z = \frac{1}{\sqrt{N-3}} \qquad (11\text{-}15)$$

Where N is the number of pairs of scores. Note that SE is not affected by anything happening in the data—the means, SDs, or the correlation itself.

Confidence Intervals

Now the 95% CI is in the same form that we've seen before:

$$CI_{95\%} = z' \pm \frac{Z_{\alpha/2}}{\sqrt{N-3}} \qquad (11\text{-}16)$$

Where $z_{\alpha/2} = 1.96$ for the 95%CI if N is over 30; if it isn't, use the table for the *t*-tests, with *N–3 df*. Now we have to take those two z'-values and turn them back into *r*s, for which we use Equation (11-17) or Table Q in the Appendix:

$$r = \frac{e^{2z'} - 1}{e^{2z'} + 1} \qquad (11\text{-}17)$$

So for our example, where $r = 0.904$,

$$z' = \frac{1}{2} \log_e \frac{1 + 0.904}{1 - 0.904} + \frac{1}{2} \log_e (19.833)$$

$$= 1.494$$

$$(11\text{-}18)$$

which means that the two ends of the interval are:

$$\left[1.494 - \frac{1.96}{\sqrt{20-3}} = 1.019 \right] \text{ and}$$

$$\left[1.494 + \frac{1.96}{\sqrt{20-3}} = 1.969 \right] \qquad (11\text{-}19)$$

Getting those back into r_s gives us:

$$\left[\frac{e^{(2 \times 1.019)} - 1}{e^{(2 \times 1.019)} + 1} = \frac{6.675}{8.675} = 0.769 \right] \text{ and}$$

$$\left[\frac{e^{(2 \times 1.969)} - 1}{e^{(2 \times 969)} + 1} = \frac{50.316}{52.316} = 0.962 \right]$$

$$(11\text{-}20)$$

so the 95% CI for the correlation is [0.769, 0.962]. Note the CI is symmetric around the z'-score, but isn't around the value of *r*. It's symmetrical when *r* is 0.50, but for all other values, it's shorter at the end

nearer to 0 or 1.

To see if the correlation is significantly different from 0, we first need the SE of *r*, which is:

$$SE_r = \sqrt{\frac{1-r^2}{n-2}} \qquad (11\text{-}21)$$

which in our case is:

$$SE_r = \frac{\sqrt{1-0.971^2}}{\sqrt{20-2}} = 0.056 \qquad (11\text{-}22)$$

Therefore, the test for statistical significance is a run-of-the-mill *t*-test; the parameter divided by the SE, with *df=N–2*:

$$t = \frac{r}{SE_r} = \frac{r}{\sqrt{(1-r^2)/(n-2)}} \qquad (11\text{-}23)$$

which is equal to $0.971 \div 0.056 = 17.340$.

For completeness, you may recall an earlier situation where we indicated that an F-value with 1 and *N df* was equal to the squared *t*-value. This case is no exception; the equivalent F-value is 17.34^2, which is just about the value (within rounding error) that emerged from our original ANOVA (Table 11-4).

Effect Size

Having just gone through all these calculations to test the significance of *r*, we should mention two things. First, you can save yourself a lot of work by simply referring to Table G in the Appendix. Second, testing whether an *r* is statistically different from 0.00 is, in some ways, a Type III error—getting the correct answer to a question nobody is asking. We have to do it to keep journal editors happy and off our backs, but the important question is rarely if *r* differs from zero; with a large enough sample size, almost any correlation will differ from zero. The issue is if it's large enough to take note of. Here we fall back on the coefficient of determination we discussed earlier; simply square the value of r. As a rough rule of thumb, if r^2 doesn't even reach 0.10 (that is, an *r* of 0.30 or so), don't bother to call us with your results.

In fact, *r* is itself a measure of effect size. The problem is that it's on a different scale from *d*, the ES for *t*-tests. *r* is constrained between −1 and +1 (although as an index of ES we can ignore the sign), whereas *d* has no upper limit. So, how can we compare them? Actually, it's quite simple; we use the formula that Cohen (1988) kindly gave us:

$$d = \frac{2r}{\sqrt{1-r^2}} \qquad (11\text{-}24)$$

to get from r to d, and

$$r = \frac{d}{\sqrt{d^2+4}} \qquad (11\text{-}25)$$

to get from d to r.

The Comparison Of Linear Regression And Linear Correlation(Table 11-6)

SPEARMAN CORRELATION

We usually encounter some data with non-normal distributed in daily work. If, for example, one variable is the Mean corpuscular volume (MCV) content in children with anemia and another variable is the signs and symptoms of anemia in children, how to test for a relationship between the rankings of the two types of program? Do children with a higher MCV content tend to have a poor physical condition? In above case, a non-parametric method—Spearman correlation could be an ideal means.

Spearman correlation coefficient, named after Charles Spearman and often denoted as r_s, is a nonparametric measure of statistical dependence between two variables. The coefficient is any of several statistics that measure the relationship between rankings of different ordinal variables or different rankings of the same variable, where a "ranking" is the assignment of the labels "first", "second", "third", etc. to different observations of a particular variable.

Spearman correlation coefficient can measure the degree of similarity between two rankings, and assess the significance of the relation between them. It, like any correlation calculation, is appropriate for both continuous and discrete variables, including ordinal variables. In essence, Spearman correlation coefficient should be defined as the Pearson correlation coefficient between the ranked variables.

For a sample of size n, the n raw scores X_i, Y_i are converted to ranks, p_i and q_i respectively, and r_s can be calculated by the Formula(11-26):

$$r_s = \frac{\sum(p_i - \bar{p})(q_i - \bar{q})}{\sqrt{[\sum(p_i - \bar{p})^2][\sum(q_i - \bar{q})^2]}} \qquad (11\text{-}26)$$

Where r_s denotes the usual Pearson correlation coefficient, but applied to the rank variables. The numerator is the covariance of the rank variables, and the denominator is simply made up of two standard deviations of the rank variables. Note that r_s has the same property as Pearson linear correlation r and is also the estimated value of the overall rank correlation coefficient ρ_s.

Table 11-7 displays is the content of MCV and signs of anemia in 10 children with anemia who were observed. To explore the correlation between the two original variables, x and y, we can compute Spearman correlation coefficient by Formula(11-26)and get $r_s = -0.741$ firstly.

Then a hypothesis testing should also be done on whether the rank correlation coefficient was statistically significant. Similar to coefficient of Pearson correlation, the Formula (11-27) can also be used.

TABLE 11-6   The Comparison of Two Linear Method

		Linear Regression	Linear Correlation
Difference	Request for Data	Random variable Y should obey a normal distribution and X is no restriction	Random variables, X and Y, should obey a bivariate normal distribution
	Application	To explain the amount of change in Y for one unit of change in X	To explain the relationship and direction between X and Y
	Coefficient	$b = \dfrac{l_{xy}}{l_{xx}}, -\infty < b < \infty$	$r = \dfrac{l_{xy}}{\sqrt{l_{xx}l_{yy}}}, -1 \leqslant r \leqslant 1$
Connection	Consistency of Direction	The signs of the two coefficients r and b, are the same for a same data set	
	Equivalence of Hypothesis Testing	For a same data set, the hypothesis test of the two coefficients are equivalent, that is, $t_r \approx t_b$	
	Coefficient of Determination	R^2 of linear regression is closer to 1,the effect of correlation will be better. Also say, it indicates that the better the regression effect is, the degree of correlation will be better	

Table 11-7   MCV content and the signs of anemia in children

Number	MCV content X	Rank p	Symptoms Y	Rank q
1	50	1	+++	10
2	58	2	++	8
3	61	3	+	6
4	73	4	+	3
5	79	5	–	8
6	80	6	+	8
7	85	7	–	3
8	87	8	–	3
9	96	9	–	3
10	102	10	–	3
total	–	55	–	55

$$t_{r_s} = \frac{r_s}{\sqrt{(1 - r_s^2)/(n-2)}} \qquad (11\text{-}27)$$

For the example above, $t_{rs} = 3.12$, and it can be considered that there is a negative correlation between the MCV content and the signs of anemia in children in the research.

SAMPLE SIZE ESTIMATION

Hypothesis Testing

In the previous chapters on ANOVA and the t-test, we determined the sample size required to determine if one mean was different from another. The situation is a little different for a correlation; we rarely test to see if two correlations are different. However, a more common situation, particularly among those of us prone to data-dredging, is to take a data base, correlate everything with everything, and then see what is significant to build a quick post-hoc ad-hoc theory. Of course, these situations are built on existing data bases, so sample size calculations are not an issue—you use what you got. However, the situation does arise when a theory predicts a correlation and we need to know whether the data support the prediction (i.e., the correlation is significant). When designing such a study, it is reasonable to ask what sample size is necessary to detect a correlation of a particular magnitude.

We construct the normal curve for the null hypothesis, the second normal curve for the alternative hypothesis, and then solve the two z equations for the critical value. However, one small wrinkle makes the sample size formula a little hairier, and it revealed itself in Equation (14-21) earlier. The good news is that the SEs of the distribution are dependent only on the magnitude of the correlation and the sample size, so we don't have to estimate (read "guess") the SE.[10] The bad news is that the dependence of the SE on the correlation itself means that the widths of the curves for the null and alternative hypotheses are different. The net result of some creative algebra is:

$$n = \left(\frac{z_\alpha + a_\beta \sqrt{1 - r^2}}{r} \right)^2 + 2 \qquad (11\text{-}28)$$

To avoid any anguish putting numbers into this equation, and also to reinforce the message that such calculations are approximate, we have put it all onto a graph (actually the two graphs in Figure 11-7).

TO READ THESE FAMILIES OF CURVES, FIRST DECIDE WHAT THE A LEVEL IS GOING TO BE: 0.05 OR 0.01; A = 0.05 PUTS YOU ON THE LEFT GRAPH; A = 0.01 PUTS YOU ON THE RIGHT. NEXT, PICK A B LEVEL FROM 0.05 TO 0.20, WHICH ORIENTS YOU ON ONE OF THE THREE CURVES ON EACH GRAPH. THE NEXT GUESS IS RELATED TO HOW BIG A CORRELATION YOU WANT TO DECLARE AS SIGNIFICANT, WHICH PUTS YOU SOMEWHERE ON THE X-AXIS. FINALLY, READ OFF THE APPROXIMATE SAMPLE SIZE ON THE Y-AXIS.

SUMMARY

✧ Simple linear regression is a method devised to assess the relationship between a single interval level independent variable and an interval level dependent variable. The method involves fitting an optimal straight line based on minimizing the sum of squares of devia-

---

[10]*Those of us who have developed sample size fabrication (oops, estimation) to an art form regard this as a disadvantage because it reduces the researcher's df.*

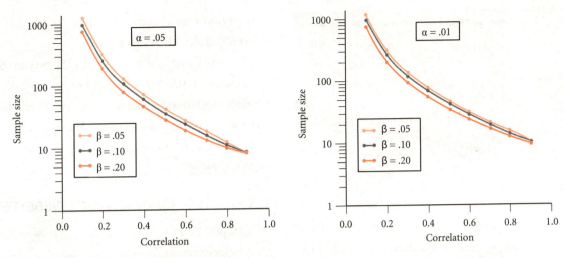

FIGURE 11-7   Sample size for correlation coefficients related to magnitude of the correlation and α and β level.

tions from the line. The adequacy of fit can be expressed by partitioning the total variance into variance resulting from regression and residual variance. The proportion of variance resulting from the independent variable is expressed as a Pearson correlation coefficient, and significance tests are derived from these components of variance. In addition, Spearman correlation is a method devised to assess the relationship between the variables expressed by rank order, discrete variables, etc.

GLOSSARY

the regression line   回归直线

least-squares analysis   最小二乘原理

residual   残差

regression coefficient   回归系数

R^2, the coefficient of determination   决定系数

covariance   协方差

Pearson correlation coefficient   Pearson 相关系数

Spearman correlation coefficient   Spearman 相关系数

EXERCISES

1. There are Age (X) and heart rate (Y) data of 12 female students. Please answer the questions as follows:

   1) Is there a relationship between age (year) and heart rate (bpm)?
   2) Please write the linear regression equation.

Age (year)	12	12	13	14	14	15	18	19	21	21
heart rate (bpm)	75	77	72	71	70	68	65	64	63	60

2. A doctor wants to explore the relationship between iodine-deficient areas of maternal TSH level, measured by immunoradiometric assay 160 pregnant women (15~17w) and cord blood TSH levels (mu/L) at birth. Some data is listed as follows. Please try to establish a linear regression equation to explain the relationship of them.

   Maternal serum TSH level   1.21,1.30,1.39,1.42, 1.47,1.56,1.68,1.72,1.98,2.10

   Umbilical cord blood TSH level   3.90,4.50,4.20, 4.83,4.16,4.93,4.32,4.99,4.70,5.20

3. How to estimate the two statistic, b_0 and b_1, in the linear regression equation $\hat{y} = b_0 + b_1 x$? What is the meaning of b_0 and b_1 respectively?

4. Please explain the difference and connection between linear regression and correlation.

5. There is a sampling data of output and unit cost of a certain product as follows. Please solve the following problems.

Output (ten thousand piece) x	unit cost (yuan/piece) y
5	56
4	58
3	60
6	54
7	52
9	50
5	55
4	57

(1) Try to calculate a correlation coefficient and to judge whether it has statistical significance.

(2) Try to establish a linear regression equation and to evaluate this equation.

(3) Point out how much the unit cost decline when the products increase 1000 yuan/piece.

How to Get the Computer to Do the Work for You

- From **Analyze**, choose **Correlate Bivariate**
- Click the variables you want from the list on the left, and click the arrow to move them into the box labeled **Variables**
- Click OK

If you want to see a scatterplot, then:

- From **Graphs**, choose **Scatter**
- If it isn't already chosen, click on the box marked **Simple**, then select the Define button
- Select the variable you want on the X-axis from the list on the left, and click the **X-axis** arrow
- Do the same for the Y-axis
- Click OK

SUGGESTED READINGS AND WEBSITES

[1] Samprit Chatterjee S, Hadi AS. Regression Analysis by example. 3rd ed. 2012.

[2] Rice JA. Mathematical Statistics and Data Analysis. 2nd ed. China Machine Press,2003.

[3] 李康 , 贺佳 . 医学统计学 . 6 版 . 北京 : 人民卫生出版社 ,2013.

[4] 方积乾 . 卫生统计学 . 6 版 . 北京 : 人民卫生出版社 ,2008.

[5] Seber GAF. Lee A. Linear Regression Analysis. World Scientific, 2009:362-363.

[6] Weisberg S. Applied linear regression. Wiley, 1985.

[7] http://www.amstat.org/publications/jse/.

Multiple Regression

In this chapter, we generalize the methods of regression analysis to cope with the situation where we have several independent variables that are all interval-level and one dependent variable.

SETTING THE SCENE

Having described (and published about) the new syndrome, Beemer Knee, and shown that it is indeed a result of a decadent lifestyle, you decide to explore further exactly what aspects of "lifestyle" are causing the problem. You want to look at all the variables in the CHICC score, both individually and together. How do you combine all these multiple measures into one regression analysis?

Our intrepid physiotherapist ventured into behavioural medicine by examining the relationship between Beemer Knee and a number of factors associated with the Yuppie lifestyle. It may have occurred to you that she was perhaps oversimplifying things by picking five variables and then ramming them all into a single total score.

You may recall that Yuppiness was codified by a **CHICC** score, defined as follows:

CARS—Number of European cars + Number of off-road vehicles—Number of Hyundai Elantras, Toyota Corollas, or Chrysler Caravans.

HEALTH—Number of memberships in tennis clubs, ski clubs, and fitness clubs.

INCOME—Total income in $10 000 units.

CUISINE—Total consumption of balsamic vinegar (liters) + number of types of mustard in the fridge.

CLOTHES—Total of all Gucci, Lacoste, and Saint Laurent labels in the closets.

Looking closer at the cause of the affliction, it seems at first blush that some of these variables may play a larger role in the disease than others. CARS is an obvious prime candidate because the disease was first recognized among Beemer drivers and appeared to be related to fast shifting or heel-and-toe braking. HEALTH might aggravate the condition, despite the label, as a result of all the twisting and knee strain

from tennis, squash, or skiing. CLOTHES might hurt too, if subjects are wearing skin-tight slacks too often, constricting the circulation in the lower extremities. But INCOME and CUISINE seem to be a bit of a stretch.

What is the effect of stuffing extra variables in the summary score? First, collecting, coding, and analyzing all these extra data costs more.[1] Second, beyond a certain point, they are likely contributing only noise to the prediction, reducing the sensitivity of the analysis. We want to keep track of the contribution made by individual variables while still allowing for the joint prediction of the dependent variable by all the variables (or, as we shall see, all the variables contributing significantly to the prediction). Although seemingly complex, the method is actually a conceptually straightforward extension of simple regression to the case of multiple variables. Not surprisingly, it goes by the name of **multiple regression**.

Multiple regression involves the linear relationship between one dependent variable and multiple (more than one) independent variables.

It is often useful to express the mean value of one variable in terms not of one other variable but of several others. Some examples will illustrate some slightly different purposes of this approach.

1. The primary purpose may be to study the effect on variable 5 of changes in a particular single

---

[1] *Although some researchers might view this as a good thing.*

variable x_1, but it may be recognized that 5 may be affected by several other variables x_2, x_3, etc. The effect on 5 of simultaneous changes in x_1, x_2, x_3, etc., must therefore be studied. In the analysis of data on respiratory function of workers in a particular industry, such as those considered in the example, the effect of duration of exposure to a hazard may be of primary interest. However, respiratory function is affected by age, and age is related to duration of exposure. The simultaneous effect on respiratory function of age and exposure must therefore be studied so that the effect of exposure on workers of a fixed age may be estimated.

2. One may wish to derive insight into some causative mechanism by discovering which of a set of variables x_1, x_2, ... , has apparently most influence on a dependent variable 5. For example, the stillbirth rate varies considerably in different towns in Britain. By relating the stillbirth rate simultaneously to a large number of variables describing the towns— economic, social, meterological or demographic variables, for instance—it may be possible to find which factors exert particular influence on the stillbirth rate (see Sutherland, 1946). Another example is in the study of variations in the cost per patient in different hospitals. This presumably depends markedly on the 'patient mix'— the proportions of different types of patient admitted—as well as on other factors. A study of the simultaneous effects of many such variables may explain mush of the variation in hospital costs and, by drawing attention to particular hospitals whose high or low costs are out of line with the prediction, may suggest new factors of importance.

3. To predict the value of the dependent variable in future individuals. After treatment of patients with advanced breast cancer by ablative procedures, prognosis is very uncertain. If future progress can be shown to depend on several variables available at the time of the operation, it may be possible to predict which patients have a poor prognosis and to consider alternative methods of treatment for them (Armitage et al., 1969).

CALCULATIONS FOR MULTIPLE REGRESSION

The first step in multiple regression is to create a new regression equation that involves all the independent variables of interest. Ours would look like:

$$\hat{Y} = b_0 + b_1 \text{CARS} + b_2 \text{HEALTH} + b_3 \text{INCOME} + b_4 \text{CLOTHES} + b_5 \text{CUISINE} \quad \text{(12-1)}$$

This is just longer than what we had before, not fundamentally different. A reasonable next step would be to graph the data. However, no one has yet come up with six-dimensional graph paper, so we'll let that one pass for the moment. Nevertheless, we will presume, at least for now, that were we to graph the relationship between ROM and each of the independent variables individually, an approximately straight line would be the final result.

We can then proceed to stuff the whole lot into the computer and press the "multiple regression" button. Note that "the whole lot" consists of a series of 20 data points on this six-dimensional graph paper, one for each of the 20 Yuppies who were in the study. Each datum is in turn described by six values corresponding to ROM and the five independent variables. The computer now determines, just as before, the value of the bs corresponding to the best-fit line, where "best" is defined as the combination of values that result in the minimum sum of squared deviations between fitted and raw data. The quantity that is being minimized is:[2]

$$\sum [ROM_i - (b_0 + b_1 \text{CA}_i + b_2 \text{HE}_i + b_3 \text{INC}_i + b_4 \text{CL}_i + b_5 \text{CU}_i)]^2 \quad \text{(12-2)}$$

We will call this sum, as before, the Sum of Squares (Residual) or SS_{res}.

Of course, two other Sums of Squares can be extracted from the data, Sum of Squares (Regression), or SS_{reg}, and Sum of Squares (Total), or SS_{tot}.

$$SS_{reg} = \sum [\overline{ROM} - (b_0 + b_1 \text{CA}_i + b_2 \text{HE}_i + b_3 \text{INC}_i + b_4 \text{CL}_i + b_5 \text{CU}_i)]^2 \quad \text{(12-3)}$$

Although this equation looks a lot like SS_{res}, the

---

[2]From here on in, the independent variables are abbreviated to conserve paper; our bit for the "green revolution" and as compensation for the contribution of all our hot air to global warming.

fine print, particularly the bar across the top of ROM instead of the i below it, makes all the difference. SS_{res} is the difference between individual data, ROM_i, and the fitted value; SS_{reg} is the difference between the fitted data and the overall grand mean $\overline{ROM}$. Finally, SS_{tot} is the difference between raw data and the grand mean:

$$SS_{tot} = \sum [ROM_i - \overline{ROM}]^2 \qquad \textbf{(12-4)}$$

And of course, we can put it all together, just as we did in the simple regression case, making an ANOVA table (Table 12-1).

TABLE 12-1   Analysis of variance of prediction of ROM from five independent variables

Source	Sum of squares	df	Mean square	F	p
Regression	4280	5	856.0	25.17	0.001
Residual	476	14	34.0		
Total	4756	19			

Several differences are seen between the numbers in this table and the tables resulting from simple regression in the previous chapter. In fact, only the Total Sum of Squares (4756.0) and the df (19) are the same. How can such a little difference make such a big difference? Let's take things in turn and find out.

1. Sum of Squares—Although the Total Sum of Squares is the same as before, the Sum of Squares resulting from regression has actually gone up a little, from 3892 to 4280. This is actually understandable. In the simple regression case, we simply added up the five subscores to something we called CHICC. Here we are estimating the contribution of each variable separately so that the overall fit more directly reflects the predictive value of each variable. In turn, this improves the overall fit a little, thereby increasing the Sum of Squares (Regression) and reducing the Sum of Squares (Residual) by the same amount.

2. Degrees of Freedom—Now the df resulting from regression has gone from 1 to 5. This is also understandable. We have six estimated parameters, rather than two, as before; one goes into the intercept. The overall df is still 19, with 5 df corresponding to the coefficients for each variable. Then, because the overall df must still equal the number of data 1, the df for the residual drops to 14.

3. Mean Squares and F-ratio—Finally, the Mean Squares follow from the Sum of Squares and df. Because Sum of Squares (regression) uses 5 df, the corresponding Mean Square has dropped by a factor of nearly four, even though the fit has improved. This then results in a lower F-ratio, now with 5 and 14 df, but it is still wildly significant.

Significant or not, this is one of many illustrations of the Protestant Work Ethic as applied to stats: "You don't get something for nothing." The cost of introducing the variables separately was to lose df, which could reduce the fit to a nonsignificant level while actually improving the fitted Sum of Squares. Introducing additional variables in regression, ANOVA, or anywhere else can actually cost power unless they are individually explaining an important amount of variance.

We can now go the last step and calculate a correlation coefficient:

$$R = \sqrt{\frac{SS_{reg}}{SS_{reg} + SS_{err}}} = \sqrt{\frac{4280}{4280 + 476}} = 0.95$$

$$\textbf{(12-5)}$$

As you might have expected, this has gone up because the Sum of Squares (Regression) is larger. Note the capital R; this is called the **Multiple Correlation Coefficient** to distinguish it from the simple correlation. But the interpretation is the same.

The *Multiple Correlation Coefficient* (R) is derived from a multiple regression equation, and its square (R^2) indicates the proportion of the variance in the dependent variable explained by all the specified independent variables.

As always, a graphical interpretation displays activities of the sums of squares. In Figure 12-1, we have shown the proportion of the Total Sum of Squares resulting from regression and residual. As we already know, a bit of difference exists, with the multiple regression taking a bit more of the pie.

So that's it so far. You might rightly ask what the big deal is because we have not done much else than improve the fit a little by estimating the coefficients singly, but at the significant cost of df. However, we have not, as yet, exploited the specific relationships among the variables.

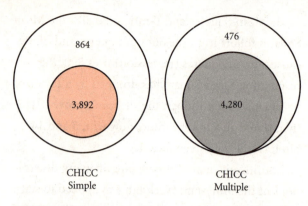

FIGURE 12-1 Proportion of variance (shaded) from simple regression of CHICC score and multiple regression of individual variables. The numbers represent the relevant Sum of Squares.

TYPES OF VARIABLES

Before we go much further, let's discuss the types of variables that we can use in multiple regression. The only requirement is that the *dependent* variable be normally distributed (to be more precise, that the errors or residuals—which we'll discuss later—are normally distributed). Other forms of regression, such as logistic regression or Poisson regression (which are discussed in the next chapter), allow for different distributions of the dependent variable. What about the predictor variables? The bad news is that it's assumed that they're measured without any error. This is like the Ten Commandments—something we all aspire to but is impossible to achieve in real life (we'll leave it to you to decide which ones to break). So, as with those injunctions, we'll acknowledge this one exists and then promptly forget about it. Its only meaningful implication is that regression is a *large sample* procedure; with small samples, the error has a large effect, but it becomes less important as the sample size increases.

The good news is that there are no assumptions about the distributions of the predictors. Want to use normally distributed variables? Great. You have dichotomous ones? Sure, go right ahead. About the only type we can't use are nominal variables, where the coding is arbitrary, but we'll tell you how to handle those later in the chapter. This means that if your predictors aren't normally distributed, you don't have to do any fancy transformations to make them normal.

RELATIONSHIPS AMONG INDIVIDUAL VARIABLES

Let's backtrack some and take the variables one at a time, doing a simple regression, as discussed previously. If you permit a little poetic license, the individual ANOVAs (with the corresponding correlation coefficients) would look like Table 12-2. These data give us much more information about what is actually occurring than we had before. First, note that the total sum of squares is always 4756, as before. But CARS alone is most of the sum of squares and has the correspondingly highest simple correlation. This is as it should be; it was clinical observations about cars that got us into this mess in the first place. HEALTH comes next, but it has a negative simple correlation; presumably if you get enough exercise, your muscles can withstand the tremendous stresses associated with Beemer Knee. INCOME is next, and still significant; presumably you have to be rich to afford cars and everything else that goes with a Yuppie lifestyle. Last, CUISINE and CLOTHES are not significant, so we can drop them from further consideration.

TABLE 12-2   ANOVA of regression of individual variables

Source	Sum of squares	df	Mean square	F	r
Cars:					
Regression	3405.0	1	3405.0	45.4	0.85
Residual	1351.0	18	75.0		
Health:					
Regression	1622.0	1	1622.0	9.31	0.58
Residual	3134.0	18	174.1		
Income:					
Regression	643.0	1	643.0	2.81	0.36
Residual	4113.0	18	228.5		
Clothes:					
Regression	214.5	1	214.5	0.85	0.21
Residual	4541.5	18	252.3		
Cuisine:					
Regression	237.0	1	237.0	0.95	0.22
Residual	4519.0	18	251.0		

Although we confess to having rigged these data so that we wouldn't have to deal with all the complications down the road, the strategy of looking at simple correlations first and eliminating from consideration insignificant variables is not a bad one. The advantage is that, as we shall see, large numbers of variables demand large samples, so it's helpful to reduce variables early on. The disadvantage is that you can get fooled by simple correlations—in both directions.

At first blush, you might think that we can put these individual Sums of Squares all together to do a multiple regression. Not so, unfortunately. If we did, the Regression Sum of Squares caused by just the three significant variables would be:

$$SS_{reg} = (3405 + 1622 + 643) = 5670 \qquad \textbf{(12-6)}$$

Not only is this larger than the Sum of Squares (Regression) we already calculated, it is also larger than the total Sum of Squares! How can this be?

Not too difficult, really. We must recognize that the three variables are not making an independent contribution to the prediction. The ability to own a Beemer and belong to exclusive tennis clubs are both related to income—the three variables are **intercorrelated**. This may suggest that income causes everything, but then *real* income may lead to a Rolls, and legroom is not an issue in the driver's seat of a Rolls.[3] We are not, in any case, concerned about causation, only correlation, and as we have taken pains to point out already, they are not synonymous. From our present perspective, the implication is that, once one variable is in the equation, adding another variable will account only for some portion of the variance that it would take up on its own.

As a possibly clearer example, imagine predicting an infant's weight from three measurements— head circumference, chest circumference, and length. Because all are measures of baby bigness, chances are that any one is pretty predictive of baby weight. But once any of them is in the regression equation, addition of a second and third measurement is unlikely to improve things that much.

We can also demonstrate this truth graphically. First, consider each variable alone and express the

proportion of the variance as a proportion of the total area, as shown in Figure 12-2. Each variable occupies a proportion of the total area roughly proportional to its corresponding Sum of Squares (Regression). Note, however, what happens when we put them all together as in the lower picture. This begins to show quantitatively exactly why the Sum of Squares (Regression) for the combination of the three variables equals something considerably less than the sum of the three individual sums of squares. As you can see, the individual circles overlap considerably, so that if, for example, we introduced CARS into the equation first, incorporating HEALTH and INCOME adds only the small new moon-shaped crescents to the prediction. In Figure 12-3 we have added some numbers to the circles.

We already know that the Sum of Squares (Regression) for CARS, HEALTH, and INCOME are 3405, 1622, and 643, respectively. But Figure 12-3 shows that the overall Sum of Squares (Regression), as a result of putting in all three variables, is only SS (Total) − SS (Err) = (4756 − 595) = 4161. [Alternatively, this equals the sum of all the individuals areas (2180 + 830 + 212 + 183 + 508 + 72 + 176)= 4161.] For thoroughness, the new multiple correlation, with

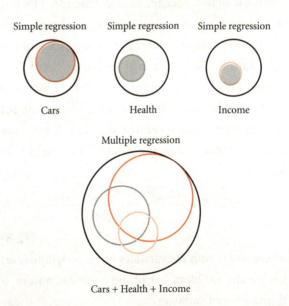

Simple regression   Simple regression   Simple regression

Cars   Health   Income

Multiple regression

Cars + Health + Income

FIGURE 12-2 Proportion of variance from simple regression of Cars, Health, and Income, and multiple regression.

---

[3]*This is not from personal experience, although if this book sells well, one day it may be.*

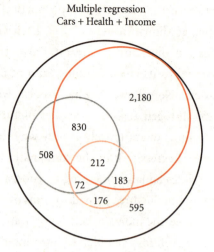

Multiple regression
Cars + Health + Income

Partial sums of squares indicated

FIGURE 12-3   Proportion of variance from multiple regression with partial sums of squares.

just these three variables, is:

$$R = \sqrt{\frac{SS_{reg}}{SS_{reg} + SS_{err}}} = \sqrt{\frac{4161}{4161 + 595}} = 0.935$$

$$(12-7)$$

PARTIAL *F*-TESTS AND CORRELATIONS

Partial *F*-Tests

We can now begin identifying the unique contributions of each variable and devising a test of statistical significance for each coefficient. The test of significance is based on the *unique* contribution of each variable after all other variables are in the equation. So, for the contribution of CARS, the unique variance is 2180; for HEALTH, it's 508; and for INCOME, it is 176. Now we devise a test for the significance; each contribution called, for fairly obvious reasons, a **partial *F*-test**. Its formula is as follows:

$$\text{Partial } F = \frac{[SS_{reg}(\text{in}) - SS_{reg}(\text{out})] / n_v}{MS_{res}(\text{in})}$$

$$(12-8)$$

where (*in*) is with the variables in the equation, (*out*) is with the variables out of the equation, and *nv* is the number of variables.

The *partial F-test* is the test of the significance of an individual variable's contribution after all other variables are in the equation.

The numerator of this test is fairly obvious: the

Sum of Squares explained by the variables added, divided by the number of variables, or the Mean Square due to variables added.

The denominator of the test is a bit more subtle. What we require is an estimate of the true error variance. As any of the Sums of Squares within the "regression" circles is actually variance that will be accounted for by one or another of the predictor variables, the best guess at the Error Sum of Squares is the SS (Err) after all variables are in the equation, in this case equal to 595. In turn, the Mean Square is then divided by the residual *df*, now equal to (19 − 3) = 16. So, the denominator for all of the partial *F*-tests is 595 ÷ 16 = 37.18, and the tests for each variable are in Table 12-3.

TABLE 12-3   Partial *F* tests for each variable

Variable	Numerator MS	Denominator MS	*F*	*P*
Cars	2180	37.18	58.63	0.0001
Health	508	37.18	13.66	0.0001
Income	176	37.18	4.73	0.05

Partial and Semipartial Correlations

Another way to determine the unique contribution of a specific variable, after the contributions of the other variables have been taken in account, is to look at the **partial** and **semipartial** (or **part**) correlations. Let's say we have a dependent variable, z, and two predictor variables, a and b. The **partial correlation** between a and z is defined as:

$$r_{az.b} = \frac{r_{az} - r_{ab}r_{zb}}{\sqrt{1 - r_{ab}^2}\sqrt{1 - r_{zb}^2}}$$

$$(12-9)$$

The cryptic subscript, $r_{az.b}$, means the correlation between a and z, partialling out the effects of b. This statistic tells us the correlation between a and z, with the contribution of b removed from *both* of the other variables. However, for our purposes, we want the effect of b removed from a, but we don't want it removed from the dependent variable. For this, we need what is called the **semipartial correlation**, which is also known by the alias, the **part correlation**. Its numerator is exactly the same as for the partial correlation, but the denominator doesn't have the SD of the partialled scores for the dependent variable:

$$sr_{az.b} = \frac{r_{az} - r_{ab}r_{zb}}{\sqrt{1 - r_{zb}^2}} \qquad (12\text{-}10)$$

Partial and semipartial correlations highlight one of the conceptual problems in multiple regression. On the one hand, the more useful variables we stick into the equation (with some rare exceptions), the better the SS_{reg}, R, and R^2, all of which is desirable. On the other hand (and there's always another hand), the more variables in the equation, the smaller the unique contribution of a particular variable (and the smaller its t-test). This is also desirable, because the contribution of any one variable is not usually independent of the contributions of others. We could, in fact, end up with the paradoxical situation that none of the predictors makes a significant unique contribution, but the overall R is "whoppingly" significant. We'll return to some of these pragmatic issues in a later section.

bS AND βS

As you may have noticed, we have been dealing with everything up to now by turning them into sums of squares. The advantage of this strategy is that all the sums of squares add and subtract, so we can draw pretty pictures showing what is going on. One disadvantage is that we have lost some information in the process. We did discuss the basic idea in Chapter 11, where we were dealing with simple regression. In particular, we have not actually talked about the b coefficients, which is where we began. In the last chapter, the significance of each individual b coefficient is tested with a form of the t-test, creating a table like Table 12-4. Further, the t-test is simply the square root of the associated partial F value, which we already determined using Equation (12-8).

TABLE 12-4 Coefficients and standard errors

Variable	b	SE(b)	β	t	p
Cars	0.135	0.0176	0.354	7.65	0.0001
Health	0.106	0.0287	0.245	3.70	0.0001
Income	0.037	0.0170	0.155	2.17	0.05

The coefficient, b, also has some utility independent of the statistical test. If we go back to the beginning, we can put the prediction equation together by using these estimated coefficients. We might actually use the equation for prediction instead of publication. For our above example, the prediction equation from the CHICC variables could be used as a screening test to estimate the possibility of acquiring Beemer Knee.

The b coefficients can also be interpreted directly as the amount of change in Y resulting from a change of one unit in X. For example, if we did a regression analysis to predict the weight of a baby in kilograms from her height in centimeters, and then found that the b coefficient was 0.025, it would mean that a change in height of 1 cm results in an average change of weight of 0.025 kg, or 25 g. Scaling this up a bit, a change of 50 cm results in an increase in weight of 1.25 kg.

Next in the printout comes a column labelled β. "Beta?" you ask. "Since when did we go from samples to populations?" Drat—an exception to the rule. This time, the magnitude of beta bears no resemblance to the corresponding b value, so it is clearly *not* something to do with samples and populations. Actually, a simple relationship is found between b and β, which looks like this:

$$\beta = b \times \frac{\sigma_x}{\sigma_y} \qquad (12\text{-}11)$$

In words, β is standardized by the ratio of the SDs of x and y. As a result, it is called a **standardized regression coefficient**. The idea is this: although the b coefficients are useful for constructing the regression equation, they are devilishly difficult to interpret relative to each. Going back to our babies, if weight is measured in grams and height in meters, the b coefficient is 10 000 times larger than if weight is measured in kilograms and height in centimeters, even though everything else stayed the same. So by converting all the variables to standard scores [which is what Equation (12-9) does], we can now directly compare the magnitude of the different βs to get some sense of which variables are contributing more or less to the regression equation.

Relative Importance of Variables

Now that we've introduced you to bs and βs, the question is which do we use in trying to interpret the relative importance of the variables in predicting the dependent variable (DV)? Let's briefly recap some of the properties of b and β. We use b with the raw data, and β with standardized data. Because the bs are affected by the scale used to measure the variable (e.g., change cost from dollars to cents and you'll decrease the b by 100), it's out of the running. So, at first glance, it may seem as if we should look at the relative magnitudes of the βs to see which predictors are more important. But—and there's always a "but"—we have to remember one thing: the βs are *partial* weights. That is, they reflect the contribution of the variable *after controlling for the effect of all of the other variables in the equation*. Previously, we used the example of predicting an infant's weight from head circumference, chest circumference, and length. Because the three predictor variables are highly correlated with one another, the *unique* contribution of each (i.e., its effect after controlling for the other two) would be relatively small. The result is that, for any given variable, its β weight may be quite small and possibly nonsignificant, even though it may be a good predictor in its own right. Indeed, it's possible that *none* of the predictors is statistically significant, but the equation as a whole has a high multiple correlation with weight.

Another consequence of the fact that βs are partial weights is that their magnitude is related to two factors: the strength of the relationship between a variable and the dependent variable (this is good), and the mix of other variables in the equation (this isn't so good). Adding or dropping any of the predictors is going to change the size and possibly the significance level of the weights. This means that we also have to look at the correlations between each independent variable (IV) and the predicted value of the DV (i.e., $\hat{Y}$); what are called *structure coefficients* (r_s). But here again, there may be problems. There are times (thankfully, relatively rare) where the structure correlation is very low, but the β weight is high. This occurs if there is a "suppressor" variable that

contaminates the relationships between the other predictor variables and the DV. For example, we may have a test of math skills that requires a student to read the problems (you remember the type: "Imagine that there are two trains, 150 miles apart. Train A is approaching from the east at 100 mph, and Train B is coming from the west traveling at 80 mph. How long will it take before they crash into each other?").[4] If some kids are great at math but can't read the back of a cereal box, then language skills[5] will suppress the relationship between other predictors and scores on a math exam.

So, which do we look at—the β weights or the r_ss? The answer is "Yes." If the predictors are uncorrelated with one another, it doesn't matter; the β and r_ss will have the same rank ordering, and differ only in magnitude. When they are correlated (and they usually are), we have to look at both. If β is very low, but r_s is high, then that variable may be useful in predicting the DV, but its shared predictive power was taken up by another IV. In other words, the variable may be "important" at an explanatory level, in that it is related to the DV, but "unimportant" in a predictive sense because, in combination with the other variables in the equation, it doesn't add much. On the other hand, if β is high but r_s^2 is low, then it may be a suppressor variable (Courville and Thompson, 2001).

But, how do we examine the correlation between a variable and $\hat{Y}$? One way is to run the regression and save the predicted values, and then get the correlations between them and all of the predictor variables. Another way, that may actually be easier, is to calculate them directly:

$$r_s = r_{YX_i} / R \qquad \text{(12-12)}$$

where r_{YX_i} is the correlation between the predictor X_i and the DV, and R is the multiple correlation. This formula also tells us two important things about the r_ss. First, notice that only the IV that we're interested in is the numerator, not any of the other IVs. That means that structure coefficients are not affected by

---

[4]*Why is it that most problems like this involve crashes or other disasters? Doe it say something about the people who were most influential during our formative years?*

[5]*What used to be called "English" in less pretentious days.*

multi-collinearity. Second, because each r_s is simply the zero-order correlation between the IV and the DV divided by a constant (R), the rank order of the r_ss is the same as that of the r_s. But, because we're dividing a number less than 1.0, r_s is "inflated" relative to r.

So, why go to the bother to calculate r_ss rather than just use r? In fact, some people (e.g., Pedhazur, 1997) argue that you shouldn't use them at all because they don't add any new information. Others argue that r_s is more informative because it tells us the relationship between a predictor variable and the *predicted* value of Y (i.e., $\hat{Y}$), which is really what we're interested in. Also, structure coefficients play important roles in interpreting other statistics based on the *general linear model* (which we'll discuss later), so it's easier to see the relationship between multiple regression and other techniques.

The bottom line, though, is that whether you use r or r_s to figure out what's important, the first step is to look at R^2 and see if it's worthwhile going any further. If it's too small to pique your interest, stop right there. Only if it is of sufficient magnitude should you look at the βs and r_ss (or r_s) and decide which variables are important in helping to predict the DV.

GETTING CENTERED

A caveat. This section is not a digression into "new age" psychobabble; there's enough nonsense written about that already without having us add our two cents' worth. Rather, it describes a technique that may make the interpretation of the results of multiple regression easier, and help alleviate some of the other problems we may encounter.

If we were to run a regression without thinking about what we're doing (i.e., the way 99.34% of people do it), we would take our raw data, enter them into the computer, and hit the Run button. When the computer has finished its work, we'll have a table of bs and βs as we described in an earlier section. Let's try to interpret these. Remember that the formula we ended up with is:

$$\hat{Y} = b_0 + b_1 CARS + b_2 HEALTH + b_3 INCOME$$

$$(12\text{-}13)$$

The intercept, b_0, is the value of Beemer Knee we'd expect when all of the IVs have a value of zero. Similarly, b_1 is the effect of Cars on Beemer Knee when the other variables are set equal to zero, and so on for all of the other b coefficients in the equation. Now, we know what it means to have no cars and no income—everyone with kids in university has experienced that. But, what does it mean to have no health? That's a meaningless concept. It would be even worse if we threw in Age as another predictor; we'd be examining a middle-aged ailment for people who have just been born!

To see how centering can help us interpret the data better, let's interpret it with the example of the C^{11} diet. Because Captain Casper Casimir's diet looks so promising, we'll do a bigger study, comparing 50 men and 50 women, half of whom use the diet and half of whom do not. After months of being or not being on the diet, we weigh these 100 people and get the results shown in Table 12-5. Now, let's run a multiple regression, where the DV is weight, and the IVs are Gender (1 = Male, 2 = Female) and Group (1 = C^{11}, 2 = Control). The bs that we get are shown in the first line of Table 12-5.

TABLE 12-5 **Weights of 50 men and 50 women, half of whom were on the C^{11} diet**

	Controls	On Diet	Average
Men	187.73	162.39	175.06
Women	141.20	114.43	127.81
Average	167.47	138.41	151.44

Going by what we said before, the intercept is the weight of a person whose gender is 0, and who was in Group 0. Now that really told us a lot, didn't it? The bs for Program and Gender are equally uninformative, because they are the differences in weight compared with groups that don't exist. So, we can use the equation to predict the average weight gain or loss for a new individual, but the coefficients don't tell us much.

Now, let's use *centering*, following the recommendations of Kraemer and Blasey (2004). *For dichotomous variables, use weights of +½ and −½ instead of* 1 and 2, or 0 and 1, or any other coding scheme. So, if we code men as $-\frac{1}{2}$ and women as $+\frac{1}{2}$; and C[11] people as $-\frac{1}{2}$ and controls as $+\frac{1}{2}$, we'll get the results shown in the second line of Table 12-6. Suddenly, the numbers become meaningful. The intercept (151.44) is the mean of the whole group, as we see in Table 12-5. The *b* for Program (29.06) is exactly the difference between the mean weights of the two programs (165.47 for the Controls, and 138.41 for the C[11] group); and that for Gender (-47.25) is the difference between the mean weights of men (175.06) and women (127.81).

TABLE 12-6   Results of a multiple regression of the C[11] study, without (line 1) and with (line 2) centering

	Intercept	Program	Gender	Interaction
Uncentered	186.44	23.92	49.39	1.43
Centered	151.44	29.06	47.25	1.43

Centering has other effects, too. With the raw data, there was a significant effect of Gender ($p = 0.023$), but neither Program nor the interaction between Program and Gender were significant. Once we center the data, though, Gender becomes even more significant ($p < 0.001$), and the effect of Program is significant ($p = 0.0002$). As you can see from Table 12-6, centering doesn't affect the *b* for the interaction between the variables, nor does it change the significance level. Another advantage, which we won't elaborate on, is that when *multicollinearity* (high multiple correlations among the predictor variables, which we'll discuss in just a bit) is present, centering reduces its ill effects.

So what do we do if the variable is ordinal or interval? Kraemer and Blasey (2004) recommend using the median for ordinal data, and the mean for interval (or ratio) variables. In fact, they argue that, unless there are compelling reasons to the contrary, we should always center the data, which will also help to center our lives.

HIERARCHICAL AND STEPWISE REGRESSION

One additional wrinkle on multiple regression made

possible by cheap computation is called **stepwise regression**. The idea is perfectly sensible—you enter the variables one at a time to see how much you are gaining with each variable. It has an obvious role to play if some or all of the variables are expensive or difficult to get. Thus economy is favored by reducing the number of variables to the point that little additional prediction is gained by bringing in additional variables. Unfortunately, like all good things, it can be easily abused. We'll get to that later.

Hierarchical Stepwise Regression

To elaborate, let's return to the CHICC example. We have already discovered that Cuisine and Clothes are not significantly related to ROM, either in combination with the other variables or alone. This latter criterion (significant simple correlation) is a useful starting point for stepwise regression because the more variables the computer has to choose from, the more possibility of chewing up *df* and creating unreproducible results.

Physiotherapy research is notoriously underfunded, so our physiotherapist has good reason to see if she can reduce the cost of data acquisition. She reasons as follows:

1. Information on the make of cars owned by a patient can likely be obtained from the Department of Motor Vehicles without much hassle about consent and ethics.[6]

2. She might be able to get income data from the Internal Revenue department, but she might have to fake being something legitimate, such as a credit card agency or a charity. This could get messy.

3. Data about health, the way she defined it, would be really hard to get without questionnaires or phonesurveys.

So if she had her druthers, she would introduce the variables into the equation one at a time, starting with CARS, then INCOME, then HEALTH. This perfectly reasonable strategy of deciding on logical or logistic grounds *a priori* about the order of entry is called **hierarchical stepwise regression**. Because it requires some thought on the part of the researcher,

---

[6]*There is no ethical behaviour on the road.*

it is rarely used.

Hierarchical stepwise regression introduces variables, either singly or in clusters, in an order assigned in advance by the researcher.

What we want to discover in pursuing this course is whether the introduction of an additional variable in the equation is (1) statistically significant, and (2) clinically important. Statistical significance inevitably comes down to some F-test expressing the ratio of the additional variance explained by the new variable to the residual error variance. Clinical importance can be captured in the new multiple correlation coefficient, R^2, or, more precisely, the change in R^2 that results from introducing the new variable. This indicates how much additional variance was accounted for by the addition of the new variable.

All this stuff can be easily extracted from Figure 12-3. We have rearranged things slightly in Figure 12-4. Now we can see what happens every step of the way. In Step 1, we have one independent variable, CARS, and the results are exactly the same as the simple regression of CARS on ROM. The Sum of Squares (Regression) is 3405, with 1 df, and the Sum of Squares (Error) is 1351, with 18 df. The multiple R^2 is just the proportion of the Sum of Squares explained, $3405 \div 4756 = 0.716$ as before, and the F-test of significance is the Mean Square (Regression) ÷ Mean Square (Error) = $(3405 \div 1) \div (1351 \div 18) = 45.37$.

Now we add INCOME. Because all the independent variables are interrelated, this adds only 248 to the Sum of Squares (Regression), for a total of 3653, with 2 df, leaving a Sum of Squares (Error) of 1103 with 17 df. Now the multiple R^2 is $3653 \div 4756 = 0.768$, and the F-test for the addition of this variable is $(248 \div 1) \div (1103 \div 17) = 3.822$. This is conventionally called the **F-to-enter** because it is associated with entering the variable in the equation. The alternative is the **F-to-remove**, which occurs in stepwise regression (discussed later). This score results from the computer's decision that, at the next step, the best thing it can do is remove a variable that was previously entered.

A subtle but important difference exists between this partial sum of squares and the partial sum of squares for INCOME, which we encountered previously. In ordinary multiple regression, the partials are always with *all* the other independent variables in the equation, so it equalled only 176. Here, it is the partial with just the *preceding* variables in previous steps in the equation; consequently, this partial sum of squares is a little larger.

Finally, we throw in HEALTH. This adds 508 to the Sum of Squares (Regression) to bring it to 4161, with 3 df. The Sum of Squares (Error) is further reduced to 595, with 16 df. The multiple R^2 is now $4161 \div 4756 = 0.875$, and the F-test is $(508 \div 1) \div (595 \div 16) = 13.66$.

All of this is summarized in Table 12-7, where we have also calculated the change in R^2 resulting from adding each variable. Addition of INCOME accounted for only another 5% of the variance. Although

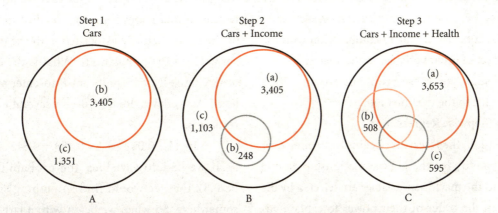

FIGURE 12-4 Proportion of variance from stepwise regression of Cars, Income, and Health. The sums of squares correspond to A, regression from the previous step, B, additional Sum of Squares from pre-sent step, and C, residual Sum of Squares.

TABLE 12-7 Stepwise regression analysis of ROM against Cars, Income, and Health

Variable	Multiple R^2	Change in R^2	F	p
Cars	0.716	—	45.37	0.0001
Income	0.768	0.052	3.82	ns
Health	0.875	0.107	13.66	0.0001

ns = not significant.

this is not too bad (most researchers would likely be interested in variables that account for 2% to 3% of the variance), this time around it is not significant. How can this be? Recognize that both the numerator and denominator of the F-test are contingent on what has gone before. The numerator carries variance in addition to that already explained by previous variables, and the denominator carries variance that is *not* explained by all the variables in the equation to this time. When we examined the partial F-tests in Table 12-3, all three variables were in the equation. The additional Sum of Squares resulting from INCOME was 176 instead of 248 because both CARS and HEALTH were in the equation. However, the denominator (the Mean Square [Residual]) was reduced further from $1103 \div 17 = 64.9$ to 37.18. The net effect was that the partial F-test for introduction of INCOME was just significant in the previous analysis.

This illustrates both the strength and limitations of the stepwise technique. By considering the combination of variables, it is possible to examine the independent effect of each variable and use the method to eliminate variables that are adding little to the overall prediction. Unfortunately, therein also lies a weakness, because the contribution of each variable can be considered only in combination with the particular set of other variables in the analysis.

As we shall see, these problems are amplified when we turn to the next method.

Ordinary Stepwise Regression

In this method, the researcher begins by turning over all responsibility for the logical relationship among variables to the machine. Variables are selected by the machine in the order of their power to explain additional variance. The mathematics are the same as used in hierarchical regression described above, ex-

cept that, at the end of every step, the computer calculates the best next step for *all* the variables that are not yet in the equation, then selects the next variable to enter based on a statistical criterion. The usual criterion is simply the largest value of the F-to-enter, determined as we did before.

The process carries on its merry way, entering additional variables with gay abandon, until ultimately the beast runs out of steam. "Out of steam" is also based on a statistical criterion, usually an F-to-enter that does not achieve significance.

Of course, we have yet one more wrinkle. It can happen (with all the interactions and interrelationships among the variables) that, once a whole bunch of variables are in the model, the best way to gain ground is to throw out a variable that went into the equation at an earlier stage but has now become redundant. The computer approaches this by determining not only what would happen if any of the variables *not* in the equation were *entered*, but also what would happen if any of the variables presently *in* the equation were *removed*. The calculation just creates another F-ratio, and if this F-to-remove is the largest, the next step in the process may well be to throw something out.

So what's the matter with letting the machinery do the work for you? Is it just a matter of Protestant Work Ethic? Unfortunately not, as several authors have pointed out (e.g., Leigh, 1988; Scailfa and Games, 1987; Wilkinson, 1979). At the center of the problem is the stuff of statistics: random variation. Imagine we have 20 variables that we are anxious to stuff into a regression equation, but in fact *none* of the 20 are actually associated with the dependent variable (in the population). What is the chance of observing at least 1 significant F-to-enter at the 0.05 level? As we have done before in several other contexts, it is:

$$1 - (1 - 0.05)^{20} = 1 - 0.358 = 0.642 \qquad \textbf{(12-14)}$$

If we had 40 variables, the probability would be 0.87 that we would find something significant somewhere. So when we begin with a large number of variables and ask the computer to seek out the most significant predictor variables, inevitably, buried somewhere among all the "significant" variables are some that are present only because of a Type I error. Actually, the situation is worse than this (bad as it may already seem). Along the way to selecting which variable should enter into the equation at each step, the program runs one regression equation for every variable that's not included, and also runs the equation taking out each of the variables that's already in (to see if removing a variable helps). Then, to compound the problem even further, the computer ups and lies to us. Strictly speaking, we should be "charged" one df for each predictor variable in the equation. If the computer is looking for the third variable to add to the mix, and screens 18 variables in the process, $df_{Regression}$ should be 20 (the 3 in the equation plus the 17 that didn't get in on this step but were evaluated). However, it will base the results on $df = 3$. So, we've lost complete control over the alpha level, because hundreds of significance tests may have been run; and the $MS_{Regression}$ will be overly optimistic, because it's based on the wrong df. One simulation found that stepwise procedures led to models in which 30% to 70% of the selected variables were actually pure noise (Derksen and Keselman, 1992). In fact, one journal has gone so far as to ban any article that uses stepwise regression (Thompson, 1995).

Stepwise regression procedures, using a statistical criterion for entry of variables, should therefore be regarded primarily as an exploratory strategy to investigate possible relationships to be verified on a second set of data. Naturally, very few researchers do it this way.

A number of procedures have been developed whereby the computer selects the 'best' subset of predictor variables, the criterion of optimality being somewhat arbitrary. There are four main approaches.

1. Step-up (forward-entry) procedure. The computer first tries all the p simple regressions with just one predictor variable, choosing that which provides the highest Regression SSq. Retaining this variable as the first choice, it now tries all the p-1 two-variable regressions obtained by the various possibilities for the second variable, choosing that which adds the largest increment to the Regression SSq. The process

continues, all variables chosen at any stage being retained at subsequent stages. The process stops when the increments to the Regression SSq cease to be (in some sense) large in comparison with the Residual SSq.

2. Step-down (backward-elimination) procedure. The computer first does the regression on all predictor variables. It then eliminates the least significant and does a regression on the remaining p-1 variables. The process stops when all the retained regression coefficients are (in some sense) significant.

3. Stepwise procedure. This is an elaboration of the step-up procedure (1), but allowing elimination, as in the step-down procedure (2). After each change in the set of variables included in the regression, the contribution of each variable is assessed and, if the least significant makes insufficient contribution, by some criterion, it is eliminated. It is thus possible for a variable included at some stage to be eliminated at a later stage because other variables, introduced since it was included, have made it unnecessary. The criterion for inclusion and elimination of variables could be, for example, that a variable will be included if its partial regression coefficient is significant at the 0.05 level and eliminated if its partial regression coefficient fails to be significant at the 0.1 level.

4. Best-subset selection procedure. Methods 1, 2 and 3 do not necessarily reach the same final choice, even if they end with the same number of retained variables. None will necessarily choose the best possible regression (i.e. that with the largest Regression SSq) for any given number of predictor variables. Computer algorithms are available for selecting the best subset of variables, where 'best' may be defined as the regression with the largest adjusted R^2 (11.46) or the related Mallows Cp statistic.

So, is there no use for stepwise regression outside of data dredging? In our (not so) humble opinion, just one. If your aim is to find a set of predictors that are optimal (i.e., best able to predict the DV with the fewest IVs), and it doesn't matter from a theoretical perspective which variables are in the equation and which are out, go ahead and step away. Other than that relatively limited situation, remember that the answer to the subtitle to Leigh's (1988) article, "Is stepwise unwise?" is most likely "Yes."

PRE-SCREENING VARIABLES

While we're on the topic of losing control over degrees of freedom, we should mention one other commonly (mis)used technique: running univariate tests between the dependent variable and each of the predictor variables beforehand to select only the significant ones to be used in the equation. This is often done because there are too many potential predictors, given the number of subjects, a point we'll discuss later under sample size. This is a bad idea for at least two reasons. The first is that, as with stepwise procedures, we're running statistical tests but not counting them and adjusting the α level accordingly, what Babyak (2004) refers to as "phantom degrees of freedom." The second reason is that there's a rationale for running multivariable procedures; we expect that the variables are related to one another, and that they act together in ways that are different from how they act in splendid isolation. Variable A may not explain much on its own, but can be quite a powerful predictor when combined with variables B and C. Conversely, B may eat up much of A's variance, so that we've lost any potential gain of testing A beforehand, but we've still used up *dfs*.

So what do you do if you have too many variables? The answer is, Think for yourself! Don't let the computer do the thinking for you. Go back to your theory (or beliefs or biases) and choose the ones you feel are most important. As the noted psychologist, Kurt Lewin (1951) once said, "There is nothing so useful as a good theory."

R^2, ADJUSTED R^2, AND SHRINKAGE

We've already introduced you to the fact that R^2 reflects the proportion of variance in the DV accounted for by the IVs. But, if you look at the output of a computer program, you'll most likely see another term, called the **Adjusted R^2**, or AdjR^2. It is always lower than R^2, so you may want to ignore it, because your results won't look as good. However, bad as the news may be, the adjusted R^2 tells us some useful information that we should pay attention to.

With rare exceptions, every time we add a variable to a regression equation, R^2 increases, even if only slightly. Thus, we may be tempted to throw in every variable in sight, including the number of letters in the subject's mother's maiden name. But, this would be a grave mistake. The reason is that statistical formulae, and the computers that execute them, are dumb sorts of animals. They are unable to differentiate between two types of variance—true variability between people, and error variance owing to the fact that every variable is always measured with some degree of error. So the computer grinds merrily away,[7] and finds a set of *b*s and *β*s that will maximize the amount of variance explained by the regression line. The problem is that if we were to perfectly replicate the study, drawing the same types of individuals and using the exact same variables, the true variance will be more or less the same as for the original sample, but the error variance will be different for each person. So, if we take the values of the variables from the second sample and plug them into the equation we derived from the first sample, the results won't be nearly as good. This reduction in the magnitude of R^2 on replication is called **shrinkage**. Another way to think of shrinkage is that it's a closer approximation of the *population* value of R^2 than is value derived from any given sample.

Now, needless to say, we'd like to know by how much the value of R^2 will shrink, without having to go through the hassle of rerunning the whole blinking study.[8] This is what the Adjusted R^2 tells us. One problem is that there are a whole slew of formulae for AdjR^2. Probably the most commonly used one is:

$$AdjR^2 = R^2 - \frac{p(1-R^2)}{N-p-1} \tag{12-15}$$

---

[7]*We're using this term metaphorically. If you do hear your computer grinding away, it's usually a sign that your hard disk is about to crash.*

[8]*Although maybe, after looking at the results, you don't really want to know.*

Where p is the number of variables in the equation and N is the sample size. In Figure 12-5, we've plotted the AdjR^2 for various values of R^2 and p, assuming a sample size of 100. As you can see, there is less shrinkage as R^2 increases and as N is larger, but we pay a price for every variable we enter into the mix. You should also note that this equation produces less of a discrepancy between R^2 and AdjR^2 than most of the other equations, so the problem is probably worse than what the computer tells you.

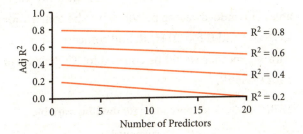

FIGURE 12-5   How adjusted R^2 is affected by R^2 and the number of predictor variables.

If you run a hierarchical or stepwise regression, you'll see that, in the beginning, both R^2 and AdjR^2 increase with each variable entered (although, as expected, AdjR^2 won't increase as much). Then, after a number of variables are in, R^2 will continue to increase slowly, but AdjR^2 will actually decrease. This indicates that the later variables are probably contributing more error than they're accounting for.

INTERACTIONS

One simple addition to the armamentarium of the regressive (oops, regression) analyst is the incorporation of *interaction* terms in the regression equation. We have already described the glories of systematic use of interactions, and the logic rubs off here as well.

As an example, there are several decades of research into the relationship between life stress and health. A predominant view is that the effect of stress is related to the accrual of several stressful events, such as divorce, a child leaving home,[9] or a mortgage

(Holmes, 1978). In turn, the model postulates that social supports can buffer or protect the individual from the vagaries of stress (Williams, Ware, and Donald, 1981). Imagine a study where we measured the number of stressful events and also the number of social relationships available, and now want to examine the relationship to doctor visits.[10] The theory is really saying that, in the presence of more stressful events, more social supports will reduce the number of visits; in the presence of less stress, social supports are unrelated to visits. In short, an *interaction* exists between stress, social supports, and visits.

How do we incorporate this interaction in the model? Nothing could be simpler—we create a new variable by multiplying the stress and support variables. So, the equation is:

$$\text{Visits} = b_0 + b_1\text{STRESS} + b_2\text{SOCSUP} + b_3(\text{STRESS} \times \text{SOCSUP}) \quad (12\text{-}16)$$

Finally, we would likely test the theory using hierarchical regression, where we would do one analysis with only the main effects and then a second analysis with the interaction term also, to see whether the interaction added significant prediction.

As you are no doubt painfully aware by this time, there ain't no such thing as a free lunch; if something looks good, you have to pay a penalty somewhere. In this case, the cost of being able to look at interaction terms is the loss of power. Jaccard and Wan (1995) pointed out that the ability of an interaction to increase R^2 is related to the reliability, and that the reliability is the product of the reliabilities of the individual variables. So, if the scale measuring STRESS has a reliability of 0.80, and that tapping SOCSUP a reliability of 0.70, then the reliability of the interaction is 0.56, meaning that its effect on R^2 is just over half of what it would be if the reliability were 1.0.

DUMMY CODING

DO NOT SKIP THIS SECTION JUST BECAUSE YOU'RE SMART! We are not casting aspersions on the intelligence of people who code data; dummy

---

[9] *In contrast to most parents, psychologists view this event as stressful.*

[10] *Actually, we don't have to imagine one, we did it (McFarlane et al., 1983).*

coding refers to the way we deal with predictor variables that are measured on a nominal or ordinal scale. Multiple regression makes the assumption that the dependent variable is normally distributed, but it doesn't make any such assumption about the predictors. However, we'd run into problems if we wanted to add a variable that captures that other aspect of "Yuppiness"—type of dwelling. If we coded Own Home = 1, Condo with Doorman = 2, and Other = 3, we would have a nominal variable. That is, we can change the coding scheme and not lose or gain any information. This means that treating DWELLING as if it were a continuous variable would lead to bizarre and misleading results; the b and β wouldn't tell us how much Beemer Knee would increase as we moved from one type of dwelling to another, because we'd get completely different numbers with a different coding scheme.

The solution is breaking the variable down into a number of *dummy variables*. The rule is that if the original variable has k categories, we will make $k - 1$ dummies. In this case, because there are three categories, we will create two dummy variables. So, who gets left out in the cold? Actually, nobody. One of the categories is selected as the reference, against which the other categories are compared. Mathematically, it really doesn't make much difference which one is chosen; usually it's selected on logical or theoretical grounds. For example, if we had coded income into three levels (for Beemer owners, that would be 1 = $150 000 to $174 999; 2 = $175 000 to $199 999; and 3 = $200 000 and up[11]), then it would make sense to have the paupers (Level 1) as the reference, and see to what degree greater income leads to more Beemer Knee. If there is no reason to choose one category over another (as is the case with DWELLING), it's good practice to select the category with the largest number of subjects, because it will have the lowest standard error. Following Hardy (1993), the three guidelines for selecting the reference level are:

1. If you have an ordinal variable, choose either the upper or lower category.

2. Use a well-defined category; don't use a residual one such as "Other."

3. If you still have a choice, opt for the one with the largest sample size.

If we chose OWN HOME as the reference category, then the two dummy variables would be CONDO (with Doorman, naturally) and OTHER. Then, the coding scheme would look like Table 12-8; if a person lives in her own home, she would be coded 0 for both the CONDO and the OTHER dummy variables. A condo-dwelling person would be coded 1 for CONDO and 0 for OTHER; and someone who lives with his mother would be coded 0 for CONDO and 1 for OTHER.[12]

TABLE 12-8   Dummy coding for dwelling variable

Dwelling	Dummy variable	
	Condo	Other
Own home	0	0
Condo	1	0
Other	0	1

Now our regression equation is:

$$\hat{Y} = b_0 + b_1 CARS + b_2 HEALTH + b_3 INCOME + b_4 CLOTHES + b_5 CUISINE + b_6 CONDO + b_7 OTHER \qquad (12\text{-}17)$$

Where b_6 tells us the increase or decrease in Beemer Knee for people who live in condos as compared with those who own a home, and b_7 does the same for the OTHER category as compared with OWN HOME.

The computer output will tell us whether b_6 and b_7 are significant, that is, different from the reference category. One question remains: How do we know if CONDO and OTHER are significantly different from each other? There are two ways to find out. The first method is rerunning the analysis, choosing a different category to be the reference. The second method is to get out our calculators and use some of the output from the computer program, namely, the variances and covariances of the regression coefficients. With these in hand, we can calculate a *t*-test:

---

[11]*Minus the yearly cost of maintaining their car, so we subtract $63 000 from each.*

[12]*There are other possible coding schemes (see Hardy, 1993), but this is the easiest.*

$$t = \frac{b_6 - b_7}{\sqrt{\sigma_{b_6}^2 + \sigma_{b_7}^2 - 2\,cov\,(b_6 b_7)}} \quad \text{(12-18)}$$

Where $cov\,(b_6 b_7)$ means the covariance between the two bs.

WHAT'S LEFT OVER: LOOKING AT RESIDUALS

Let's go back to the beginning for a moment. You'll remember that our original equation looking at Beemer Knee was:

$$\hat{Y} = b_0 + b_1\text{CARS} = b_2\text{HEALTH} + b_3\text{INCOME} + b_4\text{CLOTHES} + b_5\text{CUISINE} \quad \text{(12-19)}$$

where the funny hat over the Y means that the equation is *estimating* the value of Y for each person. But, unless that equation results in perfect prediction (i.e., R and $R^2 = 1$, which occurs as often as sightings of polka-dotted unicorns), the estimate will be off for each individual to some degree. That means that each person will have two numbers representing the degree of Beemer Knee: Y, which is his or her actual value; and $\hat{Y}$, which is estimated value. The difference between the two, $Y-\hat{Y}$, is called the **residual**. Because the equation should overestimate Y as often as it underestimates it, the residuals should sum to zero, with some variance. Another way of defining R is that it's the correlation between Y and $\hat{Y}$. When $R = 1$, Y and $\hat{Y}$ are the same for every person; the lower the value of R, the more the values will deviate from one another, and the larger the residuals will be.

One of the assumptions of multiple regression is **homoscedasticity**, which means that the variance is the same at all points along the regression line. It's a pain in the rear end if we had to calculate the variance at each value of the predictors, so we fall back

on the granddaddy of all tests, the calibrated eyeball. Take a look at the left side of Figure 12-6, which shows a scatter plot for one predictor and one dependent variable, and the regression line. The points seem to be fairly evenly distributed above and below the line along its entire length. But, we can go a step further and look to see how the *residuals* are distributed. If we plot them against the predicted values, as we've done in the graph on the right side of Figure 12-6, the points should appear to be randomly placed above and below a value of 0, and no pattern should be apparent.

Now take a look at the left side of Figure 12-7. The data seem to fall above the regression line at low values of the predictor, then fall below the line, and then above it again—a situation called **heteroscedasticity** (i.e., not homoscedastic). This is even more apparent when we plot the residuals, as in the right side of the figure; they look like a double-jointed snake with scoliosis. This is only one of the patterns that shows up with heteroscedasticity. Sometimes the variance increases with larger values of the predictors, leading to the fan-shaped pattern, with the dots further from the line as we move from left to right. In brief, any deviation from a random scattering of points between ± 2SDs is a warning that the data are heteroscedastic, and you may want to use one of the transformations outlined in Chapter 17 before going any further.

WHERE THINGS CAN GO WRONG

By now, you're experienced enough in statistics to know that the issue is never, "Can things go wrong?" but, rather, "Where have things gone wrong?" However, before you can treat a problem, doctor, you

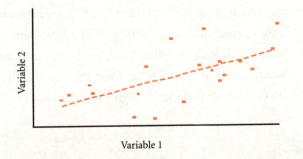
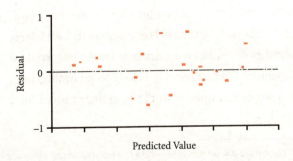

FIGURE 12-6 Scatter plot and plot of residuals when the data are homoscedastic.

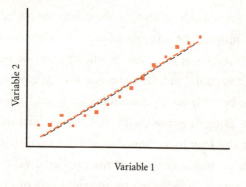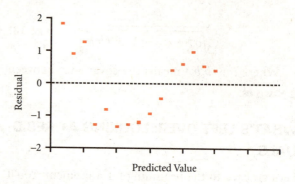

FIGURE 12-7 Scatter plot and plot of residuals when the data are heteroscedastic.

have to know what's wrong. So, we're going to tell you what sorts of aches and pains a regression equation may come down with, and how to run all sorts of diagnostic tests to find out what the problem is.[13] There are two main types of problems: those involving the cases (the specific disorders are *discrepancy*, *leverage*, and *influence*[14]) and those involving the variables (mainly *multicollinearity*).

Discrepancy

The discrepancy, or *distance*, of a case is best thought of as the magnitude of its residual, that is, how much its predicted value of Y (Y-hat, or $\hat{Y}$) differs from the observed value. When the residual scores are standardized (as they usually are), then any value over 3.0 shows a subject whose residual is larger than that of 99% of the cases. The data for these *outliers* should be closely examined to see if there might have been a mistake made when recording or entering the data. If there isn't an error you can spot, then you have a tough decision to make—to keep the case, or to trim it (which is a fancy way of saying "toss it out"). We'll postpone this decision until we deal with "influence."

Leverage

Leverage has nothing to do with junk bonds or Wall Street shenanigans. It refers to how atypical the pattern of predictor scores is for a given case. For example, it may not be unusual for a person to have a large number of clothes with designer labels; nor would it be unusual for a person to belong to no health clubs; but, in our sample, it would be quite unusual for a

person to have a closet full of such clothes *and* not belong to health clubs. So, leverage relates to combinations of the predictor variables that are atypical for the group as a whole. Note that the dependent variable is not considered, only the independent variables.

A case that has a high leverage score has the potential to affect the regression line, but it doesn't have to; we'll see in a moment under what circumstances it will affect the line. Leverage for case i is often abbreviated as h_i, and it can range in value from 0 to $(N-1)/N$, with a mean of p/N (where p is the number of predictors). Ideally, all of the cases should have similar values of h, which are close to p/N. Cases where h is greater than $2p/N$ should be looked on with suspicion.

Influence

Now let's put things together:

$$\text{Influence} = \text{Distance} \times \text{Leverage} \qquad \textbf{(12-20)}$$

This means that distance and leverage individually may not influence the coefficients of the regression equation, but the two together may do so. Cases that have a large leverage score but are close to the regression line, and those that are far from the regression line but have small leverage scores, won't have much influence; whereas cases that are high on both distance and leverage may exert a lot of influence. If you look at Figure 12-8, you'll see what we mean. Case A is relatively far from the line (i.e., it's discrepancy or distance is high), but the pattern of

---

[13] *The cure is always the same—take two t-tests and call me in the morning.*

[14] *Not to be confused with the Washington law firm of the same name.*

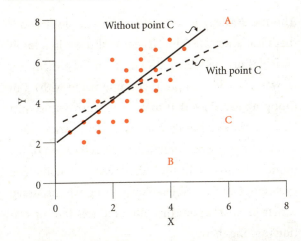

FIGURE 12-8 A depiction of cases with large values for leverage (Case A), discrepancy (Case B), and influence (Case C).

predictors (the leverage) is similar to that of the other cases. Case B has a high leverage score, but the discrepancy isn't too great. Case C has the largest influence score, because it is relatively high on both indices. In fact, Case A doesn't change the slope or intercept of the regression line at all, because it lies right on it (although it is quite distant from the other points). Case B, primarily because it is near the mean of X, has no effect on the slope, and lowers the value of the intercept just a bit. As you can see from the dashed regression line, Case C has an effect on (or "influences") both the slope and the intercept.

Influence is usually indicated in computer outputs as "Cook's distance," or CD. CD measures how much the residuals of all of the other cases would change when a given case is deleted. A value over 1.00 shows that the subject's scores are having an undue influence and it probably should be dropped.

Multicollinearity

Multiple regression is able to handle situations in which the predictors are correlated with each other to some degree. This is a good thing because, in most situations, it's unusual for the "independent variables" to be completely independent from one another. Problems arise, however, when we cross the threshold from the undefined state of "to some degree" to the equally undefined state of "a lot." We can

often spot highly correlated variables just by looking at the correlation matrix. *Multicollinearity* refers to a more complex situation, in which the *multiple correlation* between one variable and a set of others is in the range of 0.90 or higher. This is much harder to spot, because the zero-order correlations among the variables may be relatively low, but the multiple correlation—which is what we're concerned about—could be high. For example, if we measured a person's height, weight, and body mass index (BMI), we'd find that they were all correlated with each other, but at an acceptable level. However, the multiple correlation of height and weight on the BMI would be well over 0.90.

Most computer programs check for this by calculating the squared multiple correlation (SMC, or R^2) between each variable and all of the others. Some programs try to confuse us by converting the SMC into an index called *tolerance*,[15] which is defined as $(1-R)$. The better programs test the SMC or tolerance of each variable, and kick out any that exceed some criterion (usually SMC $\geq$ 0.99, or tolerance $\leq$ 0.01). We would follow Tabachnick and Fidell's (2001) advice to override this default and use a more stringent criterion. They recommend a maximum SMC of 0.90 (that is, a tolerance of 0.10), but Allison (1999) and others are even more conservative, advocating a maximum of 0.60, corresponding to a tolerance of 0.40. For once in our lives, we tend to side with the conservatives.

Yet another variant of the SMC that you'll run across is the *Variance Inflation Factor* (VIF), which is the reciprocal of tolerance. For variable i:

$$VIF_i = \frac{1}{(1 - R_i^2)} \qquad (12\text{-}21)$$

The main effect of multicollinearity is to inflate the values of the standard errors of the βs, which, in turn, drives them away from statistical significance. VIF is an index of how much the variance of the coefficients are inflated because of multicollinearity. More specifically, how much the standard error in-

[15] *No, we don't know either why this term was chosen. Perhaps it refers to the tolerance of statisticians to use terms that are seemingly meaningless.*

creases is given by the square root of the VIF; with a VIF of 9, the standard error is three times as large as it would be if the VIF were 1. This means that, in order to be significant, the coefficient would have to be three times larger. If we stick with our criterion that any R^2 over 0.90 indicates trouble, then any VIF over 10 means the same thing. Another effect of multicollinearity is the seemingly bizarre situation that some of the β weights have values greater than 1.0, which, in fact, can be used as a diagnostic test for the presence of multicollinearity.

Note that high multicollinearity doesn't violate any of the assumptions of multiple regression. All of the estimates of the coefficients will be unbiased; it's only the standard errors and confidence intervals that will be inflated and therefore the tests of significance underestimated.

There are a couple of situations that may result in multicollinearity in addition to high correlations among the predictors. One is screwing up dummy coding by not excluding one category. For example, if you divide marital status into six categories (Single, Married, Common-Law, Widowed, Divorced, and Separated) and used a dummy variable for each of them, you'll run into problems. A second situation is including a variable that's derived from other variables, and then including all of them. For instance, in some intelligence tests, the Full Scale IQ is in essence the mean of the Verbal and Performance IQs; if all three are included in a regression, you'll get multicollinearity. Third, measuring the same variable twice but using different measures of it—for example, the prothrombin ratio and the International Normalized Ratio (INR)—will give you a severe case of the multicollinearities. Finally, you can run into problems if your regression equation includes a non-linear term, something we'll discuss in Chapter 14. In essence, this means that we have a variable, such as Age, as well as Age^2. Since these two terms will be highly correlated, the result will be multicollinearity.

There are no easy ways to cure this malevolent condition. You should make sure you haven't committed one of the errors we just mentioned regarding dummy coding or measuring the same thing twice.

Another strategy is to increase the sample size, but that's not always feasible. If you've thrown in a lot of variables just to see what's going on, take them out (it was a bad idea to put them in to begin with). But dropping variables that make substantive sense just because they're highly correlated with other variables is usually a bad practice; misspecification of the model is worse than multicollinearity. Finally, you can center the variables—something we discussed earlier in the chapter; this often reduces the correlations among them.

THE PRAGMATICS OF MULTIPLE REGRESSION

One real problem with multiple regression is that, as computers sprouted in every office, so did data bases, so now every damn fool with a lab coat has access to data bases galore. All successive admissions to the pediatric gerontology unit (both of them) are there *in a data base*. Score assigned to the personal interview for every applicant to the nursing school for the past 20 years, the 5% who came here and the 95% who went elsewhere or vanished altogether, are there *in a data base*. All the laboratory requisitions and routine tests ordered on the last 280 000 admissions to the hospital are there—*in a data base*.

A first level of response by any reasonable researcher to all this wealth of data and paucity of information should be, "Who cares?". But then, pressures to publish or perish being what they are, it seems that few can resist the opportunity to analyze them, usually without any previous good reason (i.e., hypothesis). Multiple regression is natural for such nefarious tasks—all you need do is to select a likely looking dependent variable (e.g., days to discharge from hospital, average class performance, undergraduate GPA—almost anything that seems a bit important), then press the button on the old "multreg" machine, and stand back and watch the F-ratios fly. The last step is to examine all the significant coefficients (usually about 1 in 20), wax ecstatic about the theoretical reasons why a relationship might be so, and then inevitably recommend further research.

Given the potential for abuse, some checks and

balances must exist to aid the unsuspecting reader of such tripe. Here are a few:

1. The number of data (patients, subjects, students) should be a minimum of 5 or 10 times the number of variables entered into the equation—not the number of variables that turn out to be significant, which is always small. Use the number you started with. This rule provides some assurance that the estimates are stable and not simply capitalizing on chance.

2. Inevitably, when folks are doing these types of post-hoc regressions, something significant will result. One handy way to see if it is any good is to simply square the multiple correlation. Any multiple regression worth its salt should account for about half the variance (i.e., a multiple R of about 0.7). Much less, and it's not saying much.

3. Similarly, to examine the contribution of an individual variable before you start inventing a new theory, look at the *change in* R^2. This should be at least a few percent, or the variable is of no consequence in the prediction, statistically significant or not.

4. Look at the patterns in the regression equation. A gradual falloff should be seen in the prediction of each successive variable, so that variable 1 predicts, say, 20% to 30% of the variance, variable 2 an additional 10% to 15%, variable 3, 5% to 10% more, and so on, up to 5 or 6 variables and a total R^2 of 0.6 to 0.8. If all the variance is soaked up by the first variable, little of interest is found in the multiple regression. Conversely, if things dribble on forever, with each variable adding a little, it is about like number 2 above—not much happening here.

5. Remember that if you use one group of subjects to run the regression, you shouldn't make definitive statements about the model using the same data. The real test is to see if the model applies in a new sample of people. If you have enough subjects, you should split the sample in two—run the regression with half of the subjects, and test it with the other half.

SAMPLE SIZE CALCULATIONS

For once, nothing could be simpler. No one could possibly work out ahead of time what a reasonable value for a particular regression coefficient might be, let alone its SE. About all that can be hoped for is that the values that eventually emerge are reasonably stable and somewhere near the truth. The best guarantee of this is simply that the number of data be considerably more than the number of variables. Thus the "sample size calculation" is the essence of simplicity:

Sample size = 5 (or 10) times the number of variables

If you, or the reviewers of your grant, don't believe us, try an authoritative source—Kleinbaum, Kupper, and Muller (1988).

Let's point out why sample size is important. Strictly speaking, you can run a regression with as many subjects as predictors (i.e., variables and interaction terms). In fact, the results will look marvelous, with an R^2 value of 1.00 and many of the variables and interactions highly significant. This will be true even if all of the predictor variables are just random data. The model is *over-fitted*. The reason is that if we have 10 predictors and 10 subjects, we would in essence be estimating each β weight with a sample size of 1. Even doubling the number of subjects means that the sample size for each estimate is a whopping 2, not an ideal situation for ending up with a stable, replicable model. Also, the smaller the subject-to-variable ratio, the higher the rate of spurious R^2 values (Babyak, 2004). So, follow our advice—use at least 10 subjects per variable (and remember that each interaction term is another variable).

REPORTING GUIDELINES

Reporting the results of a multiple regression is a bit more complicated than for the tests we've described so far, because there are usually two sets of findings we want to communicate: those for the individual variables, and those for the equation as a whole. Let's start off with the former. What should be reported are:

1. The standardized regression weights.
2. The unstandardized regression weights.
3. The standard error of the unstandardized

weights.

4. The *t*-tests for each weight, and their significance levels.

It's often easiest to put these into tabular form, as in Table 12-4.

What should be reported for the equation as a whole is:

5. The value of R^2.

6. The adjusted R^2.

7. The overall *F*-test, with its associated *df*s and *p* level.

These can be given either within the text, at the bottom of the table, or as a separate ANOVA table like Table 12-1. Within the text, you need to state:

8. Whether there were any missing data and how they were handled (e.g., list-wise deletion, imputation).

9. Whether there were any outliers and how they were treated.

10. Whether there was any multicollinearity.

11. Whether there was any heteroscedasticity of the residuals.

12. Whether the residuals were normally distributed.

SUMMARY

✧ Multiple linear regressions is a multivariable analysis method which studies the quantitative relationship between a dependent variable and two or more independent variables. The objective of multiple linear regressions is to estimate parameters and test hypothesis for the whole model and the regression coefficients of explanatory variables. The least sum of squares method is the common technique for parameter sums of squares reflecting different sources of variability named as regression sum of squares and residual sum of squares. In addition, the coefficient of determination R^2, is interpreted as the proportion of response variation 'explained' by the independent variables in the model. Thus,

$R^2=1$ indicates that the fitted model explains all variations of *y*, while $R^2=0$ indicates no 'linear' relationship between independent variables and dependent variable. Statistical independence of observations and homoscedasticity are two assumptions for multiple linear regression.

✧ Sum of square of partial regression, reflecting the specific contribution of one or more independent variables to the regression model, is an important concept in multiple linear regression. *F* statistic is to test whether one or more explanatory variables are statistically significant and further to incorporate these explanatory variables into regression model. *t* statistic in *t*-test gives the same conclusion as *F* statistic for single variable selection. The selection methods of independent variables for multiple linear regression include optimal model selection and stepwise regression. The stepwise regression includes forward selection, backward elimination, and stepwise regression selection.

✧ The response variable in multiple linear regression is commonly continuous, but sometimes noncontinuous, like binary. The explanatory variables in multiple linear regression are distribution-free. The technique for yielding dummy variables is needed when an explanatory variable is categorical. Residual plot is often used to test whether the fitted model satisfies the assumptions.

GLOSSARY

multiple linear regression　多重(元)线性回归
multiple correlation　复相关
partial correlation　偏相关
standardized regression coefficient　标准化回归系数
adjusted R^2　调整决定系数
partial regression coefficient　偏回归系数
residual　残差

forward-entry 前进法

backward-elimination 后退法

stepwise 逐步回归法

Cook's distance 库克氏距离

multicollinearity 多重共线性

variance inflation factor (VIF) 方差膨胀因子

interaction 交互作用

Cp statistic Cp统计量

EXERCISES

1. A researcher does a study to see if he can predict success in reflexology school (measured by the average number of skull bumps the student can detect on simulated plastic heads) using several admissions variables: age, GPA, and gender (M = 0, F = 1). He does a multiple regression analysis and determines the R^2s and bs. Comment on the results shown in the several displays below.

   a. Multiple $R = 0.15$
      $R^2 = 0.0225$
      $n = 17$

Variable	b	SE (b)	t	p
Age	0.131	0.044	2.97	0.01
GPA	0.034	0.112	0.303	ns
Gender	0.003	0.017	0.176	ns

ns = not significant.

   b. Multiple $R = 0.15$
      $R^2 = 0.0225$
      $n = 1233$

Variable	b	SE (b)	t	p
Age	0.131	0.004	32.75	0.0001
GPA	0.034	0.012	2.83	0.01
Gender	0.003	0.0007	4.28	0.001

   c. Multiple $R = 0.75$
      $R^2 = 0.5625$
      $n = 5$

Variable	b	SE (b)	t	p
Age	0.561	0.424	1.32	ns
GPA	0.383	0.312	1.22	ns
Gender	0.137	0.129	1.06	ns

ns= not significant.

2. In a study of high school depression, a sample of 800 children were selected at random from city high schools.

   A questionnaire was administered, including the categories (a) stress, (b) perceived comfort in social situations, (c) attitudes to parents, (d) social support from parents, (e) socioeconomic status, and (f) a standardized measure of depression.

   A regression analysis used the depression score as dependent variable. The multiple correlation was significant ($R^2 = 0.176$, $p < 0.001$), and all the individual variables entered the regression equation. What effect would the following strategies have on the listed measures?

		R^2	Significance of R^2	Beta
A.	Increase sample size to 1600	___	___	___
B.	Select only kids from private schools	___	___	___
C.	Include family income as predictor	___	___	___
D.	Repeat study with kids who were depressed then had therapy	___	___	___

3. A study aimed to elucidate the relationship between fasting blood-glucose (FBG) and total cholesterol (TC), triglyceride (TG) of diabetes patients. One research team collected the data of FBG, TC and TG from 40 diabetes patients. The researcher ran programme of multiple regression and the results were showed as follows.

Table 1   The estimation of regression coefficient

variables	b	SE	t	P	95%CI	
constant	5.358	0.466	12.08	0.000	4.459	6.257
TC	0.172	0.055	3.14	0.003	0.061	0.282
TG	0.318	0.148	2.15	0.038	0.019	0.617

Table 2   ANOVA of the regression model

Source	SS	df	MS	F	P
Regression	4.281	2	2.141	7.69	0.001
Residual	10.293	37	0.278		
Sum	14.574	39	0.374		

Questions

(1) According to Table 1, write the equation to

estimate the relationship between FBG and TC, TG.

(2) Try to explain the meaning of b-TC=0.172.

(3) How do you explain the results of Table 2? Calculate R^2, $Adj\ R^2$ and try to explain the meaning.

4. A researcher established an equation between 4 independent variables (X_1, X_2, X_3, X_4) and 1 dependent variable (Y). He got 15 equations based on the combination of independent variables. He listed $Adj\ R^2$ and Cp of all the equations as the following table. Try to select a best equation you want and explain the reasons.

Independent variables	Adj R^2	C_p
X_2, X_3, X_4	0.546	3.15
X_1, X_2, X_3, X_4	0.528	5.00
X_1, X_3, X_4	0.488	5.96
X_1, X_2, X_4	0.447	7.97
X_1, X_4	0.441	7.42
X_2, X_4	0.440	7.51
X_3, X_4	0.435	7.72
X_1, X_2, X_3	0.408	9.88
X_2, X_3	0.408	9.14
X_1, X_3	0.375	10.78
X_4	0.347	11.63
X_1	0.284	14.92
X_1, X_2	0.275	15.89
X_3	0.231	17.77
X_2	0.179	20.53

5. After learning this chapter, you need to take the following questions into consideration.

(1) Does the regression equation really provide better than chance prediction?

(2) Out of a set of explanatory variables in a regression equation how can one select the more important ones?

(3) Having obtained a regression equation how can one judge whether adding one or more explanatory variables would improve prediction of the response?

**How to Get the Computer to
Do the Work for You**

All forms of regression are run from the same dialog box; you simply choose different options to do the different types of analyses. For a straight multiple regression:

- From **Analyze**, choose **Regression → Linear**
- Click on the dependent variable from the list on the left, and click the arrow to move it into the box marked **Dependent**
- Click on the predictor variables from the list on the left, and click the arrow to move them into the box marked **Independent**
- Click OK

To do a hierarchical regression, click the Next button to the right of **Block 1 of 1** after you've chosen the variable(s) you want to enter first; select the variable(s) in the second block and click Next , and so on, until all the variables you want are selected.

For a stepwise solution, also click on the down-arrow in the **Method** box and choose **Stepwise**.

SUGGESTED READINGS AND WEBSITES

[1] http://www.statsoft.com/textbook/multiple-regression

[2] https://statistics.laerd.com/spss-tutorials/multiple-regression-using-spss-statistics.php

[3] http://www.stat.yale.edu/Courses/1997-98/101/linmult.htm

[4] http://onlinestatbook.com/2/regression/multiple_regression.html

[5] http://www.unesco.org/webworld/idams/advguide/Chapt5_2.htm

[6] http://udel.edu/~mcdonald/statmultreg.html

[7] http://pareonline.net/getvn.asp?n=2&v=8

[8] http://www.statisticssolutions.com/what-is-multiple-linear-regression/

CHAPTER THE THIRTEENTH Logistic Regression

Logistic regression is an extension of multiple linear regression methods for use where the dependent variable (DV) is dichotomous (e.g., dead/alive), ordinal (e.g., worse/bad/good/better), or multinomial (e.g., A/B/C). The method determines the predicted probability of the outcome based on the combination of predictor variables. This chapter focuses on binary logistic regression where DV is dichotomous.

SETTING THE SCENE

A dreaded disease of North African countries is "Somaliland Camelbite Fever," which is contracted, as the name implies, from intimate contact with camels. What combination of variables related to camel contact best predicts the likelihood of contracting the scourge? Can we go even further and say what variables predict the number of cases?

Clearly, the proposed questions can not be explored using multiple linear regression, because DV (getting disease or not) in this study is a binary variable, rather than a continuous one.

In this case, a commonly used advanced nonparametric statistical method is called logistic regression. It is used when the dependent variable is dichotomous, for example, dead or alive; the independent variables are usually continuous (but they don't have to be). You will notice that the boundaries are starting to smear. Although it's an advanced nonparametric method, once you get into it, it looks an awful lot like ordinary multiple linear regression.[1]

For illustration, let's acknowledge that many of the major scourges of mankind never reach the temperate shores of Europe and North America. One of the deadliest is Somaliland Camelbite Fever [2] (SCF), which results in an involvement of multiple systems.

One intrepid epidemiologist ventured forth to determine risk factors for the disease. Four potential variables were identified: (1) number of years spent herding camels (Years); (2) size of the herd (Herd); (3) family history of SCF (Fam), which is a dichotomous variable; and (4) a buccal coliform count (BCC) from a mouth swab of the beasts (since it was thought that the disease is spread by bacteria residing in the camel's mouth—leading to the horrible odor).

Now if SCF were a continuous variable, the next step should be almost self-evident by now: Construct a regression equation to predict the probability of SCF, which we'll call z, from a linear combination of Years, Herd, Fam, and BCC. The equation would then express the risk of coming down with SCF as a weighted sum of the four factors, and would look like:

$$z = b_0 + b_1 Year + b_2 Herd + b_3 Fam + b_4 BCC + e$$

(13-1)

We can write a linear regression equation like this, but we shouldn't due to the following reasons. First, probabilities do not go in a straight line forever; they are bounded by zero and one. Second, there's a problem with that little e hiding at the end of the equation. In linear regression, the assumed distribution of that error term is normal. But, if the dependent variable is dichotomous, then the distribution of e is binomial rather than normal. That means that any significance tests we run or confidence intervals that we calculate won't be accurate. Finally, we call it multiple linear regression because we assume that the relationship between the DV and all the predictor variables is (you guessed it) linear. For a dichotomous outcome, though, the relationship is more S-

---

[1]*So if you're rusty on multiple regression, you might want to have a fresh look at Chapter 14 before you proceed.*

[2]*First brought to the attention of modern medicine in PDQ Statistics.*

shaped; the technical term is a logistic function. So, to get around all these problems, we transform things so that there's an S-shaped outcome that ranges between zero and one; Not too surprisingly, this is called a logistic (sometimes referred to as a logit) transformation:[3]

$$\hat{y} = Pr\,(SCF\mid z)=\frac{1}{1+e^{-z}} \qquad (13\text{-}2)$$

(where you'll remember that the "hat" over the y means the estimated value).

A complicated little ditty. What it is saying in the first instance is that y is the probability of getting SCF for a given value of z, that is, for a given value of the regression equation. This function does have good attributes. When $z= 0$, y is $1/(1 + e^{0}) = 1/(1 + 1) = 0.5$. When z goes to infinity (∞), it becomes $1/(1 + e^{-\infty}) = 1$. And when z goes to $-\infty$, it becomes $1/(1 + e^{\infty}) = 0$. So, it describes a smooth curve that approaches zero for large negative values of z, and goes to 1 when z is large and positive.

There are a couple of other things to note about Figure 13-1. The shape implies that there are two threshold values. There's almost no relationship between the predictor variables and the probability of the outcome for low values of z; in this figure, z can increase from –10 to about –3 without significantly changing the probability. But, once the predictors pass a certain lower threshold, there's a linear re-

lationship between them and the probability of an outcome. Then, beyond an upper threshold, the linear relationship disappears again, so that further increases in the predictors don't distinctly increase the probability any more.

Until now, the shape of the curve is not self-evidently a good thing; now, we remind ourselves about the situation we're trying to model. The goal is to estimate something about the various possible risk factors for dreaded SCF. All the predictors are set up in an ascending way, so that if z is low, you don't have any risk factors, and the probability of contracting SCF should be low, which it is—that's the left-hand side of the curve. Conversely, if you have a lot of risk factors, you're off on the right-hand side, where the probability of getting SCF should approach one, which it does. If we had tried this estimate with multiple linear regression, it would have ended up as a straight-line relationship, so probabilities would be negative on the left side, and go to infinity on the right side—definitely not a good thing.

This ability to capture a plausible relationship between risk and probability is not the only nice feature of the logistic function, but we'll save some of the other surprises until later. For the moment, it's best to realize that the job is far from done, since we have this linear sum of our original values (which is the good news) hopelessly entangled in the middle of a complicated expression. Time to mess around a bit more. First, we'll rearrange things to get the linear expression all by itself:

$$\frac{(1-\hat{y})}{\hat{y}} = e^{(-b_0 + b_1\,Years + b_2\,Herd + b_3\,Fam + b_4\,BCC)}$$

$$(13\text{-}3)$$

Now, the next bit of sleight of hand. The way to get rid of an exponent is to take the logarithm, so we now get:

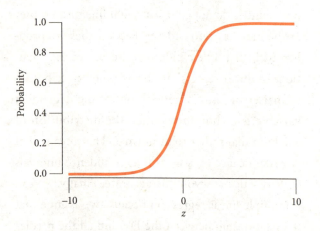

FIGURE 13-1   The logistic function.

$$ln\frac{(1-\hat{y})}{\hat{y}} = -(b_0+b_1\,Years+b_2\,Herd+b_3\,Fam+b_4\,BCC)$$

$$(13\text{-}4)$$

---

[3]*On a historical note, for those so inclined, its name comes from the fact that it was originally used to model the logistics of animal populations. As numbers increased, less food was available to each member of the herd, leading to increased starvation. As the population dropped, more food could be consumed, resulting in an increase in numbers, and so on.*

and-log $(c/d) = \log(d/c)$, so the negative sign goes away:

$$ln\frac{\hat{y}}{(1-\hat{y})} = (b_0 + b_1 Years + b_2 Herd + b_3 Fam + b_4 BCC)$$

(13-5)

We have managed to recapture a linear equation, so we can go ahead and analyze it as yet another regression problem. Here's another definition to add to the long list, by the way. The expression we just derived, $\ln[\hat{y}/(1-\hat{y})]$, is called the logit function of y. As you see, a logit is the natural logarithm (that is, a log with the base e) of an odds ratio. We'll talk later about the interpretation of this function, but first we have to figure out how the computer computes all this stuff.

We fly off to the Sahara,[4] rent the Land Rover, and wander from wadi to wadi and oasis to oasis, recruiting camel herders wherever we can find them, buying off each with a few handfuls of beads and bullets, administering a questionnaire, and swabbing their camels' mouths. After months of scouring the desert, we have found 30 herders. The pathologist does her bit and we have found that 18 herders had SCF and 12 didn't. The data for the first few are shown in Table 13-1.

TABLE 13-1   Data from the first 10 of 30 camel herders

Subject	Years of herding	Number in herd	Family history	Buccal count	SCF
1	3	22	No	300	No
2	5	3	No	350	No
3	25	344	Yes	446	Yes
4	14	28	Yes	121	No
5	2	77	No	45	No
6	16	34	No	233	Yes
7	28	66	Yes	654	Yes
8	19	100	Yes	277	No
9	13	87	Yes	321	Yes
10	33	45	Yes	335	Yes

Before we get to the output of the analysis, we should invest some time describing how the computer does its thing. One might think that, having converted the whole thing to a linear equation, we could just stuff the data into the regression program and let the beast go on its merry way, estimating the parameters and adjusting things so that the Sum of Squares (Residual) is at a minimum (see Chapter 12).

Unfortunately, things aren't quite that simple. The standard method of computing regression by minimizing the residual Sum of Squares, called the **method of least squares** for (one hopes) fairly obvious reasons, can be used only when the underlying model is linear, and the dependent variable is approximately normally distributed. Although we have done our best to convert the present problem to a linear equation, this was at the cost of creating a dependent variable that is anything but linear. So, statisticians tell us that we cannot just crash ahead minimizing the error Sum of Squares. Instead we must use an alternative, computationally intensive,[5] method called **Maximum Likelihood Estimation**, or **MLE**.

MAXIMUM LIKELIHOOD ESTIMATION PROCEDURES

To understand what MLE procedures are all about, it's necessary to first go back to basics. The whole point of logistic regression is to compute the estimated probability for each person, based on Equation (13-2). That estimate of the probability that the poor soul will have SCF is then compared with the actual probability, which is of a particularly simple form: 0 (the person don't get it) or 1 (the person does get it). Now, if the logistic regression is doing a good job, and the universe is being predictable, the estimated probabilities for those poor souls who actually have SCF will be high, and the probabilities for those who don't will be low. The **Likelihood Function** considers the fit between the estimated probabilities and the true state, computed as an overall probability across all cases.

Looking at things one case at a time, if p_i is the

---

[4]*Normally research assistants do the data gathering, but this rule is ignored when exotic travel and frequent flyer points are involved.*
[5]*Which is why logistic regression was absent from many statistical packages until recently.*

computed likelihood of disease given the set of predicting variables for person i who has the disease, then the probability of the overall function being correct associated with this person is just p_i. If person j doesn't have the disease, then the appropriate probability of a correct call on the part of the computer program is $(1-p_j)$. So the overall probability of correct calls (i.e., the probability of observing the data set, given a particular value for each of the coefficients in the model) is just the product of all these ps and $(1-p)s$:

$$L = \prod_i \hat{p}_i \prod_j (1 - \hat{p}_j) \qquad \textbf{(13-6)}$$

where the is includes all the cases, and the js includes all the non-cases, and $\prod$ (Greek letter *pi*) is a symbol meaning "product."[6] This is the **Likelihood Function**, obtained by simply multiplying the *ps* for all the cases and (1–p)s for all the non-cases together to determine the probability that things could have turned out the way they did for a particular set of coefficients multiplying the predictors. It's actually conceptually similar to the standard approach of minimizing the residual sum of squares in ordinary regression. The residual sum of squares in this case is the difference between the observed data and the fitted values estimated from the regression equation, except that we do the whole thing in terms of estimated probabilities and observed probabilities. And since the numbers of interest are probabilities, we multiply them together instead of adding them.

The rest of the calculation is the essence of simplicity. All the computer now has to do is try a bunch of numbers, compute the probability, fiddle them a bit to see if the probability increases, and keep going until the probability is maximum (the Maximum Likelihood Estimation). That's what happens conceptually, but not actually. Just as in ordinary regression, calculus comes to the rescue to find the maximum

value of the function.[7] However, this analysis is so hairy that even after using calculus, it's still necessary for the computer to use iteration to get the solution, rather than calculate it from the equation.

Unconditional versus Conditional Maximum Likelihood Estimation

Unfortunately, that's still not the whole story. What we computed above is one kind of MLE, called **Unconditional MLE.** There's still another kind, called, not surprisingly, **Conditional MLE.** Basically, they differ in that unconditional MLE takes the computed probability at face value, and goes ahead and maximizes it. The conditional MLE compares the particular likelihood with all other possible configurations of the data. What actually gets maximized is the ratio of the likelihood function for the particular set of observations conditional on all other likelihood functions for all other possible configurations of the data.

What do we mean by "all other configurations"? Assume we reorder the data so the first 13 are cases and the next 17 are controls. That's only one possibility; others include the first 12 are cases, the next one isn't, the one after that is, and the remaining 16 are not. That is, the other configurations are computed by keeping the predictors in a fixed order and reordering the cases and controls in the last column to consider all possible combinations, always keeping the totals at 13 and 17. For each one of these configurations the MLE probability is computed, and then they're all summed up.[8] Needless to say, the computation is *very* intensive and complicated.

All this would be of academic interest only, except that sometimes it really matters which one you pick. When the number of variables is large compared with the number of cases, then the conditional approach is preferred, and the unconditional MLE can give answers that are quite far off the mark. How

---

[6]*Note that we threw in a little hat over the ps ; this is the mathematical way to say that these are estimates, not the truth.*

[7]*What really happens is that the process begins by differentiating the whole thing with respect to each parameter (calculus again) resulting in a set of k equations in k unknowns, the set of coefficients for each of the predictor variables, and a constant.*

[8]*For your interest (who's still interested?), the number of possible combinations for our 30 herders is 1.786×10^{35}! If you want to see how we got there, look up the Fisher Exact Test.*

large is large? How high is up? It seems that no one knows, but perhaps the "rule of 5"—5 cases per variable—is a safe bet.

SAMPLE CALCULATION

Now that we understand a bit about what the computer is doing, let's stand back and let it do its thing. We press the button on the SCF data, sit back, and watch the electrons fly, and, in due course, a few pages come spinning out of the printer. Some of it looks familiar; some does not. Let's deal with the familiar first. A recognizable table of *b* coefficients is one of the first things we see, and it looks like Table 13-2.

TABLE 13-2   *B coefficients from logistic regression analysis of SCF data*

Variable	*B*	SE	Wald	*df*	Sig	*Exp(B)*
Family history	3.36	1.48	5.13	1	0.023	28.79
Herd	0.0073	0.010	0.547	1	0.459	0.992
Years	0.0086	0.0238	0.132	1	0.716	1.008
BCC	0.0128	0.0061	4.42	1	0.035	1.012
Constant	1.45	2.044				

Just like ordinary multiple linear regression, this table shows the coefficients for all the independent variables and their associated standard errors (SEs). However, the column to the right of SE, which one might expect to be the *t*-test of significance for the parameter [$t=b$/SE(b)] is now labelled the **Wald** test, and it doesn't look a bit like the b/SE(b) we expected.

The Wald statistic has two forms: in the first form, it is just the coefficient divided by SE, and it is distributed approximately as a *z* test (so Table A in the Appendix is appropriate). In the second form, the whole thing is squared, so it equals [b/SE(b)]^2. In the present printout, taken from SPSS, they chose to square it. So this part of the analysis, in which we have computed the individual coefficients, their SEs, and the appropriate tests of significance, is familiar territory indeed. As it turns out, Family history and

BCC are significant at the 0.05 level; Herd and Years are not.

This is almost straightforward, except for the last column. What on earth is *Exp(B)*? So glad you asked. The short answer is that is stands for "exponential of regression coefficient (B)," which leaves most folks no further ahead. Remember, however, that we began with something that had all the regression coefficients in a linear equation inside an exponential. Now we're working backward to that original equation.

Suppose the only variable that was predictive was Family history (Fam), which has only two values: 1 (present) or 0 (absent). We have already pointed out that the logistic function expresses the probability of getting SCF given certain values of the predicting variables. Focusing only on Fam now, the probability of SCF given a family history looks like:

$$\log\left[\frac{p_1(SCF)}{(1-p_1)(SCF)}\right] = b_0 + b_3 \qquad (13\text{-}7)$$

If there is no family history then Fam=0, and the formula is:

$$\log\left[\frac{p_0(SCF)}{(1-p_0)(SCF)}\right] = b_0 \qquad (13\text{-}8)$$

Now the ratio of $p/(1-p)$ is the **odds**[9] of SCF with Fam present or absent.

$$\log\left[\frac{p_1/(1-p_1)}{p_0/(1-p_0)}\right] = b_3 \qquad (13\text{-}9)$$

In words: for discrete predicting variables, the regression coefficient is equal to the log odds ratio of the event for the predictor present and absent. If we take the exponential of the regression coefficient, we can get to the interpretation of the last column:

$$\frac{p_1/(1-p_1)}{p_0/(1-p_0)} = e^{b_3} \qquad (13\text{-}10)$$

So, in the present example, the b coefficient for Fam is 3.36, and $e^{3.36}$ is 28.79; therefore, the relative odds of getting SCF with a positive family history is 28.79. That is, in this equation, a family history

[9]*Although some folks might like to convince you that this came from epidemiology, it didn't—it came from horse racing. Imagine that the odds makers work out that the probability of Old Beetlebaum winning is 20%. The odds of him winning is 0.2/(1 − 0.2) = 0.25, or turning it around, the odds against Beetlebaum are 0.8/(1 − 0.8) = 4.*

is a bad risk factor; the odds of getting SCF when you have a positive history is about 29 times what it would be otherwise. Perhaps you should stay away from your parents.

For continuous variables we can do the same calculation, but it requires a somewhat different interpretation. Now the e^b corresponds to the change in odds associated with a one-unit change in the variable of interest. So looking at BCC, the other significant predictor, the OR is 1.012, meaning that a one-unit change in BCC increases the odds of contracting SCF by about 1%.

Interpreting Relative Risks and Odds Ratios

The major problem with logistic regression is the interpretation (or rather, the *mis*interpretation) of the OR. Many people interpret them as if they were **relative risks**, which they are not. Let's go through some examples to see the difference between them. In our example, we haven't differentiated between Bactrian camels (two humps) and Dromedaries (one hump).[10] Is it possible that two humps doubles the chances of SCF? In Table 13-3, we present the results from two different regions—Somaliland itself, and that ancient emirate, Kushmir en Tuchas.[11]

TABLE 13-3   **The relationship between type of camel and SCF in two regions**

Somaliland				
	SCF			
Type of Camel	**Yes**	**No**	**Total**	***p***
Bactrian	10	40	50	0.20
Dromedary	5	45	50	0.10
Total	15	85	100	

Kushmir en Tuchas				
	SCF			
Type of Camel	**Yes**	**No**	**Total**	***p***
Bactrian	40	10	50	0.80
Dromedary	20	30	50	0.40
Total	60	40	100	

In Somaliland, the **risk** of SCF from Bactrian camels is $10/50 = 0.20$; and the risk from Dromedaries is $5/50 = 0.10$. Hence, the **relative risk** (RR) of SCF from Bactrians is $0.20/0.10 = 2$; that is, you're twice as likely to get this debilitating disorder from the two humper as compared with the unihumper. But the OR, which is calculated as:

$$Odds\ Ratio\ (OR) = \frac{ad}{bc} \qquad (13\text{-}11)$$

Where a, b, c, and d refer to the four cells, is:

$$\frac{10 \times 45}{40 \times 5} = 2.25 \qquad (13\text{-}12)$$

In Kushmir en Tuchas, the comparable numbers are again an RR of 2.0, but with an OR of 6.0. Clearly, the two are not the same. In Kushmir, you're twice as likely to get SCF from Bactrians as Dromedaries (that's from the RR); but the odds are 6 : 1 that if you got SCF, it was from a B-type beast. The important point is that the OR does *not* describe changes in probabilities, but rather in odds. With a probability, the numerator is the number of times an event happened, and the denominator is the number of times it *could have* happened. The numerator is the same in an OR, but the denominator is the number of times the event *didn't* occur.

When the numbers in cells a and c are small, the RR and OR are almost identical, as in Somaliland. As the proportion of cases in those cells increases, the OR exceeds the value of the RR. To see why, let's spell out the equation for a relative risk. It's:

$$Relative\ Risk = \frac{\left(\dfrac{a}{a+b}\right)}{\left(\dfrac{c}{c+d}\right)} = \frac{a(c+d)}{c(a+b)}$$

$$(13\text{-}13)$$

Now, when the prevalence of a disorder is very low (say, under 10%), $c+d$ isn't much different from d; and $a+b$ is just about equal to b. So, the equation simplifies to ad/bc, which is the formula for the OR we saw in Equation (13-11).

---

[10] *If you can't remember the difference, rotate the first letters 90° to the left—a B has two bumps, and a D has one. Now tell us, in what other statistics book outside of Saudi Arabia can you learn about the finer points of camel herding?*

[11] *For those of you not fluent in Yiddish, "Kush mir in tuchas" is a request to kiss my other beast of burden—a smaller one spelled with three letters, the first of which is a and the third of which is s.*

So, to summarize:

• An RR and an OR of 1 means that nothing is going on; the outcome is equally probable in both groups.

• When the prevalence of a disorder is low (under about 10%), the RR and OR are nearly the same.

• As the prevalence increases, the OR becomes larger than the RR. In fact, the OR sets an upper bound for the RR. We'll discuss ORs and RRs in greater depth in later Chapter.

GOODNESS OF FIT AND OVERALL TESTS OF SIGNIFICANCE

That was the easy part; however, missing from the discussion so far is any overall test of fit—the equivalent of the ANOVA of regression and the R^2 we encountered in multiple linear regression. Since this is a categorical outcome variable, we won't be doing any ANOVAs on these data.

At one level, goodness of fit is just as easy to come by with logistic regression as with continuous data. After all, we began with a bunch of cases of SCF and controls. We could do the standard epidemiologic "shtick" and create a 2 × 2 table of observed versus predicted classifications. To do this, since the predicted value is a probability, not 0 or 1, we must establish some cut-off value above which we'll call it a case—50% or 0.50 seems like a reasonable starting point.

If we do that for the present data set, the contingency table would look like Table 13-4.

TABLE 13-4   Observed and predicted classification

Predicted	Observed		
	Control	Case	Total
Control	9	1	10
Case	3	17	20
Totals	12	18	30

The overall agreement is 26/30 or 86.67%. We could of course calculate *kappa*s or *phi*s on the thing—but we won't. However, there are a couple of useful statistics that come out of tables like this. The *Gamma* statistic tells us how many fewer errors would be made in predicting the outcome using the equation rather than just chance. If the value were 0.532, for example, we'd make 53.2% fewer errors in predicting who will get SCF. But, it tends to overestimate the strength of the relationship. Another useful bit of information is the *c* statistic. If we take two camel herders, one of whom has SCF and the other not, how good is our equation in predicting who is the unlucky one? If *c* were 0.750, it would mean that our equation gave a higher probability of SCF to the sick herder 75% of the time. A useless equation has a *c* value of 0.50 (that is, it's operating at chance level), and a perfect one has a value of 1.00. This statistic is particularly useful when we're comparing a number of regression equations with the same data, or the same equation to different data sets—go with the one with the highest value of *c*.

While this table is a useful way to see how we're doing overall, it is not easily turned into a test of significance. We could just do the standard chi-square test on the 2 × 2 table, but this isn't really a measure of how well we're doing, because to create the table, every computed probability from 0 to 0.49999 was set equal to 0, and everything from 0.50000 to 1 was set equal to 1. So, the actual fit may well be somewhat better than it looks from the table.

In fact, the likelihood function, which we have already encountered, provides a direct test of the goodness of fit of the particular model, since it is a direct estimate of the likelihood that the particular set of cases and controls could have arisen from the computed probabilities derived from the logistic function. That is, the MLE *is* a probability—the probability that we could have obtained the particular set of observed data given the estimated probabilities computed from putting the optimal set of parameters into the equation for the logistic function (optimal in terms of maximizing the likelihood, that is). Now, the better the fit, the higher the probability that the particular pattern could have occurred, so we can then turn it around and use the MLE as a measure of goodness of fit.

It turns out that, although the programs could report this estimate, they don't—that would be too sensible. Instead, they do a transformation on the likelihood:

$$Goodness - of - Fit = -2\log\hat{L} \qquad (13\text{-}14)$$

The only reason to do this transformation is that some very clever statistician worked out that this value is approximately distributed as a chi-square statistic with degrees of freedom equal to the number of variables in the model.

In the present example, the value of the goodness-of-fit is 18.10. With 4 variables, there are 4 *df*, so the critical chi-square statistic, derived from Table F in the Appendix, is 14.86 for $p < 0.005$; so, it's highly significant.

There are a couple of tricks in the interpretation of this value. First, you have to recall some arcane high school math. For any number x less than one, the logarithm of x ($\log x$) is negative. Since the MLE is a probability (and, therefore, can never exceed 1.0), its log will always carry a negative sign, and further, the bigger the quantity (bigger negative that is), the smaller the probability, the worse fit. So, when we multiply the whole thing by "–2," it all stands on its head. Now, the bigger the quantity (this time in the usual positive sense), the lower probability, and the *worse* the fit. That is, just as you've gotten used to the idea that the bigger the test, the better, statisticians turn things "bass-ackwards" on you.

A consequence of this inversion is that, like all multiple regression stuff, the more variables in the model, the *smaller* the goodness-of-fit measure. Tracing down this logic, as we introduce more variables, we expect that the fit will improve, so the ML probability will be higher (closer to 1), the log will be smaller (negative but closer to zero), and ($-2 \log L$) will be smaller. Of course, also like multiple regression, this is achieved at the cost of an increase in the degrees of freedom, so it's entirely possible that additional predicting variables will improve the goodness of fit (make it smaller), but it will be less significant, since the degrees of freedom for the chi-squared is going up faster than is the chi-square statistic.

Faking R^2

So, with all this talk about how well the equation does or doesn't work, why haven't we mentioned R^2? For one simple reason: it doesn't exist for logistic regression. Just as the Crusaders searched high and low for the Holy Grail, statisticians have looked just as diligently, and just as fruitlessly, for an R^2-like statistic for logistic regression. The problem is that logistic regression uses MLE, rather than trying to minimize variance, so the R^2 approach doesn't work. The good news is that there are a number of other indices proposed to replace it—what are called **pseudo-R^2** statistics. The bad news is that they all differ, and nobody knows which one is best. There are three major contenders.

McFadden's R^2 tells you how much better the model is compared to one that includes only the intercept (the "null" model). Like R^2, it ranges from 0 to 1, and can be interpreted as (a) the proportion of total variance explained by the model and (b) the degree to which the model is better than the null model; it *can not* be interpreted as the square of the correlation between the DV and IVs. There's also a variant called **McFadden's adjusted R^2**, which is similar to the adjusted R^2 in least-square regression: you're penalized for adding variables to the equation, especially variables that don't contribute much. In fact, add too many of these, and the adjusted R^2 can actually be negative.

The second contender is **Cox and Snell's R^2**. It gives you the degree to which the model is better than the null, but doesn't tell you the proportion of variance explained by the model nor is it the square of the multiple correlation. Moreover, its maximum value is less than 1. In our opinion, it doesn't have much going for it. **Nagelkerke's R^2**, the third contender, overcomes the last problem with Cox and Snell's R^2 by rescaling it so that its maximum value is 1.

STEPWISE LOGISTIC REGRESSION AND THE PARTIAL TEST

All of the above suggests a logical extension along the lines of the partial *F*-test in multiple linear regression. We could fit a partial model, compute the goodness of fit, then add in another variable, recompute the goodness of fit, and subtract the two, creating a test of the last variable which is a chi-squared with one degree of freedom. In the present example, if we just include Fam, Herd, and Years on the principle that it's awfully difficult to persuade camels to "open wide" as we ram a swab down their throats, we find the goodness of fit is 25.88. So, the partial test of BCC is:

$$- 2\log L \text{ (full model)} - (-2\log L(\text{partial model}))$$
$$= 25.89 - 18.10 = 7.79 \qquad \textbf{(13-15)}$$

With $df = 1$, the critical chi-squared is 3.84, so there's a significant change by adding BCC.

One final wrinkle, then we'll stop. The *p*-value resulting from this stepwise analysis *should* be the same level of significance as that for the regression coefficient of BCC in the full model. Regrettably, it isn't quite. Looking again at Table 13-2, the computed Wald statistic yields a *p* of 0.03, which is larger but still significant.

Why the discrepancy? As near as we can figure, it's because of the magical word "approximately", which has featured prominently in the discussion. For the discrepancy to disappear, we need a larger sample size, but we have it on good authority[12] that no one seems to know how much larger it needs to be. Again, upon appealing to higher authorities than ourselves, we are led to believe that, when in doubt, we should proceed with the formal likelihood ratio test.

MORE COMPLEX DESIGNS

Now that we have this basic approach under our belts, we can extend the method just as we did with multiple linear regression. Want to include interactions? Fine. Just multiply Herd × Years to get an overall measure of exposure[13] and stuff it into the equation. Want to do a matched analysis, in which each person in the treatment group is matched to another individual in the control group? Now we have a situation like a paired *t*-test, in which we are effectively computing a difference within pairs. No big deal. Create a dummy variable for each of the pairs (so that, for example, pair 1 has a dummy variable

associated with it, pair 2 has another, and so on). Of course, in this situation, where the number of variables is going up by leaps and bounds, the use of an unconditional ML estimator is a really bad idea, and you'll have to shell out for a new software package. And on and on—*ad infinitum, ad nauseam*.

WHERE THINGS CAN GO WRONG

Independence among individuals observed values. logistic regression requires the independence among individuals or observed values. When the study subjects are measured or recorded more than once or there is clustering among study subjects within the same group (village, town, class, school, etc.), the independence assumption will be violated. In this case, longitudinal analysis models or multi-level models are preferred. Please refer to advanced statistical books.

Correlations between independent variables. When high correlations exist between independent variables included in the logistic regression, the fit of logistic regression will be greatly affected, yielding biased estimates of regression coefficient, inflated standard error, and invalid statistical test results.

Insufficiency of sample size. In case of small sample, the fit of logistic regression will be invalid. Due to the insufficiency of sample size, you cannot obtain significant statistical results despite large odds ratios.

Variable assignment. In logistic regression, continuous variable, categorical variable and ordinal variable can be independent variable of regression model. Continuous variable can participate in analysis in the original form of the data, or discretize into ordinal variable, or be described in dummy variable after discretization.

Abuse of logistic regression. The choice of independent variables and dependent variables should be determined based on clear and reasonable research assumptions. Without clear assumptions, logistic regression may yield confusing (even obviously wrong) but significant results.

---

[12]*Kleinbaum (1994), in the "To Read Further" section.*

[13]*If these were wolves, not camels, we would obviously call it a "pack-year" of exposure.*

SAMPLE SIZE

Tabachnick and Fidell state that there are problems when there are too few cases relative to the number of variables, and spend the next three paragraphs discussing the problems and possible solutions (such as collapsing categories). Unfortunately, they don't say what's meant by "too few cases." But, we do know this: logistic is a large-sample technique, so the old familiar standby of 10 subjects per variable probably doesn't work, and you'd do better thinking of at least 20 per variable.

SUMMARY

✧ Logistic regression analysis is a powerful extension of multiple linear regression for use when the dependent variable is binary (0 and 1). It works by fitting a logistic function to the cases and controls, estimating the fitted probability associated with each observed value. The test of significance of the model is based on adjusting the parameters of the model to maximize the likelihood of the observed arising from the linear sum of the variables, the so-called **MLE** procedure. Tests of the individual parameters in the logistic equation proceeds much like the tests for ordinary multiple linear regression.

REPORTING GUIDELINES

✧ There are no generally accepted ways of reporting the results of logistic regression. Some people use a table similar to the one for ordinary least squares regression, except for replacing the *t*-test with the Wald statistic and its *df* and adding an extra column called either Odds Ratio (OR) or Exp(*b*), which is the same thing. As an added fillip, you can add the confidence interval around Exp(*b*). Other journals are content for you to report the ORs and CIs. Whichever format you use, be sure

to report one or more of the pseudo-R^2 statistics for logistic regression; we'd recommend McFadden's adjusted R^2 and Nagelkerke's R^2. As we said, we don't see much use for the Cox and Snell statistic.

GLOSSARY

logistic regression   logistic 回归
logistic function   logistic 函数
logistic transformation   logistic 变换
maximum likelihood estimation, MLE   最大似然估计
likelihood function   似然函数
Wald test   Wald 检验
odds ratio, OR   优势比
goodness of fit   拟合优度

EXERCISES

1. What are similarities and dissimilarities between logistic regression and multiple linear regression?
2. What is odds ratio (OR)?
3. How to assess the significance and goodness of fit of logistic regression equation?
4. What kind of statistic data is logistic regression mainly used for?
5. A randomized trial of a new anticholesterol drug was analyzed with logistic regression (using cardiac death as an endpoint), including drug/placebo as a dummy variable, and a number of additional covariates. The output from a logistic regression reported that $Exp(b_1) = 0.5$. Given that the cardiac death rate in the control group was 10%, what is the relative risk of death from the treatment?

SUGGESTED READINGS AND WEBSITES

[1] Tripepi G, Jager KJ, Stel VS, et al. How to deal with continuous and dichotomic outcomes in epidemiological research: linear and logistic regression analyses. Nephron Clin Pract. 2011,

118(4): c399-406.

[2] Domínguez AS, Benítez PN, Gonzalez-Ramirez AR. Logistic regression models. Allergol Immunopathol (Madr). 2011, 39(5): 295-305.

[3] LaValley MP. Logistic regression. Circulation. 2008, 117(18): 2395-2399.

[4] Nick TG, Campbell KM. Logistic regression. Methods Mol Biol. 2007, 404: 273-301.

[5] Worster A, Fan J, Ismaila A. Understanding linear and logistic regression analyses. CJEM. 2007, 9(2): 111-113.

[6] Hosmer DW, Hosmer T, Le Cessie S, et al. A comparison of goodness-of-fit tests for the logistic regression model. Stat Med. 1997, 16(9): 965-980.

CHAPTER THE FOURTEENTH
Advanced Topics in Regression and ANOVA

This chapter reviews several advanced analytical strategies that look into multivariate analysis and bring together ANOVA and regression. The first section tells you all the need-to-know bases about Analysis of covariance (ANCOVA). Such method combines continuous variables (covariates) and factors and is used for assessing treatment effects while controlling for baseline characteristics. Power series analysis is a regression including higher powers of the independent variable (e.g., quadratic, cubic, or quartic terms). The second section lectures you about Multivariate analysis of variance (MANOVA). This method is an extension of ANOVA that allows for two or more dependent variables to be analyzed simultaneously. This avoids the problem of inflation of the alpha level because of multiple testing, and takes into consideration the correlations among the dependent variables. It is also useful in analyzing repeated measures.

ANCONA and Fancy GLM

SETTING THE SCENE

You have been collecting data at your PMS (Pathetic Male Syndrome) Clinic for 15 years. Despite admonitions to the contrary, you just can't resist the temptation to analyze everything in sight with multiple regression. After graphing the data, three things are evident: (1) Pathos Quotient (PQ) increases linearly with belly size, (2) middle-aged males have the highest PQ, and (3) treatment with testosterone injections appears to have some effect on the PQ. Multiple regression tells us how to deal with straight-line relationships, ANOVA works on treatment groups, but how in the world will you deal with all this complexity?

By now we have given you the conceptual tools to master nearly every complexity of ANOVA and regression. However, we have left out one small detail—namely, how to put them together. It may not be self-evident why one should bother to try to merge two good things. After all, it would seem that each is capable of handling a large class of complex problems. But reflect a moment on a simple twist to the designs we have encountered thus far.

The syndrome we investigate in this chapter, PMS, is commonly referred to as "mid-life crisis" or "male menopause" in its acute phase, but it has a more insidious onset than is implied by those terms. One sign is a gradual movement upward or downward in the belt line.

Certainly, there is some hope on the horizon. To deal with the more systemic manifestations of masculine aging, we have to revert to more traditional therapy, specifically testosterone injections.

But how does one actually measure PMS? A simple diary, wherein the PM (pathetic male) counts the number of wistful sighs, the number of unused notches on his belt and the number of ounces of Greek Formula 18 consumed in a week, which we'll call the Pathos Quotient, or PQ.

As we indicated above, PMS is related to three other variables. Pathos Quotient increases linearly with belly size—that's a job for regression. On the other hand, if males are given male sex hormones, they seem to recover a bit. That is a comparison between two groups formed on the basis of a nominal variable, and it can be handled with a *t*-test or a one-way ANOVA. As far as the relationship with age goes, it sounds like a curve peaking at about 45 and falling off on both sides, which to those of mathematical inclination might suggest a quadratic term. (*Quadratic* means a term squared, *cubic* is a term cubed, and *quartic* is to the fourth power.) But how can we put it all together?

Having gotten this far, we might like to see the appearance of these elements on graphs. Figure 14-1 shows the PQ scores for 16 subjects in comparison to belt size, age, and treatment, based on the data of Table 14-1. It is evident from the graph that the data are pretty well linearly related to belt size. We could proceed to do a regression analysis on the data in the usual way. If we did, the ANOVA of the regression looks like Table 14-2, and the multiple R^2 turns out to be 0.30, which is not all that great.

Looking at treatment, this is just a nominal vari-

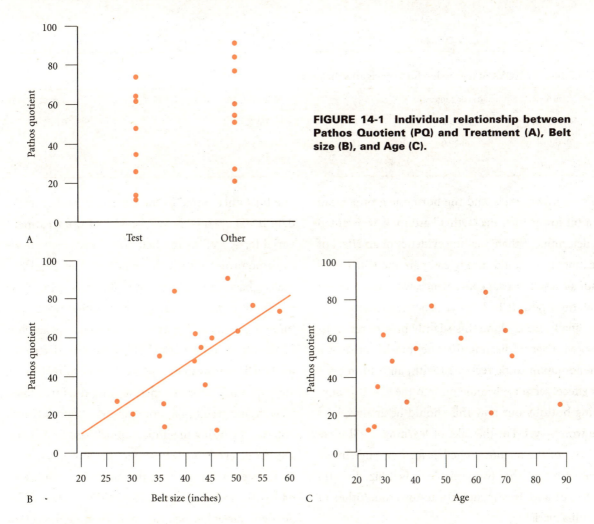

FIGURE 14-1 Individual relationship between Pathos Quotient (PQ) and Treatment (A), Belt size (B), and Age (C).

TABLE 14-1   Data for 16 PMS patients

Subject	Age	Belt size	Treatment	PQ
1	24	46	Testosterone	12
2	26	36	Testosterone	14
3	27	40	Other	27
4	88	44	Testosterone	35
5	32	36	Testosterone	26
6	29	30	Other	21
7	70	42	Testosterone	48
8	75	35	Other	51
9	37	42	Other	62

Continued

Subject	Age	Belt size	Treatment	PQ
10	65	50	Testosterone	64
11	72	45	Testosterone	60
12	55	53	Other	77
13	45	48	Other	91
14	41	38	Other	84
15	63	43	Other	55
16	40	58	Testosterone	74

TABLE 14-2   ANOVA of regression for PMS against belt size

Source	Sum of squares	df	Mean square	F	p
Regression	2893.2	1	2893.2	6.11	0.027
Residual	6629.0	14	473.5		
$R^2 = 0.303$					

able with two levels, and the hormone group mean is a bit lower than the "Other" group. If we wanted to determine if there was any evidence of an effect of treatment, we could simply compare the two means with a t-test. For your convenience, we have done just that; the t-value is 1.33, which is not significant.

Finally, we do have this slightly bizarre relationship with age, indicating that the mid-life crisis is a phenomenon to be reckoned with, an d moreover, its effects seem to dwindle on into the 60s. It is anything but obvious how this should be analyzed, so we won't—yet. For the sake of learning, we'll leave age out of the picture altogether for now and simply deal with the other two variables—Belt Size (a ratio variable) and Treatment with testosterone/other (a nominal variable).

ANALYSIS OF COVARIANCE

Again, if you've learned your lessons well, you know by now that a first approach is to graph the data, and at least this time it really isn't too hard to put three variables on two dimensions. We simply use different points for the two groups, then plot the data against belt size again. Figure 14-2 shows the updated graph.

Now we have a slightly different picture than before. If we look back at the relationship to Belt Size, we can see that the data are actually pretty tightly clustered around *two* lines, one for Testosterone and

one for Other. Some of the variability visible in the data in Figure 14-1B was a result of the treatment variable, as well as the belt size. Conversely, if we imagine projecting all the data onto the Y-axis, so that we have essentially two distributions of PQs, one for Testosterone and the other for Other, we recapture the picture of Figure 14-1A. And taking account of all of the variance from both sources, by determining two lines instead of one, we are able to reduce the scatter, or the error variance, around the fitted lines. This should result in a more powerful statistical test, both for analyzing the impact of belt size on PQ and also for determining if treatment has any effect.

Conceptually, we have the same situation as we had with multiple regression. We have two independent variables, Belt Size and Treatment, each of which is responsible for some of the variance in PQ. As a result, the residual variance, which results from other factors not in the study, is reduced. The effect of using both variables in the analysis is to reduce the error term in the corresponding test of significance, thereby increasing the sensitivity of the test.

The challenge is to figure out how to deal with both nominal and ratio independent variables. What we seem to need is a bit of ANOVA to handle the grouping factor and a dose of regression to deal with the continuous variable. Historically, the problem is dealt with by a method called **ANCOVA**, from

ANalysis of COVAriance, once again using creative acronymizing to obscure what was going on. The covariance was a product of X and Y differences that expressed the relationship between two interval-level variables, so this is a reasonable description of what might be the relationship to belt size. We then need some way to analyze the effect of the treatment variable, which amounts to looking at the difference between two groups, something we would naturally approach with an ANOVA, or a *t*-test, which is the same thing. Put it together and what have you got? Analysis of covariance.

The time has now come to turn once again from words to pictures, employing what is now a familiar refrain—parceling out the total Sum of Squares in PQ into components resulting from Belt, Treatment, and error. To see how this comes about, refer to Figure 14-3, which is simply an enlargement of Figure 14-2 around the middle of the picture. We have also included the Grand Mean of all the PQs as a large black dot, and we have thrown in a bunch of arrows (we'll get to those in a minute).

Three possible sources of variance are Treatment, Belt, and the ubiquitous error term. So far, so good, but how do they play out on the graph? Sum

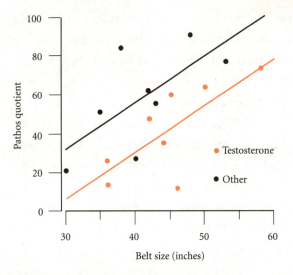

FIGURE 14-2   Relationship between PQ and Treatment and Belt size.

of Squares resulting from Treatment is related to the distance between the two parallel lines, so it expresses the treatment effect on PQ. The Sum of Squares resulting from Belt is the sum of all the squared vertical distances between the fitted points and their corresponding group mean, just as in a regression problem, except that the distances are measured to one or the other line. Sum of Squares (Error) is the distance between the original data points and the corresponding fitted data point. The better the fit between the

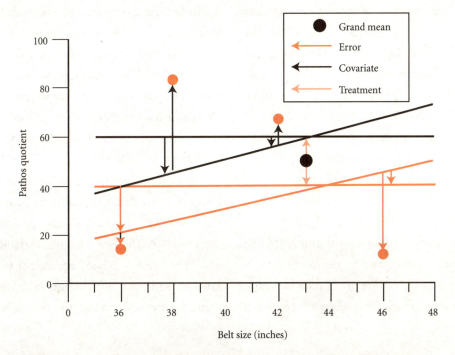

FIGURE 14-3   Relationship between PQ and Treatment and Belt size (expanded), indicating sums of squares.

two independent variables (Treatment and Belt), (1) the closer the data will fall to the fitted lines, and (2) the larger will be Sum of Squares (Belt) and Sum of Squares (Treatment) when compared with the Sum of Squares (Error).

Viewed this way, it's not such a difficult problem, showing once again that a picture is worth a few words. But we haven't actually started analyzing it numerically yet, so here we go. You will note that we have made a big deal of putting together both nominal and interval-level data, but in fact they both come down to sums of squared differences when we look at the variance components. In fact, we seem to be in the process of collapsing the distinction altogether between ANOVA and regression methods. After all, in the last chapter we got used to the idea of ANOVAing a regression problem. Perhaps we can be forgiven if we now stand things on their heads and do a regression to an ANCOVA problem.

Suppose we forget for a moment that these are a mixture of variables and just plow ahead, stuffing them into a regression equation. It might look a bit like this:

$$PQ = b_0 + b_1 \times \text{Treatment} + b_2 \times \text{Belt}$$

That looks like a perfectly respectable regression equation. But we have only one little problem. When we put Belt into the equation it's pretty clear what belt size to use—32, 34, 36 … 54 inches (or the metric equivalent). But what number do we use for Treatment? It's a nominal variable, so there is no particular relationship between any category and a corresponding number. Well … suppose we try 0 for Other and 1 for Testosterone; what happens? Then the regression equation for the control group is:

$$PQ = b_0 + b_1 \times 0 + b_2 \times \text{Belt} = b_0 + b_2 \times \text{Belt}$$

and for the treatment group it is:

$$PQ = b_0 + b_1 \times 1 + b_2 \times \text{Belt} = [b_0 + b_1] + b_2 \times \text{Belt}$$

In other words, the choice of 0 and 1 for the Treatment variable creates two regression lines with the same slope, b_2, which differ only in the intercept. In the Testosterone group, the intercept is $(b_0 + b_1)$;

in the Other group it is just b_0. So b_1 is just the vertical distance between the two lines in the graph (i.e., the effect of treatment). That is just what we want. All that remains is to plow ahead just as with any other regression analysis and determine the value and statistical significance of the bs. In the course of doing so we have actually done what we set out to do: determine the variance attributable to each independent variable.[1]

In this case, the Sum of Squares resulting from regression, for the full model, is equal to:

$$\sum[(b_0 + b_1 \times \text{Treatment}_i + b_2 \times \text{Belt}_i) - \overline{PQ}]^2 \quad \textbf{(14-1)}$$

Lest the algebra escape you, this is just the difference between the fitted point at each value of PQ_i (the whole equation in the parentheses) and the overall mean of PQ, with all the individual differences squared and summed. So this is the sum of squares in PQ resulting from the combination of the independent variables.

The Sum of Squares (Residual) is equal to:

$$\sum[PQ_i - (b_0 + b_1 \times \text{Treatment}_i + b_2 \times \text{Belt}_i)]^2 \quad \textbf{(14-2)}$$

This takes the difference between the original data, PQ_i, and the fitted values (again, the stuff in the parentheses), all squared and added. So this represents the squared differences between the original data and the fitted points.

To test the significance of each independent variable, we must actually determine three regression equations: one with just Treatment in the equation, one with just Belt in the equation, and the last with both in the equation. This way we can determine the effect of each variable above and beyond the effect of the other variables. The ANOVAs for each of the models are in Table 14-3.

We then proceed to determine the individual contributions. For Belt, the additional Sum of Squares is $(5274.5 - 1139.1) = 4135.4$ with 1 df, and the residual term is 326.8. The F-test for this variable is therefore $4135.4 \div 326.8 = 12.65$, equivalent to a t of 3.56. We'll let you work out the equivalent test for Treatment. Suffice to say that it, too, is significant, with a t

---

[1] *This is just creating dummy variables. As it turns out, ANCOVA is just a special case of multiple regression.*

TABLE 14-3   ANOVAs of regressions for Testosterone/other, Belt size, and Both

Source	Sum of squares	df	Mean square	F	p
Treatment					
Regression	1139.1	1	1139.1	1.90	0.189
Residual	8383.9	14	598.9		
R^2 0.120					
Belt size					
Regression	2893.7	1	2893.7	6.11	0.027
Residual	6629.2	14	473.5		
R^2 0.303					
Treatment and Belt size					
Regression	5274.5	2	2637.2	8.07	0.005
Residual	4248.5	13	326.8		
R^2 0.553					

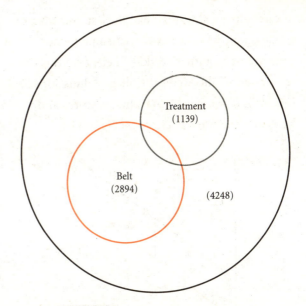

FIGURE 14-4   Variance in PQ resulting from Belt size and Treatment.

of 2.70, $p < 0.05$.

Actually, although we have structured the problem as a regression problem for continuity and simplicity, if the analysis were actually run as an ANCOVA program, the contributions of each variable would be separately identified in the ANCOVA table (Table 14-4).

TABLE 14-4   Summary ANCOVA table for Treatment and Belt size

Source	Sum of squares	df	Mean square	F	p
Covariate (Belt)	4135.4	1	4135.4	12.65	0.01
Treatment	2380.8	1	2380.8	7.29	0.01
Explained*	5274.5	2	2637.2	8.07	0.01
Residual	4248.5	13	326.8		

* Note that, in contrast to factorial ANOVA designs, here the sums of squares don't add up because there is an overlap in the explained variance. If you don't believe it yet, look at Figure 14-4.

Note that a funny thing happened when both variables went in together. Because each variable accounted for some of the variance, independent of the other, the residual variance shrank, so the test of significance of both variables became highly significant. When each was tested individually, however, Treatment was not significant, and Belt was only marginally so. For those of you with a visual bent, the situation is illustrated in Figure 14-4.

Figure 14-4 nicely illustrates one potential gain in using ANCOVA designs: the apportioning of variance resulting from covariates such as Belt can actu-

ally increase the power of the statistical test of the grouping factor(s). Of course, this is true only insofar as the covariates account for some of the variance in the dependent variable. As with regression, it can work the other way, where adding variables decreases the power of the tests.

ANCOVA for Adjusting for Baseline Differences

Actually, surprisingly few people are even aware of this potential gain in statistical power from using covariates. More frequently, ANCOVA is used in designs such as cohort studies where intact control groups are used and the two groups differ on one or more variables that are potentially related to the outcome or dependent variable.

As an example, consider the pitiless task of trying to drum some statistical concepts into the thick heads of a bunch of medical students. In an attempt to engage their humorous side, one prof decides to try a different text this year—*Bare Essentials*, naturally. He gives this class the same exam as he gave out last year and finds that the mean score on the exam is 66.1% this year, whereas it was 73.5% last year. That's not funny for him or us.

A little detective work reveals the fact that the admissions committee has also been messing around and dropped the GPA standard, replacing it with interviews and other touchy-feely stuff. So one explanation is that this class has a slightly higher incidence of cerebromyopathy[2] than had the last. But what can we do about it? Clearly we need some independent measure of quantitative skills. Let's take the physics section of the Medical College Admissions Test (MCAT). If we plot MCAT physics scores and final grades for the two classes, we get Figure 14-5.

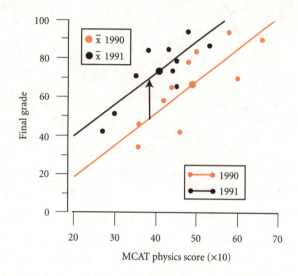

FIGURE 14-5 Relationship between MCAT physics and post-test statistics score for the classes of 1990 and 1991.

A different picture now emerges. It is clear that *Bare Essentials* delivered on the goods. The regression line for this year's class is consistently higher than last year's, by about 15%, as shown by the arrow. But what happened is that the admissions committee blew it (at least as far as stats mastery goes) by admitting a number of students with chronic cases of cerebromyopathy, so that they start off duller (i.e., to the left of the graph), and end up duller. But, relative to their starting point, they actually learn more from *Bare Essentials*.

We'll put some statistics into it (which is what we're here for), and the data for the two cohorts on MCAT and post-test are shown in Table 14-5. If we do a *t*-test on the post scores, the result is $t(18) = 0.02$, $p = 0.41$, which is a long way from significance and in the wrong direction anyway. Note that graphically, this is equivalent to projecting all the data onto the

TABLE 14-5 Mean scores (and SD) for the classes of 1990 and 1991 on MCAT physics and post-test

Test	Class	
	1990	**1991**
MCAT	48.6 (25.1)	40.8 (8.2)
Post-test	73.0 (16.0)	66.1 (28.8)

Y-axis and looking at the overlap of the two resulting distributions. However, if we bring up the heavy artillery and ANCOVA the whole thing, with MCAT as the covariate and 90/91 as the grouping factor, a whole new picture emerges.

First, the estimated effect of 90/91 (i.e., the *Bare Essentials* treatment effect) is now a super 19.75—the difference between the two lines. Further, the effect is highly significant [$t(18) = 3.60$, $p = 0.002$]. So not only did we improve the sensitivity of the test in this analysis, we also corrected for the bias resulting from baseline differences, to the extent that the estimate of the treatment effect changed direction.

This then summarizes the potential gains resulting from using ANCOVA to account for baseline differences:

1. When randomization is not possible and differences between groups exist, ANCOVA can correct for the effect of these differences on the dependent variable. However, this correction for baseline differences is fraught with bias, as we'll talk about in the next chapter, and really shouldn't be done without a lot of thought.

2. Even when you have no reason to expect baseline differences, ANCOVA can improve the sensitivity of the statistical test by removing variance attributable to baseline variables.

Extension to More Complex Designs

So far we have considered only a simple design, with one grouping factor and one covariate, but there is no theoretical limit to the extension of the basic strategy to any number of covariates, or any number of grouping factors.[3] Any legitimate ANOVA design

---

[2] *Muscle heads.*

[3] *There are, of course, practical limits, both logistical and statistical. Like all regression problems, diminishing returns are the order of the day.*

can be extended by the addition of covariates. We must, however, emphasize that this strategy is useful only to the extent that the covariates are related to the dependent variable and are unrelated to each other, as discussed earlier.

The approach is simple enough. You just continue to treat it as a regression problem, with a new b for each covariate and a new dummy variable for each grouping factor.[4] The analysis proceeds to estimate a Sum of Squares, Mean Square, and significance test for each variable, just as before.

Suppose, for example, that we were also interested in the effects of steroids on PQ. This amounts to another nominal variable in the design. As we discussed in Chapter 12, we must create a new coefficient to separately estimate the difference between steroid and placebo, and testosterone and placebo. In general, if there are k levels of a grouping factor, there will be $(k-1)$ dummy variables created.[5]

Nonlinear Regression

Whatever happened to age and PMS? We established that there was a slightly bizarre relationship between age and the PQ score, so that it peaked at about 45, but we then went on to greener pastures. Time to recycle.

If you return to Figure 14-1C, you will note that the relationship of PQ with age adopted a peculiar form, somewhat akin to a 10-gallon hat. Actually, a flashlight reflector is a more appropriate, although not as glaringly obvious, analogy. If you ever survived one of those courses in plane and solid geometry, or optics,[6] you would immediately recognize this as the curve traced out by a function of the form $y=x^2$; take our word for it.

How can we crunch out the statistics of it all? Easy, by now—just create another regression equation containing both linear ($y=bx$) and quadratic ($y=cx^2$) terms. The equation would look like:

$$PQ = b_0 + b_1 \times Age + b_2 \times Age^2$$

Now to look at the contribution of each term, it is necessary to do three regression analyses: one containing only the term in Age, one containing only Age^2, and one containing both. The corresponding ANOVA tables are shown in Table 14-6. Clearly Age alone does a fairly crummy job of fitting the data, and Age^2 is even worse, but the combination of the two is quite credible.

TABLE 14-6 Nonlinear regression with Age and Age^2

Age				
Source	Sum of squares	df	Mean square	F	p
Regression	1043	1	1043.0	1.72	0.210
Residual	8479	14	605.6		
R^2 0.109					

Age^2				
Source	Sum of squares	df	Mean square	F	p
Regression	412.6	1	412.60	0.634	ns
Residual	9110.0	14	650.7		
R^2 0.043					

$Age + Age^2$				
Source	Sum of squares	df	Mean square	F	p
Regression	6831	2	3416.0	16.49	0.0001
Residual	2692	13	207.1		
R^2 0.717					

ns = not significant.

If we then proceed to determine the individual contributions, the additional Sum of Squares for Age^2 is $(6831 - 1043) = 5788$ with one degree of freedom, and the residual term is 207.6. So, the F-test for this variable is $5788/207.6 = 27.8$, equivalent to a t of 5.27, which is significant at the 0.0001 level. For Age, the t-value is 5.57, also significant at the 0.0001 level.

Clearly the addition of the quadratic term to the

---

[4]See the section "Dummy Coding" in Chapter 12 if you forget what a dummy variable is—dummy!

[5]A more illuminating approach might have been to create a fourth group that gets both drugs. We would then likely want to examine whether there is an interaction—whether both drugs together are better than the simple additive effect. This is easily handled with yet another parameter, based on the product of the two dummy variables, so it is 1 if both are present, and 0 otherwise.

[6]Both are courses that have proven absolutely essential to your subsequent success in life—for those of you who are physicists or pure mathematicians.

linear term resulted in a much better fit than either alone. Conceptually, the analysis proceeded in familiar fashion, simply creating a multiple regression equation in which there are terms for Age and Age^2. If the model still didn't look too great, and we saw from the figure some suggestion of additional curlicues, we could easily add in a cubic or quartic term.[7]

The general strategy of creating nonlinear terms in a regression equation is called **Power Series Regression** when it involves a series of terms with increasing powers of some variable (obviously). However, there are other times we might want to depart from a straight-line relationship.

One of the most common times occurs when things are either accruing, such as serum drug levels, or falling away, as in weight-loss programs (in theory, at least). In these cases, we would likely invoke negative exponential or logarithmic terms.

General Linear Model

By now, it is apparent that we can recast just about every ANOVA problem as a regression problem by the appropriate choice of dummy variables. We can introduce interaction terms to cover all contingencies. We can also throw around nonlinear terms with gay abandon and again shove them into some regression form, then proceed with business as usual. In short, all these problems can be cast as a sum of terms, each with a coefficient to be estimated, something of the form:

$$Y_j = b_0 + \sum b_i f(X_j) \qquad (14\text{-}3)$$

where $f(X)$ indicates some mathematical function of X—linear, quadratic, exponential, logarithmic, or whatever.

At some point in the not-too-distant past, the similarity between ANOVA, ANCOVA, and regression was noted,[8] and all of these analyses are now viewed as subsets of something called the **General Linear Model** (GLM).

For a sense of closure, we'll finish off by completing the analysis of the PMS data according to the initial observations of the astute clinician. We'll fit a model of the form:

$$PQ = b_0 + b_1(Age) + b_2(Age)^2 + b_3(Belt) + b_4(Test/Other)$$

We have a nominal variable (Test/Other), a ratio variable (Belt), and a power series in Age. When the dust settles, the analysis appears as in Table 14-7.

TABLE 14-7   Analysis of Age, Age^2, Belt size, and Test/Other

Variable	b coeff.	SE	t	p
Test/Other	13.50	7.65	1.76	0.105
Age	4.71	1.32	3.56	0.004
Age^2	0.0041	0.012	3.33	0.007
Belt size	1.241	0.557	2.23	0.048

ANOVA of the regression					
Source	Sum of squares	df	Mean square	F	p
Regression	7755	4	1938.0	12.06	0.001
Residual	1768	11	160.7		

So, as before, the addition of more terms resulted in an improved fit and a reduction of the error term. Note, however, that individually the only significant contributions came from the terms in Age and Belt Size, and there is no longer an effect of Treatment.

Although the last bit looks just like we changed the name to protect the guilty, it's actually a lot more profound than that. The fact that we can lump both nominal and interval-level variables into the same equation starts to collapse the distinction between the two historical classes—regression and ANOVA. Indeed, we can see that both are just special cases of the GLM. In principle, any of the designs we have discussed in the previous chapters can be put into the form of a linear equation, in which the interval-level predictors like Belt Size are entered directly, the nominal level predictors are accommodated through the use of dummy variables, and power terms and interactions can be thrown in with gay abandon. Even repeated measures designs, in which *Subject*

---

[7] *We can't, however, add in a term in x5, because we don't know how to express it in Latin. (From long-suffering coauthor—it's quintic.)*

[8] *A similarity that we deliberately highlighted by treating ANCOVA with regression analysis, instead of drawing out the standard, and forgettable, formulae for it.*

is an explicit factor, are handled by creating whole families of dummy variables—one for each subject.[9] Including interaction terms just amounts to more terms in the equation.

Although folks don't often conduct their analyses this way, since special-purpose software to do ANOVA or regression is much simpler to use, there are two good reasons to know about GLM. First, it becomes a constant reminder that all of statistics—in fact, all of science—is really about explaining variance. Second, in some sticky situations, such as multifactor ANOVAs in which some subjects had the indecency to drop out leaving you with an unbalanced design (Oh, the shame of it!), GLM approaches must be used to avoid biased estimations.

Assumptions of ANCOVA

Unfortunately, ANCOVA comes with some costs, namely the usual raft of assumptions. Certainly one condition is that the lines are parallel. We neatly avoided this issue by cooking our data so that we always ended up with parallel lines. The two reasons why the lines must be parallel are (1) because that's what the ANCOVA packages are designed for, and (2) because that is the only way you can estimate a treatment effect. After all, if the lines are not parallel, that means that the effect of treatment (the distance between the lines) is different depending on where you are situated on the X-axis.

Actually, now that you have, through our guidance, achieved a sense of holistic serenity about the world of statistics, you may realize that this condition is not really too constraining. In the first place, many situations arise where there is no relationship between the treatment and the covariate. Patients may well respond about the same to a drug, regard-less of the initial state of the disease (or they may not). Second, as we pointed out in Chapter 7, we rather like interactions because they can be informative, and this is just another example of an interaction.

In any case, the prudent and standard action to take is to always test for an interaction first, before proceeding with the ANCOVA. This is done by performing a separate regression on each line, determining the slopes, and then testing whether the slopes are significantly different. If they are, then you don't proceed with the ANCOVA. Note that most computer programs automatically test for parallelism.

If they're not parallel, what you do is use a slightly more elaborate model, one that explicitly includes an interaction term. It involves an arcane and complex methodology called multiplication, where you multiply the treatment dummy variable and the covariate together, and then fit a new constant. Here's how. Recall that the model equation before was:

$$PQ = b_0 + b_1 \times \text{Treatment} + b_2 \times \text{Belt}$$

If we now add in an interaction term, the new equation looks like:

$$PQ = b_0 + b_1 \times \text{Treatment} + b_2 \times \text{Belt} + b_3 \times \text{Treatment} \times \text{Belt}$$

Now remember that the way we pulled this off was to use a dummy variable with values of 0 for Other or 1 for Testosterone. If we do the same stunt here, the equation for the control group, which is coded 0, is:

$$PQ = b_0 + b_2 \times \text{Belt}$$

And for the testosterone group, it is equal to:

$$PQ = b_0 + b_1 + b_2 \times \text{Belt} + b_3 \times \text{Belt}$$
$$= (b_0 + b_1) + (b_2 + b_3) \times \text{Belt}$$

So the treatment effect is contained in the b_1 coefficient as before. The two slopes are estimated separately; for the control group the line has a slope of b_2, and for the treatment group the line's slope is $(b_2 + b_3)$. So any difference in the slopes shows up in the test of significance of the b_3 term, which is done as is any other regression coefficient.

Some other constraints on the selection of the covariates exist; they are more a matter of logic than of statistics.

1. *The covariate should be* related *to the dependent variable.* Because the whole game is to remove

---

[9]*Actually one for each subject but the first one. The b coefficients for each subject express the difference between the mean of each subject (after the first one) and the first subject. The old "N – 1" routine strikes again.*

variance in the dependent variable attributed to the covariate, it should be almost self-evident (if we've been doing our jobs) why this is a good idea. But this condition does preclude the willy-nilly covarying of anything you can lay your hands on, such as age, gender, marital status, number of dogs, etc., most of which are virtually unrelated to everything. A good rule of thumb is that if the correlation between the covariate and the dependent variable is under 0.30, use ANOVA; if it's 0.30 or above, use ANCOVA.

2. *The covariate should be* unrelated *to the treatment variable*. This sounds a bit like what we were dealing with above, but it's not quite the same. Imagine, in our example, that our statistics teaching is so very good that it acts on general mathematical skills the way that teachers of yore insisted a Latin course would act on language skills and that computer science teachers still insist BASIC will act on logic skills. If so, then we might expect that *Bare Essentials* would improve not just the post-test score but also the MCAT score. Now suppose further that we didn't dream up the idea of using MCAT as a covariate until we found the first conclusion from the *t*-test, and at that point we insisted that all the little dears had to take the MCAT as a condition of getting through the course.

If all these supposes are so, then the treatment will change *both* the post-test and the MCAT score equally. The net result will be that the two groups will end up on the same regression line except that the treatment group will have moved up and to the right, reflecting improvement in both MCAT and post-test scores. Thus we would falsely conclude that treatment had no effect.

For this reason, conservative statisticians demand that any covariates be measured before treatment. We are a less severe; we'll accept that, for all its virtues, Bare Essentials is unlikely to influence height or religion, so these could be measured anytime.

3. *If multiple covariates are used, these should be unrelated to each other*. It is straightforward to extend the strategy to include the analysis of multiple covariates—straightforward and usually dumb. The reason is already familiar (we hope). As you introduce additional variables, the law of diminishing returns rapidly takes hold so that each new variable accounts for relatively little additional variance but costs 1 *df* or more. The situations where gains can be had from more than one or two covariates are rare indeed.

SAMPLE SIZE

As you might have guessed, by the time we arrive at these complexities, any attempt to make an exact sample size calculation is akin to keeping an umbrella open in a tornado. There are therefore two strategies available:

1. Add up all the independent variables (not forgetting to count dummy variables as appropriate), multiply by 10 (Kleinbaum, Kupper, and Muller, 1988), and that's the sample size.

2. Take the comparison you *really* care about and calculate a simple sample size for it. For example, in a two-group drug trial with a covariate, the comparison of real interest is drug/placebo. Use the formula for a *t*-test, indicate that the use of a covariate will add statistical power, and stop. As another example, if you wanted to measure change with ANCOVA, you could use the formula for a paired *t*-test and again indicate that it is likely conservative.

SECTION SUMMARY OF ANCOVA

This first section described several advanced methods of analysis based on regression analysis. Power series analysis and other nonlinear regressions are simply multiple regressions where coefficients are estimated for various functions of the X variable. ANCOVA methods combine continuous variables and grouping factors into a single regression equation, using dummy variables for the latter.

How to Get the Computer to
Do the Work for You

- To add covariates for both factorial and repeated-measures ANOVAs, there is just one more step: simply move the desired variable(s) from the list on the left to the box labeled **Covariates**

- To add covariates within a Regression approach, move the covariate(s) into the **Independent(s)** box

- Then press the [Next] button to the right of **Block 1 of 1**
- Enter the other predictor variables and again press [Next]

- Select **Forward** from the **Method** option
- For regression equations that include power terms and interactions, it is easiest to first create new variables using **Transform → Compute**

MANOVA

SETTING ANOTHER SCENE

Imagine yourself as a sex therapist, you want to evaluate if your clients are satisfied with the ancient missionaries. You may ask yourself: Does it really matter who's on top?! And if it does, from whose perspective do I measure satisfaction—the man's or the woman's? It is possible that what may be better for men is worse for women, and vice versa, so that the results of a study may be different depending on the choice of the outcome measure. We can get around this problem, and others, by using techniques that allow us to consider more than one dependent variable at a time; one such technique is an extension of ANOVA, called multivariate analysis of variance, or MANOVA.

To deal with your beloved clients, you shall not be in a rush. We'll start off easy, and have only two groups of subjects: a group that does "it" in the missionary position, and a second group in which the women are on top. To avoid the problem of having to make an arbitrary decision regarding whose opinion we will assess, we'll ask both partners[10] to complete a satisfaction scale that ranges from 1 ("It would have been better if I had done it myself") to 100 ("The Earth hasn't stopped moving yet"). The first (clean) question that could be asked is, Why would obtaining two measures lead to an entire chapter in a book? Why not simply do two *t*-tests and be done with it? This question is even more cogent when we realize that the mathematics of univariate statistics are relatively straightforward, but multivariate tests—those that involve two or more dependent variables—require something called ***matrix algebra***, which has its own arcane language. The answer is that once we have more than one dependent variable (DV), a host of problems arises if we treat them as if they were unrelated variables.

The first problem is one of interpretation. If we did separate *t*-tests on the measures, and found that both were significant, would it mean that the groups differed on both variables? The answer is a very definite "Yes and No." The groups did, in fact, differ on the two outcomes, but, because the two variables are likely correlated with one another (if they weren't correlated, we wouldn't bother with multivariate analyses), we can't really conclude that they differed in two discrete areas. Let's use an extreme example to illustrate this point. If the intervention were a weight reduction program, and the outcomes were both weight and the body mass index, it would be ridiculous to become ecstatic about the fact that we found change in both variables. Of course both variables changed, because they're highly correlated with one another; so, if one changes, the other must, too. His and her satisfaction scores probably aren't as highly correlated, but since we are dealing with warm, sensitive, gender-neutral, whale-loving tree-huggers, it would be highly unusual for them to engage in practices that satisfy one person and are a turnoff for the other. MANOVA takes the correlations among the DVs into account, so the results aren't distorted by having redundancies among the variables.

The second problem is that of multiple testing. The probability of finding at least one outcome significant by chance increases according to the formula.

---

[10]*We recognize that restricting this study to situations involving only two partners may impose limitations for some people, but it is necessary to keep the analysis simple.*

$$1-(1-\alpha)^N \qquad \text{(14-4)}$$

where N is the number of tests we do. If we have two outcome variables (and, hence, have performed two tests), the probability that at least one will be significant by chance at a 0.05 level is:

$$1-(1-0.05)^2=0.0975 \qquad \text{(14-5)}$$

If we have five outcomes, the probability is over 22%; by the time we have 10 outcome variables, it would be slightly over 40%. We could try to control this inflation of the alpha level with a Bonferroni correction or some other technique, but, as we discussed in Chapter 7, these tend to be overly conservative. Also, neither the estimate of how many tests would be significant by chance, nor the corrections for this would take into account the correlations among the dependent variables, which often can be considerable.

A third problem is the converse of the second: rather than finding significance where there is none, we may overlook significant relationships that are present. First, we'll show that this *can* happen and then *why* it can happen. Let's start off in the usual way, by plotting the data to help us see what's going on; the results of the males' satisfaction questionnaires are shown on the left side of Figure 14-6, and those of the females' satisfaction on the right side of the figure. Using that most sensitive of tests, the cali-

brated eyeball, it doesn't look as if much of anything is happening (insofar as the data are concerned, at least)[11]; the distributions of the two groups (positions) seem to overlap quite a bit for both variables.

The next step is to do a couple of *t*-tests on the data, and these are reported in Table 14-8. Again, the groups look to be fairly similar on the two variables; the means are relatively close together, differing by less than half a standard deviation, and only someone truly desperate for a publication would look twice at the significance levels of the *t*-tests. We could even go so far as to correlate each variable with the grouping variable, using the point-biserial correlation.[12] This doesn't help us much either; the correlation between the men's ratings and position is −0.12, and that for the women's is an equally unimpressive 0.10.

TABLE 14-8   Results of *t*-tests between the groups for both variables

Rater	Who's on top	Mean	SD	t	df	p
Male	Man	34.0	10.3	0.73	38	0.47
	Woman	31.8	8.73			
Female	Man	41.95	12.79	0.61	38	0.55
	Woman	44.2	10.37			

Now, though, we'll pull another statistical test out of our bag of tricks and analyze both dependent

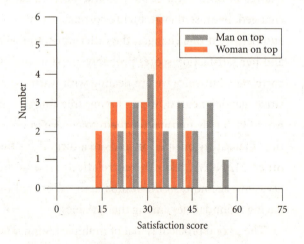
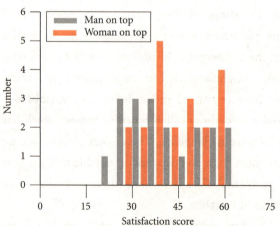

FIGURE 14-6   Men's and women's satisfaction scores, depending on who's on top.

---

[11]*Looking at the magnitudes of those evaluations, it doesn't look as if much is happening elsewhere, either.*

[12]*The point-biserial correlation was used in the situation where one variable was continuous (satisfaction scale) and the other was dichotomous (who's on top?). It is just a Pearson correlation, quite simple enough.*

variables at the same time using a **multivariate analysis of variance**(MANOVA). We won't show you the results right now, but trust us that there is now a statistically significant difference between the groups.[13] So, what's going on? Why did we find significant results using a multivariate test when it didn't look as if there was anything happening when we used a whole series of univariate tests? The reason is that the *pattern* of the variables is different in the two groups. If you go back to Table 14-8, you can see that when men do the rating, they score higher for the male superior position than for the female superior position; but when women do the rating, the situation is reversed—both physically and psychometrically. This couldn't be seen when we looked at each variable separately. It's analogous to the advantage of a factorial design over separate one-way ANOVAs: with the former, we can examine interactions among the independent variables that wouldn't be apparent with individual tests; with MANOVA, we can look at interactions among the *dependent* variables in a way that is impossible with univariate tests.

So, the conclusions are clear: when you have more than one dependent variable, you're often ahead of the game if you use multivariate procedures. At the end of this section, we'll discuss some limitations to this approach, but for now let's accept the fact that multivariate statistics are the best way of analyzing multivariate data.

WHAT DO WE MEAN BY "MULTIVARIATE"

In statisticians' world, it refers to the analysis of two or more *dependent* variables (DVs) at the same time.

Doesn't this sound simple and straightforward? That's a sure sign that something will go awry. The fly in the ointment is that statisticians aren't consistent. Some of them would call multiple regression a multivariate technique, even though there is only one

DV, and it is mathematically identical to ANOVA. Others prefer the term *multivariable* but, even here, some use the term to refer to many IVs and some just to indicate that many variables—dependent and independent—are involved. For most of us, however, multivariate means more than one DV, and that's the usage that we'll adopt.

t FOR TWO (AND MORE)

If we had only one dependent variable, the statistic we would use for this study would be the *t*-test, which starts with the null hypothesis:

$$H_0: \mu_1 = \mu_2 \tag{14-6}$$

that is, that the means of the two groups are equal. However, we have two dependent variables in the current example, so that each group has two means. In this case, then, the null hypothesis is:

$$H_0: \begin{pmatrix} \mu_{11} \\ \mu_{12} \end{pmatrix} = \begin{pmatrix} \mu_{21} \\ \mu_{22} \end{pmatrix} \tag{14-7}$$

where the first subscript after the μ indicates group membership (1 = Man on Top, 2 = Woman on Top), and the second shows the dependent variable (1 = Male Rater, 2 = Female Rater). What this indicates is that the list of means for Group 1 (the technical term for a list of variables like this is a **vector**) is equal to the vector of means for Group 2.[14] In other words, we are testing two null hypotheses simultaneously:

$$\mu_{11} = \mu_{21} \text{ and } \mu_{12} = \mu_{22} \tag{14-8}$$

When we plot the data for a *t*-test, we would have two distributions (hopefully normal curves) on the *X*-axis. The picture is similar but a bit more complicated with multivariate tests. For two variables, we would get an ellipse of points for each group, as in Figure 14-7. If we had three dependent variables, the swarm of points would look like a football (without the laces); four variables would produce a four-dimensional ellipsoid, and so on. These can be (relatively) easily described mathematically, but are

---

[13]*If you don't trust us, you can skip ahead a few pages to Table 14-10 and check for yourself. Now, aren't you sorry you doubted us?*

[14]*You've just been introduced to your first term in matrix algebra, "vector." See, that was painless, wasn't it? There actually is a link between the use of the term vector in matrix algebra and in disease epidemiology, obscure though it may be: both are represented symbolically by arrows.*

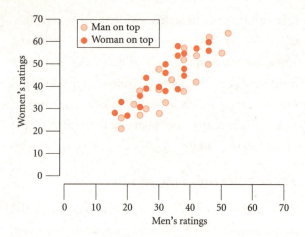

FIGURE 14-7 Scatterplot of the two DVs for both groups.

somewhat difficult to draw until someone invents three-, four-, or five-dimensional graph paper.

Sticking with the analogy of the *t*-test, we compare the groups by examining how far apart the centers of the distributions are, where each center is represented by a single point, the group mean. In the multivariate case, we again compare the distance between the centers, but now the center of each ellipse is called the **centroid**.[15] It can be thought of as the overall mean of the group for each variable; in this case, in two-dimensional space (Male's rating and Female's rating). If we had a third variable, we would have to think in three dimensions, and each centroid would consist of a vector of three numbers—the means of the three variables for that group. The logic of the statistical analysis is the same, however: the greater the distance, the more significant the results (all other things being equal).

LOOKING AT VARIANCE

Comparing the means in a *t*-test is necessary, but not sufficient; we also have to compare the differences between the means to the variances within the groups. Not surprisingly, the same applies in the multivariate case. However, there's an added level of complexity; in addition to the variances of each of the variables,

we also have the **covariances** between the variables.[16] What this means is that instead of having just one number for the variance, we now have a *matrix* of variance and covariance terms. Not surprisingly, it's referred to as the **variance-covariance matrix** (VCV) and looks like:

$$VCV = \Sigma = \begin{bmatrix} s_{11}^2 & s_{12}^2 \\ s_{21}^2 & s_{22}^2 \end{bmatrix} \tag{14-9}$$

First, note that we just stuck in a third term from matrix algebra, "matrix" itself, which is simply a rectangular array of numbers. Second, the abbreviation for a variance-covariance matrix is either VCV or the symbol. That's right, it's the same symbol we use to indicate summation. You'd think that with so many Greek letters lying around that aren't being used in statistics, statisticians would have thought to use something different, but they didn't. Usually, the context makes the meaning clear; in addition, the symbol for a matrix is usually printed in **boldface**, to avoid confusion.

In the VCV matrix, the terms along the main diagonal s_{11}^2 and s_{22}^2, where the subscripts are the same) are the variances, and those off the diagonal (s_{12}^2 and s_{21}^2, where the subscripts are different) are the covariances. Just as with a correlation matrix, the VCV is symmetrical, so the value of s_{12}^2 is the same as that for s_{21}^2. Needless to say (but we'll say it anyway), there would be more terms in the VCV matrix if we had more dependent variables: for three variables, we would have three variances and three unique covariances; for four variables, four variances and six covariances, and so on.

Testing for equivalence of the VCV matrices means that the variance of X_1 is the same across all groups; the covariance between X_1 and X_2 is the same; and so forth for all of the variances and all of the covariances. The usual test for homogeneity of the VCV matrices is **Box's *M*** statistic. After some statistical hand waving over the matrices, the number

---

[15]*That's your second term in matrix algebra.*

[16]*A covariance is similar to a correlation between two variables, except that the original units of measurement are retained, rather than transforming the variables to standard scores first, as is done with correlations. It reflects the variance shared by the two variables.*

is transformed into either an F-ratio or a x^2. If $p > 0.05$, then it's safe to proceed, because the matrices do not differ significantly from each other. However, like many other tests for homogeneity, M is unduly sensitive to differences, especially when the sample size is large. The consequence is that a significant M statistic doesn't always mean that you have to either stop with the analysis or transform the data; unfortunately, there is nothing but our "feel" for the data to tell us whether the deviation from homogeneity is worth worrying about. Tabachnick and Fidell (2013) offer the following guidelines:

- If the sample sizes are equal, don't worry about M, because the significance tests are robust enough to handle any deviations from homogeneity
- If sample sizes are not equal, and the p associated with M is greater than 0.001, it's fairly safe to proceed
- If the cell sizes are unequal, and p is less than 0.001, interpret the results of the MANOVA very cautiously

The consequence of violating the assumption of homogeneity of the VCV matrices if the sample sizes are equal is a slight reduction in the power of the MANOVA. If the sample sizes vary considerably, then a significant M can indicate that the Type I error rate may be either inflated or deflated. Because this depends on which matrices are the most different, it is almost impossible to just look at the data and figure out which it will be.

FROM ANOVA TO MANOVA

The logic of MANOVA is very similar to that of ANOVA. With the one-way ANOVA, we partition the total variance (the Sum of Squares Total, or SS_{Total}) into that due to differences *between* the groups ($SS_{Between}$) and the error variance, which is the Sum of Squares *within* the groups (SS_{Within} or SS_{Error}). Then, the F-test looks at the ratio of the explained variance (that due to the grouping factor) to the error (or unexplained) variance, after adjusting for the number of subjects and groups (the Mean Squares). With more complicated designs, such as factorial or repeated-measures ANOVAs, we "simply" split the SS_{Total} into

more sources of variance, such as that due to each factor separately, that due to the interaction between the factors, and that due to measurements over time; divide by the appropriate error term; and get more F-ratios.

We do exactly the same thing in MANOVA, except that we have more terms to worry about—the relationships between or among the DVs. This is equivalent to expanding the measurement of variance into a variance-covariance matrix when we looked at the assumption of homogeneity of variance. Similarly, we expand the Sum of Squares terms into a corresponding series of **Sum of Squares and Cross-Products** (SSCP) matrices: $SSCP_{Total}$, $SSCP_{Between}$, and $SSCP_{Within}$. That sounds somewhat formidable, but it's something we do all the time in statistics, as we'll see when we describe the Pearson correlation. A small data set, consisting of two variables (X and Y) and five subjects, is shown in Table 14-9. For each variable, the sum of squares is simply the sum of each value squared. The cross-product is the first value of X multiplied by the first value of Y; these are then added up to form the sum of cross-products. The SSCP matrix for these numbers is therefore:

TABLE 14-9 Calculating sums of squares and cross-products

	X	**Y**	**X²**	**Y²**	**(X) (Y)**
	3	9	9	81	27
	4	7	16	49	28
	5	5	25	25	25
	6	3	36	9	18
	7	1	49	1	7
TOTALS	25	25	135	165	105

$$SSCP = \begin{bmatrix} 135 & 105 \\ 105 & 165 \end{bmatrix} \qquad (14\text{-}10)$$

where the off-diagonal cells are the same, since $X \cdot Y$ is the same as $Y \cdot X$.

The F-test is now just the ratio of the $SSCP_{Between}$ to the $SSCP_{Within}$, after the usual corrections for sample size, number of groups, and the number of DVs. As we'll see, however, we will run into the ubiquitous problem of multivariate statistics—a couple of other ways to look at the ratios. So, stay tuned.

FINALLY DOING IT

Sad to say, "it" in this case means only running the test (now that we've gotten the foreplay out of the way). The first question is, what test do we run? So far, we've been referring to the test as MANOVA, and, in fact, that's how we'll continue to refer to the test. If you look at older books, however, you'll see this test is also called Hotelling's T^2. Just as a *t*-test is an ANOVA for two groups (or, in the case of the paired *t*-test, two related variables), T^2 is a MANOVA for two groups or two variables. In the years B.C.,[17] it made sense to have a separate test for the two-group case, since there were some shortcuts that could simplify the calculations, which were all done by hand. Now that computers do all the work for us, the distinction

isn't as important, and references to Hotelling's T^2 are increasingly rare, and nonexistent in the menus for some computer programs.

If we (finally) run a MANOVA on the satisfaction data, we would get an output similar to that shown in Table 14-10. As we mentioned, the multivariate equivalent of the test for homogeneity of variance is Box's *M*, which tests for equivalence of the variance-covariance matrices; this is the first thing we see in the output. The *p* level shows that the test is not significant, so we don't have any worries in this regard.

The next set of homogeneity tests belong to **Levene**, they are univariate tests that look at each of the DVs separately. The usual rule of thumb is that if they are not significant, we can use the results from the MANOVA; if they are significant, then we should

TABLE 14-10   Output from a MANOVA program

Box's	1.696	F	0.533	Df 1	3	Df 2	259 920	p	0.660

Levene's test			
	F	**df 1**	**df 2**	**Sig**
Male	0.932	1	38	0.341
Female	1.205	1	38	0.279

Multivariate tests						
Effect		**Value**	**F**	**df N**	**df D**	**Sig**
Intercept	Pillai's trace	0.936	270.24	2	37	0.001
	Wilks' lambda	0.064	270.24	2	37	0.001
	Hotelling's trace	14.607	270.24	2	37	0.001
	Roy's largest root	14.607	270.24	2	37	0.001
Group	Pillai's trace	0.159	3.49	2	37	0.040
	Wilks' lambda	0.841	3.49	2	37	0.040
	Hotelling's trace	0.189	3.49	2	37	0.040
	Roy's largest root	0.189	3.49	2	37	0.040

Tests of between-subjects effects					
		SS hyp	**df**	**Mean square**	**F**	**Sig**
Intercept	M	43 296.4	1	43 296.4	475.07	0.001
	F	74 218.225	1	74 218.225	547.614	0.001
Group	M	48.4	1	48.4	0.531	0.471
	F	50.625	1	50.625	0.374	0.545
Error	M	3463.2	38	91.137		
	F	5150.15	38	135.53		

[17]*That's Before Computers; non-Christians prefer the term B.C.E., for Before Calculating Engines.*

stick with univariate tests. In our case, there are no significant differences in the error variances between groups, so it's safe to use the output labeled **Multivariate Tests.**

To make our job easier, we can skip the first four lines of the table, those dealing with the intercept. They simply tell us that something is going on, and that the data as a whole deviate from zero.[18] Finally, we arrive where we want to be—a multivariate test of the difference between the groups based on all of the DVs at once. But, as is all too common with multivariate statistics, we don't have just one test but, rather, four of them! Actually, things aren't quite as bad as they seem, especially when we have only two groups. As you can see, **Hotelling's trace**[19] and **Roy's largest root** have the same value; **Pillai's trace**[20] and **Wilks' lambda**[21] add up to 1.0; and with appropriate transformations, all of the tests end up with the same value of *F*. These relationships don't necessarily hold true when there are three or more groups, but let's start off easy.

Because many multivariate tests use Wilks' Lambda (λ), that's where we'll start. As you no doubt remember, the *F*-ratio for the between-groups effect in an ANOVA is simply:

$$F = \frac{MS_{Between\ Groups}}{MS_{Within\ Groups}} \qquad (14\text{-}11)$$

Analogously,   is:

$$\lambda = \frac{SS_{Within\ Groups}}{SS_{Total}} \qquad (14\text{-}12)$$

Notice that, for some reason no one except Wilks understands, λ is built upside down; the smaller the within-groups sum of squares (that is, the error), the smaller the value of λ. So, unlike almost every other statistical test we'll ever encounter, smaller values are better (more significant) than larger ones. What λ

shows is the amount of variance *not* explained by the differences between the groups. In this case, about 6.4% of the variance is unexplained, which means that 93.6% *is* explained.[22] Not coincidentally, 0.936 is also the value of Pillai's trace. In the two-group case, it's simply $(1 - \lambda)$, or the amount of variance that *is* explained.[23] Because most people use either Wilks' λ or Pillai's criterion, we won't bother with the other two. When there are more than two groups, Pillai's trace does *not* equal $(1 - \lambda)$, so you'll have to choose one of them on which to base your decision for significance (assuming they give different results). If you've done just a superb job in designing your study, ending up with equal and large sample sizes in each cell, and managed to keep the variances and covariances equivalent across the groups, then use Wilks' λ. However, if you're as human and fallible as we are, use Pillai's criterion, because it is more robust to violations of these assumptions (Olson, 1976), although slightly less powerful than the other tests (Stevens, 1979). In actual fact, however, the differences among all of the test statistics are minor except when your data are *really* bizarre.

The last part of Table 14-10 gives the univariate tests. Just a little bit of work with a calculator shows that they're exactly the same as the univariate tests in Table 14-8; square the values of *t* and you'll end up with the *F*s. These tests are used in two ways. If the assumptions of homogeneity of variance and covariance aren't met, we would rely on these, rather than on the multivariate tests, to tell us if anything is significant. If we can use the results of the multivariate analysis, these tests tell us which variables are significantly different, in a univariate sense. Hence, they're analogous to post-hoc tests used following a significant ANOVA. These results are somewhat un-

---

[18]*If this ever does come out as nonsignificant, we should question whether we should be in this research game at all or become neo-postmodern deconstructionists, so that no one will ever know that our hypotheses amount to nothing.*

[19]*Also called the Hotelling-Lawley trace, or T.*

[20]*Which is also called the Pillai-Bartlett trace, or V.*

[21]*A.k.a. Wilks' likelihood ratio, or W. (Ever get the feeling that everything is called something else in this game?)*

[22]*If you didn't suspect it before, this should convince you that these are artificial data; if we did any study that accounted for 94% of the variance, our picture would show us holding Nobel prize medals, not a lousy cardboard maple leaf.*

[23]*Pillai's trace is also equivalent to η^2 (eta-squared), which is the usual measure of variance accounted for in ANOVAs.*

usual, in that the multivariate tests are significant but the univariate ones aren't, indicating that we have to compare the patterns of variables between the groups.

MORE THAN TWO GROUPS

If we had a third group,[24] the output would look very much the same as in Table 14-10. Naturally, the Sums of Squares and Mean Squares would be different, and perhaps the significance levels would also be different (depending on how much or little the participants enjoyed themselves), but the general format would be the same. The major difference in terms of interpretation is the Group effect; there will now be two degrees of freedom, reflecting the fact that there are three groups. If the Group effect is significant, then we have the same problem as with a run-of-the-mill, univariate ANOVA: figuring out which groups are significantly different from the others. Fortunately, the method is the same—post-hoc tests, such as Tukey's HSD. Most programs will do this for you, as long as you remember to choose this option.

DOING IT AGAIN: REPEATED-MEASURES MANOVA

What would be the MANOVA equivalent of a repeated-measures ANOVA? At first glance, it would seem to be two or more dependent variables, both of which are measured on two or more occasions and, in fact, this is one possible design (called a **doubly repeated MANOVA**). However, even if we have only one DV measured two or three times, it is often better to use a repeated-measures MANOVA than an ANOVA. There are two reasons for this. The first is that, although between-subjects designs are relatively robust with respect to heterogeneity of variance across groups, within-subjects designs are not, resulting in a higher probability of a Type I error than the α level would suggest (LaTour and Miniard, 1983). The second reason is that with ANOVA, there

is an assumption of **sphericity**—that for each DV, the variances are equal across time, as are the correlations (that is, the correlation between the measures at Time 1 and Time 2 is the same as between Time 2 and Time 3 and is the same as between Time 1 and Time 3). Most data don't meet the criterion of sphericity, and this is especially true when the time points aren't equally spaced (such as measuring a person's serum rhubarb level immediately on discharge, then one week, two weeks, four weeks, and finally six months later). It's more likely that there's a higher correlation between the measures at Week 1 and Week 2 than between Week 1 and Month 6. Repeated-measures MANOVA, however, treats each time point as if it were a different variable, so the assumption of sphericity isn't required.

To keep things a bit simpler, we'll go back to using two groups, and modify our study a bit by having only one rater,[25] but we'll repeat the experiment three times, so we have three time points. The design, then, is a 2 (Who's on Top) by 3 (Trials) factorial. The results are shown graphically on Figure 14-8, and the computer output appears in Table 14-11.

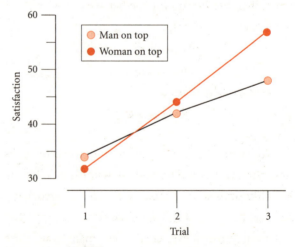

FIGURE 14-8 Repeated measures of satisfaction for the two groups.

The first part of the table gives the results for the between-subjects effect, which in this case is Group or Position. This is actually a univariate test, a one-

---

[24]*You can use your imagination for this, as long as it doesn't involve more than two people; that would require another dependent variable (and perhaps a larger bed). As a hint, a bed isn't de rigueur.*

[25]*You can determine for yourself whether the scores show it's a man or a woman doing the ratings.*

TABLE 14-11 Output from a repeated-measures MANOVA program

Tests of between-subjects effects					
Source	Sum of squares	df	Mean square	F	Sig
Intercept	219 564.08	1	219 564.08	637.20	0.001
Group	261.08	1	261.08	0.76	0.390
Error	13 093.85	38	344.58		

Multivariate tests					
Effect		Value	F	dfN	dfD	Sig
Trial	Pillai's trace	0.924	224.68	2	37	0.001
	Wilks' lambda	0.076	224.68	2	37	0.001
	Hotelling's trace	12.145	224.68	2	37	0.001
	Roy's largest root	12.145	224.68	2	37	0.001
Trial Group	Pillai's trace	0.575	25.00	2	37	0.001
	Wilks' lambda	0.425	25.00	2	37	0.001
	Hotelling's trace	1.351	25.00	2	37	0.001
	Roy's largest root	1.351	25.00	2	37	0.001

Mauchly's test of sphericity							
Within-subjects effect	W	x^2	df	Sig	Epsilon		
					Greenhouse-Geisser	Huynh-Feldt	Lower Bound
Trial	0.4	32.33	2	0	0.632	0.661	0.5
Box's 4.419			F 0.673		Df1 6	Df2 10 462		p 0.671

Tests of within-subjects effects						
Source		SS	df	MS	F	Sig
Trial	Sphericity assumed	7571.45	2	3785.73	259.16	0.001
	Greenhouse-Geisser	7571.45	1.265	5986.69	259.16	0.001
	Huynh-Feldt	7571.45	1.323	5724.38	259.16	0.001
	Lower Bound	7571.45	1	7571.45	259.16	0.001
Trial 3 Group	Sphericity assumed	612.35	2	306.18	20.96	0.001
	Greenhouse-Geisser	612.35	1.265	484.18	20.96	0.001
	Huynh-Feldt	612.35	1.323	462.97	20.96	0.001
	Lower Bound	612.35	1	612.35	20.96	0.001
Error (trial)	Sphericity assumed	1110.2	76	14.61		
	Greenhouse-Geisser	1110.2	48.06	23.10		
	Huynh-Feldt	1110.2	50.26	22.09		
	Lower Bound	1110.2	38	29.22		

way ANOVA, in which all of the trials are averaged. In this case, the F is not significant, showing that, overall, position doesn't make a difference.

Next, we see the multivariate tests for the within-subjects factors and the interactions between the within-subjects and the between-subjects factors. In this example, we have only one within-subject factor

(Trials) and one interaction term (Trials by Group). The same comments apply to this output as previously with regard to the meaning of the four different tests: they all yield the same F-test when there are two groups, and stick with Pillai's trace or Wilks' lambda. In this example, there is an overall Trials effect and a significant interaction. If we go back to Figure 14-8, it appears that when summing over Groups, the ratings increase over time; and women's ratings start somewhat lower but increase more than men's.[26]

Following this, we have univariate tests for the within-subject factor, used if Box's *M* shows us we should be concerned about the assumption of equality of the covariance matrices. The same general guidelines apply that we discussed before: don't worry about this if the sample sizes are equal or $p > 0.001$. If we do feel that it's more appropriate to use the univariate tests, then we first have to look at the test of sphericity, known as **Mauchly's** *W*. For the purposes of significance testing, *W* is transformed into an approximate x^2 test. If it is not significant (and you have a sufficient sample size), then we can proceed with abandon, using the appropriate lines in the succeeding tables. If it is significant (as it is here), then the numerator and denominator degrees of freedom for the *F*-tests are "adjusted" by some value, which is referred to as ε (epsilon). As is so often the case, we have more adjustments than we can use. The most conservative one is the **Lower Bound**, which assumes the most extreme departure from sphericity.[27] The **Huynh-Feldt** adjustment is the least conservative, with the **Greenhouse-Geisser** adjustment falling in between. Most people use the Greenhouse-Geisser value, except when the sample size is small, in which case the Huynh-Feld t value is used.

The caveat we added in the previous paragraph about *W* ("and you have a sufficient sample size") is one that holds true for every statistical test trying to prove a null hypothesis: the result may not be significant if the sample size is small, and there just isn't the power to reject the null of sphericity. The trouble is, nobody knows how much is enough,[28] so if your sample size is on the low side, you'd be safer to use one of the correction factors.

ROBUSTNESS

MANOVA is relatively robust to violations here, especially if the group sizes are equal. With that same proviso of equal sample size, it is also relatively robust to deviations from multivariate normality. "Relatively" means two things: if the degrees of freedom associated with the univariate error terms are over 20, and if the deviation from normality is due to skewness, you can get away with almost anything. However, if the df_{Error} is less than 20, or if the non-normality is due to outliers, then it would be safer to trust the results of the univariate tests, *trim* the data to get rid of the outliers,[29] or use ranks instead of the raw data (discussed below). It's also a reminder (as if one were necessary) to plot your data before you do anything else to make sure you don't have outliers or any other pathologic conditions.

Is there anything we *can't* get away with if we have large and equal groups? There are two things we can't mess around with—random sampling and independence of the observations. As with most statistical techniques, MANOVA assumes that the data come from a random sample of the underlying population, and that the scores for one person are independent of those for all other people. If you violate either of these, the computer will still blithely crunch the numbers and give you an answer, but the results will bear little relationship to what's really going on.

POWER AND SAMPLE SIZE

As we have seen, the first test that's performed when we do a MANOVA is a test for homogeneity of the VCV matrices. For this test to run, we must have more subjects than variables in every cell (Tabachnick and Fidell, 2013). But, this is an absolute minimum

---

[26]*As before, we leave it to you to figure out the meaning of this.*

[27]*It's called the Lower Bound because it is the lowest value that ε can have: $1 / (k - 1)$, where k is the number of groups. The maximum value of ε is 1.0, indicating homogeneity.*

[28]*At least in the area of statistics.*

[29]*"Trimming" is how you can get rid of data you don't want and still get published, as opposed to saying that you simply disregarded those values you didn't like.*

requirement. There are tables for estimating sample size, based on the number of groups, variables, and power (Läuter, 1978), and some of them appear in Appendix N. These tables first appeared in a very obscure journal from what was once East Germany, so we're not sure if they are legitimate or part of a conspiracy to undermine capitalist society by having the West's researchers waste their time with under-or overpowered studies. In any case, we offer them for your use. Going the other way, Appendix O (adapted from Stevens, 1980) gives the power for the two-group MANOVA (Hotelling's T^2) for different numbers of variables, sample sizes, and effect sizes.

For the most part, MANOVAs are less powerful than univariate tests. This can result in the anomalous situation that some or all of the univariate tests come out significant, but multivariate tests such as Pillai's trace are not significant.

There is one issue that has bedeviled statisticians (and us, too) ever since MANOVA was developed: if the overall F-test is significant, is it necessary to adjust the α level for the post-hoc analyses that examine which specific variables differ between or among the groups? The answer, as has been the case so often in this book, is a definitive, "Yes, no, and maybe." Some people have vehemently argued that a significant omnibus test "protects" the α levels of the post-hoc tests, so that no adjustment is necessary. There are just as many people on the other side, saying that multiple testing is multiple testing, so a Bonferroni-type adjustment is required.

The problem is that both sides are right, but under different conditions. If the null hypothesis is true for all of the DVs (a situation called the *complete null hypothesis*), then α is indeed protected, and there's no need to adjust for the fact that you are doing a number of ANOVAs on the individual variables after the fact.[30] However, if the null hypothesis is true for some of the variables but not for others (the *partial null hypothesis*), then α is not protected, and an adjustment for multiplicity is required. The problem

is that you never know which is the case, even based on the results of the univariate F-tests (Jaccard and Guilamo-Ramos, 2002). So, it's safest to assume that you're dealing with the partial null hypothesis, and make the adjustment.

WHEN THINGS GO WRONG: DEALING WITH OUTLIERS

As we've mentioned, MANOVA can't handle data with outliers very well. If you're reluctant to trim the data and still want to use a multivariate procedure, an alternative exists for the one-way test. First, transform your raw data into ranks; if there are n_1 subjects in Group 1 and n_2 subjects in Group 2, then the ranks will range from 1 to (n_1+n_2) for each variable. Then, run MANOVA on the rank scores. Finally, multiply the Pillai trace (V) by ($N - 1$), and check the results in a table of x^2, with $df = p\,(k - 1)$, where p is the number of variables and k the number of groups (Zwick, 1985).

EFFECT SIZE

There are actually at least two effect sizes; one for the MANOVA as a whole, and then one for the individual main effects. As we mentioned, Wilks' λ is a measure of how much variance is *not* accounted for, so ES is $1 - \lambda$, or Pillai's trace. For the main effects and interactions, use η^2 or ω^2, as we described in Chapter 7.

A CAUTIONARY NOTE

From all of the above, it may sound as if we should use MANOVA every time we have many dependent measures, and the more the better. Actually, reality dictates just the opposite. The assumption of homogeneity of the VCV matrices is much harder to meet than the assumption of homogeneity of variance; so, it's more likely that we're violating something when we do a MANOVA. Second, the results are often harder to interpret, because there are more things going on at the same time. Third, as we've seen, we may have less power with multivariate

---

[30] *And don't forget that if the null hypothesis is true for all DVs, you're dealing with a Type I error to begin with.*

tests than with univariate ones. The best advice with regard to using MANOVA is offered by Tabachnick and Fidell (1983), who are usually strong advocates of multivariate procedures. They write:

Because of the increase in complexity and ambiguity of results with MANOVA, one of the best overall recommendations is: Avoid it if you can. Ask yourself why *you are including correlated DVs in the same analysis. Might there be some way of combining them or deleting some of them so that ANOVA can be performed?*

If the answer to their question is "No," then MANOVA is the way to go—but, don't throw everything into the pot. The outcome variables included in any one MANOVA should be related to each other on a *conceptual* level, and it's usually a mistake to have more than six or seven at the most in any one analysis.

REPORTING GUIDELINES

For a between-subjects design, you can report the results pretty much as if it were a run-of-the-mill ANOVA. It's not really necessary to report the statistics regarding the intercept, because in most cases, it doesn't mean much. However, you should also report Wilks' λ and its transformed value of F (with, of course, the proper df). Within the text, you should report whether or not the tests for homogeneity of the variance–covariance matrix and normality were significant.

For repeated measures designs, life is a bit more complicated. In addition to what we said above, you also have to report Mauchly's W (best to report the x^2 equivalent, with its df). If it's not significant, then that's it. But, if it is significant, you must also state which adjustment you used (lower bound, Greenhouse-Geisser, or Huynh-Feldt) and its value.

SECTION SUMMARY OF MANOVA

Taking Tabachnick and Fidell's advice to heart, we should try to design studies so that MANOVA isn't needed: we should rely on one outcome variable, or try to combine the outcome variables into a global measure. If this isn't possible, then MANOVA is the

test to use. Analyzing all of the outcomes at once avoids many of the interpretive and statistical problems that would result from performing a number of separate *t*-tests or ANOVAs. We pay a penalty in terms of reduced power and more complicated results, but these are easier to overcome than those resulting from ignoring the correlations among the dependent variables.

GLOSSARY

ANCOVA	协方差分析
nonlinear regression	非线性回归
general linear model	广义线性方程
MANOVA	多变量方差分析
matrix algebra	矩阵代数
variance-covariance matrix	方差 - 协方差矩阵

How to Get the Computer to Do the Work for You

- From **Analyze**, choose **General Linear Model   Multivariate…**
- Click the variables you want from the list on the left, and click the arrow to move them into the box labeled **Dependent Variables**
- Choose the grouping factor(s) from the list on the left, and click the arrow to move them into the box labeled **Fixed Factor(s)**
- If you have more than two groups, click the **Post Hoc** button and select the ones you want [good choices would be **LSD, Tukey**, and **Tukey's-b**], and then click the **Continue** button
- Click the **Options** button and check the statistics you want displayed. The least you want is **Homogeneity Tests**; if you haven't analyzed the data previously, you will also want **Descriptive Statistics** and perhaps **Estimates of Effect Size**

EXERCISES

1. In the following designs, identify the between-subject factors, within-subject factors, and covariates.

   a. A group of students are randomized to receive

either (a) a wonderful, humorous, perceptive, brilliant, and witty new statistics book (this one, naturally), or (b) the same old boring, dull, inarticulate, condescending statistics book (any of the others) at the beginning of a stats course. The mark in their last undergraduate math course is recorded. At the end of the stats course, they complete a 60-item multiple choice test.

b. Patients with chronic leg cramps are randomized to receive either calcium supplements or a placebo. After 6 weeks, they are asked to rate whether the pain has become better or worse and by how much (on a 100 mm Visual Analog Scale).

c. The effect of transcutaneous electrical nerve stimulation (TENS) is assessed by physiotherapists. Each time patients with low back pain come in for treatment, they are given TENS at one of six different power levels assigned at random. Unbeknownst to the patient or therapist, a random device in the machine turns it on or off for a particular session. This continues until patients have completed 12 sessions—TENS/Placebo at 6 levels.

d. As in c above, but the sample is stratified on male/female.

e. Surgical performance, measured by the total time required to remove a gallstone, is predicted using the following variables: (a) Right-handed or left-handed, (b) Reaction time, (c) I.Q..

2. The "Dr. Fox Effect" demonstrates that a charming, witty speaker can suck everybody into believing his message. (That's where we get Presidents and Prime Ministers from, silly). To further explore this phenomenon, students received a series of seminars from a total of 12 speakers of varying ages. Six were dressed neatly and nattily (NN), and 6 were dressed soiled and shabbily (SS). The effect of dress and speaker age on student ratings were explored. As one final wrinkle, students were divided by gender, with 10 men and 10 women in the class.

a. What variable corresponds to "Subjects"?

b. What is the "Between Subjects" factor? How many df?

c. What is the covariate, and how many df does it have?

d. How many repeated measures are there? What is the df associated with each?

3. The "Dr. Fox Effect" demonstrates that a charming, witty speaker can suck everybody into believing his message. (That's where we get Presidents and Prime Ministers from, silly). To further explore this phenomenon, students received a series of seminars from a total of 12 speakers of varying ages. 6were dressed neatly and nattily (NN), and 6 were dressed soiled and shabbily (SS). The effect of dress and speaker age on student ratings were explored. As one final wrinkle, students were divided by gender, with 10 men and 10 women in the class.

a. What variable corresponds to "Subjects"?

b. What is the "Between Subjects" factor? How many df?

c. What is the covariate, and how many df does it have?

d. How many repeated measures are there? What is the df associated with each?

4. For the following designs, indicate whether a univariate or a multivariate ANOVA should be used.

a. Scores on a quality-of-life scale are compared for three groups of patients: those with rheumatoid arthritis, osteoarthritis, and chronic fatigue syndrome.

b. Each of these patient groups is divided into males and females as another factor.

c. All of these groups are tested every 2 months for a year.

d. The same design as 1.a, but now the eight subscales of the quality-of-life scale are analyzed separately.

e. Same design as 1.b, but using the eight subscales.

f. Same as 1.c, but with the subscales.

5. If the three groups did not differ with regard to their quality of life, and if the eight subscales were

analyzed separately, what is the probability that at least one comparison will be significant at the 0.05 level by chance?

6. Based on the results of Box's M, you should:
   a. proceed with the analysis without any concern.
   b. proceed, but be somewhat concerned.
   c. stop right now.

Box's M	22.745	F	3.240	$df1$	6	$df2$	1193	p	0.004

7. Based on the results of Levene's test, you should:
   a. use the results of the multivariate tests.
   b. use the results of the univariate tests.

Levene's test			
	F	**dfN**	**dfD**	**Sig**
Variable A	0.055	1	46	0.815
Variable B	0.155	1	46	0.695
Variable C	0.865	1	46	0.357

8. Looking at the output from the multivariate tests:
   a. Is there anything going on?
   b. Does the variable SETTING have an effect?

Multivariate tests					
Effect		**Value**	**F**	**dfN**	**dfD**	**Sig**
Intercept	Pillai's trace	0.913	154.618	3	44	0.000
	Wilk's lambda	0.064	154.618	3	44	0.000
	Hotelling's trace	10.542	154.618	3	44	0.000
	Roy's largest root	10.542	154.618	3	44	0.000
SETTING	Pillai's trace	0.060	0.941	3	44	0.429
	Wilk's lambda	0.940	0.941	3	44	0.429
	Hotelling's trace	0.064	0.941	3	44	0.429
	Roy's largest root	0.064	0.941	3	44	0.429

CHAPTER THE FIFTEENTH   **Measuring Change**

There are a number of approaches to examining the change in a variable over time. The simplest involves difference scores, and is analyzed with a paired t-test. Analysis of covariance is more appropriate, and generally leads to a more powerful test. ANCOVA can also be generalized to the situation in which there are multiple occasions of measurement.

SETTING THE SCENE

Over the years, people with arthritis have fallen prey to countless over-the-counter preparations, guaranteeing immediate relief from the pain, and charging outrageous prices considering that about 90% are just variants on aspirin. In this chapter, we examine one more of the family, Robert's Rectal Pills, which has the dubious advantage that its mode of administration is somewhat unusual, at least for an aspirin concoction. In the course of doing so, we explore a number of methods for assessing change (in this case, change in joint counts) ranging from the simple, obvious, and ubiquitous methods (difference scores and paired t-tests) to more advanced and powerful methods, including ANCOVA.

There is probably no area in statistics (and measurement theory, for that matter) that is so seemingly straightforward but at the same time so controversial as measuring change. Books can be written about it, and in fact, many have been (Collins and Horn, 1991; Collins and Sayer, 2001; Harris, 1967), and the controversy is still alive (e.g., Norman, 1989, 1998). After all, calculating a **gain score** is as simple as subtracting the preintervention score from the postintervention score. It has intuitive appeal to clinicians—something along the lines of, "We're in the business of making people better, so we should measure how much better we make them." It also seems like the proper thing to do statistically. In fact, in many situations, it is so self-evident that we do it almost without thinking about it. For example, if we were to do a study of some new diet plan by assigning everyone to a treatment or control group, no one in his or her right mind would just look at the weights after the treatment was over. Obviously, you would measure everyone before and after, find out how much each person gained or lost, then analyze these difference scores.[1] This step seems so intuitively correct that it couldn't possibly be wrong. Unfortunately, although it's not exactly wrong, it's not quite right either. In addition, it is limited to the simple case of only two measurements—a pretest and a post-test. In this chapter, we will begin with this simple case, then develop several other more powerful methods to assess change in more complex (and powerful) experimental situations.[2]

For illustration, consider briefly a disease like rheumatoid arthritis, which goes up and down with the weather, the time of day, the period of the moon, and the advancing perihelion of Mercury's orbit. Now we have a new wonder drug, called Robert's Rectal Pills (RRP)[3]. Like most over-the-counter medications, it contains mostly ASA (acetylsalicylic acid) with a mere soupçon of baking soda.

To test it, we could bring a series of patients into

---

[1] And if you want to practice your statistical prowess, the right test is an unpaired t-test on the difference scores derived from the treatment and control groups.

[2] The reason it is wrong or at least suboptimal to use difference scores has to do with a phenomenon called **regression to the mean**, which we'll talk about in due course. If there is no measurement error, which excludes every study we've ever done or read about, then difference scores are perfectly OK.

[3] Carter and Dodd beat us to the better organs.

the clinic and measure their joint counts or any of the dozen other things rheumatologists like to measure. For the moment, let's just stay with joint counts (JC). Then, like all good experimenters, we randomize them into two groups. One group would get RRP, and another would get some other pill that looks like RRP, goes in the same place, but contains only the baking soda. We would wait a month, bring them all back, measure their new JC, do some analyses, and publish. To put some meat on the bones, the JCs for 20 patients (10 in the RRP group, 10 in the placebo group), before and after treatment, are shown in Table 15-1.

TABLE 15-1 Data from a randomized trial of RRP versus placebo with a pre-test and a 1 month post-test

Subject	Group	Pre-test of JC (0 month)	Post-test of JC (1 month)	Difference
1	1	22	16	6
2	1	24	17	7
3	1	32	25	7
4	1	24	21	3
5	1	35	32	3
6	1	27	22	5
7	1	34	27	7
8	1	15	13	2
9	1	29	25	4
10	1	25	21	4
MEAN		26.7	21.9	4.8
SD		6.1	7.8	1.78
11	2	32	31	1
12	2	33	34	1
13	2	42	34	8
14	2	27	24	3
15	2	22	24	2
16	2	18	15	3
17	2	16	13	3
18	2	32	29	3
19	2	25	19	6
20	2	24	22	2
MEAN		27.1	24.5	2.6
SD		7.8	7.5	2.80

If that's all we did, then the straightforward analysis is, as we already indicated, an unpaired t-test on the difference scores for each subject in the treatment

and control groups. We did that for the data in Table 15-1, and it turns out to be 1.99, which, with $df = 18$, is not significant at the 0.05 level.

On the other hand, if you have been taking to heart all the more complicated stuff in the last few chapters, you might want to do a repeated-measures ANOVA, with one between-subjects factor (RRP group vs Placebo group) and one within-subjects repeated measure (Pre-test/Post-test). Since we expect the treatment group to get better over the time from pre-test to post-test and the control group to stay the same, this amounts to a Pre-/Post-test Group interaction. All these calculations are shown in Table 15-2 The mean scores for the RRP and control groups are about the same initially: 26.7 and 27.1. After a month, the JC of the RRP group has dropped some to 21.9, and the JC of the control group has also dropped a bit to 24.5. The Time × Group interaction resulted in an F-test of 3.96 with 1 and 18 degrees of freedom, which has an associated p-value of 0.062. This is equivalent to the t-test of the difference scores, which came out to 1.99 (the square root of 3.96) with the same probability (0.062), just as we had hoped. So the interaction term is equivalent to the unpaired t-test of the difference scores, and the F-test of the interaction is just the square of the equivalent t-test. Once again, statistics reveals itself to be somewhat rational (at least some of the time).

TABLE 15-2 ANOVA of pre-test and post-test scores for the RCT of RRP

Source	Sum of Squares	df	Mean square	F	p
Group	22.5	1	22.5	0.25	0.63
Subject: Group	1617.4	18	89.85		
Time	136.9	1	136.9	44.8	0.001
Time × Group	12.1	1	12.1	3.96	0.062
Error	55.0	18	3.05		

PROBLEMS IN MEASURING CHANGE

If it's this simple and straightforward, where's the problem? There is none, actually, if you just want to plug the numbers into the computer and were interested only if the p level is significant or not; but there are many if you want to understand what the numbers mean. The two major issues affecting the interpretation of change[4] scores are the *reliability of difference scores* and *regression to the mean*.

Reliability of Difference Scores

To understand whether there is a problem with difference scores being unreliable, we'll have to make a brief detour into measurement theory.[5] Any score that we observe, whether it's from a paper-and-pencil test, a blood pressure cuff, or the most expensive chemical analyzer in the lab, has some degree of error associated with it. The error can arise from a number of sources, such as inattention on the part of the subject, mistakes reading a dial, transposition errors entering the data, fluctuations in a person's state, and a multitude of others. Thus, the **observed score** (X_O) consists of two parts: the **true score** (X_T) and **error** (X_E). We never observe the true score; it's what would result if the person were tested an infinite number of times. The consequence is that, when we think about the total variation in a distribution of scores, it has two components, one due to real differences between people and the other due to measurement error. So the variance in a distribution of scores looks like:

$$\sigma^2_{Observed} = \sigma^2_{True} + \sigma^2_{Error} \qquad (15\text{-}1)$$

If we imagine doing a trial where we assign folks at random to a treatment or a control group, doing something (or nothing) to them, and then computing an unpaired *t*-test on the final scores, the denominator of the test, is actually based on this sum of variances.

One thing we can do to make this error term smaller is to measure everyone before the intervention and again afterward, then do an unpaired *t*-test on the difference scores. This is usually a good thing. But not always, and that's where these variance components come in; let's see why.

When we take differences, we do indeed get rid of all those systematic differences between subjects that go into σ^2_{True}. But, because we've measured everyone twice, the cost of all this is to introduce error twice. Now the error is:

$$\sigma^2_{Change} = \sigma^2_{Error} + \sigma^2_{Error} = 2\sigma^2_{Error} \qquad (15\text{-}2)$$

What does this have to do with reliability? Well, if we compare Equation (15-1) with Equation (15-2), it's pretty evident that we won't always come out ahead with change scores. If the inequality:

$$\sigma^2_{True} + \sigma^2_{Error} < 2\sigma^2_{Error} \qquad (15\text{-}3)$$

holds, or simplifying a bit, if $\sigma^2_{True} < \sigma^2_{Error}$, then the test on postintervention scores will be larger than the test on difference scores. Now, we defined reliability as:

$$Reliability = \frac{\sigma^2_{True}}{\sigma^2_{Observed}} = \frac{\sigma^2_{True}}{\sigma^2_{True} + \sigma^2_{Error}} \qquad (15\text{-}4)$$

so if $\sigma^2_{True} < \sigma^2_{Error}$, this amounts to saying that the reliability is less than 0.5. In short, measuring change is a good thing if the reliability is greater than 0.5, and a bad thing if it is less than 0.5.

Regression to the Mean

Now that we've put to rest the issue that measuring change is always a good thing, let's confront the second issue, **regression to the mean**. If you think that term has a somewhat pejorative connotation, you should see what Galton (1877) originally called it— "reversion to mediocrity." What he was referring to was that if your parents were above average in height, then most likely you will also be taller than average but not quite as tall as they are. Similarly, if their income was below average, yours will be, too, but closer to the mean. In other words, a second measure will revert (or regress) to the mean.[6]

Let's take a closer look at the data in Table 15-1. On the right side, we have displayed the difference in joint counts from pre- to post-treatment. A close inspection reveals that it seems that in both the treatment and control groups, the worse you are to begin

---

[4]*The terms difference score, change score, and gain score are synonymous, and we'll use them interchangeably. Also, it doesn't matter if we subtract the pretest score from the post-test or vice versa. The statistics don't care, and neither do we.*

[5]*For a Cook's Tour of measurement theory, see Streiner and Norman (2014).*

[6]*This is also the bane of recruiting agents for sports teams. If a batter or pitcher has had an above-average year, we can guarantee that next year's performance will be worse.*

with, the more you improve. Even in the placebo group, those with really bad joint counts initially seem to get quite a bit better after treatment. What an interesting situation. The drug and the placebo both do a world of good for severe arthritics, but don't really help mild cases; in fact, they get worse.

This is a prime example of **regression to the mean**. There are a couple of reasons it rears its ugly head: sampling, and measurement theory (which rears *its* ugly head again). From the perspective of sampling, who gets into a study looking at the effects of treatment? Obviously, those who are suffering from some condition. You won't end up as a subject in a study of RRP if you don't have arthritis, or if you have it but aren't bothered by it too much. You're a participant because you went to your family physician and said, "Help me, Doc, the pain is killing me." Now, as we said earlier, arthritis, like many other disorders, is a fluctuating condition, so the next time you're seen, it's likely the pain isn't quite as bad. If that second evaluation of your pain occurs during the post-treatment assessment, then *voilà*, you've improved! So, one explanation of regression to the mean is that people enter studies when their condition meets all the inclusion and exclusion criteria (i.e., it's fairly severe), and normal variation in the disorder will make the follow-up assessment look good. In fact, this is likely the reason "treatments" such as copper or "ionized" bracelets still continue to be bought by the truckload; people *do* get better after they've put them on. The only problem is that the improvement is due to regression effects, not the bangles.

The measurement perspective is fairly similar. Whose scores are above some cut-point (assuming that high scores are bad)? Those whose True and Observed scores are above the criterion; and those whose True scores are *below* the cut-point but, because of the error component, their Observed scores are above it. On retesting, even if nothing has intervened, a number of people in this latter group will

have scores below the criterion, and yet again, *voilà*! Furthermore, these people won't be balanced out by those whose True scores are above the mark but their Observed scores are below it; they wouldn't have gotten into the study.

Measurement theory also provides another way of looking at the problem of regression toward the mean. Let's assume that the test that we're using has perfect reliability. That means that the correlation between the pretest and post-test scores is 1.0, shown in Figure 15-1, going up at a 45° angle.[7] If a person has a pretest score of, say, 0.8 (don't forget that we are dealing with standardized scores), then he or she will have the same post-test score. But, we know that no test on the face of the earth has a reliability of 1.0, so the actual regression line between pre- and post-test scores is at a shallower angle, like the broken line in the figure. In this case, the post-test score is less than 0.8, so the person has "improved" even in the absence of any intervention. Mathematically, the expected value at Time 2 (T_2), given that the score at Time 1 (T_1) was x is:

$$E(T_2 \mid T_1 = x) = \rho \times x \qquad (15\text{-}5)$$

where the vertical line means "given that," and r (the Greek letter rho) is the test's reliability.

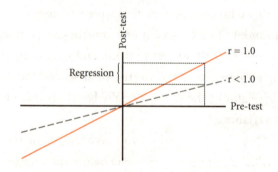

FIGURE 15-1 Relationship between pretest and post-test scores, showing regression to the mean.

This graph and equation tell us two other things. First, the less reliable the test, the greater the effect. Second, the more the score deviates from the mean, the more regression there will be. That's why in Table 15-1, the more severely impaired patients "improved"

[7]*It's at 45° only if we standardize the two scores, which we've done to make the example easier. However, the argument is the same even when the scores haven't been standardized.*

more, whereas those who had less severe scores (those below the mean) actually appeared to get worse.[8]

One solution, if people were randomly assigned to the groups, is to do an *Analysis of Covariance* (ANCOVA), with the final score as the dependent variable and the initial state as the covariate.[9] The ANCOVA fits the optimal line to the scores, in the regression sense of minimizing error, and avoids overcorrection. We have done this in Table 15-3. Now we find that the effect of treatment results in an *F*-test of 4.36, which, with 1 and 17 *df*, is significant at the 0.05 level.

TABLE 15-3   Analysis of covariance of pretest and post-test scores for the RCT of RRP

Source	Sum of Squares	df	Mean square	F	p
Group	25.2	1	25.2	4.36	0.05
Pre-test (covariate)	691.1	1	691.1	119.57	0.001
Error	98.3	17	5.78		

The use of ANCOVA in the design more appropriately corrected for baseline differences, leaving a smaller error term and a significant result. Under fairly normal circumstances, the gains from using ANCOVA instead of difference scores will be small, although, occasionally, there can be gains of a factor of two or more in power. Of course, if there is less measurement error, there is less possibility of regression to the mean, and less gain from the use of ANCOVA.

Regression to the Mean and ANCOVA

As we've just said, adjusting for baseline differences among groups with ANCOVA is definitely the way to go if the people ended up in those groups by random assignment. Through randomization, we can assume that the differences are due to chance, and ANCOVA can do its magical stuff. In fact, the daddy

of ANCOVA, Sir Ronald Fisher, took it for granted that there was random assignment. After all, he was working then at the Rothamsted Agricultural Experiment Station with plants and grains,[10] and they don't have the option of saying, "Sorry, I want to be in the other group." However, when we're dealing with cohort studies, where people end up in groups because of things they may have done (e.g., smoked or didn't smoke, did or didn't use some medication), background factors (male or female, socioeconomic status), or something else, we can't assume that about baseline differences. In fact, it's more likely that the group differences are related to those factors, and this may affect the outcome. In situations like these, the use of ANCOVA can lead to error.

The heart of the problem is something called **Lord's paradox.**[11] Let's change the example we used in the previous chapter, looking at the relation between Pathos Quotient (PQ) and belt size; instead of randomly assigning men to the treatment and incidentally measuring their PQ, we'll focus on seeing if fat and skinny men's PQ scores change to the same degree when given testosterone. So, we form one group of broomsticks and another of gravity-challenged men, put them both on the hormone, and measure them before and after treatment.

Suppose, for the sake of this example, that there really is no difference on average; everyone changes by the same amount except for random error. Consequently, the two means—for the fatties and skinnies—both lie on the same 45° line relating pretest to post-test, just as we see with the asterisks in Figure 15-2. However, the thing is, because of **regression to the mean**, the two ellipses don't quite lie with their major axis on the 45° line. In each group, those who are below the mean the first time aren't quite so low on the post-test, and vice versa. The net effect is that

---

[8] *And why batters who hit exceptionally well one year will really take a tumble the next. The good news is that those who had a very bad year will likely improve.*

[9] *If people weren't randomly assigned (e.g., in a cohort study), you have to be aware of Lord's paradox, which we will discuss shortly.*

[10] *This legacy lives on in other ways. Another variant of ANOVA, not discussed in this book, is called a split plot design, because Fisher took a plot of land and split it, planting different grains in each section, thus controlling for soil and atmospheric conditions.*

[11] *That refers to Frederick M. Lord (1967, 1969)*

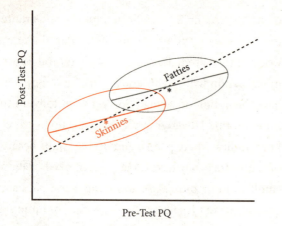

FIGURE 15-2 Analyzing the effect of testosterone in two groups using difference scores.

the footballs aren't quite as tilted at the 45° line.

If we analyze the data by using a simple difference score (post-test minus pretest), and plot the findings, we're effectively forcing the line of "best fit" to stay at 45°. We'll get the results shown in Figure 15-2, where everyone, regardless of group, sits on the 45° line. From this, we'd conclude that there is no effect of weight, and that both groups changed to the same degree.

Let's analyze the data again, this time using AN-COVA to adjust for baseline differences in weight. What we'd find is shown in Figure 15-3. Now the picture is somewhat different. The ANCOVA line for each group goes right along the major axis of the ellipse, at a slope a bit less than 1. When we project these two lines to the *Y*-axis to see whether there is a differential effect of testosterone, we find to our amazement that there *is*, equal of course, to the distance between the two regression lines. But this is a

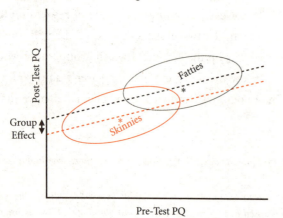

FIGURE 15-3 Analyzing the same data as in Figure 15-2, but using ANCOVA.

consequence entirely of regression to the mean and the fact that the two groups started out differently.

So, which analysis is correct? Should we use a *t*-test on the difference scores, or an ANCOVA taking baseline differences into account? As is often the case, the answer is Yes, No, Maybe, or even Neither. The trouble is that the ANCOVA is pretty clearly overestimating the effect in this case. But under different circumstances, where there was a small "treatment effect" so the two means won't lie on the 45° line, as shown in Figure 15-4, the ANCOVA, which, as we discussed, is more sensitive, will correctly say that there is a difference between groups. On the other hand, it may be that the difference score, which, as we discussed earlier, is a bit conservative, may well miss these effects. Of course, the closer the two groups are in starting values, the smaller the effect of the inequality in driving the two intercepts apart.

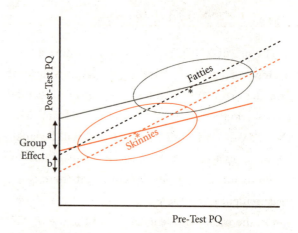

FIGURE 15-4 A similar graph, only this time showing a small treatment effect, with Fatties slightly higher than the slope = 1 line and the Skinnies lower.

The paradox was raised by Lord, but he didn't explain it. The explanation was given by Holland and Rubin (1983), and made comprehensible by Wainer (1991, 2004). Part of the problem is not just that one test is biased or the other is conservative. The reason for the equivocal answer is that the "real" answer depends on the assumptions we make, and those assumptions are untestable. What we *really* want to know is, if a person of a particular weight lost 5 Pathos Quotient points in the Skinny group, would he also lose 5 points if he were in the Fatties group? This is obviously an unanswerable question, because the same person can't be in both groups. Moreover, even if we could find a person in the Fatties group who weighed the same and looked the same as someone in the Skinnies condition, these two people are not the same in one very important sense. The person in the Fatties group is below the mean of his group, whereas the equivalent person in the Skinnies group is above the mean of his mates. So, when the Fatty gets retested, he's likely, because of measurement error, to move upward, whereas the Skinny of the same weight is more likely to move downward; what's called **differential regression toward the mean**.

We can get a good approximation of the answer with random assignment to groups, because the people are more or less similar and interchangeable.[12] This isn't the case with cohort studies, for the reasons we outlined before. The assumption we make when we use difference scores, and analyze the data with t-tests or repeated-measures ANOVA, is that the amount of change is independent of the group (if one group is a placebo condition, that the dependent variable won't change between pretesting and post-testing). The assumption with ANCOVA is that the amount of change is a linear function of the baseline, and that this relationship holds for all people in the group. In a cohort study, neither of these assumptions is testable. So, the choice of which strategy to use depends on which assumption you want to make, and then you pays your money and you takes your chances. Not very satisfying, but that's the way the world is.

MULTIPLE FOLLOW-UP OBSERVATIONS: ANCOVA WITH CONTRASTS

That's fine as far as it goes. However, it is rarely the case that people with chronic diseases have only one follow-up visit. They come back again and again, seemingly forever and ever. It seems a shame to ignore all these observations just because you can't do a t-test on them. Of course, one approach is to pick one time interval, either by design (e.g., specifying in advance that you'll look at the 12-month follow-up)

or by snooping (e.g., looking at all the differences and picking the one time period when the treatment seems to have had the biggest impact). The former is inefficient; the latter is fraudulent, although we've seen both done, with great regularity.

What's so bad about the first strategy? Two things. First, it's throwing away half the data you gathered, which is something that statisticians really don't like to do. Second, and more fundamentally, it's treating change in a very simplistic manner, kind of like a quantum change—first you're in this state, later you're in that state.[13] There's a ton of information about *how* patients are getting from one state to the other that is lost in the simple look at just the first and last measurements.

Let's take a closer look. Examine Table 15-4, in

TABLE 15-4 Data from an RCT of RRP versus placebo with post-tests at 1, 3, 6, and 12 months

Subject	Group	Pretest 0 mo	Post-test 1 mo	Post-test 3 mo	Post-test 6 mo	Post-test 12 mo
1	1	22	16	17	13	14
2	1	24	17	18	19	22
3	1	32	25	24	26	22
4	1	24	21	19	20	23
5	1	35	32	29	31	27
6	1	27	22	21	19	17
7	1	34	27	27	24	22
8	1	15	13	11	12	14
9	1	29	25	22	21	19
10	1	25	21	20	23	24
MEAN		26.7	21.9	20.8	20.8	20.4
SD		6.1	5.6	5.1	6.1	5.3
11	2	32	31	29	27	28
12	2	33	34	33	30	35
13	2	42	34	35	32	28
14	2	27	24	24	26	25
15	2	22	24	23	19	19
16	2	18	15	16	14	16
17	2	16	13	14	14	11
18	2	32	29	28	31	29
19	2	25	19	20	24	17
20	2	24	22	21	24	21
MEAN		27.1	24.5	24.3	24.1	22.9
SD		7.8	7.5	6.9	6.5	7.3

---

[12]*And also in a design called a cross-over, where the person gets both the treatment and the control intervention at different times.*

[13]*As if there's something simplistic about quantum mechanics.*

which we've thrown in some more follow-up data. We've graphed the means in Figure 15-5. As you can see, the response to the drug is pretty immediate— people in the treated group have less pain after 1 month, and more or less stay at a decreased level of pain. Those in the control group get a little better, and again, stay a little better. Of course this is only one possibility (and perhaps an unlikely one); in a while we'll examine some other possibilities. For the moment, let's think about how we can analyze the data and be true to the pattern of change.

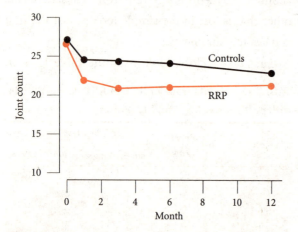

FIGURE 15-5   Joint count for the study of RRP (from Table 15-4).

Two obvious approaches come to mind, namely the two we just did: an ANOVA with five repeated measures, and an ANCOVA, using the pretest as the covariate and post-tests at 1, 3, 6, and 12 months as the repeated observations. If we do an ANOVA, we might still look for a Time × Group interaction, since we are expecting that there will be no difference at Time 0, but significant differences at 1, 3, 6, and 12 months. On the other hand, the data from the follow-up times really look like a main effect of treatment, not an interaction.

If we do an ANCOVA, things are much clearer. The baseline data are handled differently as a covariate; we would expect that the effect of treatment will simply end up as a main effect. The results of both analyses are shown in Table 15-5.

Now that's interesting! Despite the fact that we have four times as many observations of the treatment effect as before, the ANOVA now shows no overall significant effect in the main effect of Group or the Time × Group interaction, where we had an almost significant interaction before. By contrast, in the ANCOVA, the main effect of Group is now significant at the 0.012 level. What is going on here?

TABLE 15-5   ANOVA and ANCOVA of scores with multiple follow-ups at 1, 3, 6, and 12 months for the RCT of RRP

Source	Sum of Squares	df	Mean square	F	p
ANOVA results					
Group	151.3	1	151.3	0.967	0.33
Subject: Group	2815.9	18	156.44		
Time	339.3	4	84.8	20.1	0.001
Time Group	30.3	4	7.56	1.79	0.14
Error	304.0	72	4.22		
ANCOVA results					
Group	141.5	1	141.5	8.00	0.012
Pretest (covariate)	1848.8	1	1848.8	104.5	0.001
Subject: Group	300.9	17	17.7	44.8	0.001
Time	11.13	3	3.7	10.97	0.41
Time × Group	3.55	3	1.18	0.31	0.82
Time ×Pretest	20.21	3	6.74	1.76	0.17
Error	195.1	51	3.82		

The explanation lies in a close second look at Figure 15-2. When we do the ANOVA, the overall main effect of the treatment is washed out by the pretest values, which, since they occurred before the treatment took effect, are close together. Conversely, the Time × Group interaction amounts to an expectation of different differences between Treatment and Control groups at different times, and this effect happens only when you contrast the pretest values with the post-test values (which was fine when there was only one post-test value). In effect, the differences between treatments are now smeared out over the main effect and the interaction, neither of which are appropriate tests of the observed data. By contrast, the ANCOVA gives the pretest means special status and does not try to incorporate them into an overall test of treatment. Instead, it simply focuses on the relatively constant difference between treatment and control groups over the four post-test times, and appropriately captures this in the main effect of treatment.

In the situation where there are multiple follow-up observations, the right analysis is therefore an ANCOVA, with pretest as the covariate and the later observations as repeated dependent measures. Is this only the case when the treatment effect is relatively constant over time? As it turns out, no. But to see this, we have to go one further step into the analysis and also generate some new data.

MULTIPLE, TIME-DEPENDENT OBSERVATIONS

As we indicated, the situation in which the treatment acts almost instantly and does not change over time is likely as rare as hen's teeth. A more common scenario is one in which the treatment effect is slow to build and then has a gradually diminishing effect. One example of such a relationship is shown in the data of Table 15-6, where we have added some constants to the post-test observations to make the relationship over time somewhat more complex.

It is apparent that the treatment group shows continual improvement over time but with a law of diminishing returns, and the control group, as usual,

TABLE 15-6   Data from an RCT of RRP versus placebo with post-tests at 1, 3, 6, and 12 months, and linear and nonlinear changes over time

Subject	Group	Pretest 0 mo	Post-test 1 mo	3 mo	6 mo	12 mo
1	1	22	16	16	9.5	9
2	1	24	17	17	15.5	17
3	1	32	25	20	22.5	17
4	1	24	21	7	16.5	18
5	1	35	32	27	27.5	22
6	1	27	22	19	15.5	12
7	1	34	27	25	20.5	17
8	1	15	13	9	8.5	9
9	1	29	25	20	17.5	14
10	1	25	21	18	19.5	19
MEAN		26.7	21.9	17.8	17.3	15.4
SD		6.1	7.8	6.2	5.7	4.3
11	2	32	31	29	27	28
12	2	33	34	33	30	35
13	2	42	34	35	32	28
14	2	27	24	24	26	25
15	2	22	24	23	19	19
16	2	18	15	16	14	16
17	2	16	13	14	14	11
18	2	32	29	28	31	29
19	2	25	19	20	24	17
20	2	24	22	21	24	21
MEAN		27.1	24.5	24.3	24.1	22.9
SD		7.8	7.5	6.9	6.5	7.3

just rumbles along. This might be more obvious in the graph of the data shown in Figure 15-6. Here we see clearly that the relation between Time and JC in

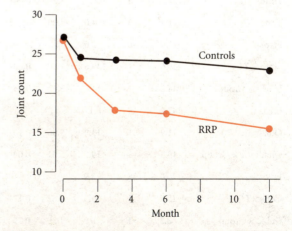

FIGURE 15-6   Joint count for the study of RRP (from Table 15-6).

the treatment group is kind of nonlinear—the sort of thing that might require a $(\text{Time})^2$ term as well as a linear term in Time. However, the control group data are still a straight horizontal line.

How do we put all this into the pot? First, we have to explicitly account for Time, since the straight ANOVA treats each X value as just nominal data—the results are the same regardless of the order in which we put the columns of data. We have somehow to tell the analysis that it's dealing with data at 0, 1, 3, 6, and 12 months. Second, it is apparent that we have to build in some kind of power series in order to capture the curvilinear change over time. Finally, we might even expect some interactions, indicating that the treated group has linear and quadratic terms but that the control group doesn't.

Believe it or not, all this happens almost at the push of a button. It's called **orthogonal decomposition.** When this button is pushed, the computer decomposes the Sum of Squares owing to Time and to the Time × Group interactions into linear, quadratic, and higher-order terms (one less term in the power series than the number of time points). The results are shown in Table 15-7.

TABLE 15-7 ANCOVA of follow-up scores with orthogonal decomposition for the RCT of RRP

Source	Sum of Squares	df	Mean square	F	p
Group	599.9	1	599.9	36.5	0.001
Pretest (covariate)	2266.1	1	2266.1	137.7	0.001
Subject: Group	279.7	17	16.5		
Time	167.1	3	55.7	9.29	0.001
Time × Group	71.9	3	24.0	4.00	0.012
Error	323.9	54	6.0		
Linear (T)	139.6	1	139.6	17.0	0.001
Linear × Group	44.2	1	44.2	5.41	0.03
Error	147.2	18	8.17		
Quadratic (T^2)	11.9	1	11.9	3.06	0.10
Quadratic × Group	19.5	1	19.5	5.01	0.04
Error	70.0	18	3.9		
Cubic (T^3)	15.5	1	15.5	2.62	0.12
Cubic × Group	8.2	1	8.2	1.39	0.25
Error	106.7	18	5.92		

Now, the first six lines of this horrendous mess should look familiar. They're completely analogous to the sources of variance we found before when we did an ANCOVA on the pretest and post-test scores. The numbers are different, of course, because we cooked the data some to yield a more complex relationship to time. In the next nine lines things get more interesting. By asking for an orthogonal decomposition, we told the computer to pay more attention to the time axis and fit the data over time to a power series regression, so we can test whether the relationship is linear, quadratic, or cubic, and so on. What emerges is an overall linear term ($F = 17.0$, $df = 1/18$, $p < 0.001$) showing that there is an overall trend downward, taking both lines into account. There is also an interaction with Group ($F = 5.41$, $df = 1/18$, $p = 0.03$), which signifies that the slopes of the two lines differ. Further down, there is a quadratic component interacting with Group ($F = 5.01$, $df = 1/18$, $p = 0.04$) showing that the line for the treated group has some curvature to it (this is not explicit in the interaction but, rather, an observation from the graph). Note that if we add up all these components, we get the three lines above that express the Time main effect and the Time × Group interaction. That is, the sum of the linear, quadratic, and cubic effects of Time ($139.6 + 11.9 + 15.5$) just equals 167.0, the main effect of Time. The interactions and error terms also sum to the Total Sums of Squares for the respective terms. We have decomposed the effects related to Time into linear, quadratic, and cubic terms that are **orthogonal**—they sum to the original. It's the same idea that we encountered when we did orthogonal planned comparisons as an adjunct to the one-way ANOVA—decomposing the Total Sum of Squares into a series of contrasts that all sum back to the original.

All this is quite neat (at least we think so), and all it requires is multiple observations over time and no missing data. Regrettably, although the multiple observations over time is easy enough to come by, persuading a bunch of patients to come back faithfully at exactly the appointed intervals, thereby missing the loving grandchild's birthday party or the free trip to Las Vegas, is as hard as Hades. This problem can be solved with another, almost magical technique, called *hierarchical linear modeling*, but for that you'll have to wait until the next chapter.

SUMMARY

✧ This chapter has explored three approaches to analyzing change. The simplest and most commonly used method is difference scores, which is analysed by a paired *t*-test. Repeated-measures ANOVA and ANCOVA can be generalized to the situation when there are three or more observations. And ANCOVA methods can usually yield more optimal and unbiased results.

GLOSSARY

regression to the mean　趋均数回归

reliability of difference scores　差分的信度

approximation　近似

differential regression toward the mean　差值趋均数回归

orthogonal decomposition　正交分解

optimal　最佳的

unbiased　无偏的

EXERCISES

1. The bane of all statistical tests is measurement error. Suppose you did a study looking at the ability of new Viagro to regenerate the hair on male scalps. You do a before/after study with a sample of 12 guys with thinning hair, before and after 2 weeks of using Viagro. Being the compulsive sort you are and desperate for something—anything—to prevent baldness, you count every single hair on their heads. Although they are thinning, the counts are still in the millions and, so, are highly reproducible from beginning to end. Regrettably, with a paired *t*-test, the differ-

ence is not quite significant, $p = 0.063$. If you proceeded to use more advanced tests, particularly repeated-measures ANOVA and ANCOVA, what might be the result?
   a. $p < 0.05$ for both ANOVA and ANCOVA
   b. $p = 0.06$ for ANOVA, $p < 0.05$ for ANCOVA
   c. $p = 0.06$ for both ANOVA and ANCOVA

2. A common practice in analyzing clinical trials is to measure patients at baseline and at follow-up visits at regular intervals until the declared end of the trial.

3. Frequently, the analysis is then conducted on the baseline and end-of-trial measures. Imagine a trial of a new antipsychotic drug, Loonix, involving measures of psychotic symptoms at baseline, 3, 6, 9, and 12 months (the declared end of the trial). The investigators report that there was a significant drop in psychotic symptoms in the treatment group (paired $t = -2.51$, $p < 0.05$), but the symptoms in the control group actually increased slightly (paired $t = +0.46$, n.s.)
   a. Is this analysis right or wrong?
   b. If the analysis was repeated, which of the following would be most appropriate? And what would be the likely result?
   i. Unpaired *t*-test on the difference scores from 0 to 12 months
   ii. Repeated-measures ANOVA on the scores at 0 and 12 months
   iii. ANCOVA on the scores at 3, 6, 9, and 12 months with time 0 as covariate

SUGGESTED READINGS AND WEBSITES

[1] Lai K,Kelley K. Accuracy in parameter estimation for ANCOVA and ANOVA contrasts: sample size planning via narrow confidence intervals. Br J Math Stat Psychol. 2012,65(2):350-370.

[2] Culpepper SA,Aguinis H. Using analysis of covariance (ANCOVA) with fallible covariates. Psychol Methods. 2011,16(2):166-178.

[3] Winkens B,van Breukelen GJ,Schouten HJ,et al. Randomized clinical trials with a pre- and a post-treatment measurement: repeated measures

versus ANCOVA models. ContempClin Trials. 2007,28(6):713-719.

[4] Van Breukelen GJ. ANCOVA versus change from baseline: more power in randomized studies,

more bias in nonrandomized studies [corrected]. J Clin Epidemiol. 2006,59(9):920-925.

[5] Peter LB. Analysis of pretest-posttest designs. New York: Chapman and Hall, 2000: 135-142.

CHAPTER THE SIXTEENTH
Analysis of Longitudinal Data: Hierarchical Linear Modeling

Techniques such as ANOVA and regression have difficulty handling missing data, differential dropouts between groups, and situations where the effect of one factor (e.g., experience of the physician) affects a number of people in the group. Hierarchical linear modeling is designed to deal with just these types of situation.

SETTING THE SCENE

In the course of running the study comparing Robert's Rectal Pills against placebo, our fearless investigator has encountered a number of problems. First, although the patients are scheduled to be assessed at 1, 3, 6, and 12 months, some have forgotten their appointments and have had to be seen at different times. Second, some patients have been unable to make the appointments at all, so their intermediate data points are missing. Third, even more troublesome, patients have dropped out of the study completely. Compounding this problem, the dropouts are unevenly distributed across groups, with more occurring in the placebo group than the RRP group. To make matters even worse, some patients in each group are seen by one physician and some by another, and it's possible that characteristics of the docs may affect the patients' responses. How on earth (or on Mars, for that matter) can all of these threats to the validity of the study be accounted for?

We wish we could say that the problems outlined in Setting the Scene are rare anomalies, owing to the incompetence of the investigative team, and that they can be avoided by careful planning and management of a study. However, they are probably more the rule in real life than the exceptions. It's very easy to write in a grant application that patients will be seen every three months, but much more difficult to actually pull this off. The study subjects may have competing demands on their time, such as an ill child at home, inability to take time off work, or even going on a vacation, so that appointments have to be rescheduled, or perhaps missed entirely. It's also quite common for there to be differential dropouts from various treatment groups. This could be because the placebo or comparison condition isn't having any effect, so the subject goes looking elsewhere for relief; or the active drug may have troubling side effects that the person doesn't feel balance the gains from the treatment.

Finally, in larger studies, subjects may be recruited from various places, and this may have an effect on the outcome. For example, a surgical trial could enroll patients from a number of hospitals, and we know that hospitals that see more patients usually have better outcomes than those that treat a smaller number of patients annually. Even within a single hospital, rates of morbidity and mortality differ from one sawbones to the next. If the study focuses on the effects of an educational intervention, then the same situation exists—schools differ from each other, and (as we all know from often bitter experience) teachers within a school range from those whom we worship to this day to those whose names are used to threaten little children. The problem is how to take these "higher level" effects into account. We could have one variable indicating the number of cases seen annually by the hospital, and another variable showing the number of cases seen by the physician, but we can't just tack these on to the records of each patient. If we did so, then all patients seen by Dr. X would have the same value, as would all patients seen in Hospital B. This violates one of the major assumptions of ANOVA and regression types of statistics, that the observations have to be independent from one another.

HIERARCHICAL LINEAR MODELING

What's in a Name?

A relatively recent technique that has been developed to deal with these issues is called **hierarchical linear modeling** (HLM). The problem is that it's also called by about half a dozen or so other names: growth curve analysis, random effects regression, mixed effects regression, multi-level models, empirical Bayes models, latent trajectory modeling, latent growth modeling, and who knows what else. All of these terms make sense, but it's like the blind men trying to describe an elephant, when one is holding its trunk, another its leg, and the third its tail—they're accurate, but only up to a point, because each is describing just one aspect of the beast. Many of these terms are the same; they are accurate but incomplete in that they're highlighting only one aspect of the technique—the statistical method (e.g., random or mixed effects regression), its usefulness in measuring change (trajectory or growth modeling), or its ability to deal with variables at different levels (hierarchical). To avoid confusion, we're going to use the term HLM throughout this chapter, but be aware that other people may be describing exactly the same technique, but use different terms to say what they're doing.

In this chapter, we'll focus primarily on one aspect of HLM, the analysis of longitudinal data. The reasons are twofold: it is probably the most widely used application, and to go beyond it would require a book in its own right. We'll also dip our toes into using HLM to account for clustering of subjects.

What Do We Need?

When using HLM to look at change over time, there are three requirements: (1) at least three data points per person, (2) an outcome that changes over time, and (3) some metric for measuring time.

1. **Three data points.** Because, as we'll see, the way HLM operates is to fit a line that best approximates each individual's change over time, there must be at least three data points per person. This may seem somewhat more restrictive than the two points

needed for simple gain scores, but it other ways, it frees us up considerably. With all other techniques that measure change over time (e.g., repeated-measures ANOVA, MANOVA, and the like), there are restrictions that hamper us in other ways. With ANOVA, the time points should be relatively evenly spaced, such as every week or every three months. Violating this plays havoc with the assumption of equal correlations across time. MANOVA relaxes this assumption, but as with ANOVA, it requires complete data for each person. Also, both of these approaches assume that all of the subjects are tested at equivalent times; you can't test one person on weeks 1, 3, 5, and 7 following an intervention; and another person at weeks 2, 4, 6, and 8 (much less 2, 6, and 12). With HLM, as long as there are at least three points, it doesn't matter when those times are. So, a person can be late for the follow-up visit, miss a visit, or even drop out of the study, and as long as there are at least three data points, HLM will easily accommodate this.

You may wonder why we need three data points, since we can fit a perfectly straight line with only two. There are three answers to this: one methodological, one statistical, and one based on measurement theory. The methodological answer is that with only two data points, we cannot determine the nature of the change. Figure 16-1 shows three of an infinite number of ways that people may change between two assessments. If the response were improvement in functioning, it makes a lot of difference whether a person improves quickly and then plateaus, starts

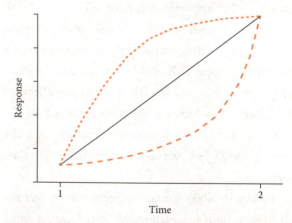

FIGURE 16-1 Three possible ways people can change between two assessments.

off slowly but shows greater improvement over time, or simply maintains improvement as a linear change with time. The more data points we have, the more accurate a picture we can get.

The statistical reason is a consequence of what we said in the first sentence—you can fit a *perfectly* straight line. That is, there is no estimate of any error, and without any error estimates, you can't run tests of significance. On the other hand, it is highly unlikely that three measures will all fall on a perfectly straight line, so there will be three estimates of how far the data points deviate from the least-squares estimate. Finally, from a measurement perspective, with only two points there is confounding between true change and measurement error. We don't know whether there was true change or whether, because of possible error, the scores were spuriously low on the first occasion and spuriously high on the second. The more time periods we have, the less likely this becomes.

2. **An outcome that changes over time.** This seems so obvious that we hesitate to mention it, but if we didn't, we can be sure that someone will use HLM with gender or hair color as the dependent variable (DV). The purpose of HLM is to determine whether different people *change* over time, and what the determinants of the rate of change may be (e.g., membership in one group or another, getting or not getting an intervention, demographic variables). If the outcome doesn't change, there ain't nothin' to model.

Another implication of this is that there must be enough time between measurements for something to have happened. If you're measuring recovery in activities in daily living following a stroke, for instance, it doesn't make sense to assess the person on days 1, 2, and 3; as we said in the previous paragraph, ain't nothin' there to model.

3. **A metric for measuring time.** Because with repeated-measures ANOVA or MANOVA we assume that everyone is tested at the same time, we don't have to keep track of when each individual is tested, except in our heads. But, the penalty for relaxing the restriction regarding when the data are

collected is that we have to let the computer know. The reason is that if a person's scores on some instrument were 5, 10, and 15, this would result in a very steep slope if the data points were only one week apart from one another; but would be a very shallow slope if the interval were years rather than weeks. Because, as we'll see, the slope is one of the main things we're interested in, we'd better get it right.

STEPPING THROUGH THE ANALYSIS

Step 1. Examine the Data

Although HLM is able to fit almost any shape of line to the data, the best place to start (and often to stop) is with a straight line. This is similar to multiple regression; we can throw in quadratic terms, cubic terms, and even try to fit the data with Shmedlap's inverse hypergeonormal function, but for the vast majority of cases, a simple linear relationship will suffice. So, it's a good idea to try fitting a straight line for each subject. In Figure 16-2, we've plotted the improvement score for the first six subjects in the RRP group, and we use that very powerful test for linearity, the eyeball check. Needless to say, not every person's data will be well fitted, but we don't want the majority of curves to look too deviant. However, if it seems as if most of the subjects' data follow a different type of curve, we should think of either transforming the data so they become linear, or using a model with a higher order time effect, such as Time. Note that Subject 5 missed the third follow-up visit, but we still have enough data to include her in the analysis.

The next thing to look at is the pattern of the correlations over time, because with the more powerful HLM programs, we'll have to specify what that pattern is. There are many possibilities. But, as a starting point, there are three that are most common; ranging from the most to the least restrictive, they are compound symmetric, autoregressive, and unstructured. With **compound symmetry**, the variances are equal across time and all the covariances are equal;[1] in simpler terms, the correlation between the data at Time 1 and Time 2 is the same as between Time 3 and

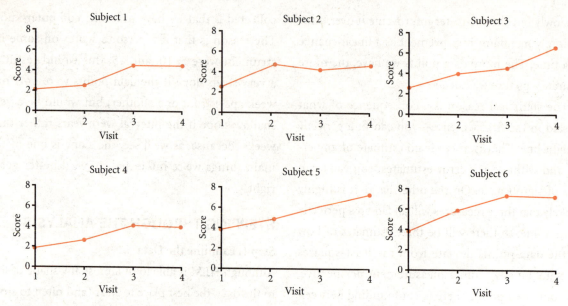

FIGURE 16-2   Checking that subjects' data are more or less linear.

Time 4. This isn't too improbable, but compound symmetry also requires them to be equivalent to the correlation between Time 1 and Time 4. [2]A more realistic picture of what really happens over time is captured by the **autoregressive model**, in which the longer the interval, the lower the correlation. So, we would find that the correlation between Times 1 and 3 is lower than between Times 1 and 2, and that between Times 1 and 4 it is lower still. If there doesn't seem to be any pattern present, we would use an **unstructured correlation matrix**. The advantage of more restrictive models is that they require fewer parameters, and this translates into more power. So, the unstructured pattern is the easiest to specify, but you pay a price for this.

At this point, it's a good idea to consider whether you should *center* the data, which we discussed in the chapter on multiple regression. As we're sure you remember, one major advantage of centering is to make the intercept more interpretable. If the time variable, for example, is the person's age or year in school, then without centering, the intercept tells you the value of the DV when the person is 0 years old,

or in Grade 0; admittedly not overly useful information. In the example of the trial of the usefulness of RRP, the time variable is the number of the follow-up visit, so it may not be worthwhile to center, since the intercept would reflect the person's status when the treatment ended.

Step 2. Fit Individual Regression Lines

The next step is up to the computer. A regression line is fitted to the data for each subject, so that we get two variables for each person, i: a slope (π_{0i}) and an intercept (π_{1i}). [3]An example for one subject is shown in Figure 16-3. It is because of this that the technique has two of its other names, *random effects regression* and *mixed effects regression*. In ordinary least squares regression (and all of its variants, such as logistic regression), we assume that the intercept and slopes that emerge from the equation apply to all individuals in the sample; that is, they're fixed for all subjects. In HLM, though, each person has his or her unique intercept and slope, so that they're *random effects*. The term *mixed effects* comes into play at the next stage, when these random effects are themselves entered into yet another regression equation, where

---

[1]*We don't know why they couldn't simply have called this constant. Guess it didn't sound intimidating enough.*

[2]*This is the assumption underlying repeated-measures ANOVA, which is why it has been replaced by MANOVA, which doesn't have this restriction.*

[3] *Here we're using πs for the slope and intercept as many other authors do so.*

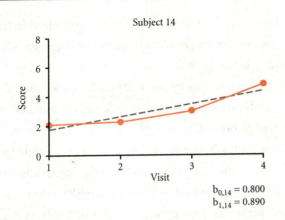

Subject 14

$b_{0,14} = 0.800$
$b_{1,14} = 0.890$

FIGURE 16-3   Fitting a straight line for each person.

the terms—the average slope and intercept for the group—are fixed.

Didn't we just violate one of the assumptions of linear regression in this step? Having the predictor variables consist of the same measurement over time for an individual most definitely violates the requirement that the errors are independent from one another. So why did we do it? Because the bible tells us we can. In this case, the bible is an excellent book on HLM by Singer and Willett (2003). The rationale is that violating the assumption of independence of the predictors plays absolute havoc with the estimates of the standard errors, but it doesn't affect the estimates of the parameters themselves. Because we're interested only in getting the parameters—the slope and intercept—for each person, and we aren't doing any significance testing, it doesn't matter.

Before continuing further with the analyses, it's a good idea to stop here and see how well the linear model fits the data for each person. With some programs, you can examine the residuals and perhaps even the value of R^2 at an individual subject level. The residual is simply the difference between the actual and predicted values of the DV, and we'd like them to be relatively small. This would mean that the values for R^2 should be moderate to large. Again, this won't hold for every person, but it should be true for most.

Step 3. Fit the Level 1 Model

At this point, we're ready to derive the model at the lowest level of the hierarchy, the individual. The form of the model is:

$$Y_{ij} = \pi_{0i} + \pi_{1i}Time_{1j} + \varepsilon_{ij} \qquad (16\text{-}1)$$

This means that person i's score at time j is a function of his or her intercept (π_{0i}), slope (π_{1i}), the value of the variable that keeps track of time or occasion ($Time_{ij}$), and the ubiquitous error (ε_{ij}). We assume that everybody has the same *form* of the equation, but that the values of π_0 and π_1 vary from one person to the next; hence the term *random effects* regression. We can even get a little bit fancy here. If, when we were eyeballing the data, we thought that they would be better described by a quadratic equation (that is, increasing ever faster as time went on), we can throw in another term, such as:

$$Y_{ij} = \pi_{0i} + \pi_{1i}Time_{ij} + \pi_{2i}Time_{ij}^2 + \varepsilon_{ij} \qquad (16\text{-}2)$$

but we'd need at least four data points per person. For now, though, we'll omit the $Time^2$ term.

We said that ε is the error term. Well, that's not entirely true. Part of what contributes to ε is indeed error, owing to all the frailties that human flesh (and its measurement tools) is heir to (W. Shakespeare, personal communication). But, in other ways, it resembles the Error terms in ANOVA, in that a better description would be "unexplained variance." With ANOVA, we try to reduce error by introducing other factors that can account for that variance. Similarly, in HLM, we may be able to reduce ε by including other factors that may account for variation between people or within people over time (Singer and Willett, 2003). Indeed, as we'll see later, we actually hope that there is unexplained variance at this stage of the game that can be reduced when we include things like group membership into the mix.

There's one very helpful implication of Equation (16-1). We've tossed all of the measurement error into the ε term, but we're using the estimates of the π terms when we move up to the next highest level. That means that these estimates *are measured separately from the measurement error* and they're not affected by attenuation caused by such errors (Llabre et al., 2004).

Step 4. Fit the Level 2 Model

Before we go any further, it's worthwhile to see if there's any variance to model in the next steps; that is, is anything going on? We do this by fitting the simplest of models:

$$\pi_{0i} = \beta_0 + \mu_{0i} \qquad (16\text{-}3)$$

$$\pi_{1i} = \beta_1 + \mu_{1i} \qquad (16\text{-}4)$$

In Equation (16-3), β_0 is the mean intercept for the group (the fixed effect), and μ_{0i} is the difference for each person between his or her intercept and the mean for the group (the random effect). Equation (16-4) is the same thing for the slope (β_1) and the residual difference between each person's slope and the mean (μ_{1i}). If the models fit, then we might as well pack up our bags and head for home, because there's nothing going on—all of the subjects have the same slope and intercept, so it's fruitless to try to determine why different people change at different rates.

If our prayers are answered and the models don't fit the data well, we can take all those parameter estimates we calculated at the individual person level and figure out what's going on at the group level. What we are interested in is whether the two groups differ over time: if their intercepts are the same (in this example, whether they are starting out at the same place after treatment), and if their slopes are the same (whether or not they're changing at the same rate over time). That means that we have to calculate two regression lines, one for each group, with an intercept and a slope for each. The way it's done is to determine the intercept for the control group, and how much the treatment group's intercept differs from it, and then do the same for the slope. Hence, we have two equations to get those four parameters. For the intercept parameters, we have:

$$\pi_{0i} = \gamma_{00} + \gamma_{01} Group_i + \zeta_{0i} \qquad (16\text{-}5)$$

where γ_{00} is the average intercept for the control subjects (γ is the Greek letter "gamma"), γ_{01} is the difference in the intercept between the control and RRP groups, $Group_i$ indicates group membership, and ζ_{0i} is the residual (ζ is the Greek "zeta").

For the slope parameters, the equation is:

$$\pi_{1i} = \gamma_{10} + \gamma_{11} Group_i + \zeta_{1i} \qquad (16\text{-}6)$$

where γ_{10} is the average slope for the control subjects, γ_{11} is the difference in the slope between the groups, and ζ_{1i} is the residual.[4]

So, before going any further, let's see what all those funny looking squiggles mean, by looking at a typical output, as in Table 16-1. The labels at first seem a bit off; the third line gives us the intercept for the slope. But realize that we're going to end up with two regression lines, one for the RRP group and one for the control group. The first line tells us that the intercept for the control group is 0.732, and the second line says that the intercept for the RRP group is $(0.732 + 1.208) = 1.940$. The third line indicates that the slope for the control group is 0.481, and the fourth tells us that the slope for the RRP group is $(0.481 + 0.421) = 0.902$. So, to summarize, what we've done is derive one regression line for the control group, and one for the RRP group. For the control group, it's:

$$0.732 + Time \times 0.481 \qquad (16\text{-}7)$$

and for the RRP group, it's:

$$1.940 + Time \times 0.902 \qquad (16\text{-}8)$$

Let's plot those and see what's going on. The results are shown in Figure 16-4.

TABLE 16-1   Output of the fixed effects of HLM

		Parameter	Estimate	SE	z
Intercept, π_{0i}	Intercept Group	γ_{00}	0.732	0.215	3.405
		γ_{01}	1.208	0.234	5.162
Slope, π_{1i}	Intercept Group	γ_{10}	0.481	0.239	2.013
		γ_{11}	0.421	0.041	10.268

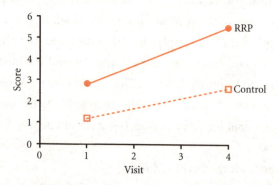

FIGURE 16-4   Plotting the fixed effects.

---

[4] As you can see, the major limit with regard to how many levels we can have in HLM is not mathematical, but the fact that we're quickly running out of Greek letters to use.

The z values in Table 16-1 are figured out the same way all z values are; they are the estimates divided by their standard errors. For reasons that we'll explain at the end of this chapter, those SEs are *asymptotic* estimates (i.e., they get more accurate as the sample size increases), so some programs label them as *ASE* rather than *SE*. In this case, they're all statistically significant, meaning that the control group began above 0 (γ_{00}); the RRP group began at a significantly higher level (γ_{01}); there is a significant change for the control group over time (γ_{10}); and that the RPP group changed at a significantly different rate (γ_{11}).

Those two residual terms, ζ_{0i} and ζ_{1i}, reflect the fact that the slopes and intercepts for individuals vary around these group estimates; again, they reflect *error* or *unexplained variance*. What we are interested in is not the actual values of those ζs but rather their variances. The amount of variance of ζ_{0i} is denoted by σ_0^2, and that for ζ_{1i} as σ_1^2. There's also a third term, σ_{01}^2, which is the covariance between ζ_{0i} and ζ_{1i}. (In this, we're following the convention of Singer and Willett (2003), but to make your life more interesting, they state that other texts and computer programs use different Greek letters and other subscripts.) To be more exact, σ_0^2 and σ_1^2 are *conditional* residual variances, because they are conditional on the predictor(s) already in the equation; in this example, they tell how much variance is left over after accounting for the effect of Group. The covariance term, σ_{01}^2, is there because it's possible that the rate of change depends on the person's starting level. We examined one aspect of this phenomenon in the previous chapter, because this covariance may be due to regression toward the mean—the greater the deviation from the mean, the more regression. Other possible reasons may be that people who start off with higher scores may be near the ceiling of the test or closer to a physiological limit, so they have less room to improve; or that those with higher scores have a head start on those with lower scores. Whatever the reason, σ_{01}^2 lets us measure its effects.

So let's take a look at those variance components and see what they tell us. In Table 16-2, we see that there's still unexplained within-person variance at Level 1 (σ_e^2). This means that we may want to go back and look for time varying predictors at the level of the individual. These are factors that could change from one follow-up visit to the next, such as the person's compliance with taking the meds or whether the person is using other, over-the-counter drugs. At Level 2, there isn't any residual variance for the intercept (σ_0^2), but there is for the slope (σ_1^2), even accounting for group membership. This tells us that we should look for other factors that may explain the variance, both time-varying ones as well as time-invariant ones, such as sex or age.[5]

TABLE 16-2 Output of variance components from HLM

		Parameter	Estimate	SE	z
Level 1	Within person, ε_{ij}	σ_e^2	15.252	1.839	8.295
Level 2	Intercept, ζ_{0i}	σ_0^2	14.745	17.722	0.832
	Slope, ζ_{1i}	σ_1^2	20.893	4.003	5.219
	Covariance between ζ_{0i} and ζ_{1i}	σ_{01}^2	−15.851	5.024	−3.155

Sidestep: Putting the Equations Together

So far, we've presented the two levels of the analysis—the individuals and the groups—as two sets of regression equations. That's both an easy way to conceptualize what's being done, and the method that was used in the far, distant past (say 10 years ago). But, let's continue to follow Singer and Willett (2003) and see how we can combine the equations, which is actually the way most HLM programs like them to be specified.

In Equation (16-1), we defined Y_{ij} in terms of π_{0i} and π_{1i}. Then, in Equations (16-5) and (16-6), we defined these two values of π in terms of different

---

[5]*We know all too well from personal experience that age actually does change—that's why we're using the photograph on the back cover we took for the first edition—but (a) it's the same change for everyone, and (b) the amount of change in age is relatively small over the course of the study compared with the whole of our lives. Hence, we're safe to consider it a time-invariant effect.*

values of γs. Putting it all together, what we get is:

$$Y_{ij} = \pi_{0i} + \pi_{li} Time_{ij} + \varepsilon_{ij}$$
$$= (\gamma_{00} + \gamma_{01} Group_i + \zeta_{0i}) + (\gamma_{10} + \gamma_{11} Group_i + \zeta_{ij})$$
$$Time_{ij} + \varepsilon_{ij} \tag{16-9}$$

where the three terms inside the first set of brackets give us the Level 1 intercept based on the Level 2 parameters, and the terms in the second set of parentheses do the same for the slope. We can go one further step by multiplying out the terms in the second set and rearranging the results, giving us:

$$Y_{ij} = [\gamma_{00} + \gamma_{10} Time_{ij} + \gamma_{01} Group_i + \gamma_{11}(Group_i \times Time_{ij})]$$
$$+ [\zeta_{0i} + \zeta_{1i} Time_{ij} + \varepsilon_{ij}] \tag{16-10}$$

This looks much more formidable than Equation (16-9), but in one way, it's actually more informative. The first part of the formula, with the γ symbols, shows the influence of the measured variables on a person's score at a given time. It consists of where the person started out (γ_{00}); the effects of Time and Group; and the interaction between the two, which allows the groups to diverge over time. It also consists of the slopes and intercepts of the RRP and control groups. The second part of the equation, with the ζs, reflects the various sources of error—around the intercept (ζ_{0i}), at each measurement over time (ζ_{1i}), and what's still unexplained (ε_{ij}).

Some Advantages of HLM

We already mentioned a few of the major advantages of analyzing change this way rather than with repeated-measures ANOVA or MANOVA—the ability to handle missing data points (as long as at least three times are left), the relaxation of the restriction about measuring at fixed times for all subjects, and the elimination of measurement error. After being so blessed, it's hard to imagine that there's even more, but there is. One of the major threats to the validity of a study is not so much people dropping out (although that can affect the sample size), but *differential dropouts from the two groups, as we men*tioned at the beginning of the chapter. That is, if more people drop out of the study from one group rather than the other, and if the reasons are related to the intervention (e.g., side effects or lack of effectiveness), then any estimate of the relative change between the

groups would be biased by this confounding.

If we're lucky, though, HLM can account for this. If, for example, people drop out because the placebo is not having an effect (duh!), then this should be reflected in a smaller slope for the dropouts than the remainers. HLM can (a) tell us if this is indeed happening, (b) retain the people in the analyses, and (c) model how much they would have changed had they remained in the study. This naturally assumes that they would have continued to change at the same rate, of course, but it's a more conservative assumption (i.e., it works against rejecting the null hypothesis) than *last observation carried forward* (LOCF). As the name implies, LOCF is a way of trying to minimize the loss of data by taking the last valid data point from a subject before he or she dropped out, and using that value for all subsequent missing values. LOCF is conservative when it's applied to the treatment group, in that it assumes that no further change occurs, but it may be too liberal when applied to the comparison group. Using HLM with both groups is probably a much better way to proceed.

Dealing with Clusters

Earlier in this chapter, we mentioned that some studies enroll participants in clusters. For example, in the Burlington Randomized Trial of the Nurse Practitioner (Spitzer et al., 1974), family physicians were randomized to have or not have a nurse practitioner (NP) assigned to their practices, and the outcome consisted of the prevalence of a number of "tracer conditions" among the patients. So, what's the unit of analysis? We can look to see how many patients in each arm of the study had these different conditions. But, we expect that people within the same family share not only the same house, but also the same food, similar attitudes toward health, and that they inhale the same germ-laden air. So, it's likely that people within a family are more similar to each other than they are to people in a different family, which means that mom, pop, and the two kids can't be treated as four separate observations. Similarly, the "philosophy" of treatment of any doc or NP— that is, when to intervene for hypertension, or how to treat otitis media—would apply to all of his or her patients, so the patients or families within any one practice aren't truly independent either. In summary, patients are *clustered* (or *nested*) within families, and families within practices.[6]

Now, HLM didn't exist back then, but these days, this would be an ideal situation in which to use it. The stretch from the previous example to this one isn't too far. With RRP, we can think of the various times as being nested within an individual; here, the clustering is within groups of people. Indeed, we can combine these by having time nested within the individual, and all of the measures for the individual nested within the groups. To keep us (and you) from going completely bonkers, though, let's restrict ourselves to one measurement of blood pressure. Now, the Level 1 (individual) model, comparable to Equation (16-1), would be:

$$Y_{ij} = \pi_{0j} + \pi_{1j} \, Family_j + \varepsilon_{ij} \qquad (16\text{-}11)$$

where Y_{ij} is the blood pressure of person i in family j, π_{0j} is the average blood pressure from family j, π_{1i} is the slope for family j, and $Family_j$ should be self-explanatory.

The Level 2 (family) model for the intercept is:

$$\pi_{0j} = \gamma_{00} + \gamma_{01} \, Group_j + \zeta_{0j} \qquad (16\text{-}12)$$

and for the slope is:

$$\pi_{1j} = \gamma_{10} + \gamma_{11} \, Group_j + \zeta_{1j} \qquad (16\text{-}13)$$

where $Group_j$ indicates whether the family is in the nurse practitioner or control group. If there were more than one family practice per condition, we would have a third level; the second level would substitute *Practice* for *Group*, and it would be this third level that would include the *Group* variable.

Whenever you're dealing with clusters, you should calculate the intraclass correlation coefficient (ICC). If you hunger for even more details about the ICC, see Streiner and Norman (2014).

SAMPLE SIZE

Although we've presented HLM as a series of multiple regressions, in fact we (or rather, the computer programs) don't use least squares regression any more. For the most part, they're calculated by a procedure called **maximum likelihood estimation** (MLE). MLE has many desirable properties, including the fact that the standard errors are smaller than those derived from other methods, it yields accurate estimates of the population parameters, and that they are normally distributed. But, these happen *asymptotically*; that is, as the sample size gets closer to infinity. So how many subjects do we need? Singer and Willet (2003) say that 10 is too few, and 100 000 may be too many. Does that give you enough guidance?

Long (1997) recommends a minimum of 100 subjects for cross-sectional studies, and says that 500 people are "adequate." Those estimates are a bit narrower, but not by much. Returning to our bible, Singer and Willett (2003) say there are too many aspects of the data and the actual ML method used to be more precise, but that p levels and confidence intervals derived from "small" samples should be regarded with caution.[7]

REPORTING GUIDELINES

In many ways, reporting the results of HLM is very similar to reporting the results of multiple regression: you need the (1) standardized and (2) unstandardized regression weights, (3) their standard error, (4) the t-tests, and (5) their significance levels; and these are best given in a table. But, because HLM is an order of magnitude more complex than regression, more has to be reported. This would include:

1. Unlike programs for ANOVA or regression, those for HLM each work somewhat differently, so you should state which program you used.

2. What method of parameter estimation was used (e.g., maximum likelihood, restricted maximum likelihood, etc.).

3. The sample size at each level of the analysis.

4. How missing data and outliers were handled at each level. (Notice that we didn't say "If there are missing data …." We assume there will be.)

---

[6] *In fact, some wags have suggested that this was one of the largest trials with N = 2.*

[7] *Without, though, ever defining what "small" is.*

5. Tests of the assumptions of the model, such as normality, homogeneity of variance, multicollinearity, and so on.

6. What pattern of correlations over time were used: compound symmetry, autoregressive, unstructured, or whatever.

7. Because the model is usually built up sequentially, from one with no predictors to the final one, each one should be described. The table should indicate how much better each more restrictive model is.

8. The table of coefficients, which we described above, for the fixed and random effects.

9. The intraclass correlation coefficients at the various levels.

SUMMARY

✧ This chapter has barely scratched the surface of HLM. We could write an entire book on it, but we won't, because many already exist. Perhaps the most readable is the one by Singer and Willett (2003), but it's limited to growth curves. The standard reference is by Bryk and Raudenbush (1992), but it's fairly rough sledding to get through. However, their program, called HLM (Bryk, Raudenbush, and Congdon, 1996) is the standard by which others are measured. Other books you can try are by Hox (2002) and Goldstein (1995). A warning, though: don't try HLM at home unless you have a knowledgeable person handy at the other end of the phone.

✧ HLM allow the analysis of between-subject and within-subject sources of variation in the longitudinal responses, because it explicitly distinguishes fixed and random effects. One very appealing aspect of HLM is its flexibility in accommodating any degree of imbalance in longitudinal data, coupled with its ability to account for the covariance among repeated measures in a relatively parsimonious way. Thus HLM is well suited for analysing inherently unbalanced longitudinal data.

GLOSSARY

hierarchical linear modeling (HLM) 多层线性模型

compound symmetry 符合对称性
autoregressive model 自回归模型
correlation matrix 相关矩阵
maximum likelihood estimation (MLE) 极大似然估计

SUGGESTED READINGS AND WEBSITES

[1] Singer JD, Willett JB. Applied longitudinal data analysis: Modeling change and event occurrence. Oxford university press, 2003.

[2] Bryk AS, Raudenbush SW. Hierarchical linear models: Applications and data analysis methods. 1992.

[3] Fitzmaurice GM, Nan ML, Ware JH. Applied Longitudinal Analysis. 2nd ed. Journal of Biopharmaceutical Statistics, 2012, 23(4):940-941.

[4] Verbeke G, Molenberghs G. Linear mixed models for longitudinal data. Springer Science & Business Media, 2009.

[5] Naumova EN, Must A, Laird NM. Tutorial in biostatistics: evaluating the impact of 'critical periods' in longitudinal studies of growth using piecewise mixed effects models. International Journal of Epidemiology, 2001, 30(6): 1332-1341.

[6] Bryk AS, Raudenbush SW, Congdon RT. HLM: Hierarchical linear and nonlinear modeling with the HLM/2L and HLM/3L programs. SSI Scientific Software International, 1996.

CHAPTER THE SEVENTEEN

Principal Components and Factor Analysis

Factor analysis looks at the pattern of relationships among variables and tries to explain that pattern in terms of a smaller number of underlying hypothetical factors.

SETTING THE SCENE

You have been appointed Dean of Admissions at the Mesmer School of Health Care and Tonsorial Trades. Your contract stipulates that you will receive a bonus of $100 000 each year that the graduation rate exceeds 75%. After signing the contract, you find the success rate for the last 5 years has averaged only 23.7%. You decide that the only way to increase this figure is to impose tighter admissions criteria, and you meet with the faculty to draw up a list of the desired attributes of successful students. They arrive at three: (1) the eyes of an eagle, (2) the hands of a woman, and (3) the soul of a Byzantine usurer. You devise a test battery for applicants, with five tests in each area, just to be sure you've covered the areas well. But, the test battery need takes 32.6 hours to administer, and you're still not sure that all of the tests in each area are tapping the right skills. Is there any way you can (1) make sure you're measuring these three areas and (2) eliminate tests that are either redundant or measuring something entirely different?

BASIC CONCEPTS

As usual, we wouldn't be asking these questions unless the answers were "yes." The technique in this chapter is called **factor analysis** (FA). It differs from other techniques that we discussed earlier in one important way: no distinction is made between independent and dependent variables; all are treated equally and the data come from one group of subjects. That is, the goal of this technique is to examine the *structure* of the relationship among the variables, not to see how they relate to other variables, such as group membership or a set of dependent variables. For this reason, some people have called the FA as an "untargeted" statistical technique.

According to the above questions, the Dean will use this procedure to: (1) explore the relationship among the variables, (2) see if the pattern of results can be explained by a smaller number of underlying constructs (sometimes called **latent variables** or **factors**), (3) test some hypotheses about the data, and (4) reduce the number of variables to a more manageable size. There is a lot of confusion regarding the terminology of FA. Some people (erroneously) make it synonymous with a related technique called **principal components analysis** (PCA). The two techniques are not identical, and you have to make sure which one is appropriate when you using them.

WHAT ARE "FACTORS?"

What he hopes to find is shown in Figure 17-1: three different attributes, labeled in the large circles on the left and each tapped by five of the tests. Strictly speaking, you can't see or measure "Soul of a Byzantine Usurer" directly; you *infer* its presence from behaviors that are supposedly based on it. We expect (based on our theory of what Byzantine usurers are like) that people who have more of this attribute would charge higher interest rates, act more "Scrooge-like," overcharge more, and so on, than would people who have less of the attribute. To give another example, we also can't see intelligence; what we see and measure are various manifestations of intelligence. If our theory of intelligence is correct, people who have more of it should have a larger vocabulary, know more facts, work out puzzles faster, and complete more school than do people with less of it. What we measure are the purported conse-

Attribute

Variable

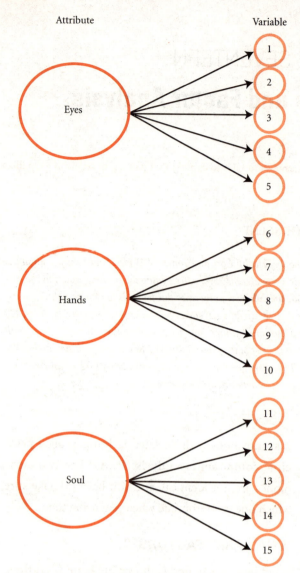

FIGURE 17-1 Three attributes (Eyes, Hands, and Soul), each measured by five tests.

quences of the attribute, and we say that the common thread that makes them all correlate with each other is the underlying attribute itself.

The 15 tests chosen by the Dean of Admissions

Eyes

1. Visual acuity
2. Color blindness
3. Nystagmus
4. Attention to detail
5. Preference for carrots

Hand

1. Fine motor dexterity
2. Gross motor dexterity
3. Pond's softness test
4. Hand tremor

5. Ability to pick up checks

Soul

1. Interest calculation
2. Scrooge factor
3. Dunning ability test
4. Overcharging index
5. Double billing

In psychological jargon, we call these attributes **hypothetical constructs;** in statistics, they are called **factors** or **latent variables**. One purpose of FA is to determine if numerous measures (these could be paper-and-pencil tests, individual items on the tests themselves, physical characteristics, or whatever) can be explained on the basis of a smaller number of these factors. In this example, the Dean wants to know if applicants' performances on these 15 tests can be explained by the 3 underlying factors; he will use these techniques to *confirm* his hypothesis (although, as we said, it's better to use *confirmatory* factor analysis to do this, which we'll explain in Chapter 18). In other situations, we may not know beforehand how many factors there are, and the object in doing the statistics is to determine this number. This is referred to as the *exploratory* use of FA.

Actually, Figure 17-1 oversimplifies the relationship between factors and variables. If variables 1 through 5 were determined solely by the Eye of an Eagle factor, they would all yield identical results. The correlations among them would all be 1.00, and only one would need to be measured. In fact, the value of each variable is determined by *two* points: (1) the degree to which it is correlated with the factor (represented by the arrow coming from the large circles); and (2) its *unique* contribution—what variable 1 measures that variables 2 through 5 do not, and so on (shown by the arrow from the boxes labelled U in Figure 17-2). We can show this somewhat more complicated, but accurate, picture in Figure 17-3.

What exactly is meant by "uniqueness"? We can best define it in terms of its converse, **communality**. The communality of a variable can be approximated by its multiple correlation, R^2, with all of the other variables; that is, how much it has in common with them and can be predicted by them. The *uniqueness*

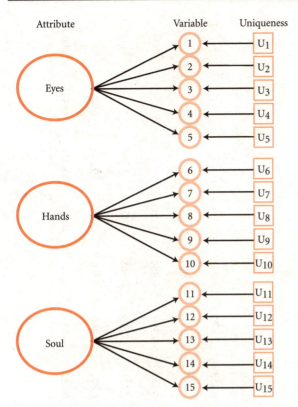

FIGURE 17-2 Adding the unique component of each variable to Figure 17-1.

for variable 1 is then simply $(1-R_1^2)$; that portion of variable 1 that cannot be predicted by (i.e., is unrelated to) the remaining variables.

Before we go on, let's look at the Figure 17-2, it assumes that Factor 1 plays a role only for variables 1 through 5; Factor 2, for 6 through 10; and Factor 3, for 11 through 15. In reality, each of the factors influences all of the variables to some degree, as in Figure 17-3. We've added lines showing these influences only for the contribution of the first factor on the other 10 variables. Factors 2 and 3 exert a similar influence on the variables, but putting in the lines would have complicated the picture too much. What we hope to find is that the influence of the factors represented by the dashed lines is small when compared with that of the solid lines.

HOW IT IS DONE

The Correlation Matrix

FA usually begins with a correlation matrix. On a technical note, we start with a correlation matrix mainly because the variables are each measured with very different units, so we convert them to standard

scores. If the variables all used a similar metric (such as when we factor analyze items on a test, each using a 0-to-7 scale), it would be better to begin with a variance-covariance matrix.

If lucky, we'd probably not need to go any further than a correlation matrix; we'd find that all of the variables that measure one factor correlate very strongly with each other and do not correlate with the measures of the other attributes (i.e., the picture in Figure 17-2). However, this is almost never the case. The correlations within a factor are rarely much above 0.85, and the measures are almost always correlated with "unrelated" ones to some degree (more like Figure 17-3). Thus we are left looking for patterns in a matrix of $[n \times (n - 1) \div 2]$ unique correlations; in our case, $(15 \times 14) \div 2$, or 105 (not counting the 1.000s along the main diagonal), as shown in Table 17-1.

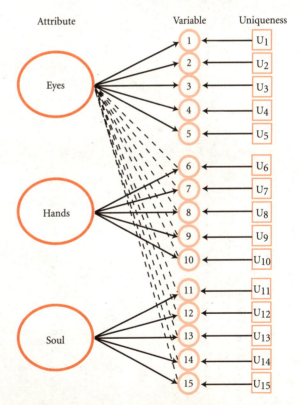

FIGURE 17-3 A more accurate picture, with each factor contributing to each variable.

Before the next step, it's worthwhile to do a few "diagnostic checks" on this correlation matrix. If no underlying factorial structure existed, resulting in the correlation matrix consisting of purely random

TABLE 17-1   Correlation matrix of the 15 tests

	Acuity	Color	Nystagmus	Detail	Carrots	Fine dexterity	Gross dexterity	Softness	Tremor	Checks	Interest	Scrooge	Dunning	Overcharge	Billing
Acuity	1.000														
Color	0.318	1.000													
Nystagmus	0.403	0.317	1.000												
Detail	0.468	0.230	0.305	1.000											
Carrots	512	0.423	0.523	0.412	1.000										
Fine dexterity	0.321	0.285	0.247	0.227	0.213	1.000									
Gross dexterity	0.335	0.234	0.268	0.327	0.275	0.622	1.000								
Softness	0.304	0.157	0.223	0.335	0.301	0.656	0.722	1.000							
Tremor	0.332	0.157	0.382	0.391	0.219	0.578	0.527	0.619	1.000						
Check	0.326	0.195	0.184	0.325	0.032	0.423	0.414	0.385	0.432	1.000					
Interest	0.116	0.057	0.075	0.099	0.105	0.311	0.203	0.246	0.285	0.370	1.000				
Scrooge	0.308	0.150	0.091	0.110	0.212	0.344	0.353	0.232	0.300	0.380	0.484	1.000			
Dunning	0.314	0.145	0.140	0.160	0.155	0.215	0.095	0.181	0.271	0.413	0.585	0.428	1.000		
Overcharge	0.489	0.239	0.321	0.327	0.222	0.344	0.309	0.345	0.395	0.480	0.408	0.535	0.512	1.000	
Billing	0.258	0.301	0.132	0.217	0.200	0.303	0.296	0.313	0.287	0.553	0.412	0.621	0.555	0.642	1.000

numbers between −0.30 and +0.30 (i.e., pretty close to 0), with 1.000s on the main diagonal (because a variable is always perfectly correlated with itself), the computer would full of numbers and graphs, signifying nothing. The extreme example of this is an **identity matrix**, which has 1.000s along the main diagonal and zeros for all the off-diagonal terms. So several tests, formal and otherwise, have been developed to ensure that something is around to factor analyze.

Some of the most useful "tests" do not involve any statistics at all, if you have only a few correlations higher than 0.30, save your paper and stop right there.

A slightly more stringent test is to look at a matrix of the **partial correlations**. This "test" is based on the variables do indeed correlate with each other because of an underlying factor structure, then the correlation between any two variables should be small *after partialing out the effects of the other variables*. Some computer programs print out the partial correlation matrix. Others, such as SPSS/PC, give you an **anti-image correlation matrix**. In either case, they're interpreted in the opposite way as is the correlation matrix; a large number of *high* partial correlations indicates you shouldn't proceed.

A related diagnostic test involves looking at the communalities. Because they are the squared *multiple* correlations, they should be above 0.60 or so, reflecting the fact that the variables are related to each other to some degree. In the SPSS/PC, the first time it prints them out, they may all be 1.00. Later in the output, there will be another column of them, with values ranging from 0.0 to 1.0; this is the column to look at.

Among the formal statistical tests, one of the oldest is the **Bartlett Test of Sphericity.** Without going into the details of how it's calculated, it yields a chi-square statistic. If chi-square value is small, and the associated *p* level is over 0.05, then the correlation matrix doesn't differ significantly from an identity matrix, and you should stop right there. However, Tabachnick and Fidell (2007) state that the Bartlett test is "notoriously sensitive," especially with large

sample sizes, so even if it is statistically significant, it doesn't mean that you can safely proceed. Consequently, Barlett's test is not a credible test.

Another test is the **Kaiser-Meyer-Olkin Measure of Sampling Adequacy** (usually called MSA), which is based on the squared partial correlations. In the SPSS/PC, the MSA value for each variable is printed along the main diagonal of the anti-image correlation matrix, and a summary value is also given. This allows you to check the overall adequacy of the matrix and also see which individual variables may not be pulling their full statistical weight. MSA is affected by four factors. It increases with (1) the number of variables, (2) the number of subjects, (3) the overall level of the correlation, and (4) a decrease in the number of factors (Dziuban and Shirkey, 1974). Kaiser (1970) gives the following definitions for values of the MSA:

Below 0.50 – Unacceptable

0.50 to 0.59 – Miserable

0.60 to 0.69 – Mediocre

0.70 to 0.79 – Middling

0.80 to 0.89 – Meritorious

Over 0.90 – Marvelous

You should consider eliminating variables with MSAs under 0.70. If, after doing this and rerunning the analysis, you find that the summary value is still low, that data set is destined for the garbage heap.

While we're on the topic of diagnostic checks of your data set, let's add one more. Take a look at the communalities for each variable; they should be above 0.50. If any variable has a value less than this, you should consider dropping it from the analysis and starting afresh.

Extracting the Factors

Assuming that all has gone well in the previous steps, we now go on to extracting the factors. The purpose of this is to come up with a series of linear combinations of the variables to define each factor. For Factor 1, this would look something like:

$$F_1 = w_{11}X_1 + w_{12}X_2 + ... + w_{1k}X_k \qquad \textbf{(17-1)}$$

where the X terms are the k (in this case, 15) variables and the w's are weights. These w terms have two subscripts; the first shows that they go with Factor 1, and the second indicates with which variable they're associated. The reason is, if we have 15 variables, we will end up with 15 factors and, therefore, 15 equations in the form of the one above. For example, the second factor would look like:

$$F_2 = w_{21}X_1 + w_{22}X_2 + ... + w_{2k}X_k \qquad (17\text{-}2)$$

If we began with 15 variables and ended up with 15 factors, what have we gained? The w's for the first factor are chosen so that they express the largest amount of variance in the sample. The w's in the second factor are derived to meet two criteria: (1) the second factor is uncorrelated with the first, and (2) it expresses the largest amount of variance left over after the first factor is considered. The w's in all the remaining factors are calculated in the same way, with each factor uncorrelated with and explaining less variance than the previous ones. So, if a factorial structure is present in the data, most of the variance may be explained on the basis of only the first few factors.

Again, returning to our example, the Dean hopes that the first 3 factors are responsible for most of the variance among the variables and that the remaining 12 factors will be relatively "weak" (i.e., he won't lose too much information if he ignores them). The actual results are given in Table 17-2. For the moment, ignore the column headed "Eigenvalue" and look at the last one, "Cumulative percent." Notice that the first factor accounts for 37.4% of the variance, the first two for over 50%, and the first five for almost 75% of the variance of the original data. So he actually may end up with what he's looking for.

TABLE 17-2 The 15 factors

Factor	Eigenvalue	Percent of variance	Cumulative percent
1	5.6025	37.4	37.4
2	2.0252	13.5	50.9
3	1.5511	10.3	61.2
4	0.8968	6.0	67.2
5	0.7888	5.3	72.4
6	0.7113	4.7	77.2
7	0.6826	4.6	81.7
8	0.5345	3.6	85.3
9	0.4514	3.0	88.3

			Continued
Factor	Eigenvalue	Percent of variance	Cumulative percent
10	0.4423	2.9	91.2
11	0.3598	2.4	93.6
12	0.3158	2.1	95.7
13	0.3015	2.0	97.8
14	0.1785	1.2	98.9
15	0.1580	1.1	100.0

What we've just described is the essence of FA. What it tries to do, then, is explain the variance among a bunch of variables in terms of uncorrelated (the statistical term is **orthogonal**) underlying factors or latent variables. The way it's used now is to try to *reduce* the number of factors as much as possible so as to get a more explanation of what's going on. In fact, though, FA is only one way of determining the factors. SPSS has seven different methods. As with most options in factor analysis, which of these methods to use has been the subject of much debate. If the data are relatively normally distributed, the best choice is probably **maximum likelihood** and, if the assumption of multivariate normality is severely violated, use **principal axis** (Fabrigar et al., 1999), which we discuss in the next section.

Principal Components Analysis and Principal Axis Factoring

To understand the differences among those techniques, we'll have to take a bit of sidestep and expand on what we've been doing. In Equations (17-1) and (17-2), we showed how we can define the factors in terms of weighted combinations of the variables. In a similar manner, we can do it the other way, and define each variable as a weighted combination of the factors. For variable X_1, this would look like:

$$X_1 = [w_{11}F_1 + w_{12}F_2 + w_{13}F_3 + ... + w_{1k}F_k] + [w_1U_1] + [e_1] \qquad (17\text{-}3)$$

Where the first subscript of the w's means variable 1, and the second refers to the factor, for the k factors we're working with. Like Gaul, then, the variance of each variable is divided into three parts, which we've highlighted by putting them in separate sets of brackets: the first reflects the influence of the factors (i.e., the variable's **communality**); the second is the variable's **unique** contribution (U); and the third is random error (e) that exists every time we measure something. Ignoring the error term for a moment, we can summarize Equation (17-3) as:

$$X_1 = Communality + Uniqueness \qquad \textbf{(17-4)}$$

The issue is what part of the variance we're interested in.

In **principal components analysis** (PCA), we're interested in all of the variance (that is, the communality plus the uniqueness); whereas in **principal axis** (PA) factoring, our interest is in only the variance due to the influence of the factors. That's the reason that PA is also referred to as **common factor analysis**; it uses only the variance that is in common with all of the variables.

In PCA, we begin with a correlation matrix that has 1.0s along the main diagonal. As a part of factor analysis, though, those 1.0s mean that we are concerned about all of the variance, from whatever source. It also means that, once we have defined the variables in terms of a weighted sum of the factors [as in Equation (17-3)], we can use those equations and perfectly recapture the original data. We haven't lost any information by deriving the factors. In terms of the computer output, it means that the table listing the initial communalities will show a 1.0 for every variable.

In PA, we're concerned only with the variance that each variable has in common with the other variables, not the unique variance. Consequently, the initial estimate of the communality for each variable (which is what's captured by the values along the main diagonal) will be less than 1.0. But, now we're in a Catch-22 situation; we use FA to determine what those communalities are, but we need some value in order to get started. So, what we do is figure out the communalities in stages. As a first step, the best estimate of a variable's communality is its **squared multiple correlation** (SMC) with all of the other variables. That is, to determine the SMC for variable X_1, we do a multiple regression with X_1 as the DV, and all of the other variables as predictors. This makes a lot of sense, since after all, R^2 (which is the usual symbol for the SMC) is the amount of variance that

the predictor variables have in common with the DV, as we discussed in the chapters on correlation and regression. This estimate is later revised once we've determined how many factors we ultimately keep.

Because we have, in essence, discarded the unique variance, this means that we can't go back and forth between the raw data and the results coming out of Equation (17-3) and expect to have exactly the same values; we've lost some information. However, from the perspective of PA, the information that was lost is information we don't care about.

So, when do we use what? If we're trying to find the optimal weights for the variables to combine them into a single measure, then PCA is the way to go. We would do this, for example, if we were concerned that we had too many variables to analyse and wanted to combine some of them into a single index. Instead of five scales tapping different aspects of adjustment, for instance, we would use the weights to come up with one number, thus reducing the number of variables by 80%. We would also use PCA if we wanted to account for the maximum amount of variance in the data with the smallest number of mutually independent underlying factors. On the other hand, if we're trying to create a new scale by eliminating variables (or items) that aren't associated with other ones or don't load on any factor, then PA (i.e., "common" FA) is the method of choice.

After we've gone to great lengths to explain the difference between PCA and PA, the reality is that it may be much ado about nothing. Because PCA uses a higher value for the communalities than FA, its estimates of something called factor loadings are a tad higher than those produced by PA. But, the differences tend to be minor, and the correlations between factor loadings coming from the two methods are pretty close to 1.0 (Russell, 2002). The reality is that FA is highly robust to the way factors are extracted and that "many of these decisions have little effect on the obtained solutions" (Watson et al.,1994, p. 20). In fact, as the number of variables increases, the differences between FA and PCA virtually disappear, since the proportion of correlations on the main diagonal decreases, and those are the only ones that differ with the two techniques.

On Keeping and Discarding Factors

We have mentioned that one of the purposes of the factor extraction phase was to reduce the number of factors, so that only a few "strong" ones remain. But first, we have to resolve what we mean by "strong," and what criteria we apply. As with the previous phase (factor extraction) and the next one (factor rotation), the problem isn't a lack of answers, but rather a surfeit of them.

At the same time, the number of factors to retain is one the most important decisions a factor analyst must make. Factor analysis is fairly robust with regard to the type of analysis (PCA versus PA), the type of rotation (stay tuned), and other details but, as we'll discuss in a bit, keeping too many or too few factors may distort the final results. With too few factors, we may lose important information; with too many factors, we may focus on unimportant ones at the expense of major ones.

The criterion that is still the most commonly used is called the **eigenvalue one** test, or the **Kaiser criterion**. It is the default option in most computer packages. We should, in all fairness, describe what is meant by an eigenvalue. Without going into the intricacies of matrix algebra, an eigenvalue can be thought of as an index of variance. In FA, each factor yields an eigenvalue, which is the amount of the total variance explained by that factor. We said previously that the w's are chosen so that the first factor expresses the largest amount of variance, and the second factor has the second largest eigenvalue, and so on. So why use the criterion of 1.0 for the eigenvalue?

The reason is that the first step in FA is to transform all of the variables to z-scores so that each has a mean of 0 and a variance of 1. This means that, with PCA, the total amount of variance is equal to the number of variables; if you have 15 variables, then the total variance within the (z-transformed) data matrix is 15. If we add up the squared eigenvalues of the 15 factors that come out of the PCA, they will sum to—that's right, class, 15. So you can think of a factor with an eigenvalue of less than 1.0 as accounting for less variance than is generated by one

variable. Obviously then, we gain nothing by keeping factors with eigenvalues under 1.0 and are further ahead if we keep only those with eigenvalues over 1.0; hence, the eigenvalue one criterion.

What most people tend to forget is that this criterion was proposed as a lower bound for the eigenvalues of the retained factors and therefore an upper bound for the number of factors to retain. In fact, this test has three problems. The first is that it's somewhat arbitrary: a factor with an eigenvalue of 1.01 is retained, whereas 0.99 is rejected. This ignores the fact that eigenvalues are measured with some degree of error. On replication, these numbers will likely change to some degree, leading to a different solution. The second problem is that the Kaiser criterion often results in too many factors when more than about 50 variables exist and in too few factors when fewer than 20 variables are considered (Horn and Engstrom, 1979). This is only logical because, with 20 variables, a factor with an eigenvalue of 1.0 accounts for 5% of the variance; whereas with 50 variables, it accounts for only 2% of the variance. The third problem is that, while this criterion may be logical in PCA, when the communalities are set equal to 1.0, it doesn't make sense in PA, since the communalities are reduced. Unfortunately, programs such as SPSS use the same criterion for both methods (Russell, 2002).

A somewhat better test is **Cattell's Scree Test**. This is another one of those very powerful statistical tests that rely on nothing more than your eyeball. We start off by plotting the eigenvalues for each of the 15 factors, as in Figure 17-4. In many cases, there's a sharp break in the curve between the point where it's descending and where it levels off; that is, where the slope of the curve changes from negative to close to zero. The last "real" factor is the one before the scree (the relatively flat portion of the curve) begins. If several breaks are in the descending line, usually the first one is chosen, but this can be modified by two considerations. First, we usually want to have at least three factors. Second, the scree may start after the second or third break. We see this in Figure 17-4; there is a break after the second factor, but it looks

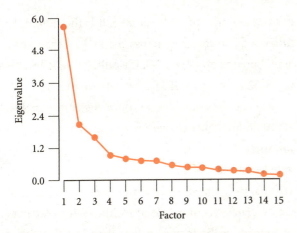

FIGURE 17-4   A scree plot for the 15 factors.

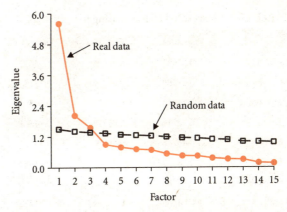

FIGURE 17-5   Results from a parallel analysis superimposed on the scree plot from Figure 17-4.

like the scree starts after the third factor, so we'll keep the first three. In this example, the number of factors retained with the Kaiser criterion and with the scree test is the same.

The fact that no statistical test exists for the scree test poses a bit of a problem for computer programs. Almost all programs use the eigenvalue as a default when they go on to the next steps of factor analysis. If you do a scree plot and decide you won't keep all the factors that have eigenvalues over 1.0, you have to run the FA in two steps: once to produce the scree plot, and again for you to override the eigenvalue criterion. You can usually do this by specifying either the minimum eigenvalue or the actual number of factors to keep.

A third method is called **parallel analysis** (Horn, 1965), and is more accurate than interpreting the scree plot by eye (Russell, 2000). You create a number of data sets of random numbers usually about 50 with the same number of variables and subjects. The random variables have the same mean and range as the corresponding variable in the real data. All of these data sets are factor analyzed, and then the means and 95% CIs of each eigenvalue are calculated. Because using the mean eigenvalue is equivalent to setting the Type I error at 50% rather than 5%, it's customary to use the value of 95th percentile rather than the mean in the next step. Finally, you superimpose these 95th percentile values from the random data on the scree plot of the real data (see Figure 17-5), and keep only those factors whose eigenvalues exceed those from the random data. In this example,

that would lead to retaining three factors.

Bear in mind that, no matter which criterion you use for determining the number of factors, the results should be interpreted as a suggestion, not as truth. What you should do is to use a couple of them (as long as one includes parallel analysis), and then run the FA a number of times; once with the recommended number, and then with one or two more and one or two fewer factors, and select the one that makes the most sense clinically. If, after using all these guidelines you still can't decide whether to keep, say, five versus six factors, go with the higher number. It's usually better (or at least less bad) to over-extract than to under-extract (Wood et al., 1996). When too few factors are extracted, the estimated factors "are likely to contain considerable error. Variables that should load on unextracted factors may incorrectly show loadings on the extracted factors. Furthermore, loadings for variables that genuinely load on the extracted factors may be distorted". The greater the degree of under-extraction, the worse the problem. Over-extraction leads to "factor splitting," and the loadings on the surplus factors have more error than on the true factors, but often, clinical judgment can alert you to the fact that the variables on these surplus factors really belong with other factors.

The Matrix of Factor Loadings

After we've extracted the factors and decided on how many to retain, the computer gives us a table (like Table 17-3) that is variously called the **Factor Matrix**, the **Factor Loading Matrix**, or the **Factor Structure**

TABLE 17-3   Unrotated factor loading matrix

	Factor1	Factor2	Factor3
Acuity	0.62684	0.28525	0.34653
Color	0.42569	0.28367	0.35186
Nystagmus	0.46046	0.51771	0.30305
Detail	0.52711	0.35772	0.14661
Carrots	0.48746	0.49096	0.43285
Fine dexterity	0.68819	0.12381	−0.44882
Gross dexterity	0.67587	0.24838	−0.46550
Softness	0.68436	0.22289	−0.51248
Tremor	0.69554	0.16367	−0.35142
Checks	0.66956	−0.24746	−0.12809
Interest	0.50922	−0.57080	−0.03457
Scrooge	0.62186	−0.42615	0.09860
Dunning	0.56544	−0.50324	0.28899
Overcharge	0.73480	−0.24955	0.23411
Billing	0.68151	−0.43433	0.19142

Matrix. Just to confuse things even more, it can also be called the **Factor Pattern Matrix**. As long as we keep the factors orthogonal to each other, the factor structure matrix and the factor pattern matrix are identical. When we relax this restriction (a topic we'll discuss a bit later), the two matrices become different.

Table 17-3 tells us the correlation between each variable and the various factors. In statistical jargon, we speak of the variables *loading on* the factors. So "Visual Acuity" loads 0.627 on Factor 1, 0.285 on Factor 2, and 0.347 on Factor 3. As with other correlations, a higher value means a closer relationship between the factor and the variable. In this case, then, "Visual Acuity" is most closely associated with the first factor.

A couple of interesting and informative points about factor loadings. First, they are *standardized regression coefficients* (β weights). In factor analysis, the DV is the original variable itself, and the factors are the IVs. As long as the factors are orthogonal, these regression coefficients are identical to correlation coefficients. (The reason is that, if the factors are uncorrelated, i.e., orthogonal, then the β weights are not dependent on one another.)

Second, the *communality* of a variable, which we approximated with R^2 previously, can now be derived exactly. For each variable, it is the *sum of the squared factor loadings* across the factors that we've kept. Looking at Table 17-3, it would be $(0.62\,684)^2 + (0.28\,525)^2 + (0.34\,653)^2 = 0.594$ for ACUITY. We usually use the abbreviation h^2 for the communality, and therefore, the uniqueness is written as $(1 - h^2)$.

Rotating the Factors

Why rotate at all?

We've simply transformed a number of variables into factors. However, if we asked for the factor matrix to include all of the factors, rather than just those over some criterion, we could without losing any information at all. It is the next step, factor rotation, that really gets the dander up among some (unenlightened) statistical folks. The reason is that we have, literally, an infinite number of ways we can rotate the factors. Which rotation we decide to use is totally a matter of choice on the analyst's part.

So, if factor rotation is still somewhat controversial, why do we do it? To us true believers, factor rotation serves some useful functions. The primary one is to help us understand what is going on with the factors.

To simplify interpretation of the factors, the factor loading matrix should satisfy four conditions:

1. The variance should be fairly evenly distributed across the retained factors.

2. Each variable should load on only one factor.

3. The factor loadings should be close to 1.0 or 0.0.

4. All the strong variables should have the same sign.

Let's see how well the factor loading matrix in Table 17-3 meets these criteria.

1. **Distribution of variance.** If we go back to Table 17-2, we can add up the eigenvalues of the first three factors. Their sum, 9.1788, shows the amount of variance explained by them (which is 61.2% of the total variance of 15). Of this amount, the first factor accounts for $(5.6025 \div 9.1788)$, or 61.0%, the second factor for $(2.0252 \div 9.1798)$ or 22.1%, and the third factor for the remaining 16.9%. So, the first factor contains a disproportionate share of the total variance explained by the three factors. We can also see this in the fact that all of the variables load strongly

on this factor (Table 17-3): 12 of the 15 have loadings over 0.50 on Factor 1, and only 2 variables (NYSTAGMUS and CARROTS) load higher on another factor than they do on Factor 1.

2. **Factorial complexity.** Whenever a variable loads strongly on two or more factors, we call it **factorially complex.** In Table 1703, NYSTAGMUS loads strongly on Factors 1 and 2, CARROTS loads on all 3 factors to comparable degrees, and so on. Factorial complexity makes it more difficult to interpret the role of the variable. INTEREST is explained by both Factor 1 and Factor 2 and, conversely, the explanation of these factors must take CARROTS into account.

3. **Magnitude of the loadings.** If a variable loads strongly on one factor, then its loadings on the other factors will be close to 0. The reason is that the sum of the squares of the loadings across factors remains constant when we rotate; so as some loadings go up, others have to go down.

4. **Unipolar factors.** If some loadings were positive and others negative, then a high score on the factor would indicate more of some variables, whereas a low score would indicate more of other variables. Again, we'd like the factor to be unipolar; that is, a higher score on the factor means more of the latent variable, and a lower score simply means less of it. This occurs when all of the factor loadings have the same sign.

A simple example. Let's see how rotating the factors can help meet the four criteria and grant us simplicity. However, because it's hard to draw three-dimensional patterns, we'll start off by forcing the FA to give us only two factors. We can then generalize the procedure to three or more factors, although we won't be able to visualize the results as readily.

By asking for two factors, our factor loading table will have just two columns. Let's plot each variable using the loading on Factor 1 as the X coordinate and the loading on the second factor as the Y coordinate. What we'll get is Figure 17-6, where we can see problems with all of the criteria: (1) all of the variables show some degree of loading on Factor 1; (2) most of the variables are in the middle portions

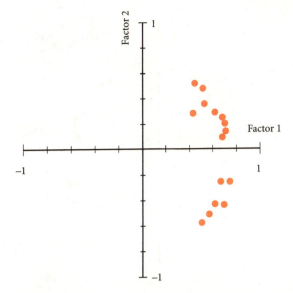

FIGURE 17-6   A factor plot of the two-factor solution.

of the quadrants, showing that they are loading on both of the factors; (3) the factor loadings all seem to fall between 0.4 and 0.8 on Factor 1, and most of them are between 0.2 and 0.6 (absolute values) on Factor 2; and (4) Factor 1 is unipolar, but Factor 2 is definitely bipolar.

Now, keeping the axes orthogonal (at right angles) to each other, let's rotate them (Figure 17-6). The new axes are labeled Factor 1' and Factor 2'. The only problem is that, if we continue to rotate the axes clockwise until Factor 1' is horizontal, all of the Factor 2' coordinates will be negative. We can correct this little annoyance simply by reversing all of the signs of the Factor 2' factor loadings. We end up with Figure 17-8.

How do our criteria fare in this picture? (1) A group of variables are showing high loadings on Factor 2 but not on Factor 1, demonstrating that not all of the variables are loading on the first factor any more. (2) The variables seem to be closer to the axes than to the middle of the quadrant, indicating reduced factorial complexity. (3) Each variable is closer to the top on one factor and closer to the origin for the other factor, showing that the loadings are nearer to 1.0 or 0.0. (4) All of the variables are in or very near to the first quadrant. This means that all of the signs are positive (or those loadings that are negative are very small), resulting in unipolar factors.

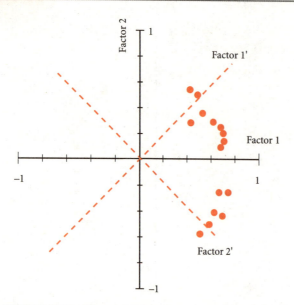

FIGURE 17-7   Figure 17-6, with the rotated axes superimposed.

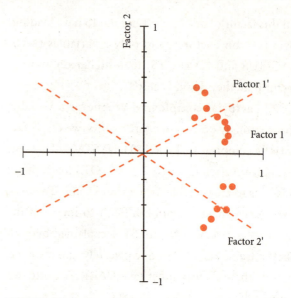

FIGURE 17-9   **An oblique rotation to the factor plot in Figure 17-6.**

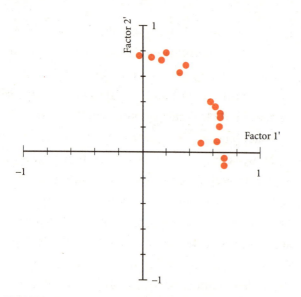

FIGURE 17-8   Figure 17-6, with the rotated axes turned more to be horizontal and vertical.

Orthogonal versus oblique rotations. You'll remember that, earlier, we said, "…keeping the axes orthogonal (at right angles) to each other, let's rotate them." However, the factors *don't have to be* orthogonal. In fact, having some degree of correlation among the factors is probably a better reflection of reality than having strictly independent ones.

When we rotated the axes in Figure 17-7, we were still left with some of the variables being near the middle of the quadrant. Because the angle between the axes was fixed at 90°, there was little we could do. But, relaxing the condition that the factors have to be orthogonal, we can draw each axis closer to the

middle of each group of variables, as in Figure 17-9. We call this an **oblique** rotation.

We said this is "*an* oblique rotation." In actuality, the best to use is called a **Promax** rotation. It begins by doing an orthogonal varimax rotation and then drops the constraint that the factors have to be uncorrelated with each other. Its advantage is that, if the factors really are uncorrelated, then the resulting factors will be pretty close to orthogonal (Fabrigar et al., 1999). Actually, though, most of the oblique rotations yield fairly similar results. The advantage is that oblique solutions often lead to greater structural simplicity than do orthogonal rotations. Instead of the relatively simple description of Figure 17-2, where the value of each variable is determined only by its "own" factor and its unique component, we have a more complicated situation (Figure 17-10).

In this case, to understand what Factor 1 is measuring, we not only have to look at the variables that have a high loading, but we also have to consider any correlation between Factor 1 and the others. The correlation among the factors leads to another issue, which we briefly mentioned earlier. As long as the factors were uncorrelated, each variable's regression coefficients for the factors were the same as the correlations between the variable and the factors; that is, the loadings could be interpreted either as simple correlations or as β weights. However, once we in-

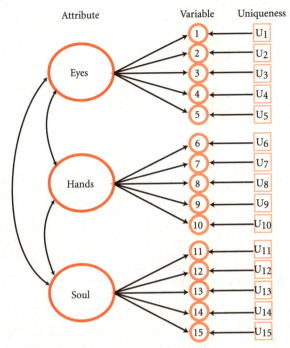

FIGURE 17-10 In an oblique rotation, the factors are correlated with each other.

ing stage because, in the absence of three-dimensional graph paper, we would have to look at three factor plots for the unrotated solution (Factor 1 vs 2; 1 vs 3; and 2 vs 3) and an equal number after the rotation. Instead, we'll focus on the factor matrix. The unrotated matrix was given in Table 17-3; the rotated one is in Table 17-4.

TABLE 17-4   Rotated factor loading matrix

	Factor1	Factor2	Factor3
Acuity	0.26607	0.18827	0.69867
Color	0.14288	0.06270	0.60095
Nystagmus	−0.02079	0.18035	0.73411
Detail	0.10065	0.29793	0.57307
Carrots	0.04798	0.09161	0.80952
Fine dexterity	0.22729	0.78554	0.14715
Gross dexterity	0.12321	0.82256	0.20833
Softness	0.13579	0.85669	0.16826
Tremor	0.22645	0.72647	0.23456
Checks	0.56992	0.43687	0.10139
Interest	0.73234	0.18696	−0.12260
Scrooge	0.72852	0.19103	0.10392
Dunning	0.79744	−0.00664	0.14328
Overcharge	0.70180	0.20167	0.35187
Billing	0.79480	0.15467	0.18470

troduce some correlation between the factors, this equivalence doesn't hold any more. The factor *structure* matrix holds the simple correlations between the variables and the factors. The coefficients in the factor *pattern* matrix are now *partial* correlations, correcting for the correlations between the factors. Consequently, the factor loadings are smaller than with the orthogonal rotation. The higher the correlation among the factors, the greater the difference between these two matrices.

So, even though oblique rotations may mirror reality more closely than orthogonal ones, most people prefer the latter. The reason is that orthogonal rotations have a number of desirable qualities. Because the factors are uncorrelated with each other (that's the mathematical meaning of "orthogonal"), any score derived from one factor will correlate 0 with scores derived from the other factors. This is a useful property if the results of a PCA or a PA are to be further analyzed with another statistical test. Also, as we've said, the interpretation of the factors is far easier if they are all independent from one another.

Back to the Dean. Before we leave the topic of rotations, let's just see how our three-factor solution fared with a varimax rotation. We'll skip the graph-

Before rotation, these three factors accounted for 61.2% of the total variance; this doesn't change. What does change is the distribution of the variance across factors. If you recall, of the variance that is explained, Factor 1 was responsible for 61.0%, Factor 2 for 22.1%, and Factor 3 for 16.9%. After rotation, these numbers become 37.0%, 33.2%, and 29.8%; obviously a much more equitable division. This is also reflected in the fact that now only five variables load strongly on Factor 1; previously, the majority of them did.

Another thing that doesn't change with rotation is the relationship among the variables. For example, the correlation between ACUITY and COLOR can be found by multiplying the coefficients for each factor and adding them up. With the unrotated solution (Table 17-3), this would be (0.627 × 0.425) + (0.285 × 0.284) + (0.347 × 0.352) = 0.470. For the rotated solution, it's (0.266 × 0.143) + (0.188 × 0.063) + (0.699 ×

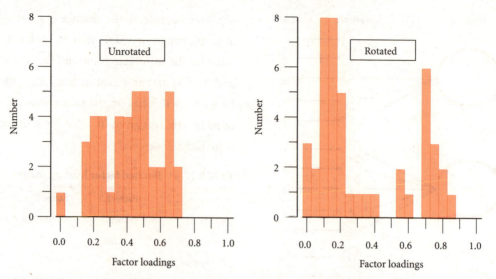

FIGURE 17-11   Plot of the factor loadings for the unrotated and rotated solutions.

0.601) = 0.470.

The other criteria did just as well. If we plot the absolute magnitudes of the unrotated factor loadings, as we did in the left side of Figure 17-11, we see that most of them fall between 0.3 and 0.7. The right side shows the same thing for the rotated loadings; the graph is much more bimodal, with relatively few values in the middle range. So we seemingly have succeeded in driving the loadings closer to 0.0 or 1.0. Also, in the unrotated solution, 12 of the 45 loadings were negative; in the rotated one, only 3 are, and they are relatively small. Last, only one variable, CHECKS, shows any degree of factorial complexity. The conclusion, then, is that rotating the axes got us a lot closer to structural simplicity.

INTERPRETING THE Principal Components and FACTORS

Now that we've got the factors, what do we do with them? The first step is to determine which variables load on each factor. To do this, we have to figure out which loadings are significant and which can be safely ignored. We know a couple of ways of doing this. One way is to adopt some minimum value, such as 0.30 or 0.40. The problem is that any number we choose is completely arbitrary and doesn't take the sample size into account; a loading of 0.38 may be meaningful if we had 1000 subjects, but it may represent only a chance fluctuation from 0 with 30 subjects.

A better method would be to retain only those loadings that are statistically significant. We can do this by looking up the critical value in a table for the correlation (see Table F in the Appendix). But which value to use? Stevens (2001) recommends (1) using the 1% level of significance, because of the number of tests that will be done, and then (2) doubling that value because the SEs or factor loadings are up to twice those of ordinary correlations. When the sample size is over 100, a good approximation to use would be:

$$CV = \frac{5.152}{\sqrt{N-2}} \qquad (17\text{-}5)$$

Where did these numbers come from? When $N > 100$, the normal curve is a good approximation for the correlation distribution, and 2.576 marks off the 1% level of significance. Following Stevens, we double this (hence, 5.152) and then multiply by the SE for a correlation, which is $\left[1 \div \sqrt{(N-2)}\right]$ and voila! So, if you want to use the 5% level, use 3.920 in the numerator. Because we had 200 most unwilling people taking the test, we would get:

$$CV = \frac{5.152}{\sqrt{198}} = 0.366 \qquad (17\text{-}6)$$

If we now go back to Table 17-4 and eliminate all loadings lower than this, we get Table 17-5. Factor 1 consists of six variables: CHECKS, INTEREST, SCROOGE, DUNNING, OVERCHARGE, and BILLING. This looks very much like the postulated Soul factor, with the addition of the CHECKS variable. Similarly, Factor 2 corresponds to the Hands attribute, and Factor 3 to Eyes.

TABLE 17-5   Matrix of significant factor loading

	Factor 1	Factor 2	Factor 3
Acuity			0.699
Color			0.601
Nystagmus			0.734
Detail			0.573
Carrots			0.810
Fine dexterity		0.786	
Gross dexterity		0.823	
Softness		0.857	
Tremor		0.726	
Checks	0.570	0.437	
Interest	0.732		
Scrooge	0.729		
Dunning	0.797		
Overcharge	0.702		
Billing	0.795		

However, there's one drawback. The CHECKS variable is both factorially complex (loading on factors 1 and 2), and its highest loading is on the "wrong" factor. So, what do we do with it? We have three options:

1. We can throw that test out of the battery because it isn't tapping what we thought it would. If there are enough variables remaining in the factors (a minimum of three), this may be a sensible option. We would also toss out variables that didn't load well on any factor. This would be the case when the variable is quite complex, loading on a number of factors, or when it loads on some factor we didn't retain.

2. We can keep the variable in both factors. However, if our aim is to achieve simplicity and end up with uncorrelated factors, this wouldn't be a good choice.

3. If the variable is one we devised, we could rewrite it. The downside of this is that we would have to repeat the whole study with a new group of subjects to see if the revised variable is better than the original. However, if we're developing a scale, and one factor has relatively few items, this may be our only alternative. In our example, because the Dean will have a new batch of 200 consenting adults next year, this option is feasible.

Table 17-5 can also help the Dean in another way. If

he wants to make the test battery shorter, he can eliminate those tests with the lowest factor loadings. Needless to say, the reduced battery will not predict the factors as well, so yet another trade off has to be made.

Before make a decision, though, we should make two last checks of the factors. A factor should consist of at least three variables. Any factor that contains fewer should be discarded. Second, it's wise to go back to the original correlation matrix and see if the variables in the factor are indeed correlated with each other. If they're not, the factor should be thrown away.

NAMING NAMES

We've been referring to the factors by using the names of Factor 1, Factor 2, and Factor 3; or Factor I, Factor II, and Factor III. These have the distinct advantages of a lack of ambiguity and telling the reader their rank order in terms of eigenvalues (and therefore the amount of variance accounted for). But, they convey absolutely no information about the underlying construct they are supposed to reflect.

Thence, the best way to go about this is to look at the three or four variables with the strongest loadings on the structure matrix (or the pattern matrix) and try to see what they have in common. When we looked at Table 17-5 in the last section, we said that Factor I looked like the Soul factor, Factor II was Hands, and Factor III was Eyes.

USING THE FACTORS

In many cases, the steps we've gone through are as far as researchers want to go. They've used PCA and FA to either explore the data or confirm some hypotheses about them, and also to eliminate variables that were either not too helpful or factorially complex. However, we can use these procedures in another way: to reduce the number of variables. We may want to do this for a few reasons.

First, subject-to-variable ratios that are too low for some multivariable procedures may still be okay in FA (see below). So we can use PCA and FA to change a large number of variables into a smaller number of factors, which we can then analyze with linear regression or something else. Second, it may be easier for us to understand what a pattern of three factors means rather than trying to juggle 15 scores in our mind all at once. What we would like to do, then, is to come up with one number for each factor. In our example, each person would have 3 scores, rather than 15, which, in essence, increases the subject/variable ratio by 5.

We mentioned earlier that the factor loadings are partial regression weights. So why not simply use them like a regression equation? The reason is that they were derived to predict the value of the *variable from the factors*. What we want to do is just the opposite, to predict the *factor from the variables*. So, if we want, we can command the computer to give us a **factor score coefficient matrix**, such as the one in Table 17-6. Each column is a regression equation, with the predicted factor score as the DV and the variables as the IVs.

So, the three-factor scores for subject 1 would be found by plugging her 15 *standardized* scores into the equations, which would then read:

$FS_1 = (0.02083)ACUITY - (0.00017)COLOR + ... + (0.26535) BILLING$

$FS_2 = (-0.06561)ACUITY - (0.09003)COLOR + ... - (0.07488)BILLING$

$FS_3 = (0.27844)ACUITY + (0.26219)COLOR + ... + (0.00191)BILLING$

TABLE 17-6   Factor score coefficient matrix

	Factor1	Factor2	Factor3
Acuity	0.02083	−0.06561	0.27844
Color	−0.00017	−0.09003	0.26219
Nystagmus	−0.08966	−0.03297	0.31804
Detail	−0.04866	0.03030	0.21378
Carrots	−0.05618	−0.09673	0.36291
Fine dexterity	−0.04008	0.30845	−0.07620
Gross dexterity	−0.08967	0.33097	−0.04558
Softness	−0.08689	0.35157	−0.07099
Tremor	−0.03831	0.26677	−0.02529
Checks	0.14474	0.10321	−0.06656
Interest	0.26002	−0.00042	−0.14349
Scrooge	0.24091	−0.03500	−0.03712
Dunning	0.29316	−0.14363	0.00856
Overcharge	0.21052	−0.06666	0.08001
Billing	0.26535	−0.07488	0.00191

Most computer programs can calculate the factor scores for us and then save them in a file, making the job of transferring the results to another program much easier.

However, we'll mention one more fact about factor scores that may actually simplify your analysis. When more than 10 variables are loading on a factor, you can probably forget about the equations entirely. If you use unit weights, set each significant loading equal to 1.00 (or −1.00 if it's negative) and the nonsignificant ones to 0.00: then all you have to do is add up the scores; forget about multiplying them by the coefficients. The reason is that, with more than 10 IVs, the b weights don't improve the predictive ability of the equation to any degree that's worth worrying about (Cohen, 1990; Wainer, 1976). Actually, this is most true when the variables are totally uncorrelated with each other; the greater the magnitude of the correlation, the greater the possible loss in efficiency when using these unit weights.

TYPES OF DATA TO USE

Most of the methods used for exploratory factor analysis are fairly robust against deviations from normality, and don't require multivariate normality (Floyd and Widaman, 1995). But, it doesn't mean that anything goes; we do have *some* standards, after all. The major no-no is dichotomous data: Yes/No, True/False, Present/Absent, 0/1, and other variables of that ilk. Comrey (1978) pointed out several problems that can arise with dichotomous data. First, if about half of the people respond True on one variable, but 95% answer True on another variable, then the maximum correlation between these two variables is about ±0.23. Second, if 99 people say False to two items, and 1 person says True, then the correlation between the items will be 1.00. However, if this one person then changes her mind and also answers False, the correlation suddenly becomes 0.00. So, correlations with dichotomous data are often unstable and will be either artificially limited or grossly inflated, depending on the situation. Just as bad as dichotomous items are nominal variables. Because their coding is arbitrary, the numbers don't really mean anything; they're just names. If we change the coding scheme, the correlations among the variables will change drastically, so any "pattern" among the variables is artifactual.

A third problem arises when one variable is a combination of others. For example, a Total variable (such as the Full Scale IQ or the Verbal and Performance IQs on Wechsler IQ tests) could be the sum of two or more other variables. If this is the case, the computer program should have a major myocardial infarct and die on the spot. The only way around this problem is to not include variables that are sums or products of other variables in the same data matrix.

ANALYZING ITEMS—A FEW MORE CAUTIONS

The example we used in this chapter involved the factor analysis of the total scores of a number of scales. Factor analysis can also be used for developing scales where the data consist of the individual items, rather than total scores. The aims are the same: to determine if there are a number of underlying factors that can explain the pattern of responses; to see if some items are redundant and can be eliminated; to find items that don't seem to belong anywhere and should be dropped; and so on. However, there are a number of problems that arise in analyzing items that go beyond the problems encountered when we analyze total scores.

We've already mentioned one issue when analyzing items: many scales use items with dichotomous responses, and factor analyzing these is a no-no. A second issue has to do with measurement theory. In classical test theory, the *reliability* of a scale is directly dependent on the number of items; *ceteris paribus*, the more items a scale has, the more reliable it is (Streiner and Norman, 2014). So when we factor analyze total scores, we're dealing with numbers that are relatively reliable. An item, though, can be seen as a "scale" having only one item, so needless to say, its reliability is going to be the pits. This means that, compared to when we factor analyze scales, we should expect to find, when we analyze items, that factor loadings may be lower, indices such as KMO

and MSA won't be as strong, and the total amount of variance explained by the factors will be lower.

A third problem involves the response formats found with some scales. Before you factor analyze such a scale, be sure to change the scoring so that high scores on all of the items mean the same thing; if you don't, then the factors will reflect the scoring direction rather than items with similar content. Some test developers try to balance the scoring by having some items worded in a positive direction (e.g., "I feel great") and others in a negative direction ("I do not feel great"). Even if the scoring is flipped for this latter item, you may still find that one factor consists of the positively worded items and a second factor of the negatively worded ones, again irrespective of content.

Finally, the correlation between any two items is affected not only by their content (which is good), but also by their statistical distributions (which is bad). Items with similar distributions tend to correlate more highly than items with dissimilar distributions (Bernstein et al., 1988). This is related to the equally unfortunate situation that easy items cluster together, as do hard ones (Nunnally and Bernstein, 1994), yet again irrespective of content.

So, the bottom line is that you can use factor analysis to analyze individual scales, but be aware of the potential problems.

SAMPLE SIZE

In factor analysis, there are no power tables to tell exactly how many subjects to use. What we *do* have are firmly held beliefs and some Monte Carlo simulations. Those simulations tell us that the sample size depends on a host of factors, such as the number of items on each factor, the average strength of the factor loadings, the communalities of the items. Very often, people who do these studies are emphatic that there are no fixed rules regarding the subject-to-variable ratio. However, in terms of planning a study, this advice fits the usual definition of an epidemiologist—he tells you something that is absolutely correct, that you already know, and that is totally useless. If we knew the magnitudes of all of these parameters, we wouldn't have to do the study to begin with! What we are left with, then, is a rule-of-thumb guideline that we've been told we shouldn't have: we must have an absolute *minimum* of five subjects per variable with the proviso that we have at least 100 subjects.

If you do a factor analysis with a subject-to-variable ratio less than 10, you'll get an output. But, there will be many problems: variables will likely load on the wrong factor; the eigenvalues will be wrong; the factor structure may be wrong; and you may end up with **Heywood cases**, in which the factor loading exceeds 1.0 (Costello and Osborne, 2005). Remember, *factor analysis is a large-sample procedure!*

Gorsuch (1983), one of the granddaddies of FA, and the person who proposed these guidelines, said that this should suffice *only if* the communalities are high and there are many variables for each factor. If you don't meet these two conditions, then you should probably at least double the subject/variable ratio, as well as the total number of subjects analyzed.

REPORTING GUIDELINES

If you run a factor analysis using any of the statistical packages, you'll get reams and reams of output. The issue is then what should you report when you write up your results. These guidelines are based on those of Henson and Roberts (2006), but modified in our usual ineffable way.

1. The sample size. We'd also suggest that, for those readers who have difficulty with division, you report the subject-to-variable ratio.

2. The method of factor extraction (e.g., principal axis, principal components analysis).

3. The criterion (ideally, the criteria) used to determine the number of factors to retain.

4. The method of factor rotation, indicating first whether it was orthogonal or oblique, and then the specific type.

5. The full factor loading matrix.

6. If an oblique rotation was used, you should also report the factor structure matrix and the matrix showing the correlations among the factors.

7. The eigenvalues of the factors before and after rotation, and the total amount of variance accounted for.

8. The communalities of each variable.

SUMMARY

✧ In the process of practical research, we should observe events or phenomena from multiple perspectives. Therefore, researchers always design many observational variables and collect mass data to look for underlying patterns. Multivariable and large samples may provide rich information for our study, but they may increase the difficulty of data acquisition and processing. Additionally, there are many related variables contributing to the overlap of information which may increase the complexity of analysis. To address this issue, we introduced PCA and FA in this chapter. The two methods could simplify the statistical model by reducing the number of highly related variables and these methods use the same factor progress in SPSS/PC, so some beginners are usually confused when faced with them. In fact, FA is to some extent considered as the promotion or development of PCA, and hence, various differences exist between them. For example, PCA may focus more on comprehensive information of original variables, while FA may stress more on explanation of the relationship between original variables. Hence, we should fully understand and correctly implement the two methods so that we obtain statistically-proven results in the practical work to address the true spirit of science.

GLOSSARY

common factor   公共因子
communality   共性方差，公共度

correlation matrix	相关矩阵
covariance matrix	协方差矩阵
eigenvalue	特征根
factor analysis, FA	因子分析
factor loading	因子载荷
factor score	因子得分
factor matrix	因子矩阵
factor rotation	因子旋转
latent variable	潜在变量
maximum likelihood	极大似然法
principal component analysis, PCA	主成分分析
partial correlations	偏相关
rate of contribution	贡献率

EXERCISES

1. The subject-to-variable ratio is:

   a. Acceptable, since it's 5 : 1.

   b. Acceptable, since they're only social workers.

   c. Too low; there should be at least 100 subjects.

   d. Too low; the ratio should be 10 : 1.

2. Using the Kaiser criterion, how many factors are there?

3. What proportion of the variance is accounted for by the retained factors?

4. Are there any items you would drop? Why (or why not, as the case may be)?

Rotated factor loadings of the 12 items

Item	Factor 1	Factor 2	Factor 3	Factor 4
1	0.53	0.33	0.27	−0.04
2	0.14	0.64	0.12	0.03
3	0.30	0.05	0.57	0.14
4	0.15	0.44	0.23	0.20
5	0.02	0.04	0.64	0.28
6	0.07	0.61	0.14	0.10
7	0.78	0.12	0.08	−0.16
8	0.80	0.15	0.17	−0.05
9	−0.06	−0.03	0.22	0.61
10	0.13	0.03	0.57	0.22
11	0.10	0.26	0.11	0.23
12	0.11	0.43	0.09	0.42
EIGENVALUES	1.709	1.380	1.323	0.828

5. **a.** What is the **communality** for Item 1?

   b. What is its **uniqueness**?

   c. What does this mean?

   d. Do you really care?

   e. Should you?

CHAPTER THE EIGHTEENTH

Path Analysis and Structural Equation Modeling

Path analysis is an extension of multiple regression, allowing us to look at the relationships among many "dependent" and "independent" variables at the same time. Structural equation modeling (SEM) takes this one step further, it has two parts: the first part is measurement model, reflecting the correlation between observed variables and latent variables; the mathematic model in this part is confirmatory factor analysis; the second part is structural model, building the structural relationship within latent variables with method analogous to path analysis.

SETTING THE SCENE

Although science has made tremendous advances in predicting which stars will become black holes instead of just flickering out, in explaining the movement of the continents over the face of the planet, and in eradicating many sources of disease, one area of knowledge has still eluded them: delineating what accounts for success in cheerleading. Dr. Yeigh Teeme has tried to solve this problem by gathering a lot of data (some say too much) about men and women who were and were not successful in this demanding task. He is bothered, however, by the fact that some variables may affect performance directly (e.g., the ability to jump high while smiling), while other variables may act indirectly (e.g., a "winning personality" may lead the coach to overvalue the person's ability). Compounding his problems, some variables are measured directly (like height and jumping ability), and others are derived from scores on two or more tests. How can Dr. Teeme tease these effects apart, take into account both measured and inferred variables, and figure out which ones are important?

PATH ANALYSIS

The two techniques we will discuss in this chapter—path analysis and structural equation modeling (SEM)—are extensions of procedures we have discussed earlier; namely, multiple regression and exploratory factor analysis.[1] So, if you feel a bit shaky about them, you may want to review those chapters first. Let's start off easy by using statistical tests we have already encountered and seeing what their limitations are and how we can get around them. We'll assume that success in cheerleading (the dependent variable) has been measured on a scale that goes from 1 ("Performance guaranteed to cause fans to root for the opposing team") to 10 ("Performance results in terminal happiness among fans"). We'll also assume that this scale, called the Cheer Leader Activ-

ity Profile/Teacher Rating of Athletic Performance or CLAP/TRAP, is normally distributed and has all of the other good qualities we would want. If Dr. Teeme wanted to predict CLAP/TRAP scores from the person's height (in inches), jumping ability (in inches), and intelligence (in IQ points), he could run a multiple regression equation, which we discussed in Chapter 12; it would look something like:

$$\text{CLAP / TRAP} = b_0 + b_1 \text{ Height} + b_2 \text{ Jumping} + b_3 \text{ Inteligence} \tag{18-1}$$

A diagram of what this equation does is shown in Figure 18-1. For reasons that will become clear soon, we've drawn a box around each of the variables and a straight arrow[2] leading from each of the predictor variables to the dependent variable (DV). This implies that we are assuming that each of the variables acts directly on the DV. But a little reflection may lead

---

[1] *In fact, path analysis is "merely" a subset of SEM, so we've just halved what you have to learn. But, because it's easier to understand, we'll start off with path analysis.*

[2] *That means a line that doesn't curve, with an arrowhead at one end; it doesn't refer to a well-scrubbed Boy Scout.*

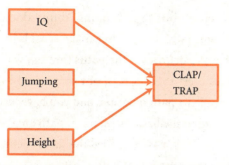

FIGURE 18-1 Model of linear regression predicting CLAP/TRAP scores from Height, Jumping Ability, and IQ.

us to feel that the story is a bit more complicated than this. A person's height may act directly on the coach's evaluation, but it may also influence jumping ability. So a more accurate picture may be the one shown in Figure 18-2. One question we may want to ask is, which model is a more accurate reflection of reality?

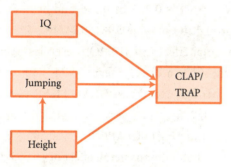

FIGURE 18-2 Modification of Figure 18-1 to show that Jumping Ability is affected by Height.

We'll begin by just looking at how the variables are correlated with each other, to get a feel for what's going on; the correlation matrix is shown in Table 18-1. As we would suspect, CLAP/TRAP has a strong positive relationship to Height and Jumping Ability, and is strongly and negatively related to IQ; Height and Jumping are positively correlated with each other and negatively related to IQ.[3]

TABLE 18-1 Correlations among the variables in predicting CLAP/TRAP scores

	CLAP/TRAP	Height	IQ	Jumping
CLAP/TRAP	1.000	0.807	−0.608	0.677
Height		1.000	−0.505	0.678
IQ			1.000	−0.433
Jumping				1.000

Interpreting the Numbers

If we now ran a multiple regression based on the model in Figure 18-1, we would get (among many other things) three standardized regression weights (betas, or βs), one for each of the predictors. In this case, β_{Height} is 0.548, $\beta_{Jumping}$ is 0.199, and β_{IQ} is −0.245. While the relative magnitudes of the β weights and their signs parallel those of the correlations, the relationship between these two sets of parameters isn't immediately obvious. The problem is that the model in Figure 18-1 shows only part of the picture; it doesn't take into account the correlations among the predictor variables themselves. To introduce a notation we'll use a lot in this chapter, we can show that the variables are correlated with each other by joining the boxes with curved, double-headed arrows. In Figure 18-3, we've added the arrows and some numbers. The numbers near the curved arrows are the zero-order correlations between the predictor variables, and those above the single-headed arrows are the correlations between the predictors and the DV. Below the arrows, and in parentheses, are the β weights. Now, believe it or not, we can see the relationship between the correlations and the β weights.

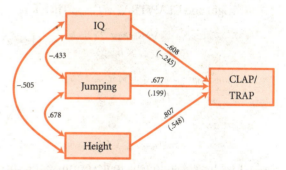

FIGURE 18-3 Figure 18-1 with the correlations among the variables and the β weights in parentheses added.

Let's start by looking at the effect of IQ on CLAP/TRAP. Its β weight is −0.245. Also, IQ exerts an indirect effect on CLAP/TRAP through its correlations with Jumping Ability and Height. Through Jumping Ability, the magnitude of the effect of IQ is the correlation between the two predictors ($r = −0.433$) times

---

[3]*The negative relationship between Height and IQ should give you some clue as to the author of this chapter. As a hint, Norman is 6'3"; Streiner is 5'8".*

the effect of Jumping on CLAP/TRAP, which is its β weight of 0.199; and so $-0.433 \times 0.199 = -0.086$. Similarly, the indirect effect of IQ through Height is -0.505×0.548, or -0.277. Adding up these three terms gives us:

$$(-0.245) + (-0.086) + (-0.277) = -0.608 \quad \text{(18-2)}$$

which is the correlation between IQ and CLAP/TRAP. Doing the same thing for Jumping Ability shows a direct effect of 0.199; an indirect effect through IQ of $-0.433 \times (-0.245)$ (which is 0.106), and an indirect effect through Height of 0.678×0.548, or 0.372. The sum of these three terms is 0.677, which, in this case,[4] is the zero-order correlation between Jumping and CLAP/TRAP.[5] Conceptually, then, r is the sum of both the direct and indirect effects between the two variables.

More formally, we can denote the correlation between pairs of predictors with the usual symbol for a correlation, r. Then, the correlation between IQ and Jumping is $r_{\text{IQ-Jump}}$, between Height and Jumping is $r_{\text{Height-Jump}}$, and between IQ and Height is $r_{\text{IQ-Height}}$. The path between each of the predictors and the dependent variable is a β weight, so that between Jumping and CLAP/TRAP is β_{Jump}, between IQ and CLAP/TRAP is β_{IQ}, and between Height and CLAP/TRAP is β_{Height}. Therefore:

$$r_{\text{IQ-CLAP/TRAP}} = \beta_{\text{IQ}} + (R_{\text{IQ-Height}} \times \beta_{\text{Height}}) \\ + (r_{\text{IQ-Jump}} \times \beta_{\text{Jump}}) \quad \text{(18-3a)}$$

$$r_{\text{Height-CLAP/TRAP}} = \beta_{\text{Height}} + (r_{\text{IQ-Height}} \times \beta_{\text{IQ}}) \\ + (r_{\text{Height-Jump}} \times \beta_{\text{Jump}}) \quad \text{(18-3b)}$$

$$r_{\text{Jump-CLAP/TRAP}} = \beta_{\text{Jump}} + (r_{\text{IQ-Jump}} \times \beta_{\text{IQ}}) \\ + (r_{\text{Height-Jump}} \times \beta_{\text{Height}}) \quad \text{(18-3c)}$$

What we have just done is to **decompose** the correlations for the predictor variables into their **direct** and **indirect effects** on the DV. Now we are in a better position to see what adding the arrow in Figure 18-2 does to our model. The main effect is that it imposes directionality on the indirect effects; we are saying that Height can affect Jumping Ability (which

makes sense), but that Jumping Ability doesn't affect Height (which wouldn't make sense). In other words, we've delineated the **paths** through which the variables exert their effects; not surprisingly, Figure 18-2 is called a **path diagram**, and you have just been introduced to the basic elements of **path analysis**.

In Figure 18-4, we've added the "path coefficients" to the second model (the one in Figure 18-2). The direct effects are changed only slightly (although they are changed), but now the indirect effects are quite different. If we follow the arrows leading out of each predictor variable, we see that Jumping has a direct effect of 0.200 and, strange as it may seem, an indirect effect through Height of 0.678×0.550 ($= 0.373$), for a total of 0.573.[6] For Height, the direct effect of 0.550 is augmented by its indirect effect through Jumping Ability of 0.678×0.200, or 0.136, and its indirect effect through IQ of $-0.505 \times (-0.247)$ ($= 0.125$), so that its total effect is 0.810. IQ is even less straightforward; it has a direct effect (-0.247), an indirect effect through Height to CLAP/TRAP ($-0.505 \times 0.550 = -0.278$), and a very indirect effect through Height to Jumping to CLAP/TRAP ($-0.505 \times 0.678 \times 0.200 = -0.068$), for an overall effect of -0.593. If you were paying attention, you will have noticed that, in this example, these numbers do not add up to equal the correlations in Table 18-2. We'll show you why they don't when we discuss how we can tell which models are better than others.

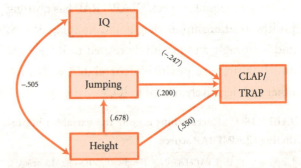

FIGURE 18-4   Figure 18-2 with path coefficients added.

---

[4] *We'll see in a bit that this is true in this model, but it doesn't necessarily hold in others. We can actually exploit this to tell us how "good" each model is.*

[5] *To test your understanding of these concepts (but mainly to save the batteries in our calculator), we'll leave the calculations for the direct and indirect effects of Height to you.*

[6] *We'll see the reason for this counter-intuitive path in the next section.*

TABLE 18-2 Original correlations in the upper triangle and reproduced correlations in the lower triangle

	CLAP/TRAP	Height	IQ	Jumping
CLAP/TRAP	1.000	0.807	−0.608	0.677
Height	0.810	1.000	−0.505	0.678
IQ	−0.593	−0.505	1.000	−0.433
Jumping	0.573	0.678	−0.342	1.000

Finding Your Way through the Paths

When we decomposed the correlations in Figures 18-3 and 18-4, there were some paths we did not travel down, and others that we took seemed somewhat bizarre. For example, in Figure 18-3, we traced the indirect contribution of IQ → Jumping → CLAP/TRAP and IQ → Height → CLAP/TRAP; we did not have a path IQ → Jumping → Height → CLAP/TRAP. Similarly, in Figure 18-4, we had Height → Jumping → CLAP/TRAP, and, strangely enough, Jumping → Height → CLAP/TRAP, even though the arrow itself actually points from Height to Jumping. Back in 1934, Sewall Wright (the granddaddy of path analysis) laid out the rules of the road:

- For any single path, you can go through a given variable only once.
- Once you've gone forward along a path using one arrow, you can't go back on the path using a different arrow.
- You can't go through a double-headed curved arrow more than one time.

Kenny (1979) added a fourth rule:

- You can't enter a variable on one arrowhead and leave it on another arrowhead.

Kenny's rule is the reason why, in Figure 18-3, we did not trace out the path IQ → Jumping → Height → CLAP/TRAP or IQ → Height → Jumping → CLAP/TRAP. These paths enter one variable on an arrowhead from IQ, and would then leave on an arrowhead to get to the other variable—maybe not a felony offense but definitely a misdemeanor with respect to the rules.

Bizarre as it may seem, the path in Figure 18-4

starting at Jumping and then going through Height to CLAP/TRAP doesn't violate any of these rules. The rule prohibits only paths that go forward and then backward, this path goes backward and then forward. This path is meaningless in terms of our knowledge of biology (the technical term for this is a **spurious** effect), but it is legitimate insofar as decomposition of the correlation is concerned. It exists because Jumping and CLAP/TRAP have a common cause—Height.

Endogenous and Exogenous Variables

The models we've discussed so far are relatively simple ones. To show what more path analysis can do, let's look at some models it can handle and, at the same time, introduce you to some of the arcane vocabulary. When we looked at Figure 18-1, we referred to the variables on the left as the predictors and CLAP/TRAP as the dependent variable. Now that we have a new statistical technique, we have new terms for these variables.[7] In path analysis (and, as we'll see, in SEM in general), the variables on the left are referred to as **exogenous variables**.

Exogenous variables have arrows emerging from them and none pointing to them.

This means that exogenous variables influence or affect other variables, but whatever influences them is not included in the model. For example, a person's height may be influenced by genetics and diet, but our model will ignore these factors.

What we had called the dependent variable, CLAP/TRAP, is an **endogenous variable** in SEM

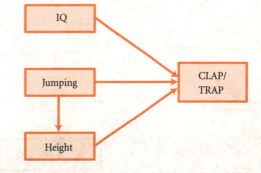

FIGURE 18-5 **Figure 18-2** with Jumping Ability affecting Height.

---

[7]*Actually, this isn't as capricious as it may first appear; for reasons we'll see shortly, keeping the original terms can lead to some confusion.*

terms, in that it has arrows pointing toward it. What about Jumping Ability in Figure 18-2? It has an arrow pointing toward it as well as one emerging from it. As long as there is at least one arrow (a path) pointing toward a variable, it is called endogenous.

Any variable that has at least one arrow pointing toward it is an **endogenous variable.**

This illustrates why the terms "independent," "predictor," and "dependent" variable can be confusing in path analysis. In Figure 18-4, Jumping is a dependent variable in relation to Height but a predictor in terms of its relationship to CLAP/TRAP. This further shows one of the major strengths of path analysis as compared to multiple regression; regression cannot easily deal with the situation in which a variable is both an independent variable (IV) and a DV.

Getting Disturbed

The models in Figure 18-6 look fairly complete and, in Part F, relatively complex. But, in fact, something is missing. A more accurate picture (and a necessary one, from the standpoint of the statistical programs that analyze path models) is to attach **disturbance terms** to each endogenous variable. These are usually denoted by the letter D (for Disturbance), E for (Error), a small circle with an arrow pointing toward

the variable, or a circle with one of the letters inside, as in Figure 18-7. This is similar to what we have in multiple regression, where every equation has an error term tacked on the end that captures the measurement error associated with each of the predictor variables. In path analysis (and in SEM in general), the disturbance term has a broader meaning; in addition to measurement error, it also reflects all of the other factors that affect the endogenous variable and which aren't in our model, either because we couldn't measure them (e.g., genetic factors) or we were too dumb to think of them at the time.

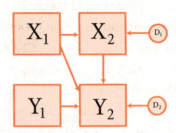

FIURE 18-7　Addition of disturbance terms to Figure 18-6F.

If we were to draw complete diagrams for the examples we've discussed, then Figure 18-3 would have a disturbance term attached to CLAP/TRAP. In Figure 18-4, there would be two disturbance terms: one associated with CLAP/TRAP and one for Jumping, since it has become an endogenous variable with the addition of the path from Height. So why didn't we draw them? Since every endogenous variable must have a disturbance term, they are superfluous to those of us who are "au courant" with path analysis. We have to draw them in when we use the computer programs, and we may put them in diagrams for the sake of completeness, but they're optional at other times.

Types of Path Models

Figure 18-6 shows a number of different path models, some of which we have already encountered. Those on the left are **direct** models, in that the exogenous variables influence the endogenous ones without any intermediary steps; in other words, the endogenous variables have arrows pointing toward them and none pointing away from them. In Part A of the figure (called an **independent** path model),

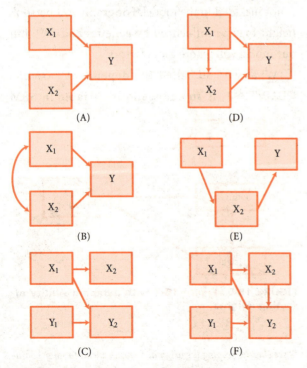

FIGURE 18-6　Different path models.

the two exogenous variables affect an endogenous one, and the exogenous variables are not correlated with each other; hence the name "independent." This situation isn't too common in research with humans, since, as Meehl said in his famous sixth law (1990), "everything correlates to some extent with everything else".[8] In part B of the figure, a **correlated** path model, is more common; it's equivalent to a multiple regression, although we often have more than two predictors, and drawing in all those arcs between pairs of variables can really make the picture look messy. The picture it portrays is what we usually deal with, in that we assume the predictors are correlated with one another to various degrees. In Part C, there are two exogenous and two endogenous variables. The interesting thing about this model is that X_1 and X_2 can be different variables, or they can be the same variable measured at two different times; the same applies to Y_1 and Y_2. For example, in one study we did (McFarlane et al., 1983), we wanted to see if stressful events in a person's life led to more illness. X_1 and X_2 were the amount of stress at time 1 and 6 months later at time 2, and Y_1 and Y_2 the number of illnesses at these two times. This model allowed us to take into account the fact that the best predictor of future behavior is past behavior (the path between Y_1 and Y_2), and then look at the added effect of stress at time 1 on illness at time 2.[9] The two endogenous variables don't have to be the same ones as the exogenous, nor do the two sets of variables have to be measured at different times, but they can be. Such is the beauty of path analysis.

The major difference between the diagrams on the left of Figure 18-6 and those on the right are that the latter have endogenous variables with arrows pointing both toward them as well as away from them. These are referred to as **indirect** or **mediated** models, because the variables with both types of arrows mediate the effect of the variable pointing to

them on the variables to which they point. In Part D of Figure 18-6, variables X_1 and X_2 both influence Y. However, X_2 also mediates the effect of X_1 on Y. In our example, Jumping (X_2) affects CLAP/TRAP directly and also mediates the effects of Height (X_1). That is, we would expect that, if two people can jump equally high, but one person is 6'3" and the other "only" 5'8",[10] we would expect the second person to get more "credit" since he's exerting himself more. In Part E of the figure, variable X_1 does not affect the endogenous variable directly, but only through its influence on X_2. For example, the height of one's father (X_1) affects a person's CLAP/TRAP score (Y) only by its effects on the cheerleader's height (X_2), which in turn affects Y.

The final model we'll show (there are infinitely many others), part F of Figure 18-6, is the same as part C, except that we've added a path between X_2 and Y_2. What this does is to turn X_2 (stress at time 2) into a mediated variable. Now we are saying that the number of illnesses measured at time 2 is affected by three things: illness at time 1, stress at time 1, and stress at time 2. Furthermore, we are saying that stress at time 1 works in two ways on illness behavior at time 2: directly (sort of a delayed reaction to stress), and by affecting stress at time 2, which, in turn, affects illness behavior immediately. The magnitude of the path coefficients tells us how strong each effect is.

Recursive and Nonrecursive Models

Although it may not be apparent at first, all of the models in Figure 18-6 are similar in two important ways. First, all the paths are unidirectional[11]; that is, they go from "cause" to "effect" (using those terms very loosely, without really meaning causation). Second, if we had drawn the disturbance terms in the models, they would all be assumed to be independent from one another; that is, we wouldn't draw curved arrows between the disturbances. For reasons

---

[8] *No one really remembers his first five laws.*

[9] *A more complete model would add a path between X_2 and Y_2, but this is a different class of model, as we'll see in a moment.*

[10] *To choose two heights, not quite at random (see note 3).*

[11] *We don't count the curved arrows, as they reflect correlations among the variables, not paths between them.*

that surpass human understanding, these models are referred to as **recursive** models.

Let's return to the example we used in Figure 18-6F and modify it a bit more. In Figure 18-8, we have added a path between X_1 and Y_1 and between X_2 and Y_2 to indicate that stress could affect illness concurrently. It could be just as logical that the relationship goes the other way and even more logical that the relationship was reciprocal: that stress at a given time affects illness and also that illness affects stress, so that Figure 18-8 may be a more accurate portrayal of what is actually occurring. A path diagram with this feedback loop is called a **nonrecursive** model.

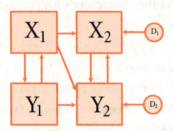

FIGURE 18-8   A nonrecursive path model.

Note that there is a difference between connecting two variables with a curved, double-headed arrow, and joining them with two straight arrows going in opposite directions. The former means that we "merely" expect the two variables to covary, such as when we use two similar measures of the same thing. Covariance may be the result of one variable affecting the other, but it may also be due to the effect of some underlying factor affecting both of them. A feedback loop, on the other hand, explicitly states that each variable directly affects the other—stress leads to illness, and illness leads to stress.

Analysis and interpretation of nonrecursive models are much more difficult than with recursive ones, and far beyond the scope of one chapter in a book. If you ever do need to analyze a nonrecursive model, we suggest two things: (1) pour yourself a stiff drink and think again, and (2) if you still want to do it, read one of the books listed under "SUGGESTED READINGS AND WEBSITES."

K.I.S.S.[12]

At first glance, it may seem as if the safest strategy to use is to draw paths connecting everything with everything else, and to let the path coefficients tell you what's going on. This would be a bad idea for two reasons. First, as we will emphasize over and over again in this chapter (and indeed in much of the book), model building should be based on theory and knowledge. One disadvantage of the more sophisticated statistical techniques is that they are too powerful in some regard; they capitalize on chance variance and, if you blithely and blindly use a computer program to replace your brain cells, you can be led wondrously astray, albeit with low p levels. The second reason is that there are mathematical limits to how many paths you can have in any one diagram.

The number of parameters (i.e., statistical effects, such as path coefficients, variances, covariances, and disturbances) you can analyze is determined by the number of observations. "Observations" here is a function of the number of variables and is *not* related to the number of subjects. That is, a given path model has the same number of observations, whether the study used 10 subjects or 10 000 subjects. If there are k variables, then:

$$Number\ of\ Observations = \frac{k \times (k+1)}{2} \qquad (18\text{-}4)$$

because there are $[k \times (k-1)/2]$ covariances among the variables, plus k variances. In Figure 18-3, we have four observed variables, so we have 10 observations. This means that we can examine at most 10 parameters. Now the problem is, How many parameters do we actually have in this model? Another way of asking this question is, What don't we know that we should know?

To answer this, we have to elaborate a bit more on the purpose of path analysis and, more generally, of structural equation modeling. We are trying to find out what affects the endogenous variables; that is, how the exogenous variables work together (the curved paths, which represent correlations or

[12]*For the two people in the world who don't know what this means, it stands for Keep It Simple, Stupid.*

covariances), and which of those paths (the straight arrows) are important. This is determined by the variances of the variables. If we had a perfect model, then knowing these variances would allow us to predict the person-to-person variation in the endogenous variables. Because the endogenous variables are, by definition, "caused" or influenced by the other variables, they are not free to vary or covary on their own but only in response to exogenous variables. Consequently, we are not interested in estimating the variances of endogenous variables but only those variances for variables that can vary. Note that the disturbance term attached to an endogenous variable is, in SEM thinking, free to vary and thus influence the endogenous variable—so it's one of those things we have to estimate.

Where does this leave us with respect to Figure 18-3? It's obvious we want to estimate the 3 path coefficients, so they're on the list of parameters to estimate. Also, we don't know the variances of the exogenous variables or the covariances among them, so that adds another 6 parameters (3 variances + 3 covariances). Finally, we have the variance of the disturbance term itself (which isn't in the figure, but is implied), meaning that there are 10 parameters to be estimated.

Now let's do the same for Figure 18-4. There are still 4 observed variables, so the limit of 10 parameters remains, but there are a different number of arrows. We have 4 path coefficients (the 3 from the variables to CLAP/TRAP, and 1 from Height to Jumping); the covariance between IQ and Height; the variances of 2 exogenous variables (IQ and Height); and 2 disturbance terms (those for Jumping and CLAP/TRAP), resulting in 9 parameters to be estimated.

If you've followed this so far, a number of questions should arise: Why didn't we count the variance of CLAP/TRAP in Figure 18-3 as one of the parameters to be estimated? Why did we count the variance of Jumping among the parameters in Figure 18-3, but not in Figure 18-4? Why can't we have more than 10 parameters? Does it make any difference that we had 10 parameters to estimate in Figure 18-3 and 9

in Figure 18-4? Is there intelligent life on Earth? If you've really been paying attention, you will have noticed that we already answered the first two questions (but we'll repeat it for your sake). Stay tuned, and the remaining questions will be answered (except perhaps the last question, which has baffled scientists and philosophers for centuries).

To reiterate what we've said, we didn't count the variance of CLAP/TRAP in either model, or that of Jumping in Figure 18-4, for the same reason: they're endogenous variables and thus not free to vary and covary on their own. Since the goal of SEM is to explain the variances of variables and the covariances between pairs of variables that can vary, we aren't interested in the parameters of variables that are determined by outside influences. Hence, endogenous variables don't enter into the count.

Why can't we examine more parameters than observations? The analogy is having an equation with more unknown terms than data. For example, if we had a simple equation:

$$a = b + c \qquad (18\text{-}5)$$

and we know that $a = 5$, then what are the values of b and c? The problem is that there are an infinite number of possible answers: $b = 0$ and $c = 5$; $b = 1$ and $c = 4$; $b = -19.32$ and $c = 24.32$; and so forth. We say that the model is **undefined** (or **under-identified**) in that there isn't a unique solution. If we had another observation (e.g., $b = -3$), then we can determine that c has to be 8; the model is now **defined** (the technical term is **just-identified**). If there were as many observations as parameters (i.e., we knew ahead of time that $a = 5$, $b = -3$ and $c = 8$), then the model would be correct, but there would be nothing left to estimate (this is referred to as being **over-identified**). This is the situation in Figure 18-3, where there are 10 observations and 10 parameters. In the next section, we'll see the implication of this.

As Good as It Gets: Goodness-of-Fit Indicators
How do we know if the model we've postulated is a good one? In path analysis, there are three things we look for: the significance of the individual paths; the **reproduced** (or **implied**) correlations; and the model as a whole. Of the three, the significance of the

paths is the easiest to evaluate. The path coefficients are parameters and, as is the case with all parameters, they are estimated with some degree of error. Again like other parameters, the significance is dependent on the ratio of the parameter to its standard error of estimate. In this case, we end up with a z-statistic:

$$z = \frac{Estimate\ of\ Path\ Coefficient}{Standard\ Error\ of\ Estimate} \qquad (18\text{-}6)$$

and (yet again like other z tests), if it is 1.96 or greater, it is significant at the 0.05 level, using a two-tailed test.[13]

A second criterion concerns the reproduced (or implied) correlation matrix. You'll remember that, when we reproduced the correlations from the path coefficients in Figure 18-3, we were able to perfectly duplicate the correlations by tracing all the paths. However, when we tried to reproduce the correlations in Figure 18-4, we found differences between the actual and implied correlations. In fact, if we look at the reproduced correlations in the lower half of Table 18-2, some of them differ quite a bit from the original correlations, which are in the upper half of the matrix. This tell us two things: (1) the model in Figure 18-3 fits the data better than the model in Figure 18-4; and (2) the model in Figure 18-3 fits the data too well, in that there is no discrepancy at all between the original and the reproduced correlations. The reason is apparent if we compare the number of observations in Figure 18-3 with the number of parameters; there are 10 of each. Like the case in which we are told ahead of time that $a = b + c$ and that $a = 5$, $b = -3$, and $c = 8$, there's nothing left to estimate, and there is a perfect fit between the model and the data. Life is usually much more interesting when we have fewer parameters than observations; we can then compare how close different models come to estimating the data.

When we look at the model as a whole, the major statistic we use is called the **goodness-of-fit χ^2** (χ^2_{GoF}), which we'll meet later in different contexts. In most statistical tests, bigger is better—the larger the

value of a t-test, F-test, r, or whatever, the happier we are. This situation is reversed in the case of the χ^2_{GoF}, where we want the result to be as small as possible. Why this sudden change of heart?

Let's go over the logic of χ^2 tests. Basically, they all reduce to the difference between what we observe and what would be expected, with "expected" meaning the values we would find if the null hypothesis were true. Thus, the larger the discrepancy between the two sets of numbers—observed and expected—the larger the χ^2. Because we usually want our results (the observed values) to be different from the null, we want the value of χ^2 to be large. However, when we use χ^2 to test for goodness-of-fit, we are not testing our observed findings against the null hypothesis, but rather against some hypothesized model, and we want our results to be congruent with it. So, the less the results deviate from the model, the better. In the case of χ^2_{GoF}, we hope to find a nonsignificant result, indicating that our results match the model.

The degrees of freedom (df) associated with the χ^2_{GoF} is the difference between the number of observations and the number of parameters. In the case of the model in Figure 18-4, we have 10 observations and 9 parameters to estimate; hence, $df = 1$. In this example, χ^2_{GoF} is 2.044, which has a p level of 0.153. Because the χ^2_{GoF} is not statistically significant, we have no reason to reject the model. Just to reinforce what we said earlier, the χ^2_{GoF} for the model in Figure 18-5, where the arrow between Jumping and Height went the "wrong" way, is also 2.044; so this statistic doesn't tell us about the "causality" of the relationship between the variables. For the sake of completeness, we also discussed a different model. This was a model where there was a path between IQ and Jumping Ability. The χ^2_{GoF} for this model (which also has $df = 1$) is 42.525, which is highly significant, and means that there is a very large discrepancy between the model and the data.

In Figure 18-3, we cannot calculate a χ^2_{GoF}, because the number of parameters is equal to the num-

---

[13]*The standard error is estimated by the computer using methods that are beyond the scope of this chapter.*

ber of observations, meaning that $df = 0$. This further illustrates that, when a model is **fully determined** (a fancy way of saying that the number of parameters and observations is the same), the data fit the model perfectly.

So, if we find that χ^2_{GoF} is not significant, does this prove that our model is the correct one? Unfortunately, the answer is a resounding "No." As we just showed, the χ^2 statistics associated with Figure 18-2 and Figure 18-5 are identical, even though one model makes sense and the other is patently ridiculous. Also, the χ^2_{GoF} is dependent on the sample size, since this influences the standard errors of the estimates. If the sample size is low (say, under 100), even models that deviate quite a bit from the data may not result in statistically significant χ^2 values. Conversely, if the sample size is very large (over 200 or so), it is almost impossible to find a model that doesn't deviate from the data to some degree. Furthermore, there is no guarantee that there is yet another, untested, model that may fit the data even better. Thus, χ^2_{GoF} can tell us if we're on the right track, but it cannot provide definite proof that we've arrived.

What We Assume

Path analysis makes certain assumptions, as do all statistical tests. Many of the assumptions are the same as for multiple regression, which isn't surprising, given that the two techniques are closely related. The first assumption is that the variables are measured without error. This is patently impossible in most (if not all) research, but it serves to remind us that we should try to use instruments that are as reliable as possible. When this rule is violated (as it always is), it results in underestimates of the effects of mediator variables (that is, the indirect paths) and overestimates of the effects of the direct paths (Baron and Kenny, 1986). The second assumption, which is much harder to detect, is that all important variables are included in the model. It's not a good idea to include variables that aren't important, but these usually become obvious from their weak path coefficients. When crucial variables are left out, though, the model fit may be poor or yield spurious results. No statistical test can tell us which variables have

been omitted; only our theory can guide us in this regard. Third, multiple regression and path analysis assume that the variables are **additive**. If there are interactions among the variables, an appropriate interaction term should be built into the model (Klem, 1995). Finally, both techniques can handle a moderate degree of correlation among the predictor variables (**multicollinearity**), but the parameter estimates become unreliable if the correlations are high (Klem, 1995; Streiner, 1994).

A Word about Sample Size

The df associated with the χ^2_{GoF} test is the difference between the number of observations and the number of parameters. So where does the sample size come into play? The sample size affects the significance of the parameter estimates—the path coefficients, the variances, and the covariances. In all cases, the significance is the ratio of the parameter to the standard error (SE), and the standard error, as we all know, is dependent on the square root of N (sample size). Having said that, how many subjects do we need? Unfortunately, there is no simple relationship between the number of parameters to be estimated and the sample size. A very rough rule of thumb is that there should be at least 10 subjects per parameter (some authors argue for 20), as long as there are at least 200 subjects. Yes, Virginia, path analysis (and SEM in general) is extremely greedy when it comes to sample sizes.

STRUCTURAL EQUATION MODELING

The major limitation with path analysis is that our drawings are restricted to circles and boxes, which become extremely monotonous. Wouldn't it be nice if we could add some variety, such as ovals? Of course the answer is "Yes"; why else would we even ask the question? This isn't as ludicrous as it first appears. In the drawing conventions of SEM, circles represent error or disturbance terms, and boxes are drawn to show **measured** variables—that is, ones we observe directly on a physical scale (e.g., Height) or a paper-and-pencil scale (e.g., CLAP/TRAP). In the chapter on factor analysis, however, we were introduced to another type of variable: **latent** variables (which we referred to in that chapter as **factors**). Very briefly, latent variables aren't measured directly; rather, they are inferred as the "glue" that ties together two or more observed (i.e., directly measured) variables. For example, if a person gets a high score on some paper-and-pencil test of anxiety (a measured variable), shows an increased heart rate in enclosed spaces (another measured variable), and uses anxiolytic medications (yet a third observed variable), we would say that these are all manifestations of the unseen factor (or latent variable) of "anxiety."

The primary difference between path analysis and SEM is that the former can look at relationships only among measured variables, whereas SEM can examine both measured and latent variables. Because we represent latent variables with ovals, there is the added advantage that our diagrams can now become more varied. Figure 18-9 illustrates the example we just used in SEM terms. Notice the direction of the arrows: they point from the latent variable *to* the measured ones, which may at first glance seem backwards. In fact, this reflects our conceptualization of latent variables—that they are the underlying causes of what we are measuring directly. Thus, the latent variable (or trait or factor) of anxiety is what accounts for the person's score on the test, his or her tachycardia, and is what leads to the use of pills. Also, since the three measured variables are endogenous, they have error or disturbance terms associated with them.

If Figure 18-9 looks suspiciously like the pictures we drew when we were discussing factor analysis, it's

not a coincidence. Exploratory factor analysis (EFA—the kind we discussed in Chapter 17) is now seen as a subset of SEM. We don't gain very much, however, if we were to use the programs and techniques of SEM to do EFA. In fact, because SEM is a model testing or confirmatory technique, rather than an exploratory one, the computer output is less helpful than from programs specifically designed to do EFA (if that's what we want to do). Despite this, we'll start off with EFA to show you how the concepts we covered in path analysis apply in this relatively simple case. This will put us in a better position to understand how SEM works in more general cases.[14]

SEM and Factor Analysis

In addition to the variables of Height, Jumping Ability, and IQ, Dr. Teeme also hypothesized that, since the first part of the word "cheerleading" is "cheer," success in this endeavor also depends on the candidate's personality. However, unable to find a questionnaire that measures Cheer directly, he had to resort to using three other tests that he felt collectively measured the same thing: one tapping extroversion (the Seller of Used Cars Scale, or SUCS); another measuring positive outlook on life (the Mary Poppins Inventory, or MPI); and a third focusing on denial of negative feelings (the We're OK Scale, or WOKS). The correlations among these scales are shown in Table 18-3. As he suspected, the correlations were moderate, but positive.

TABLE 18-3   Correlations among three tests to measure "Cheer"

	SUCS	MPI	WOKS
SUCS	1.000	0.669	0.608
MPI		1.000	0.577
WOKS			1.0000

If we now did an EFA, using a least-squares method of extracting the factor, we would find that the factor loadings were 0.840 for SUCS, 0.797 for MPI, and 0.724 for WOKS. A drawing of this using the SEM conventions is shown as Figure 18-10.

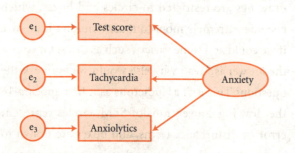

FIGURE 18-9   Relationship between three measured variables and a latent variable.

---

[14]*Notice we said "general" and not "more difficult." That's an old didactic trick we learned to make things more palatable.*

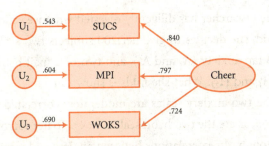

FIGURE 18-10 Factor loadings and uniqueness for the factor "Cheer" and its three measured variables.

There are a few points to note. First, the disturbance or error term in EFA is usually labeled with the letter U (which stands for "uniqueness"); the terminology is different, but the concept is the same.[15] Second, for each variable, the square of the factor loading (which is equivalent to a path coefficient) plus the square of the uniqueness equals 1.00 (e.g., $0.840^2 + 0.543^2 = 1.00$). In English, we've divided up the variance of the variable into two components: that explained by the factor (or latent variable); and that which is not explained by it (the uniqueness, error, or disturbance). Finally, the product of any two factor loadings is equal to the correlation between the variables. For example, the factor loadings for MPI and WOKS are 0.797 and 0.724, respectively; their product (i.e., 0.797×0.724) is 0.577, or their correlation.

Now, if we ran this as if it were a structural equation model, we would find exactly the same thing! So, why make such a big deal about the difference between EFA and confirmatory factor analysis (CFA—the SEM approach to factor analysis)? Leaving the math aside for the moment,[16] the major difference is a conceptual one. In traditional, run-of-the-mill EFA, we are in essence saying, "I don't know how these variables are related to one another. Let me just throw them into the pot and see what comes out." That's why it's called "exploratory," folks. In fact, when we don't know what's going on, it can be a very powerful tool that can help us understand the interrelationships in our data. The downside is that we

can end up with a set of factors that look good statistically but don't make a whole lot of sense from a clinical or scientific perspective; that is, it may not be at all obvious why the variables group together the way they do.

Confirmatory factor analysis, as is the case with all variants of SEM, is a model testing technique, rather than a model building one.[17] So, while we still get pages and pages of output (reams, if we're not careful what we ask for), the action is really at the end, where we see how well the model actually fits the data. This is a point that we've already mentioned and, as promised, we'll keep emphasizing: changes to the model to make it fit the data better should be predicated on our theoretical understanding of the phenomenon we're studying, and not based on moving arrows around to get the best goodness-of-fit index. We'll say a bit more about CFA later in the chapter.

Before we move on to discuss the steps in SEM, some other points about the advantages of using latent variables need to be discussed. In our example of the three scales to measure "Cheer," we said that none measures it exactly but that the three together more or less capture what we want; in other words, we're making a "super-scale" out of three scales. We can accomplish the same goal using other techniques, but the route would be more roundabout. We would have to run an EFA on these variables (and any other sets of variables we wanted to combine); use the output from this analysis to calculate a factor score for each person; and then use that factor score in the next stage of the analysis. With SEM, all of this can be accomplished in one step.

A second advantage arises from the use of measurement theory. Any time we measure something, for example, whether it's blood pressure or pain, some error is involved. The error can arise from a variety of sources: the person's blood pressure may

---

[15]*The reason for the difference is purely historical; EFA was developed many years before SEM, and the term was chosen to denote the unique contribution of that variable: the variance it doesn't share with the other variables (see Chapter 17).*

[16]*Actually, we're going to leave it aside as long as we can.*

[17]*And you wondered why it is called confirmatory factor analysis?*

change from one moment to the next; the manometer may not be perfectly calibrated; and the observer may round up or down to the nearest 5 mm or make a mistake recording the number. When paper-and-pencil or observer-completed tests are involved, even more sources of error exist, such as biases in responding or lapses in concentration. These errors result in a measure that is less than reliable. A problem then arises when we correlate two or more variables: the observed correlation is lower than what we would find if the tests had a reliability of 1.0. Thus, we will almost always underestimate the relationships among the variables and, if the reliabilities are "attenuated" very much, we may erroneously conclude that there is no association when, in fact, one exists (i.e., we would be committing a Type II error). The solution is to **disattenuate** the reliabilities, and figure out what the correlation would be if both tests were totally reliable. One major advantage of SEM is that this is done as part of the process.

If we had only one scale to tap some construct (that is, we would be dealing with a measured variable rather than a latent variable defined by two or more measured ones), we are sometimes further ahead if we randomly split the scale in half and then construct a latent variable defined by these two "sub-scales." We can then calculate the reliability[18] and, based on this, the disattenuated reliability.[19]

Let's see just how powerful disattenuation can be when we're testing a theory. Say we're interested in the relationship between anxiety and the compulsion to read every e-mail message as soon as it pops up on the computer screen. The usual way to test this theory is to give one anxiety inventory and one test of e-mail reading compulsion to a group of people, and see what the correlation is. But, because

the researcher has diligently digested what we've just said, she decides to give her 200 subjects two scales to tap anxiety (A_1 and A_2), and two of e-mail habits (H_1 and H_2). What she finds is shown in Table 18-4. The two anxiety scales are moderately correlated at 0.63, as are the two habit scales (0.64). To her sorrow, though, the correlations between anxiety and e-mail habits correlate only between 0.51 and 0.59; not bad, but not the stuff of which grand theories are made. However, after she creates a latent variable of anxiety, measured by the two A scales, and correlates this with the latent variable of habits, tapped by its two H scales, she finds the correlation between the traits is 0.86, and tenure are guaranteed. In this case, the technique has calculated the parallel forms reliability, used this to disattenuate the reliabilities, and found what the correlation would be in the absence of measurement error.

TABLE 18-4   Correlations among two anxiety scales (A_1 and A_2) and two scales of e-mail reading habits (H_1 and H_2)

	A_1	A_2	H_1	H_2
A_1	1.000	0.634	0.550	0.590
A_2		1.000	0.538	0.512
H_1			1.000	0.636
H_2				1.000

Now that we have a bit of background, let's turn to the steps involved in developing structural equation models. We'll follow the lead of Schumacker and Lomax (1996) and break the process down into five steps:

- Model specification
- Identification
- Estimation
- Testing fit
- Respecification

---

[18]*This would be equivalent to the split-half reliability, for those who are interested (Streiner and Norman, 2003). (Actually, it's the split-half reliability for those who aren't interested, too.) On a technical note, the reliability is corrected only for those sources of error that are captured in the model, usually due to items. If the model does not include the same scale administered on two occasions, then it cannot correct for test-retest unreliability, for example. For more details, see DeShon (1998).*

[19]*Some measurement theoreticians do not like using disattenuated reliabilities in scale development, because they are overly optimistic regarding the utility of the tests. But, in this context, they give a more accurate estimate of the relationships among the variables, which is our primary interest.*

Model Specification

To a dress designer, **model specification** may mean, "I want a woman who's 5'8" tall, weighs 123 pounds, and has a perfect 36-24-36 figure." To many men, it means stating which supercharged engine to put into a sports car, and whether to get a hard or a rag top (to attract the model of the first definition). Here, however, we are referring to something far more mundane: explicitly stating the theoretical model that you want to test. We have already discussed much of this when we were looking at path analysis. The same concepts apply, but now we will broaden them to include both measured variables (which can be analyzed with path analysis) and latent variables (which cannot be). For example, all of the diagrams in Figure 18-6 can be drawn replacing the measured variables with latent ones. In addition, we can "mix and match," using both latent and measured variables in the same diagram, as long as we don't do obviously ridiculous things, such as having two latent variables define a measured one.

Let's use these concepts to fully develop a model of success in cheerleading, which is shown in Figure 18-11. We have a latent variable, Athletic Ability, which is measured by the three observed variables IQ, Height, and Jumping; and a second latent variable, Cheer, which is measured by our scales WOKS, SUCS, and MPI. Based on what we said earlier,[20] it would make sense to randomly split CLAP/TRAP into two parallel forms (CLAP and TRAP) and have these define the latent variable, CT. Because CT is now an endogenous variable (it has arrows coming toward it from Cheer and Athletic Ability), we have to give it a disturbance term, which we've called d1.

This step of model building is called the **measurement model**, because we are specifying how the latent variables are measured. Some of the questions we could ask at this stage are as follows: (1) How well do the observed variables really measure the latent variable? (2) Are some observed variables better indices of the latent variable than are other variables? and (3) How reliable is each observed variable? (We will look at these issues in more depth and actually analyze this model when we discuss some worked-out examples of SEM and CFA.)

Identification

When we were discussing path analysis, we said that the number of parameters can never be larger than

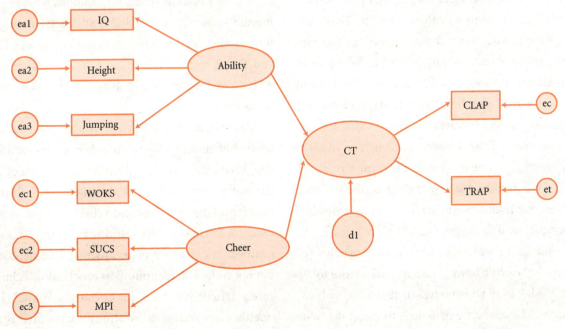

FIGURE 18-11   The full model for success in cheer-leading.

---

[20]*At least we pay attention to what we've said.*

the number of observations, and, ideally, they should be less. However, it is often the case that, once we start adding up all the variances and covariances in our pretty picture, their number exceeds the limit of $[k \times (k + 1)]/2$. The solution is to put constraints on some of the parameters. In the example we used previously, we were able to solve the equation, $5 = b + c$, by specifying beforehand that $b = -3$; that is, we made b a **fixed** parameter. We could also have solved the equation if we had said that $b = c$, in which case both b and c would have to be 2½. In this case, b and c are referred to as **constrained** parameters. So, we have three types of parameters in structural models: (1) **free** parameters, which can assume any value and are estimated by the structural equation model; (2) **fixed** parameters, which are assigned a specific value ahead of time; and (3) **constrained** parameters, which are unknown (as are free ones) but are limited to be the same as the value(s) of one or more other parameters. The joy[21] of SEM is figuring out how many parameters to leave as free and whether the remaining ones should be fixed or constrained.

Perhaps the easiest way of constraining parameters[22] is simply not to draw a path. We said that MPI loaded on Cheer and (implicitly, by not having a path) did not load on Athletic Ability. That's another way of saying that the parameter for the path from MPI to Athletic Ability is fixed to have a value of 0. Making the model as simple as possible is often the best way of avoiding "identification problems." A second method involves the latent variables. For each unobserved variable with one single-headed arrow emerging from it (such as the error terms), we must fix either the path coefficient or the variance of the error itself to some arbitrary, non-zero value; otherwise, we'd be trying to estimate b and c at the same time. But, because we don't actually measure (or observe) the error term, it doesn't make sense to assign a value to it, which leaves us fixing the path coefficient. The easiest thing to do is to give it the value

1, and this is what's usually done. In any case, assigning a different value won't affect the overall fit of the model, just the estimate of the error variance.[23]

When a latent variable has two or more single-headed arrows coming from it (as is the case with CLAP/TRAP, Cheer, and Athletic Ability), one of them must be set to be equal to 1 (i.e., be a **fixed** parameter). It doesn't really matter at all which one is chosen, but it's best to use the variable with the highest reliability, if this is known. Changing which measured variable has a coefficient of 1 will alter the unstandardized regressions of all the variables related to that latent variable (because the unstandardized regressions are relative to the fixed variable), but it does not affect the standardized regression weights. Notice that we didn't draw curved arrows between the exogenous variables. This is because we assume that the exogenous variables are correlated with themselves, and most programs, such as AMOS (Arbuckle, 1997), build this in automatically.

Finally, as we mentioned previously, there may be times when we believe that the error terms of two or more variables are identical (plus or minus some variation), and these become **constrained** parameters. This situation arises, for example, if we're giving the same test at two different times; or we give it to mothers and fathers; or, as in the case of CLAP and TRAP, split a single test in half. In programs like AMOS, we indicate this by assigning the same name to the errors.

You might think that, if you've gone to the trouble of counting up the number of observations, simplifying the model, and constraining some of the parameters, you will avoid identification problems. Such thinking is naive, and reflects a trust in the inherent fairness of the world that is rarely, if ever, justified. The steps we've just discussed are necessary but not sufficient. Identification problems will almost surely arise if you have a nonrecursive model (i.e., one that has reciprocal relationships), which is yet

---

[21]A term to be taken with a large grain of salt.

[22]The terms "constraining parameters" or "constraints" can refer to making them either fixed or constrained; confusing, ain't it?

[23]If you want a more detailed explanation of the effect of choosing different values for the path coefficient, see Arbuckle (1997).

another reason to avoid them whenever possible. You can also run into difficulty if the **rank** of the matrix[24] you're analyzing is less than the number of variables. This can occur if one variable can be predicted from one or more other variables, meaning that the row and column in a correlation matrix representing that variable is not unique. For instance, the Verbal IQ score of some intelligence tests is derived by adding up the scores of a number of subscales (six on the Wechsler family of tests). If you include the six subscale scores as well as the Verbal IQ score in your data matrix, then you will have problems, since one variable can be predicted by the sum of the others; that is, you have seven variables (the six subscales plus the Verbal IQ) but only six unique ones, resulting in a matrix whose rank is less than the number of variables. Even high correlations among variables (e.g., between height and weight) may produce problems.

Estimation

Now that you've specified the model, the time has come to estimate all of those parameters. The easy work is all of that matrix algebra—inverting matrices, transforming matrices, pre- and post-multiplying matrices, and so forth. Because it's easy, the computer does it for us. What's left for us is the hard stuff—deciding the best method to use. This requires brain cells; a commodity that is in short supply inside the computer.[25] The fact that a number of different techniques exists should act as a warning, one that we've encountered in other contexts. If there were one approach that was clearly superior, then the law of the statistical jungle[26] would dictate that it would survive, and all of the other techniques would exist only as historical footnotes. The continued survival of all of them, and the constant introduction of new ones, indicates that no clearly superior solution exists; hence, the unfortunate need to think about what we're doing.

The **unweighted least squares** (ULS) method of estimating the parameters has the distinct advantage that it does not make any assumptions about the underlying distribution of the variables. However, it is scale-dependent; that is, if one or more of the indices is transformed to a different scale, the estimates of the parameters will change. In most of the work we do, the scales are totally arbitrary; even height can be measured either in inches or centimeters. This means that the same study done in Canada and the United States may come up with different results, simply because of different measurement scales used. This becomes more of a problem when we use paper-and-pencil tests that don't have meaningful scales. This is an unfortunate property, which is one of the reasons ULS is rarely used. **Weighted least squares** (WLS) is also distribution-free and does not require multivariate normality, but it requires a very large sample size (usually three times the number of subjects whom you can enroll) to work well.

Many programs default to the **maximum likelihood** (ML) method of estimating the parameters. This works well as long as the variables are multivariate, normal, and consist of interval or ratio data. But, if the data are extremely skewed or ordinally scaled, then the results of the ML solution are suspect.

So which one do you use? If you have access to the SEM program called LISREL8, and its "front-end" program, PRELIS2, then use those. They will calculate the correct matrix, based on the types of variables you have. If you use one of the other programs (e.g., EQS, PROC CALIS, or AMOS), then it may be worthwhile to run the model with a few different types of estimators. If all of the results are consistent, then you can be relatively confident about what you've found; if they differ, you'll have to go back and take a much closer look at the data to see if you have non-normality, skewness, or some other problem. Then, either try to fix it (e.g., with transformations)

---

[24]*Roughly speaking, the rank of a matrix is the number of unique rows and columns.*

[25]*And almost as rare outside it.*

[26]*Although somehow the thought of statisticians fighting it out, "red in tooth and claw" (yes, statisticians can quote Tennyson) appears somewhat oxymoronic to us.*

or choose a method that best meets the type of data you have.

Testing the Fit

In the previous section, on estimation procedures, we lamented the fact that there were so many different approaches. While that is undoubtedly true, the problem pales into insignificance in comparison to the plethora of statistics used to estimate goodness-of-fit. We already mentioned the χ^2_{GoF} in the context of path analysis, and that test is also used in SEM. It has a distinct advantage in that, unlike all of the other GoF indices, it has a test of significance associated with it. One rule of thumb for a good fit is that χ^2_{GoF} is not significant and that χ^2_{GoF}/df should be less than two. Unfortunately, as we mentioned when we were discussing path analysis, it is very sensitive to sample size and departures from multivariate normality.

Most of the other indices we will discuss[27] are scaled to take values between 0 (no fit) and 1 (perfect fit), although what is deemed a "good fit" is often arbitrary. Usually, a value of 0.90 is the minimum accepted value, but as we just mentioned, there are no probabilities associated with these tests. Let's go over some of the more common and useful ones to show the types of indices available, without trying to be exhaustive (and exhausting).

One class of statistics is called **comparative fit indices**, because they test the model against some other model. The most widely used index (although not necessarily the best) is the **Normed Fit Index** (NFI; Bentler and Bonett, 1980), which tests, if the model is different from the null hypothesis, that all of the variables are independent from one another (in statistical jargon, that the covariances are all zero).[28] It takes the form of:

$$NFI = \frac{\chi^2_{null} - \chi^2_{model}}{\chi^2_{null}} \qquad (18\text{-}7)$$

When we discussed multiple regression, we said that the value of R^2 increases with each predictor variable we add. A similar problem exists for the NFI; it improves as we add parameters. Just as the adjusted R^2 penalizes us for adding variables, the **Normed Fit Index 2** (NFI2, also called the **Incremental Fit Index**, or IFI) penalizes us for adding parameters:

$$NFI2 = \frac{\chi^2_{null} - \chi^2_{model}}{\chi^2_{null} - df^2_{model}} \qquad (18\text{-}8)$$

Another such **parsimony** statistic (you're rewarded for being cheap when it comes to the number of parameters) is the **Comparative Fit Index** (CFI):

$$CFI = \frac{(\chi^2_{null} - df) - (\chi^2_{model} - df)}{\chi^2_{null}} \qquad (18\text{-}9)$$

Nowadays, a more popular variant of this is the **Non-Normed Fit Index** (NNFI), which is commonly called the **Tucker-Lewis Index** (TLI):

$$TLI = \frac{\chi^2_{null}/df - \chi^2_{model}/df}{\chi^2_{null}/df - 1} \qquad (18\text{-}10)$$

For any given model, a lower χ^2-to-df ratio implies a better fit. Both the CFI and TLI depend on the average correlation among the variables. Sometimes the CFI and TLI exceed 1, in which case they are set equal to 1. The CFI and TLI are highly correlated with one another, meaning that only one should be reported. When CFI is less than 1, it is always larger than TLI, which may tempt some to prefer it, but the move is toward using the TLI.

Other indices resemble R^2 in that they attempt to determine the proportion of variance in the covariance matrix accounted for by the model. One such index is the **Goodness-of-Fit Index** (GFI); fortunately for you, its formula involves a lot of matrix algebra, so we won't bother to show it.[29] The **Adjusted GFI** (AGFI) is yet a different parsimony fit index you may run across. There are a number of variants of this, all of which decrease the value of AGI proportionally to

---

[27] We will only mention a few of them; if we listed them all, this book would be thicker than the large print, illustrated version of War and Peace.

[28] As Arbuckle (1997) says, the NFI and other indices that compare your model against the null "encourage you to reflect on the fact that, no matter how badly your model fits, things could always be worse"

[29] If, for some reason you really, really want to see what it looks like, check out Tabachnick and Fidell (1996).

the number of parameters you have. Another widely used index is **Akaike's Information Criterion** (AIC) which is unusual in that smaller(closer to 0) is better[30]:

$$AIC = \chi^2_{model} - 2df_{model} \qquad \textbf{(18-11)}$$

A slight variant of it is called the Consistent AIC, or CAIC:

$$CAIC = \chi^2_{model} - (\log_e N + 1)df_{model} \qquad \textbf{(18-12)}$$

Because nobody knows what a "good" value of AIC or CAIC should be, these indices are used most often to compare models—to choose between two different models of the same data. The one with the smaller AIC or CAIC is "better"; however, there isn't any statistical test for either the indices or the difference between two AICs or two CAICs, so we can't say if one model is statistically better or insignificantly better than the other.

A more recent index, used more and more often now, is the **Root Mean Square Error of Approximation**(RMSEA, often called "Ramsey" in casual conversation). Unlike the previous indices, it takes both the df and the sample size (N) into account:

$$RMSEA = \frac{\sqrt{\chi^2 - df}}{\sqrt{df(N-1)}} \qquad \textbf{(18-13)}$$

Like the AIC and CAIC, it follows the criterion of anorectic fashion models that less is better. As with most of these indices, there's no probability level associated with it. The guidelines are that a value of 0.01 is excellent fit, 0.05 is good, and 0.08 is mediocre. (Why are these numbers?) The problem is that, as with all parameters, RMSEA is just an estimate and, when the sample size and df are low, the confidence interval can be quite wide.

Even more recent than RMSEA is the **Standardized Root Mean Square Residual** (SRMR; yes, every new dawn heralds a new index). It is the standardized difference between the observed correlations among the variables and the reproduced correlations (remember them from our discussion of path analy-

sis?). The criteria for assessing it are generally similar to those for the RMSEA. It is not a parsimony index, so it gets better (smaller) as the sample size and the number of parameters in the model increase. Indeed, it's not unusual to find values of zero.

Life is easy when all of the fit indices tell us the same thing. What do we do when they disagree? The most usual situation occurs when we get high values (i.e., over 0.90) for GFI or NFI2 and a low value for RMSEA (below 0.05), but the χ^2_{GoF} is significant. Unfortunately, here we have to use some judgment; can the significant χ^2_{GoF} be due to "too much" power?

If so, it's probably better to trust one of the other indices. If there are roughly 10 subjects per parameter, then we should look at a number of indices. If they all indicate a "good fit," then go with that. But, if the χ^2_{GoF} is significant, and the other indices disagree with one another, then we have a fit that's marginal, at best, and whether or not to publish depends on your desperation level for another article.

Respecification

Respecification is a fancy term for playing with the model to achieve a better fit with the data. If you've been paying attention, you should realize that the statistical tests play a secondary role in this; the primary role should be your understanding of the area, based on theoretical and empirical considerations. Keep chanting this mantra to yourself as you read this section.

The major reason that a model doesn't fit is that you haven't included some key variables—the ones that are really important. Unfortunately, there are no statistical tests that can help us in this regard. The statistical tests that do exist are for the opposite type of mis-specification errors: those due to variables that don't belong in the model or have paths leading to the "wrong" endogenous or exogenous variables. The easiest way to detect these is to look at the parameters. First, they should have the expected sign. If a parameter is positive and the theory states it should

---

[30]To be consistent with our nomenclature, we would call this the Twiggy criterion (also known as the "Kate Moss criterion" by the younger set).

be negative, then something is dreadfully wrong with your model. The next step is to look at the significance of the parameters. As we've said, all parameters have standard errors associated with them, and the ratio of the parameter to its standard error forms a *t*-or *z*-test. If the test is not significant, then that parameter should likely be set equal to 0. Of course, this assumes that you have a sufficient sample size, so that you're not committing a Type II error.

All of the major SEM programs, such as LISREL, CALIS (part of SAS), AMOS, and EQS, can examine the effects of freeing parameters that you've fixed (the **Lagrange multiplier test**) and dropping parameters from the model (the **Wald statistic**). *These statistical tests should be used with the greatest caution.* Whether to follow their advice *must* be based on theory and previous research; otherwise, you may end up with a model that fits the current data very well but makes little sense and may not be replicable.

Now that we've given you the basics, let's run through a couple of examples.

A Confirmatory Factor Analysis

Let's assume that we have seven measured variables that we postulate reflect two latent variables: a1 through a4 are associated with the latent variable f1, and b1 through b3 with latent variable f2. We also think that the two latent variables may be correlated with each other. We start by drawing a diagram of our model (if we're using a program such as AMOS or EQS), which is shown in Figure 18-12. The program is relatively smart,[31] so it automatically fixed the parameters from all of the error terms to the measured variables to be 1. For each of the endogenous variables, it also set the path parameter for one measured variable to be 1. We didn't like the choice the program made, so we overrode it and selected the variable in each set that, based on previous research, has the highest reliability. After we push the right button, we get the diagram shown in Figure 18-13 and reams of output, which we've summarized in

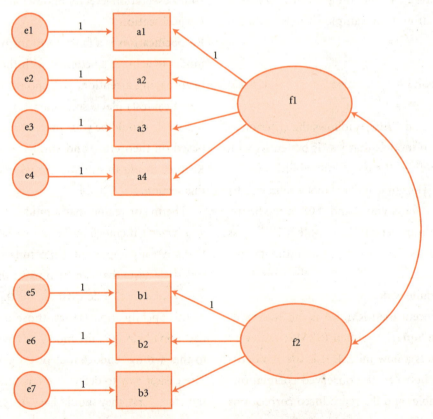

FIGURE 18-12   Input diagram for a confirmatory factor analysis.

---

[31]*With the emphasis on the term "relatively."*

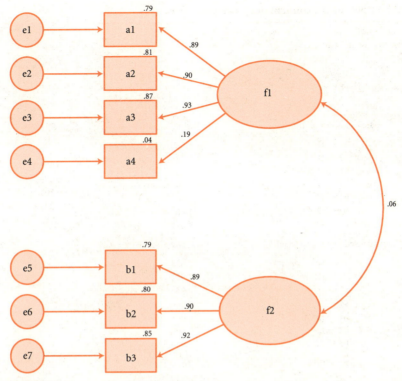

FIGURE 18-13   Output diagram based on Figure 18-12.

Table 18-5.

First, what do all those little numbers in Figure 18-13 mean? The ones over the arrows should be familiar; they're the path coefficients or standardized regression weights (either term will do), which are equivalent to the factor loadings in EFA. The numbers over the rectangles are the squared multiple correlations, which are equivalent to the communality estimates in EFA. There are two other things this figure tells us. First, we goofed when it comes to variable a4; it doesn't really seem to be caused by the latent variable f1. Note that, in contrast to EFA, we aren't told if it loads more on factor f2 or it doesn't load on either factor; yet again, that's because we're testing a model, not trying to develop one. The second fact is that factors f1 and f2 probably aren't correlated; the correlation coefficient is only 0.06.

Now let's turn to the printed output in Table 18-5 and see what else we learn. First, there are 28 "sample moments" in other words (i.e., English), 28 observations. This is based on the fact that there are

seven measured variables, so there are $(7 \times 8) / 2 =$ 28 observations. Our model specifies 15 parameters to be estimated: five regression weights (two others aren't estimated because we fixed them to be 1); the covariance between f1 and f2; and the variances of the seven error (or disturbance) terms and two latent variables.[32] There are 13 degrees of freedom, which is the difference between the number of observations and the number of parameters. The next block of output tells us that the χ^2_{GoF} is 16.392, which, based on 13 degrees of freedom, has a p level of 0.229. So, despite the fact that variable a4 doesn't work too well, the model as a whole fits the data quite well.

We then see the unstandardized and standardized regression weights. The unstandardized weights for a1 and b1 are 1.00, which is encouraging, because we set them to be equal to 1. The other five weights have standard errors associated with them, and the ratio of the weight to the SE is the **Critical Ratio**(CR) which is interpreted as a z-test. All of them are significant (at or over 1.96) except for a4, further con-

---

[32]Note that we estimate the variances of the error terms but not their path coefficients; those we constrained to be 1, since we can't estimate both at the same time.

TABLE 18-5   Selected output for the confirmatory factor analysis

Number of sample moments = 28
Number of distinct parameters to be estimated = 15
Degrees of freedom = 13

Chi-squared = 16.392
Degrees of freedom = 13
Probability = 0.229

Regression weights	Estimate	SE	CR
a1 ← f1	1.000	—	—
a2 ← f1	1.029	0.078	13.166
a3 ← f1	1.021	0.073	13.940
a4 ← f1	0.199	0.107	1.857
b1 ← f2	1.000	0.086	12.779
b2 ← f2	1.100	0.082	13.317
b3 ← f2	1.091		

Standardized regression weights	Estimate
a1 ← f1	0.888
a2 ← f1	0.901
a3 ← f1	0.934
a4 ← f1	0.190
b1 ← f2	0.888
b2 ← f2	0.897
b3 ← f2	0.920

Covariances	Estimate	SE	CR
f1↔f2	0.044	0.080	0.551

Correlations	Estimate
f1↔f2	0.059

Variances	Estimate	SE	CR
f1	0.824	0.148	5.560
f2	0.665	0.120	5.537
e1	0.220	0.044	5.050
e2	0.202	0.043	4.683
e3	0.127	0.036	3.487
e4	0.866	0.123	7.018
e5	0.178	0.037	4.854
e6	0.196	0.043	4.614
e7	0.143	0.038	3.809

Squared multiple correlations	Estimate
a1	0.789
a2	0.812
a3	0.871
a4	0.036
b1	0.789
b2	0.804
b3	0.847

Covariances	MI	Par change
e2↔e6	5.408	0.064
e3↔f2	4.173	−0.081

Regression weights	MI	Par change
a2↔b2	5.603	0.125
a3↔f2	4.157	−0.122
a3↔b2	5.749	−0.133

Model	GFI	AGFI	NFI
Your model	0.957	0.908	0.968
Saturated model	1.000		1.000
Independence model	0.454		0.000

AGFI = Adjusted GFI; CR = critical ratio; GFI = Goodness-of-Fit Index; MI = modification index; NFI = Normed Fit Index; SE = standard error.

firming that it isn't correctly specified. Similarly, the covariance (and hence the correlation) between f1 and f2 is low and has a CR of only 0.551; that is, the two latent variables or factors aren't correlated. The next sets of numbers show the variances we're estimating and the squared multiple correlations (which are also given in the figure).

Because we asked for them, we also get the **Modification Indices** (MI), which tell us how much the model could be improved if we specified additional paths. The largest one, which is listed under Regression Weights, is a3 ↔ b2. That means that, if we drew a path from b2 to a3, our fit would improve. In fact, the path coefficient between the two is −0.123,[33] and the χ^2_{GoF} (based now on $df = 12$, because we specified another path) drops to 10.028.[34] But, because there is no theoretical rationale for this path (or for the other proposed modifications), we'll just ignore them.

Finally, we've given just a few of the myriad other GoF indices. The **saturated model** represents perfection (as many parameters as observations, meaning there's nothing more to estimate), and the **independence model** is the opposite (assuming nothing correlates with anything). Fortunately, our model is close to perfection; all of the indices are over 0.90. Our model would fit even better if we dropped variable a4. Yet again, this should be dictated by theory. If we believe that the variable is a substantive one, and that the nonsignificant path coefficient may be due to sampling error or a small sample size, we would keep it; otherwise, into the trash can it goes.

Comparing Two Factor Analyses

We're sometimes in a position where we want to compare two factor structures; for example, are the results for patients and controls or for men and women alike and, if not, how do they differ? This can be done with EFA, but it is difficult, and the methods of comparing factor structures leave much to be desired. However, it's relatively easy to do it with CFA.[35]

If we don't have any hypotheses beforehand regarding the factor structure, we can start by running an EFA with one group and then use the results to fix the parameter estimates in a CFA for the second group. Conversely, if we do have some idea of what the structure should look like, we can specify it for both groups and see where it fits and doesn't fit for each.

As an example, we'll stay with the problem presented in Figure 18-13 and assume we drew another sample, one in which a4 actually does load on f1 but we don't know this beforehand. Instead of fixing just one of the paths from the latent variables to the measured ones, we'll put in the unstandardized regression weights from the first sample and again, based on our previous results, state that the covariance between f1 and f2 is 0. The output will be very similar to that in Table 18-5, with a few notable exceptions.

First, the number of parameters to be estimated drops from 15 to 9, because we've fixed an additional 6 parameters: 5 paths from the latent variables plus the covariance. Second, there will not be standard errors and critical ratios given for these 6 parameters, since we are not estimating them. The χ^2_{GoF}, now based on $df = 19$, is a whopping 144.47, indicating that the model doesn't fit the data worth a plugged nickel. If we look at the modification indices, the largest ones involve a4 and e4 in various forms, such as suggesting that we include covariance terms between e4 and f1, or paths between a4 and the three other variables associated with f1. None of these make sense theoretically, but they all point to a misspecification involving a4. We would again return to our theory and hypothesize that the path coefficient, which we fixed at 0.20 to be congruent with the results from the first sample, is wrong and perhaps should be closer to 0.80. Alternatively, we can set it free and see what the program does with it. Note (yet again) that our use of the modification indices is

---

[33]*Don't look for this in the output; it isn't there. We reran the model with this path included, just for your benefit, but we haven't shown the output.*

[34]*See note 33.*

[35]*See note 31.*

tempered by our knowledge and theory.

If the model actually fits the data, then we can conclude that the factor loadings that we found for one group would fit the second group, too. In this case, we can up the ante and make the comparison more stringent: are the variances of the error terms similar across samples? This type of analysis is very useful for determining the equivalence of questionnaires in different groups of subjects.

A Full SEM Model

Now let's return to the complete model of success in cheerleading, shown in Figure 18-11, and add what we've learned. First, we have to fix all of the paths leading to the various disturbance terms to 1, and fix one path from each latent variable to be 1. Second, because CLAP and TRAP are random halves of the same test, it is logical to assume that their variances are similar. We indicate the fact that we've constrained these terms by giving the variances the same name. The results of all of this fixing and constraining are shown in Figure 18-14; the terms vct over the disturbance terms for CLAP and TRAP tell the program that these variances should be the same. This diagram now forms the input to the program, which should run as long as the variable names in the rectangles correspond to the variable names in our data file.

The output from the program is shown in Figure 18-15. To begin, the χ^2_{GoF} is 38.225 which, based

on 19 degrees of freedom, is highly significant ($p=$ 0.006). The other GoF indices are equivocal: GFI and NFI are both just slightly above the cutoff point of 0.90, while AGFI is only 0.831. All of this leads us to believe that the model could stand quite a bit of improvement, but where? Let's start with the measurement aspect of the model—how well are we measuring the latent variables of Athletic Ability, Cheer, and CLAP/TRAP?

The answer seems to be, not too badly, thank you, but perhaps we can do better with Ability and Cheer. If we look at the Modification Indices, most of them don't make too much sense from the perspective of our theory, but one bears a closer look—the suggestion of adding a covariance between ea2 and ea3. Because Cheer as a whole seems to add little to the picture, let's leave it aside for now and rerun the model adding e2 ↔ e3. Gratifyingly, the χ^2_{GoF} ($df =$ 18) drops to 22.557, which has an associated p-value of 0.208. Because this model is a subset of the original one, the difference between their respective χ^2s is itself distributed as a χ^2. So, if we subtract the χ^2s and the dfs, we get χ^2 (1) = 15.668, meaning that there was a significant improvement in the goodness of fit. This is also reflected in an increase in the path coefficient from Ability to CLAP/TRAP, from 0.59 to 0.73; a drop in the coefficient from Cheer (from 0.02 to 0.01); and the fact that the other fit indices are in an acceptable range.

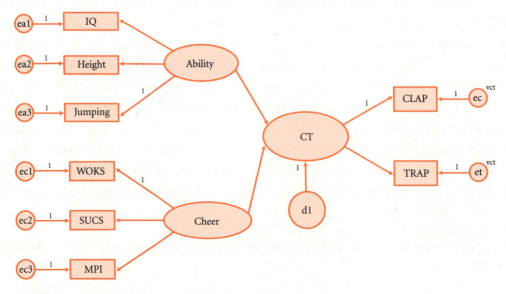

FIGURE 18-14 Figure 18-11 with the parameters constrained.

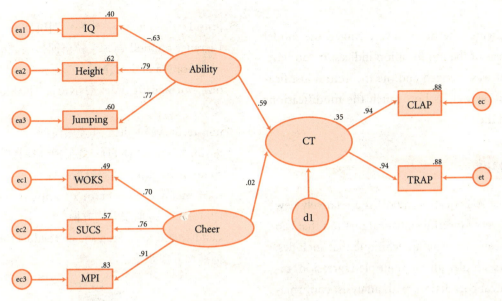

FIGURE 18-15   Output based on Figure 18-14.

Finally, because Cheer doesn't help,[36] we can have a simpler model if we just drop it. Although the change in the χ^2_{GoF} isn't significant this time around, all of the parsimony-adjusted GoF indices increase. Also, from a research perspective, it means that we don't have to administer these three tests to all people, which at least makes us more cheerful.

REPORTING GUIDELINES

Programs for SEM and CFA produce reams and reams of output. This in turn has resulted in reams and reams of guidelines for reporting the results. We have labored mightily on your behalf, reducing them to manageable size. This cannot be considered to be plagiarism, because we followed the guideline for avoiding charges for it—we stole from many sources, including McDonald and Ho (2002), Raykov et al. (1991), and Schreiber et al. (2006).

1. The most helpful thing to report is the diagram of the model, with the standardized regression weights and correlations near the arrows. You should also indicate which ones are statistically significant.

2. In the text, there should be a theoretical or research-based rationale for every arrow in the diagram, both directional (one arrowhead) and nondi-

rectional (the curved arrows with two heads).

3. There are many programs for SEM and CFA, and they differ with regard to their methods. This means that, unlike with techniques such as ANOVA or EFA, different programs can produce different results. Consequently, you must say which program you used.

4. You should indicate what kind of matrix was analyzed (covariances, covariance with means, correlation, etc.).

5. Never forget that CFA and SEM are large-sample techniques. You need to report not only the sample size but also the ratio of subjects to parameters (this implies that you know how many parameters you're estimating).

6. How did you treat outliers and missing data—did you drop those cases, impute values, or use some technique that can handle these anomalies?

7. What method did you use for parameter estimation—maximum likelihood, generalized least squares, weighted least squares, etc.—and why?

8. The model fit. As we said, there are many indices of this, but we would recommend as a minimum: (a) χ^2_{GoF} and its *df*; (b) the Tucker-Lewis Index (TLI, a.k.a. the NNFI); (c) the RMSEA; (d) SRMSR; and (e)

---

[36]*Perhaps reinforcing Woody Allen's comment, "More than any other time in history, mankind faces a crossroads. One path leads to despair and utter hopelessness. The other to total extinction. Let us pray we have the wisdom to choose correctly."*

the NFI.

9. Indicate whether you've changed the model on the basis of the modification indices. If you have, state what was changed and the theoretical justification for it, as well as how much the modifications improved the fit.

SUMMARY

✧ Structural equation model is a relatively new and very powerful statistical method that can be seen as a general technique that includes, in its simpler forms, multiple regression, canonical correlation, path analysis, confirmatory factor analysis, and other tests. Its major advantages are that it can combine measured and latent variables in the same model; it can easily handle multiple predictor and outcome variables and complicated models; and it can accommodate mediating variables as well as variables measured over time. However, despite its early name (causal analysis) it can determine causality only if the design of the study is appropriate; the statistic itself cannot assess causality from cross-sectional data.

GLOSSARY

adjusted GFI (AGFI)　调整拟合优度指数
Akaike's Information Criterion (AIC)　赤池信息量准则
comparative fit index (CFI)　比较拟合指数
consistent AIC(CAIC)　一致性赤池信息量准则
endogenous variables　内生变量
exogenous variables　外生变量
incremental fit index (IFI)　增值拟合指数

just-identified model　恰好识别模型
Lagrange multiplier test　拉格朗日乘数检验
modification indices (MI)　修正指数
non-normed fit index (NNFI)　不规范拟合指数
non-recursive model　非递归模型
normed fit index (NFI)　规范拟合指数
recursive models　递归模型
root mean square error of approximation (RMSEA)　近似误差均方根
standardized root mean square residual (SRMR)　标准均方根残差

EXERCISES

If the correlation between two predictor variables, A and B, is 0.50; the weight between A and the outcome is 0.20; and the weight between B and the outcome is 0.30; then:

1. What is the correlation between A and the outcome?
2. What is the correlation between B and the outcome?
3. Which variable(s) is (are) endogenous and which is (are) exogenous?
4. Which variable(s) should have a disturbance term?
5. How many observations are there?
6. If χ^2_{GoF} is 8.32, on $df = 2$, $p < 0.02$, does the model fit the data or not?

SUGGESTED READINGS AND WEBSITES

Streiner D,Norman G. Health measurement scales. 3rd ed. Oxford, England: Oxford University Press,2003.

CHAPTER THE NINETEENTH
Equivalence and Non-Inferiority Testing

Sometimes, the aim of a study is not to show a difference between groups, but to "prove" that two treatments are equivalent. This requires us to reverse the role of the null and alternate hypotheses, and to define what we mean by "equivalent."

SETTING THE SCENE

Now that the patent has expired on the block-buster Charm Promoter, LoveMe!, every other drug manufacturer wants to get in on the act (in a manner of speaking). To do so, they have to demonstrate to the regulatory agencies that their version of the pill is equivalent to the already approved one. That is, they have to prove that there is no difference between the drugs. However, their scientists have all taken introductory statistics and philosophy classes, and know that you can never prove the null hypothesis. How can they demonstrate the lack of difference between their pill and the approved one, in such a way as to satisfy both the regulatory bodies and the nervous males?

PHILOSOPHY 101

If I claim there are pink elephants, your natural reaction, as a highly educated, erudite, and verbally facile scientist, would be, "Oh yeah, bud? Well, prove it." Now the ball is back in my court. It's not sufficient for me to reply with, "Prove that they're not there!" If I assert the existence of something, it is incumbent on me to demonstrate its existence; not upon you to disprove it. The reason for this dates back to David Hume (1748—1999) and the philosophy of science. We can never prove the non-existence of something. If we haven't found it, it could be because we weren't looking the right place, or haven't looked hard enough or long enough, or were searching with the wrong instruments. Just because nobody has ever seen a pink elephant[1] doesn't mean that none exists. Who knows if one just might walk out of the forest tomorrow, perhaps even wearing a white tutu. As improbable as this sounds, something like this actually happened. It would seem fairly safe to say that no species that was alive 60 million years ago next Thursday would still exist today. But, in 1938 the coelacanth *Latimeria chalumnae* was pulled from the waters off South Africa.[2]

The same problem exists in medicine in trying to show that there is no difference between two agents. For example, one study "showed" that there was no difference between a type of antidepressant called a monoamine oxidase inhibitor (MAOI) and placebo.

---

[1] *At least not while sober.*

[2] *No, we're not saying that this particular fish was alive back then; only that its great, great uncle on its mother's side was.*

The difficulty was that they were using the wrong type of patients, who were given an insufficient amount of the drug for too short a period of time, and assessed with inappropriate outcome measures (Clinical Psychiatry Committee, 1965). So, their "proof" of the non-existence of a difference between the drug and placebo was simply an inability to show a difference, because of a poorly executed study. In fact, many later studies have shown that MAOIs are very effective. This seeming impossibility of showing that "nothing" exists is reflected in our language. If the results of a study show a p-level greater than 0.05, we don't say that we have proven the null hypothesis, but rather that we failed to reject it. The implication is that the next time around, we'll do things right, and get significance.

There's only one fly in the ointment; there are times when we *do* want to be able to conclude there is no difference between two treatments. For example, surgeons (or at least their administrators) would like to reduce the number of days a patient stays in hospital after surgery; in some cases, even, doing procedures on a day-hospital basis. Psychiatrists and psychologists would prefer to treat anorectic and bulimic patients as out-patients rather than in-patients. In these, and many other situations, it may be unethical to use a placebo group, because effective treatments exist. And, needless to say, drug companies want their own "me, too" versions of profitable drugs. In each of these cases, the aim is to "prove" that the alternative is not any different from the more expensive standard;[3] in other words, to prove the null hypothesis.

THE STATISTICAL RATIONALE

In order to explain how we test for equivalence, we have to go back to basics; in particular, what we mean by the null hypothesis (H_0). In almost all cases,

what we postulate with H_0 is that some parameter, θ, is the same in all groups, where θ can be a mean, a proportion, an odds ratio, or whatever; that is:

$$H_0 : \theta_1 = \theta_2 \qquad \text{(19-1)}$$

versus the alternative hypothesis (H_A) that the parameters aren't equal:

$$H_A : \theta_1 \neq \theta_2 \qquad \text{(19-2)}$$

But, the null hypothesis doesn't always have to postulate no difference between or among the groups. Null, in this case, doesn't mean "nothing," but rather *the hypothesis to be nullified*. Cohen (1994) referred to Equation (19-1) as the **null hypothesis.** In the vast majority of studies, the null hypothesis is the nil hypothesis, but it needn't be, and this is the first half of the rationale for equivalence testing.

The second half of the rationale is that there are differences between groups, and then there are differences between groups. In other words, some differences, even if they are statistically significant, are trivial from a practical perspective. Because of sampling error, we're always going to find some differences between groups, even if both groups are treated identically. Furthermore, given a sufficiently large sample size, we can show that even a tiny difference is statistically significant. For example, let's assume the systolic blood pressure in a control group is 163, and that it's 160 in the treatment group. If the SD is 15 mmHg, and there were 400 patients in each group, then this difference would be statistically significant. However, there would be precious few clinicians who would change their practice for just 3 points.[4]

TESTING FOR NO DIFFERENCE

Now let's return to the plight of the scientists at WCMM2,[5] Ltd., who have to show the federal regulatory agencies that their drug, *WonderScent*, is not different from the already-approved pill, *LoveMe!*[6] The

---

[3] *Actually, in the case of me-too drugs, to show that the more expensive alternative is no different from the cheaper standard. You figure out the logic of that.*

[4] *Maybe for a free dinner at an upscale restaurant paid for by the drug company, but not for 3 points.*

[5] *That stands for "We Can Make Money, Too."*

[6] *Notice that we're following the trendy marketing strategies of eliminating spaces between words, capitalizing in the middle, and using exclamation points with great abandon.*

issue they face is how to show this. They have two choices: an **equivalence trial**, and a **non-inferiority trial**. As we'll see, both are predicated on the two points we just discussed: the difference between the null and nil hypotheses, and the proposition that not all differences are worth writing home about.

EQUIVALENCE INTERVAL

In both types of trials, the first step is to establish an **equivalence interval**. This is simply a quantification of the second point: how close is "close enough?" We've already encountered this concept in sample size calculations, where it's necessary to stipulate ahead of time what the smallest difference is between the groups for us to pay attention to the results. The process, you'll remember, is not statistical, but judgmental: "Will I change what I do clinically if the groups differ by 1 point? If not, how about 2 points? Would you believe 3 points?" We do this until we reach a point where the difference starts to look promising, and we're interested in results *at or above this value*. In setting the equivalence interval, we go through the same process, but with a slightly different question: "Do I really care if the groups differ by 1 point? If not, how about 2 points? Would you believe 3 points?" Once we reach a level where we would care about the difference, we say that we're not interested in results *below that value*. So, for example, if people who take *LoveMe!* are rated on average as 75 on the 100-point *Social Excitement/Charm Scale* (SECS),[7] does it make a difference that those on *WonderScent* score only 74? 73? 72? If we perk up (so to speak) when the difference is five points, then we say that the equivalence interval (which we designate by *I*) is four points; that is, any difference in effectiveness of four points or less would be considered to be clinically or practically inconsequential.

Unfortunately, clinical judgment isn't the only factor that affects the width of *I*. From a clinical perspective, we want *I* to be as narrow as possible, because the smaller it is, the more similar the treatments are to one another. But, there's a trade-off. The smaller its width, the harder it is to demonstrate equivalence and the larger the sample size that's required (Kendall et al., 1999). Thus, there is great incentive, especially if a company is paying for the study, to increase the size of *I*; we'll return to this point when we discuss some of the problems with these types of trials.

EQUIVALENCE TRIAL

In an equivalence trial, we say that the new drug is equivalent to the standard if it falls within the range of $[\bar{X}_{Standard}-I_1]$ to $[\bar{X}_{Standard}+I_2]$ where I_1 is the lower equivalence interval and I_2 is the upper one. That is, there is an equivalence interval above and below the mean of the standard therapy, as shown in Figure 19-1. In this case, there are two null hypotheses:

$$H_{0_1}: \bar{X}_{New} < \bar{X}_{Standard}-I_1 \qquad (19\text{-}3)$$

$$H_{0_2}: \bar{X}_{New} > \bar{X}_{Standard}+I_2 \qquad (19\text{-}4)$$

and the alternative hypothesis is:

$$H_A: (\bar{X}_{Standard}-I_1) \leq \bar{X}_{New} \leq (\bar{X}_{Standard}+I_2) \qquad (19\text{-}5)$$

The logic is that if we can reject both null hypotheses using *t*-tests, then by default we're left with the alternative hypothesis that the mean of the new drug falls within the equivalence interval. The figure shows a symmetrical equivalence interval around the standard, but it doesn't have to be; we can set the interval to be five points below the mean and 10 points above it.

Although much has been written about equivalence testing (e.g., Blackwelder, 1982; Hatch, 1996; Rogers et al., 1993), it's rarely done in real life. The reason for this is simple; in the vast majority of cases, the second null hypothesis [Equation (19-4)] is of absolutely no interest to us. Nobody wants to prove that their intervention isn't superior to the standard, especially when the sample size needed to do so can grow alarmingly if *I* is small (Streiner, 2003). All that's necessary to keep regulatory agencies happy is to show that the new drug isn't much worse than

---

[7] *It's all right; you can go ahead and pronounce the acronym.*

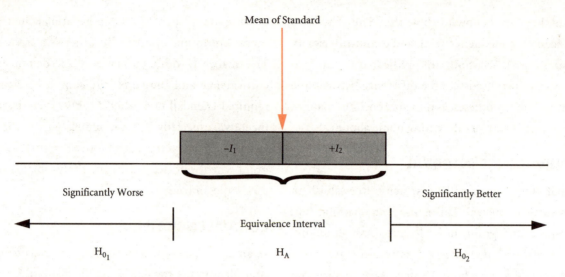

FIGURE 19-1   The equivalence intervals and hypotheses for equivalence testing.

the existing one, so why go to all that bother and expense?

The one area where equivalence testing is widely used to test for bioequivalence, where the outcome could be the blood level of some compound; we don't want the new drug to produce too little of it, but neither do we want too much. So to keep those folks happy, let's go through the exercise (although briefly). To keep our lives easier, we're going to use a symmetrical equivalence interval, so that $-I_1 = I_2$.

Because we have two null hypotheses, we have to conduct two t-tests:

$$t_1 = \frac{(\bar{X}_{New} - \bar{X}_{Standard}) - (-I)}{SE_{Difference}} \tag{19-6}$$

and

$$t_2 = \frac{(\bar{X}_{New} - \bar{X}_{Standard}) - I}{SE_{Difference}} \tag{19-7}$$

where $SE_{Difference}$ is defined the usual way:

$$SE_{Difference} = \sqrt{\left[\frac{(n_1-1)s_1^2 + (n_1-1)s_2^2}{n_1 + n_2 - 2}\right] \times \left[\frac{1}{n_1} + \frac{1}{n_2}\right]} \tag{19-8}$$

and the two subscripts refer to the two groups. If instead of means we were dealing with proportions of people in each group, we simply substitute p_{New} and $p_{Standard}$ for the $\bar{X}$s in Equations (19-6) and (19-7), and use the formula for the SE of the difference in proportions:

$$SE_{Difference} = \sqrt{\frac{p_1(1-p_1)}{n_1} + \frac{p_2(1-p_2)}{n_2}} \tag{19-9}$$

Note that, even with the same value for I, Equations (19-6) and (19-7) will have different numerators, because one has $-I$ and the other has $-(-I)$.

There is one important difference between Equations (19-6) and (19-7) and the equation for the traditional t-test. In the latter, it doesn't matter if we subtract the mean of Group 1 from the mean of Group 2, or vice versa, because we're interested only in the absolute value of the difference. But, as we'll see later on, it does make a difference in equivalence and non-inferiority testing.

In fact, though, if we calculate the t-test with the smaller numerator, we don't have to run the other one at all. The rationale is that for H_A to be true, we have to reject both tests of H_0. So if the test with the smaller numerator is not significant, it's irrelevant if the other one is or isn't; we haven't rejected both null hypotheses. On the other hand, if it is significant, then the one with the larger numerator must be even more significant. One last point: don't be deluded into thinking that, just because you're running only one t-test and it's one-tailed, you can get away with putting the entire 0.05 rejection area into that tail and use a smaller critical value for t. We keep α at 0.025, because the other test is still there, even though we don't explicitly calculate it.

To be true to our promise and keep this section (blessedly) short, we'll hold off on a worked example until the next section.[8]

NON-INFERIORITY

Getting back to our example, to get *WonderScent* on the market and pull in the dough, WCMM2 simply has to show that it isn't too much worse than *LoveMe!*, where "not too much worse" is again the equivalence interval. Now, though, we're dealing with only one interval, and a one-tailed test. The null hypothesis is:

$$H_0 : \bar{X}_{New} < \bar{X}_{Standard} - I \qquad (19\text{-}10)$$

and the alternative is:

$$H_A = \bar{X}_{New} \geq \bar{X}_{Standard} - I \qquad (19\text{-}11)$$

which is shown in Figure 19-2. Again, the logic is that if we can reject H_0, then we're left with H_A, which says that the mean of the new treatment falls at least within the equivalence interval, and may even be better.[9]

So, let's say that *WonderScent* will be considered to be equivalent if it performs (again, in a manner

of speaking) no worse than 5 points poorer than *LoveMe!* on the SECS; that is, we set I equal to –5. We take 50 (very willing) volunteers[10] and randomly divide them into two groups. Half are given *LoveMe!* and half *WonderScent*, and then we get 50 equally willing volunteers of the opposite sex to rate each person.[11] What we find is shown in Table 19-1 Now let's run those numbers through Equation (19-6). [We're using Equation (19-6) rather than Equation (19-7) because the equivalence interval is below the mean. If larger numbers reflect a worse state, as in measuring blood pressure or LDL cholesterol level, we'd use Equation (19-7).]

Trust us when we say that $SE_{Difference}$ is 4.174.[12] So, plugging those numbers into the equation we get:

$$t = \frac{(71-75)-(-5)}{4.174} = \frac{1}{4.174} = 0.240 \qquad (19\text{-}12)$$

which, with $n_1 - n_2 - 2 = 48$ *df*, is not the least bit significant. Now let's wrap our collective heads around the logic. We've failed to reject H_0 that *WonderScent*

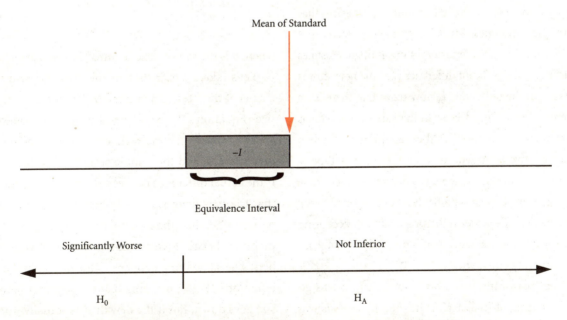

FIGURE 19-2 The equivalence interval and hypotheses for non- inferiority testing.

---

[8]*That's also a ploy to keep you reading the book.*

[9]*Although when have you ever heard of a me-too drug being better? Perhaps fewer side effects; definitely more expensive; but better?*

[10]*Who knows; they may even be willing to pay us to be in the study.*

[11]*What's the olfactory equivalent of a double-blind study? We don't know, either.*

[12]*If you don't trust us after all this time, run it yourself. See; we told you it was 4.174.*

TABLE 19-1   Results of a study comparing *Love Me!* to *Wonderscent* on the SECS

Group	$\bar{X}$	SD	n
Love Me!	75	15.2	25
Wonderscent	71	14.2	25

is worse than *LoveMe!*, so we have to conclude that they're not equivalent.

Wait a minute! Didn't we say that we'd be content if the two preparations were within five points of one another, and didn't we find that they're only four points apart? So why didn't we conclude that they're equivalent? This raises the issues of what we mean by Type I and Type II errors in non-inferiority trials, and what effect this has on power.

Type I and Type II Errors

Because we've flipped the meaning of the null and alternate hypotheses, we also have to change our thinking about the meaning of Type I and Type II errors. Type I, as you well know, is the probability of rejecting H_0 when in fact it's true. Now, in traditional significance testing, H_0 is the null hypothesis—that there's no difference—and H_A is the alternative, that there is one. In non-inferiority testing, though, H_0 states that there *is* a significant difference (i.e., the new stuff is worse than the old), and H_A now states that there is *no* difference. So, a Type I error in this case means there is no significant difference (i.e., there is equivalence) when in fact the two treatments do differ. Similarly, a Type II error means that we say there is a difference when there really isn't one (which is probably what happened here). This means that power is the probability of accepting that the groups are equivalent when they actually are the same (Hatch, 1996).

That reasoning was a bit convoluted, so let's go over the logic of it all again. Our null hypothesis was that there *is* a difference between the two substances. Because our power was low, we failed to reject H_0, so

we're left with the alternative hypothesis that there is a difference, and so we can't claim equivalence. Whew!

Another difference between traditional and non-inferiority testing is (or isn't) the z-value for the α level. One would think that, since we're doing a one-tailed test (that is, we're not testing if the difference is in favor of the new treatment), we could set z at 1.64 as both the critical value for significance and in the formula for the sample size (discussed below). This would have the effect of lowering the bar for significance, and reducing the sample size. But, some people and groups have advocated using the 2.5% level rather than the 5% level for equivalence and non-inferiority trials (e.g., Julious, 2004; Piaggio et al., 2006), so we'd be back where we started from with a z-value of 1.96. This recommendation is a bit more conservative, so it probably makes sense to follow it.

Sample Size and the Effects of I

The formula for the sample size of a non-inferiority trial is very similar to the one for a regular *t*-test, but again with the added factor of I thrown in:

$$n=2\left[\frac{(Z_\alpha+Z_\beta)s}{(\overrightarrow{X}_{New}+\overrightarrow{X}_{Standard})-I}\right]^2 \quad \textbf{(19-13)}$$

where n is the sample size required for each group.

Let's take a closer look at the effect of I on the results of the *t*-test [Equation (19-7)] and the sample size [Equation (19-13)]. When I is 0, both equations are the same as for the regular *t*-test; the value of *t* isn't affected, and the sample size remains the same. If the actual difference between the groups (Δ) shows that the new drug is actually better than the comparison one, then the numerator of Equation (19-7) increases because we're adding two positive numbers. The same thing happens to the denominator of Equation (19-13), meaning that the required sample size goes down. But if the new drug is actually worse, then Δ is negative, and, because I has a negative value, then $-I$ is positive.[13] This increases the sample

---

[13]*This is using the example where more is better. If larger numbers indicate a worsening in the condition (e.g., blood pressure), then just reverse everything. We could actually work out an example to show you that the conclusions are the same, but our fingers are getting tired.*

size very dramatically, which is why the results of our study most likely suffer from a Type II error. The unfortunate fact is that most equivalence and non-inferiority trials are underpowered (D'Agostino et al., 2003; Wiens, 2002).

Unfortunately, it also opens the door for a lot of mischief[14] on the part of nefarious commercial manufacturers. One way around the sample size problem is to make I very large. If we had chosen an equivalence interval of 10 points rather than 5, then t would have been 1.437, and the one-tailed test would be significant. So, it's easier to reject the null hypothesis and to conclude that the treatments are equivalent if we use a more liberal definition of "not worse."

There's also another potential problem, and that is that the standard may slip over time. Let's say we had actually used a sufficient sample size, and concluded that *WonderScent* was equivalent to *LoveMe!*, even though it's actually a bit worse. If *WonderScent* now becomes the gold standard against which we test an even newer preparation, the mean we're shooting for is 71 rather than 75. The newest agent could be non-significantly worse than this, and so our reference point drops yet again. Although we don't know of any examples of this, it's something to keep in mind.

More Room for MisChief

When our goal is to demonstrate that A is better than B, where B can be treatment as usual or a placebo condition, we go out of our way to design the best study we can. We do everything possible to ensure that A works, such as monitoring compliance, calling patients to remind them to take their pills, training the therapists, using manuals to guide treatment, and so on. Now, difficult as it is for you, put yourself in the mind of an unscrupulous person who is trying to demonstrate equivalence or non-inferiority. What would you do? You'd run the sloppiest study ever imagined—you'd recruit patients who are unlikely to respond, not worry about

compliance by either the patients or clinicians, allow drop-outs to occur, use an unreliable outcome measure; in short, do everything possible to dilute the effects of the intervention(s). We would never dream of accusing anyone of doing this deliberately,[15] but you get the point. Equivalence and non-inferiority can simply be the result of a badly executed study, rather than a true lack of difference between the groups (Kim and Goldberg, 2001; Streiner, 2006).

Another strategy is to blindly adhere to the received wisdom of analyzing all subjects who have been randomized, irrespective of whether or not they actually finished or even started the trial—what is called an **intention to treat** (ITT) analysis. This is what's usually done in superiority trials, because the bias is usually against finding a difference; that is, it's a conservative bias. However, because we've switched the meaning of the null and alternative hypotheses in equivalence and non-inferiority trials, the bias from ITT analyses in tilting the results toward finding no difference often (but not always) works in favor of rejecting the null, which is, in statistical parlance, a no-no (Piaggio et al., 2006). So, we're left with the position that ITT is either bad or its effects unpredictable in these types of trials.

A final bit of mischief is to try to rescue a failed superiority study by concluding that it demonstrates equivalence or non-inferiority. Unfortunately, this bit of flummery is relatively common. Greene et al. (2000) reviewed 88 studies done over a 5-year time span that claimed equivalence, and found that this conclusion was inappropriate for 67% of the articles. In order to show equivalence or non-inferiority, you have to begin by trying to demonstrate it from scratch; the lack of superiority doesn't equal equivalence.

So what's the bottom line? It's possible to conduct trials "proving" the null hypothesis, but it ain't as easy as it looks.

---

[14] *That's a polite term for pulling the wool over regulators' eyes.*

[15] *This phrase was added at the express instructions of our lawyer. Talk to her if you don't believe us.*

SUMMARY

✧ By rejecting the two H_0s of non-equivalence, equivalence testing can be used to show whether the two treatments are equivalent. The non-inferiority testing can be used to test whether a treatment is not worse than the other one. An equivalence interval should be determined before the equivalence or non-inferiority test. Although the meaning of the null and alternate hypotheses is flipped in the equivalence test, the Type I error is still defined as failing to reject the true H_0.

GLOSSARY

equivalence trial   等效性试验

non-inferiority trial   非劣效性试验

equivalence interval   等效区间

equivalence testing   等效性检验

non-inferiority testing   非劣效性检验

intention to treat (ITT)   意向性治疗

EXERCISES

1. What is the difference among the equivalence testing, non-inferiority testing and the general hypothesis testing?

2. A double-blinded clinical trial was performed to evaluate the efficacy of *cefaclor* on the treatment of children influenza. In the treatment group, 101 patients were treated with *cefaclor* with 84 of them recovered. The *cefradine* was used as the control drug. Among the 89 patients in the control group, 71 recovered after the treatment. Was the *cefaclor* not inferior to the *cefradine*? (hint: $I=10\%$)

SUGGESTED READINGS AND WEBSITES

Ng TH. Noninferiority Testing in Clinical Trials: Issues and Challenges. Chapman & Hall. 2014.

CHAPTER THE TWENTIETH — Screwups, Oddballs, and Other Vagaries of Science

Locating Outliers, Handling Missing Data, and Transformations

In this chapter, we discuss ways of locating anomalous data values, how to handle missing data, and what to do if the data don't follow a normal distribution.

SETTING THE SCENE

You've carefully planned your study and have estimated that you need 100 subjects in each of the two groups, with each subject tested before and after the intervention. With much effort, you're able to locate these 200 patients. But, at the end of the trial, you find that 8 subjects didn't show up for the second assessment; 2 subjects forgot to bring in urine samples; and you lost the sheet with all the demographic data on 1 subject. Your printout also tells you that your sample includes 2 pregnant men, a mother of 23 kids, and a 187-year-old woman. One disaster after another, some of the data distributions look about as normal as the Three Stooges.

The situation we just described is, sad to say, all too common in research. Despite our best efforts, some data always end up missing, entered into the computer erroneously; or are accurate, but reflect someone who is completely different from the madding crowd. Sometimes the fault is ours; we lose data sheets, punch the wrong numbers into the computer, or just plain screw up in some other way. Other times, the fault lies with the subjects;[1] they "forget" to show up for retesting, put down today's date instead of their year of birth, omit items on questionnaires, or are so inconsiderate that they up and die on us before filling out all the necessary paperwork. Last, what we've learned about the normal curve tells us that, although most of the people will cluster near the mean on most variables, we're bound to find someone whose score places him or her somewhere out in left field.

Irrespective of the cause, though, the results are the same. We might have a few anomalous data points that can screw up our analyses, we have fewer valid numbers and less power for our statistical tests than we had initially planned on, and some continuous variables look like they cannot be analyzed with parametric tests. Is there something we can do with sets of data that contain missing, extreme, and obviously wrong values?

Of course there is, otherwise we wouldn't have a chapter devoted to the issue. We have two broad options; grit our teeth, stiffen our upper lip, gird our loins, take a deep breath, and simply accept the fact that some of the data are fairly anomalous, wrong, or missing, and throw them out (and likely all of the other data from that case). Or, we can grab the bull by the horns and "fake it"—that is, try to come up with some reasonable estimates for the missing values. Let's start off by trying to locate extreme data points and obviously (and sometimes not so obviously) wrong data. This is the logical first step because we would usually want to throw out these data,

---

[1] *At least that's what we tell the granting agency.*

and we then end up treating them as if they were missing.

FINDING ANOMALOUS VALUES

Ideally, this section would be labeled "Finding Wrong Values," because this is what we really want to do— find the data that eluded our best efforts to detect errors before they became part of the permanent records.[2] For instance, if you washed your fingers this morning and can't do a thing with them, and entered a person's age as 42 rather than 24, you may never find this error. Both numbers are probably within the range of legitimate values for your study, and there would be nothing to tell us that you (or your research assistant) goofed. The best we can do is to look for data that are outside the range of expected values or where there are inconsistencies with a given case.

Spotting Anomalous Values for Discrete Data

The easiest type of anomaly to spot is where a number falls either into a category that shouldn't exist or above or below an expected range. For example, we can make a histogram of the subjects' gender, using one of the computer packages. If we got the result shown in Figure 20-1, we'd know we've got problems.[3]

Spotting Anomalous Values for Continuous Data

With continuous data, the two primary ways of spotting whether any data points are out of line are visually and statistically.

1. Visually   The visual way involves plotting each variable and seeing if any oddballs are way out on one of the tails of the distribution. You can use a histogram or a box-plot; with each of them, the eyeball is a good measurement tool. Figure 20-2 shows what an outlier looks like on a histogram, and Figure 20-3 shows the same data displayed in a box plot. The solid circle on the right of Figure 20-3 is a far outlier, corresponding to the blip on the right of the histogram in Figure 20-2; and the asterisk is a run-of-the-mill outlier.

Notice that the histogram did not identify this low value as an outlier. The difference is that, with a histogram, we rely on our eyeballs only to detect outliers. With box plots, outliers are defined statistically, and this may pick up some of the buggers we would otherwise have overlooked. So, box plots combine visual detection of outliers with a bit of statistics.

2. Statistically

A. Summarize a variable   You get a purely "statistical" look when you ask most computer packages

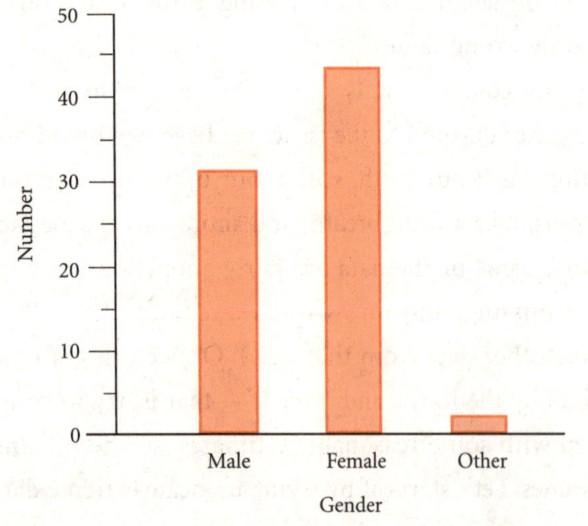

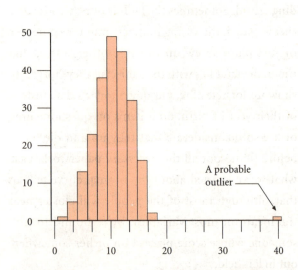

FIGURE 20-1   An obvious coding error.

FIGURE 20-2   Histogram showing an outlier.

---

[2]*We know of several ways to do this, such as entering the data twice and looking for discrepancies. But if you're reading this book to find out other ways, you've picked up the wrong volume, so go look somewhere else.*

[3]*Actually, our problems are not as serious as those of the two people labeled "Other," if the data aren't wrong.*

to summarize a variable (show the mean, SD, and the like); they will also give the smallest and largest value for each variable. So if you're studying the fertility patterns of business women, a minimum value of 2 or a maximum of 99 for age should alert you to the fact that something is awry, and you should check your data for outliers. Quite often, values such as 9 or 99 are used to indicate missing data. Again, check to see if this is the case.

B. Use *z* score   A more sophisticated approach looks at how much each score deviates from the mean. You no doubt remember that the easiest way of doing this is to transform the values into *z* scores. Each number now represents how far it is from the mean, in SD units. The cutoff point between what's expected and what's an outlier is somewhat arbitrary, but usually anything over +3.00 or under −3.00 is viewed with suspicion. Doing this, we find that the highest value is 7.33— definitely an outlier that should be eliminated from further analysis. The lowest value has a *z* score of −2.54, so even though one program[4] flagged it as suspicious, we'd probably keep it.

By eliminating the outlier(s), we've changed the distribution a bit. In this case, the mean dropped from 10.28 to 10.15, and the SD naturally got smaller (going from 4.06 to 3.54). Consequently, values that weren't extreme previously may now have *z* scores beyond ±3.00.[5] So it makes sense to go through the data a few times, eliminating the outliers on each pass, until no more come to light.

Spotting "Multivariate" Errors

More difficult to spot are "multivariate" errors. These occur when you've got two or more variables, each of which looks fine by itself, but some combinations are a bit bizarre. Imagine that we surveyed the incoming class of the Mesmer School of Health Care and Tonsorial Trades and got some basic demographic information. Take a look at the data in Table 20-1,

which summarizes what we found for the first six students. If we used all of the tricks we just outlined, none of the variables would look too much out of line: the ages go from 18 to 32, which is reasonable; the only genders listed are male (M) and female (F); and once we realize that 99 means "Not Applicable," the number of pregnancies looks okay. But wait a minute—we've got an 18-year-old female who had 5 pregnancies, and a 23-year-old man who had 2! Even in these days of more liberal attitudes toward sex, and a blurring of the distinctions between the genders, we would hazard a guess that these are, to use the statistical jargon, boo-boos.

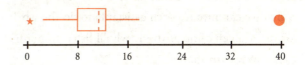

FIGURE 20-3 Box plot with one, possibly two, outliers.

TABLE 20-1   Data with some problems

Subject	Age	Gender	Number of pregnancies
1	27	M	99
2	18	F	5
3	19	F	0
4	32	M	99
5	21	F	3
6	23	M	2

The important point is that neither of these errors would have been detected if we restricted our attention to looking at the variables one at a time; they were spotted only because we took two into consideration at the same time—age and number of pregnancies, and gender and number of pregnancies. One problem, though, is that if we have *k* variables, we have $k \times (k-1) \div 2$ ways of looking at them two at a time. For these 3 variables, there are 3 combinations;

---

[4]We used Minitab in this case.

[5]We can actually figure out which, if any, values would be "revealed." Using all the original data, a z-score of 3 corresponds to a raw score of 22.46 (i.e., 10.28 + 3 × 4.06); after we eliminated the outlier, a z of 3 corresponds to a score of 20.77. So any score between these two values would not be detected the first time but would be extreme on the second pass through the data.

10 variables would have 45, and so on. Although it may not make sense to look at all of these pairs, you should still examine those where being in a certain category on one of the variables limits the range of possible categories on the other. For example, age imposes limits on marital status (few people under the age of 17 have entered into the state of matrimonial bliss), number of children, income (not too many teenagers gross over $1 000 000 a year, although they all spend money as if their parents do), and a host of other factors.

Checking the data for integrity is a boring job that is best compared to being forced to listen to politicians. But it has to be done. The only saving grace is that we can hire research assistants to do the work for us; you can't find anybody who'll listen to politicians, for love or money.

TYPES OF MISSING DATA

Missing Completely at Random (MCAR)

You would think that data that are missing are just plain missing. But life is never that simple in statistics. Data can be missing in a number of ways. The situations we just outlined, for the most part, describe data that are **missing completely at random** (MCAR), in that there's no pattern in the missingness (now isn't that one ugly statistical term). This can happen if some values are entered incorrectly and later eliminated, if some data sheets are misplaced, if the machine that gathers the data acts up in unpredictable ways, or if the research assistant acts out in unpredictable ways. And for once, a statistical term means exactly what it says; the data are truly missing completely at random.

Missing at Random (MAR)

A term that doesn't mean what it says is **missing at random** (MAR), which is different from MCAR, and doesn't exactly mean that the data are missing randomly.[6] MAR means that the probability of a score being missing for some variable is not related to the value of that variable, after controlling for other vari-

ables. For example, people with less education may be more likely to skip difficult items on a questionnaire. So, there is a definite pattern to the missingness, but it can be explained by some other variable in the data set; in this case, education level.

Not Missing at Random (NMAR) or Are Non-ignorable (NI)

Finally, the data can be **not missing at random** (NMAR) or are **non-ignorable** (NI). This is the bane of existence of all researchers and, unfortunately, the most common situation. It means that the reason for missingness is directly related to the variable of interest. For example, in a study of analgesia, those in most pain may be the ones who are most unlikely to fill out the questionnaire. Similarly, patients in intervention trials who derive the least benefit or who experience the most side-effects would be those most likely to drop out early.

So why are we bothering you with these distinctions? It's because the reason for data being missing affects how we deal with them. Some of the techniques we'll describe in the next section don't really work unless the assumptions of missingness at random or completely at random are met.

FILLING IN THE BLANKS

Just Forget about It

Once data are missing or have been eliminated as wrong or too anomalous, they are gone for good. Some statistical purists may say that any attempt to estimate the missing values either introduces a new source of error or results in biased estimations. Their solution would be to acknowledge the fact that some data are missing and then do the best with what is at hand. In fact, this is likely the most prudent path to take, especially when only a small amount of data are missing. As in other areas of statistics, the definition of "small" is subjective and arbitrary, but it probably hovers around 5% of the values for any one variable.

Even so, we still have a choice to make; to use all the available data left, or to eliminate all the data

---

[6]*You just gotta love statistical terminology.*

associated with a subject who is missing at least one data point. To illustrate the difference, let's do a study testing a hypothesis based on our years of clinical observation working in a faculty of health sciences: the major criterion used to select deans (at least for males) is height. You can be the head of the largest clinical department, pull in the most grant money, and be responsible for a scientific advance that reduced the suffering among thousands of patients, but if you ain't over 6' tall, you won't become a dean. To test this hypothesis, we'll collect five pieces of data on former chairmen from several schools: whether or not they became a dean (coded 0=No, 1=Yes); the number of people in their department; the number of grants received during the last 5 years of their chairmanships; a peer rating of their clinical competence, on a 7-point scale (1=Responsible for More Deaths than Attila the Hun, 7=Almost as Good as I Am), and of course, their height. The data for the first 10 people are shown in Table 20-2.

Each of these 10 people was supposed to have 5 scores. As you can see, though, 5 subjects have some missing data: variable X_1 (whether or not the person became a dean) for Subject 7; variable X_2 for Subject 3; variable X_3 for Subject 5, variable X_4 for Subject 4, and Subject 8 has variable X_5 missing. Assuming we want to correlate each variable with the others, how much data do we have to work with?

1. *Pairwise deletion* If we use as much data as possible, then the correlation between variables X_2 and X_3 is based on 8 subjects who have complete data for both variables (Subjects 1, 2, 4, 6, 7, 8, 9, and 10), as is the correlation between variables X_2 and X_4 (Subjects 1, 2, and 5 through 10) and similarly for all other pairs of variables. Intuitively, this approach is the ideal one to take because it makes maximum use of the existing data and makes no assumptions regarding what is missing. This way of analyzing missing data is sometimes referred to as **pairwise** deletion of data.

In *pairwise* deletion of data, a subject is eliminated from the analysis only for those variables where no data are available.

Needless to say, if anything seems logical, easy, and sensible in statistics, there must be something dreadfully wrong, and there is. Note that each of the 10 possible correlations is based on a different subset of subjects. This makes it difficult to compare the correlations, especially when a larger proportion of cases have missing data. Moreover, techniques that begin with correlation matrices (and this would include all the multivariate procedures, along with ordinary and logistic regression) may occasionally yield extremely bizarre results, such as F-ratios of less than 0 or correlations greater than 1.0. An additional problem is that it becomes nearly impossible to figure out degrees of freedom for many tests, because different parts of the model have differing numbers of subjects.

2. *Casewise deletion/ listwise deletion* The other

TABLE 20-2   Data set with missing values

Subject	Variable				
	Dean X_1	Department size X_2	Number of grants X_3	Competence X_4	Height (in.) X_5
1	0	22	12	2	70
2	0	49	5	6	69
3	1	—	8	5	76
4	0	44	10	—	68
5	1	47	—	1	72
6	0	45	15	4	66
7	—	27	9	3	67
8	0	13	1	4	—
9	1	42	12	5	71
10	0	32	7	6	68

way of forgetting about missing data is to eliminate any case that has any data missing; this is referred to as **casewise** or **listwise** deletion of data. In *casewise* or *listwise* data deletion, cases are eliminated if they are missing data on any of the variables. All of the statistics are then based on the same set of subjects.

The trade-off is the potential loss of a large number of subjects. It may seem that our example, where 50% of the subjects would be dropped from the study, is extreme. Unfortunately, it's not. One simulation found that, when only 2% of the data were missing at random, over 18% of the subjects were eliminated using listwise deletion; and with 10% of the data missing, nearly 60% of the cases were dropped (Kim and Curry, 1977). So let this serve as a warning; if values are missing throughout the data set, listwise deletion can result in the elimination of a large number of subjects. If the data are MCAR, then listwise deletion results "only" in a loss of power because of the reduced sample size. In all other cases, it may lead to biased results, depending on which subjects are eliminated from the analyses.

When in Doubt, Guess

The second way of handling missing data is by **imputing** what they should be. This is simply a fancy way of saying "taking an educated guess." Several techniques have been developed over the years, which in itself is an indication of the ubiquity of the problem and the lack of a totally satisfactory solution.[7]

1. *Deduction (the Sherlock Holmes technique)* Sometimes it is possible to deduce a logical value for a missing data point. For instance, if a person's race was missing, but we had data on the person's parents, it's a safe bet that the data would be the same. This approach is not always possible, but is actually quite useful in cases where it can be used. It does work well in one common situation, where one too many (or too few) spaces were added during data entry. If an adult has an age of 5.2 years or 520 years, it's pretty

safe to assume that the correct age is 52, but the number got moved in one direction or the other. An "age" of 502 is a bit more tricky; should it have been 50 or 52?

2. *Replace with the mean* The most straightforward method is to replace the missing data point with the mean of the known values for that particular variable. For example, the mean of the nine known values for variable X_2 is 35.7, so we could assume that the value for Subject 3 is 36. Note that this hasn't changed the value of the mean at all; it still remains 35.7 (plus or minus a tiny bit of error introduced by rounding). However, we reduced the variance somewhat; in this case, from 12.71 for the 9 values to 11.98 when we impute a value of 36. The reason is that it would be highly unusual for the missing value to have actually been the same as the mean value, so we've replaced the "real" (but lost) value with one that is closer to the mean—in fact, it is the mean. If only a small number of items are missing, the effect is negligible; once we get past 5% to 10%, however, we start to dramatically underestimate the actual variance. A good approximation of how much the variance will be reduced is n/N, where n is the number of non-missing values, and N is the total number of subjects.

Replacing the missing value with the mean would still result in an unbiased estimate of the numerator in statistics methods such as the t-test. However, the denominator may be a bit smaller, leading to a slightly optimistic test. On the other hand, correlations tend to be more conservative, by the amount:

$$\frac{\sqrt{n_x n_y}}{N} \tag{20-1}$$

Where n_x is the number of non-missing values for variable X, and n_y is the number of non-missing values for variable Y. The distribution of scores is also affected by mean replacement, tending to become more leptokurtic.

Sometimes we can be even more precise. For ex-

---

[7] *Where do all the data go when they go missing? Is there some place, equivalent to the elephants' burial ground, filled with misplaced 1s, 32s, and 999s?*

ample, departments of medicine are usually much larger than departments of radiology. So if we were missing the number of faculty members for a chairman of medicine, we'd get a better estimate by using the mean of only departments of medicine, rather than a mean based on all departments. However, because replacing the missing values with the mean lowers the SD, changes the distribution, and distorts correlations with other variables, this type of imputation should be avoided.

It's important to note that mean substitution gives an unbiased estimate of the mean only if the data are MCAR (which, as we said, is rarely the case). When the data aren't missing at random, it's quite possible that those in the middle of the distribution are the people most likely to respond to a question; it's those at the extremes who are more likely to skip items about income, for example (would you admit that your income is under $10 000 or over $50 000 a year?).

3. *Use multiple regression*   The next step up the ladder of sophistication is to estimate the missing value using the other variables as predictors. For example, if we were trying to estimate the missing value for the number of grants, we would run a multiple regression, with X_3 as the dependent variable and variables X_1, X_2, X_4, and X_5 as the predictors. Once we've derived the equation, we can plug in the values for subjects for whom we don't know X_3 and get a good approximation (we hope).

A few problems are associated with this technique. First, it depends on the assumption that we can predict the variable we're interested in from the others. If there isn't much predictive ability from the equation (i.e., if the R^2 is low), then our estimate could be way off, and we'd do better to simply use the mean value. The opposite side of the coin is that we may predict *too* well; that is, the predicted value will tend to increase the correlation between that variable and all the others, for the same reason that substitut-

ing the mean decreases the variance of the variable. The usual effect is to bias correlations toward +1 or –1. A better tactic is to add some random error to the imputed value (a method called stochastic regression). That is, instead of replacing the missing value with $\hat{y}$, it's replaced by $\hat{y}+N (0, s^2)$,[8] where s^2 is the Mean Square (Residual) of the multiple regression. This substitution preserves the mean, the variable's distribution, and its correlations with other variables. Last, multiple regressions are usually calculated using casewise deletion. Because several variables may be used in the regression equation, we may end up throwing out a lot of data and basing the regression on a small number of cases (i.e., we're shafted by the very problem we're trying to fix)! We should also note that although this technique is used widely, it should only be used when the data are MCAR or MAR (which they rarely are).

4. *Use multiple imputation*   The top step of the sophistication ladder is a technique called multiple imputation. What it does, in essence, is to impute the missing values a number of times (hence "multiple") by using somewhat different initial guesses of what's missing. Because these estimates are based on the data themselves, the final imputed values recreate the variance that was in the data. Rubin and Little (the guys who created this technique) say it can accurately impute values if up to 40% of the data are missing; and that as few as five imputations are required (Little and Rubin, 1987). That's the good news. The bad news is that multiple imputation can be difficult to carry out. It means that there are five sets of data that are analyzed, their results stored, and then all the parameters averaged across these multiple data sets. As of this writing, very few statistical packages have implemented it. If you search the web, you'll find some stand-alone packages; some are quite expensive, but others, like Amelia Ⅱ (named after the aviator who went missing) and NORM,[9] are free.

---

[8] *The term $N(0, s^2)$ is statistical shorthand for a normally distributed variable with a mean of 0 and a variance of s^2. Most statistical packages allow you to do this quite easily.*

[9] *It's called that because it assumes the data are normally distributed; it's not in honor of one of the authors, despite what he'd like to believe.*

Yet again, this technique works only for data that are MAR or MCAR, even though it's commonly used for all types of missing data.

5. *Last observation carried forward*   If the previous techniques were on a ladder of increasing sophistication, last observation carried forward (LOCF) is, in our opinion, a broken rung. It is used with longitudinal data to cover circumstances where a subject drops out before the end. As the name implies, it consists simply of using that person's last valid response to replace all the missing values. LOCF has two things going for it: it's easy to implement, and it has the imprimatur of federal drug regulatory agencies.[10] The underlying assumptions are that patients will improve while they're receiving treatment, and won't improve without therapy. If these assumptions are true, then carrying an intermediate value forward to the end is a conservative estimate of improvement that works against the study, which is good for intellectual honesty, if not for your curriculum vitae. So, what's the problem? It's with the assumptions. For example, studies of antidepressants often show that up to 40% of patients in the placebo condition improve, so assuming that they wouldn't change without therapy is unwarranted. Also, improvement is rarely linear. More often, it is more rapid in the beginning and then starts to level out (*asymptotes*, if you want to use the technical jargon), so that LOCF may not be as conservative as you might think.

Another nail in the coffin of LOCF is the fact that the last value carried forward is always the same number. That is, if the final value were 7, then all of the imputed values will also be 7. But we know from psychometric theory that there will always be error associated with any measurement, so even if the person's score actually remained 7, the measured value will vary around this number. This means that the constant value underestimates the error variance, which then leads to inflation of the statistical test; again, a bias operating in the wrong direction.

In some situations, LOCF actually *overestimates*

the actual effectiveness of an intervention. This can occur if the outcome is the slowing of a decline. For example, the "memory drugs" used with patients with Alzheimer's disease don't improve memory; they simply slow its loss over time. If people drop out of the treatment condition more than the comparison because of adverse events, then LOCF would result in an overly optimistic picture of its effectiveness, by assuming that there won't be any further decline. Similarly, you shouldn't use this technique for adverse events, because LOCF will underestimate them for the same reason it underestimates improvement.

The bottom line is that, if you have longitudinal data with at least three data points for a person, use hierarchical linear modeling, as we discussed in Chapter 16, not LOCF. If you have even more data points, you could even model non-linear change.

6. *Comparing techniques*   We did a simulation by using real data consisting of 10 variables from 174 people, and randomly deleting 20% of the values for one variable (Streiner, 2002b). These values were imputed using replacement with the mean, a regression based on the other nine variables, regression with error built in, and multiple imputation; the results are in Table 20-3. As you can see, all did a credible job of recapturing the actual mean of the variable. But, true to what we've said, replacement with the mean and with a value predicted by multiple regression underestimated the SD, and, as a result, the 95% CIs were overly optimistic. Adding in a fudge factor with multiple regression helped a bit, but multiple impu-

TABLE 20-3   Imputing means, SDs and CIs using four different methods

Method	Mean	SD	95% CI
Original data	575.93	85.32	563.25–588.61
Replace with mean	575.68	74.47	564.61–586.75
Replace with regression estimate	575.05	76.33	563.71–586.39
Replace with regression error	573.07	79.31	561.29–584.85
Multiple imputation	575.93	85.07	563.29–588.57

---

[10]*That alone should be a warning that something is amiss; it's probably simple-minded and wrong.*

tation stole the show; the confidence interval (CI) was almost identical to the original.

Over the past decade a number of other techniques have been introduced for dealing with missing data, such as **expectation maximization** and **full information maximum likelihood** (FIML). These are beyond the scope of this book,[11] except to say that FIML is slowly becoming the default standard. It can be used with sample sizes as small as 100 and doesn't require combining data sets as does multiple imputation. However, as of the writing of this edition, it hasn't been implemented in many statistical programs.

TRANSFORMING DATA

To Transform or Not to Transform

In previous chapters, we learned that parametric tests are based on the assumption that the data are normally distributed.[12] Some tests make other demands on the data; those based on multiple linear regression (MLR), for example, MLR itself, ANOVA, and AN-COVA, as the name implies, assume a straight-line relationship between the dependent and independent variables. However, if we actually plot the data from a study, we rarely see perfectly normal distributions or straight lines. Most often, the data will be skewed to some degree or show some deviation from mesokurtosis, or the "straight line" will more closely resemble a snake with scoliosis. Two questions immediately arise: (1) can we analyze these data with parametric tests and, if not, (2) is there something we can do to the data to make them more normal? The answers are: (1) it all depends, and (2) it all depends.[13]

The situations that need not to transform data

Let's first clarify what effect (if any) non-normality has on parametric tests. The concern is not so much that deviations from normality will affect the final value of t, F, or any other parameter testing the difference between means (except to the degree that extreme outliers affect the mean or SD); it is that they *may* influence the p-value associated with that parameter. For example, if we take two sets of 100 numbers at random from normal distributions and run a t-test on them using an α level of 0.05, we should find statistical significance about 5% of the time. The concern is that, if the numbers came from a distribution that wasn't normal, we'd find significance by chance more often than 1 time in 20. Several studies, however, have simulated non-normal distributions on a computer, sampled from these distributions, and tested to see how often the tests were significant. With a few exceptions that we discuss below, the tests yielded significance by chance about 5% of the time (i.e., just what they should have done). In statistical parlance, most parametric tests (at least the univariate ones) are fairly *robust* to even fairly extreme deviations from normality. This would indicate that, in most situations, it's not necessary to transform data to make them more normal. There's a second argument against transforming data, and that has to do with the interpretability of the results. For example, one transformation, called the "arc sine" and sometimes used with binomial data, is:

$$X' = 2\,sin^{-1}\sqrt{X+0.5} \qquad (20\text{-}2)$$

A colleague of ours once told us that his master's thesis involved looking at the constipative effects of medications used by geriatric patients. He reasoned (quite correctly) that because his dependent variable— the number of times the patients had a bowel movement on a given day—was binomially distributed, he should use this transformation. Proud of his deduction and statistical skills, he brought his transformed data to his supervisor, who said, "If a clinician were to ask you what the number means, are you going to tell him, 'It is two times the angle whose sine is the square root of the number of times (plus

---

[11]*Meaning that we don't understand them either.*

[12]*Some tests assume other distributions, such as the Poisson or exponential. However, because we've been successful so far in ignoring them, we'll continue to pay them short shrift.*

[13]*It's been rumored that graduate students receive their PhDs in statistics when they reflexively answer, "It all depends" to any and all questions.*

1/2) that each patient shat that day'?" Needless to say, our friend used the untransformed data.[14] The moral of the story is that, even when it is statistically correct to transform the data, we pay a price in that lay people (and we!) have a harder time making sense of the results.

The situations that need to transform the data

As the name implies, J-shaped data are highly skewed, either to the right or to the left, as in Figure 20-4. Data such as these occur when there's a limit at one end of the values that can be obtained, but not at the other end. For example, several studies have tried to puzzle out what is disturbed in the thought processes of people with schizophrenia by seeing how quickly they react to stimuli under various conditions. The lower limit of reaction time is about 200 ms, reflecting the time it takes for the brain to register that a stimulus has occurred, deciding whether or not it is appropriate to respond, and for the action potential to travel down the nerves to the finger. However, no upper limit exists; the person could be having a schizophrenic episode or be sound asleep at the key when he or she should be responding. We often run into the same problem with variables such as the number of days in hospital, or when we're counting events, such as the number of hospitalizations, times in jail, and the like. The majority of numbers are bunched up at the lower end, and then taper off

quickly at the upper end. When data like these are analyzed with parametric tests, the *p*-values could be way off, so it makes sense to transform them.

A second situation in which transforming data is helpful is when we're calculating Pearson correlations or linear regressions. Recall that these tests tell us the degree of *linear* relationship between two or more variables. It's quite possible that two variables are strongly associated with one another, but the shape of the relationship is not linear. Around the turn of the last century, Yerkes and Dodson postulated that anxiety and performance are related to each other in an inverted U (∩)-shaped fashion: not enough anxiety, and there is no motivation to do well; too much, and it interferes with the ability to perform. Who studies 10 weeks before a big exam, and who *can* study the night before? As Figure 20-5 shows, a linear regression attempts to do just what its name implies: draw a straight line through the points.

As you can see, the attempt fails miserably. The resulting correlation is 0. Although this is an extreme example, it illustrates the fact that doing correlations where the relationship is nonlinear underestimates the degree of association; in this case, fairly severely. It would definitely help in this situation to transform one or both of the variables so that a straight line runs through most of the data points.

The third situation where transformations help is similar to the previous one; when, because of the nature of the data, they are *expected* to follow a nonlinear pattern, such as logarithmic or exponential. This assumption can be tested by doing the correct transformation and seeing if the result is a straight line. For example, if the relationship between the variables is exponential, a logarithmic transformation should make the line appear straight, and vice versa.[15] This happens often when we're looking at biological variables, such as blood levels. Here, the level of serum rhubarb, for instance, may depend on a previous enzymatic reaction, which in turn is dependent on a

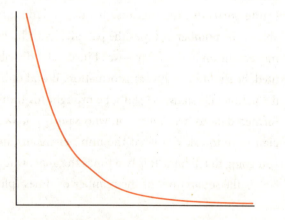

FIGURE 20-4   A J-shaped distribution.

---

[14]*And later went on to become the head of Statistics Canada.*

[15]*AHA! Finally, an explanation of the phrase, log linear. It appears linear when we take the log of one variable.*

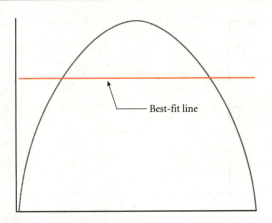

FIGURE 20-5   A straight-line fit through an inverted U (∩)-shaped distribution.

prior one. The central limit theorem tells us that the *sum* of a number of factors is normally distributed. In this situation, though, this causal chain is a result of the *product* of many influences, so the distribution is normal only if we take its log (Bland and Altman, 1996). Even if it isn't necessary to transform the variable for statistical reasons, simply seeing that the line is straight confirms the nature of the underlying relationship (Figure 20-6).

The last situation where transformations may be warranted is when the SD is correlated with the mean across groups. Way back in Chapter 4, we mentioned that one of the desirable properties of the normal distribution is that the variance stays the

same when the mean is increased. In fact, that's one of the underlying assumptions of the ANOVA; we change the means of some groups with our interventions, but homogeneity of variance is (in theory, at least) maintained. This independence of the SD from the mean sometimes breaks down when we're looking at frequency data: counts of blood cells, positive responses, and the like. If the correlation between the mean and the variance is pronounced,[16] a transformation is the way to go. A good way to check this out is visually; plot the mean along the *X*-axis and the variance along the *Y*-axis; if the line of dots is heading toward the upper right corner, as in Figure 20-7A, you've got heteroscedasticity. If the line is relatively flat, as in Figure 20-7B, there's no relationship between the two parameters.

Should we transform data or shouldn't we?

So let's get down to the bottom line: should we transform data or shouldn't we? We would propose the following guidelines[17]:

Don't transform the data if:

a. The deviation from normality or linearity is not too extreme.

b. The data are in meaningful units (e.g., kilos, mm of mercury, or widely known scales, such as IQ points).

c. The sample size is over 30.

d. You're using univariate statistics, especially

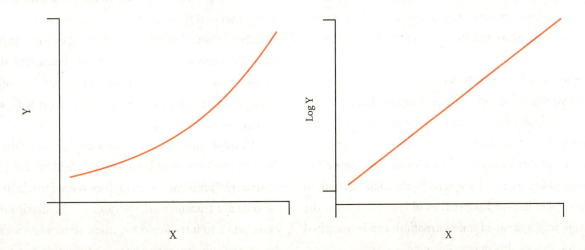

FIGURE 20-6   An exponential curve straightens out with a logarithmic transformation.

---

[16] *Yet another precise term to which we can't assign a number.*

[17] *Bear in mind that these are just guidelines. Any statistician worth his or her salt can think of a dozen exceptions, even before the first cup of coffee.*

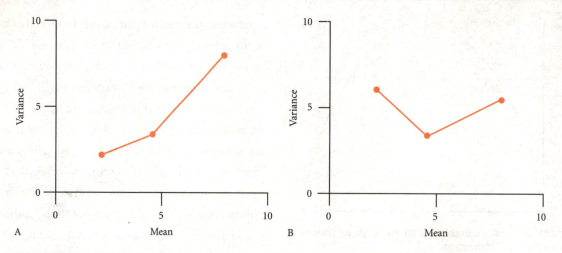

FIGURE 20-7   A situation where the means and SDs are A, correlated and B, independent.

ones whose robustness is known.

e. The groups are similar to each other in terms of sample size and distribution.

Transform the data if:

a. The data are highly skewed.

b. The measurements are in arbitrary units (e.g., a scale developed for the specific study or one that isn't widely known).

c. The sample size is small (usually under 30).

d. You'll be using multivariate procedures because we don't really know how they do when the assumptions of normality and linearity are violated.

e. A large difference exists between the groups in terms of sample size or the distribution of the scores.

f. A moderate-to-strong correlation exists between the means and the SDs across groups or conditions.

So You Want to Transform

You've made the momentous decision that you want to transform some variables. Now for the hard question: which transformation to use? We can think of distributions as ranging from extremely skewed to the right (sort of a backward J), through normal, to extremely leftward skewed, as in Figure 20-8. In the same way, a range of transformations can be matched to the shapes almost one-to-one:

Shape	Figure	Transformation
Reverse J	20-8A	$1 \div X$
Severe skew right	20-8B	$\text{Log}(X)$
Moderate skew right	20-8C	$\sqrt{X}$
Moderate skew left	20-8D	$-1 \div \sqrt{X}$
Severe skew left	20-8E	$-1 \div \text{Log}(X)$
J-shaped	20-8F	$-1 \div X$

The first transformation we'll do is on these terms, by turning them into English. In fact, we can make this task even easier for ourselves; although it looks like we have six transformations here, we really have only three[18]. The *–1* term in the last three rows serves to "flip" the curve over, so the skew left curves become skewed right, allowing us to use the top three transformations. Let's finish talking about this flip[19] before explaining the transformations themselves. It's obvious that, if we started with all positive numbers (such as scores on some test), we'll end up with all negative ones.

Although the statistical tests don't really mind, some people have trouble coping with this. We can get around the "problem" in a couple of ways. First, before the data are transformed, we can find the maximum value, add 1 to it (to avoid too many zeros when we're done), and subtract each raw value from this number.

---

[18]*There are actually many more possible transformations, including the arc sine one, but they're rarely used, so we'll ignore them.*

[19]*The correct word would be "reflect," as in a mirror— not meaning to ponder (we never do that in statistics).*

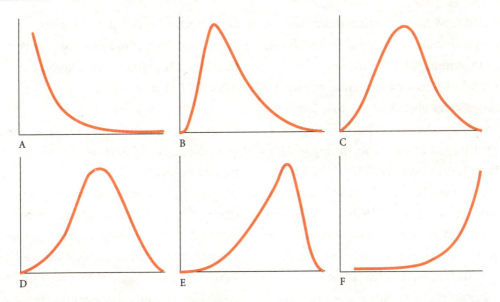

FIGURE 20-8   The "family" of distributions.

For example, if we started out with the numbers:

    1   1   2   4   8   9

then we would subtract each number from 10 (the maximum, 9, plus 1), yielding:

    9   9   8   6   2   1

We would then use the transformations for right-skewed data, rather than left-skewed; that is, this reflection takes the place of dividing into –1.

The other method of eliminating the negative numbers is fairly similar[20] but takes place after we divide the appropriate denominator into the –1 term. First, find the smallest number (i.e., the biggest number if we ignore the sign); subtract 1 from it (again to avoid too many zeros); and then add the absolute value of the number to all the data points. So, if our transformed data were:

    –0.1   –2   –3.7   –5   –6   –11

we would subtract 1 from –11, giving us –12; the absolute value is +12; and the result of the additions would be:

    11.9   10   8.3   7   6   1

(1) Reciprocal transformation

Now to explain the transformations. The first one, $1 \div X$, is simply the **reciprocal** of X; if X is 10, the transformed value is $(1 \div 10 = 0.1)$[21]. The last transformation, $-1 \div X$, is exactly the same, except that 10 now becomes –0.1 (i.e., $-1 \div 10$).

(2) The square root transformation

The **square root** transformation is similar to the log transformation in that zeros and negative numbers are taboo[22]. But, there's an additional consideration in deciding how to eliminate these unwanted numbers: we also want to get rid of all numbers between zero and one. In other words, before we transform, we want the minimum number to be 1.0. The reason is that numbers between 0 and 1 react differently to a square root transformation than numbers greater than 1: the square root of numbers over 1 are smaller than the original numbers (e.g., the square root of 4 is 2), but the square roots of numbers less than 1 get larger with a square root transformation (the square root of 0.5 is 0.71). We often use square root transformations with data that have a Poisson distribution, which are counts of things, such as the number of people dying in a given time period.

(3) The logarithm transformation

---

[20]For once, we don't get rid of the minus sign by squaring!

[21]Don't get too worried that you'll have to do all these transformations by hand; at the end of the chapter, we'll show you how to get the computer to do the work for you.

[22]This is beginning to sound like a commercial for unmentionables.

The second (and fifth) transformation involves taking the logarithm of the raw data. To refresh your memory, a logarithm (often called just a "log") is the power to which a base number must be raised to equal the original number. So, if the base number is 10, $1=10^0$ (any base to the power 0 is, by definition, 1), $10=10^1$, $100=10^2$, and $21=10^{1.32}$. So, the log of 21, to the base 10, is 1.32 [written as $\log 10(21)=1.32$]. But, we don't have to use a base of 10. For arcane reasons, we sometimes use a base of 2.71828..., which is abbreviated as e, and we write the log to base e as ln. Needless to say, the exponent is different: $\log_e(21)=\ln(21)=3.04$. In fact, we can use any number as a base, but in practice, we usually stick to bases of 2, 10, and e. Most computers can automatically figure out logs to bases of 10 and e and, with some manipulation, can handle base 2. When doing log transformations, it's often a good idea to try a few bases because, depending on the nature of the data, some will work better than others. In general, the more extreme the spread of scores ("extreme" being yet another undefined term), the larger the base you should use. The same considerations apply to logs as to the square root transformation: the computer will have a minor infarct with zeros and negative numbers, and you should avoid numbers between zero and one. Log transforms come in handy with many physiological variables, where there are many factors that act together to affect an outcome.

These rules may seem to imply that you look at your data, pick the right transformation, and you're off and running. Unfortunately, reality isn't quite like that. The curves we get in real life don't look like these idealized shapes; they always fall somewhere in between two of the models. What you have to do is try out a transformation and actually see what it does to the data (perhaps by looking at the figures for skewness and kurtosis, or at a box plot). It's possible that you chose a transformation that overcorrected and turned a moderate left skew into a moderate right one. This gains you nothing except heartache.

So, if this has happened, go back and try a less "powerful" transformation; perhaps square root rather than log, or log rather than reciprocal.

After the Transformation

(1) Interpret the results

Once we've transformed the data, our work isn't quite done. We still have to interpret the results, and that often involves undoing what we've just done. In Figure 20-9, we've plotted the serum rhubarb levels of 366 patients with hyperrhubarbemia[23]. As expected, it's highly skewed to the right, with a mean of 4.645, and an SD of 2.083. If we use a $\log_{10}$ transformation, as in Figure 20-10, the distribution isn't great, but it's a lot more normal. Its mean is 0.622, with an SD of 0.206. You may think that if you "untransform" the log mean by $10^{0.622}$, you'll be back to where you started. But if you do that, you'll get 4.190, not 4.645. The reason is that the antilog of the mean of transformed numbers is not the original arithmetic mean, but rather the geometric mean (Bland and Altman, 1996). As we pointed out in Chapter 2, the geometric mean is always smaller than the arithmetic mean. It's not that the geometric mean is wrong, but just realize what the number represents. The same argument applies to all other transformations, such as the reciprocal and square root.

(2) Figure out confidence intervals

If you want to figure out confidence intervals,

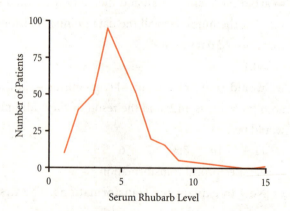

FIGURE 20-9   **Graph of the distribution of hyperrhubarbemia.**

---

[23] *You'll remember that it's a disorder marked by extreme redness of the torso and green hair.*

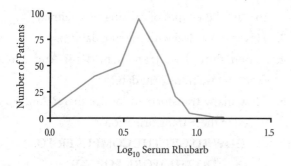

FIGURE 20-10   The distribution after a log$_{10}$ transformation.

continue working with the transformed data: calculate the standard deviation and the standard error, multiply by the correct value for the 95% or 99% interval, and then transform back to the original units at the very end (Bland and Altman, 1996). This is all very well and good for a single group. The fly in the ointment is that it breaks down when we are looking at the CI of the difference between groups (Bland and Altman, 1996); the results are either meaningless (with square root or reciprocal transformations) or very difficult to interpret (with log transforms). As much as possible, try to work in the original units when you're comparing groups.

SUMMARY

In this chapter, we discussed ways of locating anomalous data values, how to handle missing data, and what to do if the data don't follow a normal distribution.

For discrete data, we can make a histogram to spot anomalous data values. With continuous data, there are two primary ways of spotting whether any data points are out of line: (1) visually: you can use a histogram, or a box-plot. (2) statistically: you get a purely "statistical" look when you ask most computer packages to summarize a variable (show the mean, SD, and the like); they will also give the smallest and largest value for each variable. A more sophisticated approach looks at how much each score deviates from the mean. You no doubt remember that the easiest way of doing

this is to transform the values into z scores. There are three types of missing data, which are missing completely at random (MCAR), missing at random (MAR), not missing at random (NMAR) or are non-ignorable (NI). Once data are missing or have been eliminated as wrong or too anomalous, they are gone for good. The first way of handling missing data is to forget about missing data. One way of forgetting about missing data is referred to as pairwise deletion of data, in which a subject is eliminated from the analysis only for those variables where no data are available. The other way of forgetting about missing data is to eliminate any case that has any data missing; this is referred to as casewise or listwise deletion of data. The second way of handling missing data is by imputing what they should be, including six techniques: deduction, replacing with the mean, using multiple regression, using multiple imputation, Last observation carried forward (LOCF) and comparing techniques.

In previous chapters, we learned that parametric tests are based on the assumption that the data are normally distributed. Some tests make other demands on the data; those based on multiple linear regression (MLR), for example, MLR itself, ANOVA, and ANCOVA, as the name implies, assume a straight-line relationship between the dependent and independent variables. However, we rarely see perfectly normal distributions or straight lines. Most often, the data will be skewed to some degree or show some deviation from mesokurtosis, or the "straight line" will more closely resemble a snake with scoliosis. what to do if the data don't follow a normal distribution. The answer is: it all depends. We described the situations that we need to transform data or need not to transform data. There are three transformations, including reciprocal transformation, the logarithm transformation and the square root transformation.

Once we've transformed the data, our work isn't done, yet. We still have to interpret the results, and that often involves undoing what we've just done. If you want to figure out confidence intervals, continue working with the transformed data: calculate the standard deviation and the standard error, multiply by the limit value for the 95% or 99% interval, and then transform back to the original units at the very end.

GLOSSARY

anomalous value   异常值

outlier   异常值

missing data   缺失值

missing completely at random (MCAR)   完全随机缺失

missing at random (MAR)   随机缺失

not missing at random (NMAR) or non-ignorable (NI)   完全非随机缺失

pairwise deletion   成对删除

casewise deletion/listwise deletion   个案删除

imputing   插值

replace with the mean   均值填补

multiple regression   多重回归

multiple imputation   多重填补

last observation carried forward (LOCF)   末次观测值结转

comparing techniques   对比法

transformation   转换

reciprocal transformation   倒数转换

the logarithm transformation   对数转换

the square root transformation   平方根转换

EXERCISES

1. How can we find anomalous values?

2. How many types of missing data are there? And

how are these types of missingness defined?

3. How can we deal with missing data?

4. When should we transform data? And when shouldn't we transform data?

5. How many transformations are there? And how to define these transformations?

HOW TO GET THE COMPUTER TO DO THE WORK FOR YOU

Finding Cases That Are Outliers

- From **Analyze**, choose **Descriptive Statistics** → **Explore**
- Select the variables in the left column, and move them into the **Dependent List**
- Click [OK]

Imputing Missing Values

- From **Transform**, choose **Replace Missing Values**
- Select the **Method** [try Linear Trend at Point or Series Mean]
- Select the variable from the left column and click the arrow key
- Repeat this for all the variables [you can use different transformations for each variable]
- Click [OK]

[New variables are created with the imputed values replacing the missing data.]

Transforming Data

- From **Transform**, choose **Compute**
- Type in a new variable name in the **Target Variable** box
- Select or type in what you want to do in the **Numeric Expression** box; for example, to take the natural logarithm of variable

VAR1:

- Type **VAR2** in **Target Variable**
- Choose **LN(numexpr)** from the **Functions:** box and click the up arrow
- Select the variable to be transformed from the list, and click the arrow

SUGGESTED READINGS AND WEBSITES

[1] Altman DG, Bland JM. Detecting skewness from summary information. BMJ, 1996,313(7066):1200.

[2] Kim JO, Curry J. The treatment of missing data in multivariate analysis.Sociological Methods and Research, 1977.6(2):215-241.

[3] Little JR, Rubin DB. Statistical analysis with missing data.Wiley, New York. 1987:1322-1339.

[4] Streiner DL. The case of the missing data: methods of dealing with dropouts and other vagaries of research. Canadian Journal of Psychiatry, 47(1):68-75.

CHAPTER THE TWENTY-FIRST

Getting Started with SPSS

This is a brief introduction to using SPSS, both to analyze an existing data set, and for entering and analyzing your own data.

SETTING THE SCENE

*You've spent your hard-earned money buying this book and SPSS. After loading the program into your computer, you click on the icon and a screen appears. Now comes the anguished cry, "**What do I do now?**" In this chapter, we borrow a title from Moses Maimonides, and offer **A Guide for the Perplexed**.*

SPSS, like most computer programs, has a steep learning curve; it requires getting used to its quirks, conventions, and idiosyncrasies. However, once you get past these, it's a remarkably easy program to use. We can use it in two ways: to analyze data that others have given us, and to enter and play with our own data. So, let's start off with how we get those numbers into the program.

ENTERING YOUR OWN DATA

After clicking on the SPSS icon, be prepared to read a couple of chapters of War and Peace. It seems that while each generation of computers gets faster and faster, software developers use this as an opportunity to add more and more bells and whistles, so like the Red Queen in Alice, we have to run faster and faster just to stay in the same place. But eventually, SPSS will appear on your screen and shown as Figure 21-1:

Notice that in the lower left corner, there's one tab labelled **Data View** and another called **Variable View** (which is the screen we're in now). Clicking on these allows you to switch between looking at the numbers themselves (the Data View) and the properties of the variables. It's usually a good idea to start with the Variable View page, so you can name the variables and control what they look like on the screen. So, the first step is to give a name to each variable.

Defining the Variables

Name. There are a few rules for the variable names. They (1) must begin with a letter; (2) can be a mix of upper and lower case; (3) can contain the symbols @, #, _, and $; (4) cannot include a blank or any character not mentioned in (3), such as !, *, or ?; (5) cannot end with a period; and (6) cannot be more than 64 characters in length. You also have to avoid names that are used by SPSS for other purposes, such as LE (which means Less Than or Equal To), WITH, and a bunch of others. You don't have to memorize these forbidden names; SPSS will tell you if you have blasphemed. Once you've filled in a name, SPSS fills in many of the other properties, but you can change these if you like, so let's go through them.

Type. There are eight different "types" of variable. The default is **Numeric**, and this will suffice approximately 98.32% of the time. The only others you're likely to use would be **Date** and **String**. As the name implies, date variables are for things like when the person was born or seen at the clinic. Once you click it, you'll be offered a number of different ways of recording the date, such as dd.mm.yy, mm/dd/yy, and eight other formats. One advantage of using date is that, given two dates, such as birth and visit, SPSS can use a function called YRMODA[1] to calculate the

---

[1] *No, he was not a character in Star Wars. It stands for YeaR, MOnth, DAy.*

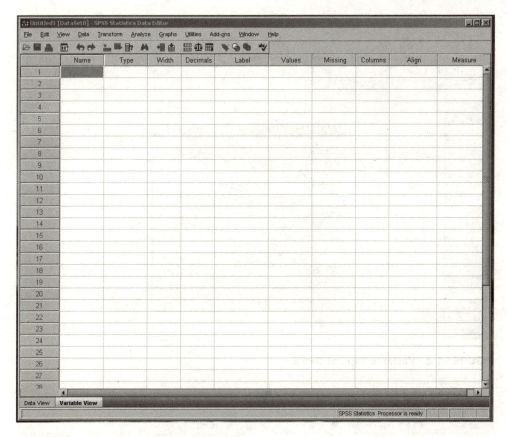

FIGURE 21-1   SPSS Statistics Data Editor

exact age of the person at the time, saving you the agony and sparing the subject the necessity of lying.[2] To most people, a string is something you use to tie up a package. But, for some strange reason, computer nerds use the term to describe a variable recorded as a word, such as "Male" or "Married."

To change the type of variable, put the cursor anywhere inside the Type box and click once. The end of the box will become a grey square with three dots inside, and a new menu will appear, as Figure 21-2.

Width. Don't worry about this unless the numbers you'll be dealing with will have more than eight digits (the default).

Decimals. This controls how many decimal places are displayed in the Variable view; it doesn't affect the storage of the data. So, if you have two decimal places (the default for numeric variables), and enter 5.249, it will appear on the screen as 5.25 but remain in memory as 5.249. We find the data easier to scan if you set it to zero for integers. As always, click anywhere inside the box, and use the arrows to modify the default. You can always change it later if you want to display more or fewer decimal places.

Label. Some variable names, such as Sex, ID Number, or Age, are sufficient to identify the contents. But, six months later, will you remember that ROMLKT3 refers to the range of motion of the left knee at time 3? Don't count on it. With *Label*, you can give an extended description of the variable in something as close to English as you like; spaces and special characters are allowed.

Values. This is used primarily for nominal and some ordinal variables. For example, if you've coded 1=Han, 2=La Hu, 3=Wa, 4=Bu lang, and 5=Dai, you can use this option to both remind you of the coding scheme, and have the values printed out with the analyses. The default is None, but if you click inside

---

[2]*Why is it that people will lie about their age, but never about their date of birth?*

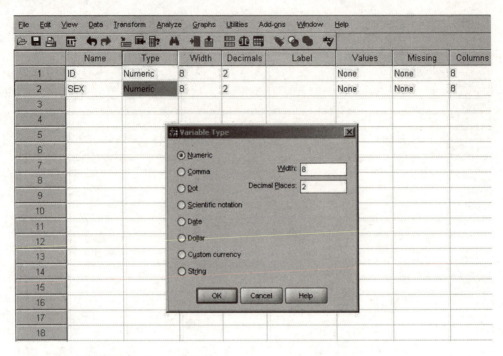

FIGURE 21-2   Variable Type of SPSS

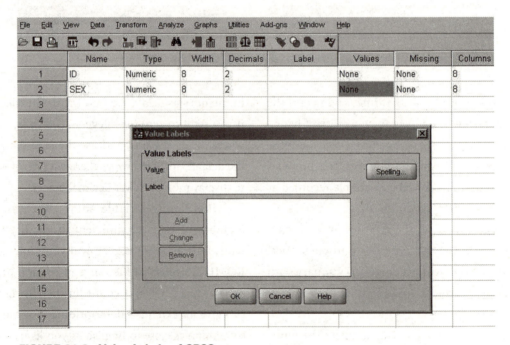

FIGURE 21-3   Value Labels of SPSS

the box, you'll get a box as Figure 21-3:

Enter *1* where it says *Value* (the u is underlined to indicate that you can also press Alt-u to get there), tab to the *Value Label* line and enter Never, and then click *Add* (or Alt-A), as Figure 21-4. Continue to do this until all the values are entered and click on OK.

Missing. *Do not forget this box if you have any missing values!* Otherwise, you'll end up with heights of 999 inches, or a lot of people who are 99 years old. Clicking inside this box brings up another dialog box:[3]

If you have anywhere from one to three different

---

[3]*Why is it called a "dialog box" when it never answers you back? Shouldn't it be a "monologue box"?*

File Edit View Data Transform Analyze Graphs Utilities Add-ons Window Help
Name Type Width Decimals Label Values Missing Columns Align
1 ID Numeric 8 2 None None 8 Right
2 SEX Numeric 8 2 {1.00, male}... None 8 Right
3 NATION Numeric 8 2 None None 8 Right
Value Labels
Value Labels
Value: 6
Label: Other
Spelling...
1.00 = "Han"
2.00 = "La hu"
3.00 = "Wa"
4.00 = "Bu lang"
5.00 = "Dai"
Add
Change
Remove
OK Cancel Help

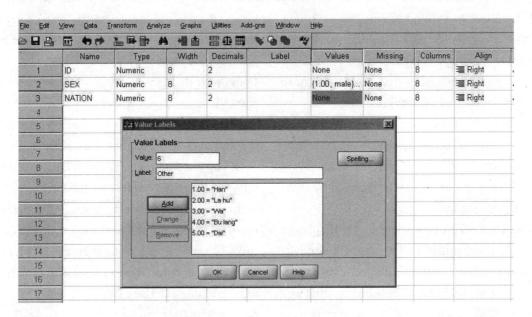

FIGURE 21-4 Value Labels Editor

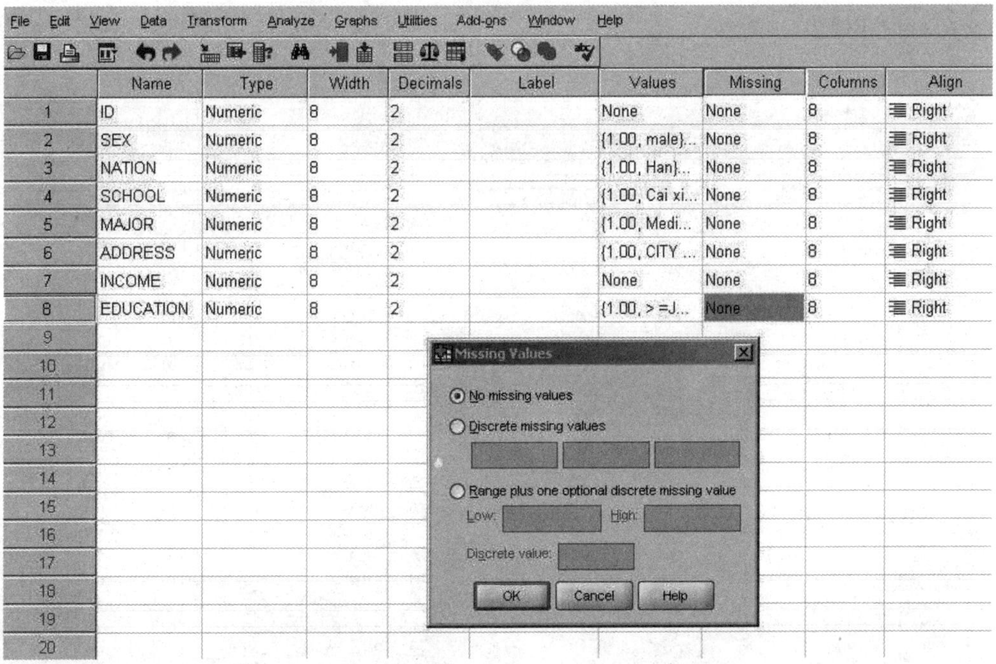

File Edit View Data Transform Analyze Graphs Utilities Add-ons Window Help
Name Type Width Decimals Label Values Missing Columns Align
1 ID Numeric 8 2 None None 8 Right
2 SEX Numeric 8 2 {1.00, male}... None 8 Right
3 NATION Numeric 8 2 {1.00, Han}... None 8 Right
4 SCHOOL Numeric 8 2 {1.00, Cai xi... None 8 Right
5 MAJOR Numeric 8 2 {1.00, Medi... None 8 Right
6 ADDRESS Numeric 8 2 {1.00, CITY ... None 8 Right
7 INCOME Numeric 8 2 None None 8 Right
8 EDUCATION Numeric 8 2 {1.00, > =J... None 8 Right
Missing Values
No missing values
Discrete missing values
Range plus one optional discrete missing value
Low: High:
Discrete value:
OK Cancel Help

FIGURE 21-5 Missing Values of SPSS

indicators for missing values, click the button next to *Discrete missing values* (or press Alt-d) in Figure 21-5 and enter the numbers. If the numbers are sequential (e.g., 7=Omitted, 8=Refused to Answer, 9=Other), you could check *Range plus one optional discrete missing value*. It's also a good idea to go back to the *Values* box and enter 7=Omitted, and so forth, so that the reasons for missingness get printed out.

Columns. This allows you to control how wide each column appears on the screen (*Width* affects the storage in memory, not the display). The default is, again, eight, and, yet again, can be changed by clicking anywhere in the box.

Align. This affects how the data are displayed. The default is right-justified for numbers and left-justified for string variables, but you can change these if you want to. Sometimes, when reading in a set of data, SPSS gets confused and interprets what should be a numeric variable as a string. If you reset the *Type* indicator, you may then want to change the justification to Right. We tend to avoid the Center option because (a) it should be spelled Centre, and (b) the decimal points don't line up, making it more difficult to read the column.

Measure. The defaults are Scale for numeric variables and Nominal for string variables. The only other option is Ordinal. Some procedures differentiate among the types of measurements, so it's a good idea to choose the right one. Change it in the usual way.

Entering the Data

If you now click on the tab in the lower left labelled **Data View**, the screen will change to reveal a spreadsheet as Figure 21-6, with the variables listed across the top, and where each line is for a new subject.

If you are entering data one subject at a time, hit <TAB> after each value, and the cursor will automatically jump to the next variable. After the last, the cursor will move to the next subject. If you're entering one variable at a time, then use <Enter> after each value, and you'll move from one subject to the next. And that's all there is to it.

Saving Your Data

Shown in Figure 21-7, click on *File* in the upper left hand corner, then *Save As....* You can change the directory in which you save the file, then enter the name under which you want to keep the file. SPSS will automatically give the file the extension *.sav*. Later, if you click on a file with this extension, it will open SPSS with

	ID	SEX	NATION	SCHOOL	MAJOR	ADDRESS	INCOME	EDUCATION	OCCUPATION	HBV	var
1	1.00	2.00	1.00	1.00	2.00	2.00	3500.00	2.00	1.00	0.00	
2	2.00	2.00	1.00	1.00	2.00	2.00	3300.00	1.00	1.00	0.00	
3	3.00	2.00	6.00	1.00	2.00	2.00	2700.00	4.00	1.00	0.00	
4	4.00	2.00	1.00	1.00	2.00	2.00	2400.00	4.00	1.00	1.00	
5	5.00	2.00	6.00	1.00	2.00	2.00	1900.00	2.00	1.00	0.00	
6	6.00	2.00	1.00	1.00	2.00	2.00	2100.00	1.00	1.00	0.00	
7	7.00	1.00	1.00	1.00	2.00	2.00	2800.00	4.00	1.00	1.00	
8	8.00	2.00	6.00	1.00	2.00	2.00	2200.00	4.00	1.00	0.00	
9	9.00	2.00	1.00	1.00	2.00	2.00	4500.00	4.00	2.00	0.00	
10	10.00	2.00	1.00	1.00	2.00	2.00	5600.00	2.00	1.00	1.00	
11	11.00	2.00	1.00	1.00	2.00	2.00	6040.00	1.00	1.00	1.00	
12	12.00	1.00	1.00	1.00	2.00	2.00	5890.00	4.00	2.00	0.00	
13	13.00	1.00	1.00	1.00	2.00	2.00	2390.00	4.00	1.00	1.00	
14	14.00	2.00	1.00	1.00	2.00	2.00	2230.00	2.00	2.00	1.00	
15	15.00	1.00	1.00	1.00	2.00	2.00	1580.00	2.00	1.00	0.00	
16	16.00	2.00	1.00	1.00	2.00	2.00	1903.00	4.00	1.00	1.00	
17	17.00	2.00	1.00	1.00	2.00	2.00	1200.00	4.00	1.00	1.00	
18	18.00	2.00	6.00	1.00	2.00	2.00	1000.00	4.00	1.00	0.00	
19	19.00	2.00	1.00	1.00	2.00	2.00	1300.00	2.00	1.00	0.00	
20	20.00	2.00	1.00	1.00	2.00	2.00	1400.00	2.00	2.00	1.00	
21	21.00	2.00	1.00	1.00	2.00	2.00	900.00	4.00	1.00	1.00	
22	22.00	1.00	1.00	1.00	2.00	1.00	800.00	2.00	2.00	1.00	
23	23.00	2.00	2.00	1.00	2.00	2.00	1500.00	4.00	1.00	0.00	

FIGURE 21-6   Data View of SPSS

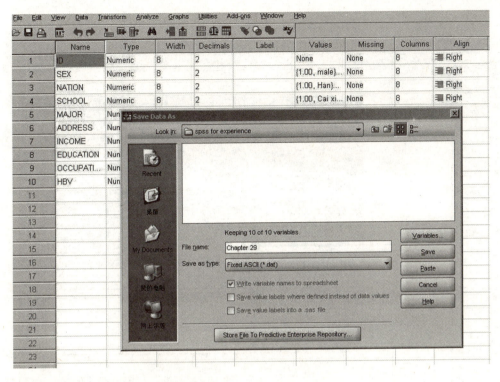

FIGURE 21-7   Save Data of SPSS

it as the active file. But, only some other statistical programs, such as SAS, will be able to read it. If you want the data saved in a format that other programs can use, then click on *Save as type* and select *Fixed ASCII (*.dat)* as the most flexible.

READING EXISTING FILES

In addition to *.sav* files, SPSS can read files created with spreadsheet programs, such as Excel, Lotus, and dBase; and some other statistical programs, such as SAS and Systat.[4] If the file was created with a word processing program, it can be read as long as the file was saved with the extension *.dat* or *.txt*.

Reading .sav Files

You can open a data file created by SPSS by simply clicking on its name, or within SPSS itself. If SPSS is already running, then click *File → Open → Data…* and click on the filename.

Reading .txt or .dat Files

After you've gone through the *File → Open → Data…* routine, click the down arrow to the right of the *Files of type:* line and choose either *Text (*.txt)* or *Data (*.dat)*, and then click on the filename. After you've done this, a "wizard" will open up,[5] guiding you through the steps necessary to import the file (Figure 21-8).

Your data most likely do not match a predefined format, so simply press *Next* and move on to Step 2 (Figure 21-9).

In most cases, the data are arranged in columns of fixed width, so change the default. Unless you entered variable names into the text file as the first row, leave that as the default. You'd possibly choose this option if you had used a spreadsheet to enter the data, and assigned names to the variables.

We can usually get through Step 3 by clicking *Next >* and accepting all the options (Figure 21-10).

In Step 4, SPSS tries to differentiate among the variables by detecting where one ends and the next one starts. In most cases, it does a pretty good job. Otherwise, click on the vertical line and move it to the correct place. You can also delete variables at this stage; just read the instructions.

---

[4]*Because there's a new version of SPSS every other year or so, this may change. You can check the types of files SPSS accepts after you've opened it, by clicking on Help → Topics, and then typing in open.*

[5]*This terminology is probably a holdover from the days when computer programmers spent all of their time playing fantasy games.*

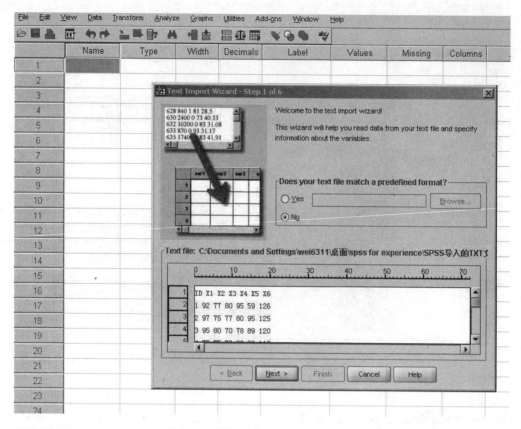

FIGURE 21-8   Text Import Wizard-Step 1 of 6

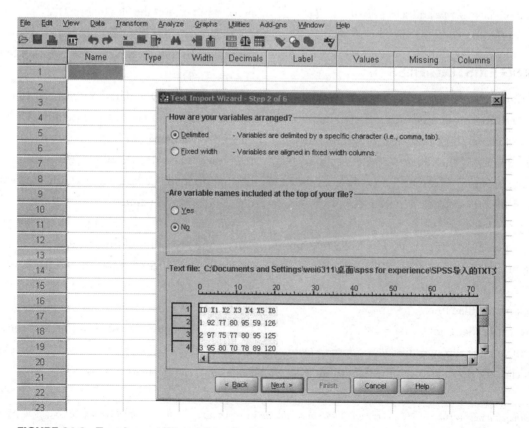

FIGURE 21-9   Text Import Wizard-Step 2 of 6

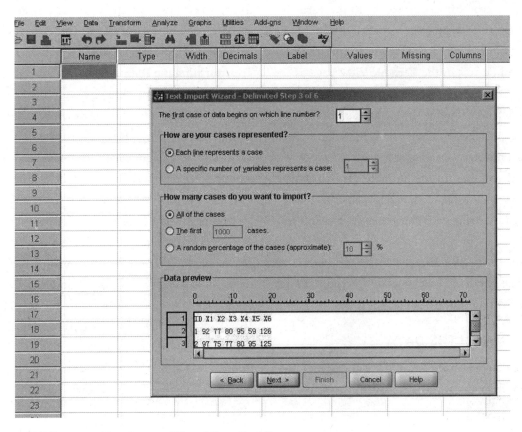

FIGURE 21-10   Text Import Wizard-Step 3 of 6

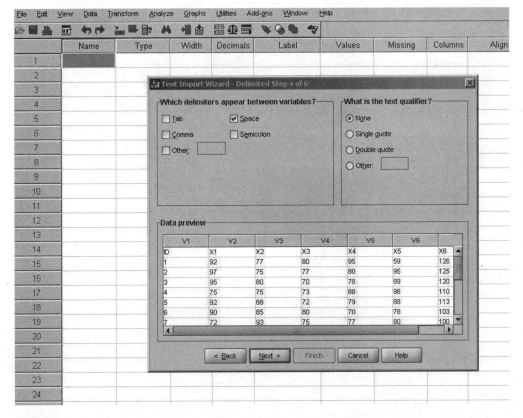

FIGURE 21-11   Text Import Wizard-Step 4 of 6

In Step 5, you can assign names to the variables and change their type (e.g., numeric, string, etc.) (Figure 21-12). Alternatively, you can just click on *Next >* and do this in the **Variable View** page as we outlined previously. If you do this, the variables will be given default names of *V1, V2*, and so on.

Our experience has been that SPSS sometimes mistakes a numeric variable for a string, so watch out for that. If you wait for the **Variable View** to change it, you may also want to change the justification to right, because string variables are entered as left justified.

For the last page, ignore the options and just click *Finish.* The data will now be ready for you to (mis) apply everything you've been taught so far.

PLAYING WITH THE DATA

Once the data are in the machine, you can manipulate them in many ways—transform them, recode them, select only subjects who meet certain criteria, and on and on. We can't show you everything,[6] but we'll tell you how to get started (Figure 21-13).

Transforming the Data

All of the commands we'll discuss in this section are accessed through the pull-down menu called *Transform* on the top line (surprise, surprise).

Compute. The *Compute...* command allows you to modify existing variables and to create new ones. When you call it up, you'll get a screen as Figure 21-14:

The first thing to do is to enter the name of the new variable you'll be creating where it says *Target Variable*. What you do next depends on what you want to do. If, for example, you want to transform the variable using one of the functions (e.g., take the log to the base 10 or base *e*; take the square root; or calculate the number of times between two dates), select that function from the (very long) list, and press the button pointing upwards. What you'll see is shown as Figure 21-15:

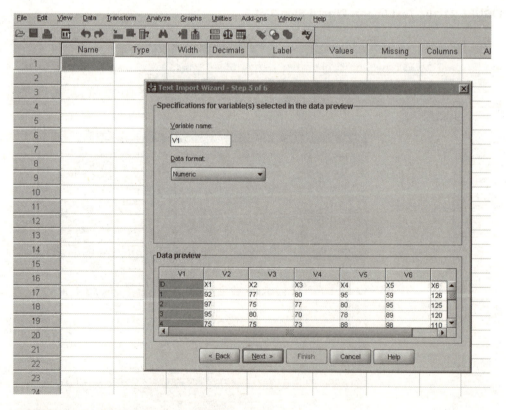

FIGURE 21-12   Text Import Wizard-Step 5 of 6

---

[6]*Actually, we can, but we won't. We have better things to do than copy the SPSS manuals. So, remember the computer nerds' saying, "RTFM!," which means "Read The Flippin' Manual!"*

FIGURE 21-13   The Display of the Saved Data

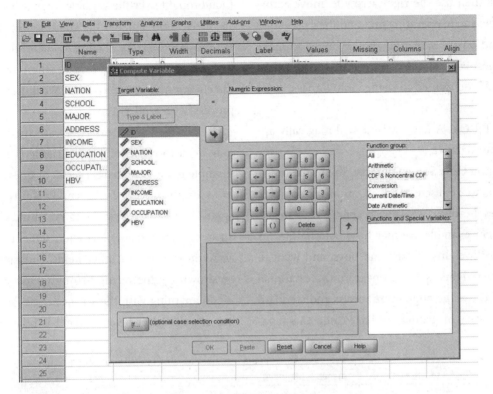

FIGURE 21-14   Compute Variable of SPSS

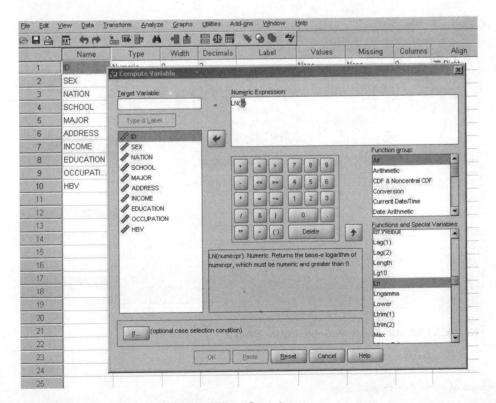

FIGURE 21-15   Compute Variable Editor-Step 1

with the cursor on the question mark. Then double-click the variable you want transformed, and you'll have created a new variable; in this case, it would be the log of the original. If you're not using one of the functions, then use the right arrow to move across the variable you're operating on,[7] and then use either the keypad on the screen or the keyboard to make the changes. For example, we recorded birthweight in grams. If you wanted to change it to ounces, you'd type in (Figure 21-16):

and then hit *OK*. A new variable will magically appear in your data set.

Changing Only Some Subjects. So far, the transformations we've discussed affect all of the subjects. Sometimes, however, we want to change only selected cases. For example, we may have national norms for the birthweights of girls and boys, and want to express the weights as deviations from these national norms. Because the population means and standard deviations vary by gender, we have to do this sepa-

rately for each group. For this, we use the button marked *If...*

The default is *Include all cases*, so we first clicked on the button for *Include if case satisfies condition*, then brought over the variable we're using as the basis of selection, entered the condition, and we'll end by pressing *Continue* (Figure 21-17). This will bring us back to the previous screen, where we can enter the equation to create *z*-scores. We'll then repeat the process, with *gender=2*.

Recoding Variables. There are times when we may need to change how a variable is coded. One example is when we have a series of questions where 1=Strongly Agree, 2=Agree, 3=Neutral, 4=Disagree, and 5=Strongly Disagree.[8] But, sometimes, Strongly Agree may reflect endorsement of the trait we're measuring; for other items, endorsement may be shown by answering Strongly Disagree. Before we do anything with the scale, such as factor analyzing it, we'd better be sure that 1 is reflecting strong

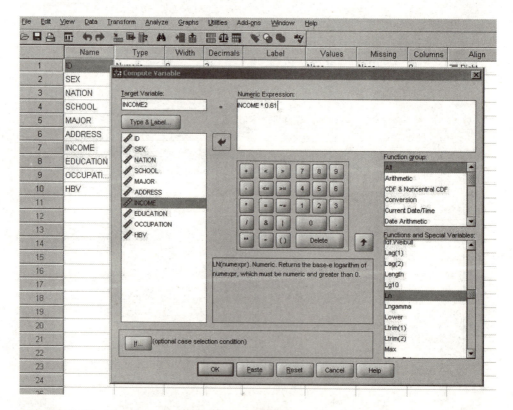

FIGURE 21-16   Compute Variable Editor-Step 2

---

[7]*In the mathematical, rather than surgical, sense.*

[8]*For those who are interested, this is called a Likert scale. It's also called a Likert scale for those who aren't interested.*

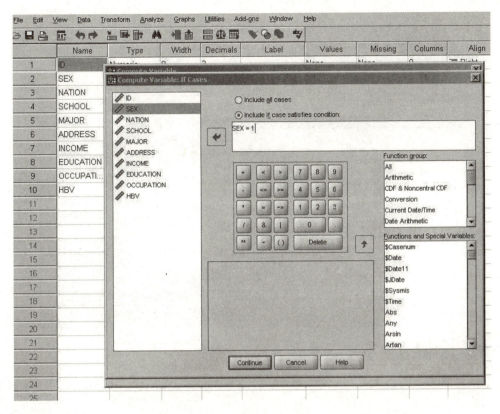

FIGURE 21-17   Compute Variable Editor-If cases edit

endorsement for all items, or else our results will be meaningless.[9] A different use of recoding is when we want to combine various categories of a nominal or interval variable. In the example we're showing, we recorded nine different types of seizures that neonates may have had. However, when it came time to analyze the data, there were too few kids in each category for us to get any idea of what was going on, so it made sense to combine them into just four types. Here's where the *Recode* command comes in.

When we pull down the Recode menu, we get two options: (1) to recode into the same variable, or (2) recode into a different variable. It's almost always a good idea to choose the latter. This is especially true if you're combining categories, because you can never go back and recapture the original data if you later change your mind and want to recode it differently. The first screen that comes up looks like Figure 21-18:

The variable *INCOME* is the name of the original variable. We entered a new name, *INCOME2*, in the box

in the upper right corner, and gave it a label to remind ourselves that it's the recoded variable. When we hit the *Change* button, the question mark in the middle box will be replaced with the new name. Then click on *Old and New Values…* to get the next screen (Figure 21-19).

Here we're about half way through the process. We began with *Range: Lowest through* and entered a 3000 into the box; put a 1 in the box in the upper right corner called *Value*, and hit *Add*. In the second step, we clicked on *Range* in the middle left, entered a 3000 through 4000, and then a 2 in the box in the upper right, and hit *Add* again. At this stage, the values of the lowest through 3000 in the original variable are combined into 1 in the new variable, and what was originally 3000 through 7000 is now coded as 2. We'll continue doing this until all of the original nine values have been recoded, and then click on *Continue*.

There are many other things you can do, but this should be enough to get you started.

---

[9] They may be meaningless even after recoding, but let's not make things even worse for ourselves.

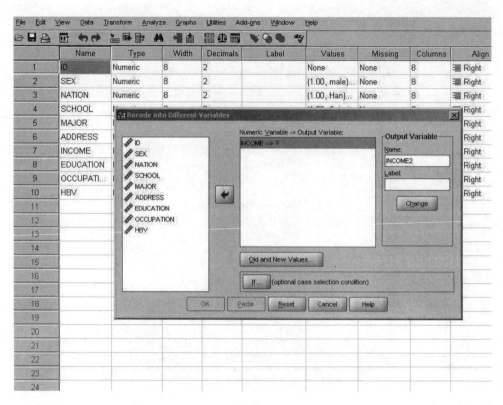

FIGURE 21-18   Recode into Different Variables-Step 1

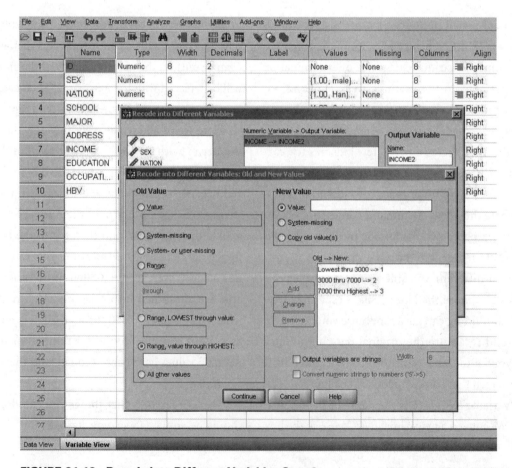

FIGURE 21-19   Recode into Different Variables-Step 2

EXERCISES

Example: Forty students of Grade 6 in a school were randomly selected as study subjects and some information on their daily life and the current condition were collected (Table 1). Please save the data into a dataset and do a descriptive analysis in SPSS.

Table 1   Daily life and the current condition of 40 students in a school

ID	Gender	Age	Height (cm)	Weight (kg)	Vital capacity (ml)	Dietary habit	Exercises	Sleep quality
1	Male	11	162	45	2300	Regularly	Sometime	Good
2	Male	12	160	58	2500	Irregularly	Never	Good
3	Female	12	158	43	2100	Regularly	Often	Well
4	Female	11	156	56	1900	Regularly	Sometime	Not good
5	Female	12	161	45	1200	Irregularly	Sometime	Not good
6	Female	11	157	52	2500	Regularly	Sometime	Good
7	Male	12	163	59	3100	Regularly	Sometime	Good
8	Male	11	163	70	2100	Irregularly	Often	Well
9	Male	10	158	41	1800	Irregularly	Never	Well
10	Female	12	154	39	1500	Irregularly	Never	Not good
11	Female	11	155	46	2100	Regularly	Sometime	Good
12	Female	12	160	51	2300	Irregularly	Sometime	Well
13	Male	11	162	52	3100	Regularly	Never	Good
14	Male	12	161	70	2100	Regularly	Never	Not good
15	Female	10	158	62	2300	Irregularly	Sometime	Not good
16	Male	12	167	54	2300	Irregularly	Sometime	Well
17	Female	11	157	54	1600	Irregularly	Sometime	Well
18	Male	12	160	62	1700	Regularly	Never	Well
19	Male	13	157	65	2700	Regularly	Sometime	Good
20	Female	10	155	57	2500	Regularly	Never	Good
21	Female	12	151	43	1700	Irregularly	Sometime	Well
22	Female	11	160	42	1400	Irregularly	Sometime	Well
23	Male	11	172	65	2600	Regularly	Sometime	Well
24	Male	12	164	70	2300	Regularly	Never	Not good
25	Male	12	161	70	1900	Regularly	Never	Not good
26	Female	11	153	41	1500	Irregularly	Sometime	Well
27	Male	13	160	58	1800	Regularly	Sometime	Well
28	Male	10	163	56	2100	Irregularly	Often	Not good
29	Female	11	152	41	2100	Regularly	Often	Not good
30	Female	12	155	56	2600	Regularly	Often	Well
31	Female	11	154	45	1700	Regularly	Sometime	Not good
32	Male	12	161	71	1900	Irregularly	Sometime	Well
33	Male	11	159	67	1600	Irregularly	Never	Well
34	Male	11	160	56	2500	Regularly	Never	Not good

Continued

ID	Gender	Age	Height (cm)	Weight (kg)	Vital capacity (ml)	Dietary habit	Exercises	Sleep quality
35	Female	11	152	52	2700	Regularly	Often	Well
36	Female	10	156	62	2900	Irregularly	Often	Well
37	Male	12	156	68	2100	Regularly	Never	Not good
38	Male	13	163	67	1900	Regularly	Never	Not good
39	Female	11	159	54	2300	Irregularly	Often	Well
40	Male	10	168	71	3400	Regularly	Often	Well

SUGGESTED READINGS AND WEBSITES

[1] http://www.spsstools.net/en/spss-tutorials/

[2] http://www.ibm.com/analytics/us/en/technology/spss/

[3] https://en.wikipedia.org/wiki/SPSS

Being a Compendium of Questions and Answers

The purpose of this section is for you to see how well you've picked up the material so far. It consists of two types of problems: abstracts of real articles, and studies we have made up for the occasion[1]. With the abstracts, we've deleted all the irrelevant stuff and any mention of the statistics they used. Your job is to figure out the correct statistical test to use to analyze the data. The answer section gives what we think should have been done, which in some cases is not what actually was done.[2] Of course, this is only our opinion, and you are at liberty to disagree.[3]

QUESTIONS

Problem 1. Andersen et al. (1990) compared the excess mortality rate following transurethral resection of the prostate versus the more traditional, open resection in men with benign hypertrophy. They used hospital data, following 38 067 cases for up to 10.5 years.[4] However, this was not a randomized trial, and the two groups differed in terms of age and previous health status. How did they do it?

Problem 2. It was found that more male patients with ocular rectitis (OR) had a family history of hemorrhoids than did the healthy controls. In addition, it was noted that such individuals tended to wear tight underwear more than did the controls. How would you analyze these data?

Problem 3. A retrospective study looked at risk factors for Chronic Fatigue Syndrome. Fifteen CFS sufferers were matched by age and sex to 15 controls in the same company. They examined three predictor variables—Life stress score (0~64), Locus of control (Internal [0] or External [1]), and White collar (1) or Blue collar (2)—to see what best predicted CFS. What analysis would you do?

Problem 4. Patients with chronic obstructive pulmonary disease were randomly assigned to either a comprehensive rehabilitation program or an educational control program. The primary outcome variable was exercise endurance, as determined by treadmill time, measured monthly over a 6-month follow-up period (Toshima, Kaplan, and Ries, 1990).

Problem 5. A scotchophile wanted to see whether other connoisseurs could really discriminate single malt from blended scotches, or well-aged from relatively young scotches. He assembled 4 scotches of each type (8 years old/12 years old, and single malt/blended) and had them rated for quality by a panel of 5 judges, each judge rating all 16 samples. Compliance exceeded 100%, although some of the later ratings were nearly indecipherable.

Problem 6. To judge the effect of this book, your intrepid authors gave away free copies to a bunch (n=34) of undergraduates on the condition that they take the test you are now taking (a) before they left the bookstore, and (b) after they read the book. Mean percent score was 23% (SD 14%) in the pretest and 45% (SD 12%) at the post-test.

Problem 7. A palm reader (of the hands, not the

---

[1]*You can tell which are real articles—a reference is given, and the clinical questions are far more mundane than the ones we made up.*

[2]*If no comments are made, we go along with how the authors handled the data.*

[3]*You are also at liberty to write your own statistics book.*

[4]*"Following" is an epidemiological term, meaning that they kept track of the cases through medical records; the authors did not hire Bulldog Drummond or Sam Spade to shadow the patients.*

dates) hears of the success of ear creases in predicting coronary artery disease and wonders if it generalizes to other body parts, specifically those she can exploit. She assembles a bunch of heart attack victims ($n=12$) from an old folks' home and also a control sample. She counts the number of wrinkles on the middle knuckle of each finger and each toe (excluding thumb and big toe) and determines whether any of these can differentiate between heart disease patients and healthy people.

Problem 8. To determine if the prevalence of phobias is different among older men and women, and if the prevalence changes with age, 512 people between the ages of 50 and 89 were given a telephone-administered questionnaire (Liddell, Locker, and Burman, 1991). Then what did the researchers do?

Problem 9. Marshall et al. (1991) compared recidivism rates among male exhibitionists who received or did not receive therapy.[5] Recidivism was a binary variable—occurring or not occurring within the follow-up period.

Problem 10. In a study of 50 mammograms, two observers classified each film as "Normal," "Suspicious— Repeat Test," or "Likely Malignant." How well do they agree with each other?

Problem 11. To test the hypothesis that sinistrality[6] is associated with decreased "survival fitness,"[7] Coren and Halpern (1981) compared the longevities of right-handed versus left-handed baseball players; how did they?

Problem 12. To see if attractiveness has any bearing on performance on oral examinations, class photographs of 50 final-year dental students were ranked by 2 patients from most to least attractive. These rankings were pooled and then compared with their class standing on the final oral examination.

Problem 13. Because "Hispanics, being a Mediterranean people, tend to put statements in relatively strong terms," Hui and Triandis (1989) hypothesized that they would be more likely to use the extreme ends of 5-point rating scales than would non-Hispanics. They also hypothesized that this difference would disappear when the scale had 10 points, rather than 5. Each subject completed 165 items, using either a 5- or 10-point rating scale.

Problem 14. In another trial of the wonder drug Clamazine, patients evaluated their itchiness on an 11-point scale before and after using the medication. For the 208 patients, their itchiness before Clamazine was 9.5 (SD=4.2) and 5.7 (SD=2.8) after the drug.

Problem 15. In the previous problem (number 14, if you've lost track), is there sufficient information to proceed to calculate the test statistic?

a. Yes, we know the means, SDs, and sample size

b. No, we don't know the comparable data for the control group

c. No, we don't know the SD of the differences

d. No, we don't know the *df*

Problem 16. The local dermatologist, building on the growing interest in clam juice for psoriasis, did a study of varying dosage regimens. He looked at 30 ml bid (twice a day), 60 ml daily, and 20 ml tid (three times a day). Twelve patients were assigned to each cohort for a 2-month period, and extent of lesions measured at the end of the trial.

Problem 17. Weiss and Larsen (1990) hypothesized that scores on the four subscales of the multidimensional Health Locus of Control (HLC) scale and a Health Value Index would individually and together predict participation in "health-protective behaviors" (HPB), such as using seat belts and undertaking vigorous exercise. HPB was measured on a 10-point scale.

Problem 18. Leary and McLuhan investigated whether any association existed between pot smoking in the 1960s and cocaine addiction in the 1990s. They did a case control study involving 50 coke ad-

---

[5]*Fortunately for the patients, treatment was not vivisection therapy, which is based on the biblical injunction, "If thine eye offend thee, pluck it out."*

[6]*That's a fancy term for left-handedness.*

[7]*Another fancy euphemism meaning they die at an earlier age.*

dicts from the Bay area and 50 normal controls, and they inquired whether these folks were potheads in the 1960s (Never, Occasional, Continuous). The association was significant (chi-squared=4.56). How could they measure the strength of association?

Problem 19. Minsel, Becker, and Korchin (1991) looked at whether "mental health" was seen the same way in four different cultures (United States, France, Germany, and Greece). The questionnaire consisted of 186 items answered on a 5-point scale. The primary aim was to look at the *relative* importance of each item, rather than the absolute value. Unfortunately, there were cultural differences, in that Greeks used the higher end of the scale more than did the other groups, and the Germans and Americans used the lower end more often.

a. How did they eliminate this "cultural bias?"

b. How did they see if the four groups had similar concepts of "mental health?"

Problem 20. A local clinician became convinced that, among other evils, smoking causes cirrhosis of the liver, because "if you go into any bar, they are all smoking." Smoking causes drinking, which causes liver damage. On reflection, it might be desirable to look at the effects of both smoking and drinking (categorized as smoker/nonsmoker, drinker/ nondrinker), on a sample of cirrhosis patients and controls.

Problem 21. To see if proxy assessments by relatives could substitute for patient assessments of physical and psychosocial health status, Rothman et al. (1991) had 275 patient-proxy pairs complete the Sickness Impact Profile. How did they evaluate the similarity?

Problem 22. College fraternities and sororities traditionally run "Dog Pools" on prom nights. All contribute and the one who ends up with the most unattractive mate wins the pool. More often than not, it seems that the winner of the fraternity dog pool is paired with the winner of the sorority dog pool. To test this scientifically, two frat rats used the graduation pictures of all concerned and rank ordered them by male or female pulchritude, as the case may be. They then determined who was paired

with whom on prom night and looked for a measure of association.

Problem 23. Bennett et al. (1987) used a randomized trial to improve students' knowledge of critical appraisal in two areas: diagnosis and therapeutics. They administered a pretest and a post-test in each area to the treatment group (which received training in critical appraisal) and the control group (which did not). For the treatment group, the paired t-test was highly significant ($p < 0.001$) for diagnosis, and it was significant for therapy ($p < 0.01$). For the control group, neither t-test was significant. They concluded that critical appraisal works. Would you have analyzed the study this way?

Problem 24. Feighner (1985) ran an RCT of patients on the new wonder drug Prozac against the old stand-by, amitriptyline. Each group had 22 patients, who were assessed at baseline on three measures—the HAM-D, the Raskin depression scale, and the Covi anxiety scale—and then weekly thereafter for 5 weeks. A one-tailed Wilcoxon signed rank test was used to compare improvement from week 0 to week 5.

Problem 25. Physicians in Ontario are all subjected to regular peer review of records, and those who have problems identified are sent for a further 2-day assessment that includes various measures—simulated patients, oral examinations, chart review, O.S.C.E. (Objective Structured Clinical Examination), and written tests. The question posed was whether some identifiable underlying components are assessed by all these measures. Can statistics help?

Problem 26. A concern was that Medicare beneficiaries who join health maintenance organizations (HMOs) were sicker than people not on Medicare. To check this out, Lichtenstein et al. (1991) looked at a 9-level functional health status measure in patients in 23 HMOs. How did they determine if health status differed between recipients and nonrecipients of Medicare?

Problem 27. To see whether reaction times (RT) in traffic situations deteriorate in low-light conditions, a simulator was set up in which the same traffic situations could be displayed under high- and low-light conditions. Subjects were tested with a series of 20 videotaped traffic situations, where 10 were in daylight and 10 were at night, and response times were measured. Because RT has a severely skewed distribution, it was analyzed with a non-parametric test.

Problem 28. Thomas and Holloway (1991) investigated whether unplanned hospital readmission was related to hospital size, length of stay, discharge to home versus an organized care facility, teaching status of the hospital, and so on.

Problem 29. Sorenson et al. (1991) wanted to compare the age of onset of any depressive disorder in the population for (a) men versus women and for (b) non-Hispanic whites versus Mexican-Americans born in the United States versus Mexican-Americans born in Mexico.

Problem 30. Does the high school yearbook have any predictive validity? To investigate this, students in the graduating class of one midwestern school were rank ordered by teachers on their likelihood of success. Ten years later, their success was assessed by educational attainment—no completed postsecondary education, bachelor's degree, or graduate degrees (this is a measure of success?).

ANSWERS

Problem 1. They used a survival analysis, with the Cox proportional hazards approach.

Problem 2. There are three variables—one dependent (OR yes/no) and two independent variables (Jockey/boxer shorts; family history yes/no). Mantel-Haenszel chi-squared or log-linear analysis; the choice is yours.

Problem 3. To examine variables individually, you could do a paired t-test on the life stress score and the McNemar chi-squared on locus of control and white/blue (remember that it is a matched design). To see what combination best predicts CFS, use logistic regression. But the matching creates real problems, as these procedures are really for independent samples. Also note that, in doing this, we have interchanged the independent and dependent variables for the purpose of analysis. Now CFS/Normal is acting like a dependent variable. This happens

often in statistics and is of no consequence, as the computer doesn't know which is which.

Problem 4. The data were analyzed using a repeated-measures ANOVA, with Treatment (rehab versus education) as a between-subjects factor and Time as a within-subjects factor.

Problem 5. The analysis is a factorial ANOVA. There are two grouping (between subject) factors: (1) young/old, and (2) single malt/blended; and one within subject factor (rater). The real trick is that "subject," in this case, is the scotch, which is the object of measurement. If you like, the design looks like this:

			Rater				
		Scotch	A	B	C	D	E
Single malt	Young	1					
		2					
		3					
		4					
	Old	5					
		.					
		8					
		9					
Blended	Young	.					
		12					
		13					
	Old	.					
		16					

Problem 6. Because it's a pretest–post-test design, a paired t-test would do. Repeated-measures ANOVA gives the same answer.

Problem 7. Repeated-measures ANOVA. There is one between-subject factor (heart attack/normal) and three repeated-measures (hand/foot, left/right, and first, second, third, little) factors, so there are $2 \times 2 \times 4$ measures on each subject. By the way, there again we have flipped the independent and dependent variables, treating heart attack/normal as an independent variable. No one cares.

Problem 8. They broke the subjects down into three age groups (50 to 64, 65 to 74, and 75+), and then used an Age × Sex ANOVA. Although correct, another approach would be to use a multiple regression, with Age and Sex as the predictors. This would preserve the ratio nature of Age and not force it into arbitrary categories.

Problem 9. The data were analyzed with a 2 × 2 chi-squared.

Problem 10. Because the films are classified in three ordinal categories, a weighted kappa is appropriate.

Problem 11. Coren and Halpern argued that a *t*-test wouldn't be appropriate because the data are highly skewed. They used the Wald-Wolfowitz Runs test, which is a nonparametric test of differences between groups. You could also do a life-table analysis on the data.

Problem 12. Two rankings on each of 50 students were compared. Use a Spearman rank correlation.

Problem 13. They used a 2 (Hispanic versus nonHispanic) × 2 (5- or 10-point scale) factorial between-subjects ANOVA, with the dependent variable being the number of times an extreme response category was chosen.

Problem 14. Because the data are continuous, forget about χ^2s, of any flavor. Because both values are collected from the same subject, we need a paired, as opposed to an unpaired, *t*-test (If you said a repeated-measures ANOVA, give yourself ½ a point; a paired *t*-test is a form of ANOVA, but it's much easier to calculate if you've got only two values).

Problem 15. The correct answer is *c*. The SDs that are given are *between* subjects. The whole point of the paired *t*-test is that it uses the *within* -subject SDs—that is, the SD of the differences, which we don't have.

Problem 16. The quantitative doses suggest a regression problem; however, the total daily dose is the same in all schedules, so the differences are qualitative. A straight one-way ANOVA is appropriate. However, the sensitivity of the experiment would be enhanced by measuring at baseline and doing ANCOVA with baseline measure as covariate.

Problem 17. They used a multiple regression, with the HLC subscales and the health value as predictors and the HPB score as the dependent variable.

The correct way to see if any interaction between HCL and health value exists would be to create a new variable that is the product of these two (i.e., an interaction term). The authors state that, "because of the unusually high multicollinearity," this could not be done; they ended up dichotomizing health value and running separate regressions for the two groups. This study was very well analyzed.

Problem 18. Several epidemiologic measures of strength of association exist, such as odds ratio or log likelihood ratio. On the statistical side, we could use one of the measures based on chi-squared (phi, Cramer's *V*, contingency coefficient). Note that we cannot use a kappa or any of the other measures that depend on a 2 × 2 table, as this is a 2 × 3 table.

Problem 19. (*a*) The data for each subject were transformed into standard scores, with a mean of 100 and an SD of 10. (*b*) The data were factor analyzed for each group separately, and the factor matrices were examined for comparability.

Problem 20. Because there are three factors and all are categorical, the choice is between Mantel-Haenszel and log-linear analysis.

Problem 21. They first correlated the two sets of scores to see if they were associated with one another and then did a paired *t*-test to look for any systematic bias. They could not have used an independent (unpaired) *t*-test because, although the two scores came from different people (patient and proxy), they were about the same person (the patient). But if you wanted to look at agreement, it would be better to use an intraclass correlation coefficient.

Problem 22. Use a measure of association for ranked data—Spearman rho or one of the alternatives.

Problem 23. Approaching the analysis this way essentially ignores the control group. They should have done an *unpaired t*-test on the difference scores, contrasting the treatment with the control group. In fact, the investigators reported both analyses.

Problem 24. First, using a nonparametric procedure on these data is unnecessary. There probably isn't much loss of power, but it does limit the analysis. Second, they threw out the data from weeks 1 to

4 to do this test. What they should have done was three ANCOVAs (one for each variable), with the baseline as the covariate and weeks 1 to 4 as repeated measures. And, by the way, the one-tailed test is really hard to justify on this occasion.

Problem 25. Factor analysis would determine whether scores group into homogeneous factors.

Problem 26. They ran t-tests between the two groups for each of the 23 HMOs. It would have been much better to do one ANOVA, with two between-subject factors: Medicare status (two levels) by HMO (23 levels). This would have allowed them to see if differences existed among the HMOs, as well as avoid the problem of running so many t-tests.

Problem 27. This is a within-subject design, with an average RT for day and night for each subject. Use a Wilcoxon signed rank test. Alternatively, as you actually have 20 RTs per subject, you might want to transform using a log transformation to reduce skewness, then do a repeated-measures ANOVA with two factors—Day/Night, and specific scenario (10 levels).

Problem 28. For each of 22 diagnosis-related groups (DRGs), they ran stepwise logistic regressions. This makes sense because admission is a binary outcome, and there is little assurance of multivariate normality among the predictor variables.

Problem 29. They began by simply looking at the median age of onset. Recognizing that, because the subjects could be any age at the time of the interview, and therefore at risk of becoming depressed for varying lengths of time, they also used a survival analysis.

Problem 30. Three groups, ordinal ranks, Kruskal-Wallis one-way ANOVA by ranks.

APPENDIX

Table A Area of the normal curve.

Table B Sample size requirements to show a difference between two means of size α/δ.

Table C Critical values for the t-test.

Table D Sample size requirements for the independent t-test.

Table E Power table for the independent t-test.

Table F Critical values for the chi-squared test.

Table G Critical values for the Pearson correlation coefficient (r).

Table H Critical values for the F test.

Table I Sample size requirements for the one-way ANOVA.

Table J Power table for the one-way ANOVA.

Table K Sample size requirements for the difference between independent proportions ($\alpha=0.05$).

Table L Required number of events per group for survival analysis (two-tailed test).

Table M Critical values of the Studentized Range test.

Table N Sample size requirements for MANOVA.

Table O Power of the two-group MANOVA.

Table P r to z' transformation.

Table Q z' to r transformation.

TABLE A   Area of the normal curve

z	Area below	z	Area below	z	Area below	z	Area below
0.00	0.0000						
0.01	0.0039	0.41	0.1591	0.81	0.2910	1.21	0.3869
0.02	0.0079	0.42	0.1627	0.82	0.2932	1.22	0.3888
0.03	0.0119	0.43	0.1664	0.83	0.2967	1.23	0.3906
0.04	0.0159	0.44	0.1700	0.84	0.2995	1.24	0.3925
0.05	0.0199	0.45	0.1736	0.85	0.3023	1.25	0.3943
0.06	0.0239	0.46	0.1772	0.86	0.3051	1.26	0.3962
0.07	0.0279	0.47	0.1808	0.87	0.3078	1.27	0.3980
0.08	0.0318	0.48	0.1844	0.88	0.3106	1.28	0.3997
0.09	0.0358	0.49	0.1879	0.89	0.3133	1.29	0.4015
0.10	0.0398	0.50	0.1914	0.90	0.3159	1.30	0.4032
0.11	0.0438	0.51	0.1950	0.91	0.3186	1.31	0.4049
0.12	0.0477	0.52	0.1985	0.92	0.3212	1.32	0.4066
0.13	0.0517	0.53	0.2019	0.93	0.3238	1.33	0.4082
0.14	0.0556	0.54	0.2054	0.94	0.3264	1.34	0.4099
0.15	0.0596	0.55	0.2088	0.95	0.3289	1.35	0.4115
0.16	0.0635	0.56	0.2122	0.96	0.3315	1.36	0.4131
0.17	0.0675	0.57	0.2156	0.97	0.3340	1.37	0.4147
0.18	0.0714	0.58	0.2190	0.98	0.3365	1.38	0.4162
0.19	0.0753	0.59	0.2224	0.99	0.3389	1.39	0.4177
0.20	0.0792	0.60	0.2257	1.00	0.3413	1.40	0.4192
0.21	0.0831	0.61	0.2291	1.01	0.3437	1.41	0.4207
0.22	0.0870	0.62	0.2324	1.02	0.3461	1.42	0.4222
0.23	0.0909	0.63	0.2356	1.03	0.3485	1.43	0.4236
0.24	0.0948	0.64	0.2389	1.04	0.3508	1.44	0.4251
0.25	0.0987	0.65	0.2421	1.05	0.3531	1.45	0.4265
0.26	0.1025	0.66	0.2454	1.06	0.3554	1.46	0.4279
0.27	0.1064	0.67	0.2486	1.07	0.3577	1.47	0.4292
0.28	0.1102	0.68	0.2517	1.08	0.3599	1.48	0.4306
0.29	0.1141	0.69	0.2549	1.09	0.3621	1.49	0.4319
0.30	0.1179	0.70	0.2580	1.10	0.3643	1.50	0.4332
0.31	0.1217	0.71	0.2611	1.11	0.3665	1.51	0.4345
0.32	0.1255	0.72	0.2642	1.12	0.3686	1.52	0.4357
0.33	0.1293	0.73	0.2673	1.13	0.3708	1.53	0.4370
0.34	0.1330	0.74	0.2703	1.14	0.3729	1.54	0.4382
0.35	0.1368	0.75	0.2734	1.15	0.3749	1.55	0.4394
0.36	0.1406	0.76	0.2764	1.16	0.3770	1.56	0.4406
0.37	0.1443	0.77	0.2793	1.17	0.3790	1.57	0.4418
0.38	0.1480	0.78	0.2823	1.18	0.3810	1.58	0.4429
0.39	0.1517	0.79	0.2852	1.19	0.3830	1.59	0.4441
0.40	0.1554	0.80	0.2881	1.20	0.3849	1.60	0.4452
1.61	0.4463	2.02	0.4783	2.43	0.4925	2.84	0.4977
1.62	0.4474	2.03	0.4788	2.44	0.4927	2.85	0.4978
1.63	0.4484	2.04	0.4793	2.45	0.4929	2.86	0.4979

Continued

z	Area below	z	Area below	z	Area below	z	Area below
1.64	0.4495	2.05	0.4798	2.46	0.4931	2.87	0.4979
1.65	0.4505	2.06	0.4803	2.47	0.4932	2.88	0.4980
1.66	0.4515	2.07	0.4808	2.48	0.4934	2.89	0.4981
1.67	0.4525	2.08	0.4812	2.49	0.4936	2.90	0.4981
1.68	0.4535	2.09	0.4817	2.50	0.4938	2.91	0.4982
1.69	0.4545	2.10	0.4821	2.51	0.4940	2.92	0.4982
1.70	0.4554	2.11	0.4826	2.52	0.4941	2.93	0.4983
1.71	0.4564	2.12	0.4830	2.53	0.4943	2.94	0.4984
1.72	0.4573	2.13	0.4834	2.54	0.4945	2.95	0.4984
1.73	0.4582	2.14	0.4838	2.55	0.4946	2.96	0.4985
1.74	0.4591	2.15	0.4842	2.56	0.4948	2.97	0.4985
1.75	0.4599	2.16	0.4846	2.57	0.4949	2.98	0.4985
1.76	0.4608	2.17	0.4850	2.58	0.4951	2.99	0.4986
1.77	0.4616	2.18	0.4854	2.59	0.4952	3.00	0.4987
1.78	0.4625	2.19	0.4857	2.60	0.4953	3.01	0.4987
1.79	0.4633	2.20	0.4861	2.61	0.4955	3.02	0.4987
1.80	0.4641	2.21	0.4864	2.62	0.4956	3.03	0.4988
1.81	0.4649	2.22	0.4868	2.63	0.4957	3.04	0.4988
1.82	0.4656	2.23	0.4871	2.64	0.4959	3.05	0.4989
1.83	0.4664	2.24	0.4875	2.65	0.4960	3.06	0.4989
1.84	0.4671	2.25	0.4878	2.66	0.4961	3.07	0.4989
1.85	0.4678	2.26	0.4881	2.67	0.4962	3.08	0.4990
1.86	0.4686	2.27	0.4884	2.68	0.4963	3.09	0.4990
1.87	0.4693	2.28	0.4887	2.69	0.4964	3.10	0.4990
1.88	0.4699	2.29	0.4890	2.70	0.4965	3.11	0.4991
1.89	0.4706	2.30	0.4893	2.71	0.4966	3.12	0.4991
1.90	0.4713	2.31	0.4896	2.72	0.4967	3.13	0.4991
1.91	0.4719	2.32	0.4898	2.73	0.4968	3.14	0.4992
1.92	0.4726	2.33	0.4901	2.74	0.4969	3.15	0.4992
1.93	0.4732	2.34	0.4904	2.75	0.4970	3.16	0.4992
1.94	0.4738	2.35	0.4906	2.76	0.4971	3.17	0.4992
1.95	0.4744	2.36	0.4909	2.77	0.4972	3.18	0.4993
1.96	0.4750	2.37	0.4911	2.78	0.4973	3.19	0.4993
1.97	0.4756	2.38	0.4913	2.79	0.4974	3.20	0.4993
1.98	0.4761	2.39	0.4916	2.80	0.4974	3.21	0.4993
1.99	0.4767	2.40	0.4918	2.81	0.4975	3.22	0.4994
2.00	0.4772	2.41	0.4920	2.82	0.4976	3.23	0.4994
2.01	0.4778	2.42	0.4922	2.83	0.4977	3.24	0.4994
3.25	0.4994	3.44	0.4997	3.63	0.4999	3.82	0.4999
3.26	0.4994	3.45	0.4997	3.64	0.4999	3.83	0.4999
3.27	0.4995	3.46	0.4997	3.65	0.4999	3.84	0.4999
3.28	0.4995	3.47	0.4997	3.66	0.4999	3.85	0.4999
3.29	0.4995	3.48	0.4997	3.67	0.4999	3.86	0.4999
3.30	0.4995	3.49	0.4998	3.68	0.4999	3.87	0.4999
3.31	0.4995	3.50	0.4998	3.69	0.4999	3.88	0.4999

Continued

z	Area below	z	Area below	z	Area below	z	Area below
3.32	0.4995	3.51	0.4998	3.70	0.4999	3.89	0.4999
3.33	0.4996	3.52	0.4998	3.71	0.4999	3.90	0.5000
3.34	0.4996	3.53	0.4998	3.72	0.4999	3.91	0.5000
3.35	0.4996	3.54	0.4998	3.73	0.4999	3.92	0.5000
3.36	0.4996	3.55	0.4998	3.74	0.4999	3.95	0.5000
3.37	0.4996	3.56	0.4998	3.75	0.4999	3.94	0.5000
3.38	0.4996	3.57	0.4998	3.76	0.4999	3.95	0.5000
3.39	0.4997	3.58	0.4998	3.77	0.4999	3.96	0.5000
3.40	0.4997	3.59	0.4998	3.78	0.4999	3.97	0.5000
3.41	0.4997	3.60	0.4998	3.79	0.4999	3.98	0.5000
3.42	0.4997	3.61	0.4998	3.80	0.4999	3.99	0.5000
3.43	0.4997	3.62	0.4999	3.81	0.4999	4.00	0.5000

TABLE B Sample size requirements to show a difference between two means of size σ/δ

σ/δ	$\alpha=0.10$			0.05			0.01		
	$\beta=0.20$	0.15	0.10	0.20	0.15	0.10	0.20	0.15	0.10
0.5	2	2	2	2	2	3	3	4	4
1.0	6	7	9	8	9	11	12	14	16
1.5	14	17	20	18	21	24	27	30	34
1.6	16	19	22	21	24	28	31	34	39
1.7	18	21	25	23	27	31	35	39	44
1.8	20	24	28	26	30	35	39	43	49
1.9	23	26	31	29	33	39	43	48	55
2.0	25	29	35	32	37	43	48	53	61
2.1	28	32	38	35	40	47	53	59	67
2.2	30	35	38	39	44	52	58	65	73
2.3	33	39	46	42	48	57	63	71	80
2.4	36	42	50	46	53	61	68	77	87
2.5	39	46	54	50	57	67	74	83	95
2.6	42	49	59	54	62	72	80	90	102
2.7	46	53	63	58	67	78	87	97	110
2.8	49	57	68	62	72	83	93	104	118
2.9	52	61	73	67	77	90	100	112	127
3.0	56	66	78	72	82	96	107	120	136
3.1	60	70	83	76	88	102	114	128	145
3.2	64	74	88	81	93	109	121	136	154
3.3	68	79	94	86	99	116	129	144	164
3.4	72	84	100	92	105	123	137	153	174
3.5	76	89	106	97	112	130	145	162	185
3.6	81	94	112	103	118	138	153	172	195
3.7	85	99	118	108	125	145	162	181	206
3.8	90	105	124	114	131	153	171	191	217
3.9	95	110	131	120	138	161	180	201	229
4.0	99	116	138	127	145	170	189	212	241

*NOTE δ=difference between means; σ=standard deviation.

TABLE C   Critical values for the *t*-test

df	α for a 1-tailed test					
	0.10	0.05	0.025	0.01	0.005	0.0005
	α for a 2-tailed test					
	0.20	0.10	0.05	0.02	0.01	0.001
1	3.078	6.314	12.706	31.820	63.656	636.615
2	1.886	2.920	4.303	6.965	9.925	31.599
3	1.638	2.353	3.182	4.541	5.841	12.924
4	1.533	2.132	2.776	3.747	4.604	8.610
5	1.476	2.015	2.571	3.365	4.032	6.869
6	1.440	1.943	2.447	3.143	3.707	5.959
7	1.415	1.895	2.365	2.998	3.499	5.408
8	1.397	1.860	2.306	2.896	3.355	5.041
9	1.383	1.833	2.262	2.821	3.250	4.781
10	1.372	1.812	2.228	2.764	3.169	4.587
11	1.363	1.796	2.201	2.718	3.106	4.437
12	1.356	1.782	2.179	2.681	3.055	4.318
13	1.350	1.771	2.160	2.650	3.012	4.221
14	1.345	1.761	2.145	2.624	2.977	4.141
15	1.341	1.753	2.131	2.602	2.947	4.073
16	1.337	1.746	2.120	2.583	2.921	4.015
17	1.333	1.740	2.110	2.567	2.898	3.965
18	1.330	1.734	2.101	2.552	2.878	3.922
19	1.328	1.729	2.093	2.539	2.861	3.883
20	1.325	1.725	2.086	2.528	2.845	3.849
21	1.323	1.721	2.080	2.518	2.831	3.819
22	1.321	1.717	2.074	2.508	2.819	3.792
23	1.319	1.714	2.069	2.500	2.807	3.768
24	1.318	1.711	2.064	2.492	2.797	3.745
25	1.316	1.708	2.060	2.485	2.787	3.725
26	1.315	1.706	2.056	2.479	2.779	3.707
27	1.314	1.703	2.052	2.473	2.771	3.690
28	1.313	1.701	2.048	2.467	2.763	3.674
29	1.311	1.699	2.045	2.462	2.756	3.659
30	1.310	1.697	2.042	2.457	2.750	3.646
35	1.306	1.690	2.030	2.438	2.724	3.591
40	1.303	1.684	2.021	2.423	2.704	3.551
45	1.301	1.679	2.014	2.412	2.690	3.520
50	1.299	1.676	2.009	2.403	2.678	3.496
55	1.297	1.673	2.004	2.396	2.668	3.476
60	1.296	1.671	2.000	2.390	2.660	3.460
70	1.294	1.667	1.994	2.381	2.648	3.435
80	1.292	1.664	1.990	2.374	2.639	3.416
90	1.291	1.662	1.987	2.368	2.632	3.402
100	1.290	1.660	1.984	2.364	2.626	3.390

TABLE D Sample size requirements for the independent *t*-test*

d	α (1-tail)=0.05 α (2-tail)=0.10 β=0.20	0.15	0.10	0.05	0.025 0.05 0.20	0.15	0.10	0.05	0.005 0.01 0.20	0.15	0.10	0.05
0.10	1237	1438	1713	2165	1570	1795	2102	2599	2337	2609	2977	3563
0.20	309	359	428	541	393	449	526	650	584	652	744	891
0.25	198	230	274	346	251	287	336	416	374	417	476	570
0.30	137	160	190	241	174	199	234	289	260	290	331	396
0.40	77	90	107	135	98	112	131	162	146	163	186	223
0.50	49	58	69	87	63	72	84	104	93	104	119	143
0.60	34	40	48	60	44	50	58	72	65	72	83	99
0.70	27	31	35	44	32	37	43	53	48	53	61	73
0.75	24	28	30	38	30	32	37	46	42	46	53	63
0.80	21	24	29	34	27	30	33	41	37	41	47	56
0.90	17	20	23	29	21	24	28	32	31	32	37	44
1.0	14	16	19	24	18	20	23	28	25	28	30	36
1.1	12	14	16	20	15	17	19	23	21	24	27	31
1.2	11	12	14	17	13	14	17	20	18	20	23	27
1.3	9	11	12	15	11	13	14	17	16	17	20	23
1.4	8	9	11	13	10	11	13	15	14	15	17	20
1.5	7	8	10	12	9	10	11	14	12	14	15	18
1.6	7	8	9	10	8	9	10	12	11	12	14	16
1.7	6	7	8	9	7	8	9	11	10	11	12	14
1.8	6	6	7	9	7	8	8	10	9	10	11	13
1.9	6	6	7	8	6	7	8	9	8	9	10	12
2.0	6	6	6	7	6	6	7	8	8	9	9	11
2.1	6	6	6	7	6	6	7	8	7	8	9	10
2.2	6	6	6	6	6	6	6	7	7	7	8	9
2.3	6	6	6	6	6	6	6	7	6	7	8	9
2.4	6	6	6	6	6	6	6	7	6	7	7	8
2.5	6	6	6	6	6	6	6	6	6	6	7	8
3.0	2	6	6	6	6	6	6	6	6	6	6	6
3.5	2	2	2	6	2	2	6	6	6	6	6	6
4.0	2	2	2	2	2	2	2	6	2	6	6	6

*NOTE: sample sizes are per group.

TABLE E Power table for the independent *t*-test

N per group d=	α (1-tail)=0.05 β (2-tail)=0.10 0.20	0.40	0.60	0.80	0.025 0.05 0.20	0.40	0.60	0.80	0.005 0.01 0.20	0.40	0.60	0.80
2	0.129	0.127	0.151	0.171	0.086	0.090	0.097	0.106	0.048	0.049	0.050	0.051
3	0.114	0.135	0.171	0.219	0.063	0.075	0.096	0.126	0.021	0.024	0.030	0.038
4	0.114	0.147	0.202	0.275	0.058	0.079	0.114	0.164	0.015	0.020	0.030	0.046
5	0.116	0.161	0.234	0.329	0.058	0.086	0.135	0.206	0.013	0.020	0.036	0.061
6	0.119	0.176	0.265	0.380	0.059	0.095	0.159	0.248	0.012	0.022	0.043	0.078
7	0.122	0.190	0.296	0.428	0.060	0.105	0.182	0.290	0.011	0.024	0.051	0.099
8	0.126	0.205	0.326	0.472	0.062	0.115	0.206	0.331	0.011	0.027	0.061	0.121

Continued

N per group d=	α (1-tail)=0.05 β (2-tail)=0.10				0.025 0.05				0.005 0.01			
	0.20	0.40	0.60	0.80	0.20	0.40	0.60	0.80	0.20	0.40	0.60	0.80
9	0.130	0.219	0.354	0.514	0.064	0.125	0.230	0.371	0.012	0.030	0.072	0.145
10	0.133	0.233	0.382	0.553	0.066	0.135	0.254	0.410	0.012	0.033	0.083	0.171
11	0.137	0.247	0.409	0.589	0.068	0.146	0.278	0.448	0.012	0.037	0.095	0.197
12	0.141	0.261	0.435	0.623	0.070	0.157	0.301	0.483	0.013	0.041	0.108	0.224
13	0.144	0.275	0.460	0.654	0.073	0.167	0.324	0.518	0.013	0.045	0.121	0.251
14	0.148	0.288	0.484	0.683	0.075	0.178	0.347	0.550	0.014	0.050	0.135	0.279
15	0.152	0.301	0.507	0.710	0.078	0.189	0.369	0.581	0.014	0.054	0.149	0.307
16	0.156	0.314	0.529	0.735	0.080	0.199	0.391	0.611	0.015	0.059	0.163	0.336
17	0.159	0.327	0.551	0.758	0.083	0.210	0.413	0.638	0.015	0.064	0.178	0.364
18	0.163	0.340	0.572	0.779	0.085	0.221	0.434	0.664	0.016	0.069	0.193	0.391
19	0.167	0.353	0.591	0.798	0.088	0.232	0.455	0.689	0.017	0.074	0.208	0.419
20	0.170	0.365	0.610	0.816	0.090	0.242	0.475	0.712	0.018	0.079	0.223	0.446
21	0.174	0.377	0.629	0.833	0.093	0.253	0.494	0.734	0.018	0.084	0.239	0.472
22	0.178	0.389	0.646	0.848	0.095	0.263	0.513	0.754	0.019	0.090	0.255	0.498
23	0.181	0.401	0.663	0.862	0.098	0.274	0.532	0.773	0.020	0.095	0.270	0.523
24	0.185	0.413	0.679	0.874	0.100	0.284	0.550	0.791	0.021	0.101	0.286	0.548
25	0.189	0.424	0.695	0.886	0.103	0.295	0.568	0.807	0.021	0.107	0.302	0.571
30	0.207	0.479	0.763	0.930	0.116	0.346	0.648	0.874	0.026	0.137	0.381	0.678
35	0.225	0.530	0.817	0.958	0.130	0.395	0.716	0.919	0.030	0.169	0.458	0.764
40	0.242	0.576	0.860	0.975	0.143	0.442	0.773	0.949	0.035	0.203	0.530	0.831
45	0.260	0.619	0.893	0.985	0.156	0.487	0.819	0.968	0.041	0.238	0.596	0.881
50	0.277	0.658	0.919	0.991	0.170	0.529	0.858	0.980	0.046	0.273	0.656	0.918
55	0.293	0.693	0.939	0.995	0.183	0.569	0.888	0.988	0.052	0.308	0.710	0.944
60	0.310	0.725	0.954	0.997	0.197	0.606	0.913	0.993	0.058	0.343	0.757	0.962
65	0.326	0.755	0.966	0.998	0.210	0.640	0.932	0.996	0.064	0.378	0.797	0.975
70	0.342	0.781	0.974	0.999	0.224	0.673	0.948	0.997	0.071	0.413	0.832	0.984
75	0.357	0.805	0.981	0.999	0.237	0.702	0.960	0.998	0.077	0.447	0.862	0.989
80	0.373	0.826	0.986	1.00	0.251	0.730	0.969	0.999	0.084	0.480	0.887	0.993
85	0.388	0.846	0.990	1.00	0.264	0.755	0.977	0.999	0.091	0.512	0.908	0.996
90	0.403	0.863	0.992	1.00	0.277	0.779	0.982	1.00	0.098	0.543	0.926	0.997
95	0.417	0.878	0.994	1.00	0.290	0.800	0.987	1.00	0.106	0.572	0.940	0.998
100	0.431	0.892	0.996	1.00	0.303	0.820	0.990	1.00	0.113	0.601	0.952	0.999

TABLE F   Critical values for the chi-squared test

df	α					
	0.10	0.05	0.025	0.01	0.005	0.001
1	2.706	3.842	5.024	6.635	7.879	10.828
2	4.605	5.992	7.378	9.210	10.597	13.816
3	6.251	7.815	9.348	11.345	12.838	16.266
4	7.779	9.489	11.143	13.277	14.860	18.467

Continued

df	0.10	0.05	0.025	0.01	0.005	0.001
			α			
5	9.236	11.071	12.833	15.086	16.750	20.515
6	10.645	12.592	14.449	16.812	18.548	22.457
7	12.017	14.067	16.013	18.475	20.278	24.321
8	13.362	15.507	17.535	20.090	21.955	26.124
9	14.684	16.919	19.023	21.666	23.589	27.877
10	15.987	18.307	20.483	23.209	25.188	29.588
11	17.275	19.675	21.920	24.725	26.757	31.264
12	18.549	21.026	23.336	26.217	28.299	32.909
13	19.812	22.362	24.736	27.688	29.819	34.528
14	21.064	23.685	26.120	29.141	31.319	36.123
15	22.307	24.996	27.488	30.578	32.801	37.697
16	23.542	26.296	28.845	32.000	34.267	39.252
17	24.769	27.587	30.191	33.409	35.718	40.790
18	25.989	28.869	31.526	34.805	37.156	42.312
19	27.204	30.144	32.852	36.191	38.582	43.820
20	28.412	31.410	34.170	37.566	39.997	45.314
21	29.615	32.671	35.479	38.932	41.401	46.797
22	30.813	33.924	36.781	40.289	42.796	48.268
23	32.007	35.172	38.076	41.638	44.181	49.728
24	33.196	36.415	39.365	42.980	45.558	51.178
25	34.382	37.652	40.647	44.314	46.928	52.620
26	35.563	38.885	41.924	45.642	48.290	54.052
27	36.741	40.113	43.195	46.963	49.645	55.476
28	37.916	41.337	44.461	48.278	50.993	56.892
29	39.087	42.557	45.723	49.588	52.336	58.301
30	40.256	43.773	46.980	50.892	53.672	59.703

TABLE G   Critical values for the Pearson correlation coefficient (r)

df	\alpha for a 1-tailed test			
	0.05	0.025	0.01	0.005
	α for a 2-tailed test			
	0.10	0.05	0.02	0.01
1	0.988	0.997	0.9995	0.9999
2	0.900	0.950	0.980	0.990
3	0.805	0.878	0.934	0.959
4	0.729	0.811	0.882	0.917
5	0.669	0.755	0.833	0.874
6	0.621	0.707	0.789	0.834
7	0.582	0.666	0.750	0.798
8	0.549	0.632	0.715	0.765

Continued

	α for a 1-tailed test			
	0.05	0.025	0.01	0.005
df	α for a 2-tailed test			
	0.10	0.05	0.02	0.01
9	0.521	0.602	0.685	0.735
10	0.497	0.576	0.658	0.708
11	0.476	0.553	0.634	0.684
12	0.458	0.532	0.612	0.661
13	0.441	0.514	0.592	0.641
14	0.426	0.497	0.574	0.623
15	0.412	0.482	0.558	0.606
16	0.400	0.468	0.543	0.590
17	0.389	0.456	0.529	0.575
18	0.378	0.444	0.516	0.561
19	0.369	0.433	0.503	0.549
20	0.360	0.423	0.492	0.537
21	0.352	0.413	0.482	0.526
22	0.344	0.404	0.472	0.515
23	0.337	0.396	0.462	0.505
24	0.330	0.388	0.453	0.496
25	0.323	0.381	0.445	0.487
26	0.317	0.374	0.437	0.479
27	0.312	0.367	0.430	0.471
28	0.306	0.361	0.423	0.463
29	0.301	0.355	0.416	0.456
30	0.296	0.349	0.409	0.449
35	0.275	0.325	0.381	0.418
40	0.257	0.304	0.358	0.393
45	0.243	0.288	0.338	0.372
50	0.231	0.273	0.322	0.354
55	0.220	0.261	0.307	0.339
60	0.211	0.250	0.295	0.325
70	0.195	0.232	0.274	0.302
80	0.183	0.217	0.257	0.283
90	0.173	0.205	0.242	0.267
100	0.164	0.195	0.230	0.254
125	0.147	0.174	0.206	0.228
150	0.134	0.159	0.189	0.208
175	0.124	0.147	0.175	0.193
200	0.116	0.138	0.164	0.181
250	0.104	0.124	0.146	0.162

TABLE Ha   Critical values for the F test*

df_1 — Numerator degrees of freedom

df_2	1	2	3	4	5	6	7	8	9	10	11	12	15	20	25	30	40	50	75	100
1	161	200	216	225	230	234	237	239	241	242	243	244	246	248	249	250	251	252	253	253
	4052	5000	5403	5625	5764	5859	5928	5981	6023	6056	6083	6106	6157	6209	6239	6261	6287	6302	6323	6334
2	18.5	19.0	19.2	19.2	19.3	19.3	19.4	19.4	19.4	19.4	19.4	19.4	19.4	19.4	19.5	19.5	19.5	19.5	19.5	19.5
	98.5	99.0	99.2	99.2	99.3	99.3	99.4	99.4	99.4	99.4	99.4	99.4	99.4	99.4	99.5	99.5	99.5	99.5	99.5	99.5
3	10.1	9.55	9.28	9.12	9.01	8.94	8.89	8.85	8.81	8.79	8.76	8.74	8.70	8.66	8.63	8.62	8.59	8.58	8.56	8.55
	34.1	30.8	29.5	28.7	28.2	27.9	27.7	27.5	27.3	27.2	27.1	27.1	26.9	26.7	26.6	26.5	26.4	26.4	26.3	26.2
4	7.71	6.94	6.59	6.39	6.26	6.16	6.09	6.04	6.00	5.96	5.94	5.91	5.86	5.80	5.77	5.75	5.72	5.70	5.68	5.66
	21.2	18.0	16.7	16.0	15.5	15.2	15.0	14.8	14.7	14.5	14.5	14.4	14.2	14.0	13.9	13.8	13.7	13.7	13.6	13.6
5	6.61	5.79	5.41	5.19	5.05	4.95	4.88	4.82	4.77	4.74	4.70	4.68	4.62	4.56	4.52	4.50	4.46	4.44	4.42	4.41
	16.3	13.3	12.1	11.4	11.0	10.7	10.5	10.3	10.2	10.2	9.96	9.89	9.72	9.55	9.45	9.38	9.29	9.24	9.17	9.13
6	5.99	5.14	4.76	4.63	4.39	4.28	4.21	4.15	4.10	4.06	4.03	4.00	3.94	3.87	3.83	3.81	3.77	3.75	3.73	3.71
	13.7	10.9	9.78	9.15	8.75	8.47	8.26	8.10	7.98	7.87	7.79	7.72	7.56	7.40	7.30	7.23	7.14	7.09	7.02	6.99
7	5.59	4.74	4.35	4.12	3.97	3.87	3.79	3.73	3.68	3.64	3.60	3.57	3.51	3.44	3.40	3.38	3.34	3.32	3.29	3.27
	12.2	9.54	8.45	7.85	7.46	7.19	6.99	6.84	6.72	6.62	6.54	6.47	6.31	6.16	6.06	5.99	5.91	5.86	5.79	5.75
8	5.32	4.46	4.07	3.84	3.69	3.58	3.50	3.44	3.39	3.35	3.31	3.28	3.22	3.15	3.11	3.08	3.04	3.02	2.99	2.97
	11.3	8.64	7.59	7.01	6.63	6.37	6.18	6.03	5.91	5.81	5.73	5.67	5.52	5.36	5.26	5.20	5.12	5.07	5.00	4.96
9	5.12	4.26	3.86	3.63	3.48	3.37	3.29	3.23	3.18	3.14	3.10	3.07	3.01	2.94	2.89	2.86	2.83	2.80	2.77	2.76
	10.6	8.02	6.99	6.42	6.06	5.80	5.61	5.47	5.35	5.26	5.18	5.11	4.96	4.81	4.71	4.65	4.57	4.52	4.45	4.41
10	4.96	4.10	3.71	3.48	3.33	3.22	3.14	3.07	3.02	2.98	2.94	2.91	2.84	2.77	2.73	2.70	2.66	2.64	2.60	2.59
	10.0	7.56	6.55	5.99	5.64	5.39	5.20	5.06	4.94	4.85	4.77	4.71	4.56	4.41	4.31	4.25	4.17	4.12	4.05	4.01
11	4.84	3.98	3.59	3.36	3.20	3.09	3.01	2.95	2.90	2.85	2.82	2.79	2.72	2.65	2.60	2.57	2.53	2.51	2.47	2.46
	9.65	7.21	6.22	5.67	5.32	5.07	4.89	4.74	4.63	4.54	4.46	4.40	4.25	4.10	4.01	3.94	3.86	3.81	3.74	3.71
12	4.75	3.89	3.50	3.26	3.11	3.00	2.91	2.85	2.80	2.75	2.72	2.69	2.62	2.54	2.50	2.47	2.43	2.40	2.37	2.35
	9.33	6.93	5.95	5.41	5.06	4.82	4.64	4.50	4.39	4.30	4.22	4.16	4.01	3.86	3.76	3.70	3.62	3.57	3.50	3.47
13	4.67	3.81	3.41	3.18	3.03	2.92	2.83	2.77	2.71	2.67	2.63	2.60	2.53	2.46	2.41	2.38	2.34	2.31	2.28	2.26
	9.07	6.70	5.74	5.21	4.86	4.62	4.44	4.30	4.19	4.10	4.02	3.96	3.82	3.66	3.57	3.51	3.43	3.38	3.31	3.27
14	4.60	3.74	3.34	3.11	2.96	2.85	2.76	2.70	2.65	2.60	2.57	2.53	2.46	2.39	2.34	2.31	2.27	2.24	2.21	2.19
	8.86	6.51	5.56	5.04	4.69	4.46	4.28	4.14	4.03	3.94	3.86	3.80	3.66	3.51	3.41	3.35	3.27	3.22	3.15	3.11

Continued

df_2	df_1—Numerator degrees of freedom																			
	1	2	3	4	5	6	7	8	9	10	11	12	15	20	25	30	40	50	75	100
15	4.54	3.68	3.29	3.06	2.90	2.79	2.71	2.64	2.59	2.54	2.51	2.48	2.40	2.33	2.28	2.25	2.20	2.18	2.14	2.12
	8.86	**6.36**	**5.42**	**4.89**	**4.56**	**4.32**	**4.14**	**4.00**	**3.89**	**3.80**	**3.73**	**3.67**	**3.52**	**3.37**	**3.28**	**3.21**	**3.13**	**3.08**	**3.01**	**2.98**
16	4.49	3.63	3.24	3.01	2.85	2.74	2.66	2.59	2.54	2.49	2.46	2.42	2.35	2.28	2.23	2.19	2.15	2.12	2.09	2.07
	8.53	**6.23**	**5.29**	**4.77**	**4.44**	**4.20**	**4.03**	**3.89**	**3.78**	**3.69**	**3.62**	**3.55**	**3.41**	**3.26**	**3.16**	**3.10**	**3.02**	**2.97**	**2.90**	**2.86**

*upper number is 5% level, lower (**in bold**) is 1%.

TABLE Hb   Critical values for the F test*

df_2	df_1—Numerator degrees of freedom																			
	1	2	3	4	5	6	7	8	9	10	11	12	15	20	25	30	40	50	75	100
17	4.45	3.59	3.20	2.96	2.81	2.70	2.61	2.55	2.49	2.45	2.41	2.38	2.31	2.23	2.18	2.15	2.10	2.08	2.04	2.02
	8.40	**6.11**	**5.18**	**4.67**	**4.34**	**4.10**	**3.93**	**3.79**	**3.68**	**3.59**	**3.52**	**3.46**	**3.31**	**3.16**	**3.07**	**3.00**	**2.92**	**2.87**	**2.80**	**2.76**
18	4.41	3.55	3.16	2.93	2.77	2.66	2.58	2.51	2.46	2.41	2.37	2.34	2.27	2.19	2.14	2.11	2.06	2.04	2.00	1.98
	8.29	**6.01**	**5.09**	**4.58**	**4.25**	**4.01**	**3.84**	**3.71**	**3.60**	**3.51**	**3.43**	**3.37**	**3.23**	**3.08**	**2.98**	**2.92**	**2.84**	**2.78**	**2.71**	**2.68**
19	4.38	3.52	3.13	2.90	2.74	2.63	2.54	2.48	2.42	2.38	2.34	2.31	2.23	2.16	2.11	2.07	2.03	2.00	1.96	1.94
	8.18	**5.93**	**5.01**	**4.50**	**4.17**	**3.94**	**3.77**	**3.63**	**3.52**	**3.43**	**3.36**	**3.30**	**3.15**	**3.00**	**2.91**	**2.84**	**2.76**	**2.71**	**2.64**	**2.60**
20	4.35	3.49	3.10	2.87	2.71	2.60	2.51	2.45	2.39	2.35	2.31	2.28	2.20	2.12	2.07	2.04	1.99	1.97	1.93	1.91
	8.10	**5.85**	**4.94**	**4.43**	**4.10**	**3.87**	**3.70**	**3.56**	**3.46**	**3.37**	**3.29**	**3.23**	**3.09**	**2.94**	**2.84**	**2.78**	**2.69**	**2.64**	**2.57**	**2.54**
21	4.32	3.47	3.07	2.84	2.68	2.57	2.49	2.42	2.37	2.32	2.28	2.25	2.18	2.10	2.05	2.01	1.96	1.94	1.90	1.88
	8.02	**5.78**	**4.87**	**4.37**	**4.04**	**3.81**	**3.64**	**3.51**	**3.40**	**3.31**	**3.24**	**3.17**	**3.03**	**2.88**	**2.79**	**2.72**	**2.64**	**2.58**	**2.51**	**2.48**
22	4.30	3.44	3.05	2.82	2.66	2.55	2.46	2.40	2.34	2.30	2.26	2.23	2.15	2.07	2.02	1.98	1.94	1.91	1.87	1.85
	7.95	**5.72**	**4.82**	**4.31**	**3.99**	**3.76**	**3.59**	**3.45**	**3.35**	**3.26**	**3.18**	**3.12**	**2.98**	**2.83**	**2.73**	**2.67**	**2.58**	**2.53**	**2.46**	**2.42**
23	4.28	3.42	3.03	2.80	2.64	2.53	2.44	2.37	2.32	2.27	2.24	2.20	2.13	2.05	2.00	1.96	1.91	1.88	1.84	1.82
	7.88	**5.66**	**4.76**	**4.26**	**3.94**	**3.71**	**3.54**	**3.41**	**3.30**	**3.21**	**3.14**	**3.07**	**2.93**	**2.78**	**2.69**	**2.62**	**2.54**	**2.48**	**2.41**	**2.37**
24	4.26	3.41	3.01	2.78	2.62	2.51	2.42	2.36	2.30	2.25	2.22	2.18	2.11	2.03	1.97	1.94	1.89	1.86	1.82	1.80
	7.82	**5.61**	**4.72**	**4.22**	**3.89**	**3.67**	**3.50**	**3.36**	**3.26**	**3.17**	**3.09**	**3.03**	**2.89**	**2.74**	**2.64**	**2.58**	**2.49**	**2.44**	**2.37**	**2.33**
25	4.24	3.39	2.99	2.76	2.60	2.49	2.40	2.34	2.28	2.24	2.20	2.16	2.09	2.01	1.96	1.92	1.87	1.84	1.80	1.78
	7.77	**5.57**	**4.68**	**4.18**	**3.86**	**3.63**	**3.46**	**3.32**	**3.22**	**3.13**	**3.06**	**2.99**	**2.85**	**2.70**	**2.60**	**2.54**	**2.45**	**2.40**	**2.33**	**2.29**

Continued

df_1—Numerator degrees of freedom

df_2	1	2	3	4	5	6	7	8	9	10	11	12	15	20	25	30	40	50	75	100
26	4.23	3.37	2.98	2.74	2.59	2.47	2.39	2.32	2.27	2.22	2.18	2.15	2.07	1.99	1.94	1.90	1.85	1.82	1.78	1.76
	7.72	**5.53**	**4.64**	**4.14**	**3.82**	**3.59**	**3.42**	**3.29**	**3.18**	**3.09**	**3.02**	**2.96**	**2.81**	**2.66**	**2.57**	**2.50**	**2.42**	**2.36**	**2.29**	**2.25**
27	4.21	3.35	2.96	2.73	2.57	2.46	2.37	2.31	2.25	2.20	2.17	2.13	2.06	1.97	1.92	1.88	1.84	1.81	1.76	1.74
	7.68	**5.49**	**4.60**	**4.11**	**3.78**	**3.56**	**3.39**	**3.26**	**3.15**	**3.06**	**2.99**	**2.93**	**2.78**	**2.63**	**2.54**	**2.47**	**2.38**	**2.33**	**2.26**	**2.22**
28	4.20	3.34	2.95	2.71	2.56	2.45	2.36	2.29	2.24	2.19	2.15	2.12	2.04	1.96	1.91	1.87	1.82	1.79	1.75	1.73
	7.64	**5.45**	**4.57**	**4.07**	**3.75**	**3.53**	**3.36**	**3.23**	**3.12**	**3.03**	**2.96**	**2.90**	**2.75**	**2.60**	**2.51**	**2.44**	**2.35**	**2.30**	**2.23**	**2.19**
29	4.18	3.33	2.93	2.70	2.55	2.43	2.35	2.28	2.22	2.18	2.14	2.10	2.03	1.94	1.89	1.85	1.81	1.77	1.73	1.71
	7.60	**5.42**	**4.54**	**4.04**	**3.73**	**3.50**	**3.33**	**3.20**	**3.09**	**3.00**	**2.93**	**2.87**	**2.73**	**2.57**	**2.48**	**2.41**	**2.33**	**2.27**	**2.20**	**2.16**
30	4.17	3.32	2.92	2.69	2.53	2.42	2.33	2.27	2.21	2.16	2.13	2.09	2.01	1.93	1.88	1.84	1.79	1.76	1.72	1.70
	7.56	**5.39**	**4.51**	**4.02**	**3.70**	**3.47**	**3.30**	**3.17**	**3.07**	**2.98**	**2.91**	**2.84**	**2.70**	**2.55**	**2.45**	**2.39**	**2.30**	**2.25**	**2.17**	**2.13**
40	4.08	3.23	2.84	2.61	2.45	2.34	2.25	2.18	2.12	2.08	2.04	2.00	1.92	1.84	1.78	1.74	1.69	1.66	1.61	1.59
	7.31	**5.18**	**4.31**	**3.83**	**3.51**	**3.29**	**3.12**	**2.99**	**2.89**	**2.80**	**2.73**	**2.66**	**2.52**	**2.37**	**2.27**	**2.20**	**2.11**	**2.06**	**1.98**	**1.94**
50	4.03	3.18	2.79	2.56	2.40	2.27	2.20	2.13	2.07	2.03	1.99	1.95	1.87	1.78	1.73	1.69	1.63	1.60	1.55	1.52
	7.17	**5.06**	**4.20**	**3.72**	**3.41**	**3.19**	**3.02**	**2.89**	**2.78**	**2.70**	**2.63**	**2.56**	**2.42**	**2.27**	**2.17**	**2.10**	**2.01**	**1.95**	**1.87**	**1.82**
75	3.97	3.12	2.73	2.49	2.34	2.22	2.13	2.06	2.01	1.96	1.92	1.88	1.80	1.71	1.65	1.61	1.55	1.52	1.47	1.44
	6.99	**4.90**	**4.05**	**3.58**	**3.27**	**3.05**	**2.89**	**2.76**	**2.65**	**2.57**	**2.49**	**2.43**	**2.29**	**2.13**	**2.03**	**1.96**	**1.87**	**1.81**	**1.72**	**1.67**
100	3.94	3.09	2.70	2.46	2.31	2.19	2.10	2.03	1.97	1.93	1.89	1.85	1.77	1.68	1.62	1.57	1.52	1.48	1.42	1.39
	6.90	**4.82**	**3.98**	**3.51**	**3.21**	**2.99**	**2.82**	**2.69**	**2.59**	**2.50**	**2.43**	**2.37**	**2.22**	**2.07**	**1.97**	**1.89**	**1.80**	**1.74**	**1.65**	**1.60**

*upper number is 5% level, lower (**in bold**) is 1%.

TABLE I Sample size requirements for the one-way ANOVA*

Effect size (f)	Number of groups	β=	α=0.05			α=0.01		
			0.30	0.20	0.10	0.30	0.20	0.10
	3		251	315	415	384	460	578
	4		217	269	351	324	386	481
0.1	5		191	237	307	283	335	415
	6		173	213	274	252	298	368
	7		148	182	235	216	256	315
	3		64	80	105	97	116	146
	4		55	68	89	82	99	121
0.2	5		49	60	78	72	85	105
	6		44	54	69	64	76	93
	7		38	46	59	55	65	80
	3		29	36	47	44	53	66
	4		25	31	40	37	44	55
0.3	5		22	27	35	33	39	48
	6		20	25	32	29	35	42
	7		17	21	27	25	30	36
	3		17	21	27	26	30	38
	4		15	18	23	22	26	32
0.4	5		13	16	20	19	22	27
	6		12	14	18	17	20	24
	7		10	12	16	15	17	21
	3		11	14	18	17	20	25
	4		10	12	15	15	17	21
0.5	5		9	11	13	13	15	18
	6		8	10	12	10	13	16
	7		7	8	10	10	12	14
	3		8	10	13	13	15	18
	4		7	9	11	11	12	15
0.6	5		7	8	10	9	11	13
	6		6	7	9	9	10	12
	7		5	6	8	8	9	10

*numbers are sample sizes per group.

TABLE J Power table for the one-way ANOVA

Number of groups	N per group	f=	α=0.05				α=0.01			
			0.10	0.20	0.30	0.40	0.10	0.20	0.30	0.40
3	5		0.059	0.088	0.140	0.218	0.012	0.202	0.037	0.067
	10		0.068	0.140	0.272	0.453	0.013	0.036	0.095	0.206
	15		0.080	0.199	0.405	0.647	0.015	0.060	0.177	0.380
	20		0.093	0.259	0.527	0.785	0.019	0.090	0.272	0.548
	25		0.107	0.320	0.632	0.875	0.023	0.124	0.372	0.689
	30		0.121	0.378	0.719	0.930	0.028	0.162	0.469	0.795
	35		0.135	0.435	0.789	0.962	0.033	0.203	0.560	0.871
	40		0.149	0.490	0.844	0.980	0.039	0.246	0.642	0.921
	45		0.164	0.541	0.886	0.990	0.045	0.289	0.713	0.954
	50		0.179	0.588	0.918	0.995	0.051	0.334	0.773	0.973

Continued

Number of groups	N per group	f=	α=0.05				α=0.01			
			0.10	0.20	0.30	0.40	0.10	0.20	0.30	0.40
4	5		0.059	0.090	0.149	0.239	0.012	0.021	0.041	0.078
	10		0.069	0.150	0.301	0.508	0.013	0.040	0.112	0.252
	15		0.082	0.216	0.454	0.717	0.016	0.069	0.215	0.463
	20		0.097	0.286	0.589	0.850	0.021	0.106	0.332	0.650
	25		0.112	0.355	0.701	0.926	0.026	0.148	0.451	0.789
	30		0.127	0.422	0.788	0.965	0.031	0.195	0.563	0.881
	35		0.143	0.487	0.853	0.985	0.037	0.246	0.661	0.937
	40		0.160	0.547	0.901	0.993	0.044	0.298	0.743	0.968
	45		0.176	0.604	0.934	0.997	0.051	0.351	0.810	0.984
	50		0.193	0.655	0.957	0.999	0.059	0.405	0.862	0.993
5	5		0.059	0.093	0.159	0.262	0.012	0.022	0.045	0.090
	10		0.071	0.160	0.332	0.562	0.014	0.045	0.131	0.301
	15		0.085	0.235	0.502	0.777	0.017	0.079	0.255	0.542
	20		0.101	0.313	0.647	0.898	0.022	0.123	0.393	0.736
	25		0.117	0.391	0.760	0.958	0.028	0.174	0.527	0.863
	30		0.135	0.466	0.843	0.984	0.034	0.230	0.647	0.934
	35		0.152	0.537	0.901	0.994	0.041	0.290	0.745	0.971
	40		0.171	0.603	0.939	0.998	0.049	0.352	0.822	0.988
	45		0.189	0.662	0.963	0.999	0.057	0.414	0.879	0.995
	50		0.208	0.714	0.978	1.00	0.066	0.474	0.920	0.998
6	5		0.060	0.097	0.170	0.286	0.012	0.023	0.049	0.102
	10		0.072	0.170	0.362	0.612	0.014	0.049	0.151	0.350
	15		0.088	0.254	0.547	0.826	0.019	0.089	0.295	0.615
	20		0.105	0.341	0.699	0.932	0.024	0.140	0.452	0.805
	25		0.123	0.427	0.810	0.976	0.030	0.200	0.597	0.913
	30		0.142	0.509	0.885	0.992	0.037	0.266	0.719	0.965
	35		0.162	0.584	0.934	0.998	0.045	0.335	0.812	0.987
	40		0.182	0.653	0.963	0.999	0.054	0.405	0.879	0.996
	45		0.202	0.713	0.980	1.00	0.064	0.474	0.925	0.999
	50		0.223	0.765	0.989	1.00	0.074	0.540	0.966	1.00

TABLE K   Sample size requirements for the difference between independent proportions ($α=0.05$)

p_S	Difference between proportions (p_L-p_S)															
	0.05	0.10	0.15	0.20	0.25	0.30	0.35	0.40	0.45	0.50	0.55	0.60	0.65	0.70	0.75	0.80
0.05	424	132	69	44	31	24	19	15	13	11	9	8	7	6	5	4
	485	151	79	51	36	27	21	17	14	12	10	9	8	7	6	5
	567	177	93	59	42	32	25	20	17	14	12	10	9	8	7	6
	702	219	115	73	52	39	31	25	21	17	15	13	11	10	8	7
0.10	681	195	96	59	41	30	23	18	15	12	10	9	7	6	5	5
	778	223	110	67	46	34	26	21	17	14	12	10	9	7	6	5
	911	261	129	79	54	40	31	24	20	17	14	12	10	9	7	6
	1127	323	159	98	67	49	38	30	25	20	17	15	12	11	9	8

Continued

p_S	Difference between proportions ($p_L - p_S$)															
	0.05	0.10	0.15	0.20	0.25	0.30	0.35	0.40	0.45	0.50	0.55	0.60	0.65	0.70	0.75	0.80
0.15	903	248	119	71	48	34	26	20	16	13	11	9	8	7	5	
	1032	283	136	81	54	39	30	23	19	15	13	11	9	7	6	
	1208	332	159	95	64	46	35	27	22	18	15	12	10	9	7	
	1494	410	196	117	79	57	43	34	27	22	18	15	13	11	9	
0.20	1092	292	137	80	53	38	28	22	17	14	12	9	8	6		
	1249	334	156	92	61	43	32	25	20	16	13	11	9	7		
	1462	391	183	108	71	51	38	29	23	19	15	13	10	9		
	1808	483	226	133	88	63	47	36	29	23	19	16	13	11		
0.25	1250	328	151	88	57	40	30	23	18	14	12	9	7			
	1429	375	173	100	65	46	34	26	21	16	13	11	9			
	1673	439	202	117	77	54	40	31	24	19	15	12	10			
	2069	542	250	145	95	67	49	38	30	24	19	15	12			
0.30	1376	356	162	93	60	42	31	23	18	14	11	9				
	1573	406	185	106	69	48	35	27	21	16	13	10				
	1842	476	217	124	80	56	41	31	24	19	15	12				
	2278	588	268	153	99	69	51	38	30	23	18	15				
0.35	1471	375	169	96	61	42	31	23	17	13	10					
	1681	429	193	110	70	48	35	26	20	15	12					
	1969	503	226	128	82	57	41	31	23	18	14					
	2434	621	280	159	101	70	51	38	29	22	17					
0.40	1534	387	173	97	61	42	30	22	16	12						
	1753	443	197	111	70	48	34	25	19	14						
	2053	518	231	130	82	56	40	29	22	17						
	2538	641	286	160	101	69	49	36	27	20						
0.45	1565	391	173	96	60	40	28	20	15							
	1798	447	197	110	69	46	32	23	17							
	2095	524	231	128	80	54	38	27	20							
	2591	648	286	159	99	67	47	34	25							
0.50	1565	387	169	93	57	38	26	18								
	1789	443	193	106	65	43	30	21								
	2095	518	226	124	77	51	35	24								
	2591	641	280	153	95	63	43	30								

NOTE 1: sample sizes calculated using the arcsine formula, with Fleiss' correction for continuity.
NOTE 2: line 1: $\beta=0.20$
line 2: $\beta=0.15$
line 3: $\beta=0.10$
line 4: $\beta=0.05$
NOTE 3: p_L=larger probability, p_S=smaller probability.

TABLE L Required number of events per group for survival analysis (two-tailed test)

δ	$\alpha=0.05$				$\alpha=0.01$			
	β				β			
	0.20	0.15	0.10	0.05	0.20	0.15	0.10	0.05
1.2	472	542	632	782	704	789	897	1075
1.4	139	159	186	230	207	232	264	316

Continued

δ	$\alpha=0.05$				$\alpha=0.01$			
	β				β			
	0.20	0.15	0.10	0.05	0.20	0.15	0.10	0.05
1.6	71	82	96	118	106	119	135	162
1.8	46	53	61	76	68	76	87	104
2.0	33	38	44	55	49	55	63	75
2.2	26	29	34	42	38	43	48	58
2.4	21	24	28	34	31	35	39	47
2.6	18	20	23	29	26	29	33	40
2.8	15	17	20	25	23	25	29	34
3.0	13	15	18	22	20	22	25	30
3.2	12	14	16	20	18	20	23	27
3.4	11	13	15	18	16	18	20	24
3.6	10	11	13	16	15	16	19	22
3.8	9	11	12	15	14	15	17	21
4.0	9	10	11	14	13	14	16	19
4.2	8	9	11	13	12	13	15	18
4.4	8	9	10	12	11	12	14	17
4.6	7	8	10	12	11	12	13	16
4.8	7	8	9	11	10	11	13	15
5.0	7	7	9	11	10	11	12	14

TABLE M   Critical values of the Studentized Range test

df	Number of steps								
	2	3	4	5	6	7	8	9	10
1	17.97	26.98	32.82	37.08	40.41	43.12	45.40	47.36	49.07
2	6.08	8.33	9.80	10.88	11.74	12.44	13.03	13.54	13.99
3	4.50	5.91	6.82	7.50	8.04	8.48	8.85	9.18	9.46
4	3.93	5.04	5.76	6.29	6.71	7.05	7.35	7.60	7.83
5	3.63	4.60	5.22	5.67	6.03	6.33	6.58	6.80	6.99
6	3.46	4.34	4.90	5.30	5.63	5.89	6.12	6.32	6.49
7	3.34	4.17	4.68	5.06	5.36	5.61	5.82	6.00	6.16
8	3.26	4.04	4.53	4.89	5.17	5.40	5.60	5.77	5.92
9	3.20	3.95	4.42	4.76	5.02	5.24	5.43	5.60	5.74
10	3.15	3.88	4.33	4.65	4.91	5.12	5.30	5.46	5.59
11	3.11	3.82	4.26	4.57	4.82	5.03	5.20	5.35	5.49
12	3.08	3.77	4.20	4.51	4.75	4.95	5.12	5.26	5.39
13	3.06	3.73	4.15	4.45	4.69	4.88	5.05	5.19	5.32
14	3.03	3.70	4.11	4.41	4.64	4.83	4.99	5.13	5.25
15	3.01	3.67	4.08	4.37	4.59	4.78	4.94	5.08	5.20
16	3.00	3.65	4.05	4.33	4.56	4.74	4.90	5.03	5.15
17	2.98	3.63	4.02	4.30	4.52	4.70	4.86	4.99	5.11
18	2.97	3.61	4.00	4.28	4.49	4.67	4.82	4.96	5.07
19	2.96	3.59	3.98	4.25	4.47	4.65	4.79	4.92	5.04
20	2.95	3.58	3.96	4.23	4.44	4.62	4.77	4.90	5.01
24	2.92	3.53	3.90	4.17	4.37	4.54	4.68	4.81	4.91
30	2.89	3.49	3.84	4.10	4.30	4.46	4.60	4.72	4.82

Continued

df	2	3	4	5	6	7	8	9	10
	Number of steps								
40	2.86	3.44	3.79	4.04	4.23	4.39	4.52	4.63	4.73
60	2.83	3.40	3.74	3.98	4.16	4.31	4.44	4.55	4.65
120	2.80	3.36	3.68	3.92	4.10	4.24	4.36	4.47	4.56
∞	2.77	3.31	3.63	3.86	4.03	4.17	4.29	4.39	4.47

Reprinted with permission from Harter HL (1979). *Order statistics and their use in testing and estimation. Vol.1: Tests based on the range and studentized range of samples from a normal distribution.* U.S. Washington DC. Government Printing Office.

TABLE Na   Sample size requirements for two-group MANOVA (T^2)

Effect size	Number of variables	$\beta=$	$\alpha=0.05$			$\beta=$	$\alpha=0.01$		
			0.30	0.20	0.10		0.30	0.20	0.10
Very large ($d=1.5$)	2		9	11	13		13	15	18
	3		10	12	15		15	17	21
	4		12	14	17		17	19	22
	5		13	15	18		18	20	24
	6		14	16	19		19	22	26
	8		16	18	22		21	24	28
	10		18	20	24		24	26	31
	15		21	24	28		28	31	36
	20		25	28	32		32	36	42
Large ($d=1$)	2		17	21	27		26	31	38
	3		20	24	31		29	34	42
	4		22	27	34		32	37	46
	5		24	29	36		35	40	48
	6		26	31	39		37	44	52
	8		29	35	44		42	48	56
	10		32	38	46		44	52	60
	15		38	46	54		52	60	70
	20		44	52	62		60	68	78
Moderate ($d=0.75$)	2		29	36	48		44	52	66
	3		34	42	54		50	58	72
	4		37	46	58		54	64	78
	5		42	50	62		58	68	84
	6		44	52	66		62	72	88
	8		48	58	72		68	80	96
	10		54	64	78		74	86	105
	15		64	74	92		86	100	120
	20		72	84	105		98	110	130
Small ($d=0.5$)	2		64	80	105		96	115	145
	3		74	90	120		110	130	160
	4		80	98	130		120	140	170
	5		88	110	135		125	150	180
	6		94	115	145		135	160	190
	8		105	125	160		150	175	210
	10		115	135	170		160	185	230
	15		135	160	195		185	220	260
	20		150	180	220		210	240	290

Abridged with permission from Läuter J (1978). Sample size requirements for the T^2 test of MANOVA (tables for one-way classification). *Biometrical Journal*, **20**:389–406.

TABLE Nb   Sample size requirements for three-group MANOVA

Effect size	Number of variables	$\beta=$	$\alpha=0.05$			$\beta=$	$\alpha=0.01$		
			0.30	0.20	0.10		0.30	0.20	0.10
Very large ($d=1.5$)	2		11	13	16		15	17	21
	3		12	14	18		17	20	24
	4		14	16	19		19	22	26
	5		15	17	21		20	23	28
	6		16	18	22		22	25	29
	8		18	21	25		24	28	32
	10		20	23	27		27	30	35
	15		24	27	32		32	35	42
	20		27	31	37		36	40	46
Large ($d=1$)	2		21	26	33		31	36	44
	3		25	29	37		35	42	50
	4		27	33	42		38	44	54
	5		30	35	44		42	48	58
	6		32	38	48		44	52	62
	8		36	42	52		50	56	68
	10		39	46	56		54	62	74
	15		46	54	66		64	72	84
	20		54	62	74		72	80	94
Moderate ($d=0.75$)	2		36	44	58		54	62	76
	3		42	52	64		60	70	86
	4		46	56	70		66	78	94
	5		50	60	76		72	82	100
	6		54	66	82		76	88	105
	8		60	72	90		84	98	120
	10		66	78	98		92	105	125
	15		78	92	115		110	125	145
	20		90	105	130		125	140	165
Small ($d=0.5$)	2		80	98	125		115	140	170
	3		92	115	145		135	155	190
	4		105	125	155		145	170	210
	5		110	135	170		155	185	220
	6		120	145	180		165	195	240
	8		135	160	200		185	220	260
	10		145	175	220		200	230	280
	15		170	210	255		240	270	320
	20		195	230	280		270	300	360

Abridged with permission from Läuter J (1978). Sample size requirements for the T^2 test of MANOVA (tables for one-way classification). *Biometrical Journal,* **20**:389-406.

TABLE Nc   Sample size requirements for four-group MANOVA

Effect size	Number of variables	$\beta=$	$\alpha=0.05$			$\beta=$	$\alpha=0.01$		
			0.30	0.20	0.10		0.30	0.20	0.10
Very large (d=1.5)	2		12	14	17		17	19	23
	3		14	16	20		19	22	26
	4		15	18	22		21	24	28
	5		16	19	23		23	26	30
	6		18	21	25		24	27	32
	8		20	23	28		27	30	36
	10		22	25	30		29	33	39
	15		26	30	36		35	39	46
	20		30	34	40		40	44	52
Large (d=1)	2		24	29	37		34	40	50
	3		28	23	42		39	46	56
	4		31	37	46		44	50	60
	5		34	40	50		48	54	64
	6		36	44	54		50	58	70
	8		42	48	60		56	64	76
	10		46	52	64		62	70	82
	15		54	62	76		72	82	96
	20		60	70	86		82	92	110
Moderate (d=0.75)	2		42	50	64		60	70	86
	3		48	58	72		68	80	96
	4		54	64	80		76	88	105
	5		58	70	86		82	94	115
	6		62	74	92		86	100	120
	8		70	84	105		96	115	135
	10		78	92	115		105	120	145
	15		92	110	130		125	145	170
	20		105	125	150		140	160	190
Small (d=0.5)	2		92	115	145		130	155	190
	3		105	130	165		150	175	220
	4		120	145	180		165	195	240
	5		130	155	195		180	210	250
	6		140	165	210		190	220	270
	8		155	185	230		220	250	300
	10		170	200	250		240	270	320
	15		200	240	290		280	320	370
	20		230	270	330		310	350	420

Abridged with permission from Läuter J (1978). Sample size requirements for the T^2 test of MANOVA (tables for one-way classification). *Biometrical Journal*, **20**:389-406.

TABLE O   Power for Hotelling's T^2 at $\alpha=0.05$ and $\alpha=0.10$*

Number of variables	N in each group	D^2			
		0.25	0.64	1.00	2.25
2	15	0.26 (0.32)	0.44 (0.60)	0.65 (0.77)	0.95
	25	0.33 (0.47)	0.66 (0.80)	0.86	0.97
	50	0.60 (0.77)	0.95	1.00	1.00
	100	0.90	1.00	1.00	1.00
3	15	0.23 (0.29)	0.37 (0.55)	0.58 (0.72)	0.91
	25	0.28 (0.41)	0.58 (0.74)	0.80	0.95
	50	0.54 (0.65)	0.93	1.00	1.00
	100	0.86	1.00	1.00	1.00
5	15	0.21 (0.25)	0.32 (0.47)	0.42 (0.66)	0.83
	25	0.26 (0.35)	0.42 (0.68)	0.72	0.96
	50	0.44 (0.59)	0.88	1.00	1.00
	100	0.78	1.00	1.00	1.00
7	15	0.18 (0.22)	0.27 (0.42)	0.37 (0.59)	0.77
	25	0.22 (0.31)	0.38 (0.62)	0.64 (0.81)	0.94
	50	0.40 (0.52)	0.82	0.97	1.00
	100	0.72	1.00	1.00	1.00

Modified from Stevens J (1980). Power of the multivariate analysis of variance tests. *Psychological Bulletin*, **88**:728–737, with permission from the author and the American Psychological Association.

*NOTE: power values at $\alpha=0.10$ are in parentheses; values of 1.00 are approximately equal to 1

TABLE P r to z' transformation

r	z'	r	z'	r	z'	r	z'
0.005	0.005	0.130	0.131	0.255	0.261	0.380	0.400
0.010	0.010	0.135	0.136	0.260	0.266	0.385	0.406
0.015	0.015	0.140	0.141	0.265	0.271	0.390	0.412
0.020	0.020	0.145	0.146	0.270	0.277	0.395	0.418
0.025	0.025	0.150	0.151	0.275	0.282	0.400	0.424
0.030	0.030	0.155	0.156	0.280	0.288	0.405	0.430
0.035	0.035	0.160	0.161	0.285	0.293	0.410	0.436
0.040	0.040	0.165	0.167	0.290	0.299	0.415	0.442
0.045	0.045	0.170	0.172	0.295	0.304	0.420	0.448
0.050	0.050	0.175	0.177	0.300	0.310	0.425	0.454
0.055	0.055	0.180	0.182	0.305	0.315	0.430	0.460
0.060	0.060	0.185	0.187	0.310	0.321	0.435	0.466
0.065	0.065	0.190	0.192	0.315	0.326	0.440	0.472
0.070	0.070	0.195	0.198	0.320	0.332	0.445	0.478
0.075	0.075	0.200	0.203	0.325	0.337	0.450	0.485
0.080	0.080	0.205	0.208	0.330	0.343	0.455	0.491
0.085	0.085	0.210	0.213	0.335	0.348	0.460	0.497
0.090	0.090	0.215	0.218	0.340	0.354	0.465	0.504
0.095	0.095	0.220	0.224	0.345	0.360	0.470	0.510
0.100	0.100	0.225	0.229	0.350	0.365	0.475	0.517
0.105	0.105	0.230	0.234	0.355	0.371	0.480	0.523
0.110	0.110	0.235	0.239	0.360	0.377	0.485	0.530

Continued

r	z′	r	z′	r	z′	r	z′
0.115	0.116	0.240	0.245	0.365	0.383	0.490	0.536
0.120	0.121	0.245	0.250	0.370	0.388	0.495	0.543
0.125	0.126	0.250	0.255	0.375	0.394	0.500	0.549
0.505	0.556	0.630	0.741	0.755	0.984	0.880	1.376
0.510	0.563	0.635	0.750	0.760	0.996	0.885	1.398
0.515	0.570	0.640	0.758	0.765	1.008	0.890	1.422
0.520	0.576	0.645	0.767	0.770	1.020	0.895	1.447
0.525	0.583	0.650	0.775	0.775	1.033	0.900	1.472
0.530	0.590	0.655	0.784	0.780	1.045	0.905	1.499
0.535	0.597	0.660	0.793	0.785	1.058	0.910	1.528
0.540	0.604	0.665	0.802	0.790	1.071	0.915	1.557
0.545	0.611	0.670	0.811	0.795	1.085	0.920	1.589
0.550	0.618	0.675	0.820	0.800	1.099	0.925	1.623
0.555	0.626	0.680	0.829	0.805	1.113	0.930	1.658
0.560	0.633	0.685	0.838	0.810	1.127	0.935	1.697
0.565	0.640	0.690	0.848	0.815	1.142	0.940	1.738
0.570	0.648	0.695	0.858	0.820	1.157	0.945	1.783
0.575	0.655	0.700	0.867	0.825	1.172	0.950	1.832
0.580	0.662	0.705	0.877	0.830	1.188	0.955	1.886
0.585	0.670	0.710	0.887	0.835	1.204	0.960	1.946
0.590	0.678	0.715	0.897	0.840	1.221	0.965	2.014
0.595	0.685	0.720	0.908	0.845	1.238	0.970	2.092
0.600	0.693	0.725	0.918	0.850	1.256	0.975	2.185
0.605	0.701	0.730	0.929	0.855	1.274	0.980	2.298
0.610	0.709	0.735	0.940	0.860	1.293	0.985	2.443
0.615	0.717	0.740	0.950	0.865	1.313	0.990	2.647
0.620	0.725	0.745	0.962	0.870	1.333	0.995	2.994
0.625	0.733	0.750	0.973	0.875	1.354		

TABLE Q   z′ to r transformation

r	z′	r	z′	r	z′	r	z′
0.025	0.025	0.775	0.650	1.525	0.910	2.275	0.979
0.050	0.050	0.800	0.664	1.550	0.914	2.300	0.980
0.075	0.075	0.825	0.678	1.575	0.918	2.325	0.981
0.100	0.100	0.850	0.691	1.600	0.922	2.350	0.982
0.125	0.124	0.875	0.704	1.625	0.925	2.375	0.983
0.150	0.149	0.900	0.716	1.650	0.929	2.400	0.984
0.175	0.173	0.925	0.728	1.675	0.932	2.425	0.984
0.200	0.197	0.950	0.740	1.700	0.935	2.450	0.985
0.225	0.221	0.975	0.751	1.725	0.938	2.475	0.986
0.250	0.245	1.000	0.762	1.750	0.941	2.500	0.987
0.275	0.268	1.025	0.772	1.775	0.944	2.525	0.987
0.300	0.291	1.050	0.782	1.800	0.947	2.550	0.988
0.325	0.314	1.075	0.791	1.825	0.949	2.575	0.988

Continued

r	z′	r	z′	r	z′	r	z′
0.350	0.336	1.100	0.800	1.850	0.952	2.600	0.989
0.375	0.358	1.125	0.809	1.875	0.954	2.625	0.990
0.400	0.380	1.150	0.818	1.900	0.956	2.650	0.990
0.425	0.401	1.175	0.826	1.925	0.958	2.675	0.991
0.450	0.422	1.200	0.834	1.950	0.960	2.700	0.991
0.475	0.442	1.225	0.841	1.975	0.962	2.725	0.991
0.500	0.462	1.250	0.848	2.000	0.964	2.750	0.992
0.525	0.482	1.275	0.855	2.025	0.966	2.775	0.992
0.550	0.501	1.300	0.862	2.050	0.967	2.800	0.993
0.575	0.519	1.325	0.868	2.075	0.969	2.825	0.993
0.600	0.537	1.350	0.874	2.100	0.970	2.850	0.993
0.625	0.555	1.375	0.880	2.125	0.972	2.875	0.994
0.650	0.572	1.400	0.885	2.150	0.973	2.900	0.994
0.675	0.588	1.425	0.891	2.175	0.975	2.925	0.994
0.700	0.604	1.450	0.896	2.200	0.976	2.950	0.995
0.725	0.620	1.475	0.901	2.225	0.977	2.975	0.995
0.750	0.635	1.500	0.905	2.250	0.978	3.000	0.995

图书在版编目（CIP）数据

医学统计学：英汉对照/（加）杰弗里·诺尔曼
（Geoffrey R. Norman）著；郝元涛主编 . —北京：人
民卫生出版社，2018

临床医学专业英文版教材

ISBN 978-7-117-27278-0

Ⅰ.①医… Ⅱ.①杰… ②郝… Ⅲ.①医学统计 – 统
计学 – 医学院校 – 教材 – 英、汉 Ⅳ.①R195.1

中国版本图书馆 CIP 数据核字（2018）第 210202 号

人卫智网	www.ipmph.com	医学教育、学术、考试、健康，购书智慧智能综合服务平台
人卫官网	www.pmph.com	人卫官方资讯发布平台

医学统计学

主　　编：郝元涛

出版发行：人民卫生出版社（中继线 010-59780011）

地　　址：北京市朝阳区潘家园南里 19 号

邮　　编：100021

E - mail：pmph @ pmph.com

购书热线：010-59787592　010-59787584　010-65264830

印　　刷：中国农业出版社印刷厂

经　　销：新华书店

开　　本：850×1168　1/16　　印张：25

字　　数：739 千字

版　　次：2018 年 3 月第 1 版　2018 年 3 月第 1 版第 1 次印刷

标准书号：ISBN 978-7-117-27278-0

定　　价：85.00 元

打击盗版举报电话：010-59787491　E-mail：WQ @ pmph.com

（凡属印装质量问题请与本社市场营销中心联系退换）